Jonathan EDWARDS

a reference guide

A
Reference
Guide
to
Literature

Everett Emerson
Editor

Jonathan EDWARDS

a reference guide

M. X. LESSER

G.K.HALL &CO.

70 LINCOLN STREET, BOSTON, MASS.

Copyright © 1981 by M. X. Lesser

Library of Congress Cataloging in Publication Data

Lesser, M   X
  Jonathan Edwards : a reference guide.

  (A Reference Guide to literature)
  "Writings about Jonathan Edwards"
  Includes index.
    1. Edwards, Jonathan, 1703-1758—Bibliography.   I.   Series: Reference guides
to literature.
Z8255.5.L47   [PS742]   016.2858'092'4   80-28540
ISBN 0-8161-7837-2

Contents

THE AUTHOR: M. X. Lesser earned his doctorate at
Columbia University--his dissertation a study of
seventeenth-century election sermons--and has taught
at the University of Delaware, Rutgers University,
and, for the past dozen years, at Northeastern
University. He has written articles on American
literature and his Modern Short Stories: The
Fiction of Experience was published by McGraw Hill.

Preface

I would have preferred a longer title for this, one Jonathan Edwards and his readers might have known, with the contents and the arguments spilled out upon the page, oddly pointed and capitalized. A note about what may be found in these pages will have to do.

First, a chronology lists Edwards's important work: dates, the short titles used in the text, and the longer titles as they were first published. Second, the introduction traces in detail the growth and direction of Edwards criticism--biographical, theological or philosophical, literary, and bibliographical--over the last 250 years. It is divided into five periods: the first deals with a century of estimates, from his assumption of the Northampton pulpit in 1729 to Sereno Dwight's massive biography in 1829; the second gathers up the work of the next seventy years or so, from the rise and fall of his successors to the "serious" retrospective begun on the eve of his bicentennial; the third opens with those celebrations in 1903 and closes, after a relatively quiet period, with the extraordinary burst of activity in the thirties; the fourth gauges Perry Miller's impact upon Edwards scholarship in his work and in the work of others, from 1941 to 1964; the fifth follows the almost exponential rise of interest in Edwards over the last fifteen years. The text itself is an annotated bibliography of books, articles, dissertations, reviews, fugitive references, and reprints--almost 1800 numbered items. A reprint is noted when an item is published under separate title or when it is ten pages or more in a larger context; in most instances, when an item has been reprinted more than five times, "frequently reprinted" follows the first and only citation. Items I have not personally examined are indicated by an asterisk preceding the entry number. The index interleaves author and title and limits the subject entries to those items of some significance.

My debts, of course, are to those in the text, only somewhat less obvious to the many others who helped me find them and put them there. To the people at the American Antiquarian Society, Andover Newton Theological School, the Atheneum, Boston Public Library, British Museum, Forbes Library (Northampton), Gordon-Conwell Theological Seminary, Library of Congress, Presbyterian Historical Society,

Preface

Princeton University, and Yale University I owe a deep debt; to those at Andover-Harvard Divinity School, a very special one; to Alistair Adamson, of Edinburgh, and Robyn Gard, an unexpected one; to Jon Lanham of Harvard's Widener Library, an unpayable one. To Lewis Leary of the University of North Carolina, Chapel Hill, and Daniel B. Shea, Jr., of Washington University, St. Louis, go my thanks for their suggestions and concern, and to Everett Emerson of the University of Massachusetts, Amherst, for that and for his patience. Nearer home, I owe much in kindness to Louise Dennett of Dodge Library, Northeastern; to my colleagues Louis Cooperstein and Gordon Pruett; and to our staff Ava Baker, Ivy Dodge, Maureen Godino, Barbara Sause and most especially, Mary Mello.

To Lee, for her untold help and our "uncommon union" this (and much else besides) is dedicated.

Chronology of Works by Edwards

1731   <u>God Glorified</u>/God Glorified in the Work of Redemption, By the Greatness of Man's Dependence upon Him, in the Whole of it.

1734   <u>Divine and Supernatural Light</u>/A Divine and Supernatural Light, Immediately imparted to the Soul by the Spirit of God, Shown to be both a Scriptural, and Rational Doctrine.

1737   <u>Faithful Narrative</u>/A Faithful Narrative Of the Surprizing Work of God In The Conversion of Many Hundred Souls in Northampton, and the Neighbouring Towns and Villages of New-Hampshire in New-England. In a Letter to the Revd. Dr. Benjamin Colman of Boston. Written by the Revd. Mr. Edwards, Minister of Northampton, on Nov. 6, 1736.

1738   <u>Justification by Faith Alone</u>/in Discourses on Various Important Subjects, Nearly concerning the great Affair of the Soul's Eternal Salvation.

1741   <u>Distinguishing Marks</u>/The Distinguishing Marks Of a Work of the Spirit of God. Applied to that uncommon Operation that has lately appeared on the Minds of many of the People of this Land: With a particular Consideration of the extraordinary Circumstances with which this Work is attended.

1741   <u>Sinners in the Hands of an Angry God</u>/Sinners In The Hands of an Angry God. A Sermon Preached at Enfield, July 8th 1741. At a Time of great Awakenings; and attended with remarkable Impressions on many of the Hearers.

1742   <u>Some Thoughts</u>/Some Thoughts Concerning the present Revival of Religion In New-England, And the Way in which it ought to be acknowledged and promoted, Humbly offered to the Publick, in a Treatise on that Subject.

1746   <u>Religious Affections</u>/A Treatise Concerning Religious Affections, In Three Parts.

Chronology of Works by Edwards

1747   Humble Attempt/An Humble Attempt To promote Explicit
        Agreement And Visible Union of God's People in
        Extraordinary Prayer For the Revival of Religion and the
        Advancement of Christ's Kingdom on Earth, pursuant to
        Scripture-Promises and Prophecies concerning the last Time.

1749   Life of Brainerd/An Account of the Life Of the late
        Reverend Mr. David Brainerd, Minister of the Gospel,
        Missionary to the Indians, from the honorable Society in
        Scotland, for the Propagation of Christian Knowledge, and
        Pastor of a Church of Christian Indians in New-Jersey.

1749   Qualifications/An Humble Inquiry Into the Rules of the Word
        of God Concerning The Qualifications Requisite to a Compleat
        Standing and full Communion In the Visible Christian Church.

1751   Farewell Sermon/A Farewel-Sermon Preached at the first
        Precinct in Northampton, After the People's publick
        Rejection of their Minister, and renouncing their Relation
        to Him as Pastor of the Church there, On June 22. 1750.
        Occasion'd by Difference of Sentiments, concerning the
        requisite Qualifications of Members of the Church, in
        compleat Standing.

1753   True Grace/True Grace, Distinguished from the Experience
        Of Devils.

1754   Freedom of the Will/A careful and strict Enquiry Into The
        modern prevailing Notions Of That Freedom of Will, Which
        is supposed to be essential To Moral Agency, Vertue and
        Vice, Reward and Punishment, Praise and Blame.

1758   Original Sin/The Great Christian Doctrine Of Original Sin
        defended; Evidences of it's Truth produced, And Arguments
        to the Contrary answered.

1765   Personal Narrative/in The Life and Character Of The Late
        Reverend Mr. Jonathan Edwards, President of the College at
        New-Jersey [by Samuel Hopkins].

1765   End of Creation and True Virtue/in Two Dissertations, I.
        Concerning the End for which God created the World.   II.
        The Nature of True Virtue.

1774   History of Redemption/A History Of the Work of Redemption.
        Containing, The Outlines of a Body of Divinity, In a
        Method entirely new.

1780   Eternity of Hell Torments/The Eternity of Hell Torments in
        Sermons on the Following Subjects.

1793   <u>Miscellaneous Observations</u>/Miscellaneous Observations On
        Important Theological Subjects, Original and Collected.

1852   <u>Charity and its Fruits</u>/Charity And Its Fruits; Or,
        Christian Love As Manifested In The Heart And Life.

1903   <u>Trinity</u>/An Unpublished Essay Of Edwards On the Trinity With
        Remarks On Edwards And His Theology, by George P. Fisher.

1948   <u>Images or Shadows</u>/Images or Shadows of Divine Things,
        edited by Perry Miller.

        Note: Several of Edwards's sermons were published
        posthumously as collections, in Hopkins's <u>Life</u> (1765.2),
        or in later "complete" editions. Only those sermons
        frequently cited in the text have been listed in the
        chronology.

Introduction

During his stay at the Allen Tates' in the autumn of 1942, Robert
Lowell was hard at work on a biography of Jonathan Edwards,
"heaping up books," he recalls, "and taking notes" (1968.13). After
a while his enthusiasm flagged, "getting more and more numb on the
subject, looking at old leatherbound volumes on freedom of the will
and so on, and feeling less and less a calling." So together with
Tate he began to collect poems for an anthology of English verse,
and he abandoned Edwards. Not quite: over the next several years
Lowell turned what he had found in Edwards into a pair of splendid
poems, "Mr. Edwards and the Spider" and "After the Surprising
Conversions" (1946.3), borrowing from him on spiders and suicides,
unacknowledged. Then, many years later, Lowell wrote two more
poems, "Jonathan Edwards in Western Massachusetts" (1964.14) and
"The Worst Sinner, Jonathan Edwards' God" (1973.19), contemplative
now and quite touched by the Stockbridge exile--"I love you faded,
old." It is a cautionary tale.

Over the last 250 years, attitudes towards Edwards, or what may
be wrung from him, have changed considerably, yet some fairly
well-marked continuities remain. Biographies of Edwards, for
example, were useful as "pious memorials" against the challenge to
orthodoxy launched in the eighteenth and early nineteenth centuries,
when the lives of ministering saints were summoned for defense;
later in the century, when his kind of strenuous belief waned, his
life became largely irrelevant or of only passing interest; now his
life is useful again but as a clue to his time and place, hardly
tutorial or, for that matter, inconsequential. In another way, as
discomfort about necessity and imputation rose in the nineteenth
century, the readers of Freedom of the Will and Original Sin came
chiefly to damn Edwards; those in the twentieth century--with
notable theological exceptions--to neglect him. And his style,
considered so wretched that some of his nineteenth-century editors
recast his prose to rescue him, becomes in recent years the unitive
instrument of his thought and the signal fact of his art.

Yet some things about Edwards do not change, or change ever so
slightly. A troublesome, and largely unresolved, duality haunted
Edwards from the start--mystic and rationalist, philosopher and

theologian, poet of the divine and scourger of the wicked—and hangs
on even now, though in our less dramatic age, there appears little
need to color him tragic. The habit of reading the American
experience as a quarrel between Edwards on one side and Franklin on
the other, first noted sometime in the nineteenth century, becomes
for twentieth-century cultural critics (and popularizers) a
recurrent, if not wholly rewarding, theme. There is a list of his
inadvertences--his antinomianism, his liberalism, his pantheism,
his republicanism--to reckon with from the eighteenth century on.
And there is, for Americans, the abiding question of his
importance to their history, their religion, their society, their
thought.

I

The first life of Edwards was published within months of his
death. The anonymous "Brief Account," a ten-page preface to
Original Sin (1758.4) ascribed to Samuel Finley and later reprinted
as "A Contemporaneous Account" (1903.24), derives the essential
facts of Edwards's life and much of the praise from the "public
Prints," the obituaries published in Boston and New York
newspapers and Gilbert Tennent's eulogy in the Pennsylvania
Gazette (1758.5). Seven years later the second and perhaps the
most frequently pirated biography appeared, Samuel Hopkins's The
Life and Character of the Late Reverend Mr. Jonathan Edwards,
President of the College of New-Jersey (1765.2). Not only is this
account more thorough than Finley's--it is, after all, ten times
as long--it is more intimate, for as a student in the Edwards home
in Northampton, Hopkins reports as an eye-witness and a friend, a
disciple and a just remembrancer.[1] Hopkins transcribes and
interleaves extracts from Edwards's Resolutions and Diary, the whole
of Personal Narrative, and several letters in a detailed history of
his forebears and his family, his habits of mind, the conduct of
his ministry and the occasion of his dismissal, his removal to
Stockbridge, and his death at Princeton; a bibliography of his
manuscripts and publications; and brief lives of his daughter
Esther Burr and his wife Sarah. Still valuable for its primary
materials--Personal Narrative, for example, is more reliable here
than in later redactions--and for its sympathetic understanding,
the Life fulfills Hopkins's intention to render a "faithful and
plain narration of matters of fact" about Edwards and to offer him
to the public as a model of Christian piety, "the greatest--best--
and most useful of men."

For the next sixty years the Hopkins life was variously edited,
revised, enlarged, or corrected, always recognizable, if seldom
attributed. Erasmus Middleton, for instance, dramatizes Hopkins's
account of the Northampton troubles--"Dismiss him! Dismiss him!
was the universal cry"--but closely follows his unnamed source
(1786.1); the anonymous compiler of another life in the preface to a

London imprint of History of Redemption (1788.1) closely follows
Middleton, again unnamed. Edward Williams and Edward Parsons,
editors of the first collected Edwards, the eight-volume Leeds
edition (1806.1), "improve" upon an acknowledged Hopkins by adding
Middleton; but Samuel Austin, editor of the first American, or
Worcester, edition of the complete Edwards two years later (1808.3),
acknowledges and prints Hopkins without change. At a farther
remove, John Hawksley adds "numerous verbal emendations" to
Williams and Parsons, in a separately published and attributed
Hopkins (1815.1).

It was left to Sereno Edwards Dwight and his 766-page Life of
President Edwards, the first of the ten-volume New York, or Converse,
edition of the complete Edwards (1829.4), to incorporate Finley,
Hopkins, and Williams and Parsons in what would become the standard
biography for more than a century. The chief advantage the Dwight
life enjoys is bulk: it collects and publishes for the first time
the juvenilia, the Miscellanies, and countless letters (especially
to and from Scots ministers), and it reprints and expands the texts
in Hopkins. Thus Dwight's 150-page account of Edwards's dismissal
includes, pari passu, a history of the changes in communion
practice; Hopkins's narration; Edwards's version of his differences
with his congregation, as noted in his journals and explained in
his letters; Joseph Hawley's belated recantation; and Dwight's
review of the matter and his recommendations. But, here as
elsewhere, Dwight must be approached with care. He so encumbers
his narrative with indiscriminate detail and with a ponderous style
that he makes it hard going indeed; more importantly, he silently
alters his manuscript sources, deleting here, correcting there. It
is a troublesome book but, until the Edwards manuscripts are
edited, a necessary one.

Criticism during the first hundred years centers on Edwards's
role in the early Northampton revivals and the Great Awakening--more
accurately, on his reporting and defense of those events--and
sometime later on Freedom of the Will and his treatises on sin and
virtue. In their preface to the first publication of Faithful
Narrative (1737.1), Isaac Watts and John Guyse recommend Edwards
to their London readers as the "pious" recorder of the "astonishing"
work of God in Northampton, though they are less pleased with his
choice of Abigail Hutchinson and Phebe Bartlet as suitable examples
of the conversion experience.[2] Within a year the preface and text
were translated into German (1738.5), within three into Dutch
(1740.1). Two years later John Willison offers Edwards's
Distinguishing Marks, another conversion testimony, to his Scots
reader as an American analogue to the Cambuslang revival (1742.3).

Though Benjamin Franklin urged his sister to read Edwards's
justification of the revival in Some Thoughts (see 1840.3), Charles
Chauncy detected in it few instances of genuine religious
experience and in the whole of the Awakening "a bad and dangerous

tendency" to excess. In his celebrated attack, <u>Seasonable Thoughts on the State of Religion in New-England</u> (1743.2), Chauncy called upon Edwards to denounce itinerant preachers and to impose strict church discipline upon his congregation, to return to proper religious practice, to distinguish passion from affection.[3] The unchecked enthusiasm Chauncy saw in the revivals was just as plain to William Rand (1743.3), who thought Edwards a dupe of Satan, unable to distinguish true from false marks of the spirit. Edwards, of course, was convinced of the soundness of his evangelical position, and, together with his overseas correspondents and some American friends, urged a universal concert of prayer in his <u>Humble Attempt</u> (1747.1). Later in the century the founders of the Baptist Missionary Society would testify to the singular influence Edwards exerted upon them, especially through his <u>Humble Attempt</u> and <u>Life of Brainerd</u>, an influence greater than that of either George Whitefield or John Wesley (see 1942.8).

Except for such commentary on his revivalist pieces and the partisan debate over his Northampton difficulties--for example, the exchange between Robert Breck (1751.1) and William Hobby (1751.2) on the conduct of the church council that dismissed him or the attack of Solomon Williams (1751.3) on his admission practices that precipitated it--public remarks about Edwards are rare during his lifetime. Of course, <u>Original Sin</u> was issued in 1758, the year of his death, <u>True Virtue</u> and <u>End of Creation</u> seven years later, and <u>History of Redemption</u> nine years after that. Still, <u>Freedom of the Will</u> garners little notice and few pages before 1770, fully sixteen years after it was first published. Then an anonymous writer charges Edwards with blasphemy and atheism in a bitter, brief polemic (1770.1), and James Dana issues the first of two full-length examinations (1770.2), an event warmly greeted by a correspondent of Edwards's Yale tutor, Samuel Johnson (see 1929.6). Dana originally deals with Edwards from a practical and experiential point of view, assessing his principles of volition and causation, charging him with atheism; three years later he focuses upon Edwards's "false" distinctions between natural and moral necessity and his "injurious misrepresentations" of God as the author of sin (1773.1). Stephen West defends Edwards against Dana's perceived errors in his earlier work (1772.2), and then, more than twenty years later, returns to Dana's second examination in a sixty-five-page rebuttal (1794.3). Three years later Edwards's son and namesake carefully an-alyzes the meanings of liberty and necessity, fixing the free-will con-troversy upon the question of causative or fortuitous volition, in the most sustained defense of the doctrine (1797.1). But the attacks go on, variously. Joseph Priestley challenges Edwards's notion that sin is a withheld act (1777.1); Elias Smith argues the legitimacy of the Arminian contention (1793.6); Samuel West twice tries Edwards for his confusion of antecedent and consequent necessity and his connec-tion of motive and action (1793.7 and 1795.2); Isaac Taylor charges Edwards with a violation of scientific reasoning in mixing meta-physics with Scripture (1827.5); and Thomas Tully Crybbace, at one with Edwards for revealing the "absurdities" of his antagonists, dismisses him for his failure to clarify liberty and necessity (1829.3). Beyond the strictly theological argument, the response is mixed. Samuel Taylor Coleridge thinks Freedom of the Will "destroys all will" (1829.2); James Boswell, who had read it, reports Dr. Johnson, who hadn't, as saying, "All theory is against the freedom of the will; all experience for it" (1791.1); William Godwin admires its "great force of reason" (1793.5), William Hazlitt its "closeness and candour" (1829.5); and Alexander Hamilton reportedly exclaimed that "nothing ever came from the human mind more in proof that man is a reasoning animal" (see 1968.35). As an English reviewer put it, his regret was that such intellectual rigor as Edwards had was in the service of "theological chimeras" (1762.1).

Attitudes about the other Edwards seem more evenly balanced, if, at times, equally vitriolic. So William Hart assails the "arbitrary" relationship between virtue and benevolence in True Virtue (1771.2), and Samuel Hopkins defends its necessity (1773.2). The younger Edwards values a newly produced History of Redemption (1774.3), only to have a reviewer find it full of "pious conundrums" (1775.1). One commentator discovers not the "remotest semblance" of physical depravity in Original Sin (1824.2), another points to its obvious, unequivocal, and total presence (1825.2).

About Edwards's style, there is no balance—it is all bad. His language is mysterious (1750.2), negligent (1758.4), uncouth (1808.5), vulgar (1811.2), inelegant (1822.4), repellent (1824.1). So pervasive is the view that his is one of "the most remarkable specimens of bad writing" of the time that one nineteenth-century editor of Religious Affections abridges the text to rid it of ambiguities and tautologies (1817.1), and another writes Sinners in the Hands of an Angry God in "other language" for the modern reader (1826.1). For all that, criticism during the first century is given over to frequent and studied denunciations of Edwards on the will.

Little of that bitterness touches the man. On Solomon Stoddard's death, there is every hope that Edwards will inherit his grandfather's mantle (1729.1 and 1731.1); at his own death, he is mourned as the "greatest pillar" of America's Zion (1758.3). Gilbert Tennent, the evangelist preacher, calls him a "great Divine" (1758.5); Isaac Backus, the New England Baptist, considers him "one of the best divines" of his age (1767.2). An anonymous poet eulogizes "Great EDWARDS--dead!" (1758.2) and two of the Connecticut wits sing his name: Joel Barlow launches him into "the realms of light" (1778.1), and Timothy Dwight extols him as "that moral Newton, that second Paul" (1788.3). Overseas, Edwards wins similar praise. John Erskine, his Scots editor, writes in 1758 of the "irreparable" loss: "I do not think our age has produced a divine of equal genius or judgment" (see 1818.3). And, as an American, he wins even more. John Ryland, the English Baptist, finds him "the greatest divine that ever adorned the American world" (1780.2), and Dugald Stewart, the Edinburgh philosopher, ranks him a peer of "any disputant bred in the universities of Europe" (1822.6). Such high praise would not come to Edwards again until, a generation later, George Bancroft warns that "he that will know the workings of the mind of New England in the middle of the last century, and the throbbings of its heart, must give his days and nights to the study of Jonathan Edwards" (1856.1). Except for a few academic theologians, the nineteenth century thought better of it.

II

"Next after the Bible, read and study Edwards," Dr. Lyman Beecher tells his son at Yale (see 1865.1), but, unlike some of the men in the Beecher family (1868.1), the women will have none of it. His wife flees his reading of Sinners in the Hands of an Angry God (see 1934.7); his daughter Catherine refutes Edwards in order to save her beloved from eternal damnation (see 1962.1); and, in The Minister's Wooing (1859.7), his daughter Harriet characterizes Edwards's sermons as a "refined poetry of torture."[4] The sermons are just as trying to other women later in the century. The heroine of Frank Samuel Child's A Puritan Wooing (1898.3) collapses upon hearing Edwards at Northampton on sin, only to recover converted. Less fortunately, the mother of the heroine in Paul Leicester Ford's Janice Meredith (1899.5) turns to stoney silence after hearing Edwards at Princeton on infant damnation. At a distance, John Greenleaf Whittier hears Edwards forging "the iron links of his argument" in a wilderness church (1866.2), as later in a Harvard commemorative ode Oliver Wendell Holmes thinks he hears Edwards's "iron heel" fall upon Princeton (1887.4).

The sound of the stern preacher of sin and damnation reverberates throughout early studies of American literature, though often it is muted by speculation of what Edwards might have been. Thus William Ellery Channing remarks at the beginning of the period that Edwards's mind was "lost" to literature by "vassalage to a false theology" (1830.2); at the end of the period, Walter C. Bronson regrets that so capable a writer was bound to a theology of any kind (1900.9). Edwards "might have been one of the first poets of his age," Edwards Amasa Park notes, "had he not chosen to be the first theologian" (1839.7). Even the redoubtable Moses Coit Tyler believes Edwards might have been "one of the world's masters" of imaginative literature but for his calling, or of the sciences for that matter (1878.7). He might have been "another Newton," according to Benjamin Silliman, the editor and founder of the American Journal of Science and Arts (1832.6), or a naturalist of "brilliance," according to Henry C. McCook, a noted arachnologist (1889.9 and 1890.6). That Edwards might be compared to Benjamin Franklin becomes part of the popular assessment--favorably, in

Introduction

Eugene Lawrence's <u>A Primer of American Literature</u> (1880.7), or unfavorably, in Brander Matthews's <u>An Introduction to the Study of American Literature</u> (1896.10)--and persists, with little change, well into the next century.

As persistent--and derivative--are biographical studies of Edwards during those seventy years. Both <u>The Life of President Edwards</u> (1832.1), issued by the American Sunday School Union, and Samuel Miller's "Life of Jonathan Edwards" (1837.1), part of Jared Sparks's <u>The Library of American Biography</u>, rely heavily upon Hopkins and Dwight; both are directed to the young--young readers in the first, young ministers in the second. Neither merit much attention, nor does the overly long evaluation of Edwards as "intellectual athlete" by Henry Rogers (1834.4).

Other lives, abbreviated and standard, appear with some frequency and concentrate predictably on the "tragedy" of Edwards's dismissal, citing one cause or another. James Wynne, for instance, attributes Edwards's intemperate handling of the bad-book episode to his envy of Samuel Buell's success with his young parishioners, a point, Wynne argues, avoided by the overly solicitous Hopkins and Dwight (1850.6). Joseph Clark indicts the "mischievous notion" that a Congregational church council is like an ecclesiastical court and holds it, and Edwards's participation in the Robert Breck affair, responsible for his troubles (1858.7). One commentator traces the cause of his dismissal to the opposition of neighboring churches (1867.2), another to his opposition to bundling (1892.2). And Arthur Latham Perry, closer to fact, discovers his difficulties at Northampton and at Stockbridge in the antagonism of the Williams family, a "selfish cabal" (1896.11) and the subject of a novel sometime later (1967.27).

More comprehensive, though far more questionable, views depend upon psychological or genetic analyses. In "Jonathan Edwards: A Psychological Study" (1890.3), Joseph Crooker diagnoses Edwards a "theological monomaniac," suffering from genetic "delusional insanity," obvious early in his <u>Personal Narrative</u> and continuing virulent in the unrealistic treatises of his mature years, a hopeless case. Edwards, according to Crooker, contributes "absolutely nothing" to an understanding of man in history, nature, or society. A bit more sanguine is the pseudonymous Felix Oldmixon (1895.5), who observes that a strong will and spirit checked incipient madness in Edwards only to crop up in his grandson Aaron Burr, a clinical view somewhat at odds with the diagnosis that Burr inherited Edwards's courage but not his conscience (1900.15). The most extensive study of the genetics of the matter is Albert Winship's <u>Jukes-Edwards</u> (1900.20), which concludes not unexpectedly that, aside from minor divagations, the Edwards clan represents the "midday" of eugenics. Though thirty years late, that would have come as no surprise to the hundreds gathered in Stockbridge in September of 1870 for a two-day reunion of the Edwards family, rendering tributes to its founder and congratulations to his heirs (1871.5).

As in the earlier period, the documents of the Great Awakening and Freedom of the Will command critical attention, but increasingly other works emerge and still other doctrines are examined as the question of the relationship of Edwards to the Edwardseans becomes more and more a matter of debate. Joseph Tracy's pioneer study of the Awakening (1842.6) gives Edwards and his Northampton revivals of the 1730s a central place in the larger movement of the 1740s and claims that his dismissal "disposed the pious to be on his side" here and abroad. Not everyone agreed: Charles Hodge earlier remarks Edwards's failure to check the unrestrained emotion and excitation the revival engendered, even though it pumped "new life" into the Presbyterian church (1839.5); William Henry Channing considers Edwards the true, albeit unlovely, exemplar of the revival and of the Protestant emphasis on individualism and sinfulness (1847.2). At the end of the period, Samuel Perkins Hayes details the "unstable" social and religious conditions that gave rise to the revivals, reports the theological struggle, and examines the "paradox" of Edwards, in an uncritical history appearing in the American Journal of Psychology (1902.5).

No such neutral ground exists for Freedom of the Will and, as Horace Bushnell notes, even the ground shifts in time (1858.6). Patrick Campbell MacDougall praises Edwards on the will, notwithstanding his "verbal ambiguity," and chastises Isaac Taylor and his failed case on necessity (1831.2). William Hazlitt considers Edwards's exhaustive study "one of the most closely reasoned, elaborate, acute, serious, and sensible among modern productions," comparing Joseph Priestley's Philosophical Necessity unfavorably with it (1836.1). Jeremiah Day defends Edwards twice (1831.1 and 1841.3), the second time in an elaborate analysis of his language and structure to prove that Edwards is best understood when read "as a whole." In a frequently cited letter, Thomas Chalmers remarks that there is "No book of human composition which I more strenuously recommend" than Edwards's Freedom of the Will (see 1857.4), and Thomas Huxley, no less fulsome, finds Edwards's argument "has never been equalled in power, and certainly has never been refuted" (1879.7). And in his dissertation at Leipzig, William Harder Squires, with singular and sustained conviction, relates Edwards's determinism to Schopenhauer's metaphysics of the will and Wundt's psychology of voluntarism and fixes his place in American intellectual history (1901.10).

Still, Freedom of the Will suffers at the hands of many. Henry Philip Tappan expends more than a thousand pages (1839.8, 1840.6, and 1841.4) refuting Edwards logically, psychologically, and ethically on matters of causality, consciousness, and moral agency. Albert Taylor Bledsoe's Examination (1845.2) consigns Edwards to dialectical perdition for his atheism, delusion, and imprecision--"he does not reason at all, he merely rambles." More than thirty years later, an unrelenting Bledsoe, now editor of the Southern Review, reprints his assault serially from October 1877 to the following October. Rowland Hazard exposes the "fallacies" of Edwards's argument in a 350-page addendum to his Freedom of the Mind in Willing (1864.3), and D. D. Whedon faults Edwards's "intellective conclusions" and those of his Princeton advocates in a broad-based argument on responsibility and accountability (1864.5). And George Park Fisher in his brief and incisive "The Philosophy of Jonathan Edwards" (1879.4) concludes that the "iron network" of his doctrine of necessity fails to satisfy "the generality of mankind." Less restrained critics call Freedom of the Will a "monstrous deformity," (1842.2), "pantheistic" (1860.2), a "quibble and logomachy" (1862.4). William Ellery Channing thinks it "pernicious" (1841.2) and Charles Grandison Finney an "injurious monstrosity and misnomer" (1851.2). A young Emerson—he was twenty at the time of the journal entry—is ambivalent about Freedom of the Will (see 1909.1), but an old Mark Twain is decidedly not: Edwards is a "drunken lunatic. . . . By God I was ashamed to be in such company" (see 1917.6).

No less caustic are critics of Original Sin and Edwards's doctrine of imputation: it is "revolting" to one (1858.5), "most revolting" to another (1868.5), just "strange" to a third (1872.1). Yet one writer defends Edwards against contemporary distortions (1831.1), and George Park Fisher considers his doctrine of a piece with Aquinas and Augustine (1868.2). Frank Hugh Foster examines Edwards's doctrine of the punishment of sin and its effect upon the eschatology of his disciples (1886.1), though unlike recent scholars he argues the theological rather than the social or political implications of it. In Edinburgh, James Iverach lectures on the "unspeakable importance" of True Grace in the Edwards canon, finding in it the key to all the major works and to his evangelical thought (1884.2) as will others much later (1975.5 and 1978.23). At Harvard, William James in the Varieties of Religious Experience (1902.6) contends that Edwards's empirical method in Religious Affections is the only way to know Christian virtue.

The question of Edwards's theological "improvements" and his successors proposed by his son in the latter's collected works (see 1842.3) and argued in its reviews (1843.1 and 1844.5), becomes the point of dispute over the years in the leaden, sometimes angry pages of the Bibliotheca Sacra (Andover), the Biblical Repertory (Princeton), and The New Englander (Yale) and is, perhaps, best summarized by Edwards Amasa Park of the first and Lyman H. Atwater of the second. In "New England Theology" (1852.9), Park holds that that strain of theology, by whatever name, is a natural outgrowth of Edwards's doctrines and that those doctrines are retained by Edwardseans but in a slightly altered form. In "Jonathan Edwards and the Successive Forms of the New Divinity" (1858.2), Atwater argues that, except for the doctrines of mediate imputation and true virtue, Edwards is a strict Calvinist and that there are "broad and irreconcilable differences" between him and those calling themselves his successors. Particularly divisive was the reaction to Edwards's doctrine of the atonement, in one instance fairly disdained by the Edwardseans for its imprecision (1859.5) and in another heartily endorsed by others for its orthodoxy (1860.4). Perhaps the most reliable treatment of the whole problem during the period--after it ceased to be one--is George Nye Boardman's A History of New England Theology (1899.2), which concludes that while both parties speak of God as sovereign, New England Theology celebrates the glory of man, Edwards the glory of God.

Claims of influence, or the lack of it, on Edwards's thought spread during the period, especially conjectures about the source of his idealism. In his L'Idéalisme en Angleterre (1888.2), Georges Lyon devotes a chapter to Edwards and immaterialism in America, discovering in Edwards similarities to Bishop Berkeley and positing his Yale tutor Samuel Johnson as the conduit. But, as Egbert Smyth points out, Edwards could not have known Berkeley through Johnson because Johnson first read Berkeley after he left Yale (1896.12); an examination of Edwards's shorthand notes confirms it (1902.14). John Henry MacCracken's Jonathan Edwards Idealismus (1899.6), a Halle doctoral dissertation, suggests Arthur Collier rather than Berkeley as the source, with no more real evidence than Lyon's study. Berkeley's editor, Alexander Campbell Fraser, takes an untenable middle position, claiming that Edwards "adopted" some of Berkeley though acknowledging that there is no proof that he ever read him, still less that he ever met him (1871.2, 1881.1, and 1901.5). The most balanced and convincing view, based on a careful reading of the juvenilia, is that of H. N. Gardiner in "The Early Idealism of Jonathan Edwards" (1900.12). Gardiner discounts the Berkeley evidence as "entirely internal" and defines Edwards's idealism as an "original expression of personal insight," influenced by the general direction of contemporary thought and sustained in a modified form throughout his later work.

That body of work grows with Tryon Edwards's edition of Charity and Its Fruits (1852.4), Alexander Grosart's Selections from the Unpublished Writings of Jonathan Edwards of America (1865.4), and Egbert Smyth's publication of Edwards's trinitarian views (1880.10). All are derived from manuscript sources--Grosart's was the only volume published of a projected complete Edwards so derived--and each speculates about the importance of them, a matter lent even more weight by Franklin B. Dexter's careful enumeration of the Yale holdings (1901.3) and Smyth's physical analysis of some early texts (1895.10). Sometime before, the manuscript problem erupted in a spate of suspicion and accusation about Edwards and the trinity: it was alleged that the keepers of Edwards suppressed a manuscript testifying to his heretical, unitarian views. Horace Bushnell early (1851.1) and Oliver Wendell Holmes late (1883.4) cried heterodoxy, which the published manuscripts and denials of Smyth (1880.10) and Park (1881.2) did little to still. Only with the publication of George Fisher's An Unpublished Essay of Edwards on the Trinity was the matter finally settled (see 1903.26).

Yet even without a definitive Trinity or a complete Edwards--the New York Times felt it was a patriotic necessity to publish one (1900.2)--critics in the nineteenth century began to take a studied look at Edwards's thought as a whole, seeking out connections rather than isolated clues. Gardiner's essay on Edwards's idealism (1900.12) and Fisher's analysis of his philosophy (1879.4) represent deliberate efforts to evaluate Edwards without partisan rancor or wonted praise, to steer, as Joseph Thompson remarks (1861.3), between "unquestioning veneration" and "empirical judgment." Popular assessments continue to run to form. Oliver Wendell Holmes is precious and iconoclastic in his rejection of "the unleavened bread" of Edwards (1880.6), though he seems to have tasted of it himself (1886.2); Principal Fairbairn is respectful and adulatory in his acceptance (1896.5). Occasionally, a more balanced, if still highly critical, view emerges in the general press, for example, Leslie Stephen's influential piece in Fraser's (1873.2). Stephen discovers irreconcilable tensions in Edwards between the "gentle mystic" and the "stern divine." T. F. Henderson's "contradictory qualities" echoes Stephen's observation (in the ninth edition of the Britannica, 1875.3), as does George Angier Gordon's "radical inconsistency" a quarter of a century later (1900.14). Williston Walker notes similar tensions in his extended study of Edwards as one of Ten New England Leaders (1901.14). Walker had already reserved a special place for Edwards as "the greatest theologian" of American Congregationalism (1894.5)--Baptist (1839.4), Presbyterian (1868.4), and Methodist (1885.1) claims notwithstanding--for his modifications and departures from historic Calvinism. But the later study juxtaposes Edwards's formidable intellect against his transforming vision and concludes that "this remarkable man" will be "reverenced" more for his spirit than his intellect. To F. B. Sanborn that intellect is even more suspect because derivative, and Edwards remains, for all his acuteness, "our Puritan Schoolman, our Father Jonathan of Connecticut" (1883.6),[5] the medieval mind of later critics. Even so sympathetic a reader as Adam Leroy Jones, who places Edwards in the forefront of early American philosophy (1893.5), is forced to admit that Edwards's considerable reasoning suffers from "imperfect analysis" and his prose from intellectual isolation, the "speculative recluse" of Leslie Stephen's analysis.

The only full-length study of Edwards during the period agrees. Alexander V. G. Allen's Jonathan Edwards (1889.1) characterizes Edwards's style as "thinking aloud," the speculative thought of his Stockbridge years as an exercise "in confusion, if not failure." That Allen was ill-suited theologically to deal fairly with Edwards as some reviewers claimed (1890.12, for instance), may be simply the carping reaction of the defense. Nevertheless, Allen does indict Edwards for the "great wrong" of his doctrine of divine sovereignty, for his dogged belief in original sin, for the "false premises" of his theology. As is often the case at the close of the century, the mystical Edwards is the valuable Edwards: Allen isolates his God-consciousness as the "imperishable element" in him and the saving remnant of his faith. In fact, in his tribute to Edwards on the sesquicentennial of his Northampton dismissal, Allen underscores the mystical and poetic in Edwards, remarking "the deepest affinity" between him and Dante, not Calvin.

That paper, "The Place of Edwards in History," formally opens Jonathan Edwards, A Retrospect (1901.6), a "serious attempt" by six scholars--Allen, Smyth, Gordon, Fisher, Henry T. Rose, and Gardiner--to gauge Edwards's thought and influence, to discover what in him is "temporary and accidental," what essential and permanent. To a man the very occasion of his dismissal is all but forgotten in a celebration of his gentleness, and the irreconcilable tensions Stephen noted twenty-five years earlier are all but relieved. By the turn of the century Edwards found a permanent niche in the American pantheon: on the first ballot, he was elected to the Hall of Fame, outdrawing Hawthorne by eight votes (1900.17).

III

Even so, twenty-six years would pass before the Charles Grafly bust of Edwards would be unveiled (1926.4), a time roughly matching a pause in the serious study of Edwards, a time of consolidation, and just a few years before a remarkable burst of creative scholarship about him. Though he takes on unexpected roles here and there--as a symbol for troubled times to President Roosevelt (not "a touch of the mollycoddle about him," 1916.6) or as a figure of comparison with that other Northampton celebrity, President Coolidge (1937.1)--Edwards remains for many readers, to borrow the unhappy phrase of Henry Bamford Parkes, "the fiery Puritan" (1930.10). Parkes portrays Edwards's times as those of "religious lunacy," his theology as "a blight upon posterity, . . . repulsive and absurd," and his person as "most tragic" and "not truly an American," in a biography short on insight and long on prejudice. In that, Parkes simply expands upon earlier sentiments and generally sums up the first three decades of the period: in order, a novelist scores Edwards as the "hoarsest of the whole flock of New World theological ravens" (1903.1); a freethinker villifies him as the purveyor of "the worst religion of any human being who ever lived on this continent" (1918.3); and a writer for the Forum decries his "false, harsh, and artificial" morality (1926.6). Others take Edwards's fire and his dogma somewhat differently: his great-great-grandson ranks Sinners in the Hands of an Angry God "second only" to the Sermon on the Mount in a privately printed short biography and poetic tribute (1922.2), and Gilbert Seldes in The Stammering Century (1928.8) finds his imprecations sufficient cause for the reformist cults and widespread madness of the nineteenth century.

Some few feel his fire not at all: the "real Edwards," according to I. Woodbridge Riley, is not the "sulphurous" Calvinist but the "philosopher of feeling," the typical mystic undergoing the traditional stages of the mystical experience (1908.2 and 1915.3).

That attitude, far less prominent during the first thirty years than that of Parkes, informs two of the three major addresses delivered at the Edwards bicentennial celebration held at Andover Theological Seminary in early October of 1903 (1904.14). John Winthrop Platner discounts Edwards's energetic Calvinism as chiefly necessary to his "un-theological" times and recommends Edwards's "beatific vision" to his own; Egbert C. Smyth considers "the innermost meaning and the climax" in Edwards's theology to be his "vivid sense" of the immediacy and mutuality of God's communicated love; but Frederick J. E. Woodbridge dissents. Edwards fails the early promise of his mystical pantheism and, more importantly, fails to resolve the "intellectual duality" of his philosophical speculations and his theological convictions, a point repeatedly raised by nineteenth-century critics. Edwards's influence is now "largely negligible," Woodbridge goes on, because he lacks "philosophical thoroughness," probably a result of the "unanalyzed" and disruptive emotions of his conversion experience, a new point.

The many other celebrations--far fewer, however, than the Emerson centennials earlier that year--sought less to understand Edwards than to praise him. At Stockbridge, the seven ministers of the Berkshire Conferences speak in one voice of the spirituality and righteous effect of the "modern" or the "other" Edwards (1903.17); at Berkeley, though the principal speaker notes a "deep, happy inconsistency" between Edwards's logic and his intuition, he celebrates him as a "prophet of God" (1904.10); and in Columbus, Ohio, the speaker forecasts Edwards's influence to "millennial times" (1903.35). In Utica, New York, a preacher begs for a "duplicate" Edwards to again fill the air with "Calvinistic ozone" (1903.33), while in Brooklyn, another preacher, not to be outdone, contemplates a world in which "everyone of us were a Jonathan Edwards!" (1903.28). Such single-minded rhetoric prevails at Yale, at Hartford, and at Northampton (1903.13). Only at the dedication of the Edwards memorial gateway to the South Windsor cemetery a quarter of a century later is there the familiar caveat. Charles Andrews, anticipating Perry Miller by twenty years, characterizes the story of Edwards as "less the history of a life than the analysis of a mind," a mind, Andrews adds, at war with itself, intellect against emotion, logic against mysticism (1929.7).

Woodbridge had described that conflict before in slightly different form, and so had Henry Churchill King. Edwards was both a "theistic idealist" and a "mystical ethical Calvinist," argues King, a pairing that brings about inconsistencies in his thought and almost "anti-Protestant" doctrines in his theology (1903.34).[6] No more sanguine than King are Lewis Mumford, who sees Edwards

xxv

impaled upon the horns of beauty and determinism (1926.5), and James Truslow Adams, who remarks the unavailing struggle in Edwards between the sweetness of his spirit and the pains of his doctrine (1927.1). Those contradictions, so much a part of the popular assessment of Edwards, also help define either New England Theology as a whole, according to a writer for the American Journal of Theology (1920.1), or the native philosophical tradition, according to a German writer on American thought (1928.10).

But the history of Edwards's life and times rather than an analysis of his mind, crowded with real or imagined contradictions, is the proper stuff of the period, and the definitive life, published at its close, is simply the last, best example of that predilection. An early, ninety-five-page book prizes the man at the expense of his worthless theology (1903.21); a four-page article extols the eugenics of the Edwards clan rather than his mostly unread books (1903.49)--Clarence Darrow, of course, would have neither man nor books (1925.2). An historian of Princeton doubts that Edwards would have made a successful president (1914.2); another of Yale doubts that he would have made a successful professor (1916.4). But all these are partial portraits. Only in Ola Elizabeth Winslow's definitive biography (1940.21) does Edwards the man emerge whole. Winslow explores the "inner curve of spiritual experience" to fasten on the essential Edwards--solitary and dignified, contentious, mystical leaning and ruthlessly logical, "neither Puritan nor fiery." Not an original mind, Edwards earns greatness by "initiating and directing" the Great Awakening and developing New England Theology, acts of "far reaching" consequences. Thus Winslow gathers together the facts of his life, gleaning information from the manuscripts and from a wide range of sources, early and late--from Thomas H. Johnson's first published work on Edwards describing his catalogue of books (1931.11) and from his second discovering the title of the bad book of Edwards's dismissal (1932.7), for instance. And Winslow arranges the whole of it with a fine narrative hand. But the analysis of Edwards's thought is left languishing in imprecision and in unrewarding speculation, in what is obviously an attempt to deal fully with the person and less thoroughly with his mind. In less than ten years Perry Miller's study will more than right the balance.

There was, of course, some important preliminary, even conclusive, work going on during the first thirty years of the century. Francis Albert Christie suggests that it was an Anglican rather than an Arminian threat that Edwards perceived in the 1730s (1912.3), the "myth" of Arminian-Calvinism a writer would call it a half century later (1968.12); Frank Hugh Foster defines Edwards's vital role in New England Theology in his Genetic History (1907.3), a valuable study eclipsing Boardman's earlier one (see 1899.2); and I. Woodbridge Riley usefully summarizes Edwards's development as a philosopher in sixty pages of his American Philosophy: The Early Schools (1907.6). Especially important is the full-length examination of Edwards's theology by the Dutch analyst Jan Ridderbos (1907.5). Edwards departs from the Reformed consensus both publicly and privately and, according to Ridderbos, develops a form of speculative thought at variance with "pure" Reformed theology, a point at issue from Miller on down. No less exceptional, if more eccentric, is The Edwardean, A Quarterly Devoted to the History of Thought in America (but actually devoted to Edwards) published, edited, and, as far as can be determined, written by William Harder Squires from October 1903 to July 1904. Squires's argument, derived from his Leipzig dissertation two years earlier, is that an "adequate" understanding of Edwards's philosophy can rest only on voluntaristic principles, a system of thought indigenous to America, free of European cant and "error," central to all worthwhile modern philosophers. And Squires is at pains to prove it, by shrill repetition. In a year's time the magazine ceased publication, leaving his patent clue to Edwards unexamined for almost seventy years (1972.9). These investigations aside, there remain only minor revisions of earlier attitudes, framed neatly enough by the Edwards entries in the eleventh and fourteenth editions of the Britannica: the assertion that Edwards was "the most influential religious thinker in America" (1910.4) yields in twenty years to the question of his "potent" influence and his "perpendicular piety" (1929.4).

Early, then, Edwards was broadly felt to have influenced the development of American philosophy or religious thought, for better or for worse, even by a few foreign critics (1904.16 and 1905.4). The collapse of New England Theology was attributed to his "morally incredible" view of man (1908.1), yet it was as well a "provincial" theology he lent little more than his name to (1914.6). Elements of Kant abound in Edwards (1906.2), elements of Einstein (1920.2), and of Freud (1920.6); he is likened to John Wesley (1913.3), thought "the very Doré of the pulpit" (1921.4). Josiah Royce ranks him with Emerson and William James (1911.2), Santayana with no one: he was "the greatest master in false philosophy" in America (1920.5). And three cultural historians continue the nineteenth-century habit of dividing America between Edwards and Franklin now between high-brow and low-brow (Van Wyck Brooks, 1915.1), spirituality and practicality (Carl Van Doren, 1920.7), and God and man (William Lyon Phelps, 1922.4). In his important essay in The Cambridge History of American Literature (1917.3), Paul Elmer More regrets Edwards's dogmatic theology kept him from literature; in his thoroughly wrong-headed one in Main Currents in American Thought (1927.2), Vernon Louis Parrington brands Edwards "an anachronism" but later goes on to suggest that his evangelism gave rise to democratic impulses among the people and that he was "the intellectual leader of the revolutionaries." Even earlier, in two of several studies of the Great Awakening, Edwards was singled out for his largely inadvertent help in creating "a conscious national unity" (1904.11) and "the foundation" for the separation of church and state in the emerging Republic (1905.2).'

Introduction

Except for Paul Elmer More's extended reading of Freedom of the Will in his Cambridge essay, critical remarks about Edwards's most widely debated treatise seem obligatory and redundant, and attention turns to other work to reclaim something of value. Williston Walker, the Congregational historian, believes True Virtue rather than Freedom of the Will to be the "most influential" of Edwards, especially as it affected missionary zeal (1908.3), and William Wallace Fenn, the Harvard theologian, concurs, calling it Edwards's "pre-eminent" contribution to New England thought (1925.3). But two Dutch scholars, following Ridderbos on Edwards and Reformed theology, regard True Virtue as a "thorough modification" of Calvinism and an error (1913.2 and 1928.9). And another critic, sifting the permanent from the passing in Edwards, tosses True Virtue (and a good deal more) into the dustbin of mistaken theology, and with particular insight salvages for a more responsive age Edwards's "penetrating and comprehensive" doctrine of grace (1903.50). George Park Fisher's An Unpublished Essay of Edwards on the Trinity, with Remarks on Edwards and his Theology issued the same year (1903.25) is another act of reclamation. With the quarrel about Edwards's "suppressed" essay all but over, Fisher recounts its history--as will a later observer (1959.15)--and concludes that Edwards was a theist, believing in the personality of God, and a trinitarian, teaching tripersonalism.

Little more was done during the period to establish texts--H. N. Gardiner reprints six sermons and an unpublished seventh (1904.7)--until Clarence H. Faust and Thomas H. Johnson publish their Representative Selections (1935.3), an important addition to the American Writers Series in the thirties and a signal contribution to Edwards scholarship since. Not only do they publish several letters from diverse manuscript sources and reprint selections of the best texts from the Austin, Dwight, and 1858 editions, they also spend over a hundred, closely argued pages on Edwards as man, thinker, and writer. The middle section of this introduction, by far the longest of the three sections and derived from Faust's Chicago dissertation (1935.2), deals serially with Edwards's psychological analysis of the Great Awakening, the major issues of the free-will controversy, and the coherent nature of his doctrines of sin, virtue, and grace. All of this, Faust shows, rests upon Edwards's "exalted and mystical" rendering of divine sovereignty, first experienced in conversion and later explained through logical constructs. Such rigorous forms, Johnson points out, may account for the "severe, undilated" style of the treatises, a style unlike that of the sermons, where clarity of expression and supple prose cadences make up for the want of "conscious artistry."

Representative Selections was only part of perhaps the most fruitful--certainly, the most promising--decade for Edwards studies. With the tricentennial of the Massachusetts Bay at hand and the tricentennial of Harvard hard upon it came a renewed, if more temperate, interest in Puritanism that led inevitably to

Edwards as its intellectual exemplar. In 1932, Rufus Suter wrote
"The Philosophy of Jonathan Edwards," the first dissertation at
Harvard on Edwards.[8] Like others before him, Suter found Edwards
torn between the opposing forces of his Calvinism and his
Neoplatonism and concluded that the unresolved conflict created in
Edwards a "deadlock." Shortly afterwards, Suter published two
papers about Edwards--one about his ethics and aesthetics in the
Journal of Religion (1934.8) and another about the problem of evil
in Monist (1934.9)--and he continued publishing about Edwards well
into the sixties (see 1961.14 and 1967.28). Less than a year before
Suter's dissertation, Harvey Gates Townsend, who was to spend a
lifetime editing and explaining Edwards, addressed the Seventh
International Congress on Philosophy on an alogical element in
Edwards's epistemology and metaphysics, calling the theory thus
engendered "unique in our history" (1931.16). And in the same
year of Suter's dissertation, Arthur Cushman McGiffert, Jr.,
published a sympathetic study of Edwards for Harper's Creative
Lives Series (1932.10).

To McGiffert, Edwards is a "philosophically minded" scholar
rather than a practical minister, a thinker relentlessly curious
about the vexing problems of his day. Edwards begins with a
theologically sovereign God but through mysticism moves on to
pantheism and from it to personalism, all "with no apparent jolt,"
all of it standard fare. McGiffert favors Edwards's early
work--Religious Affections, especially--rather than the "static"
thought of his late years and believes him to be an early example
of "modern-mindedness." Finding Edwards more American than modern,
H. Richard Niebuhr discovers less change than McGiffert in his
doctrine of divine sovereignty--Niebuhr calls it the "explicit
foundation" of Edwards's thought (and his own)--and places it at
the heart of his conversion experience, his imprecatory sermons,
his evangelical ardor, and his millennial hope, at the heart, in
short, of "the kingdom of God in America" (1937.7). Although
Herbert W. Schneider in his The Puritan Mind (1930.13) also locates
the source of Edwards's thought in his doctrine of divine
sovereignty, he does not take it and its millennial consequence as
integral to a native American tradition as Niebuhr does. On the
contrary, Schneider considers Edwards's love of God an "individual
analogue" of an earlier theocracy, devoid of public and social
concerns, far "too sentimental and pathological" to be of much use
in his America or ours. The following year brings three exceptions:
Henry Seidel Canby includes Edwards among his "classic Americans,"
a symbol of intellectuality and the first of a long line of native
"strenuous uplifters" (1931.4); Frederic Carpenter explains
Edwards's "radicalism," founded upon his deep-grained mysticism, and
draws parallels to later American writers (1931.5); and Francis
Albert Christie enshrines our "first great philosophic intelligence"
in the Dictionary of American Biography (1931.7).[9]

For all of Christie's praise and Riley's early analysis there remains the nineteenth-century reluctance to acknowledge Edwards as a philosopher. His high tribute aside--"the first and perhaps greatest philosophical thinker in America"--Harvey Gates Townsend's chapter on Edwards in his Philosophical Ideas in the United States (1934.10) is a useful counter to that attitude. Townsend considers Edwards an ethical aesthetic indebted to the Cambridge Platonists--Clarence Gohdes had earlier thoroughly examined that source of his idealism (1930.6)--and encompassed by a belief that men love God because He is beautiful, a perception that will gain full expression a generation later (see 1968.8). Still, the editors of Philosophy in America from the Puritans to James (1939.1), though they include Edwards, consider him a working theologian for whom philosophy was a "spendthrift luxury" or merely a means to solve theological puzzles. Of course, historians of religion had no difficulty with such semantic dilemmas: Edwards was a theologian. He may lack a fully developed social gospel (1940.2); he may be more separatist than Calvinist (1930.7); but he is clearly a theologian of significance, especially to the American experience--for Jacob Meyer (1930.9) and for William Warren Sweet (1930.14 and 1937.8), if not to the same extent for Lawrence Brynestad (1930.2). It is precisely as an influential theologian that Joseph Haroutunian treats Edwards in the standard interpretation of New England Theology, Piety versus Morality (1932.5), a study supplementing Foster (1907.3). Haroutunian traces the degradation of Edwardsean thought to the shift from Edwards's theology of "empirical piety" to the social morality of the Edwardseans as they responded to the ameliorating forces of social and political change in mid-century. Edwards was, as the title of an essay by Haroutunian had earlier described him, "a study in godliness," a type of theocentric Calvinist of "comprehensiveness, cogency, and profundity" (1931.10).

Other readings of Edwards gain a hearing now. Canby had dubbed Edwards a "born man of letters," an observation Thomas H. Johnson would explore in his doctoral dissertation (1934.4)--the second at Harvard in as many years--and the results of which he would add to Representative Selections. In another reading, Clarence Faust notes a "definitely theological tinge" to Edwards's scientific investigations and questions the legitimacy and spirit of such inquiries, in an essay in the first volume of American Literature (1930.4). That the new science doubtlessly affected Edwards's theology rather than the other way around is the point of three studies at the close of the period. In the first, Theodore Hornberger attributes Edwards's use of science to his desire to save God from seventeenth-century scientific materialists, saturating all but his evangelical work (1937.4); in the second, James Tufts traces the influence of Newton's Principia and Opticks upon Edwards's idealistic and relational designs of nature and suggests that he "went beyond" Newton in uniting a world of atoms and a world of ideas in the Idea and Will of God (1940.20); and in the third, Townsend demonstrates Edwards's continuing, mature interest

in natural science by making available for the first time the index
and some items in Images or Shadows (1940.19). In yet another
reading, two doctoral candidates examine Edward's sermons, one at
Iowa for his oratorical technique (1936.8), the other at Hartford
for his doctrine of saving grace (1937.5). But of immediate
significance to the growing cadre of Edwards students was the
publication of bibliographical materials during the decade.

Compared to earlier listings of between twenty-five (1905.5) and
seventy items (1902.10), the Edwards bibliography by John J. Coss
for The Cambridge History of American Literature (1917.1) of over
150 items of biography and criticism and a compilation of the locations
and holdings of manuscripts represents a qualitatively important increase. But in 1934, the Library of Congress issued a twenty-nine-
page typescript listing more than 400 Edwards items found in its main
reading room and including accession numbers (1934.11). In 1935,
as part of their Representative Selections, Faust and Johnson
appended an annotated bibliography of over a hundred Edwards items,
adding a short list of primary sources and a longer one of background
materials. (That valuable compilation was made even more so by
Stephen S. Weber's addition of another fifty items to the section
on biography and criticism for the paperback reissue twenty-seven
years later, 1962.2). And in 1940, in addition to Winslow's
extensive manuscript listing in her biography, Johnson published
The Printed Writings of Jonathan Edwards 1703 – 1758: A Bibliography
(1940.7), a descriptive bibliography of 346 numbered items
instrumental for estimating Edwards's reputation and popularity.
Just calculating the number of editions produced in Great Britain
and translated on the continent during the eighteen th century
reveals, among other things, that Edwards was "possibly better
known abroad than at home."

In December of 1940 Perry Miller published his first essay on
Edwards. He had, of course, studied Edwards in preparation for
his extraordinary analysis of American intellectual history in 1939:
Edwards's theology was "the supreme achievement of the New England
mind," he remarked then (1939.5); more Calvinist than covenantal
theologian, he had said in passing a few years earlier (1935.6).
But only in "From Edwards to Emerson" (1940.9) did he concentrate
on Edwards's particular vision, plotting the continuities between
his "implicit" pantheism and mysticism and Emerson's
transcendentalism. In time, Miller would concentrate on Edwards
even more, so that the eighteenth-century philosopher-theologian
came to dominate the twentieth-century intellectual historian.
And, in time, Miller's labors in behalf of Edwards came to dominate
the labors of others.

IV

One field Perry Miller barely worked during that very

productive season between 1941 and 1964 was biography, believing
perhaps that Ola Elizabeth Winslow's life of Edwards was fairly
well planted (1940.10). Except for some few scattered remarks,
scholars apparently agreed. There was, of course, the system of
countless references to Edwards in Clifford K. Shipton's
continuation of Sibley's Harvard Graduates (1942.9) and Roland H.
Bainton's account of Edwards's college days in Yale and the Ministry
(1957.1). Pages in the life studies of those Edwards knew at Yale
and elsewhere link him to David Brainerd (1950.5), the Williamses
(1954.16), Thomas Clap (1962.17), and Ezra Stiles (1962.8). There was
a fifty-page "Memoir" to a selection of his work that uses the standard biographical facts (1958.16); a 160-page novel, Consider My
Servant (1957.5), that takes "some liberty" with many of those facts;
and a ninety-five-page satire that prefers "ghostly" interviews to
any facts whatsoever (1959.2). There were some few public
honors--Princeton with showcases of Edwards memorabilia (1953.1)
and Yale at the college named after him (1953.2) celebrate his
birth, and H. Richard Niebuhr preaches in Northampton on the
bicentennial of his death (1958.3)--but they are pallid memorials
of turn-of-the-century tributes. Others celebrated the
bicentennial of Humble Attempt (1948.3), an early instance of
ecumenism, according to one (1958.5). Ernest A. Payne notes
Edwards's influence on the London missionary movement (1941.10),
and many more write of his influence upon revivalism: it is the
subject of articles in Congregational (1943.8), Presbyterian
(1961.9), and Baptist (1963.5) quarterlies; its lasting effects
are seen in England (1956.2), Scotland (1944.2), and Wales
(1960.18); and its adverse effects on William Ellery Channing
(1952.6) and Charles Grandison Finney (1960.12). Indeed, the life
of Edwards during this period is largely defined by his role in the
revivals, part of a general reappraisal of the Great Awakening then
underway, but readers are cautioned about whether he was the first
of revivalists.

   That accolade belongs to Theodorus Frelinghuysen and pietism,
not Edwards and Calvinism, according to the religious historian
William Warren Sweet, though Edwards forged the Northampton
revivals and, through Religious Affections, the theological and
intellectual basis for later ones (1942.10 and 1944.4). There was
"a continuity" between the revivals of 1734 and 1741, argues Edwin
S. Gaustad (1954.8), through the action of Edwards's personal piety
upon the theological defenses of indwelling grace and public emotion,
a view Gaustad elaborates later, especially as it touches the
Edwards-Chauncy dispute (1957.6). To the old argument that through
the Awakening Edwards unwittingly fostered religious liberty
though he "cared little" for politics, as Anson Phelps Stokes
repeats it (1950.18), or that Edwards may have been the
intellectual leader of the Awakening but "not really of it," as
Max Savelle puts it (1948.10), Perry Miller had a ready answer in
"Jonathan Edwards' Sociology of the Great Awakening" (1948.8).
Discovering hints of a social theory in three unpublished sermons

probably composed between 1734 and 1741, Miller maintains that
saving grace for Edwards operates within a social context as well as
a personal or psychological one. Sometime later Miller contributed
an essay to America in Crisis (1952.4) broadening the thesis.
Edwards was not only a "formulator" of political and social theories
of governance, he was also the ministerial embodiment of them. His
endorsement of experiential religion and of the need for pastoral
accommodation, Miller insists, paved the way for leaders responsive
to the public welfare and the perceived threats to it. For Miller
and for others after him, Edwards and the Awakening and the
Revolution were fully joined.

Science and Edwards, far more thoroughly documented in the
thirties than his role in the Awakening, is again looked into
during the forties and after. A natural history bulletin of the
State of Connecticut cites Edwards as the first recorder of
ballooning spiders in America (1948.6); in Scientific Monthly,
Rufus Suter cites his geometric method of inquiry and his deductive
or contradictive method of proof and mourns an "American Pascal"
lost to science (1949.15). One observer regrets that Edwards's
atomic theories of steric hindrance gave way to a "sterile"
theology (1961.5); at much the same time, another reader finds that
Edwards grasped and used the fundamental implications of science
throughout his theology (1961.13). One historian remarks the
coincidence of Edwards's explanation of lightning and Franklin's
(1941.2), a matter apparently explained when another historian
uncovers a source common to both (1950.2). But Franklin enters
more importantly as one of two "archsymbols," as Miller calls them
in the New England Mind (1953.10). who divide American culture
between them, though sometimes a third--John Woolman (1948.2) or
Thomas Jefferson (1955.9)--is added to muddle things. It is Miller
again, now in an introductory essay to selections of Edwards and
Franklin in Major Writers of America (1962.7), who comprehends these
"pre-eminently eloquent linked antagonists" in their mutual
disinterestedness and who plumbs the "basic and sundering theme"
of our literature and our intellectual heritage manifest in the
"irreconcilable" division between Edwards and Franklin. A year
later, David Levin reprints selections from both writers to
illustrate The Puritan in the Enlightenment, but there is none of
that disdain implicit in earlier pairings: here they simply share
the world (1963.14).

Other familiar activities go on. Critics again try those
tensions basic to earlier analyses, but they do it much less
frequently now and with little of that characteristic agonizing. A
British writer on American Protestantism points out the "unusual"
blend of mysticism and logic in Edwards, thinks him a "Calvinist
romanticist," and recalls his figure in the stained glass chapel
window at Mansfield College, Oxford (1949.4). Edwards's idealism,
at one time a crucial problem for critics, reduces itself to a
slight, comparative issue in Floyd Stovall's American Idealism

(1943.9), or, a bit more fully, to the standard American pattern
of Locke and Newton before the "more sophisticated" German theories
of the nineteenth century in Joseph Blau's Men and Movements in
American Philosophy (1952.2). Only in Harvey Gates Townsend's
questionable claim for unity and coherence in the juvenilia and
selected Miscellanies included in his The Philosophy of Jonathan
Edwards from his Private Notebooks (1955.10) does a substantial
argument rest upon Edwards's "radical" idealism. A better argument
could be made that it is immaterialism rather than idealism that
connects the juvenilia to later refinements in Edwards's mature
work, as Wallace E. Anderson does (1964.2).

About divine sovereignty, there is no such argument, even if
reasons differ. It explains everything: for Joseph Haroutunian,
theocentricism is the "clue" to Edwards, founded upon the
distinction between creator and created and manifest in his
aesthetic view of man (1944.1); for Ralph Barton Perry, it is his
one expression of "authentic" Puritan piety harmonizing the whole of
creation (1944.3); for Herbert W. Schneider, it is his "master
passion," enlisting empiricist and Platonic notions in its service
(1946.5); for Carl J. C. Wolf, its fusion with experimental religion
is one of the "true secrets" of revivalism (1958.29); for Henry
Stob, it is his "determinative intellectual conviction," the very
source of his ethics (1964.24); for H. Richard Niebuhr, according
to his eulogist, Edwards's theocentricism is the sometime "key" to
his own (1963.2; see also 1971.27). But the other side of
Edwards's theocentricism has to do with covenantal relations, a
point Miller had raised--and later despaired of--in "The Marrow of
Puritan Divinity" (1935.6 and 1956.8) and which he addressed again
in an essay about Solomon Stoddard (1941.7). The old man, Miller
claims, "freed" his grandson from covenant theology and taught him
revivalism, but he continued as a spectral presence in Northampton,
inhibiting the younger man and finally overtaking him. No so,
Thomas A. Schafer says: Edwards was far more independent of
Stoddard than that, even though he seems to follow the "general
outlines" of his grandfather's evangelical theology. Edwards's
conversion experience, Schafer notes, differs markedly from the
Stoddard pattern, and his major work is an attempt to resolve the
dichotomy inherent in Stoddard's formula of "preparation by man and
conversion by God" (1963.19). Earlier, Peter Y. DeJong laid the
"final eradication" of the covenant idea in New England, if not
the end of the traditional church itself, to Edwards's attack on
qualifications (1945.1); C. C. Goen called his insistence upon
parental profession "a curious blindness to history" (1962.3).
Still, Edwards's sense of the visible church as "the means" to
God's society is, for Schafer, integral to the rest of his thought,
especially in his fusion of the covenant of grace and the covenant
of redemption (1955.7)--a particularly sound defense.

There are a few desultory remarks about Edwards on original sin
and imputation at this time (1955.5 and 1957.13) and a fine piece

by Schafer on the ambiguity of justification by faith in his thought
(1951.17). True Virtue revives the old polarities--it is "pious
blasphemy" (1942.6) or an "important" contribution to American
theology (1960.13)--as well as more serious inquiries. A. O.
Aldridge details William Godwin's debt to Edwards (1947.1) and,
turnabout, Edwards's debt to Francis Hutcheson (1951.2). H.
Richard Niebuhr and Waldo Beach, editors of Christian Ethics
(1955.3), contend that Edwards's "primary" concern was ethical, that
he agrees and disagrees with both realistic and idealistic
formulations of historical Christian ethics in a radical way.
(Niebuhr would later number True Virtue fourth among ten books that
shaped his life, 1962.12.) Rufus Suter argues that the stark sense
of reality in Edwards's ethics renders his universe "strange" to
contemporary liberal theologians (1961.14); William K. Frankena, in
his introduction to the University of Michigan edition of the text,
believes it is just that sense in Edwards that appeals to
contemporary moral philosophers (1960.4).

Freedom of the Will undergoes a similar transformation. There
are still the certain cries of outrage (1942.3), though they are
heard less often now, and there are still the expected notes about
influences and sources--on Nathaniel Taylor (1942.7), in William
Ames (1959.14)--but there are more revealing studies too. Conrad
Wright in the Harvard Theological Review traces the "tangle of
verbal misunderstandings" between Edwards and the Arminians to
their similar analyses of mind (1942.13); Harvey Gates Townsend
in Church History characterizes Edwards's struggle over the will and
the understanding as "perennial" and his resolution in terms of
natural law and natural order as "realistic and objective" (1947.6);
W. P. Jeanes in the Scottish Journal of Theology discriminates
between the conviction of man in the Edwards moral system and the
sentiment of man in the Arminian one (1961.7); and three readers in
the Review of Metaphysics debate limited and unlimited determinism
in Edwards (1962.9, 1962.13, and 1962.15). In his History of
American Psychology, A. A. Roback discovers "psychoanalytical
adumbrations" in Edwards as he follows the labyrinth of comment on
Freedom of the Will in the nineteenth century (1952.8). The most
elaborate analysis of all, however, was a 128-page introduction to
a new edition of the text.

In 1957, Yale University Press published the first volume of
what has become the definitive Edwards (then under the general
editorship of Perry Miller), Paul Ramsey's painstaking edition of
Freedom of the Will (1957.14). In his prefatory essay, Ramsey
traces in grave detail its provenance; the theological issues; the
still-unresolved philosophical arguments; Edwards's "actual" debt
to Locke and the major points of his antagonists, matters given
"insufficient attention" in the past; and the effective and
eloquent style of his refutation. But Arthur E. Murphy questions
Ramsey's premises. In an important twenty-page commentary in
Philosophical Review (1959.13), Murphy claims that Ramsey confounds

Edwards by confusing voluntary action with the act of volition and
that Edwards confounds himself by confusing "the language of mental
causation with that of moral appraisal and justification." Still,
Ramsey's thorough knowledge of the problems and his skillful editing
of the text makes it a work of inestimable value and a model for
succeeding volumes. Two years later the Yale Religious Affections
appeared with an eighty-three-page introduction by John E. Smith
(1959.18). No less precise in his historical and textual analysis than
Ramsey, Smith provides as well commentary on the place of the affections in contemporary religious practice and on the "remarkable literary power" of the work, useful to a text that will become increasingly
important in later evangelical estimates of Edwards. Religious
Affections, Smith claims, restored religion to life, understanding
to experience, order to piety, and, through its methodology,
vitality to American Protestantism. That is high praise indeed (and
perhaps excessive) for a text that, as Clyde A. Holbrook points out,
was Edwards's "most discouraging and thankless job" (1960.9).

Other texts were produced, or rather built, during the period:
Townsend's The Philosophy or Jonathan Edwards from his Private
Notebooks, already noted; James A. Stewart's Jonathan Edwards: The
Narrative, an edition of Faithful Narrative interspersed with scraps
of biography, the Great Awakening, and conversion testimonies
(1957.17); Ralph G. Turnbull's Devotions of Jonathan Edwards,
select passages for weekly devotions (1959.20); and Leon Howard's
"The Mind" of Jonathan Edwards: A Reconstructed Text (1963.13), a
major contribution. Howard not only proves Edwards's early
commitment to philosophical idealism and logical determinism, to
conversion and Calvinism, but he also shows the "developing pattern"
in Edwards of a mind that balances the power of logic and the
power of emotion. Earlier Perry Miller had reprinted Observation
No. 782 from the Miscellanies on the sense of the heart as evidence
for his convincing and influential article on the relationship of
spiritual knowledge and "radical" empiricism in Edwards (1948.8).
Miller proposed that the sense of the heart, rooted in sensation
and distinct from the understanding, is "a sensuous apprehension of
the total situation" and makes possible for Edwards eternal
salvation "in the midst of time." Two years later in another
important essay, "Edwards, Locke, and the Rhetoric of Sensation,"
Miller pushed Edwards's psychology of sensation further still
(1950.13). Edwards was a "revolutionary artist," Miller asserted,
for accepting Locke's theory of language and then going beyond it.
To Edwards, an idea was "a unit of experience" sensibly apprehended,
and grace was a new simple idea learned "only from experience" and
realized in rhetoric. (This essay and four others touching Edwards
are reprinted in Errand into the Wilderness, 1956.8.) Of even
greater significance for future scholarship than these was the
publication about the same time of Miller's edition of Images or
Shadows of Divine Things, a text of 212 entries of types and tropes
(transcribed from manuscript), and his forty-one-page introduction to
it (1948.7). Edwards's typological use of nature is "a revolution in

sensibility," Miller insists, profound in its implications because it accommodated, as earlier typologists could not, the world of Newton and the world of Locke. Thus Edwards sought a coherence of nature, Scripture, history, and mind, a revelation of the divine intention in the things of this world.

Miller's large claim for Edwards, nay-sayers aside--I. A. Richards, for example, indicts Miller, Edwards, and typology for underwriting a "self-destructive" form of metaphor (1949.12)--, grows larger still in the work of others. In Symbolism and American Literature, Charles Feidelson calls Edwards a "philosophical symbolist," exploiting nature and anticipating Emerson (1953.5); in The Shaping of American Religion, Daniel D. Williams detects in Edwards's typology the "interplay of challenge and adjustment," the very mode of experience in America (1961.16); and in the Journal of the History of Ideas, Edward H. Davidson considers Edwards "the first native American symbolist," tracing his debt to Locke's "Of Words" and examining his distinctive theory of language (1963.7), as Miller had earlier suggested. With Ursula Brumm's Die Religiose Typologie in Amerikanischen Denken (1963.4, translated 1970.2), Edwards's types take a decidedly different turn. Brumm emphasizes the typological connection Edwards makes between his evangelism and his eschatology; he converts types to symbols in a program of hope for the kingdom of God in America, expectation and then fulfillment.

Some years before, Miller had remarked in "The End of the World" that the "hidden point" of History of Redemption was Edwards's placing of the millennium before the apocalypse, making possible the fulfillment of the Christian hope in America before its destruction (1951.12). There had been some mention of Edwards's History five years earlier--see L. E. Froom's The Prophetic Faith of Our Fathers for Edwards's dating of the Antichrist (1946.2)--but speculation about his eschatology begins with Miller in this period and continues into the next. It is a salient feature of Peter Kawerau's seventy-four-page treatment of Edwards and missions in his Amerika und die Orientalischen Kirchen (1958.13) and a contentious one in James P. Martin's briefer appraisal in The Last Judgment in Protestant Theology from Orthodoxy to Ritschl (1963.15). For Martin, it is Edwards's New Testament Biblicism rather than Miller's Locke and Newton that explains his eschatology. The fullest explanation for the time, however, is C. C. Goen's "Jonathan Edwards: A New Departure in Eschatology" (1959.5), and it follows Miller. Edwards's theory that a golden age would precede the coming of Christ is "a radical innovation," according to Goen, and a real departure from commonly held Protestant thought. He was, Goen claims, America's "first major post-millennial thinker," and he provides a religious context to manifest destiny and radical utopianism--questionable assertions, as it later turns out (1977.8 and 1977.17).

There are a few other new departures, a good many returns, and some that seem to partake of both. Pride, according to one reader, is the key to Edwards's thought and action (1949.13); his doctrine of the will is the "mainspring" of Emily Dickinson's creative activity, according to another (1961.15). In The American Adam, R. W. B. Lewis compares Edwards to the elder Henry James and Horace Bushnell, assigning the three to a third party between the party of hope and the party of memory (1955.5); Clyde A. Holbrook divides detractors of Edwards into two parties, those who think him an "evil force" and those who think him a "tragic figure," in a rapid survey of 200 years of Edwards criticism (1953.8); and William S. Morris, as a party of one, points to the first volume of the Yale Edwards as the "first evident sign" of a reappraisal of Edwards, in an even shorter survey (1957.12).[10] There are many more returns to earlier views. Edwards is still America's "first" philosopher (1952.7) and its "greatest," except for two or three others (1959.1); he is a saint to Austin Warren (1956.13), again to Randall Stewart (1958.23), and a tragedy to Chard Powers Smith (1954.13); he is still "thoroughly" Calvinistic, even if his successors are not (1957.7). And there are returns to familiar territory but with a difference. Edwards's style, the focus of so much apology early in the nineteenth century and of wishful thinking at its end, again becomes the subject of inquiry. Although Johnson had dealt with Edwards's style in Representative Selections, it was Edwin H. Cady in "The Artistry of Jonathan Edwards" who helped determine the shape of later studies (1949.1). By isolating a particular work (or genre)--Sinners in the Hands of an Angry God in this instance--Cady was able to demonstrate that Edwards achieves an "organic oneness" wherein thought and experience and language (homely images and kinesthetic ones) blend to move audiences--the "objective correlative" of T. S. Eliot. So Robert F. Sayre isolates Personal Narrative and finds a new form of autobiography there (1964.21); and Edward H. Davidson isolates sentences of Edwards and Emerson to examine a new metaethics (1964.9). In other studies, Ralph G. Turnbull locates the source for Edwards style in William Perkins and the English Puritans (1958.24), and Paul R. Baumgartner questions the view that Edwards, and Puritan writers generally, used rhetorical devices reluctantly (1963.3). Taking new and old together, there are several worthwhile summary statements: Thomas H. Johnson's in Literary History of the United States (1948.5) on literary continuities; Virgilius Ferm's in his edition of selections, Puritan Sage (1953.6), on his life; Sydney E. Ahlstrom in The Shaping of American Religion (1961.1) on his theology; and Loren Baritz in City on a Hill (1964.3), the most extensive of the four, on his effect on American culture and intellectual history.

At the beginning of the period, Max Otto feared that the attention lavished on Edwards in the thirties augured a general return to religious conservatism (1941.8); near the end of the period, a religious conservative believed it had come to pass (1957.2). Of course, nothing of the kind occurred, or rather the

renascence of Edwards had nothing to do with it if it did.   There
were still those who would cite Sinners in the Hands of an Angry God
and little else: a sociologist who saw Edwards as the "scourger of
the wicked" (1964.4), a poet who saw his God as "the Holy Terror"
(1960.11), clinicians who diagnosed him a "spiritual quack"
(1950.6) or a Stalinist brain-washer (1957.15).   There were others
who would cite only his evangelical sermons--for their "pure gold"
of Scripture (1952.13), for the minister who "really means business"
(1957.4)--and publish thirty-five "choice" sermon outlines to
celebrate the bicentennial of his death (1958.19).   And there was
Ralph G. Turnbull's Jonathan Edwards The Preacher (1958.25), a
sometime analysis of over 1100 mansucript sermons classified by
type--dogmatic, imprecatory, evangelistic, ethical, memorial,
vocational, and pastoral--and recommended to ministers and
seminarians as the work of an "evangelical mystic."   Turnbull says,
cryptically, that "whereas Edwards was a staunch Calvinist on his
knees, he was like an Arminianist on his feet."   Two years later,
John N. Gerstner published the most extended investigation of
Edwards's evangelism from a pastoral point of view, Steps to
Salvation (1960.5).   Limited both in scope and value--Edwards is a
"both/and" theologian who preaches "insistently and repeatedly" the
evangelical message of "seeking"--Gerstner's book is but another
indication of the considerable hold Edwards has on evangelical
America.

Yet though he remains very much alive in that tradition even
now--an academic theologian narrates three personal encounters with
Edwards (1978.17)--the published work on Edwards continues to belong
more to the study than to the pulpit.   Nothing dramatizes that more
than the direction taken by the six books devoted exclusively to
Edwards (the earlier noted novel and satire excepted).   Of them,
two are evangelical and paradigmatic--Turnbull and Gerstner--the
other four are theological or philosophical and thematic.   Arthur
Bamford Crabtree's sixty-four-page thoughtful examination, Jonathan
Edwards' View of Man: A Study in Eighteenth-Century Calvinism
(1948.1), was published by the Religious Educational Press in
England a year before Perry Miller's study.   In it Crabtree delves
into Edwards's ideas of sovereignty, satisfaction, and grace and
concludes that he fails to solve the problem of human responsibility
in a determined universe.   Though Edwards proves that inability to
do evil and human responsibility are compatible, Crabtree stresses,
he does not prove the more important proposition that inability to
do good and human responsibility are compatible.

Perry Miller's Jonathan Edwards (1949.9) in the American Men of
Letters series is the longest of the studies (363 pages); the most
provocative--Edwards is "the most modern man of his age," a
philosopher "infinitely more" than a theologian, a "major" artist;
and the most novel (the history of Edwards's mind is interleaved with
the facts of his life).   Edwards becomes for Miller representative
man, generalizing his experience into "the meaning of America,"

borrowing from and going beyond Newton and Locke, and finally, late in life, discovering that the central problem was history, that God's infinite judgment was renewed moment by moment and realized in beauty. That Miller overstated some facets of Edwards (his modernity, for instance) and neglected others (his Christianity, for instance) some readers were quick to point out. The best of that distressed (and often vituperative) lot are Vincent Tomas in "The Modernity of Jonathan Edwards" (1952.12)--he "takes orders" from Scripture--and Peter Gay in Loss of Mastery (1966.14)--"Far from being the first modern American, . . . he was the last medieval American--at least among intellectuals." Still Miller's book was then, and remains now, the best single statement of the quality of Edwards's mind and the drama of his ideas. And just as Edwards became a "center of consciousness" for Miller, as Alan Heimert put it (1964.12), so Miller became a center of consciousness for others.

Though half its length, neither as extravagent nor yet sympathetic, Alfred Owen Aldridge's Jonathan Edwards (1964.1) in the Great American Thinkers series is the only other study to approach Miller's. Aldridge begins where Miller does, but he stays put: for Aldridge, the eighteenth century explains Edwards, his success and his failure, his rigid Calvinism and the logic in its service, his inability to tailor his thought to common experience. Reason, for Edwards, became an instrument to reveal that reason itself was inadequate to moral truth or inferior to it. But for books of specialist concern or thematic nicety later on, Aldridge's study remains a fair complement to Miller's, intelligent and readable. The last of the book-length studies, unlike Aldridge's, is both sympathetic and questionable. Douglas J. Elwood's The Philosophical Theology of Jonathan Edwards (1960.3) correlates Edwards's theology to his philosophy in a synthesis of theism and pantheism, a "third way" through the "mutual immanence" of God that is panentheism or "mystical realism." Edwards's mysticism, according to Elwood, is an "extension" of his Puritan piety in the "continuous sacrament" of history; his doctrine of divine immediacy is a product of "his own direct experience" and important to contemporary theologians. That much of this begs examination is clear and forthcoming. Robert C. Whittemore carefully explains that Edwards is a Christian Neoplatonist, a "classical" theist, and a theologian of the sixth way--God is real and the universe is God's image or shadow--and goes on to characterize him as "an important philosopher" as well as "an anachronism" (1966.35).

While these books indicate the direction of Edwards scholarship, they cannot suggest its volume; other work may. From 1904 to 1938, doctoral candidates in America wrote seventeen dissertations concerning Edwards; from 1943 to 1964 they wrote thirty-nine.[11] Put another way, during the earlier period, a dissertation on Edwards was written once every two years; during the later period, a dissertation was written once every six months. Early, they were written chiefly at Boston, Temple, Yale, Chicago, and Harvard;

later, word spreads: though Yale and Chicago each turn out five
dissertations, Harvard four, Temple three, and Boston one, they are
joined by Illinois with three, and Brown, Duke, Minnesota, and
Southern California with two each. Significantly, the number of
academic degrees exceeds the number of seminary degrees, perhaps
thirty-two to seven, or by a ratio of more than four to one. Beyond
the figures lies an impressive range of subjects (taken at random):
Edwards's views on the atonement (1945.6), redemption (1949.5), the
trinity (1962.14), and election (1963.23); his anthropology
(1952.1) and his ontology (1951.16), his Calvinism (1950.1) and
Neoplatonism (1963.22), mysticism (1947.2) and idealism (1961.2);
his ethical theory (1945.2) and his theory of the will (1948.4).
Some few are published as books, more are squeezed into journals,
others bear silent witness to an extraordinary outpouring of
interest in Edwards. Over the next several years, the number and
the range of dissertations would testify to an interest even
greater.

V

From 1965 to 1978 doctoral candidates in America wrote
seventy-two dissertations concerning Edwards. Compared to the
preceding period, that is almost twice as many in about two-thirds
the time, or five dissertations a year on average rather than two.
Forty American institutions sponsored that work, twice as many as
before. Six foreign institutions joined them: Göttingen,
Pontifical Gregorian, Munich, McGill, Amsterdam, and St. Michaels.
A good handful are clearly the work of seminarians; the rest come
from a variety of disciplines, reflecting something of the breadth
of interest. Again, at random, studies include Edwards on faith
(1965.4) and Christ (1968.33), on glory (1965.14) and grace
(1973.40); his typology (1967.20) and his teleology (1969.15);
his social theories (1968.21), his educational (1973.25) and
psychological ones (1974.5); studies of continuities in the
Edwardseans (1972.25) and in Emerson (1976.33), comparisons with
Chauncy (1966.16) and with Stoddard (1970.39); and, following
earlier investigations, studies of his rhetoric (1967.7), his
literary techniques (1971.18), his symbolic system (1972.41), and
his style (1973.11). No fewer than eleven dissertations have to do
with Edwards's millennialism and its consequences, an earnest of
future publication.

Thus each of the decades since 1940 has seen almost a doubling
of the number of dissertations on Edwards over the previous one.
As much as that may be a stark reminder of the growth of doctorates
in the last generation, it speaks as well to the general tendency
and redirection of Puritan scholarship--more particularly, here, of
Edwards scholarship--over that time. And if there would be
something new and challenging in all this, there was as well the
comfort of old arguments, probably no better realized than in the

timely chore of ferreting out sources and influences. There was
the inevitable study of the "antithetical figures" of Edwards and
Franklin--apparently only one and that quite derivative, published
abroad (1967.21)--and a veritable Homeric catalogue of relationships: Edwards and the abolitionist John Brown (1970.28), the
determinist Thomas Chalmers (1971.25), the empiricist John Dewey
(1975.12), the voluntaryist Timothy Dwight (1971.30), the
evangelist Charles Grandison Finney (1969.19), the immaterialist
Samuel Johnson (1971.7), the radical monotheist H. Richard Niebuhr
(1976.41), the consistent Calvinist Edwards Amasa Park (1974.6),
and the founding Methodist John Wesley (1966.26). Edwards's habit
of mind is likened to Emily Dickinsons's "New Englandly" way of
seeing (1966.15), his orthodoxy to Emerson's (1968.32), his
"spiritual tension" and tone to Hawthorne's (1973.22 and 1976.18),
his determinism to Melville's "Bartleby" (1969.28 and 1976.19), his
"emblematic reading" of nature to Poe's (1972.35), his visionary
temper to Whitman's (1976.2), his public profession to Mailer's
(1978.2). Edwards exercised a "preponderant and perplexing"
influence over Robert Lowell for three decades (1974.13) and
fascinated Jorge Borges (1972.6); his sensationalist psychology
and rhetoric recalls Mrs. Rowlandson's A Narrative of the Captivity
(1973.31) and his account of his conversion recalls Adam's in
Paradise Lost, Book X (1969.34). Joseph P. Schultz detects
"remarkable" similarities between Edwards and the Habad masters of
Hassidism in their psychology of the religious experience (1973.29),
and Patricia Wilson-Kastner finds Edwards's theology "more
comprehensible" as an adaptation of Gregory of Nyssa's Christian
Neoplatonism (1978.24). Closer home, Hyatt Waggoner explores
similar patterns of grace in Edwards, Emerson, Hawthorne, and
Thoreau (1969.33); Mason I. Lowance extends to Thoreau the pattern
of the perception of nature and the symbolic expression of it that
Miller had found common to Edwards and Emerson (1973.18); and
William H. Parker uncovers a countervailing pattern to rationalism
in Edwards, Emerson, William James, and Reinhold Niebuhr (1973.26).
More boardly, Ellwood Johnson in American Quarterly (1970.16) links
Edwards's theory of perception to the individualism expressed by
Emerson, William James, Mark Twain, and Whitman, a case of cultural
continuity in America; and Sydney E. Ahlstrom in Church History
(1977.1) considers Edwards a "proto-Romantic" in his reformulation
of Calvinist doctrine in a natural context, part of the romantic
religion revolution world wide.

Though the hell-fire preacher dies hard--two early studies of
his "totalitarian" theology breathe little life into him (1965.1
and 1965.13)--the tragic figure of inner conflict shows even fewer
signs of being abandoned, though reasons differ. One study
attributes the antagonism between his mystical and rational selves
to the disjunction of historic Puritanism and Cambridge Platonism
(1967.8); another solves the paradox by examining his method of
preaching (1967.9), what still another study calls the
"double-edged form" of his rhetoric, a fusion of the rhetoric of

sensation and the rhetoric of intellect (1969.8). Far more
convincing than these is David C. Pierce's explanation of the two
"fundamentally contrasting" forms of God and piety found in
Personal Narrative--the first, a God of order and restraint, arising
from Edwards's devotion to divine sovereignty of orthodox Calvinism;
the second, a God of space and variety, arising from his delight in
the divine immediacy of contemporary natural enthusiasts (1968.22).
Again, the division in Edwards's successors, long an academic
quibble, is now laid to a split in Edwards himself as his early
experimental piety fell victim to his later rational metaphysics
(1974.4). John E. Smith returns to an equally old theme--Edwards
as philosopher or theologian--in an important analysis in the
Review of Metaphysics (1976.43). Smith neatly solves the "imposing
enigma" set by Edwards's Biblical absolutism and his philosophical
speculation by demonstrating that he "never" rested his arguments
on the Bible "alone" but "repeatedly" clinched them with
philosophical concepts, the mark of "a major philosophical
theologian." Perhaps neater yet is Morton White's resolution to the
duality of his work, the logic and the emotion: Edwards is in the
"middle band" of philosophy (1972.46).

The sixty-year-old issue of Edwards as covenantal theologian,
first raised by Jan Ridderbos and later by Perry Miller, gets a
careful reading at the beginning of the period and another at its
end. Conrad Cherry argues persuasively that Edwards "definitely
adhered" to covenant theology--the unequal contract between man and
God as all Puritans understood it--even though he sought, unhappily,
to mitigate the problematic nature of faith by distinguishing
between the covenant of redemption and the covenant of grace
(1965.5). A year later Cherry elaborates that thesis in The
Theology of Jonathan Edwards: A Reappraisal (1966.9), remarking
at the outset that Edwards is a Calvinist "first and last," that
faith and love are "central" to his thought, that his is a
"promise-making, promise-keeping God, . . . a covenant partner; not
the God of an inscrutable hinterland." Edwards may have stretched
Calvinism, Cherry points out, but he never broke with it;
theologizedon occasion, but invariably returned to the meaning of
faith and the covenant of grace; sensed God immediately, but was
hardly a mystic. In short, Edwards was nearly everything Miller
said he was not. Cherry's well-documented argument, like Aldridge's
two years earlier, tempers Miller's enthusiasm and excess in
complementing his study. Five years later, in his introduction to
an edition of Edwards's Treatise of Grace (1971.15), Paul Helm
reiterates much of what Cherry claimed: the concept of grace was a
"pivotal notion" for Edwards and worked "quite explicitly" within
the covenantal framework of Calvinism. But the matter did not end
there. Patricia Wilson-Kastner compares Edwards's view of
individual salvation and historic redemption with that of his
forebears and concludes that he rejects the covenantal theology of
the Puritans for the determinist theology of Calvin. It is
precisely the doctrine of divine grace that Edwards considers the

Introduction

"sole determining factor" for salvation; human autonomy in
individuals or in history finds no place in his scheme (1977.34).
In her book, Coherence in a Fragmented World: Jonathan Edwards'
Theology of the Holy Spirit (1978.23), Wilson-Kastner carries the
argument of grace one step farther: from each man's personal
relationship with God comes his sense of integral community and from
that, in turn, the notion that America is destined to be "a servant
of God's glory in the world." Such theological chauvinism finds
little room in Carl W. Bogue's Jonathan Edwards and the Covenant of
Grace (1975.5), but the problem raised by Cherry does. Bogue
agrees to the overwhelming importance of the covenant of grace but
argues that Edwards correlates it to his doctrine of redemption,
treating both as temporal aspects of the unabrogated covenant
of works--redemption is eternal, grace is becoming. Divine
sovereignty and human responsibility meet there, and, according to
an unduly hopeful Bogue, resolve the conflict and contradiction in
Edwards.

About Edwards and the half-way covenant, there seems to be more
clarification than debate. Edwards rejected his grandfather's system in
owning the covenant, thus ending the revival of sacramental piety in New
England (1972.16); he reverted to public profession either in a desper-
ate effort to moderate the excesses of the Great Awakening (1968.23)
or as a response to the "radical deviation" from covenant theology the
revivals fostered (1970.23); he failed to distinguish between conversion and regeneration in Stoddard's "ingenious" scheme, an "injustice"
to his grandfather and a "disservice" to himself (1972.40). Certainly, his dismissal hinged upon the changed qualifications he imposed;
that it was the result of a shift from a belief in the covenant of
grace to the covenant of works that apparently took place in his congregation (and in America), as one writer claims, is far from certain
(1977.4).

On matters of earlier importance--his idealism, for instance, or
his scientific pursuits--there is still occasional commentary but the
emphasis changes. In one of the few mentions of it, George Rupp details Edwards's "alleged" idealism: Edwards goes beyond Newton, Locke,
and Berkeley in stressing the dependence of every thing, being, and
event on divine energy and in connecting his physics (especially his
notions of solidity) to his metaphysics, but he fails to differentiate
sufficiently between objects and ideas. Withal, there is still a
"measure of coherence" to his metaphysics (1969.30). Another measure
of coherence can be traced in his metaphors of light derived from
Newton's Opticks and, according to Ron Loewinsohn, of greater importance for Edwards than the epistemology he derived from Locke (1973.17).
That epistemology, another reader insists, was hardly affected by the
new science, for in it, as in his theology generally, Edwards was
"embarrassingly conservative" (1973.20). While his "sophisticated"
scientific principles of causality may compare favorably with
formulations of modern physicists (1970.18), his paper on flying
spiders is simply a "felicitous and precocious" example of a

well-established genre in natural philosophy, not a unique
performance as is often claimed (1971.33). Even so, the Jonathan
Edwards College Press issues a handsome text of "Of Insects,"
transcribed from the manuscripts by Wallace E. Anderson (1974.2),
editor of the scientific papers for the sixth volume of the Yale
Edwards published in 1980.

Edwards's empiricism and Locke's, from the beginning a study in
similiarties, becomes more and more an inquiry into differences.
David Lyttle's standard argument that Edwards's idea of saving
grace as a sixth sense derives ultimately from Locke's notation of a
new simple idea finds careful emendation later on (1966.19). In
fact, any characterization of Edwards's account of the religious
experience or of the sixth sense as Lockean, Paul Helm justly
remarks, is subject to "important qualifications," for Edwards uses
Locke's empiricism as "a model" not a theory of that experience
(1969.16). Lyttle, for his part, had pointed out that the sixth
sense was "utterly different" from the natural senses, though
unified with them and not empirical. But Claude A. Smith contends
that Edwards is forced "to strike out on his own" to explain
divine revelation, that he goes beyond Locke in his "more active
view" of the mind, that he insists man actively judges and orders in
aesthetic categories the data of experience and thereby gains
"access" to the materials of revelation (1966.30). Sang Hyun Lee
elaborates upon that point in his study of Edwards's theory of
imagination (1972.23). Habit for Edwards, "drastically" different
for Locke, becomes "a mediating principle" between the activity of
the mind and the sensations it passively receives, and, without
resorting to rationalist explanations, he can describe the
indwelling of the Holy Spirit in a "fresh way." That all this may
be more readily accounted for by the Reformed tradition of which
he was "utterly captive," according to Sydney E. Ahlstrom (1972.2),
or by the "standard lexicon" of Calvinist peity, as Terrence Erdt
puts it (1978.7), was the point of J. Steven O'Malley's twenty-five-
page article in the Drew Gateway (1970.29). Still, Dennis M. Campbell
insists that it "knocked the props out from under" hierarchal
authority and civil governance in its reliance upon internal
awareness rather than Scripture or tradition (1976.14); and,
carrying on from there to the particular conditions of the
Connecticut Valley, Patricia J. Tracy claims that Edwards's
dismissal from his Northampton pastorate resulted from just such
a change in the traditional sources of authority and in the social
order (1977.31).

So the suggestion of Edwards's not inconsiderable effect upon
the changing social order, with its hint of rebellion, is
published afresh, and his role in the Great Awakening continues
to be a matter of first importance. Now, though, the very extent
of the enterprise separates current work from earlier periods. In
his controversial Religion and the American Mind from the Great
Awakening to the Revolution (1966.17), Alan Heimert asserts that the

evangelical religion of the Awakening, not the reasonable faith of
eighteenth-century liberals, stirred men to rebellion and that
Edwards helped provide "a radical, even democratic, social and
political ideology" for it. Some Thoughts becomes, for Heimert,
"the first national party platform"; Freedom of the Will, "the
Calvinist handbook of the Revolution." Aside from such distressing
hyperbole, Heimert's acknowledged practice of going "through and
beyond the lines" of his myriad texts to contrary implications
infuriates most readers (see, for instance, Edmund Morgan's review,
1967.25 or Sidney Mead's, 1968.14) if only because it so undermines
the real contributions of the Edwardseans to the founding of the
Republic (1967.22). Better for appraising Edwards's role is
Heimert's joint editorship with Perry Miller of The Great
Awakening: Documents Illustrating the Crisis and Its Consequences
(1967.15): forty-eight pages of reiterated claims introduce a
valuable compendium of source material about the revivals, much of
it from Edwards.[12] Five years later, a good deal more of Edwards
on the revivals finds its way into an important text: the fourth
volume of the Yale edition gathers Edwards's tracts and occasional
pieces together in accurate transcription and opens it with a ninety-
five-page essay by C. C. Goen (1972.11). The editor details the
changes both in Edwards and in his times from his clinical
observations in Faithful Narrative to his accomodation in
Distinguishing Marks, from his "most ambitious" defense in Some
Thoughts to his self-confessed failure in the preface to Joseph
Bellamy's True Religion. But, as Conrad Cherry notes in his
review article, Goen slights Edwards's central function as
evangelical preacher for that of dialectical theoretician,
emphasizing theology at the expense of affections and perpetuating,
however unintentionally, a split in Edwards remarked so frequently
before (1973.4). As Thomas A. Schafer had pointed out (1969.32),
Edwards affected American religious practice through his pastoral
role by empodying both doctrinal correctness and vital piety, by
demonstrating (at Stockbridge) the importance of missions, by
promoting ecumenism (and a new eschatology for it), and by
supporting voluntaryism in his rejection of the half-way covenant.
His "chief" role, Schafer concludes, may very well lie in the
theological ethics of Religious Affections and True Virtue, not
Freedom of the Will, a perception amply borne out in the work of the
following decade.

Other references to Edwards and the Awakening--and there are
quite a few--deal with the general historical importance of his
role in the movement (1965.9); his "monomania" about the devil
during it (1972.31); his effect upon American education (1970.7 and
1973.30) and upon the publication of Thomas Prince's Christian
History (1966.33); and the parallels between his Northampton and
John Cotton's Boston (1976.10) or William Williams's Hatfield
(1978.10). Three writers mention Edwards's particular appeal to
the young (1968.2, 1977.30, 1978.8), but in a useful statistical
analysis, Cedric B. Cowing shows that his preaching had wider

appeal, to men especially (1968.4). He serves as an example to evangelicals ministering to the urban masses (1966.7), of the Congregational way (1966.32), and for old Calvinism (1973.12). In two studies, Edwards emerges as a "moderate": in one, his emphasis upon the new birth at first seems radical to some, though in time opposition fades (1967.5); in the other, when he abandons steps to salvation for numbers of signs, he breaks sharply with an orthodox past and threatens his own position (1976.12). For one critic, the break-up of theological unity occasioned by Edwards's practice and defense of revivalism brings about the alternatives of modern American theology (1966.5); for another, his departure from Puritan practices of preparation generates "a new system" of New England theology (1966.23). On a related matter, Mary C. Foster skillfully defends Edwards's belief that his sermons on justification in November 1734 precipitated the revivals in Northampton a month later--Martin Marty still thinks it a surprise and the Great Awakening "accidental" (1977.22)--and she suggests, with reason, that the justification controversy was "much more fundamental" to the theological divisions following the Awakening than the more publicized debates on free will and original sin (1974.11). At the inauguration of a chaired professorship in South Africa, Edwards's role (through Brainerd) implies "the most shattering" social fact of divine grace: the elect could be men and women of Northampton and Stockbridge, colonist and Indian (1971.4). And Monroe Stearns suggests that Edwards brought the "unloved," the financially and politically oppressed of New England, to dignity through revival (1970.36), lifting them out of what Larzer Ziff calls their "inconsequential provinciality" (1973.42). By focusing on the shift in psychic make-up rather than on a rearrangement of social institutions, Ziff explains, Edwards developed the "characteristic pattern" of American rebellion against oppressive daily life.

That Edwards's psychic make-up was as much responsible for the Awakening as was his concern for the disenfranchised is the burden of the really important biographical studies during the period. There were, of course, derivative lives of Edwards, for the young (1968.35), in the Congregational tradition (1965.10), in the heroic colonial one (1966.3), or, less satisfactorily, amid the "friendly mountains" of the Connecticut Valley (1966.31). And there were local variations of it: Austin Warren plumbs Edwards's autobiographical writings for the conscience of a New England saint (1966.34); Leon Howard combs his undergraduate writings--he rejected Ramus for the Port Royal logic--to prove him a "student rebel" (1971.17); and Richard Warch in his School of the Prophets thinks him at least a non-conformist at Yale (1973.36). There were, as well, discoveries about his financial difficulties with Northampton's elders (1967.13) and his personal difficulties with Robert Breck (1978.13); the publication of the long-awaited diary of Ebenezer Parkman with its Edwards jottings (1974.16) and the publication of a newly found letter of Thomas Cutler with its disturbing picture of Edwards: "very much emaciated, and impair'd

in his health" (1973.32). There was a fictional treatment of his
problems with the Williamses of Stockbridge (1967.27) and a
"parable for the befuddled woman," a life of Sarah and Jonathan,
neither fiction nor fact (1971.6). But it was Richard L. Bushman's
two studies that add to the biographical Edwards in suggestive and
significant ways, through standard Freudian concepts in one,
"Jonathan Edwards and Puritan Consciousness" (1966.6); through
Ericksonian ones in the other, "Jonathan Edwards as Great Man"
(1969.5). In the first, Bushman traces Edwards's cycles of
depression and exhilaration, particularly during his conversion
experience, to infant-mother separation and union and to an
unresolved Oedipal crisis, warning his readers against reductive
errors. In the second, Bushman discovers in the "emotional
congruities" of Edwards and the Great Awakening--what Cushing
Strout would later call a "notable conjunction" of private and
public needs (1974.28)--Erik Erickson's model of the great man, the
natural leader. Edwards's "exceedingly aggressive" conscience, a
consequence of his father's traits and paternal demands, is
sublimated in his conversion experience and corresponds to the
pattern of larger motions of public anxiety at the time, a fortunate
coincidence (and a provocative thesis). Not nearly as useful an
explanation of Edwards's distinctiveness in the Great Awakening
or elsewhere is Philip Greven's study of the Protestant temperament
and child-rearing practices (1977.16). Here Edwards typifies the
evangelical in his abasement of self, submission to authority,
sublimation of hostility, and denial of masculinity. But the
parental role is much more complex than that, and, as William J.
Scheick points out, the family motif in Edwards is the environment
for conversion and the symbol of the integrated self (1974.18).

Personal Narrative, a text that figures prominently in such
readings, gains a different analysis in other hands. Daniel B.
Shea's "The Art and Instruction of Jonathan Edwards's Personal
Narrative" (1965.18) considers his autobiography "a mature
articulation" of his spiritual experience, coherent, affecting, and
artistic, governed by "heightened paradox" and by a narrative
technique that joins analyst to actor, public instruction to
private account. Shea's essay is first-rate, and, like Bushman's
study of Edwards as great man, frequently (and justly) reprinted.
In other studies of Personal Narrative, David L. Minter argues that
Edwards altered the pattern of Puritan spiritual autobiography in a
"radical sense," combining the interpretation of his conversion
with the divine judgment of it (1969.26); Norman S. Grabo discovers
a pattern of four concentric circles and an unconventional use of
time in the structure of his conversion (1969.13); and David L.
Weddle, using Erikson again, remarks the connection between the
primary language of identity there and the secondary language of
ideology in his treatises and finds, in the balance and synthesis
Edwards achieves, that "religious autobiography is a form of
theological argument" for him (1975.21). Earlier, Shea had taken
the "interrelatedness of things" to be the hallmark of Edwards's

thought, having traced an idea through the disparate forms of autobiography, narrative, polemic, and analysis to discover shifts in perspective, not in substance. Such coherence both within and without his personality shows that Edwards understood history in "multiple dimensions," and, as Shea suggests, that he contributed significantly to the "history of American consciousness" (1972.36).

Perusing many of the same texts, especially Religious Affections, a writer in the Journal of Psychology and Theology (1978.11) concludes that Edwards's analysis betrays an "integrated experience of seizure," a less useful observation than that it is "clearly informed" by melancholy, as Gail Thain Parker noted a decade earlier (1968.20). Yet for the most part, Religious Affections continues to be read as a manual for the uncertain Christian. The "real" Edwards for evangelicals can be found, for example, in the second sign (1966.11); the "very core" of pastoral theology (and personality theory) is there (1976.47); and, though contemporary theologians may have trouble with it, the problem of saving faith and history is solved there (1978.16). In a sense, John E. Smith's study of Religious Affections and its effect upon "all forms" of religion in America claims even more for it: by furnishing objective criteria to test genuine religion, Smith contends, Edwards pushed empiricism to pragmatism and made it possible to publicly assess private experience. Unwittingly, then, Edwards "opened the door" to an American religion of morality and good works, one following the practical bent of the American mind (1974.24).

Claims for Freedom of the Will during this period are less grand and border on the eccentric; Original Sin fares somewhat better, probably helped by the publication of the Yale text in 1970; but the critical importance of both continues to drop. One study of Freedom of the Will links Edwards's determinism to Karl Marx (1974.25), another to Friedrich Engels (1974.20), a third to B. F. Skinner (1974.22), and a fourth as a failed counter to Godel's proof, Chomsky's grammar, and D. M. McKay's model of free choice (1975.19). And in their introduction to a paperback edition of Freedom of the Will, Arnold S. Kaufman and William K. Frankena examine Edwards's defense of the compatibility theory, based on commonsense rather than metaphysical usages of words, and find that, though he shows "immense skill" and modernity, he nevertheless fails to solve the nagging question of authority (1969.20). Another unresolved question, this on the relevance of original sin today, ends Clyde A. Holbrook's study of the comparative views on punishment, imputation, and identity in Edwards and his antagonist John Taylor (1965.8), views Holbrook traces more fully five years later in his 101-page introduction to Original Sin, the third volume of the Yale Edwards (1970.15). There he carefully follows the New England controversy, the sources, the provenance of the text, and the "mixed" reaction to it, and concludes that Edwards was "haunted" by Taylor and so buried him

Introduction

"under an avalanche of criticism"--another instance of the thorough,
if unexceptional, introductions to the basic texts in the series.
Finally, the problem of identity and individuation central to
Edwards's theory of the imputation of original sin is examined once
more to good effect, this time by David Lyttle, who points out that
Edwards rejects man's uniqueness for his generic immateriality and
his common relationship to God (1972.28); the problem of sin (and
salvation) in an American context is again argued, this time by
Alice Cowan Cochran, with less effect (1976.15). And David L.
Weddle suggests that the organic metaphor of a tree Edwards uses to
describe the solidarity of sinners (and saints) differs
"significantly" from the biological and juridical metaphors of
tradition in that he identifies the common disposition of man as a
moral act in history (1974.29). That common disposition and the
modified penal theory furnished to deal with it is the subject of
Dorus Paul Rudisill's The Doctrine of the Atonement in Jonathan
Edwards and His Successors (1971.26). Edwards abandons the
traditional quantum measure of Christ's suffering and substitutes
for it the nature of the suffering Christ, an effective function
of God's chief attribute--love. "It would be scarcely possible,"
Rudisill concludes, "to glorify the suffering of Christ more than
Edwards does." Even without that single-mindedness, Harold P.
Simonson's Jonathan Edwards: Theologian of the Heart (1974.23)
comes to much the same conclusion, less effectively. A "heart-felt
pietism" lies at the core of religious experience for Edwards, and
transcends sense, reason, understanding, and aesthetics. Only
through the sense of the heart, through Christ, can man "come to
possess all things"--nothing new in that.

In a posthumous essay, Perry Miller had characterized True
Virtue as a "disturbing tract" for American Protestantism (1967.24),
and it seems to have become just that, especially as scholars began
to regard the ethical problem as an aesthetic or a political one.
Beauty, insists Roland André Delattre in his pioneer work on
aesthetics and ethics, explains more about Edwards than
particulate studies and provides the "central clue" to the nature
of reality for him, manifest and encountered as good in forms of
primary beauty of consent and as being in forms of secondary beauty
of proportion and harmony. Each of these forms, Delattre goes on,
correlate and coordinate with each other and with the order of
sensibility, so that beauty becomes the "formulative, structural,
inner first principle" of existence, of man's perception, and of
God's communication. Beauty and Sensibility in the Thought of
Jonathan Edwards (1968.8) is quite demanding--a better start might
be his adaptation for Soundings that year (1968.9)--and it may impose
too formulaic a scheme on Edwards. Still it is, by all counts, a
basic study and, as Delattre carries on the argument a decade later,
a continually intriguing one. In "Beauty and Politics: A
Problematic Legacy of Jonathan Edwards" (1977.9), Delattre discovers
in Edwards's concept of beauty, expressed in True Virtue and End of
Creation, a pattern of divine governance appropriate to human

1

governance, a political order derived from a personal one of virtue. Men govern responsively in beauty, moving through history toward the kingdom of God. Five years earlier, Ernest W. Hankamer in his published Munich dissertation (1972.15) traced Edwards's "wahre Politik" through his anthropology and his ethics, basing his findings not so much on the aesthetic but on the moral fact of True Virtue, Qualifications, and some sermons. Edwards regards the essence of man's freedom to be moral rather than social, says Hankamer, rooted in God's grace rather than secular guarantee. Taking it one step further or back (to Miller), Paul J. Nagy considers Edwards's thought to be "essentially social," though the cornerstone to it is "authentic" individualism (1971.23); Gerhard T. Alexis attributes Edwards's lack of concern for the social order of the theocratic ideal to be his otherworldliness (1966.2); and Robert B. Westbrook, returning to the center, finds Edwards's social criticism "self-consciously normative," part of his conviction that the imperfect society would yield in time to the community of saints, but such a possibility ended with the Great Awakening (1976.51).

The other major work, The Ethics of Jonathan Edwards: Morality and Aesthetics (1973.13), by Clyde A. Holbrook, takes the position that Edwards's ethics of "spontaneous virtue" can be best understood as an expression of theological objectivism rendered in "aesthetic rhetoric." Just as the Trinity represents "beauty in relationships," so moral beauty arises from consent of Being to being. Just so, Edwards in his radical theocentricism brings Calvinism and Neoplatonism together in a world of "beauteous evidences of God's presence." Though Holbrook's study is less formidable than Delattre's, it is also less exciting, for his "adventurous thinker" never gets beyond divine sovereignty--the "objective criterion" of an earlier statement (1967.16)--and Edwards's ethics and aesthetics, despite his title, are not nearly as congruent. That others find "an outstanding coherence and consistency" in Edwards is, however exaggerated, more to the point. Paul K. Conklin does in his Puritans and Pragmatists (1968.3), citing the fusion not only of ethics and aesthetics but of piety and sensationalism, "tempera- mental determinism" and holy affections--a "highly original" work of art. What is "highly original" to Paul J. Nagy is the fusion of Edwards's theories of the sense of the heart and consent to being, resulting in a unified view of man, nature, and God, "a new and interesting triad" (1970.26). For William A. Clebsch in his American Religious Thought (1973.5), Edwards's concept of unified experience rests on "turning the sense of duty to the sense of beauty," stamping the Puritan moral imagination with native American aesthetics. David L. Weddle thinks that Clebsch (and Delattre) confuse moral and aesthetic categories, for faith is consent to beauty (1976.48); Sang Hyun Lee thinks all of it a function of the integrating habit of mind (1976.32). As for sources, Charles Reynolds cites Edwards as the first to take Francis Hutcheson's ideal observer theory to strictly theological ends (1970.32) and Emily

Introduction

Stipes Watts numbers Thomas More's Enchiridion Ethicum an important
Neoplatonic basis for his ethics (1975.20).

If, as Miller said, True Virtue was a disturbing tract, then
History of Redemption is a challenging and fascinating one. Of
course, Peter Gay had taken Miller to task for his large claims for
Edwards and had used History of Redemption as obvious proof:
"reactionary and fundamentalist" it was, a calculus of mystery and
myth (1966.14). But to others, History of Redemption became the
vade mecum of the seventies and its explication and its relationships the hard work of many hands. In Redeemer Nation (1968.28),
Ernest Lee Tuveson places Edwards's scheme with those native plans
for the redemption of society, marking his theory of continuous
apocalypse and recurrent regeneration in America a radical and a
profound change. Only later in as comprehensive a study as
Tuveson's, The Sacred Cause of Liberty (1977.17), does Nathan O.
Hatch offer a corrective. Edwards's apocalyptic expectations
differ from the civil millennialists of the Revolution in this:
Edwards looked not for religious liberty but for religious piety,
a thoroughly apolitical millennium. Between these limiting
propositions several scholars--Sacvan Bercovitch, Mason I. Lowance,
John F. Wilson, and Stephen J. Stein come to mind--have worked
imaginatively and quite impressively. Bercovitch links Edward's
"gradualistic apocalypticism" to seventeenth-century jeremiads,
finding in both the necessary counterparts to the divine work of
redemption but seeing in Edwards a "new angle" of temporal
progression that, inadvertently, secularizes millennial hope into
political destiny (1970.1). In his essential Puritan Origins of the
American Self (1975.3), Bercovitch explores the peculiarly American
cast to the eschatology of Edwards--one of the "solitary keepers" of
the American dream--and his penchant for American figures. And in
"The Typology of America's Mission" (1978.4), Bercovitch remarks that
Edwards "drew out the implications" of the seventeenth-century millennialists of America's errand, differing only in his post-millennial
idea of progress of that corporate mission. Lowance traces the "gradu-
ated" development of Edwards's typological exegesis to the remarkable
Images or Shadows, wherein Edwards endows natural objects with allegorical significance leading to spiritual truth, and suggests that such
a process may account calling him a mystic or a pantheist (1970.20).
Sometime later, Lowance examines Edwards's unpublished writings on
typology and History of Redemption, uncovers an "original epistemology"
--nature, Scripture, prophecy, and millennialism in one--, and sees in
his apocalyptic dating a "radical justification" for the Great Awakening
and for an emergent nationalism (1977.20). That year saw two articles
by John F. Wilson on History of Redemption: history for Edwards, as
for church historians generally, is the "basic modality of individual
and collective existence," founded upon the crucial redemptive
process and couched in Scriptural types and prophecies, neither
modern nor medieval in character (1977.32); internal evidence in the
notebooks Edwards used to prepare History of Redemption reveals the
latter to be a synthesis of interest, his letter to the Princeton

trustees a genuine expression, and his proposed work an extraordinary possibility (1977.33). Probably the most extensive scholarship, beginning with his dissertation in 1971 and culminating in the fifth volume of the Yale Edwards six years later, is that of Stephen J. Stein's investigations of the apocalypse. His thorough and readable ninety-three-page introduction to Apocalyptic Writings: "Notes on the Apocalypse" and An Humble Attempt (1977.28) traces the tradition, theory, and sources of Edwards's apocalyptic thought, finding in it a persistent interest, "intriguing and complex, but sometimes contradictory" attitudes, and a mix of public and private records. Stein had gone over some of this material earlier in the William and Mary Quarterly (1972.39); but before the publication of the Yale edition he had examined Edwards both on the Antichrist, showing that anti-Catholicism continued unabated through the Revolution (1974.26), and on the covenant of the rainbow, revealing a "delightfully different" Edwards who combines science and theology in the traditional four-fold exegesis (1974.27). That "multiplicity of levels" informs his Biblical hermeneutics, Stein discovers in an examination of Edwards's "Blank Bible," emphasizing the spiritual as well as the literal understanding of a text and coming from efficacious grace (1977.29). Later, Stein takes issue with the growing scholarly sentiment about Edwards's eschatology, warning against "a monothematic portrayal" and offering providence as a "richer" construct than millennialism (1978.18). Not providence, as Stein suggests, but Scripture as a whole is the key--the prism, rather--that Edwards used to show "coherence of vision and variety" in history, according to Karl Dieterich Pfisterer in his published Columbia dissertation (1975.13). As the historian of the revival, Edwards used Scripture to integrate the past; as the historian of redemption, Edwards used Scripture to conceptualize history "ontologically as well as historically."

Others comment on the aesthetics in his eschatology (1971.24) and the nontraditional, asymptotic element in it (1976.27); the Lurianic strand in his gradualist millennialism (1974.19); his growing sense of himself as a prophet of "God's grand architectural design" (1975.14); and his formulation of types and antitypes common to nineteenth-century American writers (1977.18). In his detailed study of millennial thought in eighteenth-century New England, James West Davidson holds that Edwards's model of the apocalypse combines both hope and gloom in typical fashion, that external affliction and inner conviction were "inseparable" parts in his scheme of redemption, and that, though his History was New England's "greatest summary," its impact was "simply apolitical" (1977.8). But it did have another, deeper impact: inasmuch as the goal of missions is millennial realization, Edwards's History of Redemption found a singificant audience here in America (1965.15) and, together with Humble Attempt, abroad, especially in Scotland (1971.10) and England (1977.21).

Texts getting belated attention during the period--the coming

publication of the manuscript collection should help--are the
sermons, and the focus is generally on style. Future Punishment,
for example, reveals Edwards as a conscious artist, weaving Lockean
sensationalist imagery upon a Puritan plain style, according to
James C. Cowan (1969.9); if not that, his art in the sermons can be
explained as a "peculiarly heavy kind of pacing" upon the restraint
of Puritan practice, according to Willis J. Buckingham (1970.3).
Annette Kolodny finds "conscious artistic manipulation" in the
cumulative arrangement of Edwards's figurative language to "force"
listeners to respond (1972.20), and Robert Lee Stuart uncovers an
"element of comfort" in that much-maligned Enfield sermon (1972.40).
But it is Wilson H. Kimnach, in three separate and diverse studies,
who has obviously set the direction of future work on the form. In
"Jonathan Edwards' Sermon Mill" (1975.11), Kimnach concludes his
inspection of 600 sermons with the observation that Edwards was an
"ingenious manipulator" of the materials he kept "carefully
inventoried" in files and index; in "The Brazen Trumpet: Jonathan
Edwards's Conception of the Sermon" (1975.2), Kimnach traces the
development of Edwards's sermonic form from the imitations of his
father and grandfather's styles to his distinctive mature style
evident even in his major treatises; and in "Jonathan Edwards'
Early Sermons: New York, 1722-1723'· (1977.19), Kimnach discovers in
those early sermons clear promise of a later form and a growing
concern for experiential religion. To all this, Harold P.
Simonson demurs: Edwards was "first and last a Christian theologian,
not a literary artist," rooted in a theory of the imagination
consistent with revelation (1975.17). It is difficult to see why
Edwards cannot be both theologian and artist. Perhaps it may be too
much to claim, as John F. Lynen does, that Edwards is the artificer
of a "perfect harmony" between present time and eternal time by
means of a single point of view, or that he construes theology in a
world he defines "poetically" (1969.23). Still, it seems reasonable
(and demonstrable) that Edwards was both theologian and artist.

    In fact, a unified view is just what Edward M. Griffin achieves in
his forty-six-page Jonathan Edwards, one of the University of Minnesota
pamphlets on American writers (1971.13). Griffin isolates three
aspects of Edwards--"man, spokesman, and symbol"--to find Edwards
complete, discovering in the "odd turns" of his life and the
"radical distinction" between God and man at the core of his work,
the symbolic figure of "an American artist." So Edwards, in this
useful prolegomenon, shares with Melville and Hawthorne a mind that
strikes the "uneven balance" between good and evil, and he is the
dramatic realization of the struggling, hopeful pilgrim. Longer by
a hundred pages or so and less successful is Edward H. Davidson's
Jonathan Edwards: The Narrative of a Puritan Mind (1966.10),
reporting in a cumbersome style the uneven battle between orthodox
Calvinism and the new philosophy for the mind of "a Puritan baroque."
Davidson traces the structure of Edwards's mind as it comes to grips
with the sense and disposition of light--"a metaphor of the
mind"--and the symbolic value of language, charting his progressive

turning away from facts to ideas, in a dense survey of his work from
the juvenilia to his mature treatises. A lack of cogency or clarity
pervades Davidson: the intellectual triumphs over the poet in
Edwards, he remarks, because of "that inevitable wastage of sensual
delight"; Religious Affections is "deceptive" because "it assumes a
brute, mechanistic universe--and proves the spiritual autonomy of
God." By contrast, James Carse's Jonathan Edwards and the Visibility
of God (1967.6) shares none of Davidson's faults, though it is a
novel, not a standard, reading. Carse takes the central fact of
Edwards's thought and ministry to be his rejection of the "principle
of private judgment" in religious and ethical matters for the
"principle of visibility," namely, that the greatest good for man
lies in the visible Christ and that some men, through the effects of
divine grace, are made visible to others. Thus the church, the
"smaller society" of the redeemed, becomes a community of saints in
the vanguard of "the long journey toward the ultimate society."
Edwards preached "radical this-worldliness," but he failed as every
other "great American prophet" must. Although some charges against
Carse make sense--he builds a social activist minister, C. C. Goen
says (1968.11); he neglects the supernatural, Norman Grabo adds
(1969.14)--he does develop a coherent Edwards and a real one.

   That too is the aim of William J. Scheick's The Writings of
Jonathan Edwards: Theme, Motif, and Style (1975.16), and he
succeeds almost to the extent that Carse does but without his
clarity and with an argument diametrically opposed. Scheick
explores the "progressive interiorization" of Edwards's concerns and
the many implications of it for his theology, his identity, and his
art, by tracking the natural and familial images Edwards uses to
explain the inner and outer selves. That the mainspring to
Edwards's thought is his conversion experience and the uncertainty
that marks it leads Scheick to conclude that his "entire career
pivoted on this inner turmoil." At best, such a claim slights a
later Edwards for an earlier one, the treatises for the narratives;
but the book remains useful as an alternate, comprehensive reading.
Somewhat more limited--he simply attempts less--is William S. Morris
in his valuable thirty-five-page contribution to Reinterpretation in
American Church History, "The Genius of Jonathan Edwards," (1968.17)
wherein he discovers the essential Edwards to lie in his union of the
rational and the empirical, the logic of Burgersdycke (not Ramus)
and the sensationalism of Locke. Edwards's logic is "severely"
metaphysical and his philosophy and theology one of "spiritual
realism." And, as Morris aptly points out, Edwards is "a man of his
age," accepting the importance of reason but insisting it be "the
subject and not the cause of man's enlightenment," a view of
Edwards shared variously by Henry F. May in brief--he was a paradox
(1976.37); and by Donald H. Meyer at greater length--a "significant
representative figure" of the American Enlightenment (1976.38).
More limited still than Morris but fashioning another kind of unity
is John H. Gerstner's four-part series on Edwards's apologetics
appearing in successive issues of Bibliotheca Sacra (1976.22).

Gerstner argues the orthodoxy of Edwards's views--he was well within the "general" tradition of Bible and church--in his defense of faith against the assaults of nationalism, pantheism, and deism, and sustains it in tightly-knit theology. Limited even further are estimates of Edwards the "great American master of the creative paradox" of Margaret Wiley (1966.36) or the "pious frontier intellectual" of Richard Hofstadter (1971.16). Better than these are the larger, though vaguer, pronouncements of Edwards's "depth and dimension" in Ola Elizabeth Winslow's Basic Writings (1966.37) or his "cosmic sweep" in Thomas A. Schafer's Britannica piece (1974.17).

In the same year appeared David Levin's Jonathan Edwards: A Profile (1969.21) and John Opie's Jonathan Edwards and the Enlightenment (1969.27), estimates of Edwards from Samuel Hopkins to Robert Lowell--and a good deal of important scholarship in between--with serial comments by the compilers. Longer (and more valuable) comments in bibliographic essays have kept pace. In his two-part essay for A Critical Bibliography of Religion in America (1961.4), Nelson R. Burr divides comments between Edwards's role in the Awakening and his reconstruction and defense of Calvinism; divides his intellectual life into periods of "youthful speculation," theology, and "systematic writing," and warns that it would be "misleading to judge him solely by any one." Winfield J. Burggraaff in the Reformed Review (1965.3) notes Edwards's "rehabilitation" by scholars and claims that nothing new has emerged since Perry Miller's "classic"; Thomas Werge, in a supplement to Burggraaff five years later in the same jounral (1970.40), agrees with him on Miller and adds that important new work on Edwards will benefit from the general movement toward "defining the continuity" of Puritanism; and Gerald W. Gillette includes dissertations on Edwards in his checklist of doctoral work on Presbyterian and Reformed subjects from 1912 to 1965 (1967.12). But it is Everett Emerson's evaluation of bibliographies, editions, biographies, and criticism about Edwards over the last seventy-five years in Fifteen American Authors before 1900 (1971.8) that is of first importance in its completeness and fairness. Daniel B. Shea complements Emerson with his worthwhile study of the first two hundred years of Edwards criticism and of its later echoes,[14] and Donald Louis Weber unravels the history of the image and meaning of Edwards for American culture from the "guardians" of the eighteenth century to the restorers of the twentieth, in a different sort of bibliographic essay (1978.20).

Everett Emerson's call for a "general book" on Edwards, issued at the close of his essay almost a decade ago, remains unanswered. It may just be, as an anonymous writer for Zion's Herald noted during the Edwards bicentennial, that "the time is not yet fully ripe for a final estimate" of him (1903.11). Perhaps with the schedule of the Yale Edwards more firmly fixed and with much of the manuscript

collection then available at large, a synoptic book is possible.
Recalling the plight of Robert Lowell a generation ago, perhaps not.
Still, for some "wisely and skillfully searching professors," as
Edwards said taking his leave, there will always be a hope, and a
judgment later.

Notes

1. For the Edwards-Hopkins relationship see papers by Edwards
    Amasa Park (1852.8), Oliver Wendell Elsbree (1935.1), and
    David S. Lovejoy (1967.19).

2. Anne Stokely Pratt recounts the difficulties Watts had in
    securing the Edwards manuscripts (1938.3), drawing upon the
    Watts correspondence published by the Massachusetts Historical
    Society (1895.11). See also Arthur Paul Davis (1943.4).

3. Chauncy's reaction to Edwards is most completely described
    by Edward M. Griffin in his unpublished dissertation (1966.16).

4. For the details of Harriet Beecher's struggle with Edwards's
    theology see Charles Foster, The Rungless Ladder (1954.7), and
    Alice Crozier, The Novels of Harriet Beecher Stowe (1969.10).
    For the men in the family see Robert Meredith, The Politics
    of the Universe (1968.15).

5. See especially Vincent Tomas (1952.12), Peter Gay (1966.14),
    and, earlier and more briefly, Percy Boynton (1936.2).

6. Later Henry Bamford Parkes would go King one better:
    Edwards's conversion experience, for instance, is "Catholic
    and not Calvinist"; his nineteenth-century followers deny
    "the Catholic solution" to nature and grace (1932.12).

7. A few years earlier Sanford Cobb had concluded much the same
    thing in his study of religious liberty (1902.2); many years
    later Alan Heimert would explore the problem in greater detail
    and deeper controversy (see 1966.17). Winfield Burggraaff,
    The Rise and Development of Liberal Theology in America
    (1928.2), contends that Edwards's modified Calvinism ends in
    the "decidedly un-Calvinistic" doctrines of his successors,
    which contributes to the rise of religious liberalism.

8. The first American doctoral dissertation on Edwards, "The
    Philosophy of Jonathan Edwards and its Relation to his
    Theology," by Clement Elton Holmes, completed in 1904 at
    Boston University, is apparently lost. What survives in
    print is an article by Holmes in Zion's Herald on Edwards and
    Northampton (1903.31). Other firsts include Charles G. Bauer
    on Edwards and New England Theology at Temple (1912.1), also

ascribed to Howard F. Pierce (1912.6); Ralph Orin Harpole on the atonement, Yale (1924.1); Henry Bamford Parkes on the Awakening, Michigan (1929.10); Joseph G. Haroutunian on piety and moralism, Columbia (1932.4); George Noel Mayhew on Edwards and penology, Chicago (1932.11); and Rebecca D. Price on Edwards as educator, New York (1938.4). The first dissertation in English outside America was a study of Edwards's determinism by John Newton Thomas at Edinburgh (1937.9).

9. Not everyone agreed that year. Charles Angoff thought Edwards a "colossal" tragedy of American culture whose influence upon "enlightened American thought is nil" (1931.1). Apparently, Angoff had a change of heart: forty years later he officially welcomed a symposium on Edwards to Fairleigh Dickinson University (1975.2).

10. That seems a curious (and misleading) comment. The reappraisal of Edwards was evident at least twenty years earlier; the Yale Edwards is only a late product of it.

11. The span of years represents the actual awarding of degrees and so does not conform to my artificial divisions. Richard S. Sliwoski lists 124 dissertations on Edwards to 1978, including foreign ones: see "Doctoral Dissertations on Jonathan Edwards," Early American Literature 14 (Winter 1979): 318-27. Over the same period I account for 139, including eleven foreign ones: 1899.6, 1901.10, 1937.9, 1957.9, 1958.14, 1966.25, 1967.26, 1972.14, 1973.34, 1975.4, and 1976.11. The difference lies in the standards for inclusion. My list is either more generous or less rigorous than his--I include Conrad Wright's paper on Arminianism, for example, for its early and frequent references to Edwards (1943.10). Whatever the criteria or the arithmetic, the outpouring of academic interest in Edwards remains great.

12. Other collections of source material on the Great Awakening include an uneven selection from Edwards and comments to match: see 1970.4, 1970.5, 1972.30, and 1977.26. Two readers evaluate the Heimert thesis with restraint (1971.5 and 1977.23), one without it (1973.38), and a fourth as the subject of a dissertation (1976.11).

13. See the schedule of publication outlined by John E. Smith, general editor of the Yale Edwards, in Early American Literature, 14 (Winter 1979): 352-53: the first volume of the early sermons is expected "in the near future." Aside from the costs and the editorial decisions involved, some of the delay can be attributed to the enormous task of transcribing Edwards's difficult hand, as Thomas A. Schafer noted earlier (1968.25).

14.   Professor Shea kindly sent me a typescript copy; his paper
      will be published shortly.

Writings About Jonathan Edwards

1729

1 ANON. Obituary. Boston News-Letter, 13-20 February,
   pp. [1-2].
   Hopes that Edwards will prove a worthy successor to his
   grandfather, that "the Mantle of Elijah may rest upon
   Elisha," in an obituary of Solomon Stoddard.

1731

1 PRINCE, T[HOMAS], and COOPER, W[ILLIAM]. "To the Reader."
   In God Glorified in the Work of Redemption by the
   Greatness of Man's Dependence upon Him. A Sermon Preached
   on the Publick Lecture in Boston, July 8, 1731. And
   Published at the Desire of Several Ministers and Others,
   in Boston, Who Heard It. Boston: S. Kneeland & T. Green,
   pp. i-ii.
   Recommends Edwards's first published sermon for its
   "strength and clearness" and hopes that Yale will produce
   many more like the young minister--he was twenty-seven--and
   that Solomon Stoddard's principles will "shine" in his
   grandson.

1736

1 ANON. Appendix to The Duty and Interest of a People, by
   William Williams. Boston: S. Kneeland & T. Green,
   pp. 1-19.
   Reprints part of Edwards's letter to Benjamin Colman,
   explains what occasioned it, and solicits subscriptions
   for publishing the whole of it (as Faithful Narrative).

1737

1 WATTS, ISAAC, and GUYSE, JOHN. Preface to A Faithful

1

1737

Narrative of the Surprizing Work of God in the Conversion
of Many Hundred Souls in Northampton, and the Neighbouring
Towns and Villages of New Hampshire in New-England. London:
John Oswald, pp. [iii]-xvi.
Recommends Edwards's narrative of the "astonishing"
work of God in Northampton and its "pious" recorder, but
questions the aptness of Abigail Hutchinson and Phebe
Bartlet as significant illustrations of the conversion
experience. Perhaps Edwards chose the first because she
had died, the second because of the "stronger impression"
a child might make on his audience. Even so, "Childrens
Language always loses its striking Beauties at second-hand."

1738

1 SEWALL, JOSEPH, et al. Preface to A Faithful Narrative.
    Boston: S. Kneeland & T. Green; D. Henchman,
    pp. [i]-v.
       Praises Edwards for publishing this "particular and
    distinct Account" of the work of God and reports that it
    was well received in London.

2 WATTS, ISAAC, and GUYSE, JOHN. Preface to Faithful Narrative.
    Edinburgh: Thomas Lumisden & John Robertson, pp. iii-xii.
    Reprint of 1737.1.

3 _____. Preface to Faithful Narrative. 2d. ed. London: John
    Oswald, pp. [iii]-xvi.
    Reprint of 1737.1.

4 _____. Preface to Faithful Narrative. 3d. ed. Boston: S.
    Kneeland & T. Green, pp. [i]-viii.
    Reprint of 1737.1.

5 _____. Preface to Glaubwürdige Nachricht [Faithful Narrative].
    Magdeburg: C. Leberecht, pp. [x]-xxx.
       Reprint of 1731.1. Adds a history of soul-saving in
    Germany and New England by Johann Adam Steinmetz. (In
    German.)

1740

1 _____. Preface to Geloofwaardig Historisch [Faithful
    Narrative]. Amsterdam: Hendrik Van Bos.
       Reprint of 1738.5. (In Dutch.)

1741

1   COOPER, W[ILLIAM]. "To the Reader." In The Distinguishing
     Marks of a Work of the Spirit of God, Applied to the
     Uncommon Operation that has Lately Appeared on the Minds
     of Many of the People of this Land: With a Particular
     Consideration of the Extraordinary Circumstances with which
     this Work is Attended. Boston: S. Kneeland & T. Green,
     pp. i–xviii.
         Recommends Edwards's Distinguishing Marks for his
     scriptural, reasonable, and experiential arguments free of
     enthusiasm and sectarianism.

2   SIMS, STEPHEN. A Sober Reply in Christian Love to a Paragraph
     in Jonathan Edwards's Discourse, Delivered at New Haven,
     September 10th, 1741. New London, Conn.: [Timothy Green],
     p. [1].
         Attacks Edwards for his slur upon Quakers in his Divine
     and Supernatural Light, in a broadside affirming
     scriptural sanction for their true light of witness.

1742

1   COOPER, W[ILLIAM]. "To the Reader." In Distinguishing Marks.
     London: S. Mason, pp. [iii]–xii.
         Reprint of 1741.1.

2   _____. "To the Reader." In Distinguishing Marks.
     Philadelphia: Benjamin Franklin, pp. [iii]–xvi.
         Reprint of 1741.1.

3   WILLISON, JOHN. "Preface to the Scots Reader." In The
     Distinguishing Marks. Glasgow: T. Lumisden & J. Robertson,
     pp. v–vi.
         Considers Edwards's book "a most excellent, solid,
     judicious, and scriptural Performance" and compares the
     revival in Northampton to that in Cambuslang.

1743

1   ANON. Letter to the Publisher. Boston Evening Post, 13 June,
     p. [2].
         Notes the publication of Edwards's Some Thoughts in
     which he describes "Disorders, Delusions, Errors and
     Extravagances" that attended the revival.

2   CHAUNCY, CHARLES. Seasonable Thoughts on the State of

1743

Religion in New-England: A Treatise in Five Parts. Boston:
Rogers & Fowle, 472 pp.
  Attacks "a bad and dangerous tendency" to excess and
disorder in the current revivals and admonishes the
ministers fostering and sanctioning them--Edwards is cited
for the first time about a sixth of the way through--in an
historical investigation of the Great Awakening through
attestations, newspapers, and books. Edwards's Some
Thoughts produces only a few instances of genuine religious
experience, "though he had the whole Christian World before
him," and many instances of uncontrolled passion. Only as
Edwards ("so often refer'd to") and other ministers actively
oppose these excesses by condemning itinerant preaching,
imposing strict church discipline, and testifying to
misconduct can there be any remedy or relief.

3 [RAND, WILLIAM.] The Late Religious Commotions in New-England
   Considered. An Answer to the Reverend Mr. Jonathan
   Edwards's Sermon, Entitled "The Distinguishing Marks of a
   Work of the Spirit." Boston: Green, Bushell, & Allen,
   60 pp.
     Follows Edwards's method point by point in his defense
   of revival practices only to conclude that all of it
   strongly implies the contrary. Rather than evidences of
   the work of the spirit of God that Edwards discovers, his
   observations confirm enthusiastic and "gross" irregularities
   and errors. Edwards has been duped by Satan.

                              1744

1 ANON. "Some Serious Thoughts on the Late Times." Boston
   Evening Post, 30 January, pp. [1-2].
     Cites Edwards's description of "bodily Impressions"
   among his congregation following Samuel Buell's departure
   from the Northampton pulpit.

2 [PRINCE, THOMAS.] "Accounts of the Revival of Religion in
   Boston." Christian History 2 (2 February): 390-91.
     Notes Edwards's "natural Way of Delivery," free of
   agitation and full of solemnity.

                              1745

1 CLAP, THOMAS. A Letter from the Reverend Mr. Thomas Clap,
   Rector of Yale-College at New-Haven, to a Friend in Boston.
   Boston: T. Fleet, 8 pp.
     Claims that Edwards told him that he overheard George

Whitefield declare his intention of turning out "the
generality" of ministers from their pulpits and defends
himself against Edwards's denial.

2 _____. A Letter from the Reverend Mr. Clap, Rector of Yale
College in New Haven, to the Rev. Mr. Edwards of
North-Hampton. Boston: T. Fleet, 11 pp.
Argues that Edwards contradicts himself in his earlier
denial about George Whitefield and cautions him about his
"bitter Manner." (Edwards had denied Clap's charge in
Copies of the Two Letters, 1745, and pursued the matter
further in An Expostulatory Letter, 1745.)

3 WILLISON, JOHN. Preface to Sinners in the Hands of an Angry
God. A Sermon Preached at Enfield, July 8th 1741. At a
Time of Great Awakenings; and attended with remarkable
Impressions on many of the Hearers. Edinburgh: T.
Lumisden & J. Robertson, pp. iii-vi.
Acknowledges Edwards's "very alarming Title," but
insists that men need not only the invitation and promise
of the Gospel but the "Threats and Whips of the
Schoolmaster" as well. Besides, Edwards knew Enfield and
"judged it proper" to waken the lethargic souls with fire.

1747

1 SEWALL, JOSEPH, et al. Preface to An Humble Attempt to
Promote Explicit Agreement and Visible Union of God's
People in Extraordinary Prayer for the Revival of
Religion and the Advancement of Christ's Kingdom on Earth,
pursuant to Scripture Promises and Prophecies concerning
the Last Time. Boston: D. Henchman, pp. [i-iv].
Offers "this exciting Essay" of Edwards to the people
at a time of the outpouring of prayers. [The preface is
signed by Joseph Sewall, Thomas Prince, John Webb, Thomas
Foxcroft, and Joshua Gee.]

1749

1 PRINCE, THOMAS, et al. Preface and Appendix to An Humble
Inquiry into the Rules of the Word of God Concerning the
Qualifications Requisite to a Compleat Standing and Full
Communion in the Visible Christian Church. Boston: S.
Kneeland, pp. vi, 1-16.
Considers Edwards "singularly qualified" to argue the
terms of the communion and defends his break with his
grandfather's practice. In an appendix, Thomas Foxcroft

1749

answers Edwards's request for information about the
communion practice of Protestants generally and
Presbyterians in Scotland and Dissenters in England
particularly by assuring him that his view is consonant
with theirs.

1750

1 BRECK, ROBERT, et al. An Account of the Conduct of the
   Council which Dismissed the Rev. Mr. Edwards from the
   Pastoral Care of the First Church of Northampton.
   [Boston], 8 pp.
      Recounts the events and admission practices leading to
   Edwards's dismission in an "impartial and just Relation."
   The Council could find "no proper Expedient" to resolve the
   differences between Edwards and his congregation on the
   matter of qualifications. Of the 229 "certified" members
   of the church, only twenty voted to retain Edwards.

2 FIRST CHURCH OF CHRIST, Northampton, Mass. The Result of a
   Council of Nine Churches Met at Northampton, June 22, 1750,
   with a Protest against the Same by a Number of the Said
   Council. [n.p.] 8 pp.
      Records the proceedings of the church council
   recommending Edwards's dismission because of congregational
   opposition to his communion practice and the protest
   lodged against that action.

3 FROTHINGHAM, EBENEZER. The Articles of Faith and Practice,
   with the Covenant, that is Confessed by the Separate
   Churches of Christ in General in this Land. Newport, R.I.:
   J. Franklin, pp. 33-51, 411-32.
      Recommends "heartily" Edwards's Qualifications for
   questioning the right to communion and for disavowing the
   half-way covenant, but finds fault with its view of
   Separatists and with its "misterious" [sic] language.
   Edwards errs about the visibility of saints and "opens a
   door wide enough for all moral hypocrites to come into
   the Church that can parrot or say over a form of Christian
   experience." His writing appears "in such different
   shapes" that it is often difficult to know what he means.

1751

1 BRECK, ROBERT, et al. A Letter to the Reverend Mr. Hobby in
   Answer to his Vindication of the Protest, Against the
   Result of an Ecclesiastical Council, Met at Northampton.

Boston: S. Kneeland, 28 pp.
Refutes point by point William Hobby's Vindication
(1751.2), but asserts that his "Representation of the case
fully justifies us in dismissing Mr. Edwards."

2 HOBBY, WILLIAM. A Vindication of the Protest Against the
Result of the Northampton Council. Boston: S. Kneeland,
19 pp.
Attacks Robert Breck's Account of Edwards's dismissal
(1750.1) as "very partial, defective and unjust" and cites
Solomon Stoddard's changed attitude on admission, the
selection and division of the Council, the nature of the
protestations, and so on, in a sometimes witty,
page-by-page rebuttal.

3 WILLIAMS, SOLOMON. The True State of the Question Concerning
the Qualifications Necessary to Lawful Communion in the
Christian Sacraments. Boston: S. Kneeland, 150 pp.
Refutes Edwards's Qualifications point by point and
page by page and upholds Stoddard's view of the communion
as a converting ordinance. The "whole Controversy" turns
upon the visibility of saints and the necessity of
sanctifying grace prior to lawfully attending the Lord's
Supper. Despite Edwards's reasonings, Stoddard's
arguments--and the scriptural support for them--remain in
"full force." (Williams does not expect to help Edwards
stay on at Northampton because of his stand on
qualifications.)

1753

1 ASHLEY, JONATHAN. Preface to his An Humble Attempt to Give a
Clear Account from Scripture, How the Jewish and Christian
Churches were Constituted, and What Sort of Saintship is
Necessary in Order to Be a Communicant at the Lord's
Table. Boston: S. Kneeland, pp. i-iv.
Recounts an invitation extended by the Northampton
congregation to preach the Stoddardean way of communion
after Edwards was dismissed and reprints the sermons he
delivered.

1757

1 ANON. [A Memorial to Aaron Burr.] Boston News-Letter,
20 October, p. [1].
Notes that Edwards will succeed Aaron Burr as president
of Princeton.

1758

1 ANON. Obituary. Boston Gazette, 10 April, p. [3].
    Notes the death of Edwards, "a most rational, generous,
    catholick and exemplary Christian."

2 ANON. Obituary. New York Mercury, 10 April, p. [1].
    Ends a column-length encomium on the life and death of
    Edwards with a ten-line poem that begins,
        Great EDWARDS dead! how doleful is the sound?
    How vast the Stroke! how piercing is the Wound?

3 BOSTWICK, DAVID. "Self Disclaimed, and Christ Exalted: a
    Sermon Preached at Philadelphia, before the Reverend Synod
    of New York, May 25, 1758." In Peace and Union
    Recommended, by Francis Alison. Philadelphia: W. Dunlop,
    pp. 47-50.
        Considers Edwards's death the loss of the "greatest
    pillar in this part of Zion's buildings" and reprints
    Gilbert Tennent's obituary (1758.5).

4 [FINLEY, SAMUEL.] "A Brief Account of the Book and its
    Author." In The Great Christian Doctrine of Original Sin
    Defended; Evidences of its Truth Produced, and Arguments
    to the Contrary Answered. Containing, in Particular, a
    Reply to the Objections and Arguings of Dr. John Taylor,
    in his Book, Intitled, "The Scripture Doctrine of Original
    Sin Proposed to Free and Candid Examination, &c." Boston:
    S. Kneeland, pp. [i]-x.
        Recounts Edwards's life--derived from "public
    Prints"--and finds his intellect to be uncommon and his
    language to have "a noble Negligence" about it.

5 [TENNENT, GILBERT.] Obituary. Pennsylvania Gazette, 6 April,
    p. 1.
        Notes the death of Edwards, "a person of Great Eminence,
    both in respect of Capacity, Learning, Piety, and
    Usefulness; a good Scholar, and a great Divine," in a
    laudatory tribute.

1759

1 BOSTWICK, DAVID. Self Disclaimed, and Christ Exalted.
    London: T. Field, pp. 31-33; London: E. Dilly, pp. 32-34.
    Reprint of 1758.3.

1760

1   BELLAMY, JOSEPH. A Careful and Strict Examination of the
      Covenant. New Haven, Conn.: Thomas & Samuel Green,
      p. 184.
         Considers Edwards's Religious Affections "one of the
      best books...on experimental religion and vital piety
      since the days of inspiration."

1762

1   ANON. Review of Freedom of the Will. Monthly Review
      27 (December): 434-38.
         Regrets that Edwards's acuteness, dexterity, and
      subtlety of argument was in the service of the "theological
      chimeras of calvinistical orthodoxy."

2   [BELLAMY, JOSEPH.] A Dialogue on the Christian Sacraments,
      Boston: S. Kneeland, 81 pp.
         Presents a dialogue between Orthodoxus and Hereticus on
      the occasion of Edwards's dismission from the Northampton
      pulpit for denying communion to non-professing congregants.
      Orthodoxus converts to Hereticus's view of Edwards's
      doctrinal and practical soundness when confronted with an
      array of quotation from notable Puritan divines, from
      Richard Baxter to Isaac Watts.

3   _____. An Essay on the Nature and Glory of the Gospel of
      Jesus Christ. Boston: S. Kneeland, p. 191.
         Refers to Edwards's work for "the Solution of
      Difficulties" about original sin.

4   GORDON, WILLIAM. "The Preface of the Compiler of this
      Abridgement." In A Treatise Concerning Religious
      Affections. London: T. Field, pp. ix-xii.
         Finds Edwards's certain and judicious handling of
      religious affections a result of his being an eye-witness
      to the revivals, and charges Palaemon plagiarized from
      Edwards in his Letters on Theron and Aspasio.

1765

1   ANON. Preface to Two Dissertations, I. Concerning the End
      for which God created the World. II. The Nature of true
      Virtue. Boston: S. Kneeland, pp. [i]-iii.
         Finds these late pieces to be designed for "the learned
      and the inquisitive" rather than the common reader and

typical of the play of Edwards's genius.

2   [HOPKINS, SAMUEL.]   The Life and Character of the Late
    Reverend Mr. Jonathan Edwards, President of the College
    of New Jersey: Together with a Number of his Sermons on
    Various Important Subjects. Boston: S. Kneeland, 291 pp.
        Transcribes and interleaves extracts from Edwards's
    Resolution and Diary, the whole of Personal Narrative, and
    several letters, in a detailed history of his forebears and
    his family, his habits of mind, the conduct of his ministry
    and the occasion of his dismissal, his removal to
    Stockbridge, and his death at Princeton; a bibliography of
    his manuscripts and publications; and brief lives of his
    daughter Esther Burr and his wife Sarah. In its
    sympathetic understanding and eye-witness account, the
    Life fulfills Hopkins's intention to render a "faithful
    and plain narrative of matters of fact" about Edwards and
    to offer him to the public as a model of Christian piety,
    "the greatest--best--and most useful of men."
        (Reprinted in 1969.21.)

1767

1   ANON. Review of The Great Christian Doctrine of Original
    Sin. Monthly Review 36 (January): 17-21.
        Considers Edwards on original sin the "most important
    defense" against John Taylor (1694-1761) but doubts he has
    the advantage over him or that his work generally will be
    intelligible or useful to the "bulk of the people."

2   BACKUS, ISAAC. True Faith Will Produce Good Works. Boston:
    D. Kneeland, pp. 67-71.
        Notes that Edwards's changed views on public
    profession led to the dismissal from the Northampton
    pulpit of "one of the best divines that his age has seen."

3   HEMMENWAY, MOSES. Seven Sermons on the Obligation and
    Encouragement of the Ungenerate. Boston: Kneeland &
    Adams, pp. 34-35.
        Notes, contrary to Edwards in True Virtue, that a moral
    sense need not arise from self-love.

1768

1   [FINLEY, SAMUEL.] "A Brief Account of the Book and its
    Author." In Original Sin. Dublin: Robert Johnson,
    pp. iii-xvi.

Reprints of 1758.4.

2 _____. "A Brief Account of the Book and its Author." In
Original Sin. Glasgow: Robert Urie, pp. iii-xiv.
Reprint of 1758.4.

1770

1 ANON. A Preservative against the Doctrine of Fate:
Occasioned by Reading Mr. Jonathan Edwards against Free
Will, in a Book, Entitled A Careful and Strict Enquiry,
&c. Boston: Z. Fowle & I. Thomas, 31 pp.
     Calls the doctrine in Freedom of the Will "false and
blasphemous" because Edwards fails to find sin repugnant
to God nor responsibility available to man. Edwards
contradicts common sense, overthrows morality, and
encourages atheism.

2 [DANA, JAMES.] An Examination of the Late Reverend President
Edwards's "Enquiry on Freedom of Will": More Especially
the Foundation Principles of his Book, with the Tendency
and Consequences of the Reasoning therein Contained.
Boston: Daniel Kneeland, 151 pp.
     Deals with Edwards's Freedom of the Will from a
"practical view," not from a speculative or abstract one,
and discovers it to be "false, so far as our experience
reacheth," in a detailed examination of the connection
between volition and motive, cause and effect, liberty
and necessity.

3 HART, WILLIAM. A Letter to the Rev. Samuel Hopkins,
Occasioned by his Animadversions on Mr. Hart's Late
Dialogue, in which Some of his Misrepresentations of Facts,
and Other Things, are Corrected. New London, Conn.: T.
Green, pp. 11-12.
     Calls Edwards's views on true virtue and on primary and
secondary beauty "wrong, imaginary, and fatally destructive
of the foundations of morality and true religion."

4 HOLLY, ISRAEL. A Letter to the Reverend Mr. Bartholomew of
Harwinton: Containing a Few Remarks upon Some of his
Arguments and Divinity.... Hartford: Green & Watson,
pp. 3-4 passim.
     Urges repeatedly any who would discuss the halfway
covenant or determine communion participants to "Read
Edwards!"

5 HOPKINS, SAMUEL. Animadversions on Mr. Hart's Late Dialogue;

1770

in a Letter to a Friend. New London, Conn.: T. Green,
pp. 15, 17.
Recommends Edwards's True Virtue to William Hart as a
necessary corrective to the fallacies in the latter's
Brief Remarks.

6   MATHER, MOSES. The Visible Church in Covenant with God,
Further Illustrated. New Haven, Conn.: Thomas & Samuel
Green, pp. 36-39.
Ascribes to Edwards in Religious Affections the notion
that the implanting of grace in regenerate man results in
physical change--a sixth sense--and that it becomes an
unexamined assumption of New Divinity men.

1771

1   [FINLEY, SAMUEL.] "A Brief Account of the Book and its
Author." In Original Sin. Wilmington, Del.: James
Adams, pp. iii-xi.
Reprint of 1758.4.

2   HART, WILLIAM. Remarks on President Edwards's Dissertations
concerning the Nature of True Virtue. New Haven, Conn.:
T. & S. Green, 52 pp.
Insists that Edwards's notions of true virtue
overthrows Arminianism "and genuine Calvinism too," in a
polemic on Edwards's definitions, doctrines, and
inconsistencies found in True Virtue. To consider
benevolence as the root of true virtue, as Edwards does,
is "imaginary and arbitrary" and contrary to "true
divinity."

1772

1   HEMMENWAY, MOSES. A Vindication of the Power, Obligation and
Encouragement of the Unregenerate to Attend the Means of
Grace. Boston: J. Kneeland, pp. 12-22.
Considers Edwards's distinction between natural and
moral inability in Freedom of the Will to be "neither
plain nor sufficient" and couched in language contrary
to Scripture, "dark and indeterminate."

2   WEST, STEPHEN. An Essay on Moral Agency; Containing Remarks
on a Late Anonymous Publication Entitled "An Examination
of the Late President Edwards's Inquiry on Freedom of
Will." New Haven, Conn.: Thomas & Samuel Green, 255 pp.
Defends Edwards's Freedom of the Will against James

Dana's Examination (1770.2) by showing in detail that Dana fails to explain or refute "that very masterly tract."

1773

1 DANA, JAMES. The "Examination of the Late Rev'd President Edwards's Enquiry on Freedom of Will," Continued. New Haven, Conn.: Thomas & Samuel Green, 168 pp.
    Examines again (1770.2) and more thoroughly Edwards's denial of moral liberty, his distinction between natural and moral necessity, and his discriminations of the nature and cause of evil discussed in Freedom of the Will. The whole controversy is reducible to this: Edwards's scheme of necessity can be defended only by positing God as the author of sin. From such "injurious representations" the moral character of God must be vindicated.

2 HOPKINS, SAMUEL. An Inquiry into the Nature of True Holiness, with an Appendix containing an Answer to the Rev. Mr. William Hart's Remarks on President Edwards's Dissertation on the Nature of True Virtue: and Brief Remarks on Some Things the Rev. Mr. Mather has Lately Published. Also an Answer to the Rev. Mr. Hemmenway's Vindication. Newport, R.I.: Solomon Southwick, pp. 81-160, 211-13.
    Answers William Hart's Remarks (1771.2) on Edwards's True Virtue point by point on benevolence, secondary beauty, natural conscience, and the essential nature of virtue; remarks on passages in Moses Mather's The Visible Church (1770.6) about Religious Affections, the selfish heart, and the new divinity; and answers Moses Hemmenway's Vindication (1772.1) on moral inability in Edwards.

1774

1 ANON. Review of The Justice of God in the Damnation of Sinners. Monthly Review 51 (September): 246-47.
    Considers Edwards's sermon a "curious system of pious abuse" unnecessary to good Christians.

2 [CALKOEN, HENDRIK.] Preface to Een Bepaald en Nauwkeurig Onderzoek [Freedom of the Will]. Utrecht: Gisbert Timon van Paddenburg, pp. [7-23].
    Offers a brief life of Edwards and a short appraisal of the free-will argument. (In Dutch.)

3 EDWARDS, JONATHAN, the younger. Preface to A History of the

1774

> Work of Redemption, Containing Outlines of a Body of
> Divinity, in a Method Entirely New. Edinburgh: W. Gray,
> pp. [iii]-v.
>   Explains his father's imaginative plan to offer a body
> of divinity in historical form to show all recorded
> "remarkable" events as part of the work of redemption and
> identifies the source as a series of sermons Edwards
> preached in Northampton in 1739. John Erskine has shaped
> the manuscript materials, obviously never intended for
> publication in that form, into a "continued treatise"
> without changing "sentiments or composition."

4   HEMMENWAY, MOSES. Remarks on the Rev. Mr. Hopkins's Answer
    to a Tract Intitled, "A Vindication of the Power,
    Obligation and Encouragement of the Unregenerate to Attend
    the Means of Grace." Boston: J. Kneeland, pp. 28-29, 39,
    44, 150-51 passim.
        Claims Edwards's ideas on self-love in True Virtue led
    him into embarrassment and error about human nature and
    gave impetus to graver confusion in Samuel Hopkins.
    Hemmenway's extended quarrel is with Hopkins not Edwards,
    whom he regards highly.

1775

1   ANON. Review of A History of the Work of Redemption.
    Monthly Review 52 (January): 117-20.
        Reviews Edwards's History of Redemption, finds it a
    "dull, confused rhapsody," and thinks it better suited to
    a less sophisticated age of "pious conundrums."

1777

1   PRIESTLEY, JOSEPH. The Doctrine of Philosophical Necessity
    Illustrated. London: J. Johnson, pp. 122-24.
        Challenges Edwards's "not well founded" argument in
    Freedom of the Will that sin is a withheld act, not a
    positive one, and that, therefore, God is not the author
    of sin: causation is the same irrespective of the nature
    of the act.

1778

1   BARLOW, JOEL. The Prospect of Peace. New Haven, Conn.:
    Thomas & Samuel Green, p. 8.
        Addresses a long poem on the coming glory of America

to the Yale class of 1778 and includes this couplet:
While Metaphysics soar a boundless height,
And launch with EDWARDS to the realms of light.

1780

1 EDWARDS, JONATHAN, the younger. Preface to <u>Sermons on the
   Following Subjects</u>. Hartford: Hudson & Goodwin,
   pp. [iii]-v.
     Attributes the delay in publication of ten of Edwards's
   sermons to the British invasion of New Haven. Although
   the disadvantages of posthumous publication are many, the
   chosen sermons still retain their "pungency."

2 RYLAND, JOHN. Preface to <u>The Excellency of Christ: A
   Sermon Preached at Northampton, in New-England, In the
   Time of the Wonderful Work of Grace there, in the Year
   1738</u>. Northampton, England: Thomas Dicey, pp. [3]-6.
     Recommends this sermon of Edwards, "the greatest
   divine that ever adorned the American world," especially
   to promote religious knowledge among the poor.

1782

1 EDWARDS, JONATHAN, the younger. Preface to <u>History of
   Redemption</u>. Boston: Draper & Folsom, pp. [v]-viii.
     Reprint of 1774.3.

1785

1 CHAUNCY, CHARLES. <u>Five Dissertations on the Scripture
   Account of the Fall; and its Consequences</u>. London: C.
   Dilly, pp. 191-99, 260-64.
     Claims Edwards's doctrine of imputation in <u>Original Sin</u>
   is "utterly inconsistent" with reason or revelation and a
   "base slander" on a good God, and quotes extensively from
   Edwards's text to prove it.

2 [HOPKINS, SAMUEL.] <u>The Life and Character of the Late
   Reverend, Learned, and Pious Mr. Jonathan Edwards....</u>
   Glasgow: James Duncan; London: C. Dilly, 408 pp.
     Reprints of 1765.2.

1786

1 MIDDLETON, ERASMUS. "Jonathan Edwards, D.D." In his
Biographia Evangelica; or, An Historical Account of the
Lives & Deaths of the Most Eminent and Evangelical
Authors or Preachers, Both British and Foreign. London:
W. Justin, 4:294-317.
Derives a life of Edwards from the Hopkins account,
with dramatic touches--"Dismiss him, dismiss him, was the
universal cry"--and British aplomb--the vote to deny
Edwards his pulpit was one of "the blessings of an
absolute democracy!"

1787

1 [HOPKINS, SAMUEL.] "The Life of the Reverend Mr. Jonathan
Edwards." In A Treatise Concerning Religious Affections.
Elizabethtown, N.J.: Shepard Kollock, pp. [25]-116.
Reprint of 1765.2.

1788

1 ANON. "The Life and Experience of the Reverend Jonathan
Edwards." In History of Redemption. London: T.
Pitcher, pp. [3]-34.
Derives a life of Edwards from Middleton (1786.1).

*2 BREM, CORNELIS. Preface to Verhandeling Over Gods Laatste
Einde [End of Creation]. Amsterdam: Martinus de Bruyn.
Cited in Johnson, The Printed Writings...(1940.7),
item 233.

2 DWIGHT, TIMOTHY. The Triumph of Infidelity: A Poem.
"Printed in the World," p. 22.
Calls Edwards "That moral Newton, and that second Paul,"
in a mock-epic of the progress of Satan in America.

4 EDWARDS, JONATHAN, the younger. Preface to History of
Redemption. Edinburgh: M. Gray, pp. [iii]-v.
Reprint of 1774.3.

5 _____. Preface to his Observations on the Language of the
Muhhekaneew Indians. New Haven, Conn.: John Meigs,
pp. [i-ii].
Recalls the Edwards family removal to Stockbridge, his
facility with the local Indian dialect, and his father's
sending him to live among the Six Nations when he was ten
to learn their language in the hope of becoming a
missionary to them.

1789

1   BURNHAM, RICHARD. <u>Pious Memorials; or the Power of Religion</u> <u>upon the Mind, in Sickness and at Death: Exemplified in</u> <u>the Experience of Many Divines and Other Eminent Persons</u> <u>at those Important Seasons</u>. London: A. Millar, W. Law, & R. Cater, pp. 416-33.
        Summarizes the standard life of Edwards and quotes at length from <u>Personal Narrative</u>.

2   CLARK, GEORGE. <u>A Vindication of the Honor of God, and of the</u> <u>Rights of Men. In a Letter to the Rev. Mr. De Coetlogon,</u> <u>Occasioned by the Publication of Mr. Edwards's Sermon, on</u> <u>the Eternity of Hell Torments</u>. London: J. Johnson, 25 pp.
        Abhors the "awful language" of Edwards's <u>Eternity of</u> <u>Hell Torments</u> for asserting that the torments of the damned glorify God, in a point-by-point refutation of that sermon, and concludes that it is better to leave men unconverted than to "blacken" God's righteous character.

3   SUTCLIFF, JOHN. Preface to <u>An Humble Attempt</u>. Northampton, England: T. Dicey, pp. vii-x.
        Reprints the Edwards text to promote an agreement of Baptist ministers, meeting in Northampton and Leicester (England), to unite in prayer each month. "By re-publishing the following work, I do not consider myself as becoming answerable for every sentiment it contains. An author and an editor are very distinct characters."

4   [WINCHESTER, ELHANAN.] <u>A Letter to the Rev. C. E.</u> <u>DeCoetlogon, A. M. Editor of President Edwards's</u> <u>Lately-Revived Sermon, on The Eternity of Hell-Torments,</u> <u>by the Author of "Dialogues on the Universal Restoration."</u> London: [Winchester], 36 pp.
        Prepares a "short answer" to Edwards's view of endless damnation and endless misery in his <u>Eternity of Hell</u> <u>Torments</u> by showing his texts and arguments to be "insufficient" to prove the case and by suggesting that etymologically <u>aionion</u> need not mean "endless."

1790

1   ANON. "Advertisement." In <u>An Humble Inquiry into the Rules</u> <u>of the Word of God</u>. Edinburgh: William Coke, pp. [iii]-iv.
        Recommends Edwards's <u>Qualifications</u>, despite current prejudice against it, and reprints Thomas Foxcroft's essay on British admissions practices (1749.1).

1790

2   WATTS, ISAAC, and GUYSE, JOHN. Preface to <u>Faithful</u>
    <u>Narrative</u>, Elizabethtown, N.J.: Shepard Kollock,
    pp. [iii]-xiii.
        Reprint of 1737.1.

1791

1   BOSWELL, JAMES. <u>The Life of Samuel Johnson</u>. London:
    Charles Dilly, 2:227-28.
        Quotes Samuel Johnson's oblique remark on Edwards's
    <u>Freedom of the Will</u>, which he had not read: "'All theory
    is against the freedom of the will; all experience for
    it'" (15 April 1778).

2   [HOPKINS, SAMUEL.] <u>Het Leeven van den Weleerwaarden en zeer</u>
    <u>Geleerden Herr Jonathan Edwards</u>. [Life of Edwards.]
    Translated by Englebert Nooteboom. Utrecht: Willem Van
    Yzerworst, 238 pp.
        Translates 1765.2 into Dutch.

3   WATTS, ISAAC, and GUYSE, JOHN. Preface to <u>Faithful Narrative</u>.
    Elizabethtown, N.J.: Shepard Kollock, pp. [iii]-xiii.
        Reprint of 1737.1.

1792

1   EDWARDS, JONATHAN, the younger. Preface to <u>History of</u>
    <u>Redemption</u>. Worcester: Isaiah Thomas, pp. [iii]-v.
        Reprint of 1774.3.

1793

1   ANON. "The Life and Experience of the Reverend Jonathan
    Edwards." In <u>History of Redemption</u>. New York: T. & J.
    Swords, pp. [3]-34.
        Reprint of 1788.1.

2   AUSTIN, SAMUEL. Preface to <u>An Account of the Life of the</u>
    <u>Reverend David Brainerd</u>.... Worcester, Mass.: Leonard
    Worcester, pp. [3]-7.
        Vouches for the authenticity of Edwards's <u>Life of</u>
    <u>Brainerd</u> because it was published by a learned, pious man.

3   EDWARDS, JONATHAN, the younger. Preface to <u>History of</u>
    <u>Redemption</u>. Edinburgh: M. Gray, pp. [iii]-v.
        Reprint of 1774.3.

18

4   ERSKINE, JOHN.   Prefards to <u>Miscellaneous Observations On</u>
    <u>Important Theological Subjects, Original And Collected</u>.
    Edinburgh: M. Gray, pp. [i-ii].
        Values the "solid reasoning" of these fragments of
    Edwards even though they lack "the beauties of eloquence."

5   GODWIN, WILLIAM.   <u>An Enquiry Concerning Political Justice</u>.
    Dublin: Luke White, 1:279.
        Praises Edwards's <u>Freedom of the Will</u> for its "great
    force of reasoning."

6   [SMITH, ELIAS].   <u>An Essay on the Fall of Angels and Men; with</u>
    <u>Remarks on Dr. Edwards's Notion of the Freedom of the Will</u>,
    <u>and the System of Universality</u>.   Wilmington, Del.:
    Brynberg & Andrews, 76 pp.
        Attacks Edwards's <u>Freedom of the Will</u> as a work against
    reason, Scripture, and salvation, and argues that free
    agency does not lead to atheism but to Arminianism, a
    doctrine Christ and the apostles taught.

7   WEST, SAMUEL.   <u>Essays on Liberty and Necessity; in which the</u>
    <u>True Nature of Liberty is Stated and Defended; and the</u>
    <u>Principal Arguments Used by Mr. Edwards, and Others, for</u>
    <u>Necessity, are Considered</u>.   Boston: Samuel Hall, 54 pp.
        Questions Edwards's distinction between moral and
    natural necessity, his confounding of antecedent with
    subsequent necessity of volition, and his "absolutely
    denying that foreknowledge is an essential attribute" of
    God, in three essays on liberty and necessity.

1794

1   AUSTIN, DAVID.   Preface to <u>The Millennium; Or, The Thousand</u>
    <u>Years of Prosperity, Promised to the Church of God</u>, by
    Joseph Bellamy.   Elizabethtown, N.J.:   Shepard Kollock,
    pp. [iii]-viii.
        Explains that Edwards's <u>Humble Attempt</u> is joined to
    Joseph Bellamy's <u>The Millennium</u> in the same text in the
    hope that the first might bear upon the promise of the
    second.   Edwards's call for concerted prayer remains an
    "invaluable tract" today.

2   LINN, WILLIAM.   <u>Discourses on the Signs of the Times</u>.   New
    York: Thomas Greenleaf, pp. 174-75.
        Approves the plan for a concert of prayers proposed by
    a group of ministers in <u>Circular Letters</u> (1798.1) to
    carry out Edwards's <u>Humble Attempt</u>.

1794

3   WEST, STEPHEN. An Essay on Moral Agency. 2d ed. Salem,
    Mass.: Thomas C. Cushing, 313 pp.
        Reprint of 1772.2. Adds a sixty-one-page appendix to
    refute James Dana's continued examination of Edwards's
    Freedom of the Will (1773.1).

                            1795

1   [SMITH, ELIAS]. An Essay on the Fall of Angels and Men.
    Providence: Enoch Hunt.
        Reprint of 1793.6.

2   WEST, SAMUEL. Essays on Liberty and Necessity; in which the
    True Nature of Liberty is Stated and Defended; and the
    Principal Arguments Used by Mr. Edwards, and Others, for
    Necessity, are Considered. Part Second. New Bedford,
    Mass.: John Spooner, 96 pp.
        Questions Edwards again (see 1793.7) on liberty and
    necessity, refuting the "infallible connection" between
    motive and action, as Edwards had argued, and maintaining
    the self-determining power of the mind, in four essays on
    action and volition, moral agency, and God and the cause
    of sin.

                            1796

1   [SMITH, ELIAS.] An Essay on the Fall of Angels and Men.
    Middleton, Conn.: Moses H. Woodward.
        Reprint of 1793.6.

                            1797

1   EDWARDS, JONATHAN, the younger. A Dissertation Concerning
    Liberty and Necessity; Containing Remarks on the Essays
    of Dr. Samuel West, and on the Writings of Several Other
    Authors, on Those Subjects. Worcester, Mass.: Leonard
    Worcester, 234 pp.
        Defends Edwards against West's attack (1795.2) in an
    elaborate argument touching natural and moral necessity,
    inability, liberty, self-determination, motive, volition,
    foreknowledge, and responsibility. A central problem
    concerns the proper definitions of key words like liberty
    and necessity, and the "whole controversy" turns on the
    question of causative or fortuitous volition.

1798

1   Circular Letters Containing an Invitation to the Ministers
    and Churches of Every Christian Denomination in the United
    States to Unite in their Endeavours to Carry into Execution
    the "Humble Attempt" of President Edwards. Concord, N.H.:
    Geo. Hough, 32 pp.
        Urges a periodic concert of prayer like that "worthy"
    Edwards supported about fifty years ago in his Humble
    Attempt.

2   MIDDLETON, ERASMUS. Evangelical Biography. Philadelphia:
    John McCulloch.
        Reprint of 1786.1.

1799

1   EDWARDS, JONATHAN, the younger. Preface to History of
    Redemption. Edinburgh: Alexander Jardine & Edmund
    Whitehead, pp. [iii]-v.
        Reprint of 1774.3.

2   [HOPKINS, SAMUEL.] The Life and Character of the Late
    Reverend, Learned, and Pious Mr. Jonathan Edwards....
    Edinburgh: Alexander Jardine, 388 pp.
        Reprint of 1765.2.

1800

1   HALL, ROBERT. Modern Infidelity Considered with Respect to
    its Influence on Society. Cambridge: M. Watson,
    pp. 62-63.
        Notes that "many fashionable infidels" have adopted
    Edwards's definition of true virtue, as has William
    Godwin.

2   WILLIAMS, EDWARD. The Christian Preacher, or, Discourses
    on Preaching, by Several Eminent Divines. Halifax: J.
    Fawcett, p. 474.
        Recommends Edwards as "a most excellent writer, both
    practical and controversial."

1801

1   DOUGLAS, N[EIL]. Appendix to his An Antidote Against Deism.
    Edinburgh: John Taylor, pp. [259]-65.

1801

Rejects Edwards's notion, that eternal punishment is consistent with divine perfection, that misery will continue without end, and that good will come from the punishment of the wicked, found in Hell Torments by pointing out linguistic difficulties with the argument and its scriptural source.

2   GODWIN, WILLIAM. Thoughts Occasioned by the Perusal of Dr. Parr's Spital Sermon, Preached at Christ Church, April 15, 1800.... London: Taylor & Wilks, pp. 50-51.
      Acknowledges a debt to Edwards, "from a spirit of frankness," because Edwards led Godwin into a particular "train of thought" in Political Justice.

3   WATTS, ISAAC, and GUYSE, JOHN. Preface to Faithful Narrative. London: C. Whittingham, pp. [i]-xii.
      Reprint of 1737.1.

4   WESLEY, JOHN. "To the Reader." In A Treatise on Religious Affections. London: G. Story, p. 3.
      Justifies an abridgement of Edwards's Religious Affections: "much wholesome food is mixt with much deadly poison."

1803

1   HUGHS, J. Preface to The Marks of a Work of the True Spirit. Pittsburgh: John Israel, pp. iii-viii.
      Compares the revivals of Edwards's Northampton, recorded in Distinguishing Marks, to those in Kentucky and the West today and can "readily discover" similarities between them.

2   MILLER, SAMUEL. A Brief Retrospect of the Eighteenth Century. New York: T. & J. Swords, 2:30-31.
      Calls Edwards's Freedom of the Will "the greatest work which the century produced" on moral necessity but regrets that some of the uses of the doctrine have been carried to extremes unintended by Edwards and have been "illegitimately drawn."

1804

1   [HOPKINS, SAMUEL.] The Life and Character of the Late Reverend, Learned, and Pious Mr. Jonathan Edwards.... Northampton, Mass.: S. & E. Butler, 372 pp.
      Reprint of 1765.2.

1806

1   WILLIAMS, EDWARD, and PARSONS, EDWARD. "Editors' Preface."
    In Works of President Edwards, in Eight Volumes. Leeds:
    Edward Baines, 1:[iii]-vi.
        Recommends Edwards as minister and writer of numerous
    and valuable theological works of "uncommon strength" of
    intellect, in the first collected edition of Edwards,
    including the Hopkins life (1765.2) slightly revised by
    the editors and using Middleton's remarks (1786.1).

1807

1   MIDDLETON, ERASMUS. Evangelical Biography. London: I.
    Stratford.
        Reprint of 1786.1.

1808

1   ANON. "An Account of the Author's Life and Writings." In
    A History of the Work of Redemption. Edinburgh: John
    Walker, pp. [v]-xvi.
        Derives a life of Edwards from Hopkins (1765.2).

2   ANON. "Life and Character of Rev. Jonathan Edwards."
    Connecticut Evangelical Magazine and Religious
    Intelligencer 1 (May): 161-78; (June):201-12.
        Depicts the standard life of Edwards and reprints part
    of Personal Narrative.

3   AUSTIN, SAMUEL. "Editor's Address to the First American
    Edition." In The Doctrine of Original Sin Defended.
    Worcester, Mass.: Isaiah Thomas, Jr., pp. [371-72].
        Advertises the forthcoming first American edition of
    Edwards's Works, from which young ministers may learn that
    "conclusive arguing is as applicable to morals as to
    mathematics."

4   FAWCETT, J., and STEADMAN, W. "Advertisement." In A
    Faithful Narrative of the Surprising Work of God.
    Halifax: Holden & Dawson, pp. [i-ii].
        Offers an edition of Edwards's "very remarkable"
    account of divine grace for circulation among the poor and
    reprints 1737.1.

5   [FOSTER, J.]. "Edwards's Faithful Narrative." Eclectic
    Review 4 (June):548-50.

1808

> Reviews a reprinted (1808) London edition of Edwards's
> Faithful Narrative and finds it still deserving of
> publication, even with its language of "theological
> uncouthness."

6   [HOPKINS, SAMUEL].   "The Life and Character of Jonathan
    Edwards." In The Works of President Edwards. Worcester,
    Mass.: Isaiah Thomas, Jr.
        Reprint of 1806.1.

7   STYLES, JOHN.   Preface to his The Life of David Brainerd,
    Missionary to the Indians, with an Abridgement of his
    Diary and Journal. From President Edwards. London:
    Williams & Smith, pp. [iii]-iv.
        Rewrites Edwards's "copious" Life of Brainerd because it
    is redundant, filled with "much unimportant and exuberant"
    material, and presents it to "this age of antinomian
    delusion."

1809

1   ALLEN, WILLIAM.   "Edwards (Jonathan)." In his An American
    Biographical and Historical Dictionary. Cambridge, Mass.:
    William Hilliard, pp. 264-69.
        Focuses upon the causes and results of Edwards's
    dismissal in a brief biography.

1811

1   AUSTIN, SAMUEL.   Preface to An Account of the Life of the
    Rev. David Brainerd. Newark, N.J.: John Austin Crane,
    pp. [3]-8.
        Reprint of 1793.2.

2   OSGOOD, SAMUEL.   "A Review of Locke's Chapter on Power, and
    Edwards on the Freedom of the Will." In his Three Letters
    on Different Subjects. New York: Samuel Whiting & Co.,
    pp. [173]-293.
        Examines Edwards's use of terms such as power, will,
    liberty, and necessity in Freedom of the Will and finds
    that he appeals to the "vulgar sense of words" to further
    his cause at the expense of the truth. Edwards's
    argument is often self-contradictory and absurd because
    the critical terms he uses are as often destitute of
    meaning.

1812

1   ANON. "Mant's Bampton Lectures." Quarterly Review 8
      (December):356-74.
         Charges that Edwards's argument in Freedom of the Will
      rests upon the ambiguity of the word necessity, logical
      quibbles, and evasion.

2   [SMITH, ELIAS]. Essay on the Fall of Angels and Men. Boston:
      True.
         Reprint of 1793.6.

3   STYLES, JOHN. Preface to The Life of David Brainerd. Boston:
      Samuel T. Armstrong, pp. [i-ii].
         Reprint of 1808.7.

1814

1   BROWN, FRANCIS. A Sermon Delivered before the Maine
      Missionary Society at their Annual Meeting in Gorham,
      June 22, 1814. Hallowell, Maine: N. Cheever, p. 13.
         Notes the disparity between Edwards's interest in a
      concert of prayer and his failure to distribute
      translations of the Bible to the Indians or to establish
      missions among them.

2   BURDER, GEORGE. Preface to United Prayer for the Spread of
      the Gospel, Earnestly Recommended. London: R. Williams,
      pp. [3-4].
         Notes Edwards's role in the concert of prayer, in an
      abridgement of his Humble Attempt.

1815

1   HOPKINS, SAMUEL. Memoirs of the Rev. Jonathan Edwards, A. M.,
      President of the College in New Jersey. Edited by John
      Hawksley. London: James Black, 278 pp.
         Reprint of 1765.2. With "numerous verbal emendations"
      by John Hawksley.

2   WILLIAMS, SOLOMON. Historical Sketch of Northampton, from
      its First Settlement. Northampton, Mass.: W. W. Clap,
      pp. 20-21.
         Notes Edwards's Northampton pastorate, from the
      invitation to assist his grandfather on 21 August 1726 to
      his dismissal on 22 June 1750.

1816

1   MIDDLETON, ERASMUS. Evangelical Biography. London: W.
    Baynes.
        Reprint of 1786.

1817

1   ELLERBY, W. "The Editor's Preface." In his The Treatise on
    Religious Affections, by The Late Rev. Jonathan Edwards,
    A.M., Somewhat Abridged, by the Removal of the Principal
    Tautologies of the Original; and by an Attempt to Render
    the Language throughout More Perspicuous and Energetic.
    London: Longman, Hurst, Rees, Orme, & Brown, pp.[iii]-vii.
        Defends his abridgement because Edwards's style was
    "ambiguous and verbose" rendering his ideas "feeble" and
    "obscure" amid a "monstrous profusion of words." Granted
    the style of many religious works is not good, probably
    Edwards affords "the most remarkable specimens of bad
    writing" of his time.

2   [HOPKINS, SAMUEL]. "The Life and Character of Jonathan
    Edwards." In The Works of President Edwards. London:
    James Black & Son, 1:[6]-119.
        Reprint of 1806.1.

3   WHITE, WILLIAM. "An Analysis of the Rev. Jonathan Edwards's
    Interpretation of the Last Ten Verses, in the Fifth Chapter
    of the Epistle to the Romans." In his Comparative Views of
    the Controversy between the Calvinists and the Arminians.
    Philadelphia: M. Thomas, 1:373-97.
        Finds it "remarkable" that Edwards's Original Sin and
    its articulate defense of imputation is not celebrated as
    widely as Freedom of the Will among Calvinists, in an
    examination of his use of Romans 5:12-21.

1818

1   FULLER, ANDREW. Letter to John Ryland, 28 April 1815. In
    Life and Death of the Rev. Andrew Fuller, by John Ryland.
    Charlestown, Mass.: Samuel Etheridge, pp. 332-33.
        Remarks that if his detractors "preached Christ half as
    much as Jonathan Edwards did, and were half as useful as
    he was, their usefulness would be double what it is," in a
    last letter of the founding secretary to the Baptist
    Missionary Society.

2   TRUMBULL, BENJAMIN. A Complete History of Connecticut, Civil
    and Ecclesiastical. New Haven, Conn.: Maltboy,
    Goldsmith & Co., 2:145 passim.
        Offers an eye-witness account of the Enfield
    congregation by Rev. Eleazar Wheelock of Lebanon during
    the delivery of Edwards's Sinners in the Hands of an
    Angry God and quotes at length from Faithful Narrative.

3   WELLWOOD, HENRY MONCREIFF. Account of the Life and Writings
    of John Erskine, D. D. Edinburgh: Archibald Constable &
    Co., pp. 196-226.
        Recounts the correspondence between Edwards and several
    Scottish clergymen, especially John Erskine, his editor in
    Scotland, and reprints a letter, 4 August 1758, expressing
    the "irreparable" loss through Edward's death. "I do
    not think," Erskine writes, "our age has produced a divine
    of equal genius or judgment."

1820

1   ANON. "Ellerby's Abridgement of Edwards." Eclectic Review,
    n.s. 13 (March):271-75.
        Welcomes any republication of Edwards, even in
    abridgement, but questions Edwards's views on self-love
    and gratitude in Religious Affections.

2   BURNHAM, RICHARD. Pious Memorials. Bungay, England: J. & R.
    Childs.
        Reprint of 1789.1.

3   STYLES, JOHN. Preface to The Life of David Brainerd. 2d ed.
    London: A. J. Valpy, pp. [v]-viii.
        Reprint of 1808.7.

1821

1   ANON. Review of The Works of President Edwards, edited by
    Samuel Austin. Christian Spectator 3 (June):298-315,
    and 3 (July):357-65.
        Sketches the "prominent features" of Edwards as
    theologian, controversialist, and preacher by focusing
    upon his sermons and their affecting power.

2   CHALMERS, THOMAS. The Christian and Civic Economy of Our
    Large Towns. Glasgow: William Collins, 1:318-22.
        Finds Edwards ideally suited by temperament and ability
    to discern the genuine from the counterfeit in conversion

experiences in particular and in Christianity in general.

3   ELLERBY, W. "The Editor's Preface." In his abridgement of
    The Treatise on Religious Affections. Boston: James
    Loring, pp. [i]-viii.
        Reprint of 1817.1. Adds extract from Eclectic Review
    (1820.1).

4   [MIDDLETON, ERASMUS.] "A Sketch of the Life of President
    Edwards." In A Treatise Concerning Religious Affections.
    Philadelphia: James Crissy, pp. [v]-xxviii.
        Reprint of 1786.1.

5   STYLES, JOHN. Preface to The Life of David Brainerd. 2d
    American ed. Boston: Samuel T. Armstrong; Crocker &
    Brewster, pp. [v]-viii.
        Reprint of 1808.7.

                           1822

1   ANON. "Edwards on the Religious Affections." Christian
    Disciple, n.s. 4 (September-October):445-63.
        Commends Edwards's Religious Affections for its "real
    piety" and genuine concern, but denounces the "radical
    error" that runs through and deforms it. Edwards insists,
    unfortunately, that the religious affections are
    "altogether supernatural" and are not under man's control
    or direction. Such a view is but another instance--Freedom
    of the Will is the foremost--of Edward's "misdirected
    ingenuity."

2   DWIGHT, SERENO EDWARDS. "Advertisement by the Editor." In
    Memoirs of the Rev. David Brainerd. New Haven, Conn.:
    S. Converse, pp. 4-10.
        Gives a history of Edwards's text and the abridgements
    of John Wesley (1801.4) and John Styles (1808.7). Perhaps
    the explanation for Edwards's method of alternate sources,
    that is, using Brainerd's diary for some days and his
    journal for others, lies in his "delicate integrity."
    Edwards did not wish "to subject his subscribers to the
    necessity of purchasing the same matter a second time,"
    for parts of the journal had already been published. The
    text here restores the whole diary.

3   DWIGHT, TIMOTHY. Travels in New-England and New-York. New
    Haven, Conn.: Timothy Dwight, 4:323-28.
        Counters the charge of the Edinburgh Review that
    America has contributed nothing to human knowledge by
    citing the example of Edwards's work. His major treatises,
    clear and precise and sublime, rival those of England and

1823

Scotland.

4   GREEN, ASHBEL. Discourses, Delivered in the College of New
    Jersey; Addressed Chiefly to Candidates for the First
    Degree in the Arts; with Notes and Illustrations, Including
    An Historical Sketch of the College, from its Origins to
    the Accession of President Witherspoon. Trenton: E.
    Littell, pp. 313-26.
        Reproduces extracts of minutes and other records of the
    trustees of Princeton in appointing Edwards president,
    offers a "memoir" of his life and work, and recounts his
    stay at the college before his death. Though his logic
    and scriptural knowledge were unequalled in his time,
    Edwards's style lacked elegance and harmony, his language
    was unselective and repetitive.

5   H. "Original Letter from President Edwards." Evangelical and
    Literary Magazine 5 (July):365-69.
        Prefaces a letter from Edwards to Joseph Bellamy,
    25 June 1750, recounting (and reprinting) the ministerial
    council's deliberations and noting his congregation's
    approval--"most...voted for my being dismissed with great
    alacrity"--with an indictment of the liberals responsible
    for it.

6   STEWART, DUGALD. A General View of the Progress of
    Metaphysical, Ethical, and Political Philosophy, Since the
    Revival of Letters in Europe: First Dissertation. Boston:
    Wells & Lilly, part 2:124-25, 256-57.
        Suggests that Anthony Collins, A Philosophical Inquiry
    concerning Human Liberty (1715), anticipates Edwards,
    Freedom of the Will--an outline of the plan of the first
    could serve as a preface to the second--and makes this
    observation (often cited): "There is, however, one
    metaphysician of whom America has to boast, who, in
    logical acuteness and subtility, does not yield to any
    disputant bred in the universities of Europe. I need not
    say, that I allude to Jonathan Edwards."

1823

1   ANON. Review of The Justice and Impolicy of the Slave Trade,
    by Jonathan Edwards [the younger], D. D. Christian
    Spectator 5 (January):39-48.
        Draws "remarkable" parallels between the two Jonathan
    Edwardses, father and son: both were graduated early;

1823

both spent two years as tutors; both settled early as
ministers; both were dismissed for religious opinions;
both resettled in retired positions; both became college
presidents; and both died shortly thereafter.

2   WATTS, ISAAC, and GUYSE, JOHN.   Preface to Faithful Narrative.
    Bungay, England: J. M. Morris, pp. [i]-xi.
        Reprint of 1737.1.

1824

1   ORME, WILLIAM.   Bibliotheca Biblica: A Select List of Books
    on Sacred Literature, with Notices, Biographical, Critical,
    and Bibliographical.   Edinburgh: Adam Black, pp. 164-65.
        Summarizes briefly Edwards's work and asks for
    perserverance and attention to overcome his repellent
    style.

2   R., T.   "Edwards's Views of Original Sin."   Christian
    Spectator 6 (November):567-75.
        Explicates Edwards on original sin to counter claims
    that he believed in physical depravity.   The propensity to
    sin results from man's "innocent appetites and passions,"
    not from a "substantial property or attribute."   For
    Edwards, man's sinfulness, the root of which is self-love,
    is natural, native, or moral and bears not the "remotest
    semblance" to physical depravity.

1825

1   EUPOIUS.   "On a Resolution of President Edwards."   Christian
    Spectator 7 (January):14-17.
        Cites Edwards's Resolution 18 (somewhat misquoted) as
    an occasion for thinking of the importance of prayer.

2   [TAPPAN, HENRY PHILIP.]   Views in Theology, No. III:
    President Edwards' Doctrine of Original Sin: the
    Doctrine of Physical Depravity.   New York: F. & R.
    Lockwood, 104 pp.
        Contends that Edwards's Original Sin "obviously and
    unequivocally" teaches the doctrine of physical depravity
    "uniformly" throughout the text, in a detailed refutation
    of T. R.'s contrary view (1824.2).

3   [WALKER, JAMES].   "Edwards's Doctrine of Original Sin."
    Christian Examiner 2 (May-June):207-29.
        Reviews and approves Henry P. Tappan's pamphlet on

Edwards's Original Sin (1825.2) and attacks T. R.'s paper
(1824.2) as a specious defense of Edwards's language.
Edwards believed in physical depravity, a view explicit
and uniform "throughout his work."

*4   YOUNG, DAVID. "An Introductory Essay." In A Treatise
      Concerning Religious Affections. Glasgow: Chalmers &
      Collins.
          Cited in Johnson, The Printed Writings... (1940.7),
      item 118.

1826

1   CLARK, DANIEL A. Preface to "Sinners in the hands of an
     angry God." A Sermon, By The Venerated President
     Edwards, Rewritten, So As To Retain His thoughts In A
     Modern Style. Amherst: Carter & Adams, p. [2].
         Attributes the unwarranted neglect of Edwards to his
     style, and so offers Sinners in the Hands of an Angry God
     in "other language."

1827

1   BRADLEY, CHARLES, ed. Select British Divines. Jonathan
     Edwards, 27. London: L. B. Seeley & Son, pp. [v]-vii.
         Offers a biographical sketch of Edwards and considers
     Religious Affections (reprinted) unsurpassed in
     "discrimination and solidity."

2   GRINFIELD, EDWARD WILLIAM. "Appendix II: Review of Edwards's
     History of Redemption." In his The Nature and Extent of
     the Christian Dispensation, with Reference to the
     Salvability of the Heathen. London: C. & J. Rivington,
     pp. 427-58.
         Deplores Edwards's notions of the salvability of the
     heathen and the "absurdity and extravagance" of some of
     his observations, in a detailed review of History of
     Redemption.

3   M., E. "President Edwards's View of Original Sin."
     Christian Spectator, n.s. 1 (December):625-29.
         Questions T. R.'s understanding of imputation in
     Edwards on original sin (1824.2). Edwards held that man's
     sinful nature is not a consequence of imputation but
     antecedent to it. The first sin imputed to Adam was the
     same sin imputed to Adam's posterity: it was not Adam's
     sin; it was their own. In his anxiety to prove that

1827

Edwards does not believe in physical depravity, T. R. batters down Edwards's "stronghold."

4   [PORTER, NOAH]. "President Edwards on Revivals." Christian
     Spectator, n.s. 1 (June):295-308.
         Summarizes the points Edwards makes in Some Thoughts
     and concludes that his arguments are still pertinent to
     current revivals. Edwards insisted on the Scriptural
     basis of revivals; he urged the elucidation and
     application of evangelical doctrines; he counseled
     awakened sinners to seek immediate repentance; and he
     emphasized practical and social duties.

5.   TAYLOR, ISAAC, ed. "Introductory Essay." In The Modern
     Prevailing Notions Respecting That Freedom of Will Which
     Is Supposed To Be Essential to Moral Agency, Virtue and
     Vice, Reward and Punishment, Praise and Blame. Liverpool:
     Edward Howell, pp. [xvii]-clxiii.
         Argues the inapplicability of abstract propositions to
     questions of Christian doctrine, in a sometime examination
     of Freedom of the Will. Though Edwards's essay
     is justly celebrated for its analytical and logical
     powers, regarded as a "scientific treatise" it violates
     argumentation by mixing metaphyics with Scripture, moral
     truths with physiological facts. And though Edwards
     routed the sophistical Arminians, he fell before his
     "crushing engine of dogmatical exposition."

6   [WALKER, JAMES.] "The Revival under Whitefield." Christian
     Examiner 4 (November-December):464-95.
         Recounts Edwards's role in the Northampton revival and
     the Great Awakening, in a review of Charles Chauncy's
     Seasonable Thoughts and Thomas Prince's Christian
     History.

7   WESLEY, JOHN. "Thoughts upon Necessity." In The Works of
     the Rev. John Wesley. 1st American ed. New York: J. & J.
     Harper, 9:457-71.
         Notes that the "whole mistake" of the "good and
     sensible" Edwards is his holding man responsible for
     necessary acts.

1828

1   PARR, SAMUEL. The Works of Samuel Parr, LL.D. Edited by
     John Johnstone. London: Longman, Rees, Orme, Brown, &
     Green, 2:487-97.
         Contrasts Edwards's idea of gratitude in True Virtue

and William Godwin's comments on it in Political Justice.
Edwards and Godwin apply the term virtue to different
subjects, and so their ideas of gratitude, which both deny
to virtue, have "little or no resemblance."

2   R., T. "Edwards's Views of Original Sin: Reply to E. M."
Christian Spectator, n.s. 2 (January):16-18.
     Corrects E. M.'s supposition (1827.3) that Edwards
ascribes to Adam's posterity double guilt, guilt of
Adam's sin and guilt of a corrupt heart. If, as Edwards
argued, Adam knowingly sinned from a heart having no sin
in it and all men acted in Adam's act, then all men
knowingly sinned from an uncorrupt heart.

1829

1   [BEECHER, LYMAN.] "Letters on the Introduction and Progress
of Unitarianism in New England." Spirit of the Pilgrims
2 (March):121-28.
     Agrees with "the judicious Edwards" about the sources
and consequences of the Great Awakening, the good and the
bad.

2   COLERIDGE, S[AMUEL] T[AYLOR]. "Aphorisms on that which is
Indeed Spiritual Religion." In his Aids to Reflection.
Edited by James Marsh. Burlington, Vt.: Chauncey
Goodrich, pp. 105-107.
     Rejects Edwards's Freedom of the Will because it
"destroys all will" and meaning and goes beyond even
Calvin.

3   CRYBBACE, THOMAS TULLY. "Review of President Edwards's
Account of the Freedom of the Will." In his An Essay on
Moral Freedom. Edinburgh: Waugh & Innes, pp. 221-47.
     Argues that Edwards's Freedom of the Will establishes
the universality of moral causation and moral freedom and
"literally nothing" about liberty and necessity and that
its value lies chiefly in demonstrating the "fantastic
mass of absurdities" of his opponents.

4   [DWIGHT, SERENO EDWARDS], ed. Life of President Edwards.
The Works of President Edwards, vol. 1. New York: S.
Converse, 766 pp.
     Traces the life and times of Edwards, a solitary thinker
who has "changed the course of human thought and feeling,"
in the first extensive biography, derived in part from
Samuel Finley (1758.4) and Samuel Hopkins (1765.2), with
brief asides on his work and including notebooks, letters,

1829

and miscellaneous manuscripts (sometimes carelessly transcribed)--"Notes on the Mind," "Notes on Natural Science," Resolutions, Diary, Personal Narrative, and Farewell Sermon. Edwards's dismissal, "one of the most painful and surprising events" in New England church history, takes up one-quarter of the text (exclusive of appended reprints) and examines in order, the "facts" of Edwards's disagreement with Stoddardean communion practice, Hopkins's rendering of the event, Edwards's account in his journal and letters, Joseph Hawley's recantation, and Dwight's estimate: providentially, Edwards's dismissal helped reform church practice in New England and gave posterity the great works of his Stockbridge years. (Frequently reprinted.)

5 [HAZLITT, WILLIAM]. Review of Sermons and Tracts, by William Ellery Channing. Edinburgh Review 50 (October):125-44.
    Praises Edwards's reasoning, his "closeness and candour" and firmness in Freedom of the Will, in a review of Channing and other American writers.

6 JONES, THOMAS. Preface to Hanes Gwaith Y Prynedigaeth [History of Redemption]. Bala, Wales: Robert Saunderson, pp. [iii]-xii.
    Offers the standard life of Edwards and reprints parts of Personal Narrative. (In Welsh.)

7 KNAPP, SAMUEL L. Lectures on American Literature with Remarks on Some Passages of American History. New York: Elam Bliss, pp. 82-83.
    Offers a brief life of Edwards and a confession that Freedom of the Will is abstruse.

8 SMITH, JOHN PYE. "Introductory Essay." In A Narrative of the Revival of Religion in New England. Glasgow: William Collins, pp. [iii]-xlvi.
    Notes that the times demand Edwards's "judicious and comprehensive" observations--out of print for forty years--in a detailed survey of revivals, and reprints the Watts-Guyse preface (1737.1).

1830

1 ANON. "Interesting Conversions: Jonathan Edwards." Religious Monitor and Evangelical Repository 6 (February):414-16.
    Reprints part of Personal Narrative as testimony to Edwards's language of the new man.

2   [CHANNING, WILLIAM ELLERY.]   ["Remarks on National
       Literature."]   Christian Examiner 7 (January):269-95.
           Calls for a national literature and cites Edwards as
       "one of the greatest men of his age, though unhappily his
       mind was lost, in a great degree, to literature, and we
       fear to religion, by vassalage to a false theology."

1831

1   B., A.   "Edwards on the Imputation of Original Sin."
       Christian Advocate 9 (March):131-35.
           Asserts that in Original Sin Edwards attributed both
       depravity and imputation to the covenant union between
       Adam and posterity, but denies that he ever taught the
       "monstrous absurdity" that men actually or personally
       sinned before they were born.

*2   MacDOUGALL, PATRICK CAMPBELL.   "Edwards on Free Will."
       [Edinburgh] Presbyterian Review 1 (September).
           Unavailable, but reprinted in 1852.7.

3   [PORTER, NOAH.]   "Review of the Works of President Edwards."
       Quarterly Christian Spectator 3 (September):337-57.
           Praises, summarizes, and quotes from the Converse
       edition, especially from the first volume, Sereno
       Dwight's Life (1829.4).

4   [TAYLOR, ISAAC], ed.   "Introductory Essay."   In An Inquiry
       into the Modern Prevailing Notions Respecting That
       Freedom of the Will. . . .   London: James Duncan,
       pp. [xvii]-clxvi.
           Reprint of 1827.5.

5   WATTS, ISAAC, and GUYSE, JOHN.   Preface to Faithful Narrative.
       Boston: James Loring.
           Reprint of 1737.1.

1832

1   AMERICAN SUNDAY SCHOOL UNION.   The Life of President Edwards.
       Philadelphia: American Sunday School Union, 143 pp.
           Derives a life of Edwards from the accounts of Samuel
       Hopkins (1765.2) and Sereno Dwight (1829.4); advises the
       young to emulate Edwards's mental discipline and habits of
       thought; and reprints parts of Personal Narrative, all of
       Resolutions, and some of the juvenilia.

1832

2 BROWNLEE, JAMES. "Memoir." In A History of the Work of
      Redemption. Edinburgh: Stirling & Kenney, pp. [ix]-lvi.
          Recounts Edwards's career in the standard fashion.

3 COLTON, CALVIN. History and Character of American Revivals
      of Religion. London: Frederick Westley; A. H. Davis,
      pp. 48, 126-27.
          Presents Edwards and the revivals to English readers,
      his narratives of some of those "disagreeable" events
      characterized by the "artless simplicity of the child"
      but judged to be honest, exact, and sound.

4 GREGORY, OLINTHUS, ed. The Works of the Rev. Robert Hall,
      A.M. London: Holdsworth & Ball, 1:58-60; 6:99, 121.
          Cites Robert Hall's "undiminished pleasure" in Edwards's
      writings for "full sixty years." Yet in a recorded
      conversation Hall claims that Edwards found the
      distinction between liberty to will and liberty to act
      "buried" in the works of John Owen; thought it useful to
      "frighten" Arminians with; and "instead of smothering it,
      he nursed it" in Freedom of the Will.

5 MACKINTOSH, JAMES. A General View of the Progress of
      Ethical Philosophy, Chiefly during the Seventeenth and
      Eighteenth Centuries. Philadelphia: Carey & Lea,
      pp. 108-10.
          Questions Edwards's use of the word being in his
      ethical theory found in True Virtue and End of Creation.
      The term is a "mere incumbrance," cloaked in mystery and
      mysticism, obscuring his "really unmeaning" assumption
      that there are degrees of existence.

6 SILLIMAN, BENJAMIN. "Juvenile Observations of President
      Edwards on Spiders." American Journal of Science and
      Arts 21 (January):109-15.
          Speculates that had Edwards devoted himself to science
      he might have become "another Newton" and quotes from his
      early observations of spiders to support it.

7 [SPAULDING, CHARLES.] "Introductory Remarks." In Edwards
      On Revivals. New York: Dunning & Spalding, pp. [ix]-xvi.
          Recommends Edwards's Faithful Narrative as a
      discriminating record of Northampton revival of 1734,
      reviews Some Thoughts section by section as a practical
      and profound analysis of the Great Awakening, and reprints
      both for "the present revived state of things".

8 [TAYLOR, ISAAC.] Essay on the Application of Abstract
      Reasoning to the Christian Doctrines: Originally

36

Published as an Introduction to Edwards on the Will.
Boston: Crocker & Brewster, 163 pp.
    Reprint of 1827.5.

1833

1   ANON. "J. E. to M. S." Christian Examiner 14 (May):236-40.
        Concludes a fictional note from Edwards to Professor
    M. Stuart on the "invincible propensity" to evil by
    suggesting that men (and children) may more keenly feel
    their sinfulness as the "ungrateful abuse" of God's
    kindness and favor than as the result of imputation.

1834

1   ANON. "Works of President Edwards." Eclectic Review, 3rd
        ser. 12 (September):181-98.
        Reviews the London edition of Edwards's Works (1834)
    and praises Henry Rogers's analysis (1834.4) and Sereno
    Dwight's biography (1829.4).

2   BANCROFT, GEORGE. History of the United States. Boston:
        Little, Brown & Co., 3:399; 4:154-58.
        Praises Edwards's concept of universal history found in
    History of Redemption as superior to that of Vico and
    Bossuet and uses briefly the major works to comment upon
    New England religion.

3   POND, ENOCH. "Review of Edwards on the Will." Literary and
        Theological Review 1 (December):523-39.
        Praises Edwards's Freedom of the Will as a "noble
    work," in a clarification of its major points.

4   ROGERS, HENRY. "An Essay on the Genius and Writings of
        Jonathan Edwards." In The Works of Jonathan Edwards.
        Edited by Edward Hickman. London: F. Westley & A. H.
        Davis, 1:i-lii.
        Analyzes the "chief peculiarites" of Edwards's
    character and his chief productions, especially Freedom of
    the Will, in a discursive, double-columned essay on genius
    and "the most perfect specimen of the intellectual
    athlete the world has ever seen." Edwards's mind was
    logical, abstract, and deductive, "ill-adapted" to
    scientific inquiry; his style was "most repulsive,"
    prolix, inverted, "barbarous and uncouth." Freedom of the
    Will is "stupendous" but lacks originality and contains
    logical defects; Original Sin is inferior in "vigour and

1834

subtilty" to it; <u>True Virtue</u>, the "most profound" of all
of Edwards is as well the "least satisfactory;" and
<u>Religious Affections</u> is one of the "most valuable" works
on experimental piety "ever published."

*5   TODD, JOHN. <u>The Pulpit--Its Influence upon Society. A</u>
      <u>Sermon, Delivered at the Dedication of the Edwards Church</u>
      <u>in Northampton, Mass., December 25, 1833</u>. Northampton,
      Mass.: J. H. Butler, 72 pp.

6   UPHAM, THOMAS C. <u>A Philosophical and Practical Treatise on</u>
      <u>the Will</u>. Portland, Maine: William Hyde, pp. 128-29.
           Agrees with Edwards that his "learned and able"
      discussion of the will is hardly exhaustive, limited as
      it is to freedom, and ranks him intellectually with
      Joseph Butler and John Locke.

                              <u>1835</u>

1   ANON. "Life of the Rev. Jonathan Edwards, President of
      Princetown [sic] College, New Jersey." In <u>Christian</u>
      <u>Biography, Containing the Lives of Rev. George Whitefield</u>,
      <u>Rev. John Wesley, Rev. Augustus Hermann Francke, Rev.</u>
      <u>Jonathan Edwards</u>. London: Religious Tract Society,
      pp. 1-72.
           Offers a life of Edwards "selected" from the Hopkins
      (1765.2) and Dwight (1829.4) biographies.

2   ANON. "Miscellaneous and Literary Notices." <u>Biblical</u>
      <u>Repository and Quarterly Observer</u> 5 (April):486-87.
           Reprints, in part, Henry Rogers's introduction to
      Sereno Dwight's London edition of Edwards (1834.4).

3   [BRAZER, JOHN.] "Essay on the Doctrine of Divine Influence."
      <u>Christian Examiner</u> 18 (March):50-84.
           Quotes several passages from <u>Religious Affections</u> and
      <u>Personal Narrative</u> only to reject Edwards's doctrine of
      the supernatural influence of the Holy Spirit in the
      conversion of the sinner.

4   MACKINTOSH, JAMES. "Dissertation Second: Progress of Ethical
      Philosophy, Chiefly during the Seventeenth and Eighteenth
      Centuries." In <u>Dissertations on the History of</u>
      <u>Metaphysical and Ethical, and of Mathematical and Physical</u>
      <u>Science</u>. Edinburgh: Adam & Charles Black, pp. 340-41.
           Reprint of 1832.5.

5   REED, ANDREW, and MATHESON, JAMES. <u>A Narrative of the Visit</u>

to the American Churches. New York: Harper & Brothers, pp. 248-50.

Suggests that Edwards asked "too much at once" in altering the communion practice of his congregation, but that neither he nor his congregation is to blame for his dismissal.

1836

1   HAZLITT, WILLIAM. "On Liberty and Necessity." In his Literary Remains. London: Saunders & Otley, pp. 170-228.

Compares Edwards in Freedom of the Will and Joseph Priestley in The Doctrine of Philosophical Necessity Illustrated (1777) and finds the first earnest and scrupulous and the other evasive and cavalier. Edwards exhausts the subject of necessity in "one of the most closely reasoned, elaborate, acute, serious, and sensible among modern productions" and anticipates Hazlitt's own remarks. Extensive quotations show Edwards's "usual truth of feeling" for clear, unambiguous definitions of key terms.

1837

1   MILLER, SAMUEL. "Life of Jonathan Edwards." In The Library of American Biography, 8. Edited by Jared Sparks. Boston: Hilliard, Gray, & Co., pp. [1]-256.

Recounts Edwards's pastoral career and comments upon his work, in a full-length biography, derived chiefly from Samuel Hopkins (1765.2), Sereno Dwight (1829.4), and published estimates, of a ministerial model "exemplary, luminous, and useful."

1838

1   DAY, JEREMIAH. An Inquiry Respecting the Self-Determining Power of the Will; or Contingent Volition. New Haven, Conn.: Herrick & Noyes, 208 pp.

Uses Edwards's passing remarks in Freedom of the Will as an occasion to elaborate and prove that there is no contingent volition, for it is inconsistent with scriptural accounts.

1839

1   [ALEXANDER, JAMES WADDEL, and DOD, ALBERT B.]
    "Transcendentalism." Biblical Repertory and Princeton
    Review 11 (January):37-101.
        Notes the important distinction between Edwards and the
    "false" theology of his successors, in an attack on the
    German influence on American thought and the "nonsense and
    impiety" of Emerson's Divinity School address.

2   ANON. "Jonathan Edwards's Later Life." Hampshire Gazette,
    30 October, p. 1.
        Recounts briefly Edwards's Northampton years.

3   ANON. Review of A Review of Edwards's "Inquiry into the
    Freedom of the Will," by Henry Philip Tappan. American
    Biblical Repository, 2nd ser. 2 (July):257-58.
        Remarks Tappan's "veneration" for Edwards though he
    assails his Freedom of the Will.

4   BACKUS, ISAAC. Church History of New England from 1620 to
    1804. Philadelphia: [Baptist] Tract Depository,
    pp. 149-69.
        Notes, from a Baptist point of view, the controversy
    that Edwards engaged in with Charles Chauncy and others
    over revival religion. Some of Edwards's work has,
    perhaps unwittingly, a Baptist turn. In "On the Right to
    Sacraments," Edwards quotes from Romans 2:29, Philippians
    3:3, and Colossians 2:11, 12, and "though he did not design
    it, yet many others have been made Baptists by the same
    scriptures, and the same ideas from them."

5   HODGE, CHARLES. "The Great Revival of Religion, 1740-45."
    In his The Constitutional History of the Presbyterian
    Church in the United States of America. Philadelphia:
    William S. Martein, Part II, pp. 13-122.
        Traces Edwards's role in the Great Awakening--and that
    of the important revivalists, George Whitefield, the
    Tennants, Samuel Blair among them--and regards him "much
    less sensible" to the dangers of unrestrained emotions,
    bodily excitation, and nervous disorders than he was to
    become. His dismissal proves the "low state" of his
    congregation and reveals "something wrong" with the
    Awakening "from the beginning": even under Edwards,
    spurious conversions and false religion flourished.
    Nevertheless, the revivals pumped "new life" into the
    Presbyterian Church, and it is still felt within it.

6   JAMES, JOHN ANGEL, and PATTON, WILLIAM, eds. "Introductory

Preface[s]." In Edwards on Revivals. London: John Snow, pp. [iii]-xii.

Recommends Faithful Narrative and Some Thoughts as the work of a "sober" eye-witness, not a "mere speculatist," in a survey of revivals from apostolic days to the Reformation and the ministry of Edwards.

7 PARK, EDWARDS A[MASA]. "Duties of a Theologian." American Biblical Repository, 2nd ser. 2 (October), 347-80.

Eulogizes Edwards as a master theologian (with Augustine and Calvin) but wishes he had been "more of a brother" as well as the "father" of New England theology. Edwards had "a rich imagination, and might have been one of the first poets of his age, had he not chosen to be the first theologian."

8 TAPPAN, HENRY PHILIP. A Review of Edwards's "Inquiry into the Freedom of the Will." New York: John S. Taylor, 300 pp.

Begins a detailed refutation of Edwards's Freedom of the Will by restating its doctrine, by following its "legitimate" consequences, and by examining arguments against self-determination, in a formidable exercise in logic. If Edwards's psychology is right, then a self-determining power of the will is the "greatest absurdity possible"; if his doctrine of necessity is right, then folly, for instance, may be a necessary act, a consequence of infinite wisdom yet opposed to it—a manifest absurdity. And his argument of the interminable series of cause and effect makes. the whole notion of causality "equally absurd." Edwards's system is Lockean and utilitarian, pantheistic and atheistic. When Edwards keeps to religious matters like salvation, he seems "one of the old preachers of the martyr age"; but when he turns to matters philosophical, he falters. (For the continuing and concluding arguments, see 1840.6 and 1841.4.)

1840

1 [ATWATER, LYMAN H.] "The Power of Contrary Choice." Biblical Repertory and the Princeton Review 12 (October):532-49.

Uses the occasion of the publication of a new edition of Freedom of the Will to call attention to the current discussion of the power of contrary choice and Edwards's "safe and prudent" study of it.

1840

2   CAMPBELL, JOHN. <u>Maritime Discovery and Christian Missions,</u>
     <u>Considered in Their Mutual Relations</u>. London: John Snow,
     pp. 159-60.
        Refers to Edwards's powerful contribution to the union
     of prayer through his <u>Humble Attempt</u>.

3   FRANKLIN, BENJAMIN.   Letter to Mrs. Jane Mecom, 28 July 1743,
     in <u>Works</u>.   Edited by Jared Sparks.   Boston: Hilliard,
     Gray, & Co., 7:8-9.
        Recommends Edwards's <u>Some Thoughts</u> to his sister.

4   QUINCY, JOSIAH.   <u>The History of Harvard University</u>.   Cambridge,
     Mass.:   John Owen, 2:54-66.
        Cites Edwards's doctrinal basis for revivalism, his
     insinuation that colleges "should, in fact, be nurseries
     of piety" in <u>Some Thoughts</u>, and Charles Chauncy's attack
     on enthusiasm and defense of Harvard in <u>Seasonable</u>
     <u>Thoughts</u>.   Although Harvard was not "drawn into the vortex"
     of revivalist controversy until the arrival of George
     Whitefield, Edwards's "bold and uncompromising"
     metaphysics prepared the way.

5   ROBE, JAMES.   <u>Narrative of the Revival of Religion at</u>
     <u>Kilsyth, Cambuslang, and Other Places, in 1742</u>.   Glasgow:
     William Collins, p. 6.
        Notes the popularity of Edwards's <u>Distinguishing Marks</u>
     in Scotland before the revivals of 1742.

6   TAPPAN, HENRY P[HILIP].   <u>The Doctrine of the Will,</u>
     <u>Determined by an Appeal to Consciousness</u>.   New York:
     Wiley & Putnam, 327 pp.
        Continues a detailed refutation of Edwards's <u>Freedom of</u>
     <u>the Will</u> by testing his doctrine by an "appeal to
     consciousness," in a psychological investigation of reason,
     sensitivity, and will.   Edwards confounds necessity and
     contingency, though they are opposite ideas, and collapses
     reason, sensitivity, and will into one, though they are
     separate faculties.   There are two elements of necessity
     in the mind and one of freedom, acting harmoniously to
     "conditionate" one another.   Hence motives, contrary to
     Edwards, are "phenomena of the reason and sensitivity
     conditionating the will."   (For the beginning and
     concluding arguments, see 1839.8 and 1841.4.)

1841

1   ANON.   "A Review of <u>An Examination of President Edwards's</u>
     <u>Inquiry on the Freedom of the Will</u>, by Jeremiah Day."

American Biblical Repository, 2nd ser. 5 (April):500-504.
    Finds Jeremiah Day's defense (1841.3) "labored" though
"indispensible" to those who do not have the patience to
go through Edwards.

2   CHANNING, WILLIAM E[LLERY]. Works. Boston: James Munroe &
    Co., 1:xiii.
        Considers Edwards's Freedom of the Will "pernicious" if
    taken seriously, but adds that no one does.

3   DAY, JEREMIAH. An Examination of President Edwards's Inquiry
    on the Freedom of the Will. New Haven, Conn.:   Durrie &
    Peck, 352 pp.
        Analyzes the language of Edwards's argument in Freedom
    of the Will section by section and definition by
    definition in an attempt to prove his thesis, confound his
    critics, and establish a categorical defense.   There is
    in Edwards "a degree of negligence" about his style--the
    structure of his sentences, the position of relatives--and
    a lack of "nice precision" about his definitions.   Edwards
    must be read "as a whole," checking earlier parts of the
    argument for consistency and determining the different
    meanings of key terms throughout the text.   And that is
    the stuff of the inquiry: the definitions and relationship
    of will, volition, motive, necessity, contingence,
    inclination, inability, liberty, self-determination,
    indifference, foreknowledge, accountability, virtue, vice,
    fatalism, and common sense.

4   TAPPAN, HENRY P[HILIP]. The Doctrine of the Will, Applied to
    Moral Agency and Responsibility. New York: Wiley &
    Putnam, 357 pp.
        Concludes a detailed refutation of Edwards's Freedom of
    the Will by examining the doctrine in connection with moral
    agency and responsibility and by exposing the "futility of
    the distinction" between moral and natural ability.   "The
    mere natural ability as a constituted connexion between
    volition and voluntary action cannot contain freedom, if
    the volition itself be not an act of freedom."   Contrary
    to Edwards, freedom does make man responsible though not
    independent of God.   Man is made in God's image and the
    "more perfectly" he knows himself--his reason, his
    emotions, his freedom--the "more perfectly" he grows in
    knowledge.   Man thus interprets the world through his own
    self-consciousness.

5   VAIL, EUGENE A. De la Littérature et des Hommes de Lettres
    des États-Unis d'Amérique. Paris: Charles Gosselin,
    pp. 205-11.

1841

Surveys briefly Edwards's life and work.   (In French.)

1842

1   ANON. "The Great Awakening." Methodist Quarterly Review
      24 (October):594-615.
          Claims Edwards perceived that Methodists and Moravians
      held the "true doctrine" of justification, in a review of
      Joseph Tracy's The Great Awakening (1842.6). Edwards's
      sermons of "greatest effect" during the Awakening were
      Arminian or Methodistic.

2   CHEEVER, GEORGE B. "Review of Professor Tappan's Works on
      the Will." American Biblical Repository, 2nd ser.
      7 (April):411-41.
          Attacks Edwards's Freedom of the Will as contrary to
      the common consciousness and experience of man and to the
      common language of Scripture, in an essay-review of
      Henry Tappan's analysis (1839.8; 1840.6; and 1841.4).
      Edwards is like a "Boa Constrictor" in logic, his
      doctrines a "monstrous deformity."

3   EDWARDS, JONATHAN, the younger. "Remarks on the Improvements
      Made in Theology by his Father, President Edwards." In
      The Works of Jonathan Edwards, D.D. Edited by Tryon
      Edwards. Andover, Mass.: Allen, Morrill & Wardwell,
      1:481-92.
          Lists in summary form ten important theological
      contributions Edwards (and his followers) made. Edwards
      "shed much light" on the question of the end of creation;
      made "important improvements" on the doctrines of liberty
      and necessity; "happily" offered his "original" scheme of
      true virtue; clarified the origin of moral end; illustrated
      experimental religion; explained disinterested affection;
      described the "new sense" doctrine of regeneration; and,
      through his disciples, examined the doctrines of
      atonement and imputation and the state of the unregenrate.

4   EMMONS, NATHANAEL. "The Treasures of a Good and Evil Heart."
      In his Works. Edited by Jacob Ide. Boston: Crocker &
      Brewster, 5:139-40.
          Disagrees with Edwards in Religious Affections that
      religion consists of a good heart and of good affections
      flowing from it: religion consists of a good heart which
      is good affections.

5   MACINTOSH, JAMES. "A General View of the Progress of Ethical
      Philosophy." Encyclopaedia Britannica. 7th ed. 1:340-41.

Reprint of 1832.5.

6   TRACY, JOSEPH. The Great Awakening: A History of the
    Revival of Religion in the Time of Edwards and Whitefield.
    Boston: Tappan & Dennet, pp. 1-18, 213-30, passim.
        Recounts Edwards's role in the Great Awakening, the
    "immediate occasion of its commencement" being his series
    of sermons on justification in 1734. "Edwards, indeed,
    had done more than any other man to awaken the ministry
    and the churches in the first instance, and to produce the
    movement" of the 1740s, a time of "nervous diathesis."
    His indulgence about bodily agitation and unrepressed
    feeling so in evidence at Enfield became even more
    pronounced as he remarked his wife's "visitation" and her
    subsequent "improvement in practical holiness." His
    dismission from Northampton drew sympathy for his views on
    conversion both here and abroad and "disposed the pious to
    be on his side."

7   UHDEN, HERMANN F. Geschichte der Congregationalsten in
    Neu-England bis zu den erweckungen um das Jahr 1740: Ein
    Beitrag zu der kirchengeschichte Nordamerika's. Leipzig:
    L. H. Rosenberg, pp. 213-38.
        Describes the religious declension in New England and
    Edwards's hand in the revival of 1734, which is detailed
    in Faithful Narrative (In German; transl. 1858.11.)

1843

1   ANON. "Review of Tappan on the Will." Christian Review
    8 (September):367-402.
        Claims Henry Tappan misconceives Edwards on the will
    and thus is "fighting a shadow" in an essay-review of
    Tappan's three-part study (1839.8, 1840.6, and 1841.4).

2   [ATWATER, LYMAN H.] "Dr. Edwards's Works." Biblical
    Repertory and Princeton Review, n.s. 15 (January):42-65.
        Compares the thought of the elder Edwards with the
    "improvements" of the younger and finds the latter
    wanting, in a review of the Works of the son.

1844

1   ANON. "An Account of the Author's Life and Writings." In
    A History of the Work of Redemption. Edinburgh: Thomas
    Nelson, pp. [vii]-xxvii.
        Offers the standard life of Edwards.

1844

2 BAIRD, ROBERT. <u>Religion in America; or, an Account of the</u>
   <u>Origins, Progress, Relation to the State, and Present</u>
   <u>Condition of the Evangelical Churches in the United States</u>.
   New York: Harper & Brothers, pp. 197-99, 273-74.
       Characterizes Edwards's preaching just before the 1734
   revival, like all preaching that prepares the way for
   awakenings, as "doctrinal" on matters of grace,
   justification, redemption, and so on.

3 [DOD, WILLIAM ARMSTRONG.] <u>History of the College of New</u>
   <u>Jersey, from its Commencement, A.D. 1746, to 1783</u>.
   Princeton: J. T. Robinson, pp. 13-15.
       Recounts, in a short memoir, Edwards's time at Princeton
   and translates his Latin epitaph.

4 P[ARK], E[DWARDS] A[MASA]. "Original Letter of President
   Edwards." <u>Bibliotheca Sacra</u> 1 (August):579-91.
       Reprints a letter from Edwards, dated 18 November 1757,
   in Stockbridge to Joseph Hawley, a cousin who actively
   sought his dismissal and later publicly recanted, and
   remarks its candor and rectitude and the power clergymen
   formerly held over the aristocracy.

5 POND, ENOCH. Review of <u>The Works of Jonathan Edwards, D.D.</u>,
   <u>late President of Union College; with a Memoir of his</u>
   <u>Life and Character</u>, by Tyron Edwards. <u>American Biblical</u>
   <u>Repository</u>, 2nd ser. 12 (October):373-91.
       Compares the two Edwardses, father and son: the father
   is more imaginative, inventive, and emotional, more
   effective a preacher, more profound an investigator than
   the son; but the son was a better polemical theologian
   than the father.

<u>1845</u>

1 ANON. "Edwards as a Sermonizer." <u>Christian Review</u>
   10 (March):32-53.
       Claims the "cumbersome and unwieldy" structure of
   Edwards's sermons are "defective" models for candidates
   for the ministry to imitate. Even though his mode of
   sermonizing was "purely his own," Edwards uses language
   clearly and precisely, orders evidence consecutively and
   cumulatively, and ranges widely in subject and tone.

2 BLEDSOE, ALBERT TAYLOR. <u>An Examination of President Edwards'</u>
   <u>Inquiry into the Freedom of the Will</u>. Philadelphia: H.
   Hooker, 234 pp.
       Examines <u>Freedom of the Will</u> in a detailed analysis of

volition, cause and effect, indifference, action and
passion, foreknowledge, free agency, self-determination,
virtue, liberty, and necessity, and concludes that
Edwards's "whole scheme...is founded in error and
delusion." Following Edwards on moral necessity destroys
moral obligation and responsibility; applying his
principle of first cause leads "directly to Atheism." He
uses definitions with confusion and imprecision, finding
a "common nature" in a term like <u>necessity</u> where there is
"only a common name." For all his "gigantic power,"
Edwards is bound to the "treadmill of a merely dialectical
philosophy," a philosophy "essentially shallow and
superficial," and in his defense of his system, "he does
not reason at all, he merely rambles."

1846

1   ANON. "Life and Genius of Leibnitz." <u>Edinburgh Review</u>
      84 (July):[1]-47.
         Compares Leibnitz and Edwards, that "great
      Transatlantic Divine," on the rigor of their attack on
      indifference in free will.

2   EDWARDS, JONATHAN, the younger. Preface to <u>History of</u>
      <u>Redemption</u>. Philadelphia: Presbyterian Board of
      Publication, pp. iii-viii.
         Reprint of 1774.3.

3   MAHAN, A[SA]. <u>Doctrine of the Will</u>. New York: J. K.
      Wellman, pp. 228-31, passim.
         Accuses Edwards of a "fundamental error" in philosophy
      --he confounds will with sensibility--and convicts him of
      faulty logic--his argument on the will is circular; his
      argument on necessity begs the question; and his argument
      on divine foreknowledge is based on a false assumption,
      neither rational nor scriptural.

1847

1   ALBRO, JOHN A. <u>The Life of Thomas Shepard</u>. Lives of the
      Chief Fathers of New England, no. 4. Boston:
      Massachusetts Sabbath School Society, pp. 318-19.
         Calculates Edwards's debt to Thomas Shepard to be
      substantial inasmuch as 65 of 132 quotations in <u>Religious</u>
      <u>Affections</u> come from his <u>The Parable of the Ten Virgins</u>.

2   C[HANNING], W[ILLIAM] H[ENRY]. "Edwards and the Revivalists."

1847

Christian Examiner 43 (November):374-94.
Explains revivalism as the product of the general
Protestant emphasis on individualism, "a lonely pilgrimage
over deserts of sin to the tomb of the Redeemer," and
Edwards as an exemplar of it. His profound sense of his
own sinfulness resulted in a "conscious longing" for
salvation that he translated at large. Edwards
"out-Lutherized Luther and out-Calvinized Calvin" in his
depiction of the infinite sins of the finite man; he
classified, examined, and treated sin-sickness like a
clinician. But Edwards, who might have been a poet or a
saint in another time, failed to see holiness as love,
God as loving.

3 GRISWOLD, RUFUS WILMOT. The Prose Writers of America.
Philadelphia: Carey & Hart, pp. 53-56.
Offers a biography and criticism of Edwards,
accounting his style "uncommonly good," suitable and
precise but lacking harmony. After reading Samuel
Richardson's Charles Grandison, Edwards tried to write
more gracefully and succeeded in part in Freedom of the
Will and Original Sin.

4 MARTIN, BENJAMIN. "Bledsoe's Examination of Edwards's
Inquiry." New Englander 5 (July):337-47.
Finds Albert T. Bledsoe's study (1845.2) a mixture of
good and bad: though some of the analyses are vigorous
and acute, the tone is discourteous and ungracious to
Edwards, contemptuous to his advocates.

5 STEARNS, W. A. "The American Pulpit--Its Ends, Its Means, and
Its Motives," Bibliotheca Sacra 4 (May):247-70.
Compares briefly Edwards and George Whitefield, in a
survey of American pulpit orators. Edwards was eloquent
and logical, more solid and solemn than Whitefield but
not as passionately appealing.

1848

1 GREENE, W[ILLIAM] B. Remarks in Refutation of the Treatise
of Jonathan Edwards, on the Freedom of the Will. West
Brookfield, Mass.: Cooke & Chapin, 30 pp.
Examines, sentence by sentence, the second section of
the second part of Edwards's Freedom of the Will by
question and answer, quotation and comment, and concludes
that "all our volitions are produced and determined by our
will" but that the will does not possess self-determination.

2   MacCLELLAND, GEORGE. <u>Predestination and Election Vindicated</u>
     <u>from Dependence on Moral Necessity, and Reconciled with</u>
     <u>Freewill and a Universal Atonement: Preceded by an</u>
     <u>Answer to the System of Edwards</u>. Edinburgh: Bell &
     Bradfute, pp. 1-56, passim.
         Considers Edwards's influence on Thomas Chalmers in
     his treatment of moral necessity and predestination to be
     profound and "destructive to the true faith" but finds the
     contrary views of the Arminians equally repugnant.

3   O[SGOOD], S[AMUEL]. "Jonathan Edwards." <u>Christian Examiner</u>
     44 (May):367-86.
         Traces the course of Edwards's life and work, "a
     theologian great as Calvin, a logician not inferior to
     Spinoza."

1849

1   ANON. "The Life and Experience of the Author." In <u>History</u>
     <u>of Redemption</u>. London: George Virtue, pp. [3]-24.
         Offers the standard life of Edwards.

2   BELCHER, JOSEPH. <u>The Clergy of America: Anecdotes</u>
     <u>Illustrative of the Character of Ministers of Religion in</u>
     <u>the United States</u>. Philadelphia: J. B. Lippincott,
     pp. 163-65, 201-202.
         Recounts anecdotes about Edwards and particularly the
     reaction of a young man to one of his sermons on
     redemption. "He waited with deepest and most solemn
     solicitude, to hear the trumpet sound and the archangel
     call; to see the graves open, the dead arise, and the
     Judge descend in the glory of his Father, with all his
     holy angels; and was deeply disappointed when the day
     terminated, and left the World in its usual state of
     tranquility."

1850

1   BEECHER, EDWARD. "Man the Image of God." <u>Bibliotheca Sacra</u>
     7 (July):409-25.
         Questions Edwards's concept of time and space as
     illusions of the imagination set forth in <u>End of Creation</u>.
     By denying reality to time and space, Edwards compromises
     rational man's ability to know God and subverts the chief
     end of his being.

2   BLAKEY, ROBERT. "Dr. Jonathan Edwards." In his <u>History of the</u>

1850

Philosophy of Mind. London: Longman, Brown, Green, &
Longmans, 4:492–519.
　　Deals with Edwards's theological system as found in
Freedom of the Will chiefly and insists that it is based
upon a mistaken theory of causation. To argue that
nothing can exist without cause is to deny the existence
of God and the "obligatory nature of moral distinctions."
Edwards had the power of sustained reasoning but he
lacked "logical comprehension." An acute philosopher, he
was not a great one.

3　FICHTE, IMANUEL HERMANN. System der Ethik. Leipzig:
　　Dyk'sche Buchhandlung, 1:544–45.
　　　　Finds an abbreviated version of End of Creation
　　"excellent" and Edwards, that "solitary thinker" in
　　America, at the very center of the principle of morals:
　　universal benevolence is the bond of love "uniting all to
　　and in God." (In German.)

4　OSGOOD, SAMUEL. "Jonathan Edwards and the New Calvinism."
　　In his Studies in Christian Biography: or, Hours with
　　Theologians and Reformers. New York: C. S. Francis & Co.,
　　pp. 348–77.
　　　　Traces Edwards's career sentimentally and estimates his
　　work principally as that of a deductive logician
　　remorselessly pursuing Calvinist doctrines "in all their
　　intrinsic repulsiveness." But beneath Edwards the
　　metaphysican lies the poet; hence, his theology is more
　　nearly "the creature of his intellect, working at the
　　bidding of his emotions."

5　WISNER, WILLIAM C. "The End of God in Creation." American
　　Biblical Repository, 3rd ser. 6 (July):430–56.
　　　　Argues against Edwards's view of the God of creation
　　in order to establish his own doctrine. The "ultimate
　　objective end" of God in creating the universe was not,
　　as Edwards held, a celebration of His attributes and
　　perfections but was to "secure the greatest possible
　　amount of creature holiness and happiness." Edwards's
　　position ends in "absurdity"; his language and sentiment
　　"savor much of pantheism."

6　WYNNE, JAMES. "Rev. Jonathan Edwards." In his Lives of
　　Eminent Literary and Scientific Men of America. New York:
　　D. Appleton & Co., pp. 134–67.
　　　　Offers the standard life of Edwards but dwells "at
　　greater length" on the bad-book episode because Samuel
　　Hopkins (1765.2) and Sereno Dwight (1829.4) "in their
　　solicitude for [his] good name" avoid the real cause.

Edwards was in a "jaundiced state of mind," irritated at
the success Samuel Buell had with the young people of
Northampton in his pulpit appearances before them. Edwards,
"aware of the absurdity" of the charge of licentious
reading against them, acted out of pique in his ringing
condemnation. Thus began the end of "one of the ablest
reasoners and profoundest thinkers of his age," but a
writer whose style was "hideous and deformed."

1851

1   BUSHNELL, HORACE. Christ in Theology. Hartford: Brown &
    Parsons, p. vi.
        Notes that he was denied access to a newly discovered
    Edwards manuscript on the trinity because of its
    questionable orthodoxy.

2   FINNEY, CHARLES G. Lectures on Systematic Theology. Edited
    and revised by George Redford. London: William Tegg &
    Co., pp. 479-500.
        Rejects Edwards's views on natural and moral ability
    and inability and the "injurious monstrosity and
    misnomer" Freedom of the Will, in three lectures. Edwards
    made a "capital error" in adopting Locke's sensationalism.

1852

1   ANON. "President Edwards on Charity and its Fruits." New
    Englander 10 (May):222-36.
        Reviews Edwards's Charity and Its Fruits, gives a
    history of the manuscript and outline of the contents of
    his "favorite" topic, and likens his sweetness of thought
    to that of Washington Irving.

2   ANON. "Retrospective Survey of American Literature."
    Westminster Review 57 (January):288-305.
        Praises Edwards, "a missionary at Northampton" [sic],
    for his subtlety and understanding and compares him to
    William Ellery Channing, in a survey of American writers
    of philosophy and literature.

3   CHEEVER, GEORGE B. "The Manuscripts of President Edwards."
    Independent 4 (23 December):208.
        Examines the Edwards manuscripts in Tryon Edwards's
    study and finds them "deeply interesting" as clues to his
    method of composition and evidence of his biblicism.

1852

4   EDWARDS, TRYON. Introduction to <u>Charity and Its Fruits; Or,</u>
    <u>Christian Love as Manifested in the Heart and Life</u>.
    London: James Nisbet & Co., pp. [iii]-vi.
        Speculates that Edwards's habit of notetaking and
    committing his thought to paper makes his manuscripts an
    incomparable record of his intellectual life. The series
    of lectures reprinted here was delivered at Northampton
    in 1738 and was "written in full," readied for publication.
    The treatise will rank with the best of Edwards.

5   HAMILTON, WILLIAM T. <u>The "Friend of Moses"; or, A Defence of</u>
    <u>the Pentateuch</u>. New York: M. W. Dodd, p. 282.
        Remarks the fecundity of the Edwards clan.

6   HANNA, WILLIAM. <u>Memiors of the Life and Writings of Thomas</u>
    <u>Chalmers</u>. Edinburgh: Thomas Constable & Co., 1:16-17.
        Quotes a manuscript letter from Thomas Chalmers to
    his mother, 26 February 1821, acknowledging his debt to
    Edwards on the will twenty-four years earlier.

7   MacDOUGALL, PATRICK CAMPBELL. "Edwards on Free Will." In
    his <u>Papers on Literary and Philosophical Subjects</u>.
    Edinburgh: Johstone & Hunter, pp. 66-138.
        Welcomes the 1831 edition of Edwards's <u>Freedom of the</u>
    <u>Will</u>, with an introductory essay by Isaac Taylor, as an
    opportunity to praise Edwards and chastise Taylor. Though
    Edwards may rely too heavily upon conceptions independent
    of external things rather than upon the actual things
    themselves and though he may be guilty, at times, of
    "verbal ambiguity," these are but passing flaws.
    Taylor's view of Edwards on liberty and necessity is
    inconsistent, self-contradictory, and just "wrong." His
    case against Edwards fails. (Reprints 1831.2.)

8   PARK, EDWARDS A[MASA], ed. "Memoir." In <u>The Works of</u>
    <u>Samuel Hopkins, D.D</u>. Boston: Doctrinal Tract & Book
    Society, 1:9-266.
        Traces Samuel Hopkins's personal relationship and
    theological debt to Edwards, from September 1741 when he
    heard Edwards deliver <u>The Trial of Spirits</u> at Yale to his
    editorial labors following Edwards's death. Hopkins
    believed that, had Edwards lived, the two would have been
    "firmly united" in faith and in "essentially the same
    theories."

9   _____. "New England Theology; with Comments on a Third
    Article in the Biblical Repertory and Princeton Review,
    Relating to a Convention Sermon." <u>Bibliotheca Sacra</u>
    9 (January):170-220.

Defends Edwards and the Edwardseans against the attacks
of Charles Hodge and the Princetonians and defines New
England Theology. Variously called New Light Divinity,
New Divinity, Edwardsean, Hopkinsian, Berkshire Divinity,
and American Theology by the British and New England
Theology by Americans, it stands "firm for the 'three
radical principles,' that sin consists in choice, that our
natural power equals, and that it also limits, our duty."
Commentators err in dividing the edler Edwards and Joseph
Bellamy from the younger Edwards, Nathanael Emmons, and
Stephen West, for all these theologians bear witness to a
systematic orthodoxy marked by "strong, practical common
sense," a Calvinism in substance old, in form new. By
1796, two hundred ministers subscribed to the tenets of
New England Theology.

10   _____. New England Theology; with Comments on a Third
        Article in the Princeton Review, Relating to a Convention
        Sermon. Andover, Mass.: Warren F. Draper, 53 pp.
           Reprint of 1852.9.

1853

1   ANON. "Dr. Alexander's Moral Science." Bibliotheca Sacra
        10 (April):390-414.
           Takes Archibald Alexander to task for confounding the
        opinions of others with those of Edwards in his
        "illustrious" True Virtue.

2   ANON. "Jonathan Edwards and John Wesley." National Magazine
        3 (October):308-11.
           Finds Edwards and John Wesley in agreement on every
        important aspect of theology except the abstract questions
        of liberty and necessity.

3   ANON. "President Edwards's Dissertation on the Nature of
        True Virtue." Bibliotheca Sacra 10 (October):705-38.
           Defends Edwards against charges (1853.4) that he and
        Joseph Bellamy disagreed on the nature of virtue by
        citing Edwards's public endorsement of Bellamy's theory,
        by answering Edwards's principal critics, and by
        examining True Virtue in detail.

4   [ATWATER, LYMAN H.] Review of Outlines of Moral Science, by
        Archibald Alexander. Biblical Repertory and Princeton
        Review 35 (January):1-43.
           Calls True Virtue "a new adamantine barrier" that
        Edwards erected against a tide of selfish religion and

1853

argues that Joseph Bellamy followed him except when he moved "eccentric to his main orbit," in a survey of practical ethics.

5   BEECHER, EDWARD. The Conflict of Ages, or the Great Debate on the Moral Relations of God and Man. Boston: Phillips, Sampson & Co., pp. 90-95 passim.
        Praises Edwards for avoiding the "sinful propensity to self-admiration" in his Farewell Sermon. He still suspected himself of tendencies to sinfulness, but he should have realized that their source "preceded his consciousness and choice."

6   _____. "The Works of Samuel Hopkins." Bibliotheca Sacra 10 (January):63-82.
        Uses the occasion of a review of Hopkins's work to trace New England Theology to the revivals and Edwards, whose regeneration was produced "not at all by Locke" but by the Bible, and to attack the Princeton divines.

*7 BERMONDEY, E. H. Preface to his abridgement of Spiritual Pride [Some Thoughts]. London: Ward & Co.
        Cited in Johnson, The Printed Works . . . (1940.7), item 93.

8   BLEDSOE, ALBERT TAYLOR. A Theodicy; or, Vindication of the Divine Glory, as Manifested in the Constitution and Government of the Moral World. New York: Carlton & Porter, pp. 61-72, 98-110, 114-26 passim.
        Contends that Edwards's necessitarian views deny responsibility to man, make God the author of sin, and cloud moral distinctions, and posits a theodicy in which the goodness of God is consistent with the suffering of man, in a serial discussion of Freedom of the Will, Original Sin, and True Virtue.

9   BROWN, JOHN. "Prefatory Notice." In his Theological Tracts, Selected and Original. Edinburgh and London: A. Fullarton & Co., 2:293-94.
        Offers a brief life and longer praise of Edwards and reprints End of Creation.

10 [CHEEVER, GEORGE B.] "The Manuscripts of President Edwards." Littell's Living Age 36 (21 January):181-82.
        Reprint of 1852.3.

11 JAMIESON, ROBERT. Cyclopaedia of Religious Biography: A Series of Memoirs of the Most Eminent Religious Characters of Modern Times, Intended for Family Reading.

London: John Joseph Green & Co., pp. 178-80.
Offers a life of Edwards and speculates that he probably preferred to remain an academic at Yale than become a minister at Northampton.

1854

1   [ATWATER, LYMAN H.] "Modern Explanations of the Doctrine of Inability." Biblical Repertory and Princeton Review 26 (April):217-46.
Insists that Edwards's moral inability in Freedom of the Will is real inability, "invincible by the sinner," and that this view is "essentially" that of his predecessors, hardly the "novelty" some claim it to be.

2   BLEDSOE, ALBERT TAYLOR. A Theodicy. New York: Carlton & Phillips.
Reprint of 1853.8.

3   E., T. "Samuel Davies and Jonathan Edwards." Presbyterian Magazine 4 (November): 512-15.
Reprints a letter, dated 4 July 1751, from Samuel Davies (1723-1761) beseeching Joseph Bellamy to urge Edwards to take a position in Virginia and adds how different theology in America would have been had Edwards complied.

4   JONES, ELECTA F. Stockbridge, Past and Present: or, Records of an Old Mission Station. Springfield, Mass.: Samuel Bowles & Co., pp. 154-61.
Charts Edwards's career both before and during his years among the Indians at Stockbridge.

1855

1   ALLEN, WILLIAM. An Address, Delivered at Northampton, Mass., on the Evening of October 29, 1854, in Commemoration of the Second Century since the Settlement of the Town. Northampton, Mass.: Hopkins, Bridgman & Co., pp. 16-17.
Offers a brief biography of Edwards and two causes for his dismission, his rejection of Solomon Stoddard's communion practice and his rigidity in matters of discipline.

2   ANON. "Familiar Sketches of Connecticut Valley: Rev. Jonathan Edwards." Hampshire Gazette, 10 July, p.1.
Provides a short, derivative life of Edwards.

1855

3 DUYCKINCK, EVERT A., and DUYCKINCK, GEORGE L. Cyclopaedia of
   American Literature. New York: Charles Scribner,
   1:92–95.
      Offers the standard short biography of Edwards, the
   "finest product" of American Puritanism.

4 O'CALLAGHAN, E. B., ed. Documents Relative to the Colonial
   History of the State of New York. Albany: Weed, Parsons
   & Co., 6:907.
      Reproduces a letter from Thomas Cutler to Dr. Secker
   (28 August 1754) recommending Edwards on election and
   reprobation but adding that he was "odd in his principles,
   haughty and stiff and morose."

5 TYLER, WILLIAM S. "Genius." Bibliotheca Sacra
   12 (April):283–312.
      Places Edwards's genius with that of Shakespeare,
   Bacon, and Washington.

                          1856

1 [BANCROFT, GEORGE.] "Jonathan Edwards." In The New
   American Cyclopaedia. New York: D. Appleton & Co.,
   7:11–20.
      Concludes a life of Edwards and an estimate of his work
   with this frequently reprinted encomium: "he that will
   know the workings of the mind of New England in the
   middle of the last century, and the throbbings of its
   heart, must give his days and nights to the study of
   Jonathan Edwards."

2 BLEDSOE, ALBERT TAYLOR. A Theodicy. New York:
   [Carlton & Porter].
      Reprint of 1853.8.

3 CAMPBELL, JOHN McLEOD. The Nature of the Atonement.
   Cambridge: Macmillan & Co., pp. 49–112, passim.
      Attacks Edwards's (and John Owen's) idea of a limited
   atonement and his view that mercy and love are arbitrary,
   not necessary. Not only does this imply that Christ died
   for the elect rather than all men, it also substitutes
   a legal for a filial standing of Christ. Edwards, unlike
   later Calvinists, eschews moral excellence through grace
   and clemency for the "fiction" of legal or penal
   imputation.

4 CHAUNCY, CHARLES. Letter, 16 March 1742/43. New England
   Historical and Genealogical Register 10 (October):332.

Reprints a letter noting Charles Chauncy's preparation of an "antidote" to Edwards's Some Thoughts.

5   FISH, HENRY C. History and Repository of Pulpit Eloquence. New York: M. W. Dodd, 2:394-95.
     Reprints Sinners in the Hands of an Angry God and compares Edwards as a preacher to the apostles in thought, argument, and effect.

6   VAUGHAN, ROBERT ALFRED. Hours with the Mystics. London: John W. Parker & Son, 1:174.
     Faults Edwards's Religious Affections for teaching that regeneration gives a new power rather than a new disposition to the mind, thus isolating one man from another.

1857

1   ELLIS, GEORGE E. A Half Century of the Unitarian Controversy. Boston: Crosby, Nichols, & Co., pp. 98-99.
     Remarks the unnecessary contention about Edwards and the doctrine of physical depravity when it is clear that he believes in it.

2   HOLLISTER, G[IDEON] H. The History of Connecticut from the First Settlement of the Colony to the Adoption of the Present Constitution. Hartford: Case, Tiffany & Co., 2:587-94.
     Recounts Edwards's life in East Windsor amid an adoring family and a congenial natural environment.

3   LOSSING, BENSON J. Eminent Americans. New York: Mason Brothers, pp. 177-79.
     Offers a brief life and a favorable appraisal of Edwards.

4   SPRAGUE, WILLIAM B. Annals of the American Pulpit. New York: Robert Carter & Brothers, 1:329-35.
     Recounts Edwards's life and concludes with this from Thomas Chalmers's letter to "Dr. Stebbins of Northampton" (frequently reprinted): "There is no European divine to whom I make such frequent appeals in my class rooms as I do to Edwards. No book of human composition which I more strenuously recommend than his Treatise on the Will,--read by me forty-seven years ago, with a conviction that has never since faltered, and which has helped me more than any other uninspired book, to find my way through all that might otherwise have proved baffling and

1857

transcendental and mysterious in the peculiarities of
Calvinism."

5 UHDEN, HERMANN F. Geschichte der Congregationalsten in
   Neu-England. Berlin: Heinrich Schindler.
      Reprint of 1842.7.

                              1858

1 ANON. Review of History of the Church of Christ in Yale
   College, by George P. Fisher. New Englander
   16 (May):434-49.
      Praises Yale for what it has done to promote theology
   through Edwards and his successors.

2 [ATWATER, LYMAN H]. "Jonathan Edwards and the Successive
   Forms of the New Divinity." Biblical Repertory and
   Princeton Review 30 (October):585-620.
      Challenges George Fisher's account of New England
   Theology (1858.9) by arguing that, except for his
   doctrine of mediate imputation and his "eccentric" theory
   of true virtue, Edwards holds to concepts of Old
   Calvinism as his successors surely do not. There are
   "broad and irreconcilable differences" between Edwards
   and Hopkins, Emmons, Smalley, Taylor, Dwight, and the
   younger Edwards, though all have been "adroitly linked" to
   his name. But for the logical or illogical ends to which
   they take his ideas of imputation, atonement, and virtue,
   these New Divinity men show little indebtedness to Edwards.

3 BACON, LEONARD. A Commemorative Discourse on the Completion
   of Fifty Years from the Founding of the Theological
   Seminary at Andover. Andover, Mass.: W. F. Draper,
   pp. 8-12.
      Celebrates the fiftieth anniversary of the Andover
   Theological Seminary and suggests that Edwards's at-home
   study with Joseph Bellamy, Samuel Buell, and especially
   Samuel Hopkins constituted the "earliest germ" of those
   private schools for theological instruction that arose
   after the Great Awakening.

4 BAIRD, SAMUEL J. "Edwards and the Theology of New England."
   Southern Presbyterian Review 10 (January):576-92.
      Attacks Edwards's fundamental doctrine of causation,
   chiefly argued in Original Sin, which dishonors God and
   denies imputation. Edwards's "revolting fatalism" ends in
   an "inadequate" view of sin and corruption and prepared
   the way for the outbreak of Pelagianism and Socinianism

at Yale.

5 _____ . "Edwards and the Theology of New England." British and Foreign Evangelical Review 7 (July):544-62.
    Reprint of 1858.4.

6 BUSHNELL, HORACE. Nature and the Supernatural. New York: Charles Scribner, pp. 47-50.
    Notes the change in fortunes of Edwards's Freedom of the Will from its original defense of the divine order to its current defense of the irresponsibility of the "moral outcast." Bushnell also argues against Edwards's a priori knowledge of the strongest motive in choice.

7 CLARK, JOSEPH S. A Historical Sketch of the Congregational Churches In Massachusetts, from 1620-1858. Boston: Congregational Board of Publication, pp. 155-59, 178-90.
    Explains in some detail Edwards's role as a Congregationalist in the Great Awakening and focuses upon the "unreasonable and un-Congregational" handling of his dismission, attributing it to the "unsettled hostility" of some churches to revivalism and its results. At the heart of the problem lay the "mischievous notion" that a church council was like a church court to which congregants could appeal for swift, unchallenged action. Such a council, functioning in a judiciary not an advisory way, was "contrary to all rule and precedent" and assured, in its "tyrannical proceedings," Edwards's condemnation. Ironically, Edwards himself "lent sanction" to a judicial council in the much-disputed Robert Breck case some years before.

8 [CUNNINGHAM, WILLIAM]. "Sir William Hamilton on Philosophical Necessity and the Westminster Confession." British and Foreign Evangelical Review 7 (January):199-252.
    Maintains, contrary to Sir William Hamilton's view, that the philosophical necessity of Edwards, and of Thomas Chalmers as well, is consistent with the Westminster Confession.

9 FISHER, GEORGE P[ARK]. A Discourse Commemorative of the History of the Church of Christ in Yale College, during the First Century of its Existence. New Haven, Conn.: Thomas A. Pease, pp. 36-37, 80-82 passim.
    Notes that Yale College has trained many important New England divines and that they all share theological affinity with Edwards, the first of them.

10 PARTON, J[AMES]. The Life and Times of Aaron Burr. New York:

1858

Mason Brothers, pp. 25-30, 626.
Traces Edwards's career and records Aaron Burr's observation that his grandfather was "'the clearest head of America. How the race has degenerated,' he would say, with a humorous shrug." Edwards's chief contribution was to render irreconcilable church and state at a time when they were beginning to "mingle."

11 UHDEN, HERMANN F. The New England Theocracy. Translated by H. C. Conant. Boston: Gould & Lincoln. Translation of 1842.7.

1859

1 ANON. "Copy of Libel Against Jonathan Edwards." Hampshire Gazette, 29 March, p. 2.
Reprints a libel, recorded in January 1735/36, by Bernard Bartlet, of Simsbury, that Edwards was "as Great an Instrument of the Devil had on this side Hell to bring souls to Hell" [sic].

2 [ATWATER, LYMAN H.] "Jonathan Edwards and the Successive Forms of the New Divinity." British and Foreign Evangelical Review 8 (April):267-96.
Reprint of 1858.2.

3 [BYINGTON, EZRA HOYT.] "The Theology of Edwards, as Shown in his Treatise concerning Religious Affections." American Theological Review 1 (May):199-220.
Claims that there is no "higher authority" than Religious Affections to deduce Edwards's theology, that it is practical and scientific, and quotes at length from it.

4 MARVIN, A. P. "Three Eras of Revivals in the United States." Bibliotheca Sacra 16 (April):279-301.
Remarks three periods of revivalism--1740, 1797, and 1830. The first, the era of Edwards, was marked by the justification by faith and the doctrine of the new birth; the second by the doctrine of divine sovereignty; and the third by a sense of "personal duty to love and serve God." The country was saved from "total corruption" by the "Reformation of 1740."

5 PARK, EDWARDS A[MASA]. "The Rise of the Edwardean Theory of the Atonement: an Introductory Essay." In his The Atonement: Discourses and Treaties by Edwards, Smalley, Maxcy, Emmons, Griffin, Burge, and Weeks. Boston: Congregational Board of Publication, pp. xi-xxxix passim.

Charts Edward's modifications of the older Calvinist
theory of the atonement as they affect "directly or
indirectly" the more modern Edwardsean scheme proposed by
his son. Edwards "exalts" the sovereignty of God rather
than the atonement of Christ; urges a distinction between
threat and promise, penalty and merit, but denies one
between active and passive obedience; gives a "previously
unwonted prominence" to love; and uses a "peculiar
nomenclature" to argue his case. This loose, vague,
seemingly inconsistent language not only has led opposing
theologians to claim him their own but also has forced
his successors to a deliberately precise language.

6   SMITH, HENRY B. History of the Church of Christ in
    Chronological Tables. New York: Charles Scribner,
    pp. 70, 73.
        Lists, under New England polity, Edwards's vindication
    of original sin and divine sovereignty through a
    scriptural and rationalistic defense of Calvinism.
    Edwards's system has had a profound effect upon the
    theology of the churches.

7   STOWE, HARRIET BEECHER. The Minister's Wooing. New York:
    Derby & Jackson, pp. 332-38, passim.
        Scatters comments about Edwards, quotes "Sarah
    Pierrepont," and regards his sermons on sin and suffering
    as "refined poetry of torture."

8   TAYLOR, ISAAC. "Logic in Theology." In his Logic in
    Theology and Other Essays. London: Bell & Daldy,
    pp. 1-76.
        Reprint of 1827.5, revised.

                        1860

1   ANON. "Religious Revivals." Quarterly Review
    107 (January):148-68.
        Reviews books about the Irish revivals of 1857, cites
    the American counterparts of 1734 and 1741, and discusses
    Edwards's role in them.

2   BAIRD, SAMUEL J. The Elohim Revealed in the Creation and
    Redemption of Man. Philadelphia: Lindsay & Blakiston,
    pp. 47-50, 103-12, 160-64, passim.
        Considers Edwards "unscriptural," "pantheistic," and
    "antinomian," and attributes much, if not all, to his
    false theory of causation. In Freedom of the Will,
    Edwards failed to recognize in the distinctive nature of

1860

the soul an efficient cause of its volitions and so
promulgated a system hostile to his doctrine of grace.
His doctrine of identity, which depends upon his theory
of causation, is irreconcilable with his doctrine of
imputation.

3 [BYINGTON, EZRA HOYT.] "The Theology of Edwards, as shown
in his Treatise Concerning Religious Affections. British
and Foreign Evangelical Review 9 (January):119-36.
     Reprint of 1859.3.

4 COOKE, PARSONS. "Edwards on the Atonement." American
Theological Review 2 (February):97-120.
     Attacks Edwards A. Park's study of the atonement
(1859.5) for its distortions, which pits Edwardseans
against Edwards in a conflict of principles and subjects
Christian doctrine to the "cramping-irons" of rationalizing
metaphysics. Edwards has always been "an index" of
orthodox Calvinism on the atonement as on other matters,
but now by a skillful "play upon figurative language" a
new system of Edwardseanism has sprung up opposed both to
Calvin and Edwards.

5 [PORTER, NOAH]. "The Princeton Review on Dr. Taylor, and the
Edwardean Theology." New Englander 18 (August):726-73.
     Asserts that Edwards should be "properly regarded as
the founder of a new school" and that the Edwardseans are
both his successors and "important" contributors to
Christian theology. The "leading peculiarity" about
Edwards was that he was both philosopher and divine: he
brought current philosophical thinking into the
Calvinistic system when possible and rejected it on
"philosophic grounds" when it proved inconsistent. The
Princetonians, on the other hand, "believe in the
absolute perfection of the old metaphysics. The
Edwardseans believe in their imperfection, and try to
improve them."

5 SHERMAN, D[AVID]. Sketches of New England Divines. New York:
Carlton & Porter, pp. 138-82.
     Reckons Edwards the "mightiest mind" in modern times and
the "apostle of a new dispensation" in a biographical
account fulsome in its praise and casual in its details.

7 TAYLOR, ISAAC. "Logic in Theology." In his Logic in
Theology and Other Essays. New York: William Gowans,
pp. 7-69.
     Reprint of 1859.8.

1861

1 [GENERAL ASSOCIATION OF CONGREGATIONAL CHURCHES, CONNECTICUT.]
   Contributions to the Ecclesiastical History of
   Connecticut. New Haven, Conn.: William L. Kingsley,
   pp. 197-98.
   Describes Edwards's role in the Great Awakening (and
   the ripple effect upon Connecticut towns) and documents
   the terms of the Bolton settlement, which he rejects for
   Yale.

2 LAWRENCE, E[DWARD] A. "New England Theology: The Edwardean
   Period." American Theological Review 3 (January):36-68.
   Examines the immediate legacy of Edwards's thought
   found in New England Theology by returning to the
   "genuine" theology of the chief productions of its
   "master-mind," both in a logical and a chronological order.
   Some may disagree with one part of the "construction" or
   another, as they are in the "right or left wing" of New
   England Theology, the New Divinity or the Old, the Old
   Calvinists or the New. Yet it is clear that in those
   major works--Freedom of the Will, End of Creation,
   Original Sin, and True Virtue--Edwards gave "deliberation
   and explicitness" to a doctrine and a theology that
   "entitle his words to be taken without attenuation or
   apology."

3 THOMPSON, JOSEPH P. "Jonathan Edwards, his Character,
   Teaching, and Influence." Bibliotheca Sacra
   18 (October):809-39.
   Mediates between "unquestioning veneration" and
   "empirical judgment" of Edwards's character in an attempt
   to study the whole man, his life and his thought, and
   concludes that his theology is "a liberalized,
   rationalized, and harmonized" Calvinism affecting New
   England theology, Congregationalism, and Christendom.

1862

1 FROTHINGHAM, W. "The Edwards Family." Continental Monthly
   1 (January):11-16.
   Journeys through the Edwards family to Judge Ogden
   Edwards, of Staten Island, New York, and stops to extol
   the "enviable greatness" of his grandfather Jonathan.

2 _____. "Jonathan Edwards and the Old Clergy." Continental
   Monthly 1 (March):265-72.
   Recounts tales and anecdotes about the clergy of New

1862

England and about its "great light," Edwards. With all his care and frugality, Edwards was still "the largest consumer of paper and ink in New England."

3 MAURICE, FREDERICK DENISON. Moral and Metaphysical Philosophy. London: Griffin, Bohn & Co., 4:469-75.
   Claims that Edwards forsakes the very Puritans and Reformers he is heir to by exchanging a supremely righteous God for a supremely happy one. Freedom of the Will, however original or important it may still be, had a "debasing" effect on religious morality.

4 PLUES, ROBERT. "Man's Moral Freedom." In his The Rev. C. H. Spurgeon and his Brethren, Drs. Payne and Wardlaw, President Edwards, and Others, in the Crucible; or the Peculiarities of Calvinism Tested. London: G. J. Stevenson, pp. 80-105.
   Analyzes the "false and stupid" philosophy of Edwards in Freedom of the Will from the title-page onward and attacks his "usual habit of crincumism" in moral matters. Edwards's book is a "quibble and logomachy, and, indeed, nonsense" and another example of perverse Calvinism.

1863

1 LAWRENCE, EDWARD A. "The Old School in New England Theology." Bibliotheca Sacra 20 (April):311-49.
   Compares "Old School" theology of Edwards and Bellamy with the "improvements" of Hopkins and Taylor on anthropological doctrines, sin, moral agency, ability and inability, regeneration, atonement and justification, divine sovereignty, and theodicy, in an attempt to reconcile them by clearly stating their positions.

1864

1 [ATWATER, LYMAN H.] "Whedon and Hazard on the Will." Biblical Repertory and Princeton Review 36 (October):679-703.
   Refutes D. D. Whedon (1864.5) and Rowland G. Hazard (1864.3) in their attack upon Edwards and suggests that such assaults on Freedom of the Will simply add to its fame and notoriety, demonstrate its considerable influence, and prove the "futility of ail replies" to its basic arguments, notwithstanding some flaws in Edwards's logic and infelicities in his language.

2   GILLETT, E[ZRA] H[ALL]. History of the Presbyterian Church
       in the United States of America. Philadelphia:
       Presbyterian Publication Committee, 1:122-23.
          Notes Samuel Davies's offer to Edwards of a pastorate
       in Virginia and quotes the latter's approval of
       Presbyterian polity in a letter, 5 July 1750.

3   HAZARD, ROWLAND G[IBSON]. "Review of Edwards on the Will."
       In his Freedom of Mind in Willing; or, Every Being that
       Wills a Creative First Cause. New York and London: D.
       Appleton & Co., pp. 173-435.
          Exposes "the fallacies" of Edwards's Freedom of the
       Will in an extended argument on liberty, necessity,
       self-determination, causation, indifference, contingence,
       understanding, motive, and foreknowledge.

4   WATERBURY, J. B. "Rev. Jonathan Edwards." In his Sketches
       of Eloquent Preachers. New York: American Tract Society,
       pp. 151-62.
          Attributes Edwards's effectiveness as a preacher not
       to his graceful delivery, musical voice, or practical
       rhetoric, all of which he seriously lacked, but to
       God-inspired power.

5   WHEDON, D. D. The Freedom of the Will as a Basis of Human
       Responsibility and a Divine Government Elucidated and
       Maintained in its Issue with the Necessitarian Theories
       of Hobbes, Edwards, the Princeton Essayists, and Other
       Leading Advocates. New York: Carlton & Porter, 438 pp.
          Refutes the doctrine of the will of Edwards (and
       others) on the basis of human responsibility and
       accountibility, in an exhaustive analysis that first
       defines the terms; then considers the necessitarian
       argument in its causational, psychological, and
       theological aspects; and finally states the positive
       arguments of consciousness, morality, responsibility,
       freedom, and theodicy. Edwards succeeds in demonstrating
       the necessity of volition in action, but he fails
       signally to square moral intuitions with "intellective
       conclusions." His is not a judicial mind, but a forensic
       one, given to advocacy, not considered thought.

1865

1   BEECHER, LYMAN. Autobiography, Correspondence, Etc., of
       Lyman Beecher, D. D. Edited by Charles Beecher. New York:
       Harper & Brothers, 1:384 and 469-71; 2:237-38.
          Mentions Edwards in several letters, most prominently

1865

in one to his son George at Yale, 5 November 1830,
recommending "Next after the Bible, read and study
Edwards."

2   FISKE, D[ANIEL] T.   "Discourse Relating to the Churches and
Religious History of Essex North." In Contributions to
the Ecclesiastical History of Essex County, Mass.   Boston:
Congregational Board of Publication, pp. 280-81.
    Asserts that Edwards did not oppose the half-way
covenant so much as the Stoddardean form of it.

3   _____. "New England Theology." Bibliotheca Sacra
22 (July):467-512; (October):568-88.
    Traces the shifting names and central doctrines of
New England Theology--the nature of virtue, the nature of
sin, original sin, natural ability, regeneration,
atonement, and decrees--from Edwards through Hopkins to
Emmons, in an historical rather than critical estimate of
"modified" Calvinism.

4   GROSART, ALEXANDER B.   Introduction to his Selctions from the
Unpublished Writings of Jonathan Edwards of America.
[Edinburgh]: Printed for Private Circulation, pp. 11-16.
    Recounts plans to publish (with Tryon Edwards) a
complete Edwards based upon available manuscripts--the
project was interrupted by the "deplorable" Civil War--and
briefly explains the contents of the texts printed here
for the first time. The "Treatise on Grace" ranks with
Religious Affections in its "rapturous exultation";
"Annotations on Passages of the Bible" is "more richly
experimental" than the previously published "Notes on the
Bible"; "Direction for Judging of Persons' Experiences"
served as a testing-guide during the Awakening; and the
eight sermon-notes refute the charge that Edwards read
his sermons.

5   HAZARD, ROWLAND G[IBSON].   "Review of Edwards on the Will."
In his Freedom of Mind in Willing. New York: D.
Appleton and Co.
    Reprint of 1864.3.

6   POTWIN, L. S.   "Freedom of the Will: -- Edwards and Whedon."
New Englander 24 (April):285-302.
    Reviews Edwards's Freedom of the Will and D. D.
Whedon's Freedom of the Will (1864.5) and compares their
definitions of will and freedom and their causational and
psychological arguments. Whedon fails "most strikingly"
to overturn Edwards.

7   THOMAS, ROBERT. Preface to <u>Ymchwiliad Gofalus A Manwl . . .</u>
     [Freedom of the Will]. Caernarfon: H. Humphreys, pp.
     [iii]-xxix.
         Offers a life of Edwards and commentary on <u>Freedom of</u>
     <u>the Will</u>. (In Welsh.)

                              1866

1   HAZARD, ROWLAND GIBSON. "Review of Edwards on the Will." In
     his <u>Freedom of Mind in Willing</u>. New York: D. Appleton &
     Co.
         Reprint of 1864.3.

2   WHITTIER, JOHN GREANLEAF. "The Preacher." In his <u>The</u>
     <u>Poetical Works of John Greenleaf Whittier</u>. Boston:
     Ticknor & Fields, 2:386-97.
         Pictures Edwards forging "the iron links of his
     argument" in a wilderness church, in a poem about George
     Whitefield and the Great Awakening.

                              1867

1   ANON. Review of <u>The Works of President Edwards</u>.
     <u>Congregationalist and Boston Recorder</u>, 28 November, p. 242.
         Reviews a reissue of the 1843 edition of Edwards and
     calls for the release of some manuscripts preventing a
     "properly" edited text.

2   GILLETT, E[ZRA] H[ALL]. "Jonathan Edwards, and the Occasion
     and Result of his Dismission from Northampton." <u>Historical</u>
     <u>Magazine</u>, 2nd ser. 1 (June):333-38.
         Recounts the problems raised by Edwards's views on
     qualifications of church membership, the council of
     ministers met to solve them, and the resulting course of
     his dismission. <u>Qualifications</u> produced a "feeble
     impression" in Northampton and opposition in most of the
     neighboring Churches; abroad it was thought "decisive" on
     the question. His dismission a year later brought
     attention to his views throughout New England, and within
     fifty years, "one by one," the churches adopted Edwards's
     scheme.

3   G[ILLETT], E[ZRA] H[ALL]. "[Note on] the Clerical Members
     of the Council that Dismis.ed Jonathan Edwards from
     Northampton." <u>Historical Magazine</u>, 2nd ser.
     2 (September):183.
         Confirms an earlier attempt (1867.2) to list the

1867

ministers on both sides of the question of Edwards's dismission and asks for further information from readers.

4   GRIDLEY, A. D. "Diary and Letters of Sarah Pierpont." Hours at Home 5 (August):295-303; and 5 (September):417-25.
     Presents an "inside view" of the lives of Sarah and Jonathan Edwards through a fictionalized diary and letters, with observations such as this: "What has set my heart into a flutter today? Is it the air, the birds, the flowers, or the sight of tutor Edwards?"

5   HOYLE, EDWARD. An Inquiry into the Truth of Christianity, and the Doctrine of Necessity. London: Austin & Co., pp. 4-5, 14-17, 45-49, 76-82 passim.
     Believes Christianity and the doctrine of necessity to be incompatible and cites Edwards's Freedom of the Will, early and frequently, as a principal source of the necessarian argument. Edwards's idea of the necessary relation between cause and effect is "false" and his insistence on necessity is at odds with man's responsiblity. If divine foreknowledge is true, then man is not a free agent; if man is a free agent, then Christianity is "not true." Christianity is not from God.

1868

1   BEECHER, HENRY WARD. Norwood: or, Village Life in New England. New York: Charles Scribner & Co., p. 326.
     Compares Edwards to Dante in remarks on New England theologians.

2   FISHER, GEORGE P[ARK]. "The Augustinian and the Federal Theories of Original Sin Compared." New Englander 27 (July):468-516.
     Finds that Edwards "fell back" to the doctrine of original sin of Aquinas and Augustine and that his original speculations--for example, on the "first rising" of sinful inclination--do not "materially" modify those old ideas.

3   G[ILLETT, EZRA HALL]. "[Note on] the General Council that Dismissed Jonathan Edwards from Northampton." Historical Magazine, 2nd ser. 3 (January):53.
     Notes that ministers of the Council that judged Edwards were "equally divided": Edward Billings, William Hobby, David Hall, Jonathan Hubbard, and Robert Abercombie for Edwards; Joseph Ashley, Chester Williams, Timothy Woodbridge, Robert Breck, and Peter Reynolds for the Church.

4   HALSEY, L. J. "Great Preachers and Pastors, or Retrospect
of the Presbyterian Pulpit in America for One Hundred and
Fifty Years: Jonathan Edwards and George Whitefield."
North-Western Presbyterian, 16 May, p. 1.
Cites the contemporaneous influence Edwards's published
treatises on the will, the affections, and original sin
had on the "forming period" of the Presbyterian Church.
Though a Calvinist in doctrine and a Congregationalist in
practice, Edwards was a "thorough" Presbyterian in polity.

5   LECKY, W[ILLIAM] E. H. History of the Rise and Influence of
the Spirit of Rationalism in Europe. New York: D.
Appleton & Co., 1:368, 387.
Considers Edwards's Original Sin "one of the most
revolting books that have ever proceeded from the pen of
man."

1869

1   EGGLESTON, NATHANIEL H. In Memoriam. A Discourse Preached
November 1st, 1868, on the Occasion of the Erection of
Tablets in the Old Church at Stockbridge, Mass., in
Memory of its Former Pastors: John Sergeant, Jonathan
Edwards, Stephen West, and David D. Field. New York:
Baker & Godwin, pp. 19-24.
Recounts Edwards's Stockbridge years, the contrast
between the man and the place.

2   LAWRENCE, M. W. "Old-Time Minister and Parish." Putnam's
Monthly Magazine, n.s. 4 (August):166-68.
Waxes sentimental about Edwards's birthplace, his
father's ministry, and the "rustic bower" of his
meditations.

3   MAGOUN, GEORGE F. "President Edwards as a Reformer."
Congregational Quarterly, n.s. 1 (April):259-74.
Reviews the life and times of the "saintly" and
"Miltonic" Edwards, an "eminent" practical and theological
reformer.

4   STOWE, HARRIET BEECHER. Oldtown Folks. Boston: Fields,
Osgood, & Co., pp. 229, 363-65, 376-78, 458-59, passim.
Comments briefly and serially upon Edwards's
rationalistic methods and suggests that the "average" New
Englander combines the materiality of Franklin and the
spirituality of Edwards.

5   TARBOX, INCREASE N. "Jonathan Edwards." Bibliotheca Sacra

26 (April):243-68.
Details the facts of Edwards's early life and concludes
that with so little to stimulate his intellectual growth
(even at Yale), he was "the best possible refutation of
Locke's philosophy, that the mind has 'no innate ideas.'"
Central to Edwards's theology is his attempt to give
"fuller recognition" to man in a scheme of divine
sovereignty. Thus did he turn theology into "new
channels and in the right direction."

<u>1870</u>

1   ANON. "Some Notes upon the Late Edwards Meeting."
     <u>Congregationalist and Boston Recorder</u>, 13 October, p. 2.
     Relates the social side of the recent Edwards meeting
     in Stockbridge.

2   B., L. D. "The Edwards Clan." <u>New York Times</u>, 5 September,
     p. 2.
     Announces a gathering of the Edwards's clan in
     Stockbridge on the next two days to "do honor to the
     memory of their great ancestor," gives the program for
     "the great event," and offers a brief life, appraisal, and
     list of descendants.

3   IRENAEUS. "Gathering of the Tribe of Jonathan Edwards."
     <u>New York Observer</u>, 15 September, p. 290.
     Summarizes the papers and events of the Edwards
     gathering at Stockbridge. Mention of Edwards's New York
     pastorate draws question and comment from readers on
     29 September (p. 309) and 22 December (p. 403).

4   MAGOUN, GEORGE F. "Unpublished Writings of President
     Edwards." <u>Congregational Review</u> 10 (January):19-27.
     Reviews and quotes from two items--a treatise on grace
     and "Directions for Judging of Person's Experiences"--in
     Alexander B. Grosart's <u>Selections</u> (1865.4), finding both
     cogent.

5   P[ARK], E[DWARDS] A[MASA]. "Edwards, Jonathan."
     <u>Cyclopaedia of Biblical, Theological, and Ecclesiastical
     Literature</u>. Edited by John McClintock and James Strong.
     New York: Harper & Brothers, 3:63-67.
     Offers a life of Edwards and an estimate, principally
     the differing views on the questions of natural or moral
     inability in <u>Freedom of the Will</u> and the question of
     identity in <u>Original Sin</u>. In <u>True Virtue</u> and <u>End of
     Creation</u>, "like many of his other essays," Edwards sought

1870

"to reconcile reason with faith."

6 T., S. E. "Jonathan Edwards." <u>New York Times</u>, 8 September,
   p. 1.
       Reports the program and the speakers at the Edwards
   reunion at Stockbridge, including a "large number of
   outsiders," and discusses biographies, estimates, and
   portraits of him. A book about the reunion is to be
   published (1871.5).

7 TARBOX, I[NCREASE] N. "Antiquities of Stockbridge."
   <u>Congregationalist and Boston Recorder</u>, 20 October, p. 1.
       Recounts briefly the Edwards family stay in Stockbridge.

8 _____. "The Edwards Meeting." <u>Congregatonalist and Boston
   Recorder</u>, 15 September, p. 1.
       Reports the events and papers of the Stockbridge meeting
   of Edwards's descendants.

9 _____. "The Old East Windsor Burying-Ground." <u>Congregation-
   alist and Boston Recorder</u>, 22 September, p. 2.
       Describes the meeting-house, dwelling, and burial
   ground of the Edwards family in East Windsor, Connecticut.

<u>1871</u>

1 EGGLESTON, N[ATHANIEL] H. "A New England Village." <u>Harper's
   New Monthly Magazine</u> 43 (November):815-29.
       Sketches a history of Stockbridge and of Edwards's
   missionary work among the Indians, performed there
   "almost in secrecy and silence."

2 FRASER, ALEXANDER CAMPBELL, ed. <u>The Works of George Berkeley</u>,
   D.D. Oxford: Clarendon Press, 1:179.
       Notes Edwards's affinity to Berkeley's immaterialism and
   their physical proximity: "when Berkeley was in Rhode
   Island, Edwards was settled in Massachusetts."

3 SIMONS, M. LAIRD. <u>Sunday Half-hours with the Great Preachers</u>.
   Philadelphia: Porter & Coates, p. 266.
       Introduces and reprints selections from Edwards's
   "Wrath upon the Wicked."

4 WAKELEY, J. B. <u>The Prince of Pulpit Orators: A Portrature
   of Rev. George Whitefield, M. A., Illustrated by
   Anecdotes and Incidents</u>. New York: Carlton & Lanahan,
   pp. 274-78.
       Describes the relationship between Edwards and George

Whitefield. Edwards was uncertain of Whitefield's feeling for him; Whitefield "winced" at Edwards's criticism of his attitude toward "impulses." The two men parted amicably though, and Whitefield left with a deep affection for Sarah, mutually shared.

5   [WOODBRIDGE, JONATHAN EDWARDS, ed.] <u>Memorial Volume of the Edwards Family Meeting at Stockbridge, Mass. Sept. 6-7, A. D. 1870</u>. Boston: Congregational Publishing Society, 206 pp.
        Gathers together the more than twenty-five tributes to Edwards delivered during a two-day family meeting in Stockbridge, including a serial life by I. N. Tarbox, E. A. Park, John Todd, Mark Hopkins, and others, and verse lines about his descendants ("While honorables, D.D.'s, and LL.D.'s,/Lie 'mong us like the leaves in autumn breeze)" by Sarah Edwards Tyler Henshaw, and about him ("an iceberg on Time's ocean") by Frank D. Clark.

1872

1   HODGE, CHARLES. <u>Systematic Theology</u>. New York: Charles Scribner & Co., 2:217-21.
        Objects to Edwards's "strange" doctrine of original sin, for it is contrary to scripture, intuition, and reason. Edwards agrees with the realists that Adam and man are identical, but he differs from them in denying the numerical sameness of substance.

1873

1   BLAIKIE, WILLIAM GARDEN. <u>For the Work of the Ministry: A Manual of Homiletical and Pastoral Theology</u>. London: Strahan & Co., pp. 223, 325-26.
        Discovers beneath the calm manner of Edwards's preaching a "deep fountain" of emotion and recommends his <u>Faithful Narrative</u> as the single most intelligent view of the "whole subject" of revivals.

2   STEPHEN, LESLIE. "Jonathan Edwards." <u>Fraser's Magazine</u>, n.s. 8 (November):529-51.
        Accounts Edwards's effort "to live constantly" under an absolute and infinite God the source of the irreconcilable tensions within him--the "gentle mystic" of <u>Personal Narrative</u> as well as the "stern divine" of <u>Original Sin</u>--in a study of his life and major work. Edwards's theological system rests upon the "fundamental" doctrine of the light

of God imparted to man; his metaphysical system, upon the
"existence of absolute a priori truths." His style is
"heavy and languid," natural in a "speculative recluse."
His theory of morality is "ennobling"; his theory of the
universe, "elevated." There is in Edwards "genuine metal,"
then, "no less unmistakably than the refuse."

1874

1   [BLEDSOE, ALBERT TAYLOR.] "Foreknowledge and Free Will."
    Southern Review 15 (July):91-109.
        Reprints Section XI of his Examination (1845.2).

2   DWIGHT, BENJAMIN W. The History of the Descendants of John
    Dwight of Dedham, Mass. New York: John F. Trow & Son,
    2:1037-50.
        Offers a brief biography of Edwards and a genealogy.

3   PORTER, NOAH. "Jonathan Edwards." In his "Appendix I:
    Philosophy in Great Britain and America" to History of
    Philosophy from Thales to the Present Time, by Friedrich
    Ueberweg. New York: Scribner, Armstrong, 2:443-48.
        Examines briefly Edwards on the will, virtue, sin, and
    affections and notes the published arguments of both his
    friends and his critics. Edwards's work exerted a
    "powerful" influence on his successors and "trained"
    generations of Americans to "pronounced speculative tastes
    and habits."

4   STEPHEN, LESLIE. "Jonathan Edwards." Littell's Living Age
    120 (24 January):219-36.
        Reprint of 1873.2.

1875

1   ANON. "Jonathan Edwards." Presbyterian Monthly Record
    26 (August):232-35.
        Renders fulsome praise to Edwards the man and the
    preacher and traces his singular influence on a multitude
    of theologians here and abroad.

2   BLEDSOE, ALBERT TAYLOR. "The Relation of the Will to the
    Feelings." Southern Review 17 (April):435-48.
        Reprints Section VIII of his Examination (1845.2).

3   HENDERSON, T. F. "Edwards, Jonathan." Encyclopedia
    Britannica. 9th ed., 7:688-91.

Traces Edwards's career and estimates the work of "the
most distinguished metaphysician and divine of America."
Edwards had the "contradictory qualities" of the mystic and
the logician and in his isolation and retrospection was
untouched by helpful and modifying influences of his time.
His Freedom of the Will, a skillful structure, "inevitably
collapses" under the weight of irreconcilable principles.

1876

1   ATWATER, LYMAN H.   "The Great Awakening of 1740."
    Presbyterian Quarterly and Princeton Review
    5 (October):676-89.
         Derives an account of the Great Awakening from Tracy
    (1842.6) and Edwards's Some Thoughts.

2   P[ARK], E[DWARDS] A[MASA], ed.   "Jonathan Edwards' Last Will,
    and the Inventory of his Estate."   Bibliotheca Sacra
    33 (July):438-47.
         Reprints Edwards's will and inventory from records in
    the Probate Office at Northampton and finds them
    illustrative of the style of living of clergymen then.

3   STEPHEN, LESLIE.   "Jonathan Edwards."   In his Hours in a Library
    Second Series. London: Smith, Elder, & Co. pp. 44-106.
         Reprint of 1873.2. (Frequently reprinted in this form.)

4   STEWART, J[AMES] G.   Freedom of the Will Vindicated; or,
    President Edwards' Necessarian Theory Refuted. Glasgow:
    David Bryce & Son, 75 pp.
         Refutes Edwards's arguments on both the self-determining
    power of the will and the determining power of motives in
    Freedom of the Will and dismisses them as sophistical and
    unintelligible.

1877

1   ANON. "Studies and Conduct, Second Series, I. Jonathan
    Edwards--Resolutions for a Holy Life." American Journal of
    Education 27 (October):721-28.
         Recounts a brief life of Edwards, man thinking.

2   BLEDSOE, ALBERT TAYLOR.   "President Edwards' Inquiry into the
    Freedom of the Will." Southern Review 22 (October):376-404.
         Reprints the introduction and Sections I-III of his
    Examination (1845.2).

1877

3   MACLEAN, JOHN. History of the College of New Jersey, from
    its Origin in 1746 to the Commencement of 1854.
    Philadelphia: J. B. Lippincott & Co., 1:169-91.
        Documents the appointment and administration of Edwards
    as president of Princeton and offers a standard biography.
    "Probably no man ever connected with this institution has
    contributed so much to the reputation of the College,
    both at home and abroad."

4   SMITH, HENRY B. Faith and Philosophy: Discourses and Essays.
    Edited by George L. Prentiss. New York: Scribner,
    Armstrong & Co., pp. 149-51, 383-86, passim.
        Praises Edwards's work, the center of which is man's
    relation to divine grace.

5   THOMPSON, CHARLES L. Times of Refreshing: A History of
    American Revivals from 1740-1877, with their Philosophy
    and Methods. Chicago: L. T. Palmer & Co., pp. 37-40.
        Singles out Edwards's Justification by Faith Alone as
    a bulwark against the drift into spiritual lethargy in the
    1730s and as vital to experimental religion.

1878

1   ANON. "Jonathan Edwards." Hampshire Gazette, 30 April, p. 1.
        Recounts Edwards's career in Northampton.

2   BLEDSOE, ALBERT TAYLOR. "President Edwards' Inquiry into the
    Freedom of the Will." Southern Review 23 (January):5-33.
        Reprints Sections IV-VII of his Examination (1845.2).

3   _____. "President Edwards' Inquiry into the Freedom of the
    Will." Southern Review 23 (April):338-89.
        Reprints Sections VIII-XI of his Examination (1845.2).

4   _____. "President Edwards' Inquiry into the Freedom of the
    Will." Southern Review 24 (July):64-93.
        Reprints Sections XII-XIV of his Examination (1845.2).

5   _____. "President Edwards' Inquiry into the Freedom of the
    Will." Southern Review 24 (October):344-72.
        Reprints Sections XV-XVIII of his Examination (1845.2).

6   NORTHAMPTON, MASS., FIRST PARISH. First Parish, Northampton:
    Meetinghouses and Ministers from 1653-1878. Northampton,
    Mass.: Gazette Printing Co., pp. 15-17.
        Details the salary and land given Edwards during his
    pastorate in the second meetinghouse. After Edwards's

dismissal in 1750, Judah Champion was offered the church
but refused; later John Hooker accepted and was ordained
5 December 1753.

7   TYLER, MOSES COIT. A History of American Literature. New
York: G. P. Putnam's Sons, 2:177-92.
Traces Edwards's career, quotes mainly from the
juvenilia, analyzes the method of Sinners in the Hands of
an Angry God, and regrets his calling. Though
"unsurpassed" as a dialectician, Edwards could have been
"one of the world's masters" in physical science or in
imaginative literature, for he had all the virtues of a
writer--clear expression, bold imagery, and keen wit.

1879

1   ALDRICH, P. EMORY. "Report to the Council." Proceedings of
the American Antiquarian Society, no. 73 (April):9-39.
Remarks Locke's influence upon Edwards and through him
to "every school of theology" in the country, in a survey
of the influence of Locke upon philosophy, politics, and
religion in America.

2   ANON. "Jonathan Edwards." Hampshire Gazette, 11 February,
p. 1.
Reprints a report from the Providence Press of an
address to the Historical Society by Abraham Payne on
Edwards's career.

3   EASTMAN, Z. "Jonathan Edwards and About his Elms." Hampshire
Gazette, 19 August, p. 1.
Describes Edwards's career in Northampton, his house on
King Street, and the elms that still stand before it (by a
Chicago correspondent).

4   FISHER, GEORGE P[ARK]. "The Philosophy of Jonathan Edwards."
North American Review 128 (March):284-303.
Examines Edwards's major work, particularly Freedom of
the Will, and concludes that the "iron network" of his
doctrine of necessity is too confining and exclusive to
satisfy "the generality of mankind." Edwards borrows the
psychology of choice from Locke, but his failure to
identify and distinguish voluntary and involuntary
inclinations is his own and his philosophy of the will as a
whole is "not consonant" with that of most Augustinian
theologians. So, too, in True Virtue, he obviously knows
Francis Hutcheson, but much of the "scientific construction"
of theory is original with Edwards and his exchange of

1879

moral right and obligation for spiritual beauty is "most questionable."

5   HAGEMAN, JOHN FRELINGHUYSEN. <u>History of Princeton and its Institutions</u>. Philadelphia: J. B. Lippincott & Co., 2:249–53.
       Notes Edwards's short stay at Princeton but claims he lent more honor to the College than any president before or since.

6   H[UMPHREYS], Z[EPHANIAH] M. "Jonathan Edwards." In <u>Lives of the Leaders of Our Church Universal</u>. Edited by Ferdinand Piper and translated and edited by Henry Mitchell MacCracken. New York: Phillips & Hunt, pp. 547–57.
       Lauds Edwards's life and work, in superlatives.

7   HUXLEY, THOMAS HENRY. <u>Hume</u>. English Men of Letters. London: Macmillan & Co., pp. 194–95.
       Finds "curious" Edwards's handling of the authorship of sin in <u>Freedom of the Will</u>, an unavailing struggle between the theologian and the logician. But Edwards's orthodox, necessarian argument "has never been equalled in power, and certainly has never been refuted."

<u>1880</u>

1   ANON. "As to Jonathan Edwards." <u>Congregationalist</u>, 7 July, p. 4.
       Awaits the publication of Edwards's manuscript on the trinity but, unlike Holmes and the <u>Hartford Courant</u> (1880.2), believes in Edwards's orthodoxy and quotes Egbert Smyth to prove it.

2   ANON. "The Injustice to Jonathan Edwards." <u>Hartford Courant</u>, 23 June, p. 2.
       Implores Edwards A. Park (see 1881.2) to publish a "suppressed" Edwards's manuscript on the trinity so that the matter of his alleged unitarian views might be settled.

3   CHADWICK, JOHN W. "In Western Massachusetts." <u>Harper's Magazine</u> 61 (November):873–87.
       Remarks Edwards's affection for his wife-to-be and reprints "Sarah Pierrepont."

4   FISHER, GEORGE P[ARK]. "The Philosophy of Jonathan Edwards." In his <u>Discussions in History and Theology</u>. New York: Charles Scribner's Sons, pp. 227–52.

1880

Reprint of 1879.4.

5   _____. "The Religious Spirit of Jonathan Edwards." <u>Hampshire</u>
      <u>Gazette</u>, 25 May, p. 1.
           Counters Boston critics of Edwards as a man hard and
      cold with citations of his kindness from <u>Personal Narrative</u>
      and his ministering to the Indians.

6   HOLMES, OLIVER WENDELL. "Jonathan Edwards." <u>International</u>
      <u>Review</u> 9 (July):1-28.
           Sketches Edwards's life and major work, much of it like
      "the unleavened bread of the Israelite: holy it may be,
      but heavy it certainly is." His theological system itself
      is "barbaric, mechanical, materialistic, pessimistic"; his
      life's work "neglected" or "repudiated"; his intellect a
      compendium of "disorganizing conceptions." Edwards had
      come under the "misguiding influence" of the doctrine of
      the imputation of Adam's sin to man and the notion that a
      just God sanctions it. Such absurdities doomed him.

7   LAWRENCE, EUGENE. <u>A Primer of American Literature</u>. Harper's
      Half-Hour Series. New York: Harper & Brothers, pp. 32-39.
           Compares Edwards and Benjamin Franklin in a brief
      biography and notes that Edwards's fame is "once more
      rising."

8   POND, ENOCH. <u>Sketches of the Theological History of New</u>
      <u>England</u>. Boston: Congregatonal Publishing Society,
      pp. 22-48.
           Sketches the influence of Edwards and his followers
      upon "improvements" in theology, especially on the nature
      and evidence of regeneration. On the will and original sin
      Edwards still offers the most cogent defense.

9   SARGENT, MRS. JOHN T., ed. <u>Sketches and Reminiscences of the</u>
      <u>Radical Club of Chestnut Street, Boston</u>. Boston: James
      R. Osgood & Co., pp. 362-75.
           Records the reactions of several members of the Radical
      Club in Boston to Oliver Wendell Holmes's "brilliant"
      essay on Edwards (reprinted). Wendell Phillips complains
      that the portrait is incomplete, that there are other
      sides to Edwards; James Freeman Clarke praises Edwards as a
      "Protestant saint" and suggests that "a little healthy
      Concord mysticism" such as Edwards's is not a bad thing
      for New England.

10   SMYTH, EGBERT C[OFFIN]. Introduction to <u>Observations</u>
      <u>concerning the Scripture Oeconomy of the Trinity and</u>
      <u>Covenant of Redemption</u>. New York: Charles Scribner's

1880

Sons, pp. [3]-18.
Attests to Edwards's "not unorthodox" trinitarian views
and to the genuineness of the manuscript, reprinted here
after considerable debate about its suppression and
alleged heterodoxy. The text is no. 1062 of the
Miscellanies, a late, "elaborately reasoned" piece, in
which Edwards emphasizes, as do Puritans generally, the
divine covenant or social aspect of the trinity. Though
the paper is hardly a treatise on the trinity, it
anticipates modern Christology and indicates Edwards's
"peculiar genius."

1881

1   FRASER, A[LEXANDER] CAMPBELL. Berkeley. Philadelphia: J.
    B. Lippincott & Co., pp. 138-41.
       Claims Edwards "adopted" Berkeley's ideas, though he
    may not have read him. On the spiritual substance of the
    universe, their views "coincide"; on causation, they
    "fundamentally differ."

2   PARK, EDWARDS A[MASA]. "Remarks of Jonathan Edwards on the
    Trinity." Bibliotheca Sacra 38 (January):147-87;
    (April):333-69.
       Introduces and reprints, from Alexander B. Grosart's
    Unpublished Writings (1865.4), Edwards on the trinity to
    answer current (and unfounded) charges of heterodoxy.
    Even though Edwards's language here is "approximate rather
    than complete, analogical rather than exact, initiatory
    rather than plenary, rudimental rather than perfected," it
    is clear that he believes in the "special mysteriousness"
    of the trinity. Nowhere in his 500 manuscripts can be
    found a sentence expressing "any doubt" about that
    doctrine, though he will at times give more prominence to
    the simplicity than the triplicity of the divine mind.

3   _____. Remarks of Jonathan Edwards on the Trinity. Andover,
    Mass.: W. F. Draper, 40 pp.
       Reprint of 1881.2.

4   PHELPS, AUSTIN. The Theory of Preaching: Lectures on
    Homiletics. New York: Charles Scribner's Sons, pp. 560,
    587-88.
       Notes the incongruity in Edwards's preaching between
    his "subdued" delivery and his vehement words.

Writings About Jonathan Edwards

1882

1   BOARDMAN GEO[RGE] NYE. The Will and Virtue: Two Essays.
    Chicago: F. H. Revell, pp. 58-59, 120-25.
        Treats briefly Edwards's "triumphant refutation" of
    self-determinism in Freedom of the Will and his
    "unwarranted distinction" between justice and holiness and
    his degradation of conscience in True Virtue.

2   CLARK, SOLOMON. Antiquities, Historicals and Graduates of
    Northampton. Northampton, Mass.: Gazette Printing Co.,
    p. 263.
        Notes that Northampton is known for Edwards and the
    number of women marrying ministers.

3   NICHOL, JOHN. American Literature: An Historical Sketch,
    1620-1880. Edinburgh: A. & C. Black, pp. 52-55.
        Presents Edwards as a example not only of dated, grim
    Calvinism but also of "pure Colonial Puritan prose."

1883

1   [FOSTER, W. E.] "The Speculative Philosophy of Jonathan
    Edwards." Monthly Reference Lists 3 (December):42.
        Lists books and parts of books about Edwards's
    philosophy and quotes briefly from them as a short
    annotated bibliography.

2   HAZARD, ROWLAND G[IBSON]. Man a Creative First Cause: Two
    Discourses. Boston: Houghton Mifflin & Co., pp. 16-18.
        Deplores Edwards's "defective definitions" of will and
    freedom, in which choice and preference, to will and to
    choose are "identical." Based on that assumption, Edwards
    "logically infers that we are not free in willing."

3   HOLMES, OLIVER WENDELL. "Jonathan Edwards." In his Pages
    from an Old Volume of Life. Boston: Houghton Mifflin &
    Co., pp. 361-401.
        Reprint of 1880.6.

4   _____. "The Pulpit and the Pew." In his Pages from and Old
    Volume of Life. Boston: Houghton Mifflin Co., pp. 402-33.
        Questions whether Edwards's suppressed manuscript on
    the trinity has in fact been published, believing it to be
    more extensive than Egbert Smyth's text (1880.10) and
    hoping that it will be recovered to prove that Edwards was
    capable of heresy or "writing most unwisely" and to reduce
    the "validity of his judgment" on matters like infant

1883

damnation.

5   PHELPS. AUSTIN. <u>English Style in Public Discourse with</u>
    <u>Special Reference to the Usages of the Pulpit</u>. New York:
    Charles Scribner's Sons, pp. 31-32.
        Calls the meaning Edwards gives to the word <u>necessity</u>
    in <u>Freedom of the Will</u> a "pure invention," neither English
    nor popular.

6   SANBORN, F. B. "The Puritanic Philosophy and Jonathan
    Edwards." <u>Journal of Speculative Philosophy</u>
    17 (October):401-21.
        Characterizes Edwards as "the most acute and inflexible"
    of American Puritans, the "clearest manifestation" of a
    derivative philosophy that, happily, yields to democracy
    and to the philanthropists like Benjamin Franklin.
    Edwards's "nobel error" was to approach philosophy from
    received theology and to attempt speculative thought
    ignorant, for the most part, of Plato and Aristotle, the
    Schoolmen and Catholic theologians since Augustine.
    Although he shows an uncommon "subtlety of mind" and an
    awareness of the intellectual currents of his time,
    Edwards remains "our Puritan Schoolman, our Father
    Jonathan of Connecticut."

7   STOUGHTON, JOHN A. <u>"Windsor Farmes": A Glimpse of an Old</u>
    <u>Parish</u>. Hartford: Clark & Smith, pp. 76-85.
        Recaptures the life of Edwards at Windsor Farms, from
    his boyhood to his rejection of the Bolton calling, and
    concludes with an encomium to a "brilliant light."

<u>1884</u>

1   GEORGE, E. A. "Jonathan Edwards." <u>Yale Literary Magazine</u>
    50 (October):7-11.
        Studies Edwards's life and catches the two-fold nature
    of his character--his gentleness and his sternness--in
    his effeminate face and virile mind.

2   IVERACH, JAMES. "Jonathan Edwards." In <u>The Evangelical</u>
    <u>Succession: A Course of Lectures Delivered in Free St.</u>
    <u>George's Church, Edinburgh, 1883-84</u>. Third Series.
    Edinburgh: MacNiven & Wallace, pp. 109-43.
        Argues the "unspeakable importance" of <u>True Grace</u> for
    the "right apprehension" of Edwards's ideas; interprets
    his major works through his "ruling idea" of the sovereign
    grace of God; and places him, the equal of William Ames
    and John Owen, in the evangelical succession. So Edwards

explores the problem of man without grace in Original Sin;
the relationship between divine sovereign grace and man
in Freedom of the Will; the behavior of those who have
grace in Religious Affections; the outcome of grace in True
Virtue; the action of grace in human history in History of
Redemption: and the "supreme justification of the ways of
God to man" in the End of Creation. Still some difficulties
remain. For instance, in Freedom of the Will his
abstractness renders "meaningless" the "concrete realities"
of life; his determinism contradicts his doctrine of
continuing creation; his philosophical disposition
"unfortunately" cannot answer the "great question" of divine
sovereignty and human agency. For all that, Edwards
never fails to raise important questions about any topic
he treats, to set "old doctrines in new light," to offer
"fresh" points of view.

3   SHERWOOD, J. M. "Preface to the Present Edition." In his
    Memoirs of Rev. David Brainerd, Missionary to the Indians
    of North America, Based on the Life of Brainerd Prepared
    by Jonathan Edwards, D. D., and Afterwards Revised and
    Enlarged by Sereno E. Dwight, D. D. New York: Funk &
    Wagnalls Co., pp. xxv-xxvi.
       Attributes Edwards's mission to the Stockbridge Indians
    to Brainerd's influence and a world-wide missionary zeal
    to the reading of Edwards's Life of Brainerd.

4   TARBOX, I[NCREASE] N. "Jonathan Edwards as a Man; and the
    Ministers of the Last Century." New Englander, n.s.
    7 (September):615-31.
       Recounts the career of the "superlative" Edwards as an
    illustration of the life of the minister in
    eighteenth-century New England.

5   WALKER, GEORGE LEON. "Jonathan Edwards and the Half-way
    Covenant." New Englander 43 (September):601-14.
       Traces the history of the half-way covenant from
    Massachusetts Bay to the Connecticut Valley and the place
    it had in Edwards's dismission. Stoddard's church was "fully
    leavened" with his view of the Lord's Supper as a converting
    ordinance; his grandson, replacing him, seems to have
    accepted it "without hesitation." But in time "scruples"
    arose in his mind, and by 1749 he published Qualifications,
    "a masterpiece of virile, subtle, comprehensive argument."
    It is clear that Edwards had "already before his
    dismission broken with the whole half-way covenant system,
    and not simply with the Stoddardian development of it."

1885

1   BRIGGS, CHARLES AUGUSTUS. American Presbyterianism; Its
    Origin and Early History. New York: Charles Scribner's
    Sons, pp. 259-61.
        Defines Edwards as the "real" theologian of Methodism,
    though he influenced nineteenth-century Presbyterianism
    and Congregationalism in Scotland, England, and America
    as well.

2   DEXTER, FRANKLIN BOWDITCH. Biographical Sketches of the
    Graduates of Yale College with Annals of the College
    History October, 1701-May, 1745. New York: Henry Holt &
    Co., pp. 218-26.
        Sketches Edwards's life at Yale, "the most eminent
    graduate of the College, the greatest theologian of his
    century, the ablest metaphysician of the period between
    Leibnitz and Kant." Edwards earned "the highest rank" in
    his graduating class, continued two more years in theology,
    was tutor from 21 May 1721 to September 1726, and, "owing
    to the vacancy in the Rectorship for the whole of this
    period, his position was one of special responsibility."

3   PORTER, NOAH. The Two-Hundredth Birthday of Bishop George
    Berkeley. New York: Charles Scribner's Sons, pp. 71-72.
        Insists that Edwards had not read Berkeley before
    writing "The Mind."

1886

1   FOSTER, FRANK HUGH. "The Eschatology of the New England
    Divines." Bibliotheca Sacra 43 (January):1-32.
        Explains Edwards's views on the punishment of sin and
    his contribution to the development of the eschatological
    doctrines of his followers, notably his son and Joseph
    Bellamy. As a matter of practical experience, Edwards
    held to the reality of eternal punishment because of an
    "extreme sensitiveness of his soul to sin, and his
    profound conviction of the utter inexcusableness and
    vileness of the sinner." Such punishment was, therefore,
    proportional (infinite offense to an infinite God merits
    infinite punishment), proper (a perfect God demands
    proper punishment), and suitable (God hates sin and
    expresses it eternally). As in so many other instances
    of doctrine, the sovereignty of God was "sufficient
    explanation" for Edwards.

2   RICHARDSON, CHARLES F. American Literature, 1607-1885. New

York and London: G. P. Putnam's Sons, 1:139–46.
  Thinks that Edwards, as the "mouthpiece" of New England
Calvinism, is superior in style, breadth, and value to
Cotton Mather. His Freedom of the Will tries,
unsuccessfully, to solve the problem of man's free will
and God's foreknowledge and bears little upon practical
life. Yet in his "Mechanism in Thought and Morals " that
staunch anti-Calvinist Oliver Wendell Holmes "sometimes
seems to join hands" with Edwards.

3   STRONG, AUGUSTUS HOPKINS. Systematic Theology: A Compendium
    and Commonplace Book Designed for the Use of Theological
    Studies. Rochester, N.Y.: E. R. Andrews, pp. 26, 287,
    588, passim.
      Extols Edwards as the "holiest man of his time" in an
    elaborate text of quotations by and about him and his
    theology.

                          1887

1   BASCOM, JOHN. "Books that have Helped Me." Forum
    3 (May):263–72.
      Cites Freedom of the Will as the "best thing" in his
    library as a youth, though not a trace of Edwards remains
    in him now.

2   BEERS, HENRY A. An Outline Sketch of American Literature.
    New York: Chautauqua Press, pp. 41–44.
      Finds art and intensity in Edwards (though he writes
    theology, not literature) in a style simple and direct
    and contrasts him to Franklin.

3   FISHER, GEORGE PARK. History of the Christian Church. New
    York: Charles Scribner's Sons, pp. 524–27, 611–12,
    650–51.
      Notes that Edwards "mingled" logic and mysticism in a
    piety "profound and sincere," founded New England Theology,
    and was "cordial" to the Great Awakening.

4   HOLMES, OLIVER WENDELL. "Poem." In A Record of the
    Commemoration, November Fifth to Eighth, 1886, on the Two
    Hundred and Fiftieth Anniversary of the Founding of
    Harvard College. Cambridge: John Wilson & Son, pp. 237–49.
      Proclaims that "Harvard's beacon" will shed its
    reflected light upon Princeton, "Where mighty Edwards
    stamped his iron heel," in a poem celebrating Harvard's
    250th anniversary.

1887

5   MINTO, WILLIAM. A Manual of English Prose Literature. Boston:
        Ginn & Co., p. 434.
            Relates Edwards's limited appeal to his "dry" style.

1888

1   C., S. "Jonathan Edwards." Hampshire Gazette, 2 October,
        p. 3.
            Finds no evidence that Edwards ever said, "Heaven is
        being paved with infants' skulls," and demands an end to
        such slander.

2   LYON, GEORGES. "L'Immatérialisme en Amérique--Jonathan
        Edwards." In his L'Idéalisme en Angleterre au XVIIIe
        Siècle. Paris: Ancienne Librarie Germer Baillière et
        Cie, pp. 406-39.
            Compares Edwards's idealism with that of Malebranche and
        Berkeley--made available to Edwards by his Yale tutor,
        Samuel Johnson--and finds striking similarities, in a
        short life and longer examination of The Mind. (In French.)

3   SHEDD, WILLIAM G. T. Dogmatic Theology. New York: Charles
        Scribner's Sons, 2:203-209.
            Explains that Edwards's argument of identity in
        Original Sin extends the notion of inclination in Freedom
        of the Will to man's sinful disposition and guilt.

4   STRONG, AUGUSTUS H[OPKINS]. "The New Theology." Baptist
        Quarterly Review 10 (January):1-29.
            Characterizes Edwards's doctrine of the imputation of
        original sin as idealist not traducian, for the unity of
        Adam and posterity was constituted by the idea and will of
        God not by historical descent. Edwards's "radical" error
        lies in his denial of substance, and his doctrine of
        continuous creation leaves man without freedom, guilt,
        or responsibility. There is no need for the New Theology,
        for "the old is better."

5   _____. "The New Theology." In his Philosophy and Religion.
        New York: A. C. Armstrong & Son, pp. 164-79.
            Reprint of 1888.4.

1889

1   ALLEN, ALEXANDER V. G. Jonathan Edwards. American Religious
        Leaders. Boston and New York: Houghton Mifflin & Co., 412 pp.
            Examines Edwards, the "father of modern Congregationlism"

and the "greatest preacher of his age," as parish minister,
revivalist, and philosophical theologian in a full-length
study "not...devoid of sympathy" yet concluding, "The
great wrong which Edwards did, which haunts us as an evil
dream throughout his writings, was to assert God at the
expense of humanity." Thus the speculative thought of his
last phase--Freedom of the Will, Original Sin, True Virtue,
and End of Creation--ends "in confusion, if not failure,"
and his work on the trinity, however modern it seems is
"weakened, if not neutralized," by his tenets of original
sin and predestination and by his lack of interest in the
humanity of Christ. The whole of Edwards suffers from the
limits of his "solitary life" and occasions a style akin
to "thinking aloud," a prose inelegant and difficult to
interpret. The one "imperishable element" of this mystic
and rationalist, when the "false premises" and "negative
side" of his theology are discarded, is his deep-seated
God-consciousness, the reality and revelation of the
divine existence.

2   _____. Life and Writings of Jonathan Edwards. Edinburgh:
     T. & T. Clark.
         Reprint of 1889.1.

3   ANON. "Jonathan Edwards." The Nation 49 (October 17):314-15.
         Faults Alexander Allen's study (1889.1) for being "too
     apologetic" and not critical enough of Edwards.

4   BYINGTON, E[ZRA] H[OYT]. "Rev. Robert Breck Controversy."
     Papers and Proceedings of the Connecticut Valley Historical
     Society 2 (February):1-19.
         Remarks Edwards's role in the Breck affair.

5   C., S. "Have the Teachings of Jonathan Edwards Ceased to
     Exert an Influence on Religious Sentiment?" Hampshire
     Gazette, 12 February, p. 3.
         Claims Edwards's teachings still live and will continue
     to.

5   _____. "Jonathan Edwards, Senior, and Jonathan, Jr.--
     Resemblances." Hampshire Gazette, 16 April, p. 3.
         Parallels the careers of Edwards and his son.

7   HAZARD, ROWLAND G[IBSON]. "Review of Edwards on the Will."
     In his Freedom of Mind in Willing. Boston: Houghton
     Mifflin & Co.
         Reprint of 1864.3.

8   LATHE, H. W. "Historical Discourse: At the Rededication of

1889

the Fifth Meeting House of the First Church of Christ, Northampton, Mass., Nov. 24, 1889." Hampshire Gazette, 26 November, p. 2.
Recounts Edwards's career at Northampton.

9   McCOOK, HENRY C. American Spiders and Their Spinningwork. Philadelphia: Henry C. McCook, 1:68-69; 2:280-82.
Acknowledges that Edwards anticipated his original findings about spider webs by 160 years and Pierre Latreille's foundation principle of the classification of spiders by a century.

10 MARTINEAU, JAMES. A Study of Religion. Oxford: Clarendon Press, 2:260-62.
Observes that while Scripture supports Edwards's view of determinism in human actions, reason does not, in a brief examination of Edwards on divine prescience.

11 MELDEN, C. M. "Jonathan Edwards." Hampshire Gazette, 27 August, p. 7; 10 September, p. 6.
Traces Edwards's career in Northampton, focusing on "two notable events," the revivals and his dismissal, and concluding that he is now "little more than a memory."

12 RICHARDS, C. A. L. "An American Religious Leader." Dial 10 (November):166-67.
Reviews Alexander Allen's Jonathan Edwards (1889.1) and finds it unexpectedly balanced.

13 WHITE, L. "Edwards on the Will." Methodist Review 71 (January-February):9-25.
Examines Edwards's Freedom of the Will with an eye to proving anew the Arminian faith in the freedom of moral agency and its rejection of theistic necessity. Edwards was "right" in treating the question of freedom theologically, noting the "plausible advantages" of necessity, claiming for God perfect providence, refusing the self-determination of the will, restricting freedom to doing, and insisting on man's dependence. But all this does not justify Edwards's conclusions that deny man responsibility.

1890

1   ALLEN, ALEXANDER V. G. Jonathan Edwards. American Religious Leaders. Boston: Houghton Mifflin & Co.
Reprint of 1889.1.

87

2   ANON. "Jonathan Edwards." The Spectator 64 (January 11):58-59.
    Reviews Alexander Allen's Jonathan Edwards (1889.1) and
    finds the author, at odds with Edwards's views, often
    dominating the theological argument.

3   CROOKER, JOSEPH H. "Jonathan Edwards: A Psychological Study."
    New England Magazine, n.s. 2 (April):159-72.
        Examines Edwards psychologically and diagnoses him a
    "theological monomaniac" afflicted with a species of
    "delusional insanity," inherited from his grandmother and
    nurtured by his "rigid and arbitrary" father, resulting in
    an irrational dogma of divine sovereignty. Personal
    Narrative shows "incipient" symptoms of the disorder--he
    should have engaged in "healthy" sports and thoughts--and
    his later work, except for the "uncorrupted" True
    Virtue, bears little connection with reality. All in all,
    Edwards contributed "absolutely nothing" to the
    understanding of man in history, nature, or society.

4   FISHER, GEORGE P[ARK]. "The Philosophy of Jonathan Edwards."
    In his Discussions in History and Theology. New York:
    Charles Scribner's Sons.
        Reprint of 1874.4.

5   _____. Review of Jonathan Edwards, by Alexander V. G. Allen.
    New Englander and Yale Review 52 (January):85-88.
        Questions the view that Edwards was inconsistent on
    divine sovereignty, in a review of Alexander Allen's
    study (1889.1).

6   McCOOK, HENRY C. "Jonathan Edwards as a Naturalist."
    Presbyterian and Reformed Review 1 (July):393-402.
        Examines, as an arachnologist, Edwards's paper on flying
    spiders to compare it to recent investigations, to test its
    scientific value, and to rank its priority. Although
    Edwards made some expected mistakes--matters more of
    speculation than of observation--he showed "brilliance"
    as a young naturalist.

7   PALFREY, JOHN GORHAM. History of New England. Boston:
    Little, Brown & Co., 5:5-7.
        Characterizes as "unimpassioned obstinacy" Edwards's
    pursuit of the doctrines of justification by faith and the
    sovereignty of God that led to the revival of 1734 and
    quotes from Faithful Narrative.

8   SMYTH, EGBERT C[OFFIN]. "The Flying Spider--Observations
    by Jonathan Edwards When a Boy." Andover Review
    13 (January):1-19.

1890

    Dates the observations recorded in "Of Insects," by external allusions and internal evidence, to a time "not later than the summer and early autumn of 1715," and reprints the text and the "apologetic epistle" Edwards wrote to his father's English correspondent.

9   _____. "Professor Allen's 'Jonathan Edwards.' With Extracts from Copies of Unpublished Manuscripts." Andover Review 13 (March):285-304.

    Uses the occasion of a review of Alexander V. G. Allen's "stimulating and fascinating" study (1889.1) to reprint Observations in order to examine and clarify Allen's "inner connections" of Edwards's thought.

10 STEARNS, LEWIS FRENCH. The Evidence of Christian Experience. New York: Charles Scribner's Sons, pp. 84-87, passim.

    Calls it an "evil day" for theology when Edwards sought to bolster the doctrine of grace with the doctrine of determinism, when he compromised the Christian experience of Religious Affections and the moral inability of Freedom of the Will.

11 WEEDEN, WILLIAM B. Economic and Social History of New England, 1620-1789. Boston: Houghton Mifflin & Co., 2:700-706.

    Compares Edwards and Benjamin Franklin as contributors to the social and political development of eighteenth-century America. Though Edwards was hardly political, his pulpit affected the politics of the next generation: men who were ruled by an absolute divine sovereign were unlikely "to submit kindly" to a temporal viceregent.

12 WELLMAN, J. W. "A New Biography of Jonathan Edwards." Our Day, 5 (March):195-219, and (April):288-307.

    Berates Alexander Allen's study (1889.1) as the work of a scholar whose "nondescript" pantheism is "violently and even bitterly" opposed to Edwards's theology. This new biography, filled as it is with misstatements and misrepresentations, "should never have been written."

1891

1 ALLEN, ALEXANDER V. G. Jonathan Edwards. American Religious Leaders. Boston: Houghton Mifflin & Co.
    Reprint of 1889.1.

2 CLARK, SOLOMON. Historical Catalogue of the Northampton First Church, 1661-1891. Northampton, Mass.: Gazette

Printing Co., pp. 40-67.
    Lists church members and notes that Edwards's pastorate
was "attended with uncommon success," though few
conversions occurred when the Church "went into a dark
cloud" at the end of his stay.

3   HOLMES, OLIVER WENDELL. Over the Teacups. Boston: Houghton
        Mifflin & Co., pp. 249-50.
            Imagines a nursery scene with Edwards, Sarah, and their
        three-year-old to suggest her tempering effect upon his
        stubborn doctrine of infant damnation and the possiblity
        of "moral parricide."

                                1892

1   HAZARD, ROWLAND G[IBSON]. "Review of Edwards on the Will."
        In his Freedom of Mind in Willing. Boston: Houghton
        Mifflin & Co.
            Reprint of 1864.3.

2   STILES, HENRY R. The History and Genealogies of Ancient
        Windsor, Connecticut. Hartford: Case, Lockwood &
        Brainard Co., 2:195-98.
            Recounts Edwards's life and suggests the cause of his
        dismissal lay in his opposition to bundling.

3   THOMAS, REUEN. Leaders of Thought in the Modern Church.
        Boston: D. Lothrop Co., pp. 7-24.
            Charts the life of Edwards and claims that he "retired
        from his post" to the Indian mission at Stockbridge rather
        than "tolerate" the obscene books discovered among the
        young at Northampton.

4   TUPPER, KERR B. "Jonathan Edwards." In his Seven Great
        Lights. Cincinnati: Cranston & Curtis, pp. 117-39.
            Examines the life and times of Edwards, in effusion and
        in comparison to Mozart and Homer, among others.

5   WALKER, WILLISTON. "The Half-Way Covenant." New Englander
        and Yale Review 56 (February):93-117.
            Notes that Edwards's opposition to Stoddardeanism and
        the half-way covenant ultimately prevailed in New England,
        in a history of the doctrine from its beginning.

6   WENDELL, BARRETT. "Some Neglected Characteristics of the New
        England Puritans." In Annual Report of the American
        Historical Association for the Year 1891. Washington:
        Government Printing Office, pp. 245-53.

1892

Notes that in Edwards's attempt to revive orthodoxy, American Puritan theology reached its "highest point."

1893

1   DAVIDSON, J[OHN] N[ELSON]. Muh-he-ka-ne-ok: A History of the Stockbridge Nation. Milwaukee, Wisc.: S. Chapman, pp. 12-14.
    Recounts Edwards's political and theological years at Stockbridge among the Housatonic Indians. "Though he made their language the subject of a treatise [?], he never learned to preach on it."

2   TURPIE, DAVID. Jonathan Edwards: An Address Delivered at Kenyon College, June 29, 1893. Columbus, Ohio: Nitschke Brothers, 31 pp.
    Recounts Edwards's career as an historical exemplar and praises his work for its candor, good faith, and justice. Although the harsh doctrine of election no longer obtains in the form he gave it, it can be found in the theory of evolution and its "'survival of the fittest.'"

3   UNDERWOOD, FRANCIS H. The Builders of American Literature: Biographical Sketches of American Authors Born Previous to 1826. First Series. Boston: Lee & Shepard, pp. 40-44.
    Recounts Edwards's career and considers his prose to be logical, idiomatic, and bald, marked by a "beautiful simplicity beyond the reach of art."

4   WALKER, WILLISTON. The Creeds and Platforms of Congregationalism. New York: Charles Scribner's Sons, pp. 283-85.
    Points to Edwards's opposition to Stoddardeanism and the half-way covenant in a "subsidary" paragraph in his Qualifications. To Edwards, the corporate experience of the half-way covenant is at odds with his emphasis on individual experience.

5   _____. Three Phases of New England Congregational Development. Hartford Seminary Publications, 28. Hartford: Hartford Seminary Press, pp. 12-14.
    Places Edwards in the second phase of New England Congregational development, the Great Awakening. Edwards marked a shift from discussions of polity to ones of doctrine and, hence, to divisions within the church.

1894

1   BASCOM, JOHN. "Jonathan Edwards." <u>Collections of the Berk-
    shire Historical and Scientific Society</u> 2, Part 1: 1-25.
        Recounts Edwards's career, especially in Stockbridge,
    and hopes that his theology will perish with his time and
    his character will remain forever. Edwards suffered a
    "total misapprehension" of the nature of man.

2   DUNNING, ALBERT E. <u>Congregationalists in America</u>. Boston
    and Chicago: Pilgrim Press, pp. 235-41, 261-64.
        Cites Edwards's "brilliant logic and fervent appeals"
    as vital and singular instruments in the Great Awakening,
    the results of which have been profound and extensive.
    Edwards "determined" the course of religious life and
    thought in New England, challenging the half-way covenant
    and separating church from state. Though he favored
    Presbyterian polity after his dismission, in fairness he
    remains "the father of modern Congregationalism."

3   [KNEELAND, FREDERICK NEWTON]. <u>Northampton, the Meadow City</u>.
    Northampton, Mass.: F. N. Kneeland & L. P. Bryant,
    pp. 29-34.
        Prints pictures of the Edwards houses and memorials in
    Northampton with facts and observations of his life there.

4   LOWELL, JAMES RUSSELL. Letter to Leslie Stephen, 15 May 1876.
    In <u>Letters of James Russell Lowell</u>. Edited by Charles
    Eliot Norton. New York: Harper & Brothers, 2: 165.
        Acknowledges "a great sympathy" with Edwards, except in
    his notion of a physical hell, on the occasion of the
    publication of <u>Hours in a Library</u> (1876.3).

5   WALKER, WILLISTON. <u>A History of the Congregational Churches
    in the United States</u>. American Church History Series,
    no. 3. New York: Christian Literature Co., pp. 253-59,
    280-86, passim.
        Considers Edwards "the greatest theologian" of American
    Congregationalism, the founder of New England Theology,
    "the only original contribution of importance given by
    America to the development of Christian theology." Edwards
    championed Calvinism, not out of devotion to tradition but
    out of a religious experience, like Calvin's, rooted in
    divine sovereignty. But Edwards generally "modified" Cal-
    vinism by stressing man's responsibility and by fostering
    emotion and a "sense of immediate communion" between God
    and man. In particular, he emphasized four positions

"essentially a departure" from historic Calvinism: that
man had natural ability to do the will of God; that virtue
consisted of disinterested benevolence; that both salvation and damnation arise from a single, wise benevolence
to the whole universe; and that the identity and unity of
an individual is an effect of the constantly creative
activity of God.

1895

1   ANON. "Art Treasures in Connecticut." New York Times, 14
     January, p. 17.
        Gives an account of the Edwards family and reprints a
     letter, 10 May 1716, from Jonathan to his sister Molly,
     whose embroidered apron "of great beauty" remains one of
     the handiwork "treasures" of the Connecticut Historical
     Society.

2   BEERS, HENRY A. Initial Studies in American Literature.
     Cleveland: Chautauqua Press, pp. 84-86.
        Recasts 1887.2.

3   GORDON, GEORGE A. Preface to his The Christ of Today. Bos-
     ton: Houghton Mifflin & Co., pp. v-viii.
        Seeks a return to Edwards's "original principle" of the
     absolute sovereignty of God--the only insurance of conti-
     nuity and progress in American Christianity--by following
     a theological tradition which "dates" from him.

4   L., C. B. A. "Genealogy of a Famous Family." New York Times,
     27 January, p. 28.
        Corrects some "surprising statements" about the Edwards
     family which appeared in an article on New Haven treasures
     in the Times two weeks earlier (1895.1). Sarah Pierrepont
     was not Jonathan Edwards's mother.

5   OLDMIXON, FELIX [pseud.]. "Old Colonial Characters: I.
     Jonathan Edwards." Connecticut Quarterly 1, no. 1 (First
     Quarter): 33-38.
        Traces the ancestors of Edwards and his grandson, Aaron
     Burr, in order to discover what "strain of blood" could
     account for such different men. Insanity, checked in
     Edwards by a strong will, spirit, and mind, crops up again
     in his "profligate, vicious and licentious" son, Pierpont,
     and his grandson, Aaron.

1895

6 _____. "Old Colonial Characters: II. Edwards and Burr."
    Connecticut Quarterly 1, no. 2 (Second Quarter): 155-59.
        Continues the Edwards genealogy (1895.5) and presents
    a brief life of America's greatest theologian, "at least
    of the last century."

7 RANKIN, J[EREMIAH] E[AMES]. "The Jonathan Edwards Letters."
    Independent 47 (28 November): 1603.
        Offers corrections to some of his earlier notes to
    Edwards's letters (1895.8), principally that Harry is "not
    a horse, but a man, a slave."

8 _____. "New Memorials of President Edwards." Independent 47
    (22 August): 1121.
        Reprints an unpublished letter from Edwards to his
    daughter Esther, 20 November 1757, which offers a rare
    glimpse of his "tender and graceful domestic character."

9 _____. "The Second Letter of President Edwards." Independ-
    ent 47 (5 September): 1185.
        Reprints Edwards's letter to his son-in-law, Aaron Burr,
    14 March 1756, on the birth of his son Aaron, "who was to
    make the name of Burr so sadly infamous." This letter is
    "not so vivacious" as another already published (1895.8).

10 SMYTH, EGBERT C[OFFIN]. "Some Early Writings of Jonathan
    Edwards. A.D. 1714-1726." Proceedings of the American
    Antiquarian Society, n.s. 10 (October): 212-47.
        Recovers and reprints some early writings from the
    Edwards manuscripts--"The Soul," "Of the Rainbow," "Of
    Being," and "Colors"--and, through an analysis of the
    paper, ink, spelling, punctuation, and style, attempts to
    date and place them in his intellectual development as
    idealist and determinist.

11 WATTS, ISAAC. "Letters of Dr. Watts." Proceedings of the
    Massachusetts Historical Society, 2nd ser. 9 (February):
    331-410.
        Reprints letters from Isaac Watts to Benjamin Colman
    concerning the London publication of Edwards's Faithful
    Narrative, 28 February 1736/37; 2 April 1737; 13 October
    1737; 31 May 1738; 7 June 1738; and 22 September 1738.
    See 1938.3 for a continuous narrative of their exchange
    and that of Edwards.

1896

1 ALLEN, ALEXANDER V. G. <u>Jonathan Edwards</u>. American Religious
  Leaders. Boston: Houghton Mifflin & Co.
  Reprint of 1889.1.

2 BYINGTON, EZRA HOYT. "The Case of Rev. Robert Breck."
  <u>Andover Review</u> 13 (May): 517-33.
  Claims Edwards's work in the revivals of 1734-35 in
  Northampton kept him from entering "very fully" into the
  Robert Breck affair, though he signed the ministerial
  petition opposing his settlement in Springfield.

3 CURTIS, MATTOON MONROE. "An Outline of Philosophy in America."
  <u>Western Reserve University Bulletin</u> 2 (March): 3-18.
  Surveys Edwards's career to find his "objectification"
  of Calvinism and the stimulation he gave to intellectual
  life in America historically significant.

4 FAIBAIRN, A. M. "Prophets of the Christian Faith, VIII-
  Jonathan Edwards." <u>Outlook</u> 53 (23 May): 930-32.
  Characterizes Edwards not only as America's "greatest"
  thinker but also as "the highest speculative genius" of
  the century, whose remarkable achievements, carried out
  in intellectual isolation from European culture and literary elegance, speak to us "in a strange tongue."
  Edwards is a "monotheistic idealist," combining intense
  spirituality and intense rationality with John Locke's
  "imperfect" psychology. So in <u>Freedom of the Will</u>, Edwards
  advocates an "alien" doctrine and abandons his own philosophy, returning to the "exhausted charms" of Locke's
  empiricism.

5 _____. "Jonathan Edwards." In <u>The Prophets of the Christian
  Faith</u>, by the Rev. Lyman Abbott et al. New York: Macmillan
  Co., pp. 145-66.
  Reprint of 1896.4.

6 F[IELD], H[ENRY] M. "'Plain Living and High Thinking.'" <u>The
  Evangelist</u> 68 (21 May): 10-11.
  Cites terms of Edwards's settlement in Stockbridge
  where he wrote books "immortal" in American history:
  thirty-five dollars a year and a hundred sleigh loads of
  firewood. "Plain living and high thinking indeed!"

7 FIELD, HENRY M. "Plain Living and High Thinking." <u>New York
  Times</u>, 8 June, p. 5.
  Reprint of 1896.6.

1896

8   FISHER, GEORGE PARK. History of Christian Doctrine. Inter-
    national Theology Library. New York: Charles Scribner's
    Sons, pp. 395-410.
       Examines Edwards's major works in a historical survey
    of great theologians and metaphysicians. His "rare ming-
    ling" of intellect and insight, logic and mysticism
    resemble Augustine, Anselm, and Aquinas.

9   HALLIDAY, S[AMUEL] B[RYAM], and GREGORY, D[ANIEL] S[EELY].
    The Church in America and its Baptism of Fire. New York:
    Funk & Wagnalls, pp. 9-15.
       Finds the source of the Great Awakening to be Edwards's
    series of sermons on the justification of faith. His
    writings guided the course of this remarkable religious
    movement and tempered its excesses.

10 MATTHEWS, BRANDER. An Introduction to the Study of American
    Literature. New York: American Book Co., pp. 18-20.
       Recounts a short biography of Edwards, compares him to
    Franklin, and concludes that Franklin was the "more im-
    portant" of the two.

11 PERRY, ARTHUR LATHAM. "Jonathan Edwards and Ephraim Williams."
    In his Origins in Williamstown. 2nd ed. New York: Charles
    Scribner's Sons, pp. 633-41.
       Details the history of doctrinal and political conten-
    tion between Edwards and the Williams family, especially
    the Ephraim Williamses, father and son, in both Northampton
    and Stockbridge. In a letter to Jonathan Ashley on 2 May
    1751 (reprinted), the younger Williams, founder of Williams
    College, remarks, "'I am sorry that a nead so full of Divin-
    ity should be so empty of Politics,'" and then lists his ob-
    jections to Edwards's presence in Stockbridge--his coldness,
    his bigotry, his age, and "'his principles.'" The "whole
    selfish cabal" to dismiss Edwards from his pastorate, which
    had succeeded in Northampton, fails in Stockbridge.

12 SMYTH, EGBERT C[OFFIN]. "The 'New Philosophy' Against Which
    Students at Yale college were Warned in 1714." Proceedings
    of the American Antiquarian Society, n.s. 11 (October):
    251-52.
       Denies Edwards got his idealism from Berkeley. A cata-
    logue of books read by Samuel Johnson, Edwards's tutor,
    since leaving Yale shows he did not know Berkeley until
    1728.

96

13 _____. Some Early Writings of Jonathan Edwards, A.D. 1714–
1726. Worcester, Mass.: Charles Hamilton.
Reprint of 1895.10.

1897

1 BACON, LEONARD WOOLSEY. A History of American Christianity.
New York: Christian Literature Co., pp. 155–59, 169–72.
Assesses Edwards's career in the revivals of the Connecticut Valley and finds his serenity in the "agitated
scene" necessary to distinguish true from spurious affections.

2 DeWITT, JOHN. "Princeton College Administrations in the
Eighteenth Century." Presbyterian and Reformed Review 8
(July): 387–417.
Notes the "great advantage" and celebrity Princeton
gained from Edwards, his association and his name.

3 GROSART, ALEXANDER B. "The Handwriting of Famous Divines:
Jonathan Edwards, M.A." Sunday at Home 31 (May): 458–60.
Reprints Edwards's letter of 13 July 1751 to William
Hogg, Edinburgh, about his settlement in Stockbridge;
reproduces the closing lines in Edwards's handwriting; and
suggests, contrary to received opinion, that Edwards was
compassionate as evident in the many tear-stained manuscript pages of Sinners in the Hands of an Angry God.

4 MITCHELL, DONALD G. American Lands and Letters. New York:
Charles Scribner's Sons, 1: 58–70.
Comments breezily upon Edwards's life and work: Freedom
of the Will is not "a popular book for a circulating
library--nor yet one for the boudoir."

5 PAINTER, F[RANKLIN] V. N. Introduction to American Literature. Boston: Leach, Shewell, & Sanborn, pp. 51–58.
Offers a derivative biography of Edwards and remarks
his "defective" style.

6 SMYTH, EGBERT C[OFFIN]. "Jonathan Edwards." In Library of
the World's Best Literature. Edited by Charles Dudley
Warner. New York: R. S. Peale & J. A. Hill, 9: 5175–79.
Notes, in a short bibliographical essay, the "incom-
pleteness" of the definitive edition of Edwards (and the
possibility of misconstruction) and quotes passages from
his work.

1897

7 _____. "Jonathan Edwards' Idealism with Special Reference to the Essay 'Of Being' and to Writings not in his Collected Works." <u>American Journal of Theology</u> 1 (October): 950-64.
Considers Edwards's early idealism "a fitting philosophical counterpart" to his doctrine of the divine and supernatural light "variously and intimately connected" to his theory of the trinity, and a view of the universe "he never lost," and quotes extensively from "Of Being" and the <u>Miscellanies</u>.

8 WALKER, GEORGE LEON. <u>Some Aspects of the Religious Life of New England with Special Reference to Congregationalists</u>. Boston: Silver, Burdett & Co., pp. 104-12 passim.
Compares Edwards's <u>Personal Narrative</u> to Thomas Hooker's <u>The Soul's Preparation</u> in an attempt to explain the later intellectualization of the theology of conversion. Hooker was content with the "vivid announcement" of truth and saw no need to justify or explain it; Edwards felt constrained to make truth of whatever kind intellectually coherent. Systematic doctrinal theology was born in the Great Awakening and matured into New England Theology.

1898

1 ANON. "Doorstone Given to Forbes Library." <u>Hampshire Gazette</u>, 2 August, p. 6.
Reports the memorial gift of the doorstep from Edwards's King Street home to the Forbes Library, Northampton.

2 BYINGTON, EZRA HOYT. "Jonathan Edwards and the Great Awakening." <u>Bibliotheca Sacra</u> 55 (January): 114-27.
Calls Edwards the "moving spirit" of the Great Awakening and explains his role as preacher, counselor, and apologist in it.

3 CHILD, FRANK SAMUEL. <u>A Puritan Wooing: A Tale of the Great Awakening in New England</u>. New York: Baker & Taylor Co., pp. 103-14 passim.
Tells the tale of Esther Hardy, a second cousin of Sarah Pierrepont, who attends one of Edwards's imprecatory sermons, falls ill at the Edwards home, and converts under the warm affection and guidance of Sarah, in a novel of romance during the Great Awakening.

4   DeWITT, JOHN. "Historical Sketch of Princeton University."
       In <u>Princeton Sesquicentennial Celebration 1746-1896</u>. New
       York: Charles Scribner's Sons, pp. 366-67.
         Records that seventeen of twenty trustees present voted
       for Edwards to be the second president of Princeton, a
       short though advantageous association for the College.

5   JONES, ADAM LEROY. <u>Early American Philosophers</u>. New York:
       Macmillan Co., pp. 46-80.
         Examines Edwards's psychology, idealism, ethics, and
       will in a survey of early American philosophers: of his
       contemporaries only Samuel Johnson is treated comparably.
       His psychology, derived from Locke, develops beyond him
       into a formulation of the association of ideas, anticipat-
       ing Hume and indicating "independence and originality."
       His idealism was worked out "early in life" (<u>Notes on the
       Mind</u>), and though it was "never formally renounced," it
       played "a very small part" in his mature thought. His
       ethical system rests upon the notion that perfection is
       the end of conduct, his doctrine of will on necessity and
       its relationship to moral agency. In all his philosophi-
       cal speculations, Edwards's considerable reasoning suffers
       from "imperfect analysis" and his turgid style from "his
       isolation and his lack of experience in oral discussion."

6   PANCOAST, HENRY S. <u>An Introduction to American Literature</u>.
       New York: Henry Holt & Co., pp. 63-67.
         Finds the "same strange contrast" between life and work
       in Edwards and in Michael Wigglesworth, the same mix of
       strengths and weaknesses in colonial literature generally
       in Edwards.

7   [SMELLIE, ALEXANDER]. Introduction to <u>A Treatise Concerning
       the Religious Affections</u>. London: Andrew Melrose,
       pp. ix-xxxiii.
         Defends Edwards aginst the extravagant "indictment" of
       the style of <u>Religious Affections</u>, in a fulsome review of
       his life, times, and work. Despite some "ruggedness" and
       haste, Edwards's style in the text is tender, strong, and
       "melodious."

8   STARR, MARY SEABURY. "The Home of Timothy and Jonathan Ed-
       wards." <u>Connecticut Quarterly</u> 4 (January-March): 33-43.
         Offers a short history of Edwards's birthplace in South
       Windsor, his father's role in the community and at home,
       and a sketch of this "poetical, dreamy lad." (Illus-
       trated).

1898

9   STOWE, C. E. "Jonathan Edwards." In <u>Realencyklopädie für</u>
    <u>Protestantische Theologie und Kirche</u>. Edited by Albert
    Hauck. Leipzig: J. H. Hinrichs, 5: 171-75.
       Sketches Edwards's career, thought, and influence upon
    his successors. (In German).

1899

1   ALLEN, ALEXANDER V. G. <u>Jonathan Edwards</u>. American Religious
    Leaders. Boston: Houghton Mifflin & Co.
       Reprint of 1889.1.

2   BOARDMAN, GEORGE NYE. <u>A History of New England Theology</u>.
    New York: A. D. F. Randolph Co., pp. 32-70, passim.
       Traces the history of New England Theology between 1730
    and 1830, from Edwards, its "radiating centre," to its
    successive forms and modifications. The first, or Edwards,
    phase (1730-1760) provides a "permanent element" of ortho-
    doxy and evangelicalism to the scheme through his influ-
    ence in practical theology, metaphysical speculation, and
    dogmatics; through his revivalism and his pastoral poli-
    cies, his theism of "the prevalence of the Infinite Will"
    and his ethics of true virtue, and his opposition to
    Arminianism in <u>Freedom of the Will</u> and to Pelagianism in
    <u>Original Sin</u>. Yet a basic difference exists between
    Edwards and New England Theology: though both hold that
    God is the "primal source of power," the new theology
    "seems to make the end of creation the glorification of
    humanity" not the glorification of God.

3   BREWER, DAVID J., ed. <u>The World's Best Orations from the</u>
    <u>Earliest Period to the Present Time</u>. St. Louis: F. P.
    Kaiser, 5: 1976-84.
       Introduces and reprints selections from three impreca-
    tory sermons.

4   BYINGTON, EZRA HOYT. "Jonathan Edwards, and the Great Awaken-
    ing." In his <u>The Puritan as a Colonist and Reformer</u>.
    Boston: Little, Brown & Co., pp. 273-305.
       Follows the career of Edwards, "this representative
    Puritan pastor," as a revivalist of permanent influence
    and a theologian of modified Calvinism.

5   FORD, PAUL LEICESTER. <u>Janice Meredith: A Story of the Revo-</u>
    <u>lution</u>. New York: Dodd, Mead & Co., 1: 57.
       Refers to two sermons on infant damnation Edwards de-
    livered at Princeton and the profound effect it had on the
    heroine's mother, in a novel on the Revolution.

6   MacCRACKEN, JOHN HENRY. "Jonathan Edwards Idealismus."
     Ph.D. dissertation, University of Halle.
     Published as 1899.7.

7   _____. Jonathan Edwards Idealismus. Halle: C. A. Kaemmerer,
     82 pp.
     Discounts Berkeley as a source, with Locke and Newton,
     of Edwards's idealism and suggests a more likely influence
     to be Arthur Collier's Clavis Universalis. (In German;
     see 1902.7 for an English version.)

8   MINTON, HENRY COLLIN. "President Jonathan Edwards." Pres-
     byterian Quarterly 13 (January): 68-94.
     Traces the life and work of the thrice-great Edwards
     (thinker, preacher, man); more a theologian than a phil-
     osopher, more a polemicist than an apologist; a pantheist,
     a mystic, a reformer; guilty of "philosophical idiosyn-
     crasies," innocent of the "libel" that he fathered what
     is now called New England Theology.

                              1900

1   ADDISON, DANIEL DULANY. The Clergy in American Life and
     Letters. New York: Macmillan Co., pp. 39-40.
     Perceives in Edwards the theologian a genuine style
     that makes him a "literary force" in America.

2   ANON. "An American Philosopher of the Eighteenth Century."
     New York Times, 11 June, p. 6.
     Calls for a new edition of Edwards's work and a "less
     critical and more human" biography than Alexander Allen's
     (1889.1). Inasmuch as standard texts exist for Franklin,
     Locke, Berkeley, and others, so one should be published
     of the mystical and saintly Edwards, if only as "a matter
     of patriotism." (An editorial.)

3   ANON. "The Edwards Commemoration." Outlook 65 (30 June):
     476-77.
     Calls the memorial tablet unveiled 22 June necessary
     to Northampton, not to Edwards, and goes on to praise
     Edwards for his rationalism, transcendentalism, and in-
     fluence upon the Beechers, Horace Bushnell, and Phillips
     Brooks.

                              101

1900

4 ANON. "Exercises at First Church and Unveiling of Memorial
      Tablet." Hampshire Gazette, 23 June, pp. 1, 8.
         Reports the commemoration of the 150th anniversary of
      Edwards's dismissal, with program notes, pictures, and
      annotations.

5 ANON. "The Jonathan Edwards Memorial." Harper's Weekly 44
      (23 June): 574.
         Considers the "serious error" Northampton made in dis-
      missing Edwards to be corrected with the erection of a
      tablet in his honor at the First Church.

6 ANON. "Tablet to Jonathan Edwards." New York Times, 23
      June, p. 7.
         Reports the unveiling in Northampton of a tablet to
      Edwards in exercises "impressive in their simplicity."

7 BARNES, LEMUEL CALL. Two Thousand Years of Missions before
      Carey. Chicago: Christian Culture Press, pp. 412-13.
         Notes Edwards's mission to the Indians at Stockbridge.

8 BRIDGMAN, S. E. "Northampton." New England Magazine, n.s.
      21 (January): 582, 585-86.
         Offers a brief life and portrait of Edwards.

9 BRONSON, WALTER C. A Short History of American Literature.
      New York: D. C. Heath & Co., pp. 33-34.
         Offers a brief biography of Edwards and keen regret
      that his powers were wasted on theology.

10 COLE, BERTHA WOOLSEY DWIGHT. "Not Jonathan Edwards's Son-in-
      Law." New York Times, 13 June, p. 6.
         Corrects the confusion about Aaron Burr, father and
      son, in a Times editorial on Edwards (1900.2). The father,
      not the son (the vice-president), was married to Edwards's
      daughter Esther.

11 DOWNES, R. P. "Thinkers Worth Remembering: Jonathan Ed-
      wards." Great Thoughts 6 (September): 296-98.
         Recounts a brief life of Edwards, a man of genuine
      piety and "morbid self-introspection."

12 GARDINER, H[ARRY] N[ORMAN]. "The Early Idealism of Jonathan
      Edwards." Philosophical Review 9 (November): 573-96.
         Traces Edwards's idealism to his earliest speculations
      on nature and the mind, "first crudely" expressed and
      defended in "Of Being" and then in "Existence," "Substance,"

and "Excellence," an "original expression of personal
insight" sustained throughout his work though in a somewhat
altered form. Edwards was influenced directly by Locke,
Newton, and Cudworth; less directly by Descartes, Norris,
and Malebranche; and not at all by Berkeley (the evidence
to the contrary is "entirely internal"). From the beginning, Edwards tends toward a "comprehensive" idealism in
which God is all in all, communicating Himself by immediate illumination in an "uninterrupted exercise of glorious
will." With that "deeper" idealism in the making, it is
unnecessary to look for "precise expressions" of Edwards's
early speculations in his later work.

13   [GARDINER, HARRY NORMAN]. "Honoring of Jonathan Edwards."
     Hampshire Gazette, 28 March, p. 1.
         Appeals for funds for the Edwards commemorative plaque.

14   GORDON, GEORGE A. "The Significance of Edwards Today." Con-
     gregationalist 85 (28 June): 944–46.
         Likens Edwards's significance today to Dante's: both
     live, despite their obsolete thought, error, and imper-
     fections, through the "majesty" of their imaginative
     appeal. Edwards is guilty of a "radical inconsistency."
     The absolute love, being, and excellence he attributes to
     God "discredits" his doctrines of man's depravity and
     election; his "glorious" theology contradicts his "inade-
     quate" and "incredible" anthropology.

15   JOHNSON, WILLIAM SAMUEL. "Where Burr Got His Mental Force."
     New York Times, 15 June, p. 6.
         Claims that Aaron Burr, the vice-president, inherited
     from his grandfather Edwards his "tremendous" though
     "conscienceless" mentality and his "always unshaken cour-
     age." This must be true unless "in heretical defiance of
     his great ancestor's thesis, we maintain that perhaps
     Aaron Burr had a will of his own."

16   M., G. P. "In Honor of Jonathan Edwards." Congregationalist
     85 (28 June): 958.
         Recounts the celebration and summarizes the five
     speeches at the dedication of the Edwards bronze memorial
     tablet in the First Church at Northampton, 22 June.

17   MacCRACKEN, HENRY MITCHELL. "The Hall of Fame." American
     Monthly Review of Reviews 22 (November): 567–68.
         Records the votes of the first twenty-nine great Ameri-
     cans elected to the Hall of Fame: Edwards got eighty-one
     to Washington's ninety-seven and Hawthorne's seventy-three.
     (Illustrated.)

1900

18   [MEAD, EDWIN D.] "Editor's Table." New England Magazine,
       n.s. 23 (December): 475-80.
            Reviews Albert E. Winship's Jukes-Edwards (1900.20)
       and finds the Edwards family an inspiring example of the
       "contagious nature of moral health."

19   WENDELL, BARRETT. A Literary History of America. The Library
       of Literary History. New York: Charles Scribner's Sons,
       pp. 83-91.
            Accounts Edwards's distance from things practical and
       political a decided and negative influence on his theology.
       His view of sinful man arises not from an American experi-
       ence he dimly knew but from a "densely populated, corrupt"
       society he imagined. By mid-century, American religious
       thought had "divorced itself from life almost as completely
       as from politics."

20   WINSHIP, A[LBERT] E. Jukes-Edwards: A Study in Education and
       Heredity. Harrisburg, Pa.: R. L. Myers & Co., 88 pp.
            Contrasts the 1,400 descendants of Edwards with the
       1,200 descendants of Max Jukes, the "midday and midnight"
       of eugenics, in a study of the heredity of intelligence,
       morality, and character.

1901

1   ANON. "The Life and Theology of Jonathan Edwards." Presby-
       terian Quarterly 15 (April): 222-37.
            Recounts the career and theology of Edwards, "a born
       metaphysician," and doubts whether he "understood" his
       people.

2   DeNORMANDIE, JAMES. "Jonathan Edwards at Portsmouth, New
       Hampshire." Proceedings of the Massachusetts Historical
       Society, 2d ser. 15 (March): 16-20.
            Expresses disappointment with the banal and tedious
       Christ the Example of Ministers, an installation sermon
       Edwards delivered for Job Strong in Portsmouth, N.H., 28
       June 1749. Such a sermon delivered today would "greatly
       discourage" any candidate for ordination.

3   DEXTER, FRANKLIN B[OWDITCH]. "The Manuscripts of Jonathan
       Edwards." Proceedings of the Massachusetts Historical
       Society, 2d ser. 15 (March): 2-16.
            Traces the progress and disposition of the Edwards
       manuscripts--from the time of his death to August 1900,

when Yale acquired them—and describes the contents. The
collection includes "a major part" of the folios and
quartos mentioned in Edwards's will and inventory, especially the "immense" number of sermons, between 1100 and
1200 items or probably a third of the sermons he may have
written on any scrap paper that came to hand—bills and
letters, prescriptions and copybooks, and, quite frequently, the thin soft paper his wife and daughters used
in making fans to support the family. Edwards's style
here is of "great simplicity and directness, . . . unexpected freshness and modernness" and suggests not an aloof
metaphysician but a very human pastor.

4   EGGLESTON, GEORGE CARY. "Jonathan Edwards." In his The
    American Immortals. New York: G. P. Putnam's Sons,
    pp. 337-49.
        Offers a life of Edwards (and of others in the Hall of
    Fame) and judges him in the light of a time that took
    authority without question and Scripture without criticism.
    Edwards was born and lived through an "extraordinary med-
    ley of contradictions which constituted [his] creed."

5   FRASER, ALEXANDER CAMPBELL. "Appendix: Samuel Johnson and
    Jonathan Edwards." In his The Works of George Berkeley.
    Oxford: Clarendon Press, 3: 390-98.
        Argues that Edwards's concept of causation on power,
    differing from Berkeley's, ends in a God whose omnipotence
    outweighs his goodness and whose creation becomes in-
    creasingly and endlessly sinful and irresponsible. Ed-
    wards seems "unappalled" by this nor aware of the "agnos-
    tic pessimism" latent in such a view. (See also 2: 21-22,
    for similarities between Edwards and Berkeley's Alciphron
    on the sense perception of the visible world.)

6   GARDINER, H[ARRY] NORMAN, ed. Jonathan Edwards, a Retrospect;
    Being the Addresses Delivered in connection with the Un-
    veiling of a Memorial in the First Church of Christ in
    Northampton, Massachusetts, on the One Hundred and Fifti-
    eth Anniversary of his Dismissal from the Pastorate of
    that Church. Boston and New York: Houghton Mifflin & Co.,
    168 pp.
        Publishes the papers (with an introduction) delivered
    at the unveiling of a memorial to Edwards's dismissal from
    his church, in the following order:
        Gardiner, H. Norman, Introduction, pp. v-xvi. Consid-
    ers Edwards "so great, so representative, so influential"
    that a broad retrospective is necessary to account for and

interpret the crisis and conflict in New England religious life that "more than any other man" he created. The work of this volume is "a serious attempt" to assay his character and his influence, his theology and his philosophy, to discover what was "temporary and accidental," what essential and permanent.

Allen, Alexander V. G., "The Place of Edwards in History," pp. 1-31. Remarks "the deepest affinity" between Edwards and Dante--their idealized women and their idealized worlds; their intellectual, poetic imaginations; their banishments and exiles--such that Divine and Supernatural Light, Distinguishing Marks, and Religious Affections are likened in "spirit and purpose" to the Divine Comedy.

Smyth, Egbert C., "The Influence of Edwards on the Spiritual Life of New England," pp. 33-48. Characterizes Edwards's influence upon New England as indirect, as "a witness unsurpassed" of intellectual power addressing the spiritual life of man, as a "synthesist, even more than an analyst" of the sweet sense of God's glory and harmony and love. The traits that mark New England theology--independence, truth, intellect--were his.

Gordon, George A., "The Significance of Edwards To-Day," pp. 49-74. Reprint of 1900.14.

Fisher, George P. "Greetings from Yale University," pp. 75-79. Ranks Edwards "foremost in the long list" of Yale graduates and celebrates the genius and holiness of "the Saint of New England."

Ormond, Alexander T., "Greetings from Princeton University," pp. 80-86. Considers Edwards a "moulding" force on Princeton, and the College a "residuary legatee" of his fame, in a short biographical sketch.

Rose, Henry T., "Edwards in Northampton," pp. 87-111. Traces Edwards's career in Northampton and concludes that he was "not a model pastor." He was lonely and cold, tactless and humorless, a martyr and a mystic, but he was a "man for the hour" at the time of Northampton's spiritual declension.

Gardiner, H. Norman, "The Early Idealism of Edwards," pp. 113-60. Reprint of 1900.12.

7   MacCRACKEN, HENRY MITCHELL. The Hall of Fame. New York and London: G. P. Putnam's Sons, pp. 213-18.
    Offers a brief life of Edwards for the young, transcribes the inscription at the Hall of Fame, and suggests that Edwards's idealism derives from Arthur Collier's Clavis Universalis (1713).

8 McKENZIE, ALEXANDER. "Remarks." Proceedings of the Massachusetts Historical Society, 2d ser. 15 (March): 23-24.
   Ascribes Edwards's "most unhappy" reference to spiders
   in Sinners in the Hands of an Angry God to his "early and
   persistent" interest in them rather than to bad taste.

9 RANKIN, JEREMIAH EAMES. Esther Burr's Journal. Washington:
   Howard University, 100 pp. passim.
   Constructs a journal attributed to Edwards's daughter
   but almost thoroughly of Rankin's devising. Typically,
   Esther "writes" this about her father: "I have just come
   back from a most wonderful ride with my honored father,
   Mr. Edwards, through the spring woods. He usually rides
   alone. . . . Though father is usually taciturn or pre-
   occupied--my mother will call these large words,--even
   when he takes one of us children with him, today, he dis-
   coursed with me of the awful sweetness of walking with God
   in Nature. . . . Going home, my father pointed out to me
   the habits of a flying spider, that sallies forth on his
   thread as upon wings."

10 SQUIRES, WILLIAM HARDER. "Jonathan Edwards und seine Willenslehre." Ph.D. dissertation, University of Leipzig.
   Published as 1901.11.

11 _____. Jonathan Edwards und seine Willenslehre. Lucka:
   Berger & Behrend, 53 pp.
   Considers the doctrine of the will central to Edwards's
   thought and to his place in American intellectual history,
   in an examination of Freedom of the Will and a comparison
   to Schopenhauer's pure metaphysics of the will and Wundt's
   psychology of voluntarism. Edwards teaches an absolute
   determinism in his speculations on universal will, but he
   postulates a moderate determinism in his treatment of the
   human will. Edwards, Schopenhauer, and Wundt represent
   three important stages in the development and investigation of the problem of the will. (In German.)

12 STAGG, JOHN W. "Three Maligned Theologians." Presbyterian
   Quarterly 15 (January): 1-53.
   Defends Calvin, Edwards, and William Twisse against
   misrepresentations of their views on infant baptism.
   Edwards, for instance, "exempts infants dying in infancy
   from Adam's sin, the only cause of condemnation against
   them, and makes the exemption an argument for the certainty of their guilt under original sin."

1901

13 STILES, EZRA. <u>The Literary Diary of Ezra Stiles, D.D., LL.D.,</u>
    <u>President of Yale College</u>. Edited by Franklin Bowditch
    Dexter. New York: Charles Scribner's Sons, 2: 337;
    3: 275.
        Praises Edwards as a linguist, logician, and metaphysi-
    cian, but thinks his "valuable writings" will be forgotten
    in another generation and his reclusive temperament was
    unsuited to the labors of a college president.

14 WALKER, WILLISTON. "Jonathan Edwards." In his <u>Ten New Eng-</u>
    <u>land Leaders</u>. New York: Silver, Burdett & Co., pp. 217-
    63.
        Juxtaposes Edwards's formidable intellect and voiced
    "terrors of the law" against his transforming vision and
    "mystic conception" of God and claims that the beauty of
    his spirit will be more "reverenced" than the qualities
    of his mind "respected," in a life and estimate of "this
    remarkable man" and his work.

1902

1 BACON, EDWIN M[UNROE]. <u>Literary Pilgrimages in New England</u>.
    New York: Silver, Burdett & Co., pp. 433-40.
        Paraphrases Oliver Wendell Holmes's sketch of Edwards
    (1880.6) and adds biographical notes.

2 COBB, SANFORD H. <u>The Rise of Religious Liberty in America,</u>
    <u>A History</u>. New York: Macmillan Co., pp. 484-89.
        Attributes to Edwards, "more than any other man," the
    separation of church and state in America. By insisting
    on its dignity and purity, its divine charter and divine
    grace, Edwards fashioned a church greater than the state
    and hence beyond its control. Yet there is "no proof
    that he meant to do anything of the kind."

3 COOKE, GEORGE WILLIS. <u>Unitarianism in America: A History of</u>
    <u>its Origins and Development</u>. Boston: American Unitarian
    Association, pp. 38-41.
        Remarks Edwards's running battle with Arminianism and
    his role in the Robert Breck affair.

4 FISKE, JOHN. <u>New France and New England</u>. The Historical
    Writings of John Fiske, no. 9. Boston and New York:
    Houghton Mifflin & Co., pp. 222-26, 231.
        Gives a short life and estimate of Edwards, "probably
    the greatest intelligence that the western hemisphere has
    yet seen."

5   HAYES, SAMUEL PERKINS. "An Historical Study of the Edwardean
     Revivals." American Journal of Psychology 13 (October):
     550-74.
         Traces the history of American revivals, attributing
     them to "unstable" conditions and religious apathy; re-
     ports the theological struggle of the Great Awakening
     between the New Lights and the Old; notes the "paradox"
     of Edwards, insisting on both man's innate depravity and
     his duty to seek regeneration; and counters Edwards's
     defense of the "positive basis" of conversion with Charles
     Chauncy's analysis of abuses, excesses, and disorders.
     Revival activity from 1735 to 1742, in which Edwards
     played so important a part, was followed by "a half cen-
     tury of popular indifference."

6   JAMES, WILLIAM. The Varieties of Religious Experience. New
     York: Longmans, Green, & Co., pp. 20, 228-29.
         Considers Edwards's empirical method in Religious Affec-
     tions the only way available to know Christian virtue--its
     roots are "inaccessible"--and finds his "rich and delicate"
     descriptions of supernatural grace identical with those of
     an "exceptionally high degree of natural goodness."

7   MacCRACKEN, JOHN HENRY. "The Sources of Jonathan Edwards's
     Idealism." Philosophical Review 11 (January): 26-42.
         Proposes Arthur Collier's Clavis Universalis (London,
     1713) as the "intermediate link" between Locke and Edwards
     in the latter's development towards idealism. "A careful
     comparative study" reveals that "there are sufficient
     grounds for supposing that it was Collier and not Berkeley
     who turned the mind of the youthful Edwards in the direc-
     tion of idealism."

8   McCULLOCH, JAMES E. "The Place of Revivals in American Church
     History." Methodist Review 84 (September-October): 681-97.
         Ascribes the pattern of revivals in America to the "law
     of ebb and flow of spiritual life" and finds Edwards re-
     sponding to the lethargy, skepticism, heresy, and schism
     of New England. Edwards was "providentially sent" to
     restore Christ to his people in the first era of revivals
     (1734), as were Timothy Dwight and Charles Grandison Fin-
     ney in the second (1797), and Jeremiah C. Lamphier and
     Dwight L. Moody in the third (1858).

9   MALLARY, R. DEWITT. Lenox and the Berkshire Highlands. New
     York and London: G. P. Putnam's Sons, pp. 246-48 passim.
         Recounts Edwards's seven years at Stockbridge minister-
     ing to the "benighted heathen" in the heart of his beloved
     Berkshires.

1902

10   MOULTON, CHARLES WELLS, ed. "Jonathan Edwards." In <u>Library</u>
     <u>of Literary Criticism of English and American Authors</u>.
     Buffalo, N.Y.: Moulton Publishing Co., 3: 380-95.
        Quotes from more than seventy texts commenting upon
     Edwards's life and work.

11   SEARS, LORENZO. <u>American Literature in the Colonial and</u>
     <u>National Periods</u>. Boston: Little, Brown & Co., pp. 91-94.
        Remarks the direct, plain, and clear diction of Edwards's
     sermons compared to the "hard and dismal" style of the
     treatises, in an estimate of Edwards and Franklin as tran-
     sitional figures.

12   STAGG, JOHN W. <u>Calvin, Twisse, and Edwards on the Universal</u>
     <u>Salvation of Those Dying in Infancy</u>. Richmond, Va.:
     Presbyterian Committee of Publication, pp. 123-42, passim.
        Balances Edwards's views on infant reprobation with
     those of his on Christ's redemption: "All anyone can say
     is, that Edwards has made sin to appear exceedingly sinful,
     but that likewise he has made redemption to appear exceed-
     ingly glorious." (A partial adaptation of 1901.12.)

13   TRUMBULL, JAMES RUSSELL. <u>History of Northampton Massachusetts</u>
     <u>from its Settlement in 1654</u>. Northampton, Mass.: Gazette
     Printing Co., 2: 41-51, 195-234.
        Details Edwards's years in Northampton; his financial,
     political, and ministerial difficulties; and the occasion
     of his dismissal; and tempers the indictment against the
     townspeople with this: at the time of his dismissal,
     Edwards was the pastor of "an obscure country parish," not
     America's greatest theologian.

14   UPHAM, WILLIAM P. "Shorthand Notes of Jonathan Edwards."
     <u>Proceedings of the Massachusetts Historical Society</u>, 2d
     ser. 15 (February): 514-21.
        Deciphers shorthand entries appended to "Notes on Natu-
     ral Science," in which Edwards lays down rules he should
     observe in writing about philosophy and natural science.
     Inasmuch as no "special secrecy" seemed needed, Edwards,
     like other ministers then, probably used shorthand to "save
     time, space, and paper." The notes also make clear that
     Edwards did not borrow his idealism from Berkeley, for
     "he was not at that time acquainted with Berkeley's publi-
     cations."

1903

1 ALLEN, JAMES LANE. The Mettle of the Pasture. New York:
   Macmillan Co., p. 128.
   Calls Edwards the "hoarsest of the whole flock of New
   World theological ravens," in a novel set in Kentucky.

2 ANDERSON, WILBERT L. "The Preaching Power of Jonathan Edwards." Congregationalist and Christian World 88 (3 October): 463-66.
   Attributes Edwards's powerful preaching to his reason,
   his passions, and his will, to his "skilled indirection"
   and speculative daring.

3 ANON. "Churches Celebrate 200th Anniversary of Edwards's
   Birth." Hampshire Gazette, 5 October, p. 4.
   Compares the current flurry of praise for Edwards with
   the earlier villification of him and reports church celebrations in Northampton of his birth.

4 ANON. "The Edwards Bicentennial." Journal of the Presbyte-
   terian Historical Society 2 (December): 166-69.
   Summarizes "careful accounts" of celebrations of the
   Edwards bicentennial appearing in the Congregationalist
   (1903.13) and furnishes an index to some "important"
   periodical literature.

5 ANON. "Edwards's Bi-Centennial." Springfield Daily Republi-
   can, 6 October, p. 7.
   Notes celebrations of Edwards's bicentennial at South
   Windsor and Yale.

6 ANON. [The Edwards Bicentennial.] Yale Daily News, 6 October, p. 1.
   Reports the Edwards bicentennial celebration at Yale
   on 5 October, details the program, and quotes from Williston Walker's address.

7 ANON. "Edwards's Birthday." Springfield Daily Republican,
   6 October, pp. 6-7.
   Details the celebration at Stockbridge commemorating
   Edwards's birth and quotes at length from the major
   speeches on the occasion.

8 ANON. "Honor Edwards's Memory." Congregationalist and
   Christian World 88 (17 October): 531.
   Hopes the praise lavished upon Edwards now will sustain
   his memory in years to come.

1903

9   ANON. "Jonathan Edwards." Journal of the Presbyterian His-
        torical Society 2 (December): 157-60.
            Suggests that there is "enough of Edwards for both"
        Congregationalists and Presbyterians. Though born a Con-
        gregationalist, Edwards "began and ended" his ministry a
        Presbyterian, in New York and in Princeton. (An editorial.)

10   ANON. "Jonathan Edwards." Outlook 75 (3 October): 248-51.
            Praises Edwards's intellectual courage and vivid imagi-
        nation, summarizes his theology for reluctant readers, and
        dismisses it as having only an "historical existence."

11   ANON. "Jonathan Edwards." Zion's Herald 81 (30 September):
        1234-35.
            Compares Edwards to Emerson and Wesley only to suggest
        that "the time is not yet fully ripe for a final estimate"
        of Edwards. There is some gold in the "vast quarry" of
        his works, but much dross. Even so, he is a "major prophet"
        of Christianity, akin to Calvin, Dante, and St. Francis.

12   ANON. "The Jonathan Edwards Bicentennial." New York Daily
        Tribune, 4 October, Part 2: 7.
            Dwells on the personal aspects of Edwards's life,
        principally during the seven "troublesome" years in
        Stockbridge, to counter the popular notion of him as an
        "ecclesiastical machine." (Illustrated.)

13   ANON. "Jonathan Edwards Celebrations." Congregationalist
        and Christian World 88 (17 October): 537.
            Describes in detail the celebrations at Andover, New
        Haven, Hartford, South Windsor, Stockbridge, and Berkeley
        of the 200th anniversary of the birth of Edwards.

14   ANON. Review of Edwards's Unpublished Essay on the Trinity.
        Nation 77 (12 November): 384.
            Welcomes the long-delayed publication of Edwards's
        trinitarian views and finds them thoroughly orthodox and
        "singularly juiceless."

15   ANON. "Story of the Great Preacher." Hampshire Gazette,
        10 October, p. 2.
            Recounts Edwards's career but glosses over his North-
        ampton dismissal: Edwards went to Stockbridge on the
        death of John Sergeant.

16   ANON. "Why Revive Edwards." <u>Congregationalist and Christian</u>
      <u>World</u> 88 (3 October):454.
          Believes Edwards was "not a storehouse of truth but a
      dynamic force" whose theology is outdated but whose
      spiritual teaching is not.

17   [BERKSHIRE COUNTY, MASS., CONGREGATIONAL CHURCHES.] <u>Jonathan</u>
      <u>Edwards: The Two Hundredth Anniversary of his Birth.</u>
      <u>Union Meeting of the Berkshire North and South Conferences,</u>
      <u>Stockbridge, Mass., October Fifth, 1903.</u> Stockbridge,
      Mass.: Berkshire Conferences, 68 pp.
          Publishes the papers delivered at the Stockbridge bi-
      centennial celebration of Edwards's birth, in the follow-
      ing order:
          Hopkins, Henry. Introduction, pp. 5-7. Acknowledges
      the greatness of Edwards's intellect and the importance of
      his influence as well as the limits of his formal reason-
      ing and the failure of some of his theology.
          Porter, Elbert S. "Address of Welcome," pp. 8-11.
      Characterizes Edwards as a "student of deep things" and a
      prodigious user of writing paper.
          Andrews, George Wakeman. "The Edwards Family," pp. 12-
      18. Studies the Edwards family for its righteous effect
      upon the country through learned and virtuous descendants,
      and concludes that the Reformation rendered an "important
      service" by rescuing the clergy from celibacy.
          Smart, I. Chipman. "The Modern Note in Edwards,"
      pp. 19-23. Notes that Edwards's belief that God "comes
      straight to the mind" as a spiritual light is one shared
      by people today.
          Rowland, Lyman S. "The Other Side of Edwards," pp. 24-
      33. Discovers another side to Edwards's preaching, "a
      Calvary as well as a Sinai, a Paradise as well as an
      Inferno," <u>A Divine and Supernatural Light</u> as well as
      <u>Sinners in the Hands of an Angry God.</u> Edwards was poetic
      and aphoristic like Emerson, like Pascal.
          DeWitt, John. "Jonathan Edwards: A Study," pp. 34-58.
      Considers Edwards's "regnant, permeating, irradiating"
      spirituality the clue to the quality of his life and to
      the unity of his work. From spirituality Edwards con-
      cluded that aesthetic emotion was rooted not in material
      beauty but in holiness; through spirituality he stressed
      the inward state of man "in nature and in grace." Thus
      Edwards effected a shift in American theology by emphasiz-
      ing the conversion experience.
          Park, William Edwards. "Edwards at Stockbridge," pp.
      59-67. Recounts Edwards's Stockbridge years.

1903

18   CHAPELL, F. L. "Jonathan Edwards and the Movement in New
      England." In his The Great Awakening of 1740. Philadel-
      phia: American Baptist Publications Society, pp. 42–66.
           Records Edwards's role in the Great Awakening--the
      scenes of his ministry and the consequences of his career
      --from a Baptist point of view.

19   CLARK, IRENE WOODBRIDGE. "A Wifely Estimate of Edwards."
      Congregationalist and Christian World 88 (3 October): 472–
      73.
           Reprints (for the first time) a letter by Sarah Edwards
      to the council at Northampton, 22 June 1750, on the con-
      troversy surrounding public profession. She insisted that
      "what might seem a sudden caprice on her husband's part
      was in reality the first public action based on a convic-
      tion long held, which time was continually strengthening."

20   CONE, KATE M. "Jonathan Edwards." Outlook 75 (3 October):
      255–66.
           Relates the "true story" of Edwards's career by high-
      lighting the women in his life, from his mother, who
      envisioned his destiny as he lay "a rosy baby on her
      breast," to his wife, who "exquisitely" illustrated an
      emotional side denied to her intellectual husband.

21   CROOK, ISAAC. Jonathan Edwards. Cincinnati: Jennings &
      Pye, 95 pp.
           Prizes Edwards the man, not the theologian--"Thousands
      of pages are not worth the paper on which his disputations
      are written"--in a desultory reading of his life and work.

22   CROTHERS, S. M. "Jonathan Edwards." Christian Register,
      22 October, pp. 1263–64.
           Focuses on the moral philosophy of True Virtue--the
      "positive element" in Unitarianism--rather than the
      "repellent" Calvinism of Sinners in the Hands of an Angry
      God, and finds a "natural and inevitable" development
      from Edwards to Samuel Hopkins, William Ellery Channing,
      and Ralph Waldo Emerson. Edwards gave them (and us) an
      ethics impersonal and universal in which the love of
      Christ yields to the love of being in general.

23   EDWARDS, WILLIAM H., comp. Timothy and Rhoda Ogden Edwards
      of Stockbridge, Mass., and their Descendants: A Genealogy.
      Cincinnati: Robert Clarke Co., pp. 6–16.
           Derives a brief life of Edwards from standard bio-
      graphical sources; reproduces portraits, photographs,

letters, and the family coat of arms; and concludes that
Edwards was "a child in the affairs of this world."

24 [FINLEY, SAMUEL]. "A Contemporaneous Account of Jonathan
Edwards." Journal of the Presbyterian Historical Society
2 (December): 125-35.
Reprint of 1758.4.

25 FISHER, GEORGE P[ARK]. An Unpublished Essay of Edwards on
the Trinity, with Remarks on Edwards and his Theology.
New York: Charles Scribner's Sons, pp. vii-xv, 1-74.
Recounts the history and debate concerning the "hetero-
dox" views of Edwards on the trinity (see especially
1865.4 and 1881.2); concludes that the unpublished essay
reprinted here is "one of the ablest arguments . . . in
behalf of fundamental positions of the Nicene theology";
and provides an abbreviated life of Edwards, a seriatim
reading of his work, and appraisal of his influence upon
New England Theology. At the heart of Edwards's philosophy and theology is the "doctrine of the Absolute,"
giving rise to doctrines of being, necessity, and causation, and to his early formulations of idealism and immanence, with its hints of pantheism. But Edwards was a
theist, believing in the personality of God, and a trinitarian, teaching tripersonalism--the priority of the
father and the coequality of the persons.

26 _____. "The Value of Edwards for Today." Congregationalist
and Christian World 88 (3 October): 469-71.
Counts Edwards's value two-fold: as a model to ministers of a believer and thinker; as an "indispensable"
source to investigators of religious thought and speculation in New England. Like Thomas Aquinas, Edwards is
Doctor Angelicus.

27 GARDINER, H[ARRY] NORMAN, et al. "Tributes to Jonathan Edwards from Careful Students of His Writings." Congregationalist and Christian World 88 (3 October): 458.
Offers tributes to Edwards by H. Norman Gardiner (his
"attractive and tonic power"), by William Newton Clarke
("a hero in strife"), and by Egbert C. Smyth ("an entire
consecration of genius and greatness to the promotion of
Christian faith").

28 GREGG, DAVID. Jonathan Edwards, a Gift of God to the American People. Brooklyn, N.Y.: Eagle Press, 20 pp.
Reprints the first of three sermons--the others (unavailable) are "The Man--His Theological Creed and Its

1903

Influence" and "Practical Odds and Ends from the Age of
Edwards; Or the Religion for Our Day"--preached at the
Lafayette Avenue Presbyterian Church, Brooklyn, on successive Sundays, beginning 4 October 1903. The sermon
elaborates upon a text from Matthew 23:24 in praise of
prophets and wise men and concludes, "Think what it would
be . . . if every one of us were a Jonathan Edwards!"

29 HARPER, WILLIAM HUDSON. "Edwards, Devotee, Theologian,
      Preacher." Interior 34 (1 October): 1272-74.
        Offers a brief life of Edwards, a man of "profound"
      devotion and "lurid" sermons, and quotes from the latter.

30 HIGGINSON, THOMAS WENTWORTH, and BOYNTON, HENRY WALCOTT.
      A Reader's History of American Literature. Boston:
      Houghton Mifflin & Co., pp. 19-23.
        Considers Edwards's Sinners in the Hands of an Angry
      God a "form of insanity," but his description of Sarah
      Pierrepont "the high-water mark of Puritan prose."

31 HOLMES, C[LEMENT] E[LTON]. "Edwards and Northampton."
      Zion's Herald 81 (30 September): 1238-42.
        Culls some anecdotes and observations about Edwards's
      career in Northampton, from his planting of elms to the
      hiring of a horse--$2.23 to Boston and back--in a desultory
      account.

32 HOPKINS, SAMUEL. "Edwards's Habits and Tastes." Congrega-
      tionalist and Christian World 88 (3 October): 471.
        Reprints selections from 1765.2.

33 HUMPHREY, G. H. Jonathan Edwards: An Address Delivered in
      Utica, N.Y., on the 200th Anniversary of His Birth, Oct.
      5, 1903. n.p., 32 pp.
        Recounts the life and thought of Edwards, a minister
      entirely free of "pulpitish cant, or tabernacular drawl,"
      and begs for a "duplicate" Edwards to again fill the air
      with "Calvinistic ozone."

34 KING, HENRY CHURCHILL. "Jonathan Edwards as Philosopher and
      Theologian." Hartford Seminary Record 14 (November): 23-
      57.
        Considers Edwards "a thorough-going theistic idealist"
      in philosophy and "a mystical ethical Calvinist" in theol-
      ogy, in a study of the sources and parallels, strengths
      and weaknesses, and "great" inconsistencies of his thought.
      His "blinding vision" of a sovereign, arbitrary God denies

man moral initiative, makes God the author of sin, and
distorts Christ's role of love. Edwards is less than
"absolutely loyal" to his principle of benevolence in
True Virtue, almost "anti-Protestant" in his distinction
between common and special grace, "unjustifiably pantheistic" in End of Creation. Still American theology owes
him "a debt unsurpassed."

35 MORRIS, EDWARD DAFYDD. Jonathan Edwards; His Contribution to
Calvinism, to Evangelical Theology Generally, to Christian
Ethics and to Practical Religion. A paper read before
the Ministerial Association of Columbus, Ohio. [n.d.,
15 pp.]
Praises Edwards for his "precious" contributions to Calvinism, evangelism, Christian ethics, and practical religion that will continue to "millennial times." Edwards
improved Calvinism by making possible "the ultimate salvation of the whole human race" and bringing it in "closer
affiliation" with Anglicanism, Lutheranism, and Wesleyean
Arminianism. His contributions to evangelical theology
rests principally in his concept of the trinity and his
rejection of the half-way covenant; to ethics in his True
Virtue; and to practical religion in his Religious Affections.

36 MORRIS, GEORGE PERRY. "The Edwards Manuscripts." Journal of
the Presbyterian Historical Society 2 (December): 169-70.
Reprints the note on the Edwards manuscripts in his
"The Human Side of Edwards" (1903.37).

37 _____. "The Human Side of Edwards." Congregationalist and
Christian World 88 (3 October): 461-62.
Calls for a biography of Edwards that studies him not
only as a theologian and writer of "noble English prose"
but also as a lad and parent, an exile-evangelist and a
"pioneer in industrial education."

38 ORR, JAMES. "Jonathan Edwards; His Influence in Scotland."
Congregationalist and Christian World 88 (3 October): 467-
68.
Estimates Edwards's influence upon John McLeod Campbell
to be "really profound," even though few outside of "serious circles" in Scotland--or New England, for that matter--
ever heard of Edwards.

39   PALMER, B. P.   "'No Grander Life Since Plato's.'"   Boston
       Sunday Globe, 4 October, p. 44.
           Recounts Edwards's career, with quotations and pic-
       tures, and catalogues his descendants.

40   PATTISON, T. HARWOOD.   The History of Christian Preaching.
       Philadelphia: American Baptist Publishing Society, pp.
       354-59.
           Asserts that Edwards begins the "powerful era" of
       preaching in America and that his greatness lies in a
       "rare combination" of insight, imagination, logic, will,
       intellect, and feelings to glorify God and save souls.

41   RANKIN, JEREMIAH EAMES.   Esther Burr's Journal.   Washington:
       Woodward & Lothrop.
           Reprint of 1901.9.

42   SELLERS, MONTGOMERY P.   "New England in Colonial Literature."
       New England Magazine, n.s. 28 (March): 100-107.
           Places Edwards "far above" all others in colonial
       letters, including Anne Bradstreet and Cotton Mather, even
       though his theology was "artificial" and his influence
       will rest upon his "wonderful personality."

43   SIMPSON, SAMUEL.   "Jonathan Edwards--A Historical Review."
       Hartford Seminary Record 14 (November): 3-22.
           Offers "in rapid review" the events of Edwards's
       career, derived from Sereno Dwight's Life (1829.4), and
       "hurried side glances" of social and religious conditions
       important to it.

44   [SQUIRES, WILLIAM HARDER.]   The Edwardean, A Quarterly De-
       voted to the History of Thought in America.
           Examines (and endorses) voluntarism in a periodical
       devoted exclusively to Edwards and written by the editor,
       William Harder Squires, professor of philosophy at Hamil-
       ton College, Clinton, New York.   The Edwardean was pub-
       lished quarterly for a year, from October 1903 to July
       1904, and includes serially the following articles in the
       first (October) issue:
           "The Edwardean," pp. 1-3.   Intends to write a history
       of philosophy in America by reviewing with "modified
       prejudice" the voluntarism of Edwards, a theism reflecting
       the religious spirit of its people.
           "Glimpses into Edwards' Life," pp. 4-12.   Calls Edwards
       "the foremost thinker [America] has ever produced," a
       mystic, a pantheist, an "open-minded" man, in a short
       biography.

"The Seventy Resolutions," pp. 13-23. Defends Edwards's "classic" Resolutions against charges that they are the "weird creations of a morbid imagination" by reprinting the text of this "sane, inquistive, and conscientious inquirer."

"President Edwards as Thinker," pp. 24-31. Praises Edwards's thought, arising as it does from the isolation of a "primitive wilderness," and centered as it is on the "idea and being" of God.

"Some Estimates of President Edwards," pp. 32-50. Cites and quotes from a variety of commentators here and abroad and concludes that Edwards is Hume, Kant, Schopenhauer, and Wundt "in one."

"Edwards' Methaphysical Foundations," pp. 51-64. Contends that an "adequate" understanding of Edwards's metaphysics can rest only upon pure voluntarism. Edwards is a "volitional pantheist, and the absolute monist." (Continued 1904.15)

45 THOMPSON, ROBERT ELLIS. "A Centenary View of Jonathan Edwards." Sunday School Times 45 (3 October): 494.
Judges Edwards's greatness as a pious man and strenuous Christian to have "disentangled" itself from a past of doctrinal and sectarian dispute.

46 W[ALKER], W[ILLISTON]. "Edwards's Recovered Treatise." Yale Alumni Weekly 13 (4 November): 106-107.
Reviews George Fisher's An Unpublished Essay of Edwards on the Trinity (1903.25), recounts the provenance of the manuscript, and concludes that Edwards shows not a "hint" of heterodoxy. Indeed, Edwards seems more orthodox, more Athanasian in his trinitarian views than had been suspected.

47 WARD, WILLIAM HAYES. "Jonathan Edwards." Independent 55 (1 October): 2321-27.
Proclaims Edwards the "broadest, grandest" man of the American pulpit, in a tribute of like superlatives.

48 WINSHIP, EDITH A. "The Descendants of Edwards." Journal of the Presbyterian Historical Society 2 (December): 170-71.
Summarizes 1903.49.

49 _____. "The Human Legacy of Jonathan Edwards." World's Work 6 (October): 3981-84.
Marvels at the 1400 descendants of Edwards, among them college professors and presidents, writers and preachers,

1903

doctors and lawyers, judges and businessmen, and public officials--mayors, governors, congressmen, senators, ambassadors. Though Edwards's theology is "dead, and his books are unread," he lives in his descendants.

50   ZENOS, ANDREW C. "The Permanent and the Passing in the Thought of Edwards." Interior 34 (1 October): 1274-75.
        Delineates Edwards's influence on American theological thought as either permanent or passing. His doctrines of original sin and freedom of the will no longer hold their places, his doctrine of virtue only negatively. But his "penetrating and comprehensive" doctrine of salvation, exemplified in The Satisfaction of Christ, will continue its profound effect, for it best accounts for "Scripture facts."

<u>1904</u>

1   ANON. "Jonathan Edwards." New York Times, 6 August, p. 540.
        Reviews both Edwards's Sermons (1904.7) and the bicentennial Exercises at Andover (1904.14).

2   BACON, LEONARD WOOLSEY. The Congregationalists. The Story of the Churches. New York: Baker & Taylor Co., pp. 117-21, 135-39.
        Remarks Edwards's role in the Great Awakening and in the founding of New England Theology, a "distinctly American" theodicy.

3   BEARDSLEY, FRANK GRENVILLE. A History of American Revivals. New York: American Tract Society, pp. 22-29, passim.
        Evaluates Edwards's role in the revivals of the Connecticut Valley and traces the "first manifestation" of the revival impulse in the 1730s to his sermons on justification, damnation, excellency, and duty.

4   CANDLER, WARREN A. Great Revivals and the Great Republic. Nashville and Dallas: Publishing House of the M. E. Church, South, pp. 43-47, 90.
        Quotes from Faithful Narrative marking the beginning of the Great Awakening but sees Edwards's role in it as secondary to George Whitefield's. Edwards became president of Princeton, "the child of the revival," because he was an evangelist.

5   COLE, SAMUEL VALENTINE. "A Witness to the Truth." New Eng-
       land Magazine, n.s. 29 (January): 583-86.
           Reprint of 1904.14.

6   DeWITT, JOHN. "Jonathan Edwards: A Study." Princeton
       Theological Review 2 (January): 88-109.
           Reprint of 1903.17.

7   GARDINER, H[ARRY] NORMAN. Introduction to his Selected
       Sermons of Jonathan Edwards. New York: Macmillan Co.,
       pp. vii-xxix.
           Considers Edwards as preacher--his "chief public work
       and his chief reputation in his lifetime"--and reprints
       six of ten sermons published during his lifetime and an
       unpublished seventh, in a brief biography and estimate.
       Edwards's sermons are "singularly clear, simple and un-
       studied" in style, of value as history, as personal expres-
       sion, and as literature.

8   HAZLITT, WILLIAM. "Of Persons One Would Wish to Have Seen."
       In Collected Works. Edited by A. R. Waller and Arnold
       Glover. London: J. M. Dent & Co., 12: 26-38.
           Lists six metaphysicians of modern times--Hobbes,
       Berkeley, Butler, Hartley, Hume, and Leibnitz--"and per-
       haps Jonathan Edwards, a Massachusetts man."

*9 HOLMES, CLEMENT ELTON. "The Philosophy of Jonathan Edwards
       and Its Relation to His Theology." Ph.D. dissertation,
       Boston University.
           Cited in Comprehensive Dissertation Index 1861-1972,
       32:379.

10 KINGMAN, HENRY. Jonathan Edwards: a Commemorative Address
       in Observance of the Bicentenary of His Birth, at the
       First Congregational Church, Berkeley, California, October
       5, 1903. E. T. Earl Lecture Foundation, no. 1. [San
       Francisco:] Pacific Theological Seminary, 22 pp.
           Offers a biography of Edwards and estimates his signi-
       ficance to be less as a theologian or philosopher than as
       a "prophet of God." There was in Edwards a "deep, happy
       inconsistency" between his dialectical thought and his
       spiritual intuition.

11 MILLER, EDWARD WAITE. "The Great Awakening and its Relation
       to American Christianity." Princeton Theological Review
       2 (October):545-62.
           Surveys the Great Awakening, the changes it wrought on
       American Christianity, and Edwards's role in it,

accounting his ministry simply a return to the "themes and
style" of earlier Puritan preachers. Edwards showed
"singular insight" in understanding the critical nature
of the revival for America if not its profound effects,
the destruction of unified New England Congregationalism
and the creation of "a conscious national unity," a change
in church and state.

12 MORE, PAUL ELMER. "The Solitude of Nathaniel Hawthorne." In
his Shelburne Essays. First Series. New York: G. P.
Putnam's Sons, pp. 22-50.
    Relates Hawthorne's "Ethan Brand" and the abject lone-
liness of the guilty to Edwards's Sinners in the Hands of
an Angry God and his "extravagant sense" of the individual
soul.

13 ORMOND, ALEXANDER T. "Jonathan Edwards as Thinker and Phil-
ospher." Philosophical Review 13 (March):183-84.
    Summarizes a paper delivered at a meeting of the Ameri-
can Philosophical Association at Princeton University,
29-31 December 1903. The "key" to Edwards's philosophy
lies in the 58th section of his "treatise on Decrees and
Election" where he discusses God and the ideal and real
worlds. Edwards "anticipates" Rudolf Hermann Lotze in
his Metaphysik (1841) and denies to God and man "the freedom of indifference."

14 [PLATNER, JOHN WINTHROP, ed.] Exercises Commemorating the
Two-Hundredth Anniversary of the Birth of Jonathan Edwards,
Held at Andover Theological Seminary, October 4 and 5,
1903. Andover, Mass.: Andover Press, 191 pp.
    Publishes the papers delivered at the Edwards bicenten-
nial celebration at Andover and appends some unpublished
miscellanies, in the following order:
    Platner, John Winthrop. "Religious Conditions in New
England in the Time of Edwards," pp. 29-45. Sketches the
religious surroundings in which Edwards lived and thought
and preached. Edwards found New England "morally deca-
dent" and "un-theological," church discipline "relaxed"
under the half-way covenant; he "redeemed" the church
from secularization, overthrew the half-way covenant,
awakened men to conviction and conversion, and left New
England with "all the apparatus for an energetic theological life." But it is not his Calvinist theology that
serves now; it is his spirituality and mysticism and
"beatific vision."

Woodbridge, Frederick J. E. "The Philosophy of Jonathan Edwards," pp. 47-72. Reckons Edwards's influence
"largely negligible" now, though he dominated New England
thought for 150 years, and accounts his work a failure
"not through refutation, but through inadequacy," through
the lack of "philosophical thoroughness." Edwards was a
thinker of promise and originality--see the mystical
pantheism of his "Notes on the Mind"--who never developed
his possibilities. He failed to link his philosophical
speculations to his theological convictions, failed to
resolve his "intellectual duality," even though his late
work on teleology and virtue reveals a conscious effort to
simplify and unify. Clearly, the "unanalyzed" and "potent" emotions of his conversion experience so disrupted
Edwards intellectually that philosophy and theology were
"almost completely divorced and unrelated."

Smyth, Egbert Coffin. "The Theology of Edwards,"
pp. 73-93. Discovers the core of Edwards's theology in
his "vivid sense" of the reality, immediacy, and peace of
God, made intelligible for him in the trinity and manifest
in the creation. God's absolute perfection implies "self-
impartation, reciprocity, mutual Love"; He creates out of
plenitude in order to communicate. As the glory of God is
to give, so the end of man is to give himself to God.
This is "the innermost meaning and the climax" of Edwards's
theology.

Cole, Samuel Valentine. "A Witness to the Truth,"
pp. 95-103. Praises Edwards as "This Dante of New England" in a poem of 166 lines.

Orr, James. "The Influence of Edwards," pp. 105-26.
Attributes Edwards's powerful influence to the "inseparable union" of intellectual power and spiritual perception,
even though there were "strange contrasts" within him.

15   [SQUIRES, WILLIAM HARDER]   The Edwardean, A Quarterly Devoted
to the History of Thought in America.
Continues the examination of Edwards's thought, especially his voluntarism (see 1903.44) and includes
serially the following articles:
"Jonathan Edwards as Philosopher," (January) pp. 65-77.
Considers Edwards's voluntarism the "natural product" of
his time, linked to the political philosophy and spirit
of America, and the "prototype" of all succeeding systems.
As a speculative philosopher--there is no desire to
resurrect his theology--Edwards is "teacher" to all modern
philosophers. The "exalted" theme of his philosophy is
the unified will of nature, man, and God.

"A Revival of Edwards," pp. 78-83. Rejoices that the bicentennial celebration signals the revival of Edwards's philosophy, which will "emancipate" American thought from European "error," and gives renewed attention to his theology, "free from the hamperings of a pulpit prejudice."

"Edwards' Psychology of the Will," pp. 84-108. Validates Freedom of the Will, Edwards's "great masterpiece of his life," in contemporary psychological terms and proposes that his theological argument is simply "confirmatory" of the metaphysical and psychological arguments. Edwards replaces the "fatalistic element" in the volitional processes of traditional Calvinism with psychological motives of character, habit, disposition, prior conduct, and present circumstance, and makes them efficient causes of volitional processes of consciousness.

"Edwards' Relation to Voluntarism," pp. 109-15. Claims that all of Edwards's work, whether philosophical or psychological, ethical or theological, gives "minute expression" to voluntarism.

"A Glance at Edwards' View of Reason," pp. 116-28. Calls Edwards an "uncompromising rationalist" though a "consistent voluntarist," anticipating Kant in the limits he places on reason and fostering rationalism in America by giving reason priority in his philosophy.

"Edwards as Theologian," (April) pp. 129-61. Rescues Edwards's theology from the "New Phariseeism" of liberal religionists and reprints parts of End of Creation. Edwards must be viewed both as a metaphysician of the absolute will of God and as a "practical teacher" and psychologist of the will of man. Thus his metaphysical theology leads to the "elimination of the will of man from the problem of human and divine relation," and results in his being considered "the most cordially hated thinker" of all time.

"Edwards's Inferno," pp. 162-74. Compares Edwards's hell to Dante's and Milton's, suggests his health and his hell were "interrelated facts," acknowledges the dramatic impact of his description, but questions its literalness for him (it would involve grave contradictions).

"A Passage from Edwards' Speculative Metaphysics," pp. 175-92. Reprints parts of "Of Being," comments upon Edwards's ideas of nothing and space, and concludes that he "affirms the objective reality and validity of space." The foundation of the visible universe is God, the only, absolute, and ultimate reality, "the first and last idea" of his metaphysics.

"Edwards' Philosophy of History and Religion," (July) pp. 193-256. Reprints parts of History of Redemption; compares Edwards's theistic philosophy of history and religion to the "psycho-physical," the "individualistic," and the "gastro-centric"; finds it not only superior in its Christo-centricity but of a piece with his "plain and voluntaristic system"; and concludes the final issue of the journal with this: "The philosophy of Jonathan Edwards is America's first and grandest contribution to the thought of the world. . . . Edwards has come nearest of all the world's metaphysicians to reconciling philosophy and religion. . . ."

16 Van BECELAERE, [EDWARD GREGORY] L[AWRENCE]. La Philosophie en Amérique depuis les Origines jusqu'à nos Jours (1607-1900). New York: Eclectic Publishing Co., pp. 33-48.
Notes Edwards's importance to the development of American philosophy—he introduced philosophical elements into Calvinist doctrine and inaugurated an era of intellectual speculation in America—in a general treatment of his life and work. (In French.)

17 WATKINS, WALTER KENDALL. "English Ancestry of Jonathan Edwards." New England Historical and Genealogical Register 58 (April):202-203.
Verifies a family tradition that Edwards's great-grandfather William Edwards, of Hartford, was brought to New England in childhood by his mother, Ann, wife of James Cole.

18 WOODBRIDGE, FREDERICK J. E. "Jonathan Edwards." Philosophical Review 13 (July):393-408.
Reprint of 1904.14.

1905

1 ANON. "Edwards Tablets." Hampshire Gazette, 6 October, p. 3.
Reports the gift of a memorial tablet at the Edwards home on King Street by the Betty Allen Chapter of the Daughters of the American Revolution and the reception following.

2 DAVENPORT, FREDERICK MORGAN. "The New England Awakening Originating with Jonathan Edwards." In his Primitive Traits in Religious Revivals: A Study in Mental and Social Evolution. New York: Macmillan Co., pp. 94-132.

1905

Traces sociologically the "abnormal development" of
religious emotion in New England and the role of Edwards,
the "ardent apologist" for terror during the Great Awakening. Generally, New Englanders are dogmatic types capable
of outbursts of emotions; Edwards, a mixture of Celtic and
Saxon strains, shows traits of "oriental imagination" and
practical common sense. Such a person in such a place and
time was bound to produce "much mental and nervous disorder" and must bear responsibility for it. Still, Edwards's
attack on the half-way covenant, as part of his revival
activity, "laid . . . the foundation" for the separation
of church and state for the emerging Republic.

3   GREENE, M[ARIA] LOUISE. The Development of Religious Liberty
     in Connecticut. Boston and New York: Houghton Mifflin &
     Co., pp. 245-48, 302-304, passim.
         Recounts Edwards's role in the Great Awakening and
     notes that the doctrinal change he brought about resulted
     from a fusing of his conservative theology to his restless
     evangelism.

4   MACPHAIL, ANDREW. "Jonathan Edwards." In his Essays in
     Puritanism. London: T. Fisher Unwin, pp. 1-52.
         Considers that superstitious and immoral New England
     was "ripe" for Edwards, a "preacher of righteousness" who
     "never was able to distinguish between thought and emotion,"
     in a general estimate of his career and the development of
     English and American Puritanism. His philosophical writ-
     ings are part of "the rubbish of libraries," their sub-
     jects "strange," their method "obscure," their conclusions
     "unintelligible," their style "involved." Edwards "knew
     little" of this world, still less of people; an intuitive
     and apocalyptic thinker, there is something "irresistibly
     comic" in the idea of Edwards among the Housatonics.

5   RAND, BENJAMIN. "Edwards, Jonathan (1703-1758)." Dictionary
     of Philosophy and Psychology. Edited by James Mark Baldwin.
     New York and London: Macmillan, 3:188-89.
         Offers an Edwards bibliography of primary sources and
     over twenty-five critical items.

1906

1   BACON, EDWIN M[UNROE]. The Connecticut River and the Valley
     of the Connecticut. New York and London: G. P. Putnam's
     Sons, pp. 434-47.
         Describes Edwards's birthplace and his genealogy.

1906

2   CURTIS, MATTOON MONROE. "Kantean Elements in Jonathan
    Ewards." In Philosophische Abhandlungen: Festschrift
    für Max Heinze. Berlin: Ernst Siegfried Mittler & Sohn,
    pp. 34-62.
        Compares Edwards and Kant on morality and religion,
    sin and grace, God and man, God and Christ, church and
    state, nature and history, and concludes that they either
    "agree" or have "essentially the same" doctrines or con-
    cepts, in a point-by-point examination of Edwards's work.
    They differ in this: Kant is "more cold, formal, and
    schematic," less feeling than Edwards; so too, Edwards has
    a more "overwhelming" sense of the sovereignty of God
    than Kant.

3   LOWELL, D. O. S. "The Descendants of Jonathan Edwards."
    Munsey's Magazine 35 (June):263-73.
        Traces Edwards's descendants and finds fourteen college
    presidents--of Amherst, Carnegie, Columbia, Hamilton,
    Johns Hopkins, Princeton, Rutgers, Union, University of
    California, and Yale--in six generations, "a remarkable
    instance of intellectual heredity."

1907

1   ANON. "The Edwards Memorial." Hampshire Gazette, 7 October,
    p. 6.
        Dedicates the site of Edwards's house on King Street as
    the home of the Northampton Historical Society and reprints
    an address by President Seelye of Smith.

2   ANON. "The 'Narrative' of Jonathan Edwards." Chautauqan 49
    (December):124-25.
        Praises Edwards's "spiritual insight" and quotes from
    Personal Narrative.

3   FOSTER, FRANK HUGH. A Genetic History of the New England
    Theology. Chicago: University of Chicago Press, pp.47-
    103 passim.
        Details Edwards's contributions to the development of
    New England Theology, in an examination of the systematic
    and thematic connections in theology over two centuries--
    in the work of Bellamy, Hopkins, and Taylor; in questions
    of eschatology, atonement, and will; in controversies of
    unitarianism and universalism; in schools of theology at
    Yale, Oberlin, and Andover. Not only did Edwards try to
    solve the problem of divine sovereignty, the doctrine

central to New England Theology, but he exerted considerable influence through his practical work as revivalist
and pastor and through "the temper of his mind," independent and restless and daring. His Freedom of the Will,
a "classic" of the Theology, engendered a series of
treatises, each trying to prove agreement; his Original
Sin bears the marks of a leader, one who "innovates as he
writes"; and his True Virtue, slow to be appreciated,
gave rise to a school of ethics and theology.

4 HOSKINS, JOHN PRESTON. "German Influences on Religious Life
   and Thought in America during the Colonial Period."
   Princeton Theological Review 5 (January):49-79.
      Numbers Edwards's Faithful Narrative one of the "imme-
   diate" sources of John Wesley's evangelism, German pietism
   a latent source.

5 RIDDERBOS, JAN. De Theologie van Jonathan Edwards. The
   Hague: Johan A. Nederbragt, 334 pp.
      Contends that Edwards diverges from the Reformed con-
   sensus and develops an unusual form of Reformed theology,
   in a study of his life and work. The source of Edwards's
   difference with the tradition is both public and private:
   he was a born Congregationalist (and remained one) and
   he was independent-minded, an original thinker. An analysis of his rationalism, ambivalence, and individuality,
   and a careful examination of his work on the will, virtue,
   grace, and the trinity indicate serious qualifications to
   "pure" Reformed theology. (In Dutch.)

6 RILEY, I. WOODBRIDGE. "Jonathan Edwards." In his American
   Philosophy: The Early Schools. New York: Dodd, Mead &
   Co., pp. 126-87.
      Traces Edwards's idealism and mysticism, their sources,
   phases, and relationship; connects these internal develop-
   ments to his external career and to his published works;
   and concludes that though he was "a precocious idealist
   and a profound mystic, he was not a consistent philosopher."
   Edwards moves through the idealism of his years at Windsor
   and at Yale, to the determinism of his Northampton ministry, to the "tentative" pantheism of his Stockbridge
   thought, when a return to his early idealism results in "an
   almost monistic" immanency. Through it all runs the
   "common element" of his mysticism, affecting each state in
   a characteristic way. His idealism, rooted in his intuition more than his logic or his learning--he did not know
   Berkeley--, finds "precocious convincement of insubstan-
   tiality" in Of Being, "tentative expression of a kindred

immaterialism" in Notes on the Mind, "rational advocacy
of the mystical principle of intuitive apprehension" in
Divine and Supernatural Light, and "laboured vindication
of the dialectic of the heart" in Religious Affections.
Edwards's later work, Freedom of the Will and True Virtue,
suffers from ambiguity, from an unresolved dualism of
Calvinism and pantheism, his theology overshadowing his
philosophy.

1908

1   GORDON, GEORGE A. "The Collapse of the New England Theology."
    Harvard Theological Review 1 (April): 127-68.
        Ascribes the collapse of New England Theology to a
    "structural defect" in the system: the humanism of
    Edwards's God is "external, subordinate, temporal."
    Edwards was a "speculative genius" with a mind of "uncom-
    mon acuteness, massiveness, and depth," but his philosophy
    of man's world is "morally incredible." Neither Edwards
    nor his successors ever gained "the least insight" into
    the nature of revelation or reason in the Bible.

2   RILEY, I. WOODBRIDGE. "The Real Jonathan Edwards." Open
    Court 22 (December): 705-15.
        Suggests that the "real Edwards" is not, as is commonly
    held, the "odious" and "sulphurous" Calvinist theologian,
    but a "philosopher of feelings, a fervent exponent of the
    dialect of the heart," a poet, a mystic. In Personal
    Narrative Edwards details the traditional stages of the
    mystical experience, the purgative, the illuminative, and
    the unitive. But in the End of Creation, "the most
    boldly imaginative" of his work, Edwards embodies and
    enlivens the thoughts of the mystic and idealist in
    figures and metaphors.

3   WALKER, WILLISTON. Great Men of the Christian Church.
    Constructive Bible Studies: Advanced and Supplementary
    Series. Chicago: University of Chicago Press, pp. 339-
    53.
        Ranks Edwards as "the ablest theologian and most power-
    ful thinker that colonial New England produced," in a
    brief biography and estimate of his work. True Virtue,
    though not as famous as Freedom of the Will, was probably
    the "most influential" of his work in New England because
    it taught disinterested love, the motive spirit of evan-
    gelism. "No wonder that the earliest American foreign
    missionaries came from the ranks of Edwards' disciples."

1909

1 EMERSON, RALPH WALDO. Journals. Edited by Edward Waldo
   Emerson and Waldo Emerson Forbes. Boston and New York:
   Houghton Mifflin Co., 1:286-87.
       Recounts a conversation with William Withington, a
   classmate, on 5 October 1823, about Edwards's error in
   Freedom of the Will of including the proposition to be
   proved with the definition. Emerson, however, praises
   Edwards's clarity in opening up the truth of the subject
   and wonders that "it ever was disputed."

2 FOSTER, FRANK HUGH. "Jonathan Edwards." In The New Schaff-
   Herzog Encyclopedia of Religious Knowledge. Edited by
   Samuel MacCauley Jackson. New York and London: Funk &
   Wagnalls, 5:80-82.
       Traces the career of Edwards.

3 POWELL, LYMAN P. Heavenly Heretics. New York: G. P. Putnam's Sons, pp. 1-29.
       Marks the scene, the manner, and the effect of Edwards's
   Sinners in the Hands of an Angry God at Northampton in
   June 1741 and accounts him "orthodox from first to last"
   for he lacked originality. Out of the pulpit this passionate revivalist exemplified piety and humility, as his
   life reveals.

1910

1 DAVENPORT, FREDERICK MORGAN. "The New England Awakening
   Originating with Jonathan Edwards." In his Primitive
   Traits in Religious Revivals. New York: Macmillan Co.
       Reprint of 1905.2.

*2 ELLIS, C. G. "The Ethics of Jonathan Edwards." Ph.D. dis-
   sertation, New York University.
       Cited in Comprehensive Dissertation Index, 1974 Supple-
   ment, 4:713.

3 FOSTER, FRANK HUGH. "New England Theology." In The New
   Schaff-Herzog Encyclopedia of Religious Knowledge. Edited
   by Samuel MacCauley Jackson. New York and London: Funk
   & Wagnalls, 8:130-40.
       Traces the development of New England Theology, "origi-
   nating" with the constructive theology of Edwards in 1734
   and ending with the Andover summaries of Edwards Amasa
   Park in the 1880s.

4   GARDINER, HARRY NORMAN, and WEBSTER, RICHARD. "Edwards,
        Jonathan." In Encyclopaedia Britannica. 11th ed. 9:3-6.
        Traces Edwards's career and estimates the work of "the
    most able metaphysician and the most influential religious
    thinker in America." Edwards's philosophy is mixed with
    his theology in a way that is "never thoroughly combined"
    and with the result that, for example, the pantheism of
    his philosophy is never reconciled with the individuality
    of his moral theology. His Freedom of the Will is "de-
    fective" in its abstract concepts.

                            1911

1   BROWN, W. ADAMS. "Covenant Theology." In Encyclopaedia of
        Religion and Ethics. Edited by James Hastings. New York:
        Charles Scribner's Sons, 4:223.
        Suggests that Edwards's interest in the "eternal law
    of things" kept him from the covenant idea.

1A McGIFFERT, ARTHUR C[USHMAN]. Protestant Thought Before Kant.
        New York: Charles Scribner's Sons, pp. 175-85.
        Considers Edwards a "profound" theologian, subtle and
    dialectical, more than the generally remembered evangeli-
    cal Pietist or rigid Calvinist. His last works, especially
    True Virtue and End of Creation, are unequalled in modern
    theology for their significance and intelligence.

2   ROYCE, JOSIAH. William James and Other Essays on the Philos-
        ophy of Life. New York: Macmillan Co., pp. 3-8.
        Ranks Edwards with Ralph Waldo Emerson and William
    James as one of only three representative American phi-
    losophers and the first in order of time. Edwards arti-
    culated ideas fundamental to our religious life by
    discovering the nature of man and God in his profound
    religious experience.

3   SMITH, FRANCES M. "Historic Lineages in America--First
        Builders of the Western Hemisphere: Edwards Foundations
    in American History." Journal of American History 5
    (April-June):298-99.
        Traces the Edwards family from England to America and
    to its "world-famous" son.

1912

*1   BAUER, CHARLES G. "Jonathan Edwards and His Relation to the
New England Theology." S.T.D. dissertation, Temple University.
[Also ascribed to Howard F. Pierce, 1912.6.] Cited in
Comprehensive Dissertation Index 1861-1972, 32:379.

2   CAIRNS, WILLIAM B. A History of American Literature. New
York: Oxford University Press, pp. 76-81.
Claims that Edwards had "perhaps the finest poetic
sensibilities" of the colonial era, though he wrote no
poetry, and that his diction was pure and simple, though
his subjects were "dry or repellent."

3   CHRISTIE, FRANCIS ALBERT. "The Beginnings of Armianism in
New England." In Papers of the American Society of Church
History. Second series, vol. 3. Edited by William
Walker Rockwell. New York and London: G. P. Putnam's
Sons, pp. 151-72.
Identifies Episcopalianism, rather than Arminianism, as
the real threat to Congregationalism that Edwards saw and
feared in 1734. Edwards fought a "myth," probably
created by George Whitefield in his "rash" denunciations
of the Congregational clergy, and attacked Arminian lit-
erature, foreign, not local, in origin. Perhaps, Sereno
Dwight's (1829.4) misreading of Edwards's letter to John
Erskine, 31 August 1748, accounts for the historical confusion.

4   DeWITT, JOHN. "Jonathan Edwards: A Study." In Biblical
and Theological Studies, by the Members of the Faculty of
Princeton Theological Seminary. New York: Charles
Scribner's Sons, pp. 109-36.
Reprint of 1904.6.

5   PERRY, BLISS. The American Mind. New York: Houghton Mifflin Co., pp. 18, 95.
Ranks Edwards with Pascal, Augustine, and Dante.

*6   PIERCE, HOWARD F. "Jonathan Edwards and His Relation to New
England Theology." S.T.D. dissertation, Temple University.
Cited in Comprehensive Dissertation Index 1861-1972,
32:379.

7   WARFIELD, BENJAMIN B[RECKINRIDGE]. "Edwards and the New
England Theology." In Encyclopaedia of Religion and
Ethics. Edited by James Hastings. New York: Charles
Scribner's Sons, 5:221-27.

Traces Edwards's career from his early preparation at home and at Yale to his pastorate in Northampton and his theology in Stockbridge and follows his influence on doctrinal and practical matters from Joseph Bellamy to Edwards Park. Edwards was a man "of thought rather than learning," a subtle analyst who "strove after no show of originality" (save in True Virtue), and a "convinced defender" of standard Calvinism. It was Edwards's "misfortune" to lend his name to the "provincial" theology of his successors whose best doctrines were a "far cry" from his Calvinist teachings.

1913

1   ANON. "Famous Old Elm Gone." New York Times, 22 August, p. 7.
       Recounts the history of the Edwards elms and the recent loss of the last one.

2   DeJONG, YMEN PETER. De Leer den Verzoening in de Amerikaanshe Theologie. Grand Rapids, Mich.: Eerdmans-Sevensma, pp. 21-25.
       Claims that Edwards's doctrine of disinterested benevolence detracts from God's being and virtue, that his doctrine of divine sovereignty reduces the role of Christ, and that his revival theology not only counters historical Calvinism but invites Arminianism. (In Dutch.)

3   HENDRIX, E. R. "Jonathan Edwards and John Wesley." Methodist Quarterly Review 62 (January):28-38.
       Draws parallels between two great revivalists, Edwards and John Wesley--both were born in the same year, both were sons of educated ministers and strong mothers, both were tutors in college, and so on--to show that the American "profoundly" influenced the Briton, that the Methodist was indebted to the Presbyterian.

4   LONG, WILLIAM J. American Literature. Boston: Ginn & Co., pp. 70-77.
       Considers Edwards "incomparably the greatest of all our early writers," in a brief survey of his life and work.

5   MABIE, HAMILTON WRIGHT. American Ideals, Character, and Life. New York: Macmillan Co., pp. 115-16.
       Notes the contrast between Edwards's mysticism and his harsh doctrines.

1913

6   SANTAYANA, G[EORGE]. <u>Winds of Doctrine</u>. New York: Charles
     Scribner's Sons, p. 191.
          Remarks how strange Edwards's sense of sin is in modern
     America, in "The Genteel Tradition in America."

1914

1   ANON. "Jonathan Edwards." <u>Hampshire Gazette</u>, 9 April, p. 12.
          Notes the moral climate of Edwards's Northampton during
     the Awakening.

2   COLLINS, VARNUM LANSING. <u>Princeton</u>. New York: Oxford Uni-
     versity Press, pp. 50-52.
          Doubts that Edwards would have made a successful college
     administrator, given his demonstrated lack of discretion
     and practicality at Northampton, nor that he left "any
     impress" on Princeton.

3   KNEELAND, HARRIET J. "Jonathan Edwards." In <u>Early North-
     ampton</u>. Edited by the Betty Allen Chapter, Daughters of
     the American Revolution. Northampton, Mass.: Betty Allen
     Chapter, pp. 71-87.
          Balances Edwards's "stern theology" against the "won-
     derful beauty" of his family life and "keen appreciation"
     of nature, in a brief narrative of his career in North-
     ampton.

4   MOFFETT, THOMAS C. <u>The American Indian on the New Trail:
     The Red Man of the United States and the Christian Gospel</u>.
     New York: Missionary Education Movement of the United
     States and Canada, pp. 71-72.
          Notes briefly Edwards's missionary work among the
     Mohicans of the Housatonic.

5   STOKES, ANSON PHELPS. <u>Memorials of Eminent Yale Men: A
     Biographical Study of Student Life and University Influ-
     ences During the Eighteenth and Nineteenth Centuries</u>.
     New Haven, Conn.: Yale University Press, 1:19-29.
          Recounts Edwards's life, especially those "most forma-
     tive" eight years he spent as student and tutor at Yale,
     and reprints letters.

1915

1   BROOKS, VAN WYCK. <u>America's Coming-of-Age</u>. New York: B. W.
     Huebsch, pp. 8-14.
          Typifies the rift in America between highbrow and low-
     brow in the "transcendental theory" of Edwards and the

"catchpenny realities" of Franklin, two philosophers who
"share the eighteenth century between them." The unreality,
inflexibility, aloofness, and refinement of American culture stems from Puritan piety and Edwards; flexibility,
opportunism, business ethics, and American humor, from
Puritan practicality and Franklin. There is no middle
ground.

2   BUCKHAM, JOHN WRIGHT. Mysticism and Modern Life. New York:
     Abingdon Press, pp. 81-82.
        Compares Edwards, that "austere" mystic, to William
     Wordsworth in their shared communion with nature deeper
     than pantheism.

3   RILEY, [I.] WOODBRIDGE. American Thought from Puritanism to
     Pragmatism. New York: Henry Holt & Co., pp. 28-36.
        Discerns in the private Edwards a poet and a mystic, a
     divine far different from the "pitiless professional"
     theologian of the public Edwards and perhaps more valuable.
     For Edwards there were three stages to the mystical proc-
     ess: "first, comes by great and violent inward struggles
     the gaining of a spirit to part with all things in the
     world; then, a kind of vision or certain fixed ideas and
     images of being alone in the mountains or some solitary
     wilderness far from all mankind; finally, a thought of
     being wrapt up in God in heaven, being, as it were,
     swallowed up in Him forever." This progression generally
     follows that of the "ancient manuals"--purgative, illumi-
     native, unitive or intuitive--as well as that detailed by
     William James--ineffability, noetic, transiency, passivity.

                              1916

*1   ALLISON, OSCAR ETHAN. "Jonathan Edwards: A Study in Puri-
     tanism." Ph.D. dissertation, Boston University.
        Cited in Comprehensive Dissertation Index 1861-1972,
     32:379.

2   ANON. "Jonathan Edwards Vindicated." New York Times, 9
     February, p. 10.
        Takes Roosevelt to task for the "tardy justice" he
     renders Edwards (1916.6). "It is a notable posthumous
     honor to have won approbation of our most renowned
     eclectic scholar and politician." (An editorial.)

1916

3 BRIGGS, CHARLES AUGUSTUS. <u>History of the Study of Theology</u>.
New York: Charles Scribner's Sons, 2:171-73.
Considers Edwards the "father" of modern English and
American religious thought: the teacher of Methodists in
Great Britain and the theologian of Presbyterianism and
Congregationalism in America and abroad.

4 OVIATT, EDWIN. <u>The Beginnings of Yale (1701-1726)</u>. New
Haven, Conn.: Yale University Press, pp. 415-17, 425-26.
Details Edwards's two years as tutor at Yale (1724-
1726). Although the college "decidedly prospered" under
his direction, Edwards found his life among the students
"somewhat irksome."

5 REDFIELD, CASPER L. "Education Extended." <u>Journal of Educa-
tion</u> 84 (October 19):[369]-71.
Calculates the amount of education in twelve immediate
ancestors of Edwards, shows the positive effect it had on
his natural ability, and insists that generational im-
provement rests upon education only.

6 ROOSEVELT, THEODORE. Letter to Marjorie Sterrett, 5 February
1916. <u>New York Tribune</u>, 8 February, p. 1.
In a photocopy of a letter to "little Miss Marjorie,"
the thirteen-year-old founder of a battleship fund, Roosevelt singles out Edwards as a symbol for troubled times.
Edwards "always acted in accordance with the strongest
sense of duty, and there wasn't a touch of the mollycoddle
about him." (See also "Roosevelt Joins Battleship Fund,"
pp. 1 and 9.)

7 WATERS, WILLIAM O., JR. "Yale Claims Jonathan Edwards." <u>New
York Times</u>, 12 February, p. 10.
Adds to the statement in the <u>Times</u> (1916.2): though a
"'Princeton worthy,'" Edwards was a Yale man first.

<u>1917</u>

1 COSS, JOHN J. "[Bibliography of] Jonathan Edwards." In <u>The
Cambridge History of American Literature</u>. Edited by
William Peterfield Trent et al. New York: G. P. Putnam's
Sons, 1:426-38.
Lists locations and holdings of Edwards manuscripts,
collected and separate works, and over 150 items of bio-
graphy and criticism.

2   DAVENPORT, FREDERICK MORGAN. "The New England Awakening
     Originating with Jonathan Edwards." In his Primitive
     Traits in Religious Revivals. New York: Macmillan Co.
         Reprint of 1905.2.

3   MORE, PAUL ELMER. "Edwards." In The Cambridge History of
     American Literature. Edited by William Peterfield Trent
     et al. New York: G. P. Putnam's Sons, 1:57-71.
         Regrets that Edwards's dogmatic theology kept him
     from being "one of the very great names in literature,"
     though he remains a towering intellect and a master of
     religious psychology, in an estimate of his life and work,
     especially Freedom of the Will. (Frequently reprinted.)

4   NORRIS, EDWIN MARK. The Story of Princeton. Boston: Little,
     Brown & Co., pp. 33-36.
         Recounts Edwards's Princeton days and the influence he
     exerted upon the college before and after his death. Ed-
     wards was the "natural" choice to follow Aaron Burr: "no
     other name was even considered."

5   PLATNER, JOHN WINTHROP. "The Congregationalists." In The
     Religious History of New England. King's Chapel Lectures.
     Cambridge, Mass.: Harvard University Press, pp. 42-45
     passim.
         Places Edwards at the beginning of a new era in American
     religious history, at once evangelical and sectarian.

6   TWAIN, MARK. Letter to Rev. Joseph H. Twichell, February
     1902. In Mark Twain's Letters. Edited by Albert Bigelow
     Paine. New York: Harper & Brothers, 2:719-21.
         Reprints Mark Twain's letter, dated "February '02," to
     the Rev. Joseph H. Twichell concerning Twain's reading of
     Edwards's Freedom of the Will lent him by Twichell. Ed-
     wards is a "drunken lunatic," a "resplendent intellect
     gone mad--a marvelous spectacle. . . . By God I was
     ashamed to be in such company."

7   WARNER, CHARLES F. Representative Families of Northampton:
     A Demonstration of What High Character, Good Ancestry and
     Heredity have Accomplished in a New England Town. North-
     ampton, Mass.: Picturesque Publishing Co., 1:19-35.
         Recounts the life of Edwards (and his descendants) as
     an example of character building and useful citizenship.

1918

1   DEXTER, FRANKLIN BOWDITCH. "The Manuscripts of Jonathan
     Edwards." In his A Selection from the Miscellaneous
     Historical Papers of Fifty Years. New Haven, Conn.:
     Tuttle, Morehouse & Taylor Co., pp. 235-46.
          Reprint of 1901.3.

2   PERRY, BLISS. The Spirit of American Literature. New Haven,
     Conn.: Yale University Press, pp. 48-52.
          Traces the "tragedy" of Edwards's career and the changes
     in his literary reputation, both the result of unforeseen
     events.

3   RICKER, MARILLA M. Jonathan Edwards: The Divine Who Filled
     the Air with Damnation and Proved the Total Depravity of
     God. New York: American Freethought Tract Society, 8 pp.
          Villifies Edwards as a mad minister who "believed in
     the worst God, preached the worst sermons, and had the
     worst religion of any human being who ever lived on this
     continent."

1919

1   BUCKHAM, JOHN WRIGHT. Progressive Religious Thought in
     America: A Survey of the Enlarging Pilgrim Faith. Boston:
     Houghton Mifflin Co., pp. 6-8, passim.
          Reveals the "true American theological apostolic suc-
     cession" to be Edwards, Horace Bushnell, and George Angier
     Gordon.

2   LEROUX, EMMANUEL. "Le Développement de la Pensée Philoso-
     phique aux États-Unis." Revue de Synthèse Historique 29
     (August-December):[125]-49.
          Considers Edwards "le puritanisme originel," in a short
     history of American philosophical thought. (In French.)

1920

1   BUCKHAM, JOHN WRIGHT. "The New England Theologians." Ameri-
     can Journal of Theology 24 (January):19-29.
          Suggests that Edwards, in an effort to "square" Calvin-
     ism with reason and morality, helped define the three
     central metaphysical issues of New England Theology: the
     conflict between sovereignty and benevolence, determinism

and freedom, total depravity and true virtue. It was left
to his followers to reconcile these contradictory doctrines
and to modern theology to withdraw from them.

2   [CATTELL, J. McKEEN]. "Jonathan Edwards on Multidimensional
     Space and the Mechanistic Conception of Life." Science,
     n.s. 52 (29 October):409-10.
         Calls Edwards "the spiritual father" of Albert Einstein's
     geometry of multidimensional space because of his remarks
     on the similarity of the various parts of time and space
     in Freedom of the Will, Part IV, Section 8.

3   GORDON, GEORGE A. Humanism in New England Theology. Boston
     and New York: Houghton Mifflin Co., 113 pp.
         Recasts 1908.1.

4   MAXSON, CHARLES HARTSHORN. The Great Awakening in the Middle
     Colonies. Chicago: University of Chicago Press, pp. 19-
     20 passim.
         Contrasts Edwards's changing views on qualifications
     for admission to T. J. Frelinghuysen's early and continued
     insistence on profession, in a study of the effect of
     German pietism on the Awakening in the Raritan Valley and
     throughout the middle colonies.

5   SANTAYANA, GEORGE. Character & Opinion in the United States.
     New York: Charles Scribner's Sons, p. 9.
         Notes that Edwards, "the greatest master in false
     philosophy" in America, was abondoned by his own sect in
     his own time.

6   SLOSSON, EDWIN E. "Jonathan Edwards as a Freudian." Science,
     n.s. 52 (24 December):609.
         Cites Edwards's Diary for 2 May and 10 August 1722 as
     instances of the psychoanalytic method. "Not only did
     Edwards use dream analysis for the discovery of secret
     sins, but he also employed the Freudian therapeutics of
     frank self-examination starting with random reverie and
     following the thread of association until he reached the
     complex that he desired to eradicate by confession and
     sublimation."

7   Van DOREN, CARL. Introduction to his Benjamin Franklin and
     Jonathan Edwards: Selections from their Writings. The
     Modern Students Library. New York: Charles Scribner's
     Sons, pp. ix-xxxiv.
         Compares Edwards and Franklin as "protagonists and sym-
     bols of the hostile movements which strove for mastery"

in the eighteenth century. Generally, Franklin seems
"contemporaneous, fresh, full of vitality"; Edwards seems
to speak of "forgotten issues in a forgotten dialect."
Yet Edwards was the better theoretical scientist, the
more imaginative philosopher, an "impressive mystic"
capable of a thrilling subtlety and intense power (in
Religious Affections) or the "true lyric and elegy" of
Puritanism (in Personal Narrative). Edwards offers illumination that lifts the spirit; Franklin offers the "indispensible wisdom" of the human experience. "They divide
the world, but so do they multiply it."

1921

1   ADAMS, JAMES TRUSLOW. The Founding of New England. Boston:
    Atlantic Monthly Press, p. 82.
        Regrets that Edwards devotes the "finest" American
    prose to the tortures of the damned.

2   CADMAN, S. PARKES. Ambassadors of God. New York: Macmillan
    Co., p. 70.
        Calls Edwards a philosopher, not a theologian, and
    that at another time this "misunderstood ambassador" might
    have become a Hume or a Kant.

3   CHRISMAN, LEWIS H. "Jonathan Edwards." In his John Ruskin,
    Preacher, and Other Essays. New York: Abingdon Press,
    pp. 25-45.
        Considers Edwards's career a vain attempt to save a
    dying Calvinism and Freedom of the Will a "cowardly sur-
    render" to it.

4   HOYT, ARTHUR S. "Jonathan Edwards." In his The Pulpit and
    American Life. New York: Macmillan Co., pp. 19-39.
        Measures Edwards against the three dimensions of any
    preacher--personality, message, manner--and finds him
    "the very Doré of the pulpit." Edwards was an ascetic,
    an idealist, a mystic; intense and spiritual, speculative
    and rational. His message was a vivid, old-line Calvinism
    rendered "boldly and terribly" in a manner plain and
    direct through arguments scriptural and experiential.
    "This quiet, philosophic preacher had greater mastery over
    his audiences than Whitefield."

5   MORE, PAUL ELMER. "Jonathan Edwards." In his A New England
      Group and Others. Shelburne Essays, 11th series. Boston
      and New York: Houghton Mifflin Co., pp. 35-65.
               Reprint of 1917.3. (Frequently reprinted in this form.)

1922

1   ANON. "Jonathan Edwards." In Hand-Book of the Hall of Fame.
      New York: Publications of the Hall of Fame, p. 23.
               Offers a brief life of Edwards, elected to the Hall of
      Fame in 1900 by eighty-two votes.

2   EDWARDS, A. J. Short Sketches of the Life and Service of
      Jonathan Edwards. Fort Worth, Tex.: A. J. Edwards, 18 pp.
               Recounts a brief life of Edwards; reprints Sinners in
      the Hands of an Angry God, a sermon "second only" to the
      Sermon on the Mount; and adds an "inspiring" poem. (By a
      great-great-grandson of Edwards.)

3   MORE, PAUL ELMER. "Jonathan Edwards." In A Short History of
      American Literature. Edited by William Peterfield Trent
      et al. New York: G. P. Putnam's, pp. 1-15.
               Reprint of 1917.3.

4   PHELPS, WILLIAM LYON. "Edwards and Franklin--the Man of God
      and the Man of the World: A Dramatic Contrast." Ladies'
      Home Journal 39 (November):16-17, 160, 163, 164, 167.
               Contrasts "those giant contemporaries," Edwards and
      Franklin, the duty to God of one, the duty to man of the
      other; the mysticism of one, the worldliness of the other;
      and suggests that in the combination of the traits of
      both we would have the "ideal" American and in a host of
      such Americans, the millennium.

1923

1   HANEY, JOHN LOUIS. The Story of Our Literature. New York:
      Charles Scribner's Sons, pp. 18-20.
               Characterizes Edwards's style as simple, pure, and
      imaginative, though his subjects were often "harrowing."

2   PHELPS, WILLIAM LYON. "The Man of the World and the Man of
      God: A Dramatic Contrast." In his Some Makers of American
      Literature. Boston: Marshall Jones Co., pp. 1-33.
               Reprint of 1922.4.

1924

1   HARPOLE, RALPH ORIN. "The Development of the Doctrine of
    Atonement in American Thought from Jonathan Edwards to
    Horace Bushnell." Ph.D. dissertation, Yale University.
        Shows that Edwards's theory of atonement is a "natural
    product" of his Calvinism, mysticism, and idealism, and
    that it is similar to Anselm's, though more formal. But
    his doctrine of satisfaction by punishment and transfer
    of merit made the atonement "more commercial" than that
    of the "great" Reformed theologians.

2   LINDERHOLM, EMANUEL. Pingströrelsen, dess forutsättningar
    och uppkomst. Stockholm: Albert Bonniers, pp. 141-45.
        Notes Edwards's role in the revival of 1734 and the
    Great Awakening, in a brief survey of the evangelical
    spirit in America. (In Swedish.)

3   OSGOOD, HERBERT L. The American Colonies in the Eighteenth
    Century. New York: Columbia University Press, 3:411-17,
    435-38, 448-50.
        Considers Edwards a brilliant apologist for an anti-
    quated Calvinism and, therefore, his career "a tragedy,"
    in a detailed account of the Great Awakening and his
    central role in it. His Some Thoughts "quivers with
    holy passion."

4   ROWE, HENRY KALLOCH. The History of Religion in the United
    States. New York: Macmillan Co., pp. 46-48.
        Characterizes Edwards as the apologist for a "partially
    humanized" Calvinism, the "apostle" against liberalism,
    the "prince" of Great Awakening revivalists. Combining
    the "severe piety" of the seventeenth-century fathers and
    the "mystical fervor" of an eighteenth-century prophet,
    Edwards clarified and spiritualized a waning Puritanism.

5   WIGGAM, ALBERT EDWARD. The Fruit of the Family Tree. In-
    dianapolis: Bobbs-Merrill Co., pp. 16-20.
        Traces the genealogy of the Edwards family, notes the
    "splendor of the bread," and cites famous members, Grant,
    Cleveland, and Churchill among them.

1925

1   ANON. "Princeton Gets Old Table." New York Times, 4 Novem-
      ber, p. 22.
          Reports that Mrs. John W. Manning, a great-great-great-
      granddaughter of Edwards, gave Princeton a mahogony drop-
      leaf table owned by Edwards till his death.

2   DARROW, CLARENCE. "The Edwardses and the Jukeses." American
      Mercury 6 (October):147-57.
          Decries the "utter absurdity" of eugenics and finds
      "amazing" that anyone would want to be traced to Edwards.
      His theology was "weird and horrible," his mind "distorted
      and diseased." It is a "not unreasonable guess that the
      ancestors of the Edwardses and the Jukeses were mixed."

3   FENN, WILLIAM WALLACE. "The Christian Way of Life in the
      Religious History of New England." In Freedom and Truth:
      Modern Views of Unitarian Christianity. Edited by Joseph
      Estlin Carpenter. London: Lindsey Press, pp. 249-80.
          Considers True Virtue, with its "glorious definition"
      of the Christian way, to be Edwards's "pre-eminent" con-
      tribution to New England religious thought but that it
      influenced "comparatively few" churches and ministers, in
      a short history of Edwards's battle against Arminianism
      and the rise of Unitarianism.

4   MUDGE, LEWIS SEYMOUR. "Jonathan Edwards and the Hall of
      Fame." Presbyterian Advance 30 (22 January):2.
          Calls for contributions totalling $3,000 to place a
      bust of Edwards in the Hall of Fame, New York, and offers
      a brief account of his career.

5   WINSHIP, ALBERT E. Heredity: a History of Jukes-Edwards
      Families. Boston: [New England] Journal of Education,
      88 pp.
          Reprint of 1900.20.

1926

1   ANON. "The Hall of Fame." Outlook 143 (26 May): 128.
          Notes the unveiling of the bust of Edwards at the Hall
      of Fame of New York University on 12 May. (Illustrated.)

1926

2   ANON. "Jonathan Edwards Honored Anew." <u>Hampshire Gazette</u>,
         19 May, p. 14.
             Notes Edwards's induction in the Hall of Fame in New
         York and a proposal to name a hotel after him in North-
         ampton.

3   ANON. "Unveil Nine Busts of Nation's Great." <u>New York Times</u>,
         13 May, p. 14.
             Reports the ceremony at the Hall of Fame at which a
         bust of Edwards, a gift of the Presbyterian Church, was
         unveiled, as were those of Daniel Boone and seven others.

4   MUDGE, LEWIS SEYMOUR. "Jonathan Edwards and the Hall of Fame."
         <u>Presbyterian Magazine</u> 32 (June):264,274.
             Notes the installation of a bust of Edwards by Charles
         Grafly at the Hall of Fame, New York, on 12 May, and
         offers a brief account of Edwards's career.

5   MUMFORD, LEWIS. "Origins of the American Mind." <u>American
         Mercury</u> 8 (July):345-54.
             Calls Edwards the "last great expositor" of Calvinism
         in America, unfortunately caught between his love of beauty
         of the soul and the needs of determinism. After him,
         Protestantism lost its "intellectual backbone."

6   NORDELL, PHILIP GREGORY. "Jonathan Edwards and Hell Fire."
         <u>Forum</u> 75 (June):860-69.
             Decries Edwards's allegiance to a "false, harsh, and
         artificial" morality, his imprecatory sermons that "reek
         and seethe" with God's implacable wrath, his pitiful lack
         of humanity.

7   SEITZ, DON C. "Jonathan Edwards, Consistent Theologian."
         <u>Outlook</u> 143 (30 June):315-16.
             Reads Edwards "rather casually" and concludes that at
         least he was a "consistent" theologian of man's depravity,
         but that he could have been "a rival" to Newton, Tyndall,
         Huxley, and Darwin.

8   WILLIAMS, STANLEY THOMAS. <u>The American Spirit in Letters</u>.
         The Pageant of America, no. 11. New Haven, Conn.: Yale
         University Press, pp. 43-44.
             Considers Edwards "the supreme Puritan," but stripped
         of his Calvinism, a transcendentalist. (Illustrated.)

1927

1   ADAMS, JAMES TRUSLOW. <u>Provincial Society, 1690-1767</u>. A History of American Life, no. 3. New York: Macmillan Co., pp. 282-83.

Cites the paradox of Edwards's sweetness of mind and character and his imprecatory sermons of damnation.

2   PARRINGTON, VERNON LOUIS. "The Anachronism of Jonathan Edwards." In his <u>The Colonial Mind, 1620-1800</u>. <u>Main Currents in American Thoughts</u>, vol. 1. New York: Harcourt, Brace & Co., pp. 148-63.

Decries Edwards's conservative stance in the midst of growing liberal tendencies, in a brief study of "the last and greatest of the royal line of Puritan mystics." Edwards's doctrine of the sovereignty of God is a return to an "absolutist past," his <u>Freedom of the Will</u> a "stifling" of New England intellectual life, his <u>Faithful Narrative</u> a collection of "repulsive records" of conversion. Ironically, reactionary Edwards hastened an end to "Puritan formalism" and old-order Presbyterian polity by espousing religious emotionalism and democratic Congregationalism. Thus Edwards, "an anachronism" in Ben Franklin's America, became "the intellectual leader of the revolutionaries." (Frequently reprinted.)

3   WORTLEY, GEORGE FRANCIS. "The Status of the Child in New England Congregationalism from Jonathon [sic] Edwards to Horace Bushnell." Ph.D. dissertation, Hartford School of Religious Education.

Traces historically the theological status of the child from the "clear crystal" of Edwards's Calvinism to the Christian nature theory of Horace Bushnell. For Edwards, the child has a dual status, at once Adamic and parental, sinful and covenanted; for his successors, the former status is "bitterly assailed"; for Bushnell, the child is "to grow up a Christian and never know himself as otherwise."

1928

1   ANON. "Recalls Life of Edwards in City." <u>Hampshire Gazette</u>, 28 July, p. 6.

Sketches the life of Edwards, "the patron saint" of Northampton.

1928

2   BURGGRAAFF, WINFIELD [J.] <u>The Rise and Development of Liberal
    Theology in America</u>. New York: Board of Publication &
    Bible-School Work of the Reformed Church in America,
    pp. 110-25, passim.
        Claims that Edwards (and through him, New England Theol-
    ogy generally) contributed to the rise of liberal religious
    thought in America by shifting theological ground from the
    objective to the subjective. In distinguishing between
    natural and moral ability, he created "deserts of specula-
    tion" in which New England Theology "died" and Pelagianism
    was born; in shifting from God as sovereign to God as
    moral governor, he limited His "totality." Thus the modi-
    fied Calvinism of Edwards ended in "decidedly un-Calvinistic"
    doctrines, preparing the way for the Arminianism of his
    successors.

3   ELSBREE, OLIVER WENDELL. <u>The Rise of the Missionary Spirit in
    America, 1790-1815</u>. Williamsport, Pa.: Williamsport
    Printing & Binding Co., pp. 135-36.
        Links the organization in 1792 of the Particular Baptist
    Society for the Propagation of the Gospel among the Heathen
    to the London reissue in 1789 of Edwards's <u>Humble Attempt</u>.

4   KUIPER, HERMAN. Appendix to his <u>Calvin on Common Grace</u>.
    Goes, Netherlands: Oosterbaan & Le Cointre, pp. iv-v.
        Notes Edwards's distinction between common or restrain-
    ing grace in natural man and saving grace in regenerate
    man.

5   LOUD, GROVER C[LEVELAND]. <u>Evangelized America</u>. New York:
    Dial Press, pp. 10-31.
        Traces Edwards's evangelical impulse to his early life
    as a "spiritual hypocondriac" and to his endless concern
    with sin. His pastoral work during 1734-35 in Northampton
    heralded the Great Awakening throughout the colonies, the
    effects of which are still broadly felt. "He spoke little
    of heaven, he cared nothing for this world, but he cer-
    tainly knew his hell."

6   ROWE, HENRY KALLOCH. "Jonathan Edwards." In his <u>Modern
    Pathfinders of Christianity: The Lives and Deeds of Seven
    Centuries of Christian Leaders</u>. New York: Fleming H.
    Revell Co., pp. 102-13.
        Recounts Edwards's career as an example of a self-
    stimulating mind productive of original thought.

7   SELDES, GILBERT. "Jonathan Edwards." Dial 84 (January):37-46.
     See 1928.8 for an expanded version of this.

8   _____. "A Stormer of Heaven." In his The Stammering Century.
     New York: John Day Co., pp. 13-35.
           Traces the plethora of cults, fads, reforms, movements,
     social crazes, and political experiments of nineteenth-
     century America to the revivalist spirit and method fos-
     tered by Edwards. Sinners in the Hands of an Angry God
     offers the "promise of libertarian religion" and Edwards's
     doctrine of direct communion with God, the hope of personal
     salvation. Thus Edwards undercut the authority of both
     minister and church and "cleared the way" for cults and
     madness.

9   VISSER'T HOOFT, WILLEM A. The Background of the Social Gospel
     in America. Haarlem: H. D. Tjeenk Willink & Zoon, pp. 89-
     97, 172-73.
           Locates the center of Edwards's thought in True Virtue,
     a "thorough modification" of traditional Calvinism.   In
     Edwards, God becomes the focus of speculation and a subject
     of understanding; the legal ethics of the past gives way
     to a mutual benevolence. Such rational theocracy, unfor-
     tunately, subordinates a mysterious and inscrutable God to
     human reasoning.

10   VOEGELIN, ERICH. Ueber die Form des Amerikanischen Geistes.
     Tübingen: J. C. B. Mohr, pp. 109-19.
           Traces the relationship of Calvinist dogma and mystical
     pantheism in Edwards, from "Of Being" and Personal Narra-
     tive to the posthumous works, and suggests links to Peirce,
     William James, and Santayana. (In German.)

11   WEIGLE, LUTHER A. American Idealism. The Pageant of America:
     A Pictorial History of the United States, no. 10. New
     Haven, Conn.: Yale University Press, pp. 64-66.
           Treats briefly Edwards as theologian, philosopher,
     mystic, and family man, and claims that he was responsible
     "indirectly" for religious freedom in America.

12   WILLIAMS, STANLEY T[HOMAS]. "Six Letters of Jonathan Edwards
     to Joseph Bellamy." New England Quarterly 1 (April):226-
     42.
           Reprints six Edwards letters in the Yale collection to
     Joseph Bellamy from 1741 to 1756, revealing the public
     man--his reading for Freedom of the Will, his friendship

with David Brainerd, his dismissal from Northampton, his mission at Stockbridge—and the personal one—his purchase of sheep.

1929

1 ANDREWS, CHARLES M. Jonathan Edwards. [New Haven, Conn.: Yale University Press], 17 pp.
    Reprint of 1929.7.

2 BACON, BENJAMIN WISNER. The Theological Significance of Jonathan Edwards. [New Haven, Conn.: Yale University Press], 33 pp.
    Reprint of 1929.7.

3 BILLINGS, THOMAS HENRY. "The Great Awakening." Essex Institute Historical Collections 65 (January):89-104.
    Surveys the Great Awakening and notes that the process of conversion outlined in Edwards's Religious Affections becomes "stereotyped" among evangelicals throughout New England, though Salem, Massachusetts, was hardly touched by the movement or the book.

4 BROWN, CHARLES REYNOLDS. "Edwards, Jonathan." Encyclopaedia Britannica, 14th ed., 8:19-21.
    Regrets Edwards's lack of concern for the poor, the "broken-hearted," and the Indians, in a brief life and estimate, and accounts his "perpendicular piety" unfeeling and his "potent" influence surprising.

5 BURT, STRUTHERS. "Jonathan Edwards and the Gunman." North American Review 227 (June):712-18.
    Offers Puritanism as a possible source for the rise in crime: gunmen "eagerly participate in the perverted remnants" of Edwards's philosophy.

6 CHANDLER, THOMAS. Letter, 14 March 1771. In Samuel Johnson: His Career and Writings. Edited by Herbert W. and Carol Schneider. New York: Columbia University Press, 1:476.
    Reprints a letter from Thomas Chandler to Samuel Johnson remarking his pleasure upon learning of James Dana's attack on Edwards's Freedom of the Will (1770.2). "If the Dissenters will confute one another, it will save us the trouble."

7   CONNECTICUT SOCIETY OF THE COLONIAL DAMES OF AMERICA. Pro-
     ceedings of the Dedication of the Memorial Gateway to
     Jonathan Edwards at the Old Burying Ground South Windsor,
     25 June 1929. New Haven, Conn.: Yale University Press,
     61 pp.
         Publishes the papers delivered at the dedication of a
     memorial gateway to Edwards at his birthplace, in the
     following order:
         Andrews, Evangeline Walker. Foreword, pp. [3]-5.
     Recounts the history of the Edwards memorial gateway, from
     the first discussions of the Landmark Committee in 1912 to
     the request for plans in October 1928, and describes it.
         Soule, Sherrod. "The Birthplace of Jonathan Edwards,"
     pp. [13]-14. Describes Edwards's birthplace in East
     Windsor.
         Williams, Mrs. James S. "The Family of Jonathan Ed-
     wards," pp. [15]-23. Traces Edwards's immediate family,
     their marriages and their deaths.
         Bacon, Benjamin Wisner. "The Theological Significance
     of Jonathan Edwards," pp. [24]-38. Marks the "crucifixion"
     by his Northampton congregation and the end of his evan-
     gelism as the beginning of the theology of Edwards. That
     theology was a "vital expression" of both his deep, mysti-
     cal experience and his eyewitness to the conversion of
     others during the revivals. His significance is that "he
     took Paul and Calvin in deadly earnest in the midst of a
     generation that did not."
         Andrews, Charles M. "Jonathan Edwards," pp. [39]-55.
     Contends that the story of Edwards is "less the history of
     a life than the analysis of a mind." Edwards's mind is in
     conflict--the logical and intellectual on one side, the
     emotional and mystical on the other--which he seeks to
     resolve by tempering Calvinism with a sense of the imme-
     diacy of God. Such is Edwards's contribution to religious
     thought.

8   JORDAN, DAVID STARR, and KIMBALL, SARAH LOUISE. Your Family
     Tree. New York: D. Appleton & Co., pp. 235-43.
         Traces Edwards's family back to Isabel de Vermandois
     and forward to such college presidents as Timothy Dwight
     and Theodore Dwight Woolsey of Yale, Sereno Dwight of
     Hamilton, and Merrill Edwards of Amherst, Oberlin, and
     Rutgers.

9   LEISY, ERNEST ERWIN. American Literature: An Interpretative
     Survey. New York: Thomas Y. Crowell, pp. 22-25.
         Suggests that students of literature will prefer
     Edwards's "prose rhapsody" on Sarah Pierrepont to his
     polemic on free will.

1929

10   PARKES, HENRY BAMFORD. "New England and the Great Awakening:
     A Study in the Theory and Practice of New England Calvin-
     ism." Ph.D. dissertaion, University of Michigan.
          See 1930.10.

11   POTTER, CHARLES FRANCIS. "Jonathan Edwards (1703-1758) and
     the Great Awakening." In his The Story of Religion as
     Told in the Lives of its Leaders. Garden City, N.Y.:
     Garden City Publishing Co., pp. 512-19.
          Relates Sarah's religious experiences, her photistic
     theophany and profound ecstasy, to Edwards's sense of
     God-consciousness and to the psychology of religion, in a
     biography of "one of the shortest-lived" religious leaders,
     and connects the circulation of obscene books in Northamp-
     ton to the emotionalism of the Great Awakening, inasmuch
     as revivals are often accompanied by "waves of sexual
     immorality."

12   WHITE, TRENTWELL MASON, and LEHMAN, PAUL WILLIAM. Writers of
     Colonial New England. Boston: Palmer Co., pp. 112-15.
          Recounts Edwards's career and finds his simple and
     direct prose superior to the "abstruse and asinine poly-
     syllablizing" of many colonial writers.

1930

1   ANON. Review of Jonathan Edwards: The Fiery Puritan, by
     Henry Bamford Parkes. Bookman 72 (October):181-82.
          Questions Henry Bamford Parkes's "lively" biography of
     Edwards (1930.10) for its "dogmatic" generalities and
     insufficient scholarship.

2   BRYNESTAD, LAWRENCE E. "The Great Awakening in the New Eng-
     land and Middle Colonies. Part II." Journal of the
     Presbyterian Historical Society 14 (September):104-41.
          Conceives the influence of Edwards on the Great Awaken-
     ing to be indirect and suggestive, "preparing the way"
     rather than shaping it, in a history of the revival, its
     sources and consequences, from a Presbyterian point of
     view. Edwards's 1734 revival had "no direct bearing" on
     the Awakening because it was so short, but it (and other
     local ones) did show that a spirit of reform was "taking
     root" everywhere. The Awakening itself developed a per-
     manent schism in Presbyterianism, though the religious
     liberties arising from it "inspired" political liberties
     of union a generation later.

3   CHAMBERLAIN, JOHN. "Jonathan Edwards, a Forebear of Modern
    Puritanism." New York Times, 28 September, Section 4,
    p. 4.
        Reviews Jonathan Edwards: The Fiery Puritan, by Henry
    Bamford Parkes (1930.10) and finds that more on the river
    gods and less on "clerical and family bickering" would
    have better served the study.

4   FAUST, CLARENCE H. "Jonathan Edwards as a Scientist."
    American Literature 1 (January):393-404.
        Questions the possibility that Edwards could have been
    a scientist, though there was a "thin vein" of such inter-
    est in him, because even his early "Notes on the Mind" and
    "Notes on Natural Science" show a "definite theological
    tinge." His path from the juvenile observations on flying
    spiders to the mature thought of Freedom of the Will was
    "surprisingly straight." What scientific promise he had
    has been "overestimated," for he all too frequently
    "disregards the truth of his premises in the enjoyment of
    his argument." Such is the way of the logician, not the
    scientist.

5   GEWEHR, WESLEY M. The Great Awakening in Virginia 1740-1790.
    Durham, N.C.: Duke University Press, p. 89.
        Notes the efforts of Samuel Davies to persuade Edwards
    to settle in Virginia after his Northampton dismissal and
    his failure: word came from Virginia after Edwards re-
    moved to Stockbridge.

6   GOHDES, CLARENCE. "Aspects of Idealism in Early New England."
    Philosophical Review 39 (November):537-55.
        Uncovers "traces" of influence of the Cambridge
    Platonists in the "much discussed" early idealism of Ed-
    wards. Ralph Cudworth's The True Intellectual System of
    the Universe (1678) seems to have found its way into Ed-
    wards's "The Mind," and he seems to have "frequently"
    borrowed from Theophilus Gale to "clinch an argument"
    in Religious Affections.

7   HALL, THOMAS CUMING. The Religious Background of American
    Culture. Boston: Little, Brown & Co., pp. 148-53,
    passim.
        Connects Edwards and the Great Awakening to the early
    English reformation of the fifteenth century and to John
    Wycliffe rather than to the Continental movement of John
    Calvin, even though there is no evidence that Edwards had
    first-hand knowledge of Wycliffe or his work. Both

Wycliffe and Edwards focus upon individual redemption
rather than the Church Universal and upon sermons rather
than the eucharist as the agency of conversion. Edwards
can "only be really understood" in a tradition of congregational Protestantism and separatist Dissent. So the
Great Awakening "breathed the air" of that movement and
prepared the way for revolution.

8   KERSHNER, FREDERICK D. Pioneers in Christian Thought.
       Indianapolis: Bobbs-Merrill Co., p. 299.
       Refers to Edwards as the "most brilliant interpreter"
    of Calvin in America.

9   MEYER, JACOB C. Church and State in Massachusetts, from 1740
       to 1833: A Chapter in the History of the Development of
       Individual Freedom. Cleveland: Western Reserve University
       Press, pp. 20-23.
       Suggests that the revival in America promoted indivi-
    dual freedom in religion, diminished Congregationalism,
    and was, for Edwards at least, a reaction against the
    "commercialism, materialism, and rationalism" of Boston.

10 PARKES, HENRY BAMFORD. Jonathan Edwards: The Fiery Puritan.
       New York: Minton, Balch & Co., 271 pp.
       Portrays Edwards, the "father of American Puritanism,"
    as student, parish minister, and exile, in a full-length
    study that details his life amid warring ministers and
    feuding families, his times of God's spirit and "religious
    lunacy," and his theology of "blight upon posterity."
    Edwards "rescued" Calvinism from its death through the
    new philosophy and rendered it "impregnable" for a cen-
    tury, but, in doing so, he "fastened upon the necks" of
    Americans a theology either "repulsive or absurd."
    Puritanism "satisfied his own psychological need," lending
    a "breathtaking sublimity" to his vision of the world, yet
    he "lacked the wisdom" to reject it for a kinder Chris-
    tianity. And so his "baneful," posthumous influence con-
    tinued through his "intolerant" and unimaginative disci-
    ples, and so this "biggest intellect" of American
    religious thought, this "most tragic" figure, this "fiery
    Puritan" is "not truly an American."

11 RILEY, [I.] WOODBRIDGE. The Meaning of Mysticism. New York:
       Richard R. Smith, pp. 90-93.
       Tempers Edwards's rationalism with his mysticism: "the
    fetters of his iron creed were loosened by his love of
    nature." Edwards's reading of the Cambridge Platonists
    proved the "antidote" to his Calvinism and to his "sorry

view" of the world and marks the distinction between his
public, professional ministry and his private, personal
belief.

12   SCHNEIDER, HERBERT WALLACE. "Jonathan Edwards." Nation 131
     (26 November):584-85.
          Reviews Jonathan Edwards: The Fiery Puritan, by Henry
     Bamford Parkes (1930.10). "The facts of Edwards's life
     and environment which Mr. Parkes has sketched so skill-
     fully bear little relation to the crude generalizations of
     the prologue and epilogue," where he traces Edwards's
     "'blight upon posterity.'"

13   _____. The Puritan Mind. Studies in Religion and Culture:
     American Religion Series, no. 1. New York: Henry Holt
     & Co., pp. 102-55.
          Attributes Edwards's success and failure to the private
     nature of his love of a sovereign God, an "individual
     analogue of the theocracy" of an earlier New England
     Puritanism and a radical departure from its public and
     social concerns, in an estimate of his career and thought
     and his role in the Great Awakening. Just as his belief
     in the Awakening was rooted in the efficacy of his struggle
     for personal conversion, so his philosophy of aesthetic
     idealism was "essentially the product of his own experi-
     ence." But the application of that "sentimental and
     pathological" love of God rendered his Puritanism "imprac-
     tical" in his day and "absurd" in ours.

14   SWEET, WILLIAM WARREN. The Story of Religions in America.
     New York and London: Harper & Brothers, pp. 185-90, 192-
     99.
          Places Edwards "at the very center" of the Great Awak-
     ening and traces the effects of revivalism upon subsequent
     doctrinal disputes and upon church polity, the New Lights
     and the Old, the orthodox Congregationalists and the
     liberal. Although Edwards held "staunchly" to divine sov-
     ereignty, he sought "larger recognition" for man's respon-
     sibility, thus preparing the way, if inadvertently, for a
     permanent theological rift in New England.

                              1931

1   ANGOFF, CHARLES. A Literary History of the American People.
     New York: Alfred A. Knopf, 1:289-310.
          Concludes, after a survey of his life and work, that
     Edwards was one of the "colossal tragedies" of American

culture, a promising philosopher and theologian "ruined completely" by Calvinism and left a "somewhat more intelligent Cotton Mather." A "theistic idealist" and "pagan pantheist," Edwards's influence upon "enlightened American thought is nil."

2   ANON. Review of Jonathan Edwards: The Fiery Puritan, by Henry Bamford Parkes. Saturday Review of Literature 7 (23 May):851.
    Notes that Henry Bamford Parkes fails to give sufficient emphasis to the effect on Edwards of the Episcopal succession at Yale, in an otherwise "well-informed" biography (1930.10).

3   BLANKENSHIP, RUSSELL. American Literature as an Expression of the National Mind. New York: Henry Holt & Co., pp. 120-25.
    Calls Edwards "the most melancholy example in American literature of a brilliant and capable man wholly dominated by an environment that was fated soon to disappear," in a brief estimate of his life, significance, philosophy, and mysticism. Behind Edwards's "unlovely" Calvinism lay a "thorough" mystic.

4   CANBY, HENRY SEIDEL. Classic Americans. New York: Harcourt, Brace & Co., pp. 9-22.
    Chooses Edwards as a "symbol of the dynamic force of New England intellectuality" that was to shape the American mind and considers him a "born man of letters." Through the primacy he gave to the will to be saved, the will to improve and to succeed, Edwards became the first of a long line of "strenuous uplifters" in America. And except for the practical necessity of his times and his critical Yale years, he could have turned his intuitive, mystic genius to literature.

5   CARPENTER, FREDERIC I. "The Radicalism of Jonathan Edwards." New England Quarterly 4 (October):629-44.
    Discovers the radicalism of Edwards in the "quality" of his thought; his "utter pantheism"; his emphasis upon Justice or Satan as the "fourth person" of God; his psychology of the will; and, most importantly, his deep-grained mysticism. "All of Edwards's work was founded on a psychology of mysticism, which was radically different from the theology of Calvinism." Parallels to Walt Whitman and the Transcendentalists in the nineteenth century and Robinson Jeffers and Theodore Dreiser in the twentieth

are "perhaps accidental," but those to William James are
"indubitable." So, too, Edwards "unconsciously helped"
the Revolution by insisting that all men were equal before
a sovereign God.

6   CASKEY, ELLEN. "If They Were Alive Today: Jonathan Edwards--
     The First American Philosopher." Thinker 4 (October):34-
     35.
         Compares Edwards's insistent belief in the horrors and
     reality of hell with the lack of such a belief today.
     Perhaps we should have a "healthy fear" of more than bore-
     dom or unemployment.

7   CHRISTIE, FRANCIS A[LBERT]. "Jonathan Edwards." In Diction-
     ary of American Biography. Edited by Allen Johnson and
     Dumas Malone. New York: Charles Scribner's Sons, 6:30-37.
         Traces the life of Edwards, America's "first great
     philosophic intelligence," and examines the major works.
     In his "Notes on the Mind," Edwards begins a study of ex-
     cellency--"the master idea of his career"--which finds its
     mature expression in True Virtue and End of Creation.
     Perhaps Edwards delayed publication of these treatises
     because the aesthetic joy voiced there is "incongruous"
     with his rational, ethical Calvinism.

8   DEWEY, EDWARD HOOKER. "Jonathan Edwards." In American
     Writers on American Literature. Edited by John Macy.
     New York: Horace Liveright, pp. 13-24.
         Considers Edwards "no less a poet" than a theologian,
     in a brief estimate of his life and work. His "admirable"
     phrasing and "memorable" words, his symbolic imagination
     breathed life into the moribund and "repellent" doctrines
     of Calvinism. "There is no question that American letters
     suffered a vital loss in Edwards's defection to his
     sleeveless cause."

9   EDWARDS, MAURICE DWIGHT. Richard Edwards and His Wife
     Catherine Pond May: Their Ancestors, Lives, and Descend-
     ants. [St. Paul, Minn.: Webb Publishing Co.], pp. 17-21.
         Outlines a life of Edwards, an "equally eminent"
     thinker and saint.

10   HAROUTUNIAN, JOSEPH G. "Jonathan Edwards: A Study in Godli-
     ness." Journal of Religion 11 (July):400-19.
         Details the "essentials" of Edwards's life and work,
     without apology for his faults, and discovers the "funda-
     mental motif" of both to be his "supreme passion" for the

glory and sovereignty of God. Holiness is a "new quality of experience": analyzable into elements; identical, like true virtue, with excellence; and, with knowledge of God, another aspect of the same experience. Although there is in Edwards "a healthy agnosticism and a genuine 'radical empiricism'"--God's love, grace, wrath, and justice are "facts" of daily life--he is not a pantheist but a "radically theocentric" Calvinist. As a doctrinal innovator Edwards is "insignificant," but his vision and type of godliness are "unique in comprehensiveness, cogency, and profundity."

11   JOHNSON, THOMAS H[ERBERT]. "Jonathan Edwards' Background of Reading." Publications of the Colonial Society of Massachusetts 28 (December):193-222.
     Traces Edwards's reading habits through his Diary, notes, and letters, but principally through his "Catalogue," a manuscript journal of forty-three brown-paper pages, begun in his early twenties and continued until within a year of his death, containing about 500 items read (and noted) or to be read. Edwards's literary interests included theology, religion--Catholic, Jewish, and Deist, as well as Protestant--contemporary philosophy, science, history, travel, and literature--fiction and poetry, but not drama--, a literary background "phenomenal" for a provincial minister. "Of all the Americans of his day--perhaps of any day--none had more notable endowments for pure scholarship or a more original metaphysical mind, yet none has left monuments so crumbled and overgrown."

12   JOHNSON, T[HOMAS] H[ERBERT]. Review of Jonathan Edwards: The Fiery Puritan, by Henry Bamford Parkes. New England Quarterly 4 (April):354-56.
     Expresses disappointment with Henry Bamford Parkes (1930.10) because he repeats the canard of the past-- Edwards was a "fiery" Puritan--and because he fails to take advantage of available biographical materials--the study is "incomplete and sensational."

13   MUIRHEAD, JOHN H. The Platonic Tradition in Anglo-Saxon Philosophy: Studies in the History of Idealism in England and America. London: George Allen & Unwin, p. 307.
     Credits Edwards as the first philosophical idealist in New England, inspired probably by the "subtle air" of Malebranchean mysticism coming from England.

14 PARRY, MARK H. "The Theology of the Great Awakening."
    Th.D. dissertation, Drew University.
        Studies the life and theological views of Edwards,
    George Whitefield, and Samuel Davies in their relation
    to the evangelicalism of the Great Awakening.

15 SCHNEIDER, HERBERT WALLACE. The Puritan Mind. London:
    Constable & Co.
        Reprint of 1930.13.

16 TOWNSEND, H[ARVEY] G[ATES]. "An Alogical Element in the
    Philosophy of Edwards and Its Function in His Metaphysics."
    In Proceedings of the Seventh International Congress of
    Philosophy. Edited by Gilbert Ryle. Oxford: Oxford
    University Press, pp. 495-500.
        Discovers in End of Creation and True Virtue the "syn-
    thetic principle" in Edwards to be ethico-aesthetic, more
    Platonic than Berkeleian, more metaphysical than epistemo-
    logical. Edwards's doctrine of the divine and supernatural
    light or "immediate awareness" links his theory of knowl-
    edge to his metaphysics and relates existence to an
    otherwise abstract logic. Being and knowing unite in a
    principle of order that is apprehended intuitively--a
    theory "unique in our history."

*17 WIDENHOUSE, ERNEST CORNELIUS. "The Doctrine of the Atonement
    in the New England Theology from Jonathan Edwards to
    Horace Bushnell." Th.D. dissertation, Hartford Seminary.
        Cited in Comprehensive Dissertation Index 1861-1972,
    32:378.

                            1932

1   CALVERTON, V. F. The Liberation of American Literature.
    New York: Charles Scribner's Sons, pp. 77-79, 173-74.
        Associates Edwards with a dying theology and a growing
    commerce. Edward's dismissal is a turning point in the
    mid-century crisis between the wealthy bourgeoisie and the
    New England clergy and marks a symbolic shift from the
    theocratic to the civil state.

2   CARPENTER, FREDERIC I. Review of Jonathan Edwards, by Arthur
    C. McGiffert. New England Quarterly 5 (April):395-97.
        Recommends Arthur C. McGiffert's study (1932.10) for
    its accuracy, clarity, and insight in interpreting
    Edwards to the modern world.

1932

3   DICKINSON, THOMAS H. <u>The Making of American Literature</u>. New
      York: Century Co., pp. 156-58.
         Considers Edwards "a kind of anachronism," in a brief
      estimate.

4   HAROUTUNIAN, JOSEPH G. "Piety versus Morality: The Passing
      of the New England Theology." Ph.D. dissertation, Colum-
      bia University.
         Published as 1932.5.

5   _____. <u>Piety versus Moralism: The Passing of the New Eng-
      land Theology</u>. Studies in Religion and Culture: American
      Religion Series, no. 4. New York: Henry Holt & Co.,
      329 pp.
         Attributes the decline of New England Theology after
      Edwards to the lack of his "profound piety" and "intellec-
      tual vigor" in his successors and to the modifying influ-
      ence of eighteenth-century political and social realities
      and humanitarian impulses, in a history of the shift from
      the theology of Edwards to the theology of the Edwardseans,
      from piety to moralism. Edwards erected his Calvinism
      upon concepts of divine sovereignty and "empirical piety,"
      grounded in nature and scripture, philosophical and
      rational, a systematic theology separate from temporal
      concerns and of "permanent human significance." But it
      was "a delicate matter" to reconcile human responsibility
      with theocentric piety and frequently the Edwardseans
      failed. The history, therefore, of New England Theology
      is a "history of degradation."

6   _____. Review of <u>Jonathan Edwards</u>, by Arthur C. McGiffert.
      <u>Church History</u> 1 (September):174-75.
         Regrets that Arthur C. McGiffert's study (1932.10)
      emphasizes the "mystical and practical" in Edwards at the
      expense of the rational and the realistic and that it
      fails to explore the "essential unity" of his thought.

7   JOHNSON, THOMAS H[ERBERT]. "Jonathan Edwards and the 'Young
      Folks' Bible.'" <u>New England Quarterly</u> 5 (January):37-54.
         Checks the manuscript notes of Edwards's inquiry into
      the reading of "'unclean'" books by certain young people
      of Northampton in 1744 and discovers the text to be "quite
      evidently" from the pseudonymous Aristotle, <u>The Midwife
      Rightly Instructed</u>, not some scandalous novel. Referred
      to mockingly as the "'young folks' Bible'" by one of the
      accused, it was a compendium of medical information put to
      "pornographic uses" by young men in mixed company. Ed-
      wards's impolitic handling of the matter probably was
      "contributory" to his dismissal six years later.

8   KNIGHT, GRANT C. <u>American Literature and Culture</u>. New York:
      Ray Long & Richard B. Smith, pp. 34-41.
          Ranks Edwards the "foremost figure" in American litera-
      ture before Franklin, in a short survey of his career.

9   LEWISOHN, LUDWIG. <u>Expression in America</u>. New York and Lon-
      don: Harper & Brothers, pp. 17-18.
          Thinks Edwards is properly neglected: he was a "baf-
      fled poet, a sick and corrupted soul."

10 McGIFFERT, ARTHUR CUSHMAN, JR. <u>Jonathan Edwards</u>. Creative
      Lives Series. New York: Harper & Brothers, 225 pp.
          Presents a full-length study of the "well-balanced"
      character and impressive thought of Edwards, "essentially
      a student" given to "relentless curiosity" and love of
      beauty, whose approach to the vexing problems of his time
      was that of a "historically and philosophically minded"
      scholar rather than a practical minister and whose reputa-
      tion continues as "one of the most stimulating and forceful
      minds America has produced." Central to his thought is his
      belief, based on youthful intuition and confirmed in later
      observation, that God was at once "majestic and holy,
      beautiful and loving," the absolute sovereign, the "Supreme
      Connoisseur." So Edwards, in his "critical mysticism,"
      moves from pantheism to personalism in his interpretation
      of God "with no apparent jolt." And Edwards, the "sacred
      gadfly" of Northampton, moves from the stylistic mastery
      of <u>Faithful Narrative</u> and from America's "most notable
      single discussion" of religion in <u>Religious Affections</u> to
      the significant, though at times "marred," works of his
      exile in Stockbridge. <u>Freedom of the Will</u>, for example,
      emphasizes the intellect at the expense of the subconscious
      processes of the mind and is typical of "static" eighteenth-
      century thought. Still Edwards remains "one of the earli-
      est representatives of modern-mindedness" in American
      religious thought.

11 MAYHEW, GEORGE NOEL. "The Relation of the Theology of Jona-
      than Edwards to Contemporary Penological Theory and Prac-
      tice." Ph.D. dissertation, University of Chicago.
          Published, in part, as 1935.5.

12 PARKES, HENRY BAMFORD. "The Puritan Heresy." <u>Hound & Horn</u> 5
      (January-March):165-90.
          Speculates on the Catholic elements in Edwards, "the
      only original thinker" of Puritan New England, and traces
      briefly his ideas and his influence. Edwards's belief

1932

that God is beauty and is revealed in nature and his conversion experience were "Catholic and not Calvinist."
And when his nineteenth-century followers denied "the
Catholic solution" to nature and grace, "the Puritan
heresy ended in the complete disappearance of Christianity
as a religion" and survived only as a "practical philosophy."

13 SUTER, RUFUS ORLANDO, JR. "The Philosophy of Jonathan Ed-
    wards." Ph.D. dissertation, Harvard University.
       Examines the philosophy of Edwards under two main
    divisions, man and the world. The first details both his
    psychological system about the understanding, the will,
    and the instincts, and his ethical theory about depravity,
    value, beauty, and virtue; the second deals with his meta-
    physics and epistemology. But in both categories Edwards
    is "rent" by loyalties to his Calvinism and his Neo-
    platonism, and the conflict creates in him a "deadlock."

14 WARFIELD, BENJAMIN BRECKINRIDGE. "Edwards and the New England
    Theology." In his Studies in Theology. New York: Oxford
    University Press, pp. 513-38.
       Reprint of 1912.7.

15 WARREN, AUSTIN. Review of Jonathan Edwards: The Fiery Puri-
    tan, by Henry Bamford Parkes; Jonathan Edwards, by Arthur
    Cushman McGiffert, Jr.; and "The Philosophy of Jonathan
    Edwards," a dissertation by Rufus Suter. American Litera-
    ture 4 (November):314-18.
       Finds that Henry Bamford Parkes's valuable study
    (1930.10) is more concerned with the New England mind than
    the mind of Edwards; Arthur Cushman McGiffert's unpreten-
    tious study (1932.10), while it does not supersede
    A. V. G. Allen's "exhaustive" theological analysis (1889.1),
    reflects a Neocalvinistic admiration for Edwards's work;
    and Rufus Suter's "painstaking" study (1932.13) is dis-
    tinctive in its emphasis on the Neoplatonism in Edwards's
    posthumous treatises.

1933

1 ANON. "From Jonathan Edwards Who Married Sarah Pierrepont in
    1727 have Descended. . . ." Philadelphia Evening Bulletin,
    11 August, [no pp.].

Considers Edwards's 853 male descendants, among them college presidents and professors, judges and governors, congressmen and senators, to be "the most valuable contribution to American blood."

2 FLEMING, SANDFORD. Children and Puritanism: The Place of Children in the Life and Thought of the New England Churches, 1620-1847. Yale Studies in Religious Education. New Haven, Conn.: Yale University Press, pp. 99-101, 163-65, passim.
    Discovers no difference between Edwards's sermons to children and his sermons to adults and notes his failure (and the failure of his age) to understand children. Yet a "remarkable number" of children participated in the revivals and showed, to a great degree, the physical effects of them.

3 SHIPTON, CLIFFORD KENYON. "The New England Clergy of the 'Glacial Age.'" Publications of the Colonial Society of Massachusetts 32 (December):24-54.
    Cites Edwards as perhaps the "last of the very great who entered the ministry because there was no other suitable outlet for his abilities" and as an example of an impoverished clergyman in eighteenth-century New England.

1934

1 ANON. "Jonathan Edwards." New York Times, 30 August, p. 18.
    Calls Edwards's ministry the "chief public interest" of the bicentennial celebration of the Stockbridge Congregational Church. Though cast out of Northampton and upon the frontier of Stockbridge, Edwards showed "his kindliness and beauty of soul . . . even to his primitive congregation." (An editorial.)

2 DEWEY, EDWARD HOOKER. "Jonathan Edwards." In American Writers on American Literature. Edited by John Macy. New York: Tudor Publishing Co.
    Reprint of 1931.8.

3 HORTON, WALTER MARSHALL. Realistic Theology. New York: Harper & Brothers, pp. 18-21.
    Rests Edwards's defense of Calvinism upon his originality in responding to his time and the thought of Locke, Leibnitz, Malebranche, Berkeley, and Wesley. His theology is marked by logic, piety, and mysticism.

4   JOHNSON, THOMAS HERBERT. "Jonathan Edwards as a Man of Let-
      ters." Ph.D. dissertation, Harvard University.
         Traces the "literary and bibliographical history" of
      Edwards's prose chiefly through an examination of the
      methods, sources, and development of his sermon style,
      his effectiveness as a preacher and a polemicist, and his
      precocity in the juvenilia, diaries, resolutions, and
      notebooks. Edwards should rank higher in American letters
      than he does, but the "quality and scope are frequently
      much less than the capacity of the man."

5   MECKLIN, JOHN M. The Story of American Dissent. New York:
      Harcourt, Brace & Co., pp. 60, 213-15, 251.
         Relates Edwards (and the Great Awakening) to the rising
      tide of political and social dissent in New England and
      Virginia, pointing out that his emphasis upon individual
      experience contained "a deadly menace" to the establish-
      ment, religious and secular.

6   NELSON, ROSCOE. "Jonathan Edwards." In Founders and Leaders
      of Connecticut, 1633-1783. Edited by Charles Edward Perry.
      Boston: D. C. Heath & Co., pp. 147-50.
         Offers a brief biography and insists that Edwards the
      mystic and saint will outlive his musty theology.

7   STOWE, LYMAN BEECHER. Saints, Sinners and Beechers. Indi-
      anapolis: Bobbs-Merrill, pp. 45-46.
         Reports the reaction of Lyman Beecher's wife to his
      reading of Edwards's Sinners in the Hands of an Angry God:
      "'Dr. Beecher, I shall not listen to another word of that
      slander on my Heavenly father!' and swept out of the room."

8   SUTER, RUFUS [ORLANDO, JR.] "The Concept of Morality in the
      Philosophy of Jonathan Edwards." Journal of Religion 14
      (July):265-72.
         Underscores the importance of ethics to Edwards, "first
      of the American philosophers"; compares it to Kant's em-
      phasis on ideal morality; and contrasts it to ethics as
      "applied sociology" of his contemporaries, as conformity
      to nature of Aristotle, and as pleasant sensation of Walter
      Pater. For Edwards, true virtue is "a sacrosanct ideal,"
      which is rooted in faculties given over to "a stupendously
      glorious emotional attachment" to being in general (God)
      and indistinguishable from God's love of Himself. Ed-
      wards's ethical system is inextricably linked to his
      theology and is generally expressed in aesthetic terms.

9   _____. "The Problem of Evil in the Philosophy of Jonathan
       Edwards." Monist 44 (July):280-95.
           Claims that Edwards tried to reconcile "two violently
       opposed philosophies"--Calvinism, with its insistence on
       the depravity of man, and Platonism, with its insistence
       on the overflowing goodness of God--and that he "struggled
       heroically" with the problem of evil throughout his
       career. At one time or another, he suggested five differ-
       ent "solutions" to the problem: one, that evil is inevi-
       table in an actual world; two, that evil is necessary to
       the possibility of good; three, that evil events do not
       exist inasmuch as consequences of those events are good;
       four, that evil events or things in and of themselves do
       not exist; five, that evil is mysteriously compatible with
       good because reality is rational. There is no intellectual
       solution to Edwards's self-created problem; "ultimately,"
       where a solution is possible, it rests upon "an act of
       faith."

10   TOWNSEND, HARVEY GATES. "Jonathan Edwards." In his Philo-
       sophical Ideas in the United States. New York: American
       Book Co., pp. 35-62.
           Considers Edwards "the first and perhaps the greatest
       philosophical thinker in America" by virtue of the origi-
       nal, systematic, and influential nature of his thought,
       in an analysis of his major work and principal concepts.
       Indebted to the Cambridge Platonists and a "sturdy" ideal-
       ist from the start, Edwards found revelation and reason
       "inseparable" and, with Locke, rooted knowledge in sensa-
       tion and reflection. Of a "sensitive aesthetic nature,"
       Edwards is more nearly a poet than a mystic. His justly
       praised logical constructs are ultimately aesthetic cate-
       gories, and the "real heart" of his ethics is his belief
       that men love God because He is beautiful. Hence the
       finite, ordered world tends to infinite wisdom and beauty
       through the divine light or love.

11   U.S. LIBRARY OF CONGRESS. A List of Printed Materials on
       Jonathan Edwards, 1703-1758, to be Found in the Library of
       Congress Reading Room. Washington: Office of the Super-
       intendent of the Reading Room, 29 pp.
           Lists approximately 400 Edwards items--biographies,
       appreciations, criticism, and fugitive references--in the
       Library of Congress. (Typescript.)

1935

1   ELSBREE, OLIVER WENDELL. "Samuel Hopkins and his Doctrine
of Benevolence." <u>New England Quarterly</u> 8 (December):534-
50.
    Attributes Edwards's influence on Samuel Hopkins to
their two years together in Northampton and the proximity
of Great Barrington, where Hopkins settled, to Stockbridge.
For all their theological similarities, Hopkins differs
from Edwards on the extent of the atonement, the existence
of free choice, and the nature of "true holiness."

2   FAUST, CLARENCE H. "Jonathan Edwards' View of Human Nature."
Ph.D. dissertation, University of Chicago.
    Reprinted as part of 1935.3 (and published separately
by the University of Chicago Libraries).

3   FAUST, CLARENCE H., and JOHNSON, THOMAS H[ERBERT]. Introduction to their <u>Jonathan Edwards: Representative Selections,
with Introduction, Bibliography, and Notes</u>. American
Writers Series. New York: American Book Co., pp. xi-
cxvii.
    Examines Edwards as man, thinker, and writer in a
closely argued three-part introduction to selections from
the standard texts and manuscript sources and an annotated bibliography. The middle part (by Faust) deals
serially with Edwards's psychological analysis of the
Great Awakening, the major issues of the free-will controversy, and the coherence of his doctrines of sin, virtue,
and grace--all a product of Edwards's "exalted and mystical" rendering of divine sovereignty, first experienced in
conversion and later explained through logical constructs.
The first part outlines Edwards's career, the third his
art (both by Johnson). His rigorous logic accounts for
the "severe, undilated" style of the treatises; the freedom from eccentricity accounts for the prose cadences and
clarity of the sermons and makes up for any want of
"conscious artistry."

4   JAMES, HENRY, SR. Letter, 11 May 1843. In <u>The Thought and
Character of William James</u>, by Ralph Barton Perry. Boston: Little, Brown & Co., p. 47.
    Remarks in a letter to Emerson that Edwards would make
"the best possible reconciler and critic of philosophy"
since his time.

5   MAYHEW, GEORGE NOEL. "The Pattern of Sovereignty in Relation
     to Punishment." In his The Relation of the Theology of
     Jonathan Edwards to Contemporary Penological Theory and
     Practice. Chicago: University of Chicago Libraries,
     pp. 47-70.
         Contends that Edwards's idea of God develops from the
     political patterns of sovereignty inherent in feudalism
     and sixteenth-century monarchy and that his sense of
     punitive justice so derived runs counter to the more
     redemptive process of democratic penology "dawning in
     his day." Edwards deals with the problem of punishment
     through the Anselmic conception of sin as a violation
     of private right or honor and through the Grotian con-
     ception as a violation of the dignity and authority of the
     law. His God is ruler, lawgiver, and judge, perfect in
     all, for whom justice is equated with punishment and
     sinners with rebels. (A twenty-three page reprint of
     chapter 3 of 1932.11.)

6   MILLER, PERRY. "The Marrow of Puritan Divinity." Publica-
     tions of the Colonial Society of Massachusetts 32
     (February):247-300.
         Concludes a study of New England convenental theology
     with this sentence: "It was Jonathan Edwards who went
     back to the doctrine from which the tradition had started;
     went back, not to what the first generation of New
     Englanders had held, but to Calvin, and who became,
     therefore, the first consistent and authentic Calvinist
     in New England." (Reprinted in 1956.8.)

                                1936

1   ANON. "Making Gavels from Stair Railing of Edwards House Is
     Idea of Rev. R. D. Scott." Hampshire Gazette, 25 January,
     pp. 1, 2.
         Recounts events that led to the making of gavels from
     the mahogany railing recovered from the dismantled
     "Edwards" house on King Street.

2   BOYNTON, PERCY H. Literature and American Life. Boston:
     Ginn & Co., pp. 84-88.
         Characterizes Edwards as a "medieval mind" given to
     reconciling the beneficent God of Personal Narrative
     with the stern God of Sinners in the Hands of an Angry
     God.

1936

3　CARPENTER, FREDERIC I. Review of Jonathan Edwards: Representative Selections, edited by Clarence H. Faust and Thomas H. Johnson. New England Quarterly 9 (March):174-75.
　　　Calls Clarence H. Faust and Thomas H. Johnson's introduction (1935.3) a "masterpiece of erudition" destined for the desks of scholars, not students, because of its dissertation-like qualities.

4　CROSBY, C. R., and BISHOP, S. C. "Aeronautic Spiders with a Description of a New Species." Journal of the New York Entomological Society 44 (March):43-44.
　　　Regrets that Edwards became a theologian of damnation instead of our first arachnologist. "It was a loss to science and a doubtful gain for religion."

5　DEAN, CHARLES J. "Finds Whitney House and the Jonathan Edwards House Were Not the Same." Hampshire Gazette, 14 February, pp. 9, 13.
　　　Describes Edwards's house in Northampton, its subsequent owners, and its razing in 1830. Josiah Dwight Whitney built a larger house on the same site, which gave rise to some local confusion about the Edwards "mansion."

6　GEROULD, JAMES THAYER. Review of Jonathan Edwards: Representative Selections, edited by Clarence H. Faust and Thomas H. Johnson. Modern Philology 34 (August):102-103.
　　　Finds "illuminating" the editors' introductory remarks on Edwards's thought and style and particularly useful the bibliography (1935.3).

7　GRAY, JOSEPH M. M. "Jonathan Edwards, His God." In his Prophets of the Soul. New York: Abingdon Press, pp. 37-61.
　　　Counts Edwards's terrible and implacable God a misrepresentation and an "immense disservice" to man, in an estimate of his life and work. Though Edwards's stern view of divinity may explain the reality of sin and may answer a human need for authority, it lacks Christian love and misconceives Scripture. Ultimately, it yields to a more liberal faith, and God the sovereign is no longer tyrant but friend.

8　HITCHCOCK, ORVILLE A. "A Critical Study of the Oratorical Technique of Jonathan Edwards." Ph.D. dissertation, State University of Iowa.
　　　Considers Edwards "a speaker first" and analyzes 1200 sermons for their speech premises, preparation and

delivery, organization, persuasion, style, and effect upon
an audience of "good, honest country folk." Edwards is a
prominent colonial speaker whose carefully prepared sermons were delivered in "tense, precise tones" and in a
style plain and simple. "The sermons are a combination of
compact, irresistible reasoning and fervent, vivid
pathetic appeals."

9   MÜLLER, GUSTAV E. Amerikanische Philosophie. Stuttgart:
F. Frommann, pp. 17-39.
Calls Edwards the first and last philosophical Puritan
in America whose originality and boldness stand in
tragicomic incongruity to his limited education and views,
in a narration of his life and an explanation of his systematic, logical, and apolitical thought. (In German.)

10 S[CHNEIDER], H[ERBERT] W[ALLACE]. Review of Jonathan Edwards:
Representative Selections, edited by Clarence H. Faust and
Thomas H. Johnson. Journal of Philosophy 33 (4 June):327.
Finds only "occasional slips"--the emphasis on Edwards's
mysticism in his doctrine of love of God, for instance--in
Clarence H. Faust and Thomas H. Johnson's "distinguished"
text (1935.3).

11 TAYLOR, WALTER FULLER. A History of American Letters. Boston: American Book Co., pp. 29-36.
Suggests that Personal Narrative is Edwards's "enduring
literary work" and mysticism his chief trait.

1937

1   ANON. "Wills of Two Famous Local Men Recalled." Hampshire
Gazette, 6 July, p. 7.
Reprints and compares wills of two local celebrities,
Edwards and Calvin Coolidge.

2   BERKHOF, LOUIS. Reformed Dogmatics. Grand Rapids, Mich.:
Wm. B. Eerdmans Publishing Co., pp. 161-63.
Sketches Edwards's modification of Reformed views in
New England in his rejection of efficiency in God's connection with the fall of man, his overemphasis of the
determinate character of the will, and his adoption of
the realistic theory of the transmission of sin.

1937

3 GAMBRELL, MARY LATIMER. <u>Ministerial Training in Eighteenth</u> <u>Century New England</u>. New York: Columbia University Press, pp. 31-35, passim.

Finds typical of the clergy of the time Edwards's pastoral role in "remote" Northampton and his tutorial one to Joseph Bellamy and Samuel Hopkins at home. Though Edwards valued learning and preaching in the ministry, his <u>True Excellency</u> centers upon "mastery of doctrine."

4 HORNBERGER, THEODORE. "The Effect of the New Science upon the Thought of Jonathan Edwards." <u>American Literature</u> 9 (May):196-207.

Traces the influence of the new science on Edwards and suggests that he incorporated science in his theology "to save God" from seventeenth-century scientific materialists. His Yale notebooks show that science "definitely affected" his idea of God; his work of the 1730s reveal "a new synthesis" of science, philosophy, and theology; but his work during the Awakening is "singularly free" of scientific argument. The impact of science returns, however, after his dismissal. <u>Freedom of the Will</u> is "saturated" with science; <u>Original Sin</u> is "equally impregnated"; and <u>End of Creation</u>, his "final statement," demonstrates the "rather close" relationship of science to his "burning and mystical" concept of God.

5 KNÖPP, WALTHER. "Jonathan Edwards: der Weg der Heiligung." Ph.D. dissertation, Hartford Theological Seminary.

Discovers in Edwards's doctrine of saving grace, found especially in his sermons, the key to his theology and a clue to American church history, in a study of his ideas of holiness, sovereignty, rebirth, and the coming kingdom. (In German.)

6 LYMAN, CLIFFORD H. <u>Northampton in the Days of Jonathan</u> <u>Edwards 1727-1750</u>. Northampton, Mass.: Metcalf Printing & Publishing Co., 14 pp. [unpaged].

Reviews Edwards's life "here in Northampton" and the memorials to him. There are two monuments in the Bridge Street Cemetery and a tablet in the First Church. Two other churches, the Edwards Congregational Church, Northampton, and the Edwards Congregational Church, in Davenport, Iowa, are "living memorials of this great and good man."

7 NIEBUHR, H. RICHARD. The Kingdom of God in America. Chicago:
    Willet, Clark & Co., pp. 101-103, 113-16, 135-45.
        Underscores divine sovereignty as the "explicit founda-
    tion" of Edwards's thought, from his conversion experience
    in Personal Narrative to his millennial hope in History of
    Redemption, in a survey of the Great Awakening and its
    impact upon the idea of the coming of the kingdom of God
    in America. Seen in the context of divine sovereignty,
    Edwards's hell-fire sermons represent an "intense aware-
    ness" of man's precarious poise between disintegration and
    harmony, not the frightening need of conventional morality
    often depicted. And his quickened sense of God's power
    in the revivals led him (and other ministers) to the real-
    ization of Christ's coming kingdom and man's "everlasting
    hope." That conviction is in a native, American tradi-
    tion.

8 SWEET, WILLIAM WARREN. Makers of Christianity from John
    Cotton to Lyman Abbott. New York: Henry Holt & Co.,
    pp. 75-87.
        Accounts Edwards's "personalized" Calvinism the source
    of "new life" in New England theology and the "vital
    spark" to religious life generally, in a survey of colo-
    nial awakeners. Edwards's mystical, inner experience (and
    Sarah's) translates the doctrines of Calvinism from a
    social and political philosophy to individual experience
    and searches out kindred experience in his congregation,
    especially in the young. Through his disciples over the
    next century, Edwards bequeaths to individuals and society
    "motives of great ethical value."

*9 THOMAS, JOHN NEWTON. "Determinism in the Theological System
    of Jonathan Edwards." Ph.D. dissertation, University of
    Edinburgh.
        Not seen except for Table of Contents.

1938

1 ANON. "Yale Gets Collection on Jonathan Edwards." New York
    Times, 4 November, p. 20.
        Reports a bequest of Edwards materials--contemporary
    portraits, manuscript sermons, letters, and such--to Yale
    from the will of Eugene Phelps Edwards, of Stonington,
    Connecticut. "A Hebrew Bible printed in Amsterdam in 1753
    has on the flyleaf records of the family."

1938

2   BEARDSLEY, FRANK GRENVILLE. The History of Christianity in
    America. New York: American Tract Society, pp. 60-62
    passim.
        Lists Edwards among the prominent figures of the Great
    Awakening--Frelinghuysen, Whitefield, the Tennents, and Dav-
    enport--in a general appraisal of the man and the movement.

3   PRATT, ANNE STOKELY. Isaac Watts and his Gifts of Books to Yale
    College. New Haven, Conn.: Yale University Press, pp. 32-47.
        Recounts in detail the provenance of Faithful Narrative;
    the correspondence of Isaac Watts, Benjamin Colman, and
    Edwards on its publication; and the corrections Edwards
    made in the text from the English to the American edition.

4   PRICE, REBECCA R. "Jonathan Edwards as a Christian Educator."
    Ph.D. dissertation, New York University.
        Traces Edwards's teaching career as a student at Yale, a
    pastor at Northampton, and a missionary at Stockbridge;
    evaluates both the weaknesses and strengths of his Chris-
    tian educational principles (aims, agencies, leadership,
    techniques, and curriculum); and estimates his influence
    on theology, personal religion, social religion, polity,
    and education.

5   RUSTERHOLTZ, WALLACE P. American Heretics and Saints. Bos-
    ton: Manthorne & Burack, pp. 76-87.
        Gives a brief life of Edwards and a discussion of his
    imprecatory sermons and contrasts his concept of God to
    that of the Universalist minister Hosea Ballou (1796-
    1861). Edwards's God was Old Testament, monarchial,
    thundering the law; Ballou's was New Testament, democrat-
    ic, "the still small voice" of love.

                            1939

1   ANDERSON, PAUL RUSSELL, and FISCH, MAX HAROLD, eds. Philoso-
    phy in America from the Puritans to James with Representa-
    tive Selections. The Century Philosophy Series. New
    York: D. Appleton-Century Co., pp. 74-82.
        Suggests that for Edwards systematic philosophy was
    probably a "spendthrift luxury," for he early abandoned
    metaphysical and epistemological investigations for theo-
    logical ones. Although his idealism, more Platonic than
    Berkeleian, is evident "from the first" and "implicit in
    all" his work, Edwards appears publicly an evangelist and a
    theologian from his first treatise to his last. Neverthe-
    less, he often uses "the equipment of a philosopher," how-
    ever apologetically, to help clarify his theology.

1940

2 BEARDSLEY, FRANK GRENVILLE. "Jonathan Edwards, the Great New
   England Divine." In his Heralds of Salvation: Biographi-
   cal Sketches of Outstanding Soul Winners. New York:
   American Tract Society, pp. 11-24.
       Recounts Edwards's career and cites the "initial im-
   pulse" he gave to the Great Awakening in the Connecticut
   Valley through his preaching and the publication of
   Faithful Narrative.

3 FAY, JAY WHARTON. American Psychology before William James.
   New Brunswick, N.J.: Rutgers University Press, pp. 43-46
   passim.
       Locates the roots of Edwards's psychology in the sensa-
   tionalism of Locke and the scholastic division of the
   operations of the mind. Psychologically, Edwards identifies the will with the inclination in Freedom of the Will
   and illustrates, as well, a logic founded upon "imperfect
   observation and inadequate analysis."

4 MALONE, DUMAS. Saints in Action. New York: Abingdon Press,
   p. 39.
       Refers to Edwards as a "major saint" of American
   Congregationalists.

5 MILLER, PERRY. The New England Mind: The Seventeenth
   Century. New York: Macmillan Co., pp. 176-77.
       Notes that Edward's theology, "the supreme achievement
   of the New England mind," differs markedly from that of
   the seventeenth century in its logic, metaphysics, and
   cosmology.

6 SWEET, WILLIAM WARREN. The Story of Religion in America.
   New York and London: Harper & Brothers.
       Reprint of 1930.14.

1940

1 ANON. "Precursor of Whitefield: Jonathan Edwards and his
   Ministry." Times Literary Supplement, 12 October, p. 516.
       Singles out George Whitefield's debt to Edwards in a
   review of Ola Elizabeth Winslow's "authorative" biography
   (1940.21).

2 BATES, ERNEST SUTHERLAND. "Jonathan Edwards and the Great
   Awakening." In his American Faith: Its Religious,
   Political, and Economic Foundations. New York: W. W.
   Norton & Co., pp. 207-17.

1940

Traces the career of Edwards, the "Puritan saint," and
his successors in the Great Awakening. Edwards's thought
hangs upon the two poles of subjectivism and idealism and
neglects the "intermediate stages of social activity" for
a limited theology of conscience. Unlike Roger Williams
or William Penn, Edwards failed to bridge the gap between
God and man. But for his mystical, personal experience,
his absolute and abstract ideal would be "barren and color-
less."

3   FAUST, C[LARENCE] H. Review of Jonathan Edwards, by Ola
    Elizabeth Winslow. New England Quarterly 13 (December):
    723-26.
        Compares Ola Elizabeth Winslow's biography (1940.21)
    to the full-length studies of Edwards by Alexander Allen
    (1889.1), Arthur C. McGiffert (1932.10), and Henry Bamford
    Parkes (1930.10). Although none treat Edwards's personal
    history as "fully and precisely" as Winslow does, she
    reduces and blurs his system of ideas, the very arguments
    necessary to define him. A study is still needed to "make
    clear the nature of his genius by an analysis rather than
    a translation."

4   GILMORE, ALBERT F. "Miss Winslow Presents a Humanized Por-
    trait of Jonathan Edwards." Christian Science Monthly,
    4 May, p. 10.
        Reviews Ola Elizabeth Winslow's Jonathan Edwards
    (1940.21) and finds it an undistorted, humanized portrait
    of a "potent preacher."

5   HAMMAR, GEORGE. Christian Realism in Contemporary Thought.
    Uppsala: A. B. Lundequistska Bokhandeln, pp. 85-90.
        Explains Edwards as the "portal" figure in American
    church history as he sought to fuse the theocentricity
    of Calvin with the subjectivism of the revivals. Such a
    "transitional" theology was only a momentary stay against
    a rising individualism in America and an anthropocentric
    religion.

6   HAWLEY, C. A. "America's Unforgettable Philosopher: Re-
    view of Jonathan Edwards, by Ola Elizabeth Winslow."
    Unity, 125 (17 June):127.
        Predicts a wide audience for Ola Elizabeth Winslow's
    Jonathan Edwards (1940.21).

7   JOHNSON, THOMAS H[ERBERT]. The Printed Writings of Jonathan
    Edwards 1703-1758: A Bibliography. Princeton, N.J.:
    Princeton University Press, pp. vii-xiv.
       Gauges Edwards's reputation and popularity in an intro-
    duction to a descriptive bibliography of 346 numbered
    items of Edwards's printed writings. The number of
    editions published in London, Edinburgh, and Glasgow
    during the eighteenth century and translated into Dutch,
    French, and German suggests that Edwards was "possibly
    better known abroad than at home," though he was not a
    "'leading light'" in either. About sixty items were
    separately printed, twenty-four of them during his life-
    time. Most frequently published (exclusive of reprints)
    were Life of Brainerd, Religious Affections, Faithful
    Narrative, and History of Redemption, about thirty edi-
    tions each. Sinners in the Hands of an Angry God went
    through twenty-three editions, Freedom of the Will twenty,
    Original Sin thirteen, and Some Thoughts twelve; ten
    works were translated, most frequently into Dutch and Welsh,
    but also into French, German, Arabic, Gaelic, and Choctaw.
    Since 1900, five works have been separately printed.

8   _____. Review of Jonathan Edwards, 1703-1758: A Biography,
    by Ola Elizabeth Winslow. American Literature 12 (May):
    251-52.
       Recommends Ola Elizabeth Winslow's sympathetic bio-
    graphy (1940.21) for its "competent and lucid" judgement.

9   MILLER, PERRY. "From Edwards to Emerson." New England
    Quarterly 13 (December):589-617.
       Explores continuities of the Puritan tradition by
    relating Edwards's perception of the "overwhelming pre-
    sence" of God in the soul and in nature to Emerson's
    transcendentalism and by finding "implicit in the texture"
    of End of Creation mysticism and pantheism. Edwards
    strained his Calvinism to the "breaking point," but
    Emerson, without the restraints of dogma and external
    law, was free to conceive of man and nature as divine.
    (Reprinted in 1956.8 and 1959.9.)

10 _____. "Speculative Genius." Saturday Review of Literature
    31 (30 March):6-7.
       Considers Ola Elizabeth Winslow's biography (1940.21),
    though limited in its aims, "our best introduction" to
    Edwards.

1940

11   MUELDER, WALTER G, AND SEARS, LAURENCE. The Development of
     American Philosophy: A Book of Readings. Boston:
     Houghton Mifflin Co., pp. 2-4.
         Calls Edwards our first "real" philosopher and his
     idealism "largely" his own invention. Edwards grafted
     the new philosophy of Newton and Locke onto the old theo-
     logy of Calvin and subjected both to an "intense"
     emotional peity.

12   NICHOLS, ROBERT HASTINGS. Review of Jonathan Edwards, by Ola
     Elizabeth Winslow. Church History 9 (June):180-82.
         Believes Ola Eliazabeth Winslow's estimate of Edwards
     (1940.21) would have been "truer" had she not considered
     his theology "a mistake and a misfortune."

13   POTTER, DAVID. "O Pioneers!" Yale Review 30 (Autumn):174-
     79.
         Recommends Ola Elizabeth Winslow's study (1940.21)
     for its astute understanding and accurate rendering of
     Edwards, in a review of books on Ethan Allen, Daniel
     Boone, and others.

14   S[CHNEIDER], H[ERBERT] W[ALLACE]. Review of Jonathan Edwards,
     by Ola Elizabeth Winslow. Journal of Philosophy 37
     (4 July):390.
         Finds that Ola Elizabeth Winslow's "excellent" bio-
     graphy (1940.21) "unfortunately throws little new light"
     on Edwards's philosophy and confuses the source of his
     conversion experience: it was intellectual, not
     mystical.

15   SHEPARD, ODELL. Review of Jonathan Edwards, by Ola Elizabeth
     Winslow. New York Times Book Review, 10 March, p. 4.
         Finds Ola Elizabeth Winslow "somewhat shy" to call
     Edwards a mystic, although the evidence is this "wise"
     book (1940.21) shows he was a mystic of "high rank."

16   SMITH, ELIZUR YALE. "The Descendants of William Edwards."
     New York Genealogical and Biographical Record 71 (July):
     217-24; (October):323-33; 72 (January):56-61; (April):
     124-32; (July):213-20; (October):320-31.
         Chronicles Edwards's life, his forebears and his pro-
     geny, as a persuasive example of eugenics. (See especially
     April, pp. 124-32.)

17   _____. Review of Jonathan Edwards, 1703-1758, by Ola
     Elizabeth Winslow. New York Genealogical and Biograph-
     ical Record 71 (April):97-98.

Calls Ola Elizabeth Winslow's <u>Jonathan Edwards</u>
(1940.21) "by far the most dynamic and absorbing of
all the books on Edwards."

18 _____. Review of <u>The Printed Writings of Jonathan Edwards,</u>
<u>1703-1758</u>, by Thomas H. Johnson. <u>New York Genealogical</u>
<u>and Biographical Record</u> 71 (October):403.
Calls Thomas H. Johnson's <u>Printed Writings</u> (1940.7) "a
valuable addition to the generally growing amount of data
on Edwards."

19 TOWNSEND, HARVEY G[ATES]. "Jonathan Edwards' Later Observations of Nature." <u>New England Quarterly</u> 13 (September):
510-18.
Inspects the manuscript of <u>Images or Shadows</u> (and by
cross-references, the <u>Miscellanies</u>) to show Edwards's
continued, mature interest in natural science and reprints the complete index and some dozen entries. The
later entries in the manuscript are "more bookish" than
the early ones and stress the analogy between the
material and the spiritual worlds.

20 TUFTS, JAMES H. "Edwards and Newton." <u>Philosophical Review</u>
49 (November):609-22.
Considers the general view of the universe commonly
held by Newton and Edwards and then examines in more
detail Edwards's ideas of atoms, solidity, and gravitation.
There can be "no doubt" about the influence of the
<u>Principia</u> and the <u>Opticks</u> on Edwards: Newton's laws of
nature "admirably" suited his sense of the "universal
interconnection of things and events," and Newton's
discoveries in color appear in his "idealistic line of
thought and in his physical analyses." But in his
theistic argument Edwards "went beyond" Newton (and
Locke) in uniting a world of atoms and a world of
ideas in the Idea and Will of God, a "swift" solution
unavailable to science and philosophy since then.

21 WINSLOW, OLA ELIZABETH. <u>Jonathan Edwards, 1703-1758: A</u>
<u>Biography</u>. New York: Macmillan Co., 418 pp.
Portrays Edwards through the "inner curve of spiritual experience" in a full-length biography that focuses
upon the details of his career--his foundations at home
and at Yale, his success and failure at Northampton, and
his new beginnings at Stockbridge and at Princeton--rather
than the details of his thought. Edwards was a lonely
figure, solitary, detached, single-minded, with a sense
of "inexorable justice" and "unassailable dignity"; a

1940

theologian with "mystical leanings," though not a mystic;
a "compelling" preacher, though "neither Puritan nor
fiery"; a religious thinker of the "vital" emotion of
personal conversion (his own), though enclosed "in the
husk of a dead idiom." For Edwards to confute was
"more important" than to tell; to be logical, precise,
legal, discriminating, tenacious, more important than
to cultivate the "delicacy of human relations." Hence,
his Farewell Sermon is chiefly a "biographical document
of importance," and Misrepresentations Corrected, more
than his major works, illustrates the "detective quality"
of his mind, his certainty and "ruthlessness." Edwards's
greatness lies not in his originality--his mind was
"strictly in the New England mold"--but in his "initiating and directing" the Great Awakening and in his
developing New England Theology, both acts of "far
reaching" consequences.

1941

1   ANON. Review of The Printed Writings of Jonathan Edwards
        1703-1758: A Bibliography, by Thomas H. Johnson. Times
        Literary Supplement, 25 October, p. 536.
            Finds Thomas H. Johnson's "admirable" bibliography
        (1940.7) follows the "exhaustive American method."

2   COHEN, I. BERNARD. Benjamin Franklin's Experiments. Cambridge,
        Mass: Harvard University Press, pp. 110-11.
            Remarks the similarity of Edwards's explanation of
        lightning in his diary to Franklin's "at about the same
        time" in the Pennsylvania Gazette, 15 December 1737.

3   DAY, RICHARD W. "Sinner in the Hands of an Angry Logic."
        Sewanee Review 49 (July-September):405-407.
            Commends Ola Elizabeth Winslow's biography (1940.21)
        as an "excellent introduction" to Edwards, a figure of
        grave importance to the development of American Christ-
        ianity and to contemporary, wayward man.

4   FAUST, C[LARENCE] H. Review of The Printed Writings of Jona-
        than Edwards 1703-1758: A Bibliography, by Thomas H.
        Johnson. New England Quarterly 14 (September):566-68.
            Calls Thomas H. Johnson's bibliography (1940.7)
        "admirably complete and accurate" and another indication
        of the need for a new edition of Edwards.

5   GOHDES, CLARENCE. Review of Jonathan Edwards, by Ola Eliza-
        beth Winslow. South Atlantic Quarterly 40 (January):89-90.
        Praises Ola Elizabeth Winslow's "pure" biography
        (1940.21), but calls for another book that deals with
        Edwards's thought and its place in eighteenth-century
        theology and psychology.

6   HORNBERGER, THEODORE. Review of The Printed Writings of
        Jonathan Edwards 1703-1758: A Bibliography, by Thomas H.
        Johnson. American Literature 13 (May):179-80.
        Judges that Thomas H. Johnson's accurate and detailed
        study (1940.7) supersedes John J. Coss's primary bibliog-
        raphy in the Cambridge History of American Literature
        (1917.1).

7   MILLER, PERRY. "Solomon Stoddard, 1643-1729." Harvard
        Theological Review 34 (October):277-320.
        Concludes that Edwards's grandfather, Solomon Stoddard,
        "had freed him from the mechanical theology of the Cove-
        nant, had brought back freshness and vigor to religion,
        had taught him how to manage revivals and to bring souls
        to conversion." For all that, Edwards failed in Northamp-
        ton not simply because he returned to an earlier way of
        church membership but because "the still domineering
        personality of Solomon Stoddard" overwhelmed him and his
        congregation.

8   OTTO, MAX C. "A Lesson from Jonathan Edwards." Humanist 1
        (Summer):37-40.
        Fears the attention given Edwards in the last decade
        augurs a return to religious conservatism.

9   PARKES, HENRY BAMFORD. "The Puritan Heresy." In his The
        Pragmatic Test: Essays on the History of Ideas. San
        Francisco: Colt Press, pp. 10-38.
        Reprint of 1932.12.

10 PAYNE, ERNEST A. The Prayer Call of 1784. London: Baptist
        Laymen's Missionary Movement, pp. 4-11.
        Acknowledges the influence of Edwards's Humble Attempt
        on later prayer calls, the founding of the Baptist Mis-
        sionary Society, the advance of the Northampton Associa-
        tion, and the start of other evangelical movements.

11 SCHNEIDER, HERBERT W[ALLACE]. Review of Jonathan Edwards, by
        Ola Elizabeth Winslow. American Historical Review 46
        (January):417-18.

1941

Praises Ola Elizabeth Winslow's "complete and scholarly" study (1940.21), but finds that if Edwards's career is
"a chapter in the Presbyterianizing" of New England, then
his pastorate in New York is more critical than his bio-
grapher allows.

12 TOWNSEND, H[ARVEY] G[ATES]. Review of <u>Jonathan Edwards</u>, by
Ola Elizabeth Winslow. <u>Philosophical Review</u> 50 (July):
450-51.
Praises Ola Elizabeth Winslow's "thorough, dependable,
modern" biography (1940.21), but notes it takes "little
account" of Edwards's philosophy or theology.

1942

1 ATKINS, GAUIS GLENN, and FAGLEY, FREDERICK L. <u>History of
American Congregationalism</u>. Boston and Chicago: Pilgrim
Press, pp. 104-14.
Traces Edwards's career, especially in the Great Awakening, and its effects on Congregationalism. Though
Edwards was "first" in a long line of important Congregational theologians, his impatience with a polity that
fostered his dismissal had personal consequences for him
and his "neo-orthodoxy" had profound doctrinal consequences
for the church.

2 CUNNINGHAM, CHARLES E. <u>Timothy Dwight, 1752-1817: A Bio-
graphy</u>. New York: Macmillan Co., pp. 348-51.
Draws "interesting parallels" between Timothy Dwight
and Edwards--both were precocious, metaphysicians, ministers, college presidents--but notes as well "significant
differences." Dwight's attack upon infidelity was "more
glorious" than Edwards's upon Arminianism, and in his influence Dwight may have "surpassed the record" of Edwards.

3 DAVIDSON, M[ARTIN]. <u>The Free Will Controversy</u>. London:
Watts & Co., pp. 55-56.
Asserts that the logic of <u>Freedom of the Will</u> would
"scarcely convince the theologian in modern times" and
that the conclusions Edwards draws from his assumptions of
God's sovereignty and man's depravity are "repulsive."

4 EDDY, [GEORGE] SHERWOOD. <u>Man Discovers God</u>. New York:
Harper & Brothers, pp. 150-59.
Traces Edwards's career as he fulfills and terminates
the mission of Calvinism, thus "opening the door to domes-
ticating God" in America.

5 KELLER, CHARLES ROY. <u>The Second Great Awakening in Connecti-
   cut</u>. New Haven, Conn.: Yale University Press, pp. 29-31,
   229-30.
      Cites Edwards's influence upon Timothy Dwight and
   Nathaniel Taylor as a force for moderation in the Second
   Awakening in Connecticut.

6 MACINTOSH, DOUGLAS CLYDE. <u>Personal Religion</u>. New York:
   Charles Scribner's Sons, pp. 191-92, 196-200, 280-81.
      Sketches, with distaste, the arguments of Edwards, the
   excesses of the Great Awakening, and the theology of his
   followers. Edwards is guilty of "pious blasphemy" for,
   among other things, suggesting disinterested love for an
   arbitrary and terrible God. As well, the development of
   Universalism may be read as a reaction to the awful vision
   of judgment in <u>Sinners in the Hands of an Angry God</u>.

7 MEAD, SIDNEY EARL. <u>Nathaniel William Taylor, 1786-1858: A
   Connecticut Liberal</u>. Chicago: University of Chicago
   Press, pp. 100-108, passim.
      Finds Edwards's distinction between moral and natural
   ability and inability in <u>Freedom of the Will</u> a "subtle
   tool" that enabled him to "force . . . together" as revealed facts God's sovereignty and man's freedom. In
   rejecting Edwards, Nathaniel Taylor (1786-1858) does not
   "outlogic" him but does place human reason before divine
   revelation, "'a rational faith of rational beings.'"

8 PAYNE, ERNEST A. "'. . . From India's Coral Strand.'"
   <u>Christian Science Monitor</u>, 25 July, pp. 5, 12.
      Calls Edwards, rather than John Wesley and George
   Whitefield, the "decisive" influence upon the founders of
   the Baptist Missionary Society in 1792.

9 SHIPTON, CLIFFORD K[ENYON]. <u>Sibley's Harvard Graduates:
   Biographical Sketches of Those Who Attended Harvard Col-
   lege</u>. Vol. 6, <u>1713-1721</u>. Boston: Massachusetts Historical Society, pp. 355-56 passim.
      Reports that Solomon and Elisha Williams joined to-
   gether to attack their "'good Kinsman, and Brother
   Edwards'" on the matter of the half-way covenant, in one
   of many references to Edwards and the Williams family,
   Charles Chauncy, Thomas Clap, Joseph Dwight, David Hall,
   Robert Breck, and other Harvard graduates throughout subsequent volumes of the work.

10 SWEET, WILLIAM WARREN. Religion in Colonial America. New
York: Charles Scribner's Sons, pp. 281-84.
Questions the primacy of Edwards in American revivalism. Priority and source belong to Theodorus Frelinghuysen and New Jersey, not Edwards and Massachusetts, to
pietism not Calvinism. Still the "Great New England
Awakening" begins with Edwards in Northampton in 1734, and
though he was not a revivalist "in the usual sense of the
word," he managed the emotional outpouring with "dignified
common sense" and kept excesses to a minimum. Out of that
experience came Faithful Narrative, probably his "most
potent" work, and Religious Affections, "more self revealing" than any of his other writing.

11 TSANOFF, RADOSLAV A. Moral Ideals of Our Civilization. New
York: E. P. Dutton & Co., pp. 454-57.
Praises Edwards's analytical power and "mystical inti-
macy" and considers his later major works on theodicy and
ethics to be theistic expressions of Neoplatonism. Edwards idealism persists in the "varieties" of transcendentalism in New England, especially in the thought of
Emerson.

12 WINSLOW, OLA ELIZABETH. Review of The Printed Works of
Jonathan Edwards, by Thomas H. Johnson. Modern Language
Notes 57 (March):230-31.
Recommends Thomas H. Johnson's informative, accurate,
and suggestive bibliography (1940.7) and wishes for a
companion volume listing the "whole panorama" of criticism
that Edwards's thought evoked.

13 WRIGHT, [CHARLES] CONRAD. "Edwards and the Arminians on the
Freedom of the Will." Harvard Theological Review 35
(October):241-61.
Suggests that "a tangle of verbal misunderstandings"
about moral agency lies at the bottom of Edwards's attack
on the Arminians, that his analysis of mind is really "not
very different" from theirs, and that both neglect the
crucial issue of original sin in their confused polemics
on will. Edwards's notions about the self-determining
power of the will that he ascribes to Arminians comes not
from their tracts but from an anonymous book by a "moderate Calvinist," Isaac Watts, An Essay on Free Will (1732);
for their part, the Arminians attacked Edwards's misrepresentation in Freedom of the Will as if it were true.

The whole controversy could have been "vastly simplified" if the Arminians had recognized that Edwards was "not wrong, but irrelevant" and if they had concentrated on original sin. "Moral necessity without total depravity loses all its sting."

1943

*1   BARNETT, DAS KELLEY. "The Doctrine of Man in the Theology of Jonathan Edwards (1703-1758)." Th.D. dissertation, Southern Baptist Theological Seminary.
Cited in Gillette, "A Checklist of Doctoral Dissertations . . ." (1967.12), p. 207.

2   BEARDSLEY, FRANK GRENVILLE. Religious Progress Through Religious Revivals. New York: American Tract Society, pp. 4-7.
Calls Edwards the "chief instrument" in the Great Awakening for his effective, if at times abhorrent, sermons in that lethargic age.

3   CURTI, MERLE. The Growth of American Thought. New York: Harper & Brothers, pp. 75-77.
Defines Edwards's "significant" place in American thought and disagrees that he was an anachronism, as V. L. Parrington held (1927.2). Edwards responded to the intellectual challenges of the Enlightenment, providing at once an "amazingly logical" defense of Calvinism and an important place within it for aesthetics and emotion.

4   DAVIS, ARTHUR PAUL. Isaac Watts: His Life and Works. New York: Dryden Press, pp. 51-52.
Calls Isaac Watts a "stout defender" of Edwards and the Awakening even though he toned down some parts of the London edition of Faithful Narrative.

5   DAVIS, JOE LEE. "Mystical Versus Enthusiastic Sensibility." Journal of the History of Ideas 4 (June):301-19.
Classifies Edwards as a mystic, not an enthusiast, in an historical analysis of the "fundamental divergencies" between mysticism and enthusiasm in Christian religious thought.

6   HITCHCOCK, ORVILLE A. "Jonathan Edwards." In A History and Criticism of American Public Address. Edited by William Norwood Brigance. New York and London: McGraw-Hill Book Co., 1:213-37.

1943

> Examines Edwards's sermons: the speaking situation;
> his training for them; the ideas, organization, and types
> of proof in them; his plain, unadorned style; his prepa-
> ration and delivery; and the effect they had upon his
> listeners. Edwards was "a speaker first and a writer
> afterward," a Calvinist and a mystic who stressed logic
> at the expense of emotion. His language was that of his
> audience--the average word was four letters--and his style
> decidedly oral--repetitive, parallel, cumulative, direct.

7   PARK, CHARLES EDWARDS. The Beginnings of the Great Awakening.
    Lancaster, Mass.: Society of the Descendants of the
    Colonial Clergy, pp. 15-29.
      Traces the career of Edwards, a "thorough-going" mystic
    and a "thorough-going" Calvinist. His sense of duty to
    the awful power and sovereignty of God "elbowed" his
    mysticism out of the way but also gave rise to a "re-
    crudesence of Puritanism" with its emphasis on moral obli-
    gation, immediate responsibility, and individual con-
    science. Edwards stands as both "sponsor" and symbol of
    the "sublime motive" of the Great Awakening.

8   PAYNE, ERNEST A. "The Evangelical Revival and the Beginings
    of the Modern Missionary Movement." Congregational Quar-
    terly 21 (July):223-36.
      Details the theological, devotional, and practical in-
    fluences Edwards exerted upon the founders of the Baptist
    missionary movement, especially William Carey, through
    the widely circulated Humble Attempt and Life of Brainerd.

9   STOVALL, FLOYD. American Idealism. Norman: University of
    Oklahoma Press, pp. 12-15, 17-18.
      Considers Edwards's idealism to be for the self rather
    than for society (like Franklin's), in a short explanation
    of his determinism and his "cautious mysticism."

10 WRIGHT, CHARLES CONRAD. "Arminianism in Massachusetts, 1735-
    1780." Ph.D. dissertation, Harvard University.
      Includes 1942.13; revised and published as 1955.12.

1944

1   HAROUTUNIAN, JOSEPH G. "Jonathan Edwards: Theologian of the
    Great Commandment." Theology Today 1 (October):361-77.
      Locates the center of Edwards's theology in his pas-
    sionate devotion to the beauty, excellency, and glory of

God, the "clue" to his life and work and a valuable counter to the "profound indifference" to God today. Edwards's theocentricism is grounded in a distinction between creator and created: his joy arises from God's communication of His glory to man; his despair from man's blindness (his sin) to it. In a time of Calvinistic legalism and Arminian moralism, Edwards's view of man was aesthetic, asserting "the integrity of man as a thinking, feeling, willing being."

2   HENDERSON, G. D. "Jonathan Edwards and Scotland." Evangeli-
      cal Quarterly 16 (January):41-52.
           Suggests that the relationship between Edwards and
      Scotland, based upon evangelical concerns, was intimate and
      reciprocal. Edwards kept in close correspondence with such
      Scottish theologians as John Erskine, Thomas Gillespie,
      and John McLaurin, and was "not uninfluenced" by them. On
      the other hand, Edwards's theology "undoubtedly left a
      permanent impression" upon the work of John McLeod Camp-
      bell, Thomas Chalmers, and George Hill.

3   PERRY, RALPH BARTON. Puritanism and Democracy. New York:
      Vanguard Press, pp. 75-77, 100-104, passim.
           Characterizes Edwards not as a dogmatic theologian but
      as a "speculative genius" responsive to the past and
      "quickened" by the Enlightenment and explains his place
      in Puritanism and evangelism. Central to Edwards's
      thought is the sovereignty of God, apprehended in "mysti-
      cal moments" and accepted without question, an expression
      of "authentic" Puritan piety. For Edwards, all parts of
      creation, from original sin to redemption, are harmonized
      by the whole, and, unlike covenant theologians, his God
      needs no justification.

4   SWEET, WILLIAM WARREN. Revivalism in America: Its Origin,
      Growth and Decline. New York: Charles Scribner's Sons,
      pp. 30-31, 78-85.
           Discovers the roots of American revivalism and its
      emotional source in the "personalizing" of Calvinism and
      the pattern for it set by Edwards in his imprecatory
      sermons. Through his preaching and pastoral work and,
      especially, in his Religious Affections, Edwards made
      religious emotion "theologically and intellectually re-
      spectable. This fact is basic to any adequate under-
      standing of the course of revivalism in America."

1945

1   DeJONG, PETER Y.   "Jonathan Edwards: The Half-Way Covenant
     Attacked."   In his The Covenant Idea in New England
     Theology, 1620-1847.   Grand Rapids, Mich.:   Wm. B. Eerd-
     mans Publishing Co., pp. 136-52, passim.
         Regards Edwards's attack on the half-way covenant a
     "turning point" in the history of Congregational thought
     and considers him instrumental in preparing for the "final
     eradication" of the covenant idea from New England reli-
     gious life.   By excluding all but the regenerate from
     church membership, Edwards effectively barred children
     from the covenant of grace, stressing their obligations
     more than their privileges.   By insisting on individualism
     and voluntarism through revivals, Edwards left "little
     room" for traditional, "organic" relations, secured by
     covenant and maintained by Calvinists elsewhere.   Thus in
     an attempt to revitalize a church fixed for so long in
     "dead formalism," Edwards unwittingly helped bring about
     its downfall.

2   HOLBROOK, CLYDE AMOS.   "The Ethics of Jonathan Edwards: A
     Critical Exposition and Analysis of the Relation of Moral-
     ity and Religious Conviction in Edwardean Thought."   Ph.D.
     dissertation, Yale University.
         Claims that Edwards's objectivism produced a dogmatic
     theory of virtue that resulted in an "unwarranted depreci-
     ation" of natural morality.   Yet his ethical theory
     repudiates theological utilitarianism and legalism, con-
     centrates upon the sinful nature of man, grounds itself
     on the ultimately real, and couples radical subjectivism
     to radical objectivism, thus making the highest morality
     identical with religious faith.

3   MILLER, RAYMOND CLINTON.   "Jonathan Edwards and His Influence
     upon Some of the New England Theologians."   S.T.D. disser-
     tation, Temple University.
         Examines Edwards's life, world, sources, and thought
     to demonstrate his influence upon his pupils and associ-
     ates, Joseph Bellamy and Samuel Hopkins; younger New
     England theologians, Stephen West, John Smalley, Nathaniel
     William Taylor; and later New England theologians, Bennet
     Tyler, Horace Bushnell, and the Oberlin group.   As pastor
     and theologian, Edwards remains an inspiration and influ-
     ence for any aspiring minister.

4   MUNCY, W[ILLIAM] L[UTHER], JR. A History of Evangelism in
        the United States. Kansas City, Kan.: Central Seminary
        Press, pp. 27–38.
            Claims Edwards's series of sermons on justification
        were coincidental to the spirit of God that moved North-
        ampton into the Great Awakening.

*5   RHOADES, DONALD HOSEA. "Jonathan Edwards: Experimental
        Theologian." Ph.D. dissertation, Yale University.
            Cited in Gillette, "A Checklist of Doctoral Disserta-
        tions . . ." (1967.12), p. 207.

6   RUDISILL, DORUS PAUL. "The Doctrine of the Atonement in
        Jonathan Edwards and his Successors." Ph.D. dissertation,
        Duke University.
            Published as 1971.26.

7   SCHRAG, FELIX JAMES. "Pietism in Colonial America." Ph.D.
        dissertation, University of Chicago.
            Traces pietism from the continent to colonial America
        in the revivalism of Theodorus Frelinghuysen, Gilbert
        Tennent, George Whitefield, and Edwards. Edwards differs
        from the orthodox Puritan tradition by ignoring the social
        and political principles of theocracy and by emphasizing
        the primacy of personal religious experience. Both at-
        titudes bespeak a debt to pietism.

8   SPERRY, WILLARD L. Religion in America. Cambridge, England:
        University Press, pp. 142–45.
            Considers Edwards's work the "mature sophistication"
        of Calvinism in America, only "once removed" in excellence
        from the Institutes.

1946

1   BLAU, JOSEPH L., ed. American Philosophic Addresses, 1700–
        1900. New York: Columbia University Press, pp. 517–36.
            Reprints God Glorified and suggests that the religious
        individualism of Edwards and his followers sapped the
        congregational system, weakened the church covenant,
        and encouraged the Presbyterians, a group "less democratic
        and less philosophical" than New England Puritans.

1946

2   FROOM, LEROY EDWIN. <u>The Prophetic Faith of Our Fathers: The</u> <u>Historical Development of Prophetic Interpretation</u>. Washington, D.C.: Review & Herald, 3:181-85.
      Explains Edwards's dating of the 1260-year reign of the papal Antichrist through the arithmetic of <u>Humble Attempt</u> and <u>History of Redemption</u>.

3   LOWELL, ROBERT. "Mr. Edwards and the Spider" and "After the Surprising Conversions." In his <u>Lord Weary's Castle</u>. New York: Harcourt, Brace & Co., pp. 58-61.
      Bases two poems about Edwards upon his writing. "Mr. Edwards and the Spider" draws chiefly from "On Insects" and <u>Sinners in the Hands of an Angry God</u>. "After the Surprising Conversions" draws from the account of Joseph Hawley's suicide in Edwards's letter to Benjamin Colman.

4   PITKANEN, ALLAN. "Jonathan Edwards--Scourger of the Wicked." <u>Social Studies</u> 37 (October):269-71.
      Recounts a short life of Edwards, an intellectual and moral force for eight generations but now largely unread and forgotten.

5   SCHNEIDER, HERBERT W[ALLACE]. <u>A History of American Philoso-</u> <u>phy</u>. New York: Columbia University Press, pp. 11-21.
      Characterizes the sovereignty of God as Edwards's "master passion," leading him to cast the idea of holy love into empiricist arguments and Platonic form and to attempt to reconcile Puritan grace and European pietism, in a survey of idealism and immaterialism in American philosophy. Edwards's doctrine asserts that matter and human will exist and operate in God as Being, just as it denies substance and mechanical causation. Hence the "immediate antithesis" of his idealism is Arminianism, not materialism.

6   WERTENBAKER, THOMAS JEFFERSON. <u>Princeton, 1746-1896</u>. Princeton, N.J.: Princeton University Press, pp. 42-43.
      Notes with regret the brief presidency of Edwards, an "ardent friend" of Princeton.

1947

1   ALDRIDGE, ALFRED OWEN. "Jonathan Edwards and William Godwin on Virtue." <u>American Literature</u> 18 (January):308-18.
      Reprints the dispute between Samuel Parr and William Godwin on Edwards's <u>True Virtue</u> and the place of gratitude

in his scheme. Godwin acknowledged a debt to Edwards in
Political Justice and perceived the "nihilistic tendencies" of his system; Parr argued in his Spital Sermon
that Edwards recognized two levels of virtue. An analysis
of Edwards gives comfort to both Godwin and Parr: gratitude is not a part of true virtue, but gratitude is a
virtue.

2   ALEXIS, GERHARD THEODORE. "Calvinism and Mysticism in Jona-
     than Edwards." Ph.D. dissertation, University of Minne-
     sota.
        Attempts to resolve the paradox of Edwards's "clearly
     recognized" mysticism and his orthodox Calvinism: though
     they are not irreconcilable, they do oppose each other on
     scriptural, ecclesiastical, and social grounds. Yet
     Edwards managed to harmonize them through a process of
     "extension and limitation," particularly in matters of
     conversion and grace. For him, the mystic's way was "the
     way of the Christian pilgrim . . . routed through North-
     ampton and Geneva."

3   EGBERT, DONALD DREW. Princeton Portraits. Princeton, N.J.:
     Princeton University Press, pp. 40-42, figs. 12-15.
        Reproduces and notes four Edwards items at Princeton:
     a portrait by Henry Augustus Loop (1860) believed to be a
     copy of one by Joseph Badger (c. 1748); a bronze relief
     by Herbert Adams (1900); a wood statuette by Irving and
     Casson (1928); and a portrait, oil on wood, by John
     Potter Cuyler (1929).

4   PARKES, HENRY BAMFORD. The American Experience: An Integra-
     tion of the History and Civilization of the American
     People. New York: Alfred A. Knopf, pp. 78-85.
        Takes Edwards to be a representative American in his
     repudiation of authority, confidence in the common man,
     exaltation of the will, and refutation of evil. Edwards
     "unconsciously Americanized" Calvinist theology, pitting
     the will against the environment and redefining conversion
     as a verifiable, emotional experience, in doctrines with
     "strongly liberal implications." Most significantly, the
     inner inconsistencies of Edwards's God "mirror with re-
     markable clarity the conflicting tendencies that run
     through the history of the American spirit."

1947

5   SWAIM, J. CARTER. "Jonathan Edwards: The Eloquent Theolo-
    gian." In his Messengers Upon the Mountains. New York:
    Evangelism Board of National Missions of the Presbyterian
    Church in the U.S.A., pp. 3-5.
        Recounts Edwards's life as a revivalist.

6   TOWNSEND, HARVEY G[ATES]. "The Will and the Understanding in
    the Philosophy of Jonathan Edwards." Church History 16
    (December):210-20.
        Deems Edwards's struggle over the relationship of the
    will and the understanding "as perennial as philosophy
    itself" and his resolution, especially to the problem of
    human freedom, "realistic and objective." Edwards sees
    human understanding and will as parts of the natural order
    and subject to natural laws--those of the understanding to
    the laws of inference, those of the will to the laws of
    choice. But man is limited by "the determinate nature of
    totality." Therefore, according to Edwards, man can
    understand but not perfectly, can choose but cannot deter-
    mine the consequences.

7   TWITCHELL, MARY EDWARDS, and EDWARDS, RICHARD HENRY. The
    Edwards Family in the Chenango Country. Lisle, N.Y.:
    Richard Henry Edwards, pp. 10-12.
        Offers a brief biography and traces the later Edwards
    family as it moves west.

8   WITHAM, W. TASKER. Panorama of American Literature. [New
    York]: Stephen Daye Press, pp. 28-30.
        Notes Edwards's career. (Illustrated.)

                            1948

1   CRABTREE, ARTHUR BAMFORD. Jonathan Edwards' View of Man: A
    Study in Eighteenth Century Calvinism. Wallington,
    England: Religious Education Press, 64 pp.
        Locates Edwards's view of man in his concepts of the
    absolute sovereignty of God, the mediatorial satisfaction
    of Christ, and the efficacious grace of the Spirit, and
    concludes that he fails to solve the problem of human
    responsibility in a system of "rigid" determinism. Ed-
    wards's formulation of man's depravity and Adam's in
    Original Sin is "singularly ill-starred"; his failure to
    prove the axiom of causation in Freedom of the Will is but
    "another instance of the fallacy of petitio principii."

He proves that inability to do evil and human responsibility are compatible, but he does not prove the more important proposition that inability to do good and human
responsibility are compatible. Like Calvin before him,
Edwards's "devotion to the system" went beyond Scripture
and his "very clarity [of reason] betrays a lack of that
awed wonder" in the presence of divine mysteries.

2 DAVIDSON, FRANK. "Three Patterns of Living." American
   Association of University Professors Bulletin 34 (Summer):
   364-74.
      Compares the autobiographical statements of Edwards,
   Franklin, and Woolman as possible models for living.
   Edwards's strength, unfortunately "deflected" into an
   apology for Calvinism, lies in his piety and spirituality,
   his idealism and mysticism.

3 FOSTER, JOHN. "The Bicentenary of Jonathan Edwards' 'Humble
   Attempt.'" International Review of Missions 37 (October):
   375-81.
      Recounts the genesis and influence of Edwards's Humble
   Attempt, a book not only "prophetic of the Missionary
   Awakening" but also a "main factor in the progress toward
   it."

*4 HOLTROP, ELTON. "Edwards's Conception of the Will in the
   Light of Calvinistic Philosophy." Ph.D. dissertation,
   Western Reserve University.
      Cited in Comprehensive Dissertation Index 1861-1972,
   32:57.

5 JOHNSON, THOMAS H[ERBERT]. "Jonathan Edwards." In Literary
   History of the United States. Edited by Robert E. Spiller
   et al. New York: Macmillan Co., 1: 71-81.
      Considers Edwards "the first American Calvinist" in
   his rejection of the covenantal theology of his forebears
   and his emphasis upon divine sovereignty and the reality
   of sin, in an examination of the consistent and original
   metaphysics that gave "permanent direction to spiritual
   culture in America." From his early speculations in
   "Notes on the Mind," which attempts "to harmonize emotion
   and reason, mercy and justice, fate and free will," to the
   late treatises of the Stockbridge years, Edwards wrought
   a coherent, if not systematic, "living philosophy." Edwards imparted love to Calvinist dogma--his "unique contribution"--and harmonized pantheism and mysticism with
   it while maintaining a "tragic intensity" about sin. Both

1948

his idealism and his pessimism find their way into
nineteenth-century America, in the work of Hawthorne,
Melville, Emerson, Whitman, and Adams. (Frequently reprinted.)

6   KASTON, BENJAMIN JULIAN. Spiders of Connecticut. State
      Geological and Natural History Survey, Bulletin no. 70.
      Hartford: State of Connecticut, p. 31.
         Notes that Edwards made the earliest recorded observa-
      tions of the ballooning or parachuting spiders in America
      (1715).

7   MILLER, PERRY, ed. Introduction to Images or Shadows of
      Divine Things. New Haven, Conn.: Yale University Press,
      pp. [1]-41.
         Discovers in Edwards's typological use of nature "a
      revolution in sensibility" profound in its implications,
      in a short history and analysis of types and tropes
      prefatory to a reprinted manuscript notebook of 212
      entries. To Edwards, the spiritualizing of nature common
      at the time (in Cotton Mather's Agricola, for instance)
      falsified the world of Newton and Locke. Thus "the most
      sensitive stylist in American Puritanism" sought in the
      perception of the images or shadows of divine things a
      coherence of nature, scripture, history, and mind, and a
      revelation of the divine intention, the "ultimate way"
      of knowing.

8   MILLER, PERRY. "Jonathan Edwards on the Sense of the Heart."
      Harvard Theological Review 41 (April):123-45.
         Likens Edwards's Miscellanies to Pascal's Pensées,
      reprints Observation No. 782 on the sense of the heart,
      and relates it to Edwards's "radical" empiricism. Ed-
      wards's fragment on spiritual knowledge "takes flight"
      from Locke's "Of Words" (An Essay Concerning Human Under-
      standing, III, i, 1) by asserting that in regenerate man
      the word, naturally detached from the sensation it de-
      scribes, vividly and fully identifies with the sensation.
      Hence Edwards's sense of the heart, distinct from the
      understanding of the head, is simply "a sensuous appre-
      hension of the total situation," and thus "eternal salva-
      tion becomes possible in the midst of time."

9   _____. "Jonathan Edwards' Sociology of the Great Awakening."
      New England Quarterly 21 (March):50-77.
         Discovers hints of Edwards's social theory in "crucial"
      sections of three unpublished revival sermons probably

written between 1734 and 1741--on texts from Matthew
25:24-28, II Samuel 20:19, and Matthew 22:9-10--and
reprints them. The first is a discussion of colonial
cultural dependence; the second, a "terrifying picture"
of a rural New England town; and the third, a "sociologi-
cal analysis" of Northampton. Clearly, a "major premise"
in Edwards's thinking is that grace operates within a
social context as well as through individual psychology.

10 SAVELLE, MAX. Seeds of Liberty: The Genesis of the American
    Mind. New York: A. A. Knopf, pp. 47-53, 64-66, 161-64,
    passim.
        Ranks Edwards's mystical idealism as the first "great"
    philosophical system to have come "natively" from American
    soil and experience, but considers his evangelism "rela-
    tively incidental and unimportant," in an intellectual
    history of the United States. For Edwards, the Great
    Awakening was not "a democratic emotional drive for salva-
    tion" but another occasion to combat rationalism and
    Arminianism in his defense of Calvinist orthodoxy. Though
    Edwards was the intellectual leader of the revival, he was
    "not really of it."

11 SCHNEIDER, HERBERT W[ALLACE]. "The Puritan Tradition." In
    Wellsprings of the American Spirit. Edited by F. Ernest
    Johnson. Religion and Civilization Series. New York:
    Institute for Religious and Social Studies, pp. 1-13.
        Considers that Edwards represents "only a passing
    phase" of Puritanism, one in which a Puritan is not a
    Yankee. Religion in New England had early accommodated
    to commerce; Edwards and the Awakening succeeded only
    briefly in divorcing them.

12 SQUIRES, J. RADCLIFFE. "Jonathan Edwards." Accent 9
    (Autumn):31-32.
        Closes Edwards's "American monologue," a thirty-three-
    line poem, with this:
            Do not open the chest
        In the attic, which is filled with something,
        Either apples or Satan. You do not wish to know.

13 TOWNSEND, H[ARVEY] G[ATES]. Review of Images or Shadows of
    Divine Things, edited by Perry Miller. Philosophical
    Review 57 (November):622-23.
        Questions Perry Miller's far-reaching claims for Ed-
    wards's typology in his edition of Images or Shadows of
    Divine Things (1948.7). Edwards's notes are intelligible
    "simply as memoranda" of an eighteenth-century New England
    preacher and scholar.

1948

14 WYCKOFF, D. CAMPBELL. "Jonathan Edwards' Contributions to
    Religious Education." Ph.D. dissertation, New York Uni-
    versity.
        Examines Edwards's theories of knowledge and responsi-
    bility, traces their influence (especially upon theologi-
    cal liberalism), and evaluates them in the light of
    contemporary religious education. Edwards addresses
    himself to the metaphysical basis, function, validity,
    and limits of knowledge and to man's inherent nature and
    its relationship to society, nature, and God, issues
    central to Christian education today.

1949

1 CADY, EDWIN H. "The Artistry of Jonathan Edwards." New
    England Quarterly 22 (March):61-72.
        Argues that the "organic oneness" in Sinners in the
    Hands of an Angry God, achieved by blending thought and
    imagery, allusion and experience, "testifies" to Edwards's
    artistry. Although he was "addicted" to biblical allusion,
    Edwards's most successful images arise "natively" from
    his imagination and tally with those of his listeners,
    homely images of fire and ice and water. Probably his
    "freshest" images are kinesthetic not visual, expressed
    in symbols of tension-pressure and suspension-heaviness,
    most notably as he adds to the suspended sinner "a night-
    marish feeling of his fatal weight." Thus Edwards finds
    an "'objective correlative'" to move his callous audience.

2 CHASE, MARY ELLEN. Review of Jonathan Edwards, by Perry
    Miller. New York Times Book Review, 11 December, p. 4.
        Considers Perry Miller's study (1949.9) "a unique and
    major contribution to American letters, thought and
    history."

3 DeVOTO, BERNARD. "Our Contemporary, Jonathan Edwards." New
    York Herald Tribune Book Review, 20 November, p. 4.
        Reviews Perry Miller's Jonathan Edwards (1949.9), a
    triumph of literary and philosophical criticism though it
    fails to examine Edwards in contemporary psychological
    terms.

4 DRUMMOND, ANDREW LANDALE. Story of American Protestantism.
    Edinburgh and London: Oliver & Boyd, pp. 107-11, 124-27,
    passim.
        Places Edwards, an "unusual" blend of dogmatism and
    speculation, mysticism and logic, within the revivalist

tradition in America, the "dominant" religious pattern
there. A "Calvinist romanticist," Edwards was "altogether
too Puritanical" to sustain the fever pitch of the Awakening. Although his theology is all but forgotten, he is
remembered as the "'greatest of New England theologians'"
in a stained glass procession at Mansfield College Chapel,
Oxford.

5   FEAVER, JOHN CLAYTON. "Edwards' Concept of God as Redeemer."
     Ph.D. dissertation, Yale University.
         Finds Edwards's concept of God as redeemer to have both
     a Christocentric and anthropological emphasis and to be
     founded upon the unresolved tensions between man's insuf-
     ficiency and his ability, God's sovereignty and His holi-
     ness, and Christ's satisfaction and His beauty. Although
     salvation is open to all, man must actively respond to the
     divine offer: faith must be "inevitably accompanied" by
     good works. Through Christ comes redemption and the Holy
     Spirit, God's love and gift to man.

6   HICKS, GRANVILLE. Review of Images or Shadows of Divine
     Things, edited by Perry Miller. New York Times Book
     Review, 30 January, pp. 4, 18.
         Suggests that Edwards's notes do not live up to Perry
     Miller's account (1948.7): if some suggest "unmistakably"
     a post-Newtonian universe, most are "'spiritualized com-
     monplaces.'"

7   HORTON, ROD W., and EDWARDS, HERBERT W. Backgrounds of
     American Literary Thought. Rowayton, Conn.: Rod W.
     Horton & Herbert W. Edwards, p. 59.
         Considers Edwards's Sinners in the Hands of an Angry
     God an "awful sermon" and his death the end of "the last
     great attempt" to save Calvinism.

8   HOWARD, PHILIP E., JR., ed. "A Biographical Sketch of the
     Life and Work of Jonathan Edwards." In The Life and Diary
     of David Brainerd. Chicago: Moody Press, pp. 11-42.
         Derives a life of Edwards from that of Samuel Miller
     (1837.1) and quotes a good deal from Edwards's works.

9   MILLER, PERRY. Jonathan Edwards. The American Men of Let-
     ters Series. [New York:] William Sloane Associates,
     363 pp.
         Considers Edwards "intellectually the most modern man
     of his age," a speculative philosopher "infinitely more"
     than a theologian, a "major" artist rather, a psychologist

and a poet in the native tradition, in a full-length study
of the "drama of his ideas"--on inherent and objective
good, Arminianism, revivalism, naturalism, conversion and
communion, free will, original sin, true virtue, teleology,
and history--interleaved with facts of external biography
and notes on historical conditions. If Edwards's success
lies in his unique ability to generalize his experience
into "the meaning of America," his importance lies in his
"inspired definitions," derived from Newton and Locke, and
not in his often "pathetic" and unsophisticated answers.
So his sermons, for example, are "immense and concentrated
efforts" to define the religious life in America after
Newton reduced nature to fixed laws and Locke reduced mind
to vagrant sensations. In late life Edwards came to believe that the complete, eternal work of God could be perceived only in finite, successive insights in time, that
the central problem was history, and that God's infinite
judgment was renewed moment by moment, realized in beauty.

10   MURDOCK, KENNETH B.   Literature and Theology in Colonial New
       England.   Cambridge, Mass.:   Harvard University Press,
       p. 183.
          Notes the "transparent clarity" of Edwards's prose.

11   NIEBUHR, REINHOLD.   "Backwards Genius."   Nation 169 (31 Decem-
       ber):648.
          Praises Perry Miller's "brilliant" and "artful" intel-
       lectual biography (1949.9) but finds its claim for
       Edwards's modernity somewhat suspect.

12   RICHARDS, I. A.   Review of Images or Shadows of Divine Things,
       edited by Perry Miller.   New England Quarterly 22 (Septem-
       ber):409-11.
          Uses the publication of Perry Miller's edition of
       Images or Shadows (1948.7) to indict typology (and Ed-
       wards's "proofs of divine design") as a limited and "self-
       destructive" form of metaphor. What is wrong with Ed-
       wards's mode and typology in general is "not extravagance
       but timidity": both refuse to "accept the responsibilities
       of poetic autonomy."

13   SCHAFER, CHARLES H.   "Jonathan Edwards and the Principle of
       Self-love."   Papers of the Michigan Academy of Science,
       Arts, and Letters 35:341-48.
          Considers self-love or pride to be central to Edwards's
       thought, from his earliest speculations (The Mind) to his
       latest (True Virtue), and important to his dismissal from

Northampton. Edwards believed in "the pleasures of humility" and preached it, but when he attacked the self-esteem
of his parishioners over the "bad book" and the new communion qualifications, he was dismissed.

14 SULLIVAN, FRANK. "Jonathan Edwards, the Contemplative Life,
    and a Spiritual Stutter." Los Angeles Tidings, 11 March,
    p. 27.
        Cites a spiritual analogy to physical stuttering in the
    tension between Edwards's disposition to the contemplative
    life and the active life he was thrust into. Personal
    Narrative records his growing hysteria about religion--his
    "spiritual stutter"--as he is deprived of opportunities to
    meditate.

15 SUTER, RUFUS [ORLANDO, JR.]. "An American Pascal: Jonathan
    Edwards." Scientific Monthly 68 (May):338-42.
        Examines Edwards's "brilliantly" conceived scientific
    thought and regrets that, like Pascal before him, a
    "lugubrious" religion cut short a promising career in
    theoretical physics. Edwards's method of inquiry was
    geometrical, using definitions, axioms, postulates, corol-
    laries, lemmata, diagrams, and such; his method of proof
    either deductive or contradictive, proving, as he later
    would in theology, that the opposite proposition was un-
    tenable. His "most exciting" thought involves an analysis
    of the indiscerptibility of atoms, the conclusion that
    matter is solid.

16 TRINTERUD, LEONARD J. The Forming of an American Tradition:
    a Re-examination of Colonial Presbyterianism. Philadel-
    phia: Westminster Press, pp. 127-28, 221-27.
        Refers to the loss of influence of New England Theology
    upon Princeton and academic Presbyterianism with the death
    of Edwards and the presidency of John Witherspoon.

17 TYLER, MOSES COIT. A History of American Literature.
    Ithaca, N.Y.: Cornell University Press, pp. 414-26.
    Reprint of 1878.7.

18 WERKMEISTER, W[ILLIAM] H. A History of Philosophical Ideas
    in America. New York: Ronald Press Co., p. 32.
        Calls it a "strange irony" that the orthodox Edwards
    brought about the separation of church and state through
    the Great Awakening and so destroyed hopes for a Puritan
    theocracy in America.

1949

19   WINSLOW, OLA ELIZABETH. Review of Images or Shadows of Divine
        Things, edited by Perry Miller. William and Mary Quar-
        terly, 3d ser. 6 (January):144-47.
           Recommends Perry Miller's "excellent" introduction
        (1948.7) and welcomes these "private jottings," because
        during his lifetime Edwards printed "some of the wrong
        things." His unpublished work is vital to an evaluation
        of his contribution to religion and philosophy.

1950

1   AIJIAN, PAUL M. "The Relation of the Concepts of Being and
        Value in Calvinism to Jonathan Edwards." Ph.D. disserta-
        tion, University of Southern California.
           Traces the concepts of being and value from the medieval
        to the Calvinistic to the Edwardsean synthesis. To Ed-
        wards, divine sovereignty and power (being) are forms of
        good (value), which man appreciates in essentially aes-
        thetic terms. Edwards's thought reflects a Ramist-Cambridge
        Platonic bent that imparts to his Calvinism a "dynamism of
        movement" permanently affecting American theology.

2   ALDRIDGE, ALFRED OWEN. "Benjamin Franklin and Jonathan Ed-
        wards on Lightning and Earthquakes." Isis 41 (July):162-
        64.
           Claims that Edwards and Franklin did not influence each
        other's ideas on lightning, as I. Bernard Cohen maintained
        (1941.2), but that both had a common source in Ephraim
        Chambers's Cyclopaedia (London, 1728). Edwards seems the
        more original thinker of the two, for he does not limit
        himself to the theories in Chambers.

3   BALDWIN, ALICE M. Review of Jonathan Edwards, by Perry
        Miller. South Atlantic Quarterly 49 (October):520-22.
           Finds Perry Miller's study (1949.9) rewarding but not
        "easy" to read.

4   C., L. "Q1." Explicator 9 (November).
           Asks for the source of Robert Lowell's "After Surprising
        Conversions."

5   DAY, RICHARD ELLSWORTH. Flagellant on Horseback: The Life
        Story of David Brainerd. Philadelphia: Judson Press,
        pp. 171-201.
           Contends that Edwards "blue-penciled with severity"
        David Brainerd's diary to hide the younger minister's

"sacred" love for Jerusha from the public, to chart his
spiritual ups and downs, and to reveal his abject unworthiness and total surrender to God. Edwards's life dominated
Brainerd's and his Life of Brainerd is but an extension of
his own. "For Brainerd was Edwards all over again, a sort
of khaki edition of a Morocco classic."

6   GODWIN, GEORGE. The Great Revivalists. Boston: Beacon
    Press, pp. 113-23 passim.
        Diagnoses Edwards as a psychopath, a "spiritual quack,"
    and the Great Awakening as a classic case of mass hysteria.
    Edwards was sadistic and "half insane," instrumental in
    bringing fear and terror, suicide and melancholia to the
    "simple folk" of New England. Only forced solitude kept
    this "self-tortured prophet" from doing even more harm.

7   HORNBERGER, THEODORE. Review of Images or Shadows of Divine
    Things, edited by Perry Miller. Modern Language Notes 65
    (April):292.
        Finds these paragraphs of Edwards, brought together by
    Perry Miller (1948.7), a "fascinating study" in symbolism
    and psychology, because Edwards "delighted in such unnat-
    ural history as the charming powers of serpents and he
    had a pathological distaste for normal animal functions,
    not to mention pleasures."

8   JOHNSON, THOMAS H[ERBERT]. "Artist in Ideals." Saturday
    Review of Literature 33 (7 January):17-18.
        Praises Perry Miller's acute, deft, and sympathetic
    analysis of Edwards's thought (1949.9) but finds that the
    portrait "lacks immediacy," that Edwards's spirituality,
    humanity, and tragedy are "disembodied." Still this is
    the first time "the artist working with ideas, emerges
    as a world figure."

9   KNOX, R[ONALD] A. Enthusiasm. New York: Oxford University
    Press, pp. 494, 526.
        Calls the "redoubtable" Edwards a "flinty-minded Cal-
    vinist."

10 LARRABEE, HAROLD A. Review of Jonathan Edwards, by Perry
    Miller. New England Quarterly 23 (March):106-109.
        Considers Perry Miller's study (1949.9) a "masterly
    treatise" on colonial American culture, if a somewhat
    exalted view of Edwards.

1950

11   LEWIS, R[ICHARD] W[ARRINGTON] B[ALDWIN]. "The Drama of
      Jonathan Edwards." Hudson Review 3 (Spring):135-40.
         Weighs Perry Miller's "splendid," dramatic intellectual
      history (1949.9) against the "enormous" reservations it
      raises against Edwards's theology, "one of the great false
      philosophies." For all of Miller's art and knowledge Ed-
      wards dwells in "learned ignorance," and his "implacably
      theocentric" theology invites either "immobility or ex-
      cess."

12   MEAD, FRANK S. "Fire Under the Boiler." Presbyterian Life
      3 (September 16):8-10.
         Claims the fiery revival sermons of the "great level-
      lers," Edwards and George Whitefield, "planted the seeds
      of democracy," personalized religion, and founded col-
      leges.

13   MILLER, PERRY. "Edwards, Locke, and the Rhetoric of Sensa-
      tion." In Perspectives in Criticism. Edited by Harry
      Levin. Harvard Studies in Comparative Literature, no. 20.
      Cambridge, Mass.: Harvard University Press, pp. 103-23.
         Characterizes Edwards as a "revolutionary artist" for
      his early and serious acceptance of Locke's theory of
      language--a word is an idea separable from reality or the
      thing itself--in a study of sensationalist psychology
      and rhetoric. But Edwards goes beyond Locke (and Berkeley)
      by insisting that an idea could be comprehended emotion-
      ally as well as intellectually, that it is "a unit of
      experience" sensibly apprehended. Grace becomes, for
      Edwards, a new simple idea learned "only from experience"
      and rhetoric an instrument, however inadequate, to define
      it. (Reprinted in 1956.8.)

14   _____. Review of Jonathan Edwards, The Life and Diary of
      David Brainerd, edited by Philip E. Howard, Jr. New
      England Quarterly 23 (June):277.
         Commends the publication of Philip E. Howard's redac-
      tion of a "classic" of evangelicals (1949.8) as testimony
      of the influence Edwards's text continues to have on the
      American character, an influence "far vaster" probably
      than anything else he wrote.

15   MÜLLER, GUSTAV E. Amerikanische Philosophie. Stuttgart:
      F. Frommann.
         Reprint of 1936.9.

1950

16 ROBERTS, PRESTON. Review of Jonathan Edwards, by Perry
    Miller. Journal of Religion 30 (October):267-70.
        Values Perry Miller's "most important" study (1949.9)
    but finds ambiguous his argument that Edwards based his
    theological insights "wholly within nature" and yet re-
    quired "a transcendent reference" beyond it. How can there
    be a "'history of redemption' and yet no 'redemption in
    history'"?

17 SMITH, H[ILRIE] SHELTON. Review of Images or Shadows of
    Divine Things, edited by Perry Miller. American Litera-
    ture 22 (May):192-94.
        Doubts the evidence sufficient to justify Perry Miller's
    claim in his "brilliant" and imaginative introduction
    (1948.7) that Edwards intended to subordinate Scripture to
    nature, divine revelation to natural images.

18 STOKES, ANSON PHELPS. Church and State in the United States.
    New York: Harper & Brothers, 1:240-43.
        Claims that the Great Awakening "aided" the cause of
    religious liberty and that Edwards, though he "cared little"
    for politics, "contributed mightily" to it. Edwards
    stressed the importance of individual conversion, the
    contrary ends of church and state, and the responsibility
    of man to God alone. These ideas and his return to ortho-
    doxy in his rejection of the half-way covenant "indirectly"
    encouraged religious liberty by forcing a split among
    Congregationalists and by rendering a dominant church
    impossible.

19 SWEET, WILLIAM WARREN. The Story of Religion in America.
    New York: Harper & Brothers.
        Reprint of 1930.14.

20 WACH, JOACHIM. Review of Images or Shadows of Divine Things,
    edited by Perry Miller. Church History 19 (March):66-68.
        Welcomes Perry Miller's study of Edwards's aphorisms
    (1948.7) as a key to his hermeneutics, as a typological
    counter to the then current grammatico-historical inter-
    pretation of Scripture, and as an aid in understanding
    the Christian kerygma today.

21 WADE, MASON. Review of Jonathan Edwards, by Perry Miller.
    Commonweal 51 (27 January):444-45.
        Recommends Perry Miller's "masterly" synthesis (1949.9)
    to Catholics for whom Edwards is a "transitional figure"
    between the medieval schoolmen and Newton and Locke.

1950

22   WALLACE, ETHEL. "A Colonial Parson's Wife, Sarah Pierrepont
     Edwards, 1710-1758, 'And a Very Eminent Christian.'"
     Review and Expositor 47 (January):41-56.
          Describes the holy affection between Edwards and his
     "exceptional" wife in their years together.

23   WINSLOW, OLA ELIZABETH. Review of Jonathan Edwards, by Perry
     Miller. William and Mary Quarterly, 3d ser. 7 (April):279-
     82.
          Considers Perry Miller's "distinguished" study of the
     essential Edwards (1949.9) a "new chance" to measure his
     intellectual stature, his originality, and his modernity.

24   WISH, HARVEY. Society and Thought in Early America. Society
     and Thought in America, no. 1. New York: David McKay Co.,
     pp. 156-58, 166-67.
          Attributes Edwards's methods in the Northampton revival
     to the German Pietists and his dismissal to this tactless-
     ness.

                              1951

1   AKEY, JOHN. "Lowell's 'After Surprising Conversions.'"
     Explicator 9 (June):53.
          Suggests that the date in Lowell's poem, 22 September,
     might be an oblique reference to 2 Kings 22, the text for
     the sermon.

2   ALDRIDGE, ALFRED OWEN. "Edwards and Hutcheson." Harvard
     Theological Review 44 (January):35-53.
          Discovers the "most pronounced" influence on the re-
     lationship between beauty and virtue in Edwards's True
     Virtue to be Francis Hutcheson's An Inquiry into the
     Original of Our Ideas of Beauty and Virtue (1725).
     Edwards's paper is "literally a commentary" on Hutcheson,
     and though he goes further than Hutcheson--putting the
     affections before reason and his faith almost in panthe-
     ism--he concludes "much like" Hutcheson on the prevalence
     in man of a sense of the basis of good and evil.

3   BRADY, MOTHER GERTRUDE V. "Basic Principles of the Philos-
     ophy of Jonathan Edwards." Ph.D. dissertation, Fordham
     University.
          Finds the basic principles of Edwards's philosophy
     "rooted" in the medieval and early Christian tradition and
     "linked" to seventeenth- and eighteenth-century currents
     of thought. Such "tremendous truths" like God's immanence

and imaging, historical providence, theocentrism, and
Christocentrism are developed in Edwards from earlier
sources in profound and brilliant ways and are "indispensable for our time."

4   GAUSTAD, EDWIN S[COTT]. "The Great Awakening in New England,
     1741-1742." Ph.D. dissertation, Brown University.
     Published as 1957.6.

5   GIOVANNI, G. "Lowell's 'After Surprising Conversions.'"
     Explicator 9 (June):53.
         Points to Lowell's "word-for-word copy" of Edwards's
     Faithful Narrative and identifies the suicide as Edwards's
     uncle, Joseph Hawley.

6   HARCOURT, JOHN B. Review of Jonathan Edwards, by Perry
     Miller. American Quarterly 3 (Spring):86-87.
         Reviews six volumes in the American Men of Letters
     Series--Cooper, Edwards, Hawthorne, Melville, Robinson,
     and Thoreau--only to find that Perry Miller's study
     (1949.9), the "most distinguished" of them all, does not
     belong in the series: "Edwards was not a literary artist
     in any meaningful sense of the term."

7   JOHNSON, THOMAS H[ERBERT]. "Jonathan Edwards," Princeton
     University Library Chronicle 12 (Spring):159:60.
         Reports on two Edwards "rarities" at Princeton: the
     ordination sermon for Jonathan Judd, The Great Concern of
     a Watchman for Souls (1743); and a German translation of
     Faithful Narrative (1738), "an instance of Edwards' con-
     tinental reputation."

8   LEARY, LEWIS. Review of Jonathan Edwards, by Perry Miller.
     American Literature, 23 (November):382-84.
         Contends that Perry Miller's Jonathan Edwards (1949.9)
     is "good intellectual biography" but "dangerous intellec-
     tual history" because it slights the background.

9   McLUHAN, JOHN, JR. "Lowell's 'After Surprising Conversions.'"
     Explicator 9 (June):53.
         Calls Lowell's poem an "expansion" of Edwards's letter
     to Benjamin Colman.

*10 McCREARY, EDWARD DANIEL, JR. "Representative Views of the
     Atonement in American Theology; A Study of Jonathan
     Edwards, Horace Bushnell, and Reinhold Niebuhr, Including
     the Major Trends in 18th, 19th and 20th Century American
     Theology." Th.D. dissertation, Union Theological Seminary
     in Virginia.

1951

        Cited in Richard S. Sliwoski, "Doctoral Dissertations on Jonathan Edwards." <u>Early American Literature</u> 14 (Winter 1979):323.

11   MARX, LEO. Review of <u>Jonathan Edwards</u>, by Perry Miller, <u>Isis</u> 42 (June):153–56.
        Characterizes Perry Miller's study (1949.9) as "a surprisingly personal book" about Edwards's "merciless dissection" of Enlightenment beliefs.

12   MILLER, PERRY, "The End of the World." <u>William and Mary Quarterly</u> 3d ser. 8 (April):171–91.
        Notes that the "hidden point" of <u>History of Redemption</u> is Edwards's placement of the millennium before the apocalypse, thus refuting the mechanical-moral model of Thomas Burnet and William Whiston, in a survey of ideas about the end of the world, from Newtonians of the seventeenth century to atomic physicists of the twentieth. (Reprinted in 1956.8.)

13   MURDOCK, KENNETH B. "Jonathan Edwards and Benjamin Franklin." In <u>The Literature of the American People</u>. Edited by Arthur Hobson Quinn. New York: Appleton-Century-Crofts, pp. 106–23.
        Explores Edwards's work and finds some of his best passages to be of "enduring literary importance" even though his "aesthetic perception often outran his stylistic capacity.

14   NICHOLS, JAMES H. Review of <u>Jonathan Edwards</u>, by Perry Miller. <u>Church History</u> 20 (December):75–82.
        Considers Perry Miller's "brilliant apology" (1949.9) "not wholly satisfying" because the focus shifts from Edwards in his time to Miller in ours.

15   PEARCE, ROY HARVEY. "Lowell's 'After Surprising Conversions.'" <u>Explicator</u> 9 (June):53.
        Suggests that "After Surprising Conversions" views the failure of Edwards's mind, and New England Protestant thought generally, in the light of Robert Lowell's "apocalyptic Catholicism."

16   SCHAFER, THOMAS ANTON. "The Concept of Being in the Thought of Jonathan Edwards." Ph.D. dissertation, Duke University.
        Isolates the "purely" ontological element in Edwards

in order to examine its influence upon his theology and ethics. For Edwards, the ontological proof was a "favorite" one, central to understanding the divine outflow in End of Creation or the human response in True Virtue. And though there are unsolved problems and inconsistencies—the heirarchy of being, the ambiguous concept of causality, the conflict between benevolence and complacence, and so on—Edwards's concepts of being and excellence, at the heart of his thought, have "grandeur and beauty."

17 _____. "Jonathan Edwards and Justification by Faith." Church History 20 (December):55-67.

Suggests that Edwards's doctrine of justification by faith occupies "an ambiguous and somewhat precarious place" in his thought, especially in the work of the Stockbridge years, and in the Arminian controversy. Edwards places love or consent at the center of man's salvation, thus bridging the gap between faith and works and avoiding the Arminian disjunction. In his later works, he departs from the early justification by faith alone by defining will to include acts of faith and obedience determined by antecedent inclination; by defining original sin as the initial inclination away from the love of God; and by defining true virtue as a new principle of love identical with God's grace.

18 VAN SCHELVEN, A. A. Het Calvinisme Gedurende Zijn Bloeitijd: Schotland, Engeland, Noord-Amerika. Amsterdam: Uitgeverij W. Ten Have, pp. 396-99.

Notes Edward's role in the Awakening and his interest in spiders, contributions to the pioneer instinct of religion and science in America. (In Dutch.)

19 WHITE, EUGENE E. "Decline of the Great Awakening in New England: 1741 to 1746." New England Quarterly 24 (March):35-52.

Notes that even Edwards's Sinners in the Hands of an Angry God (1741), "probably the most famous discourse in American homiletics," could not stay the decline of religious emotionalism in New England. In five years the Awakening was "practically dead."

1952

1 BAKER, NELSON BLAISDELL. "Anthropological Roots of Jonathan
   Edwards' Doctrine of God." Ph.D. dissertation, University
   of Southern California.
      Discovers Edwards's anthropology rooted in his theology,
   which is conditioned by his familial and intellectual
   experience, his personal needs and religious conversion,
   and his observation of others in the revivals. Upon these
   Edwards founds his anthropological and theological judgments, namely, that he and all men were sinners in God's
   hands and that God is absolute and arbitrary in His saving
   grace. Edwards's doctrine of God reflects "both his psychological needs and the anthropological formulation of his
   solution."

2 BLAU, JOSEPH L. Men and Movements in American Philosophy.
   New York: Prentice-Hall, pp. 12-27, passim.
      Surveys Edwards's philosophy of Lockean-Newtonian ideal-
   ism from the "teasing promise" of his Notes on the Mind to
   his mature treatises and concludes that while there is
   "little vitality" left in his thought, Edwards's "ingenious"
   use of Locke and Newton "set the pattern" of American
   idealism until it was supplanted by a "more sophisticated"
   German idealism in the nineteenth century. Locke remained
   a "strong influence" upon Edwards throughout his career,
   but Newton left only the principle of causation and an
   occasional, sermonic metaphor. Edwards's psychological
   version of Puritanism derives from Locke (Religious
   Affections), his ethical theory from the "durable spring"
   of self-interest (True Virtue), and theology from the
   "keystone" of necessity (Freedom of the Will).

3 LEISY, ERNEST E[RWIN]. Review of Jonathan Edwards, by Perry
   Miller. Southwest Review 37 (Spring):173-74.
      Praises Perry Miller's study (1949.9) of a "greatly
   misunderstood American," even though it stresses Edwards's
   debt to Locke at the expense of Calvin--in a review of five
   volumes in the American Men of Letters series.

4 MILLER, PERRY. "Jonathan Edwards and the Great Awakening."
   In America in Crisis. Edited by Daniel Aaron. New York:
   Alfred A. Knopf, pp. 3-19.
      Contends that Edwards was the "formulator" of political
   and social theories of governance through his work as the
   "most acute definer" of the terms of the Great Awakening.
   By urging experiential religion--the people "had to speak
   up, or else they were lost"--and by insisting that ministers

had to accommodate to the changing congregational reality,
Edwards showed "in political terms" that a public leader
had to adapt to "public welfare and calamity." Such
propositions helped put an end to the reign of "European
and scholastical" theories of social organization and
authority. Americans were now free and capable to judge
for themselves their welfare and threats to it. (Reprinted in 1956.8.)

5   MOSIER, RICHARD D. The American Temper: Patterns of Our
     Intellectual Heritage. Berkeley and Los Angeles: Uni-
     versity of California Press, pp. 79-81.
         Considers Edwards's "creative compromise" in Freedom of
     the Will between the sovereignty of man and the sover-
     eignty of God a crucial statement for both Puritanism and
     republicanism. Edwards's defense, though couched in mod-
     ern, empirical theories, rests upon aristocratic and
     arbitrary principles of governance. Yet he made possible
     at the same time "a kind of democracy in the redemption of
     man by which the aristocracy of Christian grace was quite
     effectively whittled away."

6   PATTERSON, ROBERT LEET. The Philosophy of William Ellery
     Channing. New York: Bookman Associates, pp. 10-15, 39-41,
     passim.
         Characterizes William Ellery Channing's relationship to
     Edwards as one of respect but of deep disagreement.
     Channing studied Edwards--the many references to him bears
     that out--but he was "profoundly antagonized" by Edwards
     on the will and his own thoughts owe little to him. Even
     so, Edwards's intellect and spirituality engaged Channing,
     and he found his mystical insight "extremely congenial."

7   RHOADES, DONALD H[OSEA]. "Jonathan Edwards: America's First
     Philosopher." Personalist 33 (Spring):135-47.
         Summarizes the "basic" philosophy of Edwards, America's
     "least-known philosophical genius," into categories of
     being, causation, value, knowledge, and methodology.
     Edwards's thought, "essentially aesthetic" in nature,
     begins in an "idealistic monism" and becomes in his mature
     years a "naturalistic absolutism," where whatever is, is
     "ultimately" right. But his real service to both religion
     and philosophy lies in his "uneasy and pragmatic compound
     of empiricism, rationalism, and confessional symbolism in
     high Calvinism."

1952

8   ROBACK, A. A. History of American Psychology. New York:
    Library Publishers, pp. 24-31, 105-16.
        Discovers "psychoanalytical adumbrations" in Edwards
    and traces the two-hundred-year-old psychological debate
    occasioned by Freedom of the Will in the studies of James
    Dana (1770.2), Stephen West (1794.3), Thomas Upham
    (1834.6), Henry P. Tappan (1839.8), Jeremiah Day (1841.4),
    Asa Mahan (1846.3), D. D. Whedon (1864.5), Rowland Hazard
    (1864.3). In Man Naturally God's Enemies Edwards "anti-
    cipated" Freud's notion of the Oedipal challenge to the
    ᵴmbolic father; in Original Sin he fashioned a recurrence
    tʰeory "analogous" to Freud's. Like Edwards, Freud is a
    determinist, "the first over determinist in psychology."

9   SCHERMAN, DAVID E., and REDLICH, ROSEMARIE. Literary America:
    A Chronicle of American Writers from 1607-1952 with 173
    Photographs of the American Scene that Inspired Them.
    New York: Dodd, Mead & Co., pp. 20-21.
        Characterizes Edwards as an all-but-forgotten creative
    intellect of the eighteenth century.

*10 SCOTT, LEE OSBOURNE. "The Concept of Love as Universal Dis-
    interested Benevolence in the Early Edwardseans." Ph.D.
    dissertation, Yale University.
        Cited in Comprehensive Dissertation Index 1861-1972,
    32:287.

11 STEPHENSON, GEORGE M. The Puritan Heritage. New York:
    Macmillan Co., pp. 50-55.
        Recounts Edwards's role in the Great Awakening and
    notes the "terrible consistency" in his preaching, from
    the early Justification by Faith Alone to the late Sinners
    in the Hands of an Angry God.

12 TOMAS, VINCENT. "The Modernity of Jonathan Edwards." New
    England Quarterly 25 (March):60-84.
        Attacks Perry Miller's Jonathan Edwards (1949.9), "an
    intellectual biography written as if it were a novel,"
    for obscuring (and falsifying) the real Edwards. For
    "underneath the salad dressing," when Edwards is looked
    at in the generic and specific characteristics of his
    thought, he is, despite Newton and Locke, "a medieval
    philosopher," not the modern empiricist Miller claims
    him to be. This is no more obvious than in Edwards's
    treatment of the "crucial" issue of the source of truth,
    found, for example, in Original Sin. It is from Scrip-
    ture, not experience, that Edwards "'takes orders,'"
    a practice medieval, not modern.

13   TURNBULL, RALPH G. "Jonathan Edwards--Bible Interpreter."
       Interpretation 6 (October):422-35.
          Details the range, use, style, structure, and effects
       of Edwards's sermons, expositions of the "pure gold" of
       Scripture. Edwards "restored" the sermon to its "primacy
       in the centrality" of the worship service because he held
       conversion to be the privilege of the elect, not the
       consequence of the sacraments. A "master" of approaches
       to the will, skilled in "soul surgery," Edwards was a
       passionate advocate of experimental religion then and an
       inspiration to evangelicals today.

<u>1953</u>

1   ANON. "Edwards Anniversary." Princeton Alumni Weekly 54
       (6 November):7-8.
          Traces Edwards's career--at East Windsor, Northampton,
       Stockbridge, and Princeton--in a memorial exhibition at
       Princeton Library of his books, manuscripts, and memora-
       bilia. But the study of his work in university class-
       rooms two centuries after his death is his real memorial.

2   ANON. "Jonathan Edwards is Honored at Yale." New York
       Times, 17 October, p. 17.
          Reports the celebration of Yale's Jonathan Edwards
       College of the 250th anniversary of Edwards's birth and
       the opening at the Library of a special exhibit, "The
       Life and Works of Jonathan Edwards."

3   BRAUER, JERALD C. Protestantism in America: A Narrative
       History. Philadelphia: Westminster Press, pp. 49-50,
       54-55.
          Depicts Edwards's role in the revival of 1734 and in
       the Great Awakening as he "carefully guided" souls to
       comfort and conversion.

4   FAUST, CLARENCE H. "The Decline of Puritanism." In Transi-
       tions in American Literary History. Edited by Harry
       Hayden Clark. Durham, N.C.: Duke University Press,
       pp. 22-26, 30-32, 47.
          Concludes that Edwards's "heroic efforts" to halt the
       decline of Puritanism by revivifying Calvinism with the
       new philosophy failed as political, social, and economic
       changes swept America, in a brief survey of his thought.

1953

5 FEIDELSON, CHARLES, JR. <u>Symbolism and American Literature</u>.
   Chicago: University of Chicago Press, pp. 99–101.
      Asserts that Edwards "anticipated the symbolic con-
   sciousness of Emerson" by reading nature as figuratively
   as he had Scripture. Edwards, a "philosophical symbolist,"
   extended typology to the natural and empirical world of
   the eighteenth century, thus joining religion to science.

6 FERM, VERGILUS. "Editor's Introduction." In his <u>Puritan</u>
   <u>Sage: Collected Writings of Jonathan Edwards</u>. New York:
   Library Publishers, pp. xiii–xxvii.
      Prefaces selections from Edwards, a Puritan sage who
   had "an inherently self-discovered wisdom," with a biography and with serial comments on his work. The "last
   bulwark" of Calvinism before modern thought and a prac-
   ticed mystic withal, Edwards used Newton to support
   causation in the first and Locke to define perception in
   the second. His was a speculative genius haunted by "the
   ghost of theology."

7 _____. "Jonathan Edwards: Puritan Sage." <u>Christian Century</u>
   70 (September 30):1104–1106.
      Offers a brief life and estimate of Edwards, a "puritan
   sage" whose God was aristocratic and parochial and whose
   philosophy was built upon "a plot too narrow" for an
   expanding America of free men.

8 HOLBROOK, CLYDE A[MOS]. "Jonathan Edwards and His Detractors." <u>Theology Today</u> 10 (October):384–96.
      Divides Edwards's critics into those who consider him
   an "evil force" and those who define him as a "tragic
   figure," in an historical survey of his detractors over
   the last two hundred years. The first group indicts
   Edwards for his imprecatory sermons and unyielding theocentrism; the second group deals "more gently" with him,
   decrying the unresolved tensions within him, the scientist
   lost to theology, the irrelevant genius in a changing
   America. The fault, however, lies with his critics:
   either they are predisposed to a liberal theology or they
   are unable to meet his "flaming conviction" of divine
   sovereignty.

9 MacGREGOR, CHARLES P. "The Life and Service of Jonathan
   Edwards and His Message to the Church of Our Day."
   Th.D. dissertation, Boston University.
      Traces Edwards's career, remarks his theology, and
   suggests that what he taught two hundred years ago "needs
   to be emphasized today."

10   MILLER, PERRY. The New England Mind: From Colony to Prov-
       ince. Cambridge, Mass.: Harvard University Press,
       pp. 343-44.
            Contrasts Edwards's experience in New York with Frank-
       lin's in Boston and speculates about the New England
       strain in these two "archsymbols."

11   PARKES, HENRY BAMFORD. The United States of America: A
       History. New York: Alfred A. Knopf, pp. 82-83.
            Sketches Edwards as a child of the Enlightenment, a
       "significant figure" in American cultural history.

*12   SMITH, ALECK L. "Changing Conceptions of God in Colonial New
       England." Ph.D. dissertation, University of Iowa.
            Cited in Comprehensive Dissertation Index 1861-1972,
       32:418.

13   SNYDER, RICHARD L. Letter to the Editor. Christian Century
       70 (28 October):1233.
            Questions Virgilius Ferm's (1953.7) oversimplification
       of Edwards's role in America by citing Perry Miller's
       (1949.9) social and political reading of the matter.

14   STOWE, DAVID M. Letter to the Editor. Christian Century 70
       (28 October):1233-34.
            Disagrees with Vergilius Ferm's (1953.7) anthropomorphic
       characterization of Edwards's God. His "absolute ideal-
       ism" rendered God the perfection of being, not a "gracious
       Christian gentleman."

1954

1   AARON, DANIEL. "Jonathan Edwards." In The Northampton Book.
       Edited by Lawrence E. Wikander et al. Northampton, Mass.:
       Tercentenary Committee, pp. 15-21.
            Recounts Edwards's career in Northampton, an "isolated
       river town," for its tercentenary celebration. Edwards's
       difficulties there stemmed from personal and doctrinal
       rather than political or social differences, as is some-
       times claimed. As a man he was tactless and rigid, as a
       thinker "uncompromising."

2   _____. "Jonathan Edwards's Finely Wrought Sermons Held Real
       Memorial to 'Greatest Theologian and Philosopher Yet Pro-
       duced in Century.'" Hampshire Gazette, 2 March, p. 7.
            Recounts Edwards's career in Northampton, on the oc-
       casion of its tricentennial, and suggests that his

1954

dismissal had more to do with his personal and doctrinal differences than with political or social ones.

3   BOORMAN, JOHN ARTHUR. "A Comparative Study of the Theory of Human Nature as Expressed by Jonathan Edwards, Horace Bushnell and William Adams Brown, Representative American Protestant Thinkers of the Past Three Centuries." Ph.D. dissertation, Columbia University.

Locates Edwards's theory of human nature in his Calvinist doctrine of absolute sovereignty and his idea of "radical" conversion, derived in part from Locke, Newton, and Hutcheson. Bushnell rejects Calvinism and so his theory is "more optimistic and moralistic" than Edwards's. Brown subscribed to Darwinism and sees progress for man through church participation.

4   CHESLEY, ELIZABETH. "Ode to Jonathan Edwards." Woman's Home Companion 81 (July):49.

Composes nine stanzas about Edwards's view of infant damnation and closes with "That you think them vipers may not be odd,/But speak for yourself, John--not for God."

5   CUNLIFFE, MARCUS. The Literature of the United States. London: Penguin Books, pp. 32-33.

Refers to Edwards as an eighteenth-century philosopher with a "pantheistic tinge."

6   FLYNT, WILLIAM T. "Jonathan Edwards and His Preaching." Th.D. dissertation, Southern Baptist Theological Seminary.

Studies Edwards's personality and environment as forces that affect his message and manner as a preacher; comments upon his use of Scripture, his sermonic style and structure, and the intellectual and imaginative qualities of selected sermons; and measures his contributions to religious thought, social and humanitarian movements, preaching, and modern missions.

7   FOSTER, CHARLES H. The Rungless Ladder: Harriet Beecher Stowe and New England Puritanism. Durham, N.C.: Duke University Press, pp. 179-84, 189-93 passim.

Traces Edwards's influence, often contrary, upon Harriet Beecher Stowe and her work, especially The Minister's Wooing and Oldtown Folks. Edwards became a figure she struggled with, an archetype of orthodoxy in the theology of sin and grace, though it is obvious that she seriously misread his role in the intellectual history of New England.

8   GAUSTAD, EDWIN S[COTT]. "The Theological Effects of the
Great Awakening in New England." Mississippi Valley Historical Review 40 (March):681-706.
    Discovers in Edwards "a continuity" between the reviv-
als of 1734 and 1741--he was an "amazed spectator and
reporter" of the first, a "vigorous apologist and leading
theologian" of the second--and explores the "very significant" effects revivalism had upon his work and his
school, New England Theology, in a serial history of the
Awakening. Edwards's personal piety and the many cases
of conscience he witnessed and recorded made divine grace
"an immediate indwelling reality" and a focus of his
theology and that of his disciples, Joseph Bellamy and
Samuel Hopkins. The Great Awakening, by calling attention
to his theological views, "forced" Edwards to unexpected
conclusions--Religious Affections and Qualifications, for
example--and effected a protracted defense of Calvinism
and absolute sovereignty in his later years--Freedom of
the Will, Original Sin, and True Virtue.

*9   LAVENGOOD, LAWRENCE G. "The Great Awakening and New England
Society." Ph.D. dissertation, University of Chicago.
    Cited in Comprehensive Dissertation Index 1861-1972,
35:614.

10   McNEILL, JOHN T. The History and Character of Calvinism.
New York: Oxford University Press, pp. 361-63.
    Points out that while Edwards added "humane" elements
to Calvin, he thought (and preached) of hell as physical
torment rather than as the spiritual alienation Calvin
understood.

11   PERSONS, STOW. "The Cyclical Theory of History in Eighteenth
Century America." American Quarterly 6 (Summer):147-63.
    Notes that Edwards's theory of history as the "unfold-
ing revelation of divine purpose" is at odds with others
in the eighteenth century.

12   RICE, HOWARD C., JR. "Jonathan Edwards at Princeton."
Princeton University Library Chronicle 15 (Winter):69-89.
    Recounts Edwards's connections to Princeton and re-
prints eight Edwards letters and manuscripts and describes
all other items--"waifs and strays"--acquired chiefly
through gift to the College.

1954

13   SMITH, CHARD POWERS. Yankees and God. New York: Hermitage
        House, pp. 244-53, 259-63.
            Discusses the rise and fall of American Puritanism and
        distinguishes between first and second forms of it, the
        first tending toward Arminianism under Thomas Hooker until
        1650, the second toward Antinomianism under Edwards until
        1750. Edwards accepted the materialism of Newton and
        the sensationalism of Locke, developed an idealism in
        which God was "incomprehensible" to reason, and fashioned
        a creative aesthetic akin to the experience of grace.
        The "tragedy" of our first "major modern mind" was a
        failure to find in men an imagination comparable to his.
        A decade later, emotion spent, all fell before reason.

14   SMITH, JOHN E. Review of Jonathan Edwards: Puritan Sage,
        by Virgilius Ferm. Arizona Quarterly 10 (Spring):83.
            Condemns the price, printing, and binding of Virgilius
        Ferm's "boon" to students of Edwards (1953.6).

15   STROMBERG, ROLAND N. Religious Liberalism in Eighteenth-
        Century England. New York: Oxford University Press,
        pp. 114, 118, 121.
            Notes Edwards's lonely, Calvinist battle against
        Arminianism and the optimism of the eighteenth century
        and likens him to Bernard Mandeville in his denial of
        virtue to natural, selfish man.

16   TAYLOR, ROBERT J. Western Massachusetts in the Revolution.
        Providence: Brown University Press, pp. 45-51.
            Recounts the history of opposition between the Williams
        family and Edwards, especially Israel Williams's role in
        Edwards's dismissal. With the death in 1748 of Colonel
        Stoddard, Williams openly challenged the minister's
        authority on profession and communion, put the question
        of church membership to a precinct meeting, and forced
        neighboring churches to call a council. At Williams's
        urging, Joseph Hawley viciously attacked Edwards at these
        meetings; five years later he recanted, publicly asked
        forgiveness from Edwards, and became a political enemy of
        Williams.

17   YODER, DONALD HERBERT. "Christian Unity in Nineteenth-Century
        America." In A History of the Ecumenical Movement, 1517-
        1948. Edited by Ruth Rouse and Stephen Charles Neill.
        Philadelphia: Westminster Press, pp. 221-59.
            Cites Edwards as an example of the "unitive influence
        of revivalism" through his desire for a concert of prayer

and notes his influence on revival practice in the nineteenth, but not the eighteenth, century.

1955

1   ANON. "Jonathan Edwards's Works to be Published by Yale."
    Hampshire Gazette, 29 January, pp. 1, 11.
        Notes the forthcoming Yale Edwards and an earlier
    display of memorabilia there.

2   ANON. "Services Sunday to Mark Edwards' 252nd Birthday."
    Hampshire Gazette, 6 October, p. 21.
        Notes the coming celebration of his birth at the Ed-
    wards Congregational Church, Northampton.

3   BEACH, WALDO, and NIEBUHR, H. RICHARD, eds. Christian Ethics:
    Sources of the Living Tradition. New York: Ronald Press
    Co., pp. 380-89.
        Maintains that Edwards's "primary" concern was ethical,
    that his unitive system of thought agrees and disagrees
    with naturalistic and idealistic movements of historical
    Christian ethics, and reprints selections from True Vir-
    tue. Edwards is both "radically realistic," accepting
    self-interest and moral relativity, and "radically ideal-
    istic," insisting upon possibilities beyond man's achieve-
    ment. History, for Edwards, traces man's progress of
    redemption from self-love to love of being, from self-
    glorification to glorification of God, from parochial
    views of theology and politics to "wide vistas" of uni-
    versal society and love of God.

4   DAVIES, A. MERVYN. The Foundation of American Freedom.
    New York: Abington Press, p. 196.
        Notes that Edwards was the only "authentic" Calvinist
    of his time.

5   LEWIS, R[ICHARD] W[ARRINGTON] B[ALDWIN]. The American Adam:
    Innocence, Tragedy, and Tradition in the Nineteenth Cen-
    tury. Chicago: University of Chicago Press, pp. 62-66.
        Compares Edwards to the elder Henry James and Horace
    Bushnell on original sin and finds Edwards's doctrine
    "out of harmony" with his times and his scientific defense
    of it "too far advanced." Edwards was trying to revital-
    ize a dying Puritanism with the theories of Locke and
    Newton: he was "not trying to set the clock back, he
    was trying to set it right." And unlike the Edwardseans,

213

> who were precursors of the party of Memory, or their
> opponents, who were precursors of the party of Hope,
> Edwards (and James and Bushnell) had "the more flexible
> outlook of the tertium quid."

6 MORRIS, WILLIAM SPARKES. "The Young Jonathan Edwards: A
   Reconstruction." Ph.D. dissertation, University of Chicago.
      Demonstrates "as conclusively as possible" that the
   "major part" of Edwards's metaphysics derives from the
   Dutch scholastic Calvinists and logicians Franciscus
   Burgersdicius and Adrian Heereboord, in an extensive
   reconstruction of how Edwards came to think what he did,
   from his years at home to his months in New York, and how
   he integrated theology and philosophy.

7 SCHAFER, THOMAS A[NTON]. "Jonathan Edwards' Conception of
   the Church." Church History 24 (March):51-66.
      Defends Edwards's ecclesiology against the charge that
   his revivalist impulses sundered the Church by showing
   that his ontology, cosmology, and eschatology support its
   central role in redemption as the society of the elect
   and the body of Christ. Edwards merges the covenant of
   grace in the covenant of redemption, considering the
   visible church, with its worship, preaching, and sacraments, to be "the means by which God inducts men" into
   His society. A Presbyterian more than a Congregationalist
   in church polity, Edwards advocated church unity and
   ecumenical worship in his Humble Attempt.

8 SMITH, H[ILRIE] SHELTON. Changing Conceptions of Original
   Sin: A Study in American Theology Since 1750. New York:
   Charles Scribner's Sons, pp. 27-36, passim.
      Claims that Edwards's "unusually penetrating polemic"
   against John Taylor was instrumental in keeping the
   original sin controversy alive for many years, even
   though his "spectacular" theory of imputation and personal identity "fell flat" with his theological successors, and recounts the argument of Original Sin, in a
   survey of the doctrine over the last two centuries.

9 SPILLER, ROBERT E. The Cycle of American Literature: An
   Essay in Historical Criticism. New York: Macmillan Co.,
   pp. 10-12.
      Divides Edwards's work and life into three periods:
   the philosophical inquiries of the Yale years, the
   emotional sermons of the revival years, and the logical

treatises of the Stockbridge years. Edwards adumbrates
later American writers--Poe, Hawthorne, Melville, O'Neill,
Eliot, and Faulkner--in his "structure of tragic realization," and ranks with Franklin and Jefferson as one of
three "architects" of America.

10 TOWNSEND, HARVEY G[ATES]. Introduction to his The Philosophy
of Jonathan Edwards from His Private Notebooks. University of Oregon Monographs: Studies in Philosophy, no. 2.
Eugene, Ore.: University Press, pp. v-xxi.
Offers "a coherent body of the philosophical opinions"
of Edwards by printing Of Being, The Mind, and selections
from the Miscellanies, early and private work that ex-
presses his "radical idealism." The source for Edwards's
idealism is a "long line" of Christian Platonists and
John Locke, not Bishop Berkeley; the source for his
rationalism and his belief in the "absolute reign of
universal law," the very "basis" of his philosophy, is
Isaac Newton.

11 WINN, RALPH B. "Jonathan Edwards." In his American Philosophy. New York: Philosophical Library, pp. 233-34.
Offers a brief life of Edwards, a question about his
originality, and a commendation for his polemics.

12 WRIGHT, [CHARLES] CONRAD. "The Freedom of the Will." In
his The Beginnings of Unitarianism in America. Boston:
Starr King Press, pp. 91-114.
Reprint of revised 1942.13.

1956

1 ALBERT, FRANK J. Review of The Philosophy of Jonathan Edwards from His Private Notebooks. Edited by Harvey G.
Townsend. Encounter 17 (Winter):86-87.
Finds that Harvey G. Townsend's book (1955.10) succeeds
in establishing Edwards as an important philosopher.

2 BERG, JOHANNES Van Den. Constrained by Jesus' Love: An
Inquiry into the Motives of the Missionary Awakening in
Great Britain in the Period between 1698-1815. Kampen
[the Netherlands]: J. H. Kok, pp. 83, 91-93 passim.
Ascribes to Edwards a great deal of the stimulus given
the missionary spirit in England and Scotland through his
work in the Great Awakening and his publication of Humble
Attempt and the Life of Brainerd. To Edwards as well

1956

belongs the "positive function" eschatology played in the
development of missionary thought here and abroad.

3   BROWN, ARTHUR W. Always Young for Liberty: A Biography of
    William Ellery Channing. Syracuse, N.Y.: Syracuse Uni-
    versity Press, pp. 98-101.
        Recounts William Ellery Channing's mixed reactions to
    Edwards. Channing was unnerved by enthusiasm but approved
    Edwards's religious affections; he was impressed by his
    logical consistency on the will but appalled by his doc-
    trine of necessity.

4   CLARK, GEORGE PIERCE. "An Unpublished Letter by Jonathan
    Edwards." New England Quarterly 29 (June):228-33.
        Reprints a letter, 7 May 1750, from Edwards to Peter
    Clark, pastor at Salem Village; notes that it is quoted
    at length in the preface to Farewell Sermon; and cites
    its "relevancy to the controversy" of his dismissal the
    following month.

5   COLLMER, R. G. "Two Antecedents for a Metaphor from Jonathan
    Edwards." Notes and Queries, n.s. 3 (September):396.
        Cites two antecedents--there may be more--to Edwards's
    metaphor of the dangling sinner: the medieval mystic
    William Hinton in his Scale of Perfection and the counter-
    reformer Luis de Granada in his Of Prayer and Meditation.

6   GERSTNER, JOHN H. Review of The Philosophy of Jonathan
    Edwards from His Private Notebooks, edited by Harvey G.
    Townsend. New England Quarterly 29 (September):422-24.
        Considers Harvey G. Townsend's study (1955.10) "useful
    and essential" but cites the need for an "adequate state-
    ment" of Edwards's philosophical system.

7   HITCHCOCK, ORVILLE [A]. Review of The Philosophy of Jonathan
    Edwards from His Private Notebooks, edited by Harvey G.
    Townsend. Quarterly Journal of Speech 42 (December):440.
        Welcomes Harvey G. Townsend's collection (1955.10) for
    the help it affords the critics of colonial rhetoric and
    the student of Edwards's oratory.

8   MILLER, PERRY. Errand into the Wilderness. Cambridge, Mass.:
    Harvard University Press, pp. 48-98, 153-66, 167-83, 184-
    203, 217-39.
        Reprints "The Marrow of Puritan Divinity" (1935.6);
    "Jonathan Edwards and the Great Awakening" (1952.4);

"Edwards, Locke, and the Rhetoric of Sensation" (1950.13);
"From Edwards to Emerson" (1940.9); and "The End of the
World" (1951.12).

9   _____. Review of The Philosophy of Jonathan Edwards from His
       Private Notebooks, edited by Harvey G. Townsend. American
       Literature 28 (May):236-37.
           Dismisses Harvey G. Townsend's study (1955.10) for his
       "capricious principles of selection and his ignorance of
       the general bearing of the entries" in a misconceived
       attempt to prove Edwards a philosopher rather than "a
       major religious figure."

10   OBERHOLZER, EMIL, JR. Delinquent Saints: Disciplinary Action
       in the Early Congregational Churches of Massachusetts.
       New York: Columbia University Press, pp. 19-21, 23-24.
           Claims that Edwards introduced "real Calvinism" to
       Congregational churches in Massachusetts and that he
       eschewed the covenant theology of his Puritan forebears.

11   SMITH, H[ILRIE] SHELTON. Review of Jonathan Edwards: Puritan
       Sage, by Virgilius Ferm. South Atlantic Quarterly 55
       (January):119-20.
           Faults Virgilius Ferm's introduction (1953.6) for being
       too sketchy to be of much worth, his selections for being
       too short to be of much significance. Faust and John-
       son's text (1935.3) is better on both counts.

12   TAYLOR, WALTER FULLER. The Story of American Letters.
       Chicago: Henry Regnery Co., pp. 27-33.
           Revises 1936.11.

13   WARREN, AUSTIN. New England Saints. Ann Arbor: University
       of Michigan Press, pp. 25-26.
           Counts Edwards among "our few American saints," a
       philosopher, ascetic, mystic.

14   WRIGHT, [CHARLES] CONRAD. Review of The Philosophy of Jona-
       than Edwards from His Private Notebooks, edited by Harvey
       G. Townsend. William and Mary Quarterly, 3d ser. 13
       (July):411-12.
           Questions the value for scholars of Harvey G. Town-
       send's selections from the Miscellanies (1955.10), for
       his justification of Edwards as philosopher rather than
       theologian seems unnecessary and unrewarding.

1957

1   BAINTON, ROLAND H. Yale and the Ministry. New York: Harper
    & Brothers, pp. 15-24, 52-56, passim.
        Describes the effect Yale had upon the young Edwards
    and the influence he later exerted at Yale. Both his
    knowledge of the depravity of man and the new sense of
    the glory of God come from his Yale years. His theology,
    a fusion of Calvin, Cudworth, and Newton, and "enriched"
    with pietism, is of that time and that place. Later,
    through Samuel Hopkins and Timothy Dwight, the Beechers
    and Horace Bushnell, Edwards found his way back to Yale.

2   BARNHOUSE, DONALD GREY. "The Restoration of Jonathan Ed-
    wards." Eternity 8 (September):4-5, 46-47.
        Views with pleasure the "remarkable" restoration of
    Edwards, for it is part of the general movement away from
    liberal Christianity to a more conservative position.

3   BELKNAP, GEORGE N. "Letter to the Editor." American Litera-
    ture 28 (January):525.
        Corrects Perry Miller's misunderstanding of Harvey
    Townsend's comment in his The Philosophy of Jonathan
    Edwards (1955.10) on the importance of End of Creation
    and True Virtue.

4   CONRAD, LESLIE, JR. "Jonathan Edwards' Pattern for Preach-
    ing." Church Management 33 (September):45-47.
        Offers Edwards's sermonic pattern to today's minister
    who "really means business." The pattern always begins
    with subject, text, and introduction but then develops
    into either doctrinal discussion and application or
    three to nine sections of argument.

5   COOMBE, JACK DUNCAN. Consider My Servant: A Novel Based
    upon the Life of Jonathan Edwards. New York: Exposition
    Press, 160 pp.
        Fashions a novel of the "human" Edwards in his North-
    ampton years, from his ordination to his farewell sermon,
    by getting beneath "the traditional veneer of his schol-
    arliness and Puritan composure," by taking "some liberty
    with the facts," and by inventing some events and charac-
    ters. So Sarah never really hears the whole of his ordi-
    nation sermon. "She was too much in her own secret world.
    Her thoughts were too sacred to be jarred by some theo-
    logical discourse--even if it was from her lover." And
    so Samuel Sewall hears Edwards's God Glorified delivered
    in Boston 8 July 1731, though he died 1 January 1730.

6 GAUSTAD, EDWIN SCOTT. The Great Awakening in New England.
New York: Harper & Brothers, pp. 18-24, 81-101, 134-139
passim.
Narrates the struggle over the meaning of the Great
Awakening by the two "great champions" of reason and
faith, Charles Chauncy and Edwards, in a study of revivalism and its institutional and theological effects. To
Edwards religion was an empirical affair of the heart and
the Awakening "a large and timely laboratory of experience"; to Chauncy the emotion of the Awakening contra-
dicted the reasonableness of religion. In 1741 there was
"no sharp clash" theologically between the two; by 1742
their views began to harden; by 1743 their separation was
"fully apparent," first expressed in Edwards's Some
Thoughts and then answered in Chauncy's Seasonable Thoughts.
"The intellectual bifurcation, began as a dispute over
the significance and propriety of 'Shriekings and Scream-
ings,' was soon to become a contest over the nature of God
and the constitution of man."

7 GERSTNER, JOHN H. "American Calvinism until the Twentieth
Century Especially in New England." In American Calvinism: A Survey. Edited by Jacob T. Hoogstra. Grand
Rapids, Mich.: Baker Book House, pp. 13-39.
Refutes the charge that Edwards was "guilty of more or
less deviation" from orthodox Calvinism and the source of
New England defection and finds his work on the will, for
example, "utterly Calvinistic" and that on justification
"pure Calvinism." What deviation did take place was a
reaction to his strict Calvinism: the Arminian reaction
gave rise to Unitarianism; the Pelagian reaction led to
either hyper-Calvinism or hypo-Calvinism; and the Princetonians developed a peculiar brand of Edwardsean Calvinism, that of Alexander, Hodge, Patton, and Warfield.
Contrary to W. J. Burggraaff in his study of liberal
theology (1928.2), Edwards was "thoroughly" Calvinistic.

8 HENDERSON, G. D. "Jonathan Edwards and Scotland." In his
The Burning Bush: Studies in Scottish Church History.
Edinburgh: Saint Andrew Press, pp. 151-62.
Reprint of 1944.2.

*9 HOFFMAN, GERHARD. "Seinsharmonie und Heilsgeschichte bei
Jonathan Edwards." Th.D. dissertation, Göttingen Univer-
sity.
Cited in James Woodress, Dissertations in American
Literature, 1891-1966 (Durham, N.C.: Duke University
Press, 1968), item 641.

1957

10 JOHNSON, THOMAS H[ERBERT]. Review of Freedom of the Will,
    edited by Paul Ramsey. New York Times Book Review, 23
    June, p.7.
        Hopes the rest of the Yale Edwards will adhere to Paul
    Ramsey's standard of editing (1957.14).

11 McGRAW, JAMES. "The Preaching of Jonathan Edwards."
    Preacher's Magazine 32 (August):9-12.
        Praises Edwards's preaching more for its thought than
    its eloquence, more for its logic than its rhetoric.

12 MORRIS, WILLIAM S[PARKES]. "The Reappraisal of Edwards."
    New England Quarterly 30 (December):515-25.
        Recites a short history of Edwards criticism--from the
    theological concerns of the eighteenth and nineteenth
    centuries to the philosophical ones of the early twenti-
    eth to the biographical of the last twenty-five years--and
    suggests that the initial volume of the Yale Edwards,
    Paul Ramsey's edition of Freedom of the Will (1957.14),
    is the "first evident sign" of the necessary reappraisal
    of Edwards, America's "greatest genius of her native
    intellectual heritage." Although Ramsey's introduction
    is strained at times and more analytical than psychologi-
    cal, it remains an "archtype" of editorial work, especially
    in the "masterly" historical analyses of the relationship
    of Edwards to John Locke and to the Arminians.

13 MURRAY, JOHN. "The Imputation of Adam's Sin: Third Article."
    Westminster Theological Journal 19 (May):141-69.
        Distinguishes Edwards's view of the imputation of
    original sin from that of New England Theology--Dwight,
    Emmons, Hopkins, and Taylor, and later, Hodge--as one
    between immediate and mediate. In Original Sin,
    Edwards held that hereditary corruption is consequent upon
    and is a penal consequence of Adam's sin and insisted
    that the sin as imputed includes, like Adam's, both the
    sinful disposition prior to the act and the act itself.

14 RAMSEY, PAUL. "Editor's Introduction." In Freedom of the
    Will. The Works of Jonathan Edwards, vol. 1. New Haven
    and London: Yale University Press, pp. 1-128.
        Traces the provenance, the theological issues, and the
    still-unresolved philosophical arguments of Freedom of
    the Will--liberty and necessity, responsibility and self-
    determination, moral and natural necessity; Edwards's
    relationship to Locke and to his antagonists; and his
    effective and eloquent style, in an introduction to the
    first volume of the Yale Edwards. Edwards defines
    liberty, analyzes acts of volition, and interprets

responsibility in such a way--"Edwards merely places in
brackets . . . his belief in divine determination"--
that he can show that universal causation applies to the
will, just as every event is caused or determined, though
not, he points out, compelled. Edwards's "philosophical
lineage" begins in Locke's Essay Concerning Human Understanding, especially "Of Power," but ends in his rejection of key definitions and language, of the
disjunction between faculties of the mind, and of the
distinction between object and act, as Locke revised
his text and Edwards's matured his thought. If "insufficient attention" has been given to the "actual" influence
of Locke, still less has been given to Edwards's detailed
refutation of Thomas Chubb, Daniel Whitby, and Isaac
Watts, men who represented the deist, Anglican, and
dissenting points of view, and regarded by Edwards as
necessary to his attack upon Arminianism on all fronts.

15   SARGANT, WILLIAM. Battle for the Mind: A Physiology of
     Conversion and Brain-Washing. Garden City, N.Y.:
     Doubleday & Co., pp. 140-41, 148-52.
        Culls passages from Faithful Narrative to illustrate
     the physiological mechanisms Edwards exploited in
     controlling thought and eliciting confessions and finds
     the practice reprehensible. Such methods of brain-
     washing and behavior modification found in Stalinist
     Russia are no more rigid nor intolerant than those in
     Edwardsean Northampton.

16   STALLKNECHT, NEWTON P. Review of Freedom of the Will, edited
     by Paul Ramsey. Indiana Magazine of History 53 (December):
     449-52.
        Questions the "uncritically enthusiastic" attitude of
     both Paul Ramsey (1957.14) and Perry Miller (1949.9) in
     granting Edwards philosophical significance and modernity.
     Edwards is, rather, a brilliant apologist who "plundered"
     Newton and Locke to serve his religious convictions.

17   STEWART, JAMES A., ed. Jonathan Edwards: The Narrative.
     Grand Rapids, Mich. Kregel Publications, 82 pp.
        Interleaves comments in an abridgment of Edwards's
     letter to Benjamin Colman and adds a biography, the
     story of the Great Awakening, and case histories of
     conversion. Faithful Narrative is a "priceless document"
     for evangelists, a "veritable gold mine," a "helpful
     textbook," a "spiritual classic."

1957

18   WEBBER, F. R.   A History of Preaching in Britain and America.
        Northwestern Publishing House, Part 3, pp. 83-90.
            Lays Edwards's troubles at Northampton to his
        unremitting preaching of the severity of the law with-
        out the tempering influence of the gospel. Yet his
        effect on New England theology and on the American
        pulpit was lasting: both were now subject to a
        clergy not only intellectually trained but spiritually
        alive.

                                1958

1   ANON. "Famous Theologian's Church Honors Former Pastor
        Sunday; Descendant to Attend Rites." Hampshire Gazette,
        2 October, p. 1.
            Notes that Edwin Sponseller, minister of the First
        Church, will pay tribute to Edwards and that Edwards's
        great-great-great-great-great-great-granddaughter will
        attend.

2   ANON. "Jonathan Edwards Reinstated." Christian Century 75
        (2 April):397.
            Notes the bicentennial tribute to Edwards at North-
        ampton, a belated penance and reinstatement that "would
        not have meant too much to him."

3   ANON. "Jonathan Edwards to be Honored Today by Bay State
        Church that Ousted Him." New York Times, 9 March,
        p. 59.
            Reports the coming memorial service for Edwards at
        the First Church of Christ, Congregational, in North-
        ampton, and offers a brief life and the cause for his
        dismissal from the founding church. H. Richard
        Niebuhr will preach at a special afternoon service.

4   BEACH, WALDO. "The Recovery of Jonathan Edwards: A Review."
        Religion in Life 27 (Spring):286-89.
            Welcomes the Yale edition of Freedom of the Will
        (1957.14) as an indication of the recovery of Edwards
        and praises Paul Ramsey's cogent, if prolix, introduction.
        "That the general editorial committee is headed by a
        Harvard Professor and this volume edited by a Prince-
        ton professor is the mark of a kind of intellectual
        ecumenicity in the Ivy League, and of its common roots
        in New England Calvinism."

5   BEAVER, R. PIERCE. "The Concert for Prayer for Missions:
An Early Venture in Ecumenical Action." Ecumenical
Review, 10 (July), 420-27.
       Claims Edwards's Humble Attempt, instrumental in
promoting world-wide prayer days in the nineteenth
century, fostered common action and suggested millennial
consequences.

6   BROWN, CHARLES T. "Jonathan Edwards in 1958." Minister's
Quarterly 14 (Summer):34-35.
       Cites the need for Edwards's "burning concept of sin"
to bring contemporary man to redemption, in a notice
of Edwards's death 200 years ago.

7   FAUST, CLARENCE H. Ideological Conflicts in Early American
Books. Syracuse, N.Y.: Syracuse University Press, pp.
13-14.
       Notes that emotion mattered more to Edwards than
abstract reasoning.

8   FERM, ROBERT O. Cooperative Evangelism. Grand Rapids, Mich.:
Zondervan Publishing House, pp. 49-51.
       Likens the censure of Edwards as an evangelist, though
not a major one, to that suffered by Billy Graham at the
hands of the orthodox.

*9   GRAZIER, JAMES LEWIS. "The Preaching of Jonathan Edwards:
A Study of his Published Sermons with Special Reference
to the Great Awakening." Ph.D. dissertation, Temple
University.
       Cited in Gillette, "A checklist of Doctoral Disserta-
tions . . ." (1967.12) p. 207.

10   [HENRY, CARL F. H.] "Jonathan Edwards' Still Angry God."
Christianity Today 2 (6 January):20-21.
       Urges sinful man to heed again Edwards's still angry
God, on the bicentennial of that prophet's death.

11   HUGHES, PHILIP EDGCUMBE. "Jonathan Edwards on Revival."
Christianity Today 2 (15 September):3-4.
       Asks evangelicals, on the bicentennial of Edwards's
death, to turn to his study of the revivals--Faithful
Narrative, Distinguishing Marks, Some Thoughts, Religious
Affections--for his scriptual insight is as "relevant to
our day as it was to his."

1958

12   JONES, ADAM LEROY. <u>Early American Philosophers</u>.   New York:
        Frederick Ungar Publishing Co.
           Reprint of 1898.5.

13   KAWERAU, PETER. "Jonathan Edwards (1703-1758)." In his
        <u>Amerika und die Orientalischen Kirchen: Ursprung und</u>
        <u>Anfang der Amerikanischen Mission unter den Nationalkirchen</u>
        <u>Westasiens</u>. Berlin: Walter de Gruyter & Co., pp. 1-74.
           Traces the doctrine of the divine light and its effect
        upon the nature of fallen man and workings of redemptive
        history, in a detailed examination of Edwards's view of
        the clergy and the revivals, covenant and sacrament, the
        millennium and the concert of prayer. As the old conti-
        nent gave physical birth to Christ, Edwards argued, so the
        new continent would give spiritual birth to Him through a
        wise and pure ministry spreading the Word. Thus the hopes
        of <u>History of Redemption</u> and <u>Humble Attempt</u> would be real-
        ized and America's mission fulfilled. (In German.)

*14 LONG, GEORGE W., JR. "Jonathan Edwards, 1703-1758: His
        Theory and Practice of Evangelism." Ph.D. dissertation,
        University of Edinburgh.
           Not seen except for Table of Contents.

15   METCALF, GEORGE REUBEN. "American Religious Philosophy and
        the Pastoral Letters of the House of Bishops." <u>Historical</u>
        <u>Magazine of the Protestant Episcopal Church</u> 27 (March):
        10-84.
           Deals briefly with Edwards and Samuel Johnson as early
        "representative" philosophers in a history of Episcopali-
        anism in America. Both were immaterialists and idealists,
        yet one was a Congregationalist and the other an Anglican.

16   MURRAY, IAIN H. "A Memoir of Jonathan Edwards." In his <u>The</u>
        <u>Select Works of Jonathan Edwards</u>. London: Banner of
        Truth Trust. 1:13-62.
           Offers a brief life of Edwards, an estimate of his pub-
        lications--the "most valuable" today are <u>Distinguishing</u>
        <u>Marks</u>, <u>Religious Affections</u>, and <u>Some Thoughts</u>--and a
        plea to return to his "fearless" ministry.

17   PERSONS, STOW. <u>American Minds: A History of Ideas</u>. New
        York: Holt, Rinehart & Winston, pp. 106-109 passim.
           Fits Edwards into the intellectual development of
        eighteenth-century America through his part in the "con-
        tinuing vitality" of religion then. Religion, to the
        enlightened mind, was either reasonable or a fact of

experience; to Edwards it was both. Though he remained "impervious" to some ideas of the time, he was not the anachronism Parrington depicts (1927.2).

18 PRATT, GLENN RALPH. "Jonathan Edwards as a Preacher of Doctrine." S.T.D. dissertation, Temple University.

Refutes the view of Edwards as an imprecatory preacher of hell-fire and finds his sermons "remarkable" for their biblical and doctrinal balance. Edwards renders doctrines from both the Old and the New Testaments and balances systematically his preaching of 1300 sermons in theology, anthropology, Christology, soteriology, ethics, ecclesiology. Of 655 sermons, 500 stress "hope, joy, and blessing"; only 155 center on damnation and hell.

19 QUINCER, SHELDON B., ed. Jonathan Edwards' Sermon Outlines. The World's Great Sermons in Outline, vol. 5. Grand Rapids, Mich.: William B. Eerdmans Publishing Co., 164 pp.

Reprints thirty-five "choice" sermon outlines of Edwards and quotes with approval B. B. Warfield's dictum, "'It was in his sermons that Edwards' studies bore their richest fruit.'"

20 RILEY, I. WOODBRIDGE. "Jonathan Edwards." In his American Philosophy: The Early Schools. New York: Russell & Russell.

Reprint of 1907.6.

21 SCHNEIDER, HERBERT WALLACE. The Puritan Mind. Ann Arbor: University of Michigan Press.

Reprint of 1930.13.

22 SETTLE, RAYMOND W. "Colonial Religious Awakenings: The New England Revival, 1734." Christianity Today 2 (15 September):15–17.

Recounts Edwards's efforts in 1734 to awaken religious interest among the young of Northampton, his sermon series on justification by faith, the revival's subsequent spread to nearby communities, and its development into the Great Awakening.

23 STEWART, RANDALL. American Literature and Christian Doctrine. Baton Rouge: Louisiana State University Press, pp. 8–15.

Extols Edwards as "our first Protestant American saint." Not only is he America's greatest theologian and philosopher, but in his logic and ordonnance, tenderness and beauty, our greatest writer before the nineteenth

century, a rare balance of head and heart. Edwards is an
"un-Emersonian" transcendentalist whose Divine and Supernatural Light is the "finest statement" of experiential
religion to date.

24 TURNBULL, RALPH G. "Jonathan Edwards and Great Britain."
Evangelical Quarterly 30 (April–June):68–74.
Indicates that Edwards was "profoundly influenced" by
such English Puritans as William Ames and William Chappell,
John Preston and Richard Sibbes and that William Perkins's
The Art of Prophecying (1618) had a "greater influence" as
a literary model for his sermons than any other text.
After his dismissal from Northampton, friends in Great
Britain and Scotland urged Edwards to accept a settlement
there.

25 _____. Jonathan Edwards The Preacher. Grand Rapids, Mich.:
Baker Book House, 192 pp.
Insists that Edwards's theological treatises spring
from the pastoral experiences and reflections of his sermons; analyzes them in outline and classifies them by
types--dogmatic, imprecatory, evangelistic, ethical,
memorial, vocational, and pastoral--; and concludes that
"whereas Edwards was a staunch Calvinist on his knees, he
was like an Arminianist on his feet." Edwards's sermons
are the work of "an artist, a craftsman," written in a
plain and modest style, limited and Biblical in imagery,
logical, rhythmical, and balanced, and "seldom controversial, and never contentious." They are evangelical and
ethical, agencies of redemption and psalms to God's
sovereignty. Edwards stands in the "first rank" of
preachers throughout time, an example to other preachers
and to theological students, an "evangelical mystic" who
knew and felt God's spirit in the soul and who believed
that "he was a voice for God."

26 _____. "Jonathan Edwards: A Voice for God." Christianity
Today 2 (6 January):8–9.
Observes in Edwards the paradox of the "convinced"
Calvinist and the "persuasive Arminianist," the theologian
of divine sovereignty and the preacher of man's responsibility. God's foreknowledge of man's end balances His will
to have ministers preach "as a means of urging" men to
press into the Kingdom. Thus, Edwards is "a voice for
God."

27 WEISBERGER, BERNARD A. They Gathered at the River: The Story of the Great Revivalists and Their Impact upon Religion in America. Boston: Little, Brown & Co., pp. 54-57.
Notes Edwards's role in the Great Awakening. Important as it was, Sinners in the Hands of an Angry God was almost Edwards's undoing: most Americans forgot the "keen psychologist" and "brilliant philosopher" for the hell-fire preacher.

28 WINSLOW, OLA ELIZABETH. Review of Freedom of the Will, edited by Paul Ramsey. American Literature 30 (March):121-22.
Regards Paul Ramsey's "admirable" introduction (1957.14) a rare and valuable instance of reading Edwards as if he were still a contemporary.

29 WOLF, CARL J. C. Preface to his Jonathan Edwards on Evangelism. Grand Rapids, Mich.: Wm. B. Eerdmans Publishing Co., pp. vii-xii.
Emphasizes Edwards's theocentricism as the key to his thought, suggests that his correlation of the doctrine of divine sovereignty and experimental religion may be one of the "true secrets" of revivalism, and reprints selections from his evangelical writings.

1959

1 BURANELLI, VINCENT. "Colonial Philosophy." William and Mary Quarterly, 3d ser. 16 (July):343-62.
Ranks Edwards first among "genuine" (and neglected) colonial philosophers--Samuel Johnson, Cadwallader Colden, and John Witherspoon--and, with two or three others, the "greatest" American philosopher. Edwards's place derives chiefly from his emphasis upon experience and his "creative originality."

2 DUFF, WILLIAM BOYD. Jonathan Edwards, Then and Now: A Satirical Study in Predestination. Pittsburgh: Guttendorf Press, 95 pp.
Offers a "small book" of the life and times of Edwards-- with asides on Thomas Henry Huxley and Charles Darwin, Albert Einstein and Marilyn Monroe--in an attempt to define, defend, and restore Edwards's Presbyterian orthodoxy to these parlous times. So in a "ghostly inverview," Edwards is made to say of Einstein, "'Rather than accept the theory of curved space, I had as soon believe that a curved mind concocted the theory.'" Later he adds,

1959

"'Communism is not a perversion but the most logical outgrowth of Darwinism.'" Hence, "the future trend" of
philosophy lies with Edwards, as does "the most nearly
correct answer to the riddle of the universe."

3   FERM, ROBERT O. The Psychology of Christian Conversion.
    Westwood, N.J.: Fleming H. Revell Co., pp. 113-15.
       Finds Edwards's distinction between true and false
    conversions a modern instance of psychological attitudes
    and methods in the service of religion.

4   FERM, VERGILIUS, ed. Classics of Protestantism. New York:
    Philosophical Library, pp. 180-81.
       Introduces and reprints part of Edwards's Freedom of
    the Will and Sinners in the Hands of an Angry God.

5   GOEN, C[LARENCE] C[URTIS]. "Jonathan Edwards: A New Depar-
    ture in Eschatology." Church History (March):25-40.
       Characterizes Edwards's eschatological doctrine that
    a golden age of the Church and a time for earthly bliss
    would precede the final consummation and the coming of
    Christ "a radical innovation" and "counter" to commonly
    held Protestant opinion that unprecedented grief and
    darkness would usher in the millennium. Edwards argues
    from his belief in rational man, a just and merciful God,
    and an historically realized process of redemption, though
    the "immediate" source of his speculations was probably
    the Daniel Whitby-Moses Lowman exegesis. With Qualifica-
    tions and History of Redemption Edwards becomes our "first
    major post-millennial thinker," providing a religious
    context to manifest destiny and radical utopianism in
    America.

6   HALL, THOMAS CUMING. The Religious Background of American
    Culture. New York: Frederick Ungar.
       Reprint of 1930.7.

7   KAWERAU, PETER W. "Johann Adam Steinmetz als Vermittler
    zwichen dem deutschen und amerikanischem Pietisums im 18.
    Jahrhundret." Zetschrift für Kirchengeschichte 70, no.
    1-2:75-88.
       Recounts the provenance of Edwards's Faithful Narrative
    and Steinmetz's role in making the text available to a
    German audience. (In German.)

8   LUDWIG, RICHARD M. "Jonathan Edwards." In Literary History
    of the United States. Edited by Robert E. Spiller et al.
    New York: Macmillan Co., 3:110-11.
       Supplements the bibliography in 1948.5.

9   MILLER, PERRY. "From Edwards to Emerson." In <u>Interpretations</u>
     <u>of American Literature</u>. Edited by Charles Feidelson, Jr.,
     and Paul Brodtkorb, Jr. New York: Oxford University
     Press, pp. 114-36.
                    Reprint of 1940.9.

10   _____. <u>Jonathan Edwards</u>. Cleveland and New York: World
     Publishing Co.
                    Reprint of 1949.9.

11   _____. <u>Jonathan Edwards</u>. New York: Meridian Books.
                    Reprint of 1949.9.

12   MOULTON, CHARLES WELLS, ed. "Jonathan Edwards." In <u>Library</u>
     <u>of Literary Criticism of English and American Authors</u>.
     Gloucester, Mass.: Peter Smith, 3:380-95.
                    Reprint of 1902.10.

13   MURPHY, ARTHUR E. "Jonathan Edwards on Free Will and Moral
     Agency." <u>Philosophical Review</u> 68 (April):181-202.
              Questions Paul Ramsey's reading of <u>Freedom of the Will</u>
     (1957.14)--Ramsey confuses voluntary action (the effect)
     with the act of volition (the cause) and confounds Edwards--
     and suggests that the real problem lies in the relationship
     between the determination of the will and moral agency and
     Edwards's failure to solve it. By making nonsense of the
     Arminian position on the determination of the will, Edwards
     makes "equal" nonsense of moral agency, because he confuses
     "the language of mental causation with that of moral ap-
     praisal and justification." The will does not perform
     acts of mental causation, an agent does. To have it any
     other way destroys freedom of the will, the will itself,
     and man as moral agent.

14   PICKELL, CHARLES N. "The Freedom of the Will in William Ames
     and Jonathan Edwards." <u>Gordon Review</u> 5 (Winter):168-74.
              Discovers "no essential difference" between Edwards and
     William Ames on free will (contrary to what "many scholars"
     hold) and points out "noteworthy" similarities in their
     careers and theology. Both were "adamant" on determinism,
     election, and calling, but Ames stressed preparation for
     salvation and the means of grace in his <u>The Marrow of</u>
     <u>Sacred Divinity</u> (1623), a critical text to New England
     Puritans, although he "studiously avoided any hint" that
     man might save himself. "What may appear to be theological
     differences between them are in reality only differences
     in emphasis."

1959

15   PIERCE, RICHARD D. "A Suppressed Edwards Manuscript on the
     Trinity." Crane Review 1 (Winter):66-80.
          Traces the controversy surrounding the suppressed Ed-
     wards manuscripts on the trinity (1903.25)--through con-
     temporary newspaper accounts and the correspondence between
     his heirs and his editors--and posits a reason for it.
     Edwards accepted the Nicene doctrine of the eternal gen-
     eration of the Son, a view generally abandoned and at
     times held in derision by later New England divines. To
     keep his theology in conformity with theirs, the Edwardsean
     custodians of his manuscripts withheld publication of his
     trinitarian views until forced to and then only to protect
     him from the charge of "even greater" heresy. In fact,
     the heterodoxy of the text is "slight," but it is ample
     testimony to fifty years of "exaggerated rumor and partisan
     theology."

16   ROOT, ROBERT WALTER. "The Religious Ideas of Some Major Early
     Writers of America." Ph.D. dissertation, Syracuse Univer-
     sity.
          Classifies Edwards as a conservative in a 1000-page
     study of the relation of early American religious ideas to
     American literature and culture.

17   SIZER, THEODORE. "The Story of the Edwards Portraits." Yale
     University Library Gazette 34 (October):82-88.
          Tells of the acquisition of the Edwards portraits now
     at Edwards College, Yale, in a tale of academic intrigue
     and the great hurricane of 1938.

18   SMITH, JOHN E. "Editor's Introduction." In Religious Affec-
     tions. The Works of Jonathan Edwards, vol. 2. New Haven
     and London: Yale University Press, pp. 1-83.
          Traces the provenance and historical background of Re-
     ligious Affections; examines in detail each of the twelve
     signs of the affections and each of the sixteen documented
     sources of Edwards's reading; and comments upon the place
     of the affections in contemporary religion and the "re-
     markable literary power" of the work, in an introduction
     to the second volume of the Yale Edwards. Central to
     Edwards's view of the affections and "invariably missed"
     by commentators is the unitive relationship between head
     and heart: judgment or inclination involves both the will
     and the mind--it is called will when it is expressed
     through action, heart when it is expressed through the
     mind. "Affections, then are lively inclinations and
     choices which show that man is a being with a heart." Thus
     Edwards contibuted to his time and to ours: he restored
     religion to life, showed that a form of understanding was

1960

closely related to individual experience, and provided a
rational means for validating piety. And his interpretation contributed in no small way to the "robust sense of
activity" of American Protestantism.

19 SUTER, RUFUS [ORLANDO, JR.] "A Note on Platonism in the
    Philosophy of Jonathan Edwards." Harvard Theological
    Review 52 (October):283-84.
        Recounts the view of Professor William Wallace Fenn of
    Harvard Divinity that Edwards was the "protagonist of a
    New England Tragedy" because he was self-consciously
    aware of being "unable to reconcile Platonism with his
    Calvinism."

20 TURNBULL, RALPH G. Preface to his Devotions of Jonathan
    Edwards. Grand Rapids, Mich.: Baker Book House, pp. 5-6.
        Reprints passages from the "riches" of Edwards's crea-
    tive, experimental thought as weekly devotions.

21 WEEKS, J[OHN] STAFFORD. A Review of Jonathan Edwards The
    Preacher, by Ralph G. Turnbull. Church History 28 (June):
    213-14.
        Considers Ralph G. Turnbull's study of a "master"
    preacher (1958.25) useful to today's ministers but frag-
    mented in form and without a sense of the "profound integ-
    rity" of Edwards's sermons.

22 WILLIAMS, GEORGE HUNTSTON. "The Wilderness and Paradise in
    the History of the Church." Church History 28 (March):
    3-24.
        Notes that Edwards "largely interiorized" the meaning
    of wilderness and held the promised land to be heaven, not
    a holy commonwealth, in a history of the idea of wilder-
    ness and paradise from Biblical to New England times.

23 WINTERICH, JOHN T. Review of Jonathan Edwards, by Perry
    Miller. New York Herald Tribune Book Review, 20 December,
    p. 9.
        Reviews the paperback publication of Perry Miller's
    Jonathan Edwards (1959.11) as an "admirable presentation
    by a Middle Western Scholar."

1960

1 CONRAD, LESLIE, JR. "The Importance of Preaching in the
   Great Awakening." Lutheran Quarterly 12 (May):111-20.

1960

Makes passing reference to Edwards's pulpit style in his
theory that the "main benefits" of a sermon come at first
hearing, not through later reflection.

2   DILLENBERGER, JOHN. Protestant Thought and Natural Science:
     A Historical Interpretation. New York: Doubleday &
     Co., pp. 161-62.
          Slights Edwards's contribution because, while the
     analogy he drew between Newtonian causation and faith and
     regeneration was astute, it had little lasting effect.

3   ELWOOD, DOUGLAS J. The Philosophical Theology of Jonathan
     Edwards. New York: Columbia University Press, 232 pp.
          Locates the correlation between Edwards's theology and
     his philosophy in his doctrine of the immediacy of God,
     a synthesis of elements of theism and pantheism, Calvinism
     and mysticism into a "third way" of describing the rela-
     tionship of God and the world as one of "mutual immanence:
     God in the world and the world in God." Edwards recon-
     structs Calvinism along Neoplatonic lines, stressing the
     aesthetic element rather than the moral or legal one and
     conceiving of God as absolute power. Divine immediacy,
     for Edwards, becomes not only awareness but also the self-
     movement and self-revelation of God in creation and
     history as a "continuous sacrament" and represents perhaps
     the most "authentic" element of Puritanism in his thought.
     Man passively receives from God this "new sense of things"
     as a "new simple idea" and can then grasp the "spiritual
     dimension" of life, a dimension higher and deeper than
     that afforded the unregenerate. Thus Edwards's mysticism
     is an "extension" of Puritan piety, conceiving the union
     of the soul and God as continuous rather than fugitive and
     identifying grace with "the actual presence of God in the
     human heart." Isolated as Edwards was, such ideas were
     probably the product of "his own direct experience," yet
     they have "relevancy" to a Christian understanding of God
     in our time.

4   FRANKENA, WILLIAM K., ed. Foreword to The Nature of True
     Virtue. Ann Arbor: University of Michigan Press, pp. v-
     xiii.
          Recommends Edwards's True Virtue as a well-made treatise
     on ethics, with a special appeal to neofundamentalists and
     to contemporary moral philosophers, and as an important
     item of intellectual history, in a brief explanation of
     his distinction between the two moralities, their nature
     and source.

5   GERSTNER, JOHN H. Steps to Salvation: The Evangelistic
     Message of Jonathan Edwards. Philadelphia: Westminster
     Press, 192 pp.
         Traces the steps to salvation in the published and un-
     published sermons of Edwards, a "both/and" theologian, both
     a convenant theologian and a Calvinist, both a presdesti-
     narian and an evangelist. The "keystone" to Edwards's
     evangelistic theory of salvation is seeking, a way for
     sinful man Edwards "never wearies of pleading," a doctrine
     Edwards preaches "insistently and repeatedly." Unregen-
     erate man might not be able to find the salvation he
     sought--the two are not causal--but God might reveal it
     to him if he did, Edwards thought, if he prepared,
     especially during revivals or communion, "red-letter days
     for redemption." Illumination and regeneration occur
     simultaneously at the "sovereign pleasure" of God, bring-
     ing about true faith; justification is by faith alone
     but not by "the faith that is alone"; and, because the
     signs of salvation are so "meticulous," assurance is a
     "relatively rare thing." All this Edwards holds in a
     convenantal frame of reference, distinguishing the covenant
     of redemption from the covenant of grace. By insisting
     that a sinner can do something, Edwards agrees somewhat
     with the Arminians and disagrees with such Calvinists as
     say he can do nothing. "According to Edwards, he can do
     something nonsaving but promising and hopeful: namely,
     seek."

6   GOEN, CLARENCE CURTIS. "Revivalism and Separatism in New
     England, 1740-1800: Strict Congregationalists and Sepa-
     rate Baptists in the Great Awakening." Ph.D. disserta-
     tion, Yale University.
         Published as 1962.3.

7   HEIMERT, ALAN EDWARD. "American Oratory: From the Great
     Awakening to the Election of Jefferson." Ph.D. disserta-
     tion, Harvard University.
         Published in part as 1966.17.

8   HITCHCOCK, ORVILLE A. "Jonathan Edwards." In A History and
     Criticism of American Public Address. Edited by William
     Norwood Brigance. New York: Russell & Russell.
         Reprint of 1943.6.

9   HOLBROOK, CLYDE A[MOS]. "Edwards Re-examined." Review of
     Metaphysics 13 (June):623-41.

1960

Characterizes both Paul Ramsey's introduction to
Freedom of the Will (1957.14) and John E. Smith's to
Religious Affections (1959.18) "insightful and provocative," though Ramsey finds more consistency in Edwards
and Smith more accuracy in his language than is so in
the texts, in an essay-review.

10 HOWARD, LEON. Literature and the American Tradition.
Garden City, N.Y.: Doubleday & Co., pp. 44-49.
Locates Edwards among the Cartesian logicians who re-
jected the Ramists and were opposed by the Baconians.
His dependence on a chain of causation and his "severe"
rationalism in argument exemplify his devotion to the
Port-Royal logic.

11 McGINLEY, PHYLLIS. "The Theology of Jonathan Edwards." In
her Times Three. New York: Viking Press, p. 19.
Portrays Edwards's woeful congregation during an imprecatory sermon and his "whimsical" deity, "Not God the
Father or the Son/But God the Holy Terror," in a twenty-
four-line poem.

12 McLOUGHLIN, WILLIAM G., ed. Introduction to Lectures on
Revivals of Religion, by Charles Grandison Finney.
Cambridge, Mass.: Harvard University Press, pp. x-xiii
passim.
Notes critical differences between Edwards and Finney
on matters of revivalism and theology, even though Finney
frequently quotes from Edwards, in a history of Finney's
attack on Calvinism and the "Presbygational" churches of
the nineteenth century.

13 OLMSTEAD, CLIFTON E. History of Religion in the United
States. Englewood Cliffs, N.J.: Prentice-Hall, pp. 162-
67, 170-71.
Distinguishes Edwards's theology from Calvin's as one
more concerned with man's unworthiness than with God's
sovereignty and cites his True Virtue as an "important"
contribution to American theology. Edwards's "valiant
battle" to save Calvinism and its "intellectual respect-
ability" was bound to fail: frontier optimism was at
odds with divine determinism; Arminianism was at one
with a free man's responsibility. Yet Edwards's rigorous
thought lent "backbone and stamina" to American theology
for "generations to come."

14   ROBERTS, CECIL ALBERT, JR. "The Apologetic Significance of
      Jonathan Edwards' Doctrine of Religious Experience."
      Th.D. dissertation, Southwestern Baptist Theological
      Seminary.
          Examines Edwards's defense of experiential religion,
      the background that contributed to it and the effects
      that flowed from it. Edwards's apologetic for religious
      experience reestablished the place of emotion in religion
      and revitalized the regenerate church. Though it is
      "tragic" that Edwards had to speak through a harsh Calvin-
      ism, his belief in God's active revelation and man's
      appropriation of it through emotion remains a "fundamental
      insight."

15   SMITH, H[ILRIE] SHELTON, HANDY, ROBERT T., and LOETSCHER,
      LEFFERTS A. American Christianity: An Historical Inter-
      pretation with Representative Documents. New York:
      Charles Scribner's Sons, 1:339-40.
          Reprints selections from Religious Affections and sug-
      gests that the "changing tone" in Edwards's four defenses
      of the revivals arises from excesses within the movement
      and criticism without. The first of these, Faithful Nar-
      rative, is more nearly objective and sympathetic; the
      last, Religious Affections, is critical and cautionary.

16   WHITEFIELD, GEORGE. George Whitefield's Journals. Edited by
      Iain Murray. London: Banner of Truth Trust, pp. 476-79.
          Recounts George Whitefield's meeting with Edwards in
      late October 1740--"I think I have not seen his fellow in
      all New England"; his stay at the family home--"A sweeter
      couple I have not yet seen"; and preaching to the North-
      ampton congregation--"good Mr. Edwards wept during the
      whole time of exercise."

17   WINSLOW, OLA ELIZABETH. Review of Religious Affections,
      edited by John E. Smith. American Literature 32 (Novem-
      ber):330-31.
          Praises John E. Smith's "enlightening" introduction to
      Religious Affections (1959.18), the "central core" of
      Edwards's thought.

18   WOOD, A. SKEVINGTON. The Inextinguishable Blaze: Spiritual
      Renewal and Advance in the Eighteenth Century. Grand
      Rapids, Mich.: Wm. B. Eerdmans Publishing Co., pp. 53-66.
          Connects Edwards to the 1735 revival in Wales--"part of
      American aid to Britain"--and considers him rather than
      George Whitefield the "true leader" of the Great Awakening
      and its "foremost" theologian, in a survey of the revival
      spirit in the eighteenth century.

1960

19 WOODWARD, ROBERT H. "Jonathan Edwards as a Puritan Poet."
    Exercise Exchange 8 (October-December):5-6.
        Compares Edwards's Personal Narrative with several
    poems by Edward Taylor to show another Puritan "poetic
    temperament" at work.

                            1961

1   AHLSTROM, SYDNEY E. "Theology in America: A Historical
    Survey." In The Shaping of American Religion. Edited by
    James Ward Smith and A. Leland Jamison. Religion in
    American Life, no. 1. Princeton, N.J.: Princeton Uni-
    versity Press, pp. 243-51 passim.
        Characterizes Edwards as a "Doritian philosophe," a
    Reformed theologian adapting the basic ideas of the En-
    lightenment to the Christian experience. Four "salient"
    features of his system of thought stand out: the full,
    scriptural rendering of the Reformed Christian message
    in the sermons; the empirically based apologia for the
    Christian faith in Religious Affections, Freedom of the
    Will, and Original Sin; the essentialist ontology derived
    from Christian Platonism in End of Creation and True
    Virtue; and the "ultimate mode" of expressing the meaning
    of Christianity in History of Redemption.

2   ANDERSON, WALLACE EARL. "Mind and Nature in the Early
    Philosophical Writings of Jonathan Edwards." Ph.D. dis-
    sertation, University of Minnesota.
        Studies the successive stages of Edwards's development
    of idealism from "Of Atoms and Perfectly Solid Bodies"
    to notes on "The Mind" and identifies the "dominant
    themes" to be the immateriality of the natural world and
    its immediate and continuous dependence upon God. Edwards
    draws upon Henry More's Immortality of the Soul, Newton's
    third book of Opticks, and Locke's Essay Concerning Human
    Understanding.

3   BARITZ, LOREN. "The Idea of the West." American Historical
    Review 66 (April):618-40.
        Notes that Edwards's eschatology was "partly determined
    by the idea that God faced west."

4   BURR, NELSON R. A Critical Bibliography of Religion in
    America. Religion in American Life, no. 4. Princeton,
    N.J.: Princeton University Press, pp. 132-37, 976-87.
        Provides a critical, bibliographical essay on Edwards
    in two parts: the first concerns his role in the New

                            236

England Awakening, the second his reconstruction and defense of Calvinism--the origins of his thought, his
theology, his idealism and pantheism, and commentaries.
There are three "major periods" in Edwards's intellectual
life: his "youthful speculations" before Northampton;
his "theological period" before Stockbridge; and his
"systematic writing" before Princeton. "It is misleading
to judge him solely by any one of these periods."

5 HORNE, R. A. "The Atomic Theory of Jonathan Edwards."
   Crane Review 3 (Winter):65-72.
      Considers "quite novel" for his time Edwards's atomic
   theory in "Notes on Natural Science," anticipating as it
   does ideas of "collision effectiveness" and "steric hindrance," and regrets that so inventive a scientific mind
   fell before "sterile doctrine."

6 ILLICK, JOSEPH E., III. "Jonathan Edwards and the Historians."
   Journal of the Presbyterian Historical Society 39 (December):230-46.
      Compares the studies of Edwards by V. L. Parrington
   (1927.2), Herbert W. Schneider (1930.13), Ola Elizabeth
   Winslow (1940.21), Perry Miller (1949.9), and Edwin S.
   Gaustad (1957.6) and finds them wanting. Edwards is
   "somewhat mishandled," sometimes by methodology, sometimes
   by political or philosophical assumptions. All deny
   Edwards his complexity by focusing upon only one aspect
   of him--in American thought or in religious history, in
   his personal life or his intellectual one, in his contribution to the Awakening.

7 JEANES, W. P. "Jonathan Edwards's Conception of Freedom of
   the Will." Scottish Journal of Theology 14 (March):1-14.
      Explicates Edwards's arguments of free agency, fore-
   knowledge, certainty, and necessity, and contrasts the
   moral systems of Edwards and the Arminians. Edwards re-
   moves his theocentric concept of freedom of the will from
   mechanical necessity, which would preclude responsibility;
   from contingency, which would preclude certainty; and from
   a self-determined will, which would preclude reason,
   conscience, and inclinations. Of the moral systems, it is
   "conviction" that separates Edwards from the "sentiment"
   of the Arminians, or it is the difference between man's
   conviction of his duty to God's law, irrespective of his
   feelings, and man's sentiment (or feelings) of his ability
   to determine his moral state. The centrality of God in
   Edwards's scheme lends "stability and strength" to it, at
   times "stubborness and harshness."

1961

8   LASSER, MICHAEL L. "Addendum to an Exercise on Jonathan
    Edwards." Exercise Exchange 9 (November):31.
        Cites Edwards's "Sarah Pierrepont" as evidence of a
    "poetic tendency" in Edwards and suggests a useful con-
    trast to Anne Bradstreet's "To My Dear and Loving Husband"
    and "A Letter to her Husband, Absent upon Public Employ-
    ment."

9   MacCORMAC, EARL R. "Jonathan Edwards and Missions." Journal
    of the Presbyterian Historical Society 31 (December):
    219-29.
        Finds Edwards "vitally interested" in missions--see,
    for example, his post-millennial eschatology in History of
    Redemption and his doctrine of universal imputation in
    Original Sin--contrary to the "popular assumption" that a
    theocentric, deterministic theology like his prohibits
    them. While Edwards's ministry among the Indians at
    Stockbridge was not impressive, he did exert considerable
    influence for missions upon his successors through his
    theology and upon others, here and abroad, through his
    Life of Brainerd.

10 McGRAW, JAMES. Great Evangelical Preachers of Yesterday.
    New York and Nashville: Abingdon Press, pp. 50-55.
        Judges the strength of Edwards's preaching to rest in
    his thought and argument rather than his voice and manner.
    Edwards develops the points and major sections of his
    sermons in a "smooth continuity," offering few anecdotes
    but frequent metaphors.

11 OLMSTEAD, CLIFTON E. Religion in America. Englewood Cliffs,
    N.J.: Prentice-Hall, pp. 43-45.
        Recasts 1960.13.

12 SCHAFER, THOMAS A[NTON]. Review of The Philosophical Theology
    of Jonathan Edwards, by Douglas J. Elwood. American
    Literature 33 (November):379-80.
        Considers Douglas J. Elwood's explication (1960.3)
    "rightly centered and basically correct," though it
    "underplays" Edwards's rationalistic theism and gradual-
    istic metaphysics.

13 SMITH, JAMES WARD. "Religion and Science in American Philos-
    ophy." In The Shaping of American Religion. Edited by
    James Ward Smith and A. Leland Jamison. Religion in
    American Life, no. 1. Princeton, N.J.: Princeton Uni-
    versity Press, pp. 414-17.

Claims that Edwards grasped the fundamental implications
of the scientific spirit, not simply the superficial adapta-
tions of it; that his understanding was profound and mature,
not experimental and puerile. All his later theology--Reli-
gious Affections, Freedom of the Will, True Virtue--reveals
a "monumental" effort to read Calvinist axioms in terms of
the "scientifically oriented philosophical spirit." That
philosophical spirit remains constant in Edwards, but "the
whole tone and tenor" of the Calvinist axioms do not.

14   SUTER, RUFUS [ORLANDO, JR.] "The Strange Universe of Jonathan
     Edwards." Harvard Theological Review 54 (April):125-28.
     Suggests that Edwards's universe is "strange" to contem-
     porary, liberal Protestants not because of his uncompromis-
     ing biblicism but because of his stark sense of the reality
     of ethical concepts. The goodness of virtue, the beauty of
     holiness, the necessity of justice--all are real in a lit-
     eral, cosmic sense, for they comprise the "warp and woof" of
     the universe eternally. The reality of the physical uni-
     verse is secondary to them.

15   WHEATCROFT, JOHN. "Emily Dickinson's Poetry and Jonathan Ed-
     wards on the Will." Bucknell Review 10 (December): 102-27.
     Considers Edwards's doctrine of the will to be the "main-
     spring" of Emily Dickinson's creative activity and his Con-
     necticut Valley orthodoxy the cultural context of her life
     and work. Dickinson was "born and bred" amid Edwardseans
     and owes a significant part of her "inner life" to the Rev-
     erend Charles Wadsworth, a "product" of New England Theology.
     Even the familiar opening lines of one of her "greatest"
     poems--"Because I could not stop for Death/He kindly stopped
     for me"--remain "dark" without Edwards's doctrine of will
     and necessity.

16   WILLIAMS, DANIEL D. "Tradition and Experience in American The-
     ology." In The Shaping of American Religion. Edited by
     James Ward Smith and A. Leland Jamison. Religion in Ameri-
     can Life, no. 1. Princeton, N.J.: Princeton University
     Press, pp. 448-53.
     Cites Edwards as a good example of the place experience
     holds in knowing God, the first of five categories of empir-
     icism found in the method and content of American Christian
     thought. Edwards's typology attempts to find divine truths
     in nature and in man, to see both in a "constant interplay
     of challenge and adjustment," and so illustrates the very
     condition of experience in America. His interest in the
     varieties of religious experience is "not a very long step"
     from William James and nineteenth-century empirical theology.

1961

17 WINSLOW, OLA ELIZABETH. Jonathan Edwards, 1703-1758. New
     York: Collier Books, 375 pp.
          Reprint of 1940.21.

18 _____. Review of The Philosophical Theology of Jonathan
     Edwards, by Douglas J. Elwood. New England Quarterly 34
     (June):255-57.
          Finds "exhilarating" Douglas J. Elwood's fresh approach
     (1960.3) and particularly "exciting" his inclusion of
     Edwards in the pantheon of theologians ancient and modern.

1962

1 BACON, MARTHA. "Miss Beecher in Hell." American Heritage 14
     (December):28-31, 102-105.
          Recounts the tragic "triangle" of Catherine Beecher, a
     leader in women's education in nineteenth-century America;
     Alexander Metcalf Fisher, a Yale professor; and Edwards,
     "the dark giant who gave shape to the American conscience."
     Beecher refutes Edwards in order that Fisher, a non-
     professing Christian who drowned at twenty-eight, be saved
     from eternal damnation.

2 FAUST, CLARENCE H., and JOHNSON, THOMAS H., eds. Introduc-
     tion to Jonathan Edwards: Representative Selections.
     Rev. ed. American Century Series. New York: Hill &
     Wang, pp. xi-cxvii.
          Reprints 1935.3 with a revised and updated annotated
     bibliography of over 200 items by Stephen S. Webb,
     pp. cxix-cxlii.

3 GOEN, C[LARENCE] C[URTIS]. Revivalism and Separatism in New
     England, 1740-1800: Strict Congregationalists and
     Separate Baptists in the Great Awakening. New Haven and
     London: Yale University Press, pp. 13-15, 45-46, 160-64,
     209-10.
          Distinguishes Edwards's views of conversion as experi-
     ence during the revivals and as profession for church
     membership. Edwards shaped the "normative pattern" of
     experiential conversion in the Great Awakening into
     three "well defined" stages characterized by distress,
     conviction, and assurance. Later, in Qualifications, he
     endorsed sincere profession of faith for church member-
     ship, though he opposed the separation between professing
     and real saints then in vogue. His insistence upon
     parental profession as a prerequisite to the baptism of
     their children reveals a "curious blindness to history."

4   HARLAND, GORDON. "The American Protestant Heritage and the
         Theological Task." Drew Gateway 32 (Winter):71-93.
             Notes that Edwards and Franklin divide the Puritan
         soul, setting the stage for America's subsequent religious
         history.

5   LITTELL, FRANKLIN HAMLIN. From State Church to Pluralism: A
         Protestant Interpretation of Religion in American History.
         Garden City, N.Y.: Doubleday & Co., pp. 18-19.
             Considers Edwards's career an "inevitable conflict"
         between evangelism and the parish system, symbolic of the
         transition from establishment to voluntaryism. Edwards's
         emphasis upon conversion and grace points to "a more live
         initiative" of the faithful and away from the "standing
         order."

6   LÖWE, WOLFGANG EBERHARD. "The First American Foreign Mission-
         aries: 'The Students,' 1810-1820. An Inquiry into their
         Theological Motives." Ph.D. dissertation, Brown University.
             Attributes "strong" incentives of the first American
         foreign missionaries for their work to particular ideas
         they found in Edwards, especially those on eschatology and
         benevolence, and to the general evangelical thrust of his
         theology.

7   MILLER, PERRY. "Benjamin Franklin--Jonathan Edwards." In
         Major Writers of America. Edited by Perry Miller et al.
         New York: Harcourt, Brace & World, 1:83-98.
             Contends that Edwards and Franklin, "the pre-eminently
         eloquent linked antagonists in American culture," express
         in differing ways the Protestant ethic common to both, in
         a comparison of their careers and ideas introductory to a
         selection of their work. Though both share that code as
         well as an uncommon disinterestedness about personal suc-
         cess, the division between Edwards and Franklin is "ir-
         reconcilable," and provides "the basic and sundering
         theme" of American literature and our intellectual herit-
         age.

8   MORGAN, EDMUND S. The Gentle Puritan: A Life of Ezra
         Stiles, 1727-1795. New Haven and London: Yale University
         Press, pp. 33-40, passim.
             Recounts the tense relationship between Edwards and
         Isaac Stiles over their Yale days, the Bolton settlement,
         the New Haven parish, and the Great Awakening, and con-
         tinuing with Stiles's son Ezra over the widow Sergeant at
         Stockbridge.

1962

9 MOTHERSILL, MARY. "Professor Prior and Jonathan Edwards."
    Review of Metaphysics 16 (December):366-73.
       Questions whether it is necessary or appropriate to
    seek sufficient causal conditions for contingent events
    as A. N. Prior suggests in his analysis (1962.13) and
    whether his analysis of limited and unlimited determinism
    is in fact an "alternative" to Edwards. "The only differ-
    ence then between Edwards and Prior has to do with whether
    or not there are 'non-determinate' dispositions, and on
    this point Prior is unclear."

10 MOYER, ELGIN S. "Jonathan Edwards." In his Who Was Who in
    Church History. Chicago: Moody Press, pp. 129-30.
       Traces the career of Edwards.

11 NEWLIN, CLAUDE M[ILTON]. Philosophy and Religion in Colonial
    America. New York: Philosophical Library, pp. 25-31,
    85-102, 135-94 passim.
       Characterizes Edwards's thought as the use of "novel
    philosophical material to protect old theological doc-
    trines," in a survey of his work from his Yale to his
    Stockbridge days, based principally upon extended quota-
    tion and brief comment and related to contemporary debates
    on the Awakening and Arminianism.

12 NIEBUHR, H. RICHARD. "Ex Libris." Christian Century 79
    (13 June):754.
       Numbers Edwards's True Virtue fourth among the ten books
    that have shaped his vocation and "philosophy of life."

13 PRIOR, A. N. "Limited Indeterminism." Review of Metaphysics
    16 (September):55-61.
       Contends that Edwards's inversion of approach in seek-
    ing the cause for "the beginning-to-exist of a 'thing,'"
    not for the event (see Freedom of the Will, Part II,
    Section III) is of "the very first importance" to his
    thought and argument because it assumes that the world
    does not consist of events but of things and that how
    things behave is determined partly by their natures and
    partly by what happens to them. Edwards distinguishes
    between limited and unlimited determinism dependent upon
    a "metaphysic of substances endowed with capacities."
    Hence it seems "prima facie possible" to distinguish
    between limited and unlimited indeterminism.

14   RICHARDSON, HERBERT WARREN. "The Glory of God in the Theology
      of Jonathan Edwards (a Study in the Doctrine of the
      Trinity)." Ph.D. dissertation, Harvard University.
         Considers Edwards the "first important modern" theolo-
      gian because he attempted to join Christian doctrine to
      scientific doctrine in his ontology, epistemology, and
      trinitarian views. For Edwards, the universe and the mind
      of man are the "external manifestations of the internal
      holiness" of God; the work and the Word of God are one.
      Historically, Edwards, and the Reformed thought he contin-
      ues, "self-consciously" bases his theological thinking on
      the doctrine of the trinity.

15   SCHNEEWIND, J. B. "Comments on Prior's Paper." Review of
      Metaphysics 16 (December):374-79.
         Resolves the issue between A. N. Prior (1962.13) and
      Edwards into one in which Prior makes room for the "possi-
      bility" of limited determinism and Edwards finds such a
      condition a contradiction in terms. For Edwards, "occur-
      ences of exercises of capacities" are determined by
      antecedent and linked causes; for Prior, exercises of
      capacities occur in "an utterly random fashion." If that
      were true, Edwards might be forced to conclude that such
      exercises were causeless; but, as in the case of disposi-
      tions, "it need not force him to that conclusion."

16   SMITH, ELWYN ALLEN. The Presbyterian Ministry in American
      Culture: A Study in Changing Concepts, 1700-1900.
      Philadelphia: Westminster Press, pp. 61-67, 145-47
      passim.
         Explains Edwards's definitions of natural ability and
      moral inability in Freedom of the Will and imputation in
      Original Sin and the effect his teachings had at Princeton
      and on the Presbyterian clergy into the nineteenth
      century.

17   TUCKER, LOUIS LEONARD. Puritan Protagonist: President
      Thomas Clap of Yale College. Chapel Hill, N.C.: Univer-
      sity of North Carolina Press, pp. 136-38, 147-49, passim.
         Charts the deterioration of Edwards's relationship to
      Thomas Clap, rector of Yale (1740-1766). Clap perceived
      a threat to orthodoxy and ministerial function in Edwards's
      (and Whitefield's) New Lightism and moved to eliminate it.
      Distinguishing Marks, the commencement address of 1741,
      marked the last time Edwards was invited to his alma mater.

1962

18   WIEBE, DALLAS E. "Mr. Lowell and Mr. Edwards." Wisconsin
        Studies in Contemporary Literature 3 (Spring-Summer):21-31.
            Explicates Robert Lowell's "Mr. Edwards and the Spider"
        and "After the Surprising Conversions" to show that the
        poems follow the "historical" Edwards.

                                1963

1   ABEL, DARREL. "The Great Awakening: Jonathan Edwards." In
        his American Literature: Colonial and Early National
        Writing. Great Neck, N.Y.: Barron's Educational Series,
        1:122-41.
            Calls Edwards "one of the world's great figures of
        transition" and "an archetype of the whole intellectual
        and literary development of America," in an examination
        of his role in the Great Awakening and an explanation of
        Freedom of the Will, Original Sin, and Images or Shadows.
        From his earliest speculations on, Edwards tried to unify
        all knowledge by "synthesizing" the science of Newton and
        Locke with the theology of Calvin, though in time his
        interest in science became "ancillary" to his interest
        in theology. For us his claim to intellectual greatness
        rests not upon his "decadent" theology and admired logic
        but upon his systematic and coherent view of reality and
        moral man.

2   AHLSTROM, SYDNEY E. "H. Richard Niebuhr's Place in American
        Thought." Christianity and Crisis 23 (25 November):213-17.
            Claims H. Richard Niebuhr rescued Edwards from the
        "Puritan dungeon" to make his theology of theocentrism
        and benevolence available to twentieth-century moralists,
        in a eulogy for Niebuhr. Edwards is the "key" to The
        Kingdom of God and Radical Monotheism but not the "sole
        catalyst," as some have urged.

3   BAUMGARTNER, PAUL R. "Jonathan Edwards: The Theory behind
        His Use of Figurative Language." Publications of the
        Modern Language Association 78 (September):321-25.
            Challenges the view that figurative language for Edwards,
        as for Puritans generally, is an "accommodation" to fallen
        man or a rhetoric reluctantly used. Rather it is "natural
        and happy," a necessary device to enable man to apprehend
        by analogy beauty and truth founded in the consent to
        being and an "appropriate" means for God to communicate
        to man through the senses. Such language is consistent
        with Edwards's theories of sensation and religious affec-
        tions and results in figures that are immediate and natural.

                                244

4   BRUMM, URSULA. "Jonathan Edwards und Ralph Waldo Emerson."
     In her Die Religiose Typologie in Amerikanischen Denken.
     Studien zur Amerikanischen Literatur und Geschichte, no. 2.
     Leiden: E. J. Brill, pp. 73-86, passim.
         Claims that Edwards finds "typical configurations" in
     the connection between the revivals and the eschatological
     hope of America and that he uses types "almost exclusively"
     to refer to spiritual correspondences than to traditional,
     concrete antitypes in Christ. Thus Edwards's mode becomes
     allegorical, his types symbols, and the natural world an
     expression and product of an analogous spiritual world in
     harmony with it. His world picture is "consistent and
     comprehensive," but it is "typico-transcendent" rather
     than "mechanico-causal." With Emerson, there is a "shift
     in accent"--nature becomes centrally important--and though
     "in a direct line" from Edwards, he goes "a step further"
     in "modifying Calvinism." (In German; transl. 1970.2.)

5   CLIPSHAM, ERNEST F. "Andrew Fuller and Fullerism: A Study
     in Evangelical Calvinism." Baptist Quarterly 20 (July):
     99-114.
         Cites Edwards as the "principal" theological influence
     on Andrew Fuller (1754-1851), the Baptist missionary, and
     Freedom of the Will as the "most powerful" book to him
     apart from the Bible.

6   CRABTREE, ARTHUR BAMFORD. The Restored Relationship, A Study
     in Justification and Reconciliation. London: Carey
     Kingsgate Press, pp. 151-55.
         Compares Edwards and Wesley on justification: Edwards's
     doctrine of faith alone is "shrouded in obscurity";
     Wesley's faith that works through love has "Excellent
     biblical balance!"

7   DAVIDSON, EDWARD H. "From Locke to Edwards." Journal of the
     History of Ideas 24 (July-September):355-72.
         Traces Edwards's debt to John Locke's principles of the
     mind and theory of language and his singular development
     of them, considering him "the first native American sym-
     bolist" in the "great tradition" of American literature.
     Edwards took Locke's notion that words were unreal forms
     functioning in real time and place and argued that they
     conveyed real ideas in the mind, that they could be commu-
     nicated to others, and that they were part of "the cove-
     nanted phenomenology of God's universe"--words were willed
     by God. Thus the variable and potential world may be

known through the experience of language, and the "vivid
and nebulous association" of self and nature made real in
the word (Word). Much of this is exemplified in the
"masterly" Sinners in the Hands of an Angry God.

8   DUGGAN, FRANCIS X. "Paul Elmer More and the New England
     Tradition." American Literature 34 (January):542-61.
         Recounts Paul Elmer More's view of Edwards's dualism:
     though clear and profound, it ends in a confusion of per-
     sonifications and principles and illustrates the danger
     of joining "a rigid philosophy to a daring mythology."

9   FOSTER, FRANK HUGH. A Genetic History of the New England
     Theology. New York: Russell & Russell.
         Reprint of 1907.3.

10   FOSTER, MARY. "Called to Her Husband." His 23 (February):
     15-16, 21-22.
         Depicts Sarah Edwards's "hidden ministry" as companion
     and helpmeet in spiritual things to her husband.

11   _____. "Puritan Genius." His 23 (January):30-34.
         Remarks the career of Edwards as theologian, philosopher,
     evangelist, and mystic, and quotes his dying words as the
     "truest summary" of his life.

12   HOFSTADTER, RICHARD. Anti-Intellectualism in American Life.
     New York: Random House, pp. 64-65.
         Comments upon the combination of intellectualism,
     piety, and creativity in Edwards, unique among colonial
     ministers, and notes that the Great Awakening marked the
     first time the educated clergy in America was "roundly
     repudiated."

13   HOWARD, LEON. "The Mind" of Jonathan Edwards: A Recon-
     structed Text. University of California English Studies,
     no. 28. Berkeley and Los Angeles: University of Califor-
     nia Press, 163 pp.
         Reconstructs the text of Edwards's "Notes on the Mind"
     to make this remarkable and "rebellious" document more
     comprehensible than Sereno Dwight's transcription from
     the manuscript (now lost) and provides an introduction,
     running commentary, and supplemental texts. Edwards's
     notes challenge the "whole intellectual system" at Yale
     and "consistently attack" Locke's Essay; they show him
     committed early to philosophical idealism and to logical
     determinism; and they prepare for his religious conversion
     and for his "complete conversion to Calvinism." But more

importantly, the new arrangement of the text reveals the
"developing pattern" of his rational conviction of supernatural causes and effects and of the balanced quality of
the mind between the power of logic and the power of
emotion.

14   LEVIN, DAVID, ed.   The Puritan in the Enlightenment: Franklin
     and Edwards. The Berkeley Series in American History.
     Chicago: Rand McNally & Co., pp. 1-2.
        Suggests that selections from Edwards and Benjamin
     Franklin exemplify the effect of the Enlightment on Puri-
     tanism, the contrast between piety and morality.

15   MARTIN, JAMES P.   The Last Judgment in Protestant Theology
     from Orthodoxy to Ritschl. Grand Rapids, Mich.: William
     B. Eerdmans, pp. 55-86.
        Locates the source of Edwards's eschatology in his
     biblicism, not in Locke's sensationalism or Newton's
     mechanism (as Perry Miller would have it), in an examina-
     tion of Orthodox, Pietist, and Puritan concepts of the
     millennium, judgment, and salvation. Edwards's History of
     Redemption shows "more affinity" to the New Testament than
     to Calvinist dogma; End of Creation, though orthodox in
     its conclusions, is a "mixture of ideas," both philosophi-
     cal and Biblical. Edwards "integrated" the idea of the
     millennium with that of the coming of the kingdom by
     developing an organic view of Christ's work, so that his
     various comings, from incarnation to parousia, are seen
     as divine revelation in history. The end of the world,
     therefore, was continuous with Christ, and the Last Judg-
     ment "could not be separated from the time process."

16   MORGAN, EDMUND S.   Visible Saints: The History of a Puritan
     Idea. New York: New York University Press, pp. 151-52.
        Notes that Edwards's Qualifications, a return to the
     century-old system of admission, began a "new cycle" in
     the history of the idea of visible saints.

17   PLUMSTEAD, A. W.   "Puritanism and Nineteenth Century American
     Literature." Queen's Quarterly 70 (Summer):209-22.
        Considers New England Puritanism "a major unifying
     force" in the development of American literature and
     Edwards's Images or Shadows of Divine Things the "most
     intense record" of that Puritan metaphorical mind, an
     artist's notebook comparable to Nathaniel Hawthorne's
     American Notebook. Edwards's poetic vision is "amazing";
     his text should be "required reading" for students of
     American literature.

1963

18   ROBINSON, LEWIS MILTON. "A History of the Half-Way Covenant."
      Ph.D. dissertation, University of Illinois.
          Traces the history of the half-way covenant and compares
      the theory and practice of Solomon Stoddard and Edwards.
      Stoddard took the theory of continuity to its "logical
      conclusion"; Edwards contributed to the eventual abolition
      of the half-way covenant.

19   SCHAFER, THOMAS A[NTON]. "Solomon Stoddard and the Theology
      of the Revival." In A Miscellany of American Christianity.
      Edited by Stuart C. Henry. Durham, N.C.: Duke University
      Press, pp. 328-61.
          Considers Edwards's attitude to Solomon Stoddard and to
      the Great Awakening one of "independence and critical
      appraisal," even though it is clear that Edwards followed
      the "general outlines" of his grandfather's evangelistic
      theology and practice and was undoubtedly his "main influ-
      ence" upon the revivals. But Edwards's conversion experi-
      ence differed markedly from the Stoddard pattern, and his
      ideas of spiritual light, true virtue, and divine love
      were attempts to resolve the dichotomy inherent in Stod-
      dard's formula of "preparation by man and conversion by
      God."

20   SMITH, CLAUDE ARCHIBALD. "A Sense of the Heart: The Nature
      of the Soul in the Thought of Jonathan Edwards." Ph.D.
      dissertation, Harvard University.
          Focuses upon a central concern in Edwards, his under-
      standing of man's nature as a religious being, through an
      exploration of his own piety and through Locke's Essay
      Concerning Human Understanding. But Edwards goes beyond
      Locke and offers an empirical basis to his concept rooted
      in man's sense of beauty.

21   VISSER'T HOOFT, WILLEM A. The Background of the Social Gospel
      in America. St. Louis: Bethany Press.
          Reprint of 1928.9.

22   WATTS, EMILY STIPES. "Jonathan Edwards and the Cambridge
      Platonists." Ph.D. dissertation, University of Illinois.
          Traces the influence of certain Cambridge Platonists
      upon Edwards's philosophical and theological theories.
      Ralph Cudworth "certainly" influenced Edwards's idealism;
      John Smith "contributed" to Edwards on the affections and
      on the dual end of creation; and Henry More in his
      Enchridion Ethicum "may be the source" for Edwards on
      excellency and virtue in Notes on the Mind.

*23 WEEKS, JOHN STAFFORD. "A Comparison of Calvin and Edwards on
      the Doctrine of Election." Ph.D. dissertation, University
      of Chicago.
          Cited in Gillette, "A Checklist of Doctoral Disserta-
      tions . . ." (1967.12), p. 207.

24   WEEKS, ROMONA. Review of Jonathan Edwards: Representative
      Selections, edited by Clarence H. Faust and Thomas H.
      Johnson. New Mexico Quarterly 33 (Summer):236-37.
          Notes the extensive selections in Clarence H. Faust and
      Thomas H. Johnson's reprinted text (1962.2).

                              1964

1   ALDRIDGE, ALFRED OWEN. Jonathan Edwards. The Great American
      Thinkers Series. New York: Washington Square Press,
      181 pp.
          Locates the source of both the failure and the success
      of Edwards's philosophical enterprise in Calvinist dogma,
      which "he accepted bodily" and which he defended tireless-
      ly, in a full-length study of the life and work of "the
      greatest, and virtually only, philosopher of the American
      colonies." What consistency there is in Edwards derives
      from the rigidity of Calvinism in its "last stand" and an
      extraordinary logic in its service; what beauty there is
      derives from the belief in divine sovereignty so profound
      that God could be realized only mystically or understood
      only intuitively. Reason thus became for Edwards an
      instrument to reveal that reason was inadequate to moral
      truth or inferior to it. Though Edwards provides the
      "most literate contemporary commentary" on eighteenth-
      century American theology, especially in the systematic,
      if not original, religious psychology of Religious Affec-
      tions, he left "no major school and imposed no new direc-
      tion." Aside from his generally anachronistic beliefs and
      ways, the "main trouble" with Edwards was his inability to
      fit his thought to common experience.

2   ANDERSON, WALLACE E[ARL]. "Immaterialism in Jonathan Edwards'
      Early Philosophical Notes." Journal of the History of
      Ideas 25 (April-June):181-200.
          Discovers in the juvenilia--"Of Atoms," "Of Being,"
      "The Mind," "Notes on Natural Science"--a commitment by
      Edwards not so much to idealism as to immaterialism.
      The concept of solidity or resistance founded in God's
      action or divine power that he developed at that time

underwent empirical and phenomenalistic refinement later.
But Edwards never seriously questioned his initial identi-
fication of body with resistance.

3 BARITZ, LOREN. "Theology: Jonathan Edwards." In his <u>City
on a Hill: A History of Ideas and Myths in America</u>. New
York: John Wiley & Sons, pp. 47-89.
Examines Edwards's work for its effect on American
ideas, myths, and religion. So <u>Sinners in the Hands of an
Angry God</u>, the "perfect" revival sermon, does "permanent
damage" to our future social history by influencing scores
of mindless tub-thumpers; <u>Some Thoughts</u> manages a chilias-
tic nationalism "more extreme" than any before or since;
and <u>Religious Affections</u>, his "gentlest" work, demands
that Americans abandon formula, convention, and ritual and
seek knowledge in themselves, rejecting their traditional
"intellectual posture." In <u>Freedom of the Will</u> Edwards,
New England's "most thoroughgoing" Calvinist, rebuilt the
"entire intellectual framework" of Puritanism and created
a "masculine theological cosmos" devoid of "feminine
mercy." This "quintessential Protestant mind," sharing
with the early Puritans a "fear and hatred of person" and
a love of abstraction, "helped to set both the tone and
substance of much of America's future intellectual history."

4 BARTH, J. ROBERT. "Faulkner and the Calvinist Tradition."
<u>Thought</u> 34 (Spring):100-20.
Places William Faulkner in a "direct line" of tradition
with Edwards and Cotton Mather, Nathaniel Hawthorne and
Herman Melville, in his preoccupation with determinism and
depravity.

5 BECKER, WILLIAM HARTSHORNE. "The Distinguishing Marks of
the Christian Man in the Thought of Jonathan Edwards."
Ph.D. dissertation, Harvard University.
Surveys Edwards on ontology, excellency, Scripture, and
the Christian life, principally in his work on revivals,
<u>Faithful Narrative</u>, <u>Distinguishing Marks</u>, <u>Some Thoughts</u>,
and <u>Religious Affections</u>. In the course of his thought,
Edwards redefines Christian manhood: from his personal
observation of the conversion experience to the scriptural
account of the saint in heaven, from what a Christian
"actually is" to what a Christian "knows he <u>ought</u> to be."

6   BOURKE, VERNON J. Will in Western Thought: An Historico-
       Critical Survey. New York: Sheed & Ward, pp. 41-42,
       141-43.
          Views Edwards on the will as "somewhat intellectual-
       istic" and perhaps "no more deterministic" than Thomas
       Aquinas. In the nineteenth century, faculty psychologists
       like Bledsoe, Burton, and Day took Edwards to task for
       neglecting "the characteristic of activity which they
       thought essential to the meaning of will."

7   CLAGHORN, GEORGE S. "The Manuscripts of Jonathan Edwards."
       Manuscripts 16 (Spring):38-42.
          Appeals to members of the Manuscript Society to help
       the editors of the Yale Edwards track down all letters and
       papers "by, to, and about" him. Among the missing manu-
       scripts are True Grace, Faithful Narrative, Resolutions,
       and The Mind.

8   CLOUGH, WILSON O. The Necessary Earth: Nature and Solitude
       in American Literature. Austin: University of Texas
       Press, pp. 92-94.
          Considers Edwards's introspective response to the
       wilderness in Personal Narrative typical of American
       "frontier innocence" and solitude and his accommodation
       of Locke and Newton an attempt to reconcile an inherited
       European tradition with a native American one through
       nature.

9   DAVIDSON, EDWARD H. "American Romanticism as Moral Style."
       Emerson Society Quarterly, no. 35, Part 1 (Second Quarter):
       10-14.
          Compares sentences by Edwards and Emerson as revealing
       examples of metaethics, the relation of moral thought to
       its expression. For Emerson, a sentence is wholly private
       and organizing; for Edwards, a sentence is a "steady
       interchange" between the private and the phenomenal. The
       mind comes into "exquisite conformity" with the world of
       substance and spirit, and the sentence becomes a moral
       action.

10 GAER, JOSEPH, and SIEGEL, BEN. The Puritan Heritage:
       America's Roots in the Bible. New York: New American
       Library of World Literature, pp. 28, 179-81.
          Notes that Edwards saw "no conflict" between the Bible
       and the Enlightenment, between philosophy and science,
       but that for him, as for all Puritans, reason followed
       revelation.

1964

11   HAROUTUNIAN, JOSEPH [G]. Piety versus Moralism. Hamden,
        Conn.: Shoe String Press.
              Reprint of 1932.5.

12   HEIMERT, ALAN [EDWARD]. "Perry Miller: An Appreciation."
        Harvard Review 2 (Winter-Spring):30-48.
              Cites Perry Miller's use of Edwards as a "center of
        consciousness" in his attempt to understand revival
        phenomena (in a eulogy of Miller).

13   JONES, HOWARD MUMFORD. O Strange New World. New York:
        Viking Press, p. 200.
              Notes the complementary ethics of Edwards and Franklin.

14   LOWELL, ROBERT. "Jonathan Edwards in Western Massachusetts."
        In his For the Union Dead. New York: Farrar, Straus &
        Giroux, pp. 40-44.
              Reflects upon Edwards's life and faith, in a 102-line
        poem:
                    I love you faded,
                    old, exiled and afraid
                    to leave your last flock, . . .
                    afraid to leave
                    all your writing, writing, writing,
                    denying the Freedom of the Will.

15   MILLER, PERRY. Errand into the Wilderness. Cambridge, Mass.:
        Harvard University Press; and New York: Harper & Row.
              Reprint of 1956.8.

16   OPIE, JOHN, JR. "Conversion and Revivalism: An Internal
        History from Jonathan Edwards through Charles Grandison
        Finney." Ph.D. dissertation, University of Chicago.
              Studies the American "preoccupation" with conversion in
        a century of revivalism (1735-1835) led by Edwards, Joseph
        Bellamy, Samuel Hopkins, Timothy Dwight, Nathaniel William
        Taylor, Asahel Nettleton, Lyman Beecher, and Charles
        Grandison Finney. Conversion and revivalism mutually
        explain and enhance one another and give "a unique orien-
        tation" to Protestantism in America.

17   OUTLER, ALBERT C., ed. John Wesley. New York: Oxford
        University Press, pp. 15-16, passim.
              Notes the Great Awakening as an effectual cause of the
        Wesleyan Revival and Edwards as "a major source" of John
        Wesley's evangelical theology, especially Faithful Narra-
        tive and Distinguishing Marks.

18   PATRIDES, C. A.   "Renaissance and Modern Views on Hell."
      <u>Harvard Theological Review</u> 57 (July):217-36.
         Regrets that the undue attention given the hell-fire of
      Edwards (and other New Englanders) "detracts" from parallel
      instances of such description in earlier Western European
      and English literature.

19   ROBACK, A. A.   <u>History of American Psychology</u>. New York:
      Collier Books.
         Reprint of 1952.8.

20   SAVELLE, MAX.   <u>The Colonial Origins of American Thought</u>.
      Princeton, N.J.: D. Van Nostrand Co., pp. 48, 56-58,
      65-66, passim.
         Labels Edwards an original though transitional figure
      in American thought whose influence upon later philosophy,
      particularly transcendentalism, was "enormous." Edwards
      achieved a "literary and philosophical synthesis" of
      Newton and Locke's contribution to science and philosophy
      in a vain defense of a dying Calvinism.

21   SAYRE, ROBERT F.   <u>The Examined Self: Benjamin Franklin, Henry
      Adams, Henry James</u>. Princeton, N.J.: Princeton University
      Press, pp. 34-39.
         Discovers in Edwards's <u>Personal Narrative</u> a new form of
      autobiography, unconventional and typically American.
      Edwards's grim self-discovery is managed in the "terrifying"
      isolation of a desolate world. Such American loneliness
      differs markedly from European romanticism and demands a
      radical form of autobiography to deal with it. Before
      Franklin and Adams, Edwards used his own life as "the
      starting point and the ultimate test of speculation."

22   SCHLAEGER, MARGARET CLARE.   "Jonathan Edwards' Theory of
      Perception." Ph.D. dissertation, University of Illinois.
         Traces Edwards's theories of perception. With his
      conversion experience, Edwards rejects his earlier and
      "vastly inferior" natural perception for his new spiritual
      vision, rejects the "corrupt and mutable" world of man for
      the "whole scheme" of God. His later, speculative work
      calls for the participation of human consciousness with
      the divine act of perception to perceive order.

23   SINGER, C. GREGG.   <u>A Theological Interpretation of American
      History</u>. Nutley, N.J.: Craig Press, pp. 26-29.
         Notes that Edwards's appropriation of Lockean empiricism
      helped "unwittingly" in the triumph of the American

1964

Enlightenment and permanently changed Puritanism. His
metaphysical idealism was "quite foreign" to Calvinism,
his doctrine of benevolence a "contributing factor" in
the rise of clerical liberalism after 1730.

24   STOB, HENRY. "The Ethics of Jonathan Edwards." In Faith and
      Philosophy: Philosophical Studies in Religion and Ethics.
      Edited by Alvin Plantinga. Grand Rapids, Mich.: William
      B. Eerdmans Publishing Co., pp. 111-37.
            Considers Edwards's ethics to arise from his doctrine
      of divine sovereignty, his "determinative intellectual
      conviction." Edwards "invariably" defines sovereignty in
      ethical terms in which God is "pre-eminently the ultimate
      and absolute moral reality, the supreme ground of moral
      obligation, and the final guarantor of virtue." As exist-
      ence and morality are "fundamentally social" in man, so on
      the highest level God as triune is both absolute and
      social: God's perfect idea of Himself is Christ, His pure
      act of will and love, the Holy Spirit.

25   WHITTEMORE, ROBERT CLIFTON. "Jonathan Edwards." In his
      Makers of the American Mind. New York: William Morrow &
      Co., pp. 32-45.
            Depicts Edwards's role in the Great Awakening and the
      place of the religious affections. In God Glorified,
      Edwards omits mention of assurance of mercy through the
      convenant of grace and, therefore, reveals, in fallen
      man's utter dependence upon God, a God free of convenant
      and obligation.

26   WINSLOW, OLA ELIZABETH. Review of "The Mind" of Jonathan
      Edwards, edited by Leon Howard. American Literature 36
      (March):79-81.
            Values Leon Howard's edition of "The Mind" (1963.13)
      for the light it sheds on the "originality and independ-
      ence" of Edwards's early thought, the basis of "everything
      else" he was to write.

27   WOODWARD, ROBERT H. "Jonathan Edwards and the Sweet Life."
      Fellowship in Prayer 15 (August):11-13.
            Urges that Edwards be known and valued for his sweetness
      rather than his wrath, "'ejaculatory prayer'" rather than
      imprecatory sermon, Personal Narrative rather than Sinners
      in the Hands of an Angry God.

1965

1 BALLINGER, MARTHA. "The Metaphysical Echo." English Studies
in Africa 8 (March):71-80.
Characterizes Edwards as a "terrible mouthpiece" of a
wrathful God who gave his congregation a "poetic experience" and American poetry an inescapable metaphysics.

2 BARKER, SHIRLEY. Builders of New England. New York: Dodd,
Mead & Co., pp. 68-89.
Recounts the life of Edwards for young readers, a self-
righteous logician and pious mystic.

3 BURGGRAAFF, WINFIELD J. "Jonathan Edwards: A Bibliographical
Essay." Reformed Review 18 (March):19-33.
Reviews selected studies of Edwards and concludes that
each formulates "afresh" Edwards's contribution to theology. Since the particularly sharp attacks of liberals and
Unitarians in the 1920s and 1930s, Edwards has had a
"rehabilitation" and the emphasis has been upon his
"positive and original" contributions to theology and
letters. Yet nothing new about his genius has turned up
since Perry Miller's "classic" study (1949.9).

4 CHERRY, CHARLES CONRAD. "The Nature of Faith in the Theology
of Jonathan Edwards." Ph.D. dissertation, Drew University.
Published as 1966.9.

5 CHERRY, C[HARLES] CONRAD. "The Puritan Notion of the Covenant in Jonathan Edwards' Doctrine of Faith." Church
History 34 (September):328-41.
Corrects Perry Miller's misreading of both covenant
theology and Edwards's doctrine of faith (1935.6).
Edwards "definitely adhered" to covenant theology and
understood, as did his Puritan forebears, that the con-
tractual agreement was simply a way of construing Revelation and did not bind God to man, for the covenant was
between sinful believer and a gracious sovereign God, not
between equals. God, in Christ, promises salvation and
assures His gift for which prayerful man might sue. But
the "demanding act of faith" is possible only so long as
God condescends to it. Edwards sought, unhappily, to
mitigate the problematic nature of faith by distinguishing
between a covenant of redemption and one of grace, but he
always maintained that the relation of faith was a
covenant-relation. He may have "narrowed" the importance
of the saint's role socially and politically, but he
never repudiated covenant theology.

1965

6   CHRISTIAN, CURTIS WALLACE. "The Concept of Life after Death
    in the Theology of Jonathan Edwards, Friedrich Schleier-
    macher, and Paul Tillich." Ph.D. dissertation, Vanderbilt
    University.
        Compares Edwards, a "thoroughgoing teleologist," to
    Schleiermacher, a less overt eschatologist, and Tillich,
    a more "static" ontologist. Edwards's doctrine rests on
    the "divine creative intention" and the self illuminated
    by grace and arises from his idealism, pantheism, and
    determinism. He encounters some difficulty in reconciling
    the love of God with the idea of reprobation.

7   GAUSTAD, EDWIN SCOTT. The Great Awakening in New England.
    Gloucester, Mass.: Peter Smith.
        Reprint of 1957.6.

8   HOLBROOK, CLYDE A[MOS]. "Original Sin and the Enlightenment."
    In The Heritage of Christian Thought: Essays in Honor of
    Robert Lowry Calhoun. Edited by Robert E. Cushman and Egil
    Grislis. New York: Harper & Row, pp. 142-65.
        Examines Edwards's view of original sin and that of his
    antagonist, John Taylor, and finds that "in depth and
    thoroughness" Edwards's treatment has not been matched
    until recently. His argument from infinite sin to infinite
    debt to infinite punishment and his doctrines of imputation
    and identify are skillfully handled and apt. Whether his
    insights are more relevant today than those of his Enlight-
    enment opponent "remains a question."

9   HUDSON, WINTHROP S. Religion in America. New York: Charles
    Scribner's Sons, pp. 64-69, 77-79.
        Sees Edwards's role in the Great Awakening as a vital
    one and his theological contribution to the debate about
    the revival and its effects "most impressive." His Faith-
    ful Narrative not only stimulated and inspired revivals
    elsewhere but, more importantly, provided a model for
    subsequent revivals through its "precise and detailed"
    rendering of the Northampton experience.

10 LOBINGIER, JOHN LESLIE. Pilgrims and Pioneers in the Congre-
    gational Christian Tradition. Philadelphia: United Church
    Press, pp. 50-66.
        Considers Edwards "the absentminded thinker" whose
    three positions at Northampton, Stockbridge, and Princeton
    offer an "interesting study in contrast." In all three,
    however, he emerges as an earnest, uncompromising, asocial,
    God-fearing scholar, "'the man of the century'" in American
    religious life.

11 LYTTLE, DAVID JAMES. "Jonathan Edwards' Symbolic Structure of
    Experience." Ph.D. dissertation, Pennsylvania State Uni-
    versity.
        Analyzes Edwards's conversion experience in Freudian
    terms as a "victory" of superego over id and suggests
    analogical implications. Edwards saw correspondence
    between the three persons of the trinity and the three
    elements of empirical experience, between a symbolic
    universe with a real Hell and the human personality with
    its equally real unconscious.

12 MAZZARO, JEROME. The Poetic Themes of Robert Lowell. Ann
    Arbor: University of Michigan Press, pp. 65-71.
        Compares Edwards's phrasing to Lowell's in "Mr. Edwards
    and the Spider" and "After the Surprising Conversions."

13 OLIVER, ROBERT T. History of Public Speaking in America.
    Boston: Allyn & Bacon, pp. 31-36.
        Focuses upon Sinners in the Hands of an Angry God to
    explain Edwards's "totalitarian" theocracy and his manner
    of preaching it. He preached, without "personalized"
    warmth or fervor, a dying system of divine sovereignty.

14 PIERCE, DAVID CLARENCE. "Jonathan Edwards and the New Sense
    of Glory." Ph.D. dissertation, Columbia University.
        Traces two sorts of piety in Edwards, one founded in
    divine sovereignty and election, the other in the immediacy
    of divinity. In Personal Narrative, both kinds of piety
    are "juxtaposed"--the new sense of glory confirms God's
    sovereignty; in the Northampton of the Great Awakening,
    one "mingled" with the other; and in a Stockbridge without
    a church-covenant way, the new sense of glory had "the
    last word."

15 ROOY, SIDNEY H. The Theology of Missions in the Puritan
    Tradition: A Study of Representative Puritans: Richard
    Sibbes, Richard Baxter, John Eliot, Cotton Mather, and
    Jonathan Edwards. Grand Rapids, Mich.: William B. Eerd-
    mans Publishing Co., pp. 285-309.
        Attributes Edwards's significance for missions to his
    influence in the Great Awakening, to his inspiration of
    later missionaries through his writings, and to his first-
    hand experience at Stockbridge among the Indians. Mission-
    ary work, for Edwards, was bound to his millenarianism,
    expressed particularly in History of Redemption: the goal
    of missions is the realization, in three stages, of God's

1965

purpose and the establishment of his eternal kingdom.
Northampton was but an "earnest" of the growing grace that
will, in time, become evident reality.

16 SAVELLE, MAX. Seeds of Liberty. Seattle: University of
    Washington Press.
         Reprint of 1948.10.

17 SELDES, GILBERT. The Stammering Century. New York: Harper
    & Row.
         Reprint of 1928.8.

18 SHEA, DANIEL B., JR. "The Art and Instruction of Jonathan
    Edwards's Personal Narrative." American Literature 37
    (March):17-32.
         Considers Edwards's Personal Narrative "a mature arti-
    culation" of his spiritual experience, an artistic account
    of his conversion, coherent in form, selective in detail,
    and affecting in language. With little of the intensity
    of the day-to-day struggle of the Diary about it, Personal
    Narrative makes its way through "heightened paradox" and
    a narrative technique that joins analyst to actor, reason
    to feeling, and instruction to autobiography. "He could
    scarcely have added a word to the experiential summing-up
    of all he ever thought on all that finally mattered."
    (Reprinted in 1974.21 and 1977.27.)

19 SWEET, WILLIAM WARREN. Revivalism in America. Gloucester,
    Mass.: Peter Smith.
         Reprint of 1944.4

1966

1 ALDRIDGE, ALFRED OWEN. Jonathan Edwards. New York: Washington Square Press, 181 pp.
         Reprint of 1964.1.

2 ALEXIS, GERHARD T[HEODORE]. "Jonathan Edwards and the Theocratic Ideal." Church History 35 (September):328-43.
         Speculates that Edwards's lack of concern for the
   social order or the theocratic ideal probably lies in his
   otherworldliness, his belief in the "eternal ostracism of
   the damned" and the millennial expectation of the saints.
   Hence in his thinking there is little to suggest that the
   saints would work to change the political order, none that
   Edwards advocates the theocratic ideal.

3   ANDERSON, COURTNEY. "Jonathan Edwards: Rational Mystic."
     In Heroic Colonial Christians. Edited by Russell T. Hirt.
     Philadelphia and New York: J. B. Lippincott Co., pp. 13-
     105.
         Derives from a study of the life and works of Edwards
     two conclusions about the nature and genesis of his
     thought: first, underneath all his logic, Edwards was
     a mystic; second, as a theologian, Edwards was "formed
     almost all at once" by the time he became a minister. So
     his mind simply made logical what his heart felt, and so
     his theological formulations were "determined" by his
     father in the "critical first dozen years" of his life.

4   BEAVER, R. PIERCE, ed. Pioneers in Mission: The Early
     Missionary Ordination Sermons, Charges, and Instructions.
     Grand Rapids, Mich.: William B. Eerdmans Publishing Co.,
     pp. 24, 78-79.
         Corrects the standard view of Edwards's Stockbridge
     years--he was a reluctant sojourner among the Indians--by
     insisting that he was "vitally concerned about missions
     for many years" and by quoting from his Life of Brainerd.

5   BROCKWAY, ROBERT. "Theological Parties in New England and
     the Middle Colonies in the Early Eighteenth Century."
     Crane Review 8 (Spring):125-37.
         Defines four theological parties at the time of the
     Great Awakening--Old Calvinist or conservative: Arminian
     or liberal; New Divinity or Edwardsean; and New Light
     Radical or antinomian--and suggests that modern American
     theology is "rooted" in such alternatives. "To some
     degree," Niebuhr's neo-orthodoxy and Tillich's existential-
     ism are "restatements" of Edwards's New Divinity, the
     theologicaly important center of the Awakening.

6   BUSHMAN, RICHARD L. "Jonathan Edwards and Puritan Conscious-
     ness." Journal for the Scientific Study of Religion 5
     (Fall):383-96.
         Reconstructs Edwards's "dominant states of mind" in
     order to recover Puritan consciousness and to render it
     psychoanalytically, but cautions against reductive errors
     of the method. Edwards's cycle of depression and exhila-
     ration is "reminiscent" of infant-mother separation and
     return; though his conversion experience, "on one level,"
     may be an effort to master the Oedipal crisis by "re-
     linquishing the ambition to overcome" the father (so common
     in Puritan theology), it may also be an expression of the
     "selfless union" of mother and child. Yet to leave it at

that is "grossly" to distort: unresolved is why Oedipal
problems in Edwards and the Puritan consciousness were "so
prominent" and "why their resolution took the form it did."
(Reprinted in 1977.6.)

7   CAIRNS, EARLE E.   "Jonathan Edwards, Challenge for Evangelism
Today." Moody Monthly 66 (January):60-62.
Presents Edwards's evangelical work in the Great Awakening as a ministerial pattern to follow in meeting the
needs of the urban masses in America today.

8   CARSE, JAMES PEARCE.   "The Christology of Jonathan Edwards."
Ph.D. dissertation, Drew University.
Published as 1967.6.

9   CHERRY, [CHARLES] CONRAD.   The Theology of Jonathan Edwards:
A Reappraisal. Garden City, N.Y.: Doubleday & Co.,
270 pp.
Contends that Edwards is "first and last" a Calvinist,
insisting that faith, with love at its core, is "central"
to his thought and "germane" to his major work, in a full-
length study of his theology in four parts: the act of
faith, the reality of faith, the life of faith, and the
controversy over faith. Although Edwards broadens and
sometimes alters his Calvinism, he never transcends it,
preferring to "feed new life" into it with the new learning. Hardly a mystic--the mantle fits him "loosely at
best"--Edwards is a covenant theologian, convinced his God
of faith to be "a promise-making, promise-keeping God who
may be 'dealt with' in faith as a covenant partner; not
the God of an inscrutable hinterland." Edwards theologized
"as the occasion demanded," yet his theology is "coherent,"
if not systematic, resting as it does on the meaning of
faith and the covenant of grace. For contemporary American
Protestants, Edwards reinterprets the Puritan tradition,
especially as it bears upon "his own portenteous historical
situation," and as it demonstrates that faith is "a vital
union of heart with a sovereign, transcendent God who yet
covenants in history."

10 DAVIDSON, EDWARD H.   Jonathan Edwards: The Narrative of a
Puritan Mind. Riverside Studies in Literature. Boston:
Houghton Mifflin Co., 161 pp.
Reports the uneven battle between orthodox Calvinism
and the new philosophy for the mind of Edwards, "'a
Puritan baroque,'" in a full-length study of the major
works. Edwards crucially apprehends the sense and

disposition of light--"a metaphor of the mind"--and uses
language symbolically, as he moves progressively from a
world of facts to a world of ideas. In time the intellectual triumphs over the poet in Edwards--the "inevitable
wastage of sensual delight" accounts for it in part--and
he defines in himself the impact of Locke and Newton on
a Puritan sensibility.

11 DEAN, LLOYD F. "Salvation and Self-Interest: Edwards' Concept of Love and Its Relevance to Modern Evangelism."
Gordon Review 9 (Winter):101-10.
    Discovers the "real" Edwards for evangelicals can be
found in the second sign of Religious Affections, namely,
those affections that arise selflessly out of love for the
excellencies of God. Edwards argues that sinners are
elected on God's initiative alone, and he documents it
with "extensive" biblical citations. This is so far a cry
from the "bargain-sale" and "domesticated" process of
today's conversion experience that evangelicals must "re-
discover" Edwards.

12 DELATTRE, ROLAND ANDRÉ. "Beauty and Sensibility in the Thought
of Jonathan Edwards: An Essay in Aesthetics and Ethics."
Ph.D. dissertation, Yale University.
    Published as 1968.8.

13 GAUSTAD, EDWIN SCOTT. A Religious History of America. New
York: Harper & Row, pp. 61-62.
    Cites Edwards's earlier defense of the Great Awakening
as the source of his later examination of the "whole
question of the nature of religion itself" in Religious
Affections.

14 GAY, PETER. A Loss of Mastery: Puritan Historians in Colonial America. Berkeley and Los Angeles: University of
California Press, pp. 88-117.
    Marks Edwards the "greatest," perhaps the only, "tragic
hero" of American Calvinism, a "brilliant scholar" whose
tragedy "illuminates" the failure of the Puritan experiment and the "lost mastery" over society and whose History
of Redemption is "reactionary and fundamentalist." For
Edwards, history is a calculus of mystery and myth proving
the accuracy of the Bible, not the record of a real past
urged and rendered by eighteenth-century philosophes.
Edwards uses the ideas and rhetoric of Newton and Locke
simply to "confirm" long-held religious convictions. "Far

1966

from being the first modern American, therefore, he was the
last medieval American--at least among intellectuals."

15   GELPI, ALBERT J. Emily Dickinson: The Mind of the Poet.
      Cambridge, Mass.: Harvard University Press, pp. 57-59,
      90-91 passim.
          Relates Edwards's vision (and Emerson's) to Emily Dick-
      inson's habit of seeing "'New Englandly.'" Although there
      is no evidence that Dickinson read Edwards, he typifies
      for her the Puritan mind and heart of the fathers.

16   GRIFFIN, EDWARD MICHAEL. "A Biography of Charles Chauncy
      (1705-1787)." Ph.D. dissertation, Stanford University.
          Compares Edwards's treatment of Phebe Bartlet in Faith-
      ful Narrative with Charles Chauncy's treatment of Elizabeth
      Price in Early Piety; the image of the sinner over Hell in
      Sinners in the Hands of an Angry God with the same image
      in The New Creature; and the nature and meaning of the
      Great Awakening in Some Thoughts with that in Seasonable
      Thoughts. "Disorder, not Jonathan Edwards, was the main
      target for Chauncy's criticism of the Great Awakening."
      (Revision published by the University of Minnesota Press,
      1980.)

17   HEIMERT, ALAN [EDWARD]. Religion and the American Mind from
      the Great Awakening to the Revolution. Cambridge, Mass.:
      Harvard University Press, pp. 95-158, passim.
          Contends that the evangelical religion of the Great
      Awakening--the "watershed in American history"--rather than
      the reasonable faith of eighteenth-century liberals gave
      impetus and shape to the Revolution and its democratic
      ideas; and quite frequently cites Edwards, the "most not-
      able formal expression" of experimental Calvinism, to
      prosecute the argument. Evangelical religion challenged
      the elitist and conservative ideology of "the standing
      order"; Edwards, for his part, helped provide "a radical,
      even democratic, social and political ideology" and helped
      promote American nationalism. Some Thoughts, for instance,
      was "the first national party platform in American history"
      and, in "a vital respect," America's declaration of inde-
      pendence from Europe; and Freedom of the Will became "the
      Calvinist handbook of the Revolution."

18   LYTTLE, DAVID [JAMES]. Review of Jonathan Edwards, by Alfred
      Owen Aldridge. Seventeenth-Century News 24 (Winter):63-64.
          Praises A. O. Aldridge's "valuable" explications of
      Edwards's ethics (1964.1) but faults his insensitivity to
      Edwards's personality, theology, and "literary genius,
      which is what really keeps him alive."

19   _____. "The Sixth Sense of Jonathan Edwards." Church Quar-
        terly Review 167 (January):50-59.
            Explains that Edwards used Locke's empirical terminology
        of sense experience to describe orthodox grace as a new
        "simple idea," and so the experience of the saint is
        "unique" and "radically different" from that of natural
        man. The difference lies in the way saving ideas are held:
        the saint "in the depth" of the supernatural light, the
        natural man apart from it. The saint knows the supernatu-
        ral light by a sixth sense--a spiritual, innate, non-
        cognitive perception--and though "utterly different" from
        the natural senses, unified with them in him. Thus Edwards
        the empirical philosopher of Perry Miller (1949.9) is
        joined to Edwards the medieval theologian of Vincent Tomas
        (1952.12).

20   MALEFYT, CALVIN STERLING. "The Changing Concept of Pneumatol-
        ogy in New England Trinitarianism, 1635-1755." Ph.D.
        dissertation, Harvard University.
            Devotes a chapter to Edwards, especially to the "impres-
        sive apologetic" for affectional evangelism found in Reli-
        gious Affections, in a history of the role of the holy
        spirit in New England trinitarianism and of assurance in
        the theory of salvation.

21   MAURER, ARMAND A. "Jonathan Edwards." In Recent Philosophy:
        Hegel to the Present. Edited by Etienne Gilson, Thomas
        Langan, and Armand A. Maurer. A History of Philosophy,
        no. 4. New York: Random House, pp. 559-64.
            Places Edwards's philosophical inquiries in the tradi-
        tion of Hobbes and Locke on the will, Shaftesbury and
        Hutcheson on virtue, and the Cambridge Platonists and
        Newton on being. Although the source of his idealism is
        still in dispute, Edwards "never retracted" his early
        views and they remain "implicit in much that he wrote."

22   MORGAN, EDMUND S. "The Historians of Early New England." In
        The Reinterpretation of Early American History. Edited by
        Ray Allen Billington. Essays in Honor of John Edwin
        Pomfret. San Marino, Cal.: Huntington Library, pp. 41-63.
            Surveys work on early New England and recommends Perry
        Miller's study (1949.9) and Ola Elizabeth Winslow's
        biography (1940.21) of Edwards, "the most creative
        eighteenth-century New England thinker in the Puritan
        tradition."

1966

23   PETTIT, NORMAN. The Heart Prepared: Grace and Conversion in
       Puritan Life. New Haven, Conn.: Yale University Press,
       pp. 208-12.
           Remarks Edwards's views on preparation, conversion, and
       assurance, and compares them to earlier doctrines and
       local practices. Edwards differs from the early Puritans--
       conversion, to him, is one of the signs of election not the
       start of the process to it--and agrees with Solomon Stod-
       dard in rejecting the concept of gradual assurance. But
       he would not, like his grandfather, "extend the covenant
       seal as a measure of pure expediency," and thus he began
       "a new system of theology" in New England.

24   POWERS, WILLIAM JENNINGS. "The Narrative Concept and American
       Consciousness." Ph.D. dissertation, University of Illinois.
           Uses Franklin's Autobiography and Edwards's Personal
       Narrative as early instances of a continuing narrative
       division between the city and the self or the public and
       the private utterance found in the work of Thoreau, Cooper,
       and Hawthorne.

*25   PRICE, WILLIAM WINFIELD. "The Eschatology of Jonathan Ed-
       wards." Ph.D. dissertation, University of Göttingen.
           Cited in Richard S. Sliwoski, "Doctoral Dissertations
       on Jonathan Edwards," Early American Literature 14 (Winter
       1979):324.

26   ROGERS, CHARLES A. "John Wesley and Jonathan Edwards." Duke
       Divinity School Review 31 (Winter):20-38.
           Compares Edwards and John Wesley principally to illumi-
       nate the agreements and conflicts Wesley had with doctri-
       naire Calvinism. On matters like election, perfection,
       and the perserverence of the saints the two were "unalter-
       ably opposed"; on matters like the human condition, sal-
       vation, and assurance they were "not a 'hair's-breadth'
       apart." Though Wesley was widely acquainted with Edwards
       and his work--he had much of it reprinted--Edwards had
       "only a single response, and that negative," to Wesley.

27   SARACENO, CHIARA. "Un Pensatore Puritano del Diciottesimo
       Secolo: Jonathan Edwards." Rivista di Filosofia Neo-
       Scolastica 58 (May-June):347-55.
           Traces the influence of Locke's empiricism and Newton's
       mechanism on Edwards's concept of experience and the prob-
       lem of freedom, in a brief explanation of Religious Affec-
       tions and Freedom of the Will, his major work. (In Ital-
       ian.)

28 SELLERS, JAMES. Theological Ethics. New York: Macmillan
    Co., pp. 14, 42-43.
        Suggests that Edwards's idea of benevolence to being in
    True Virtue lends ethical dimensions both to the American
    ethos and to the Reformation motif of justification by
    faith. For Edwards, every doctrine of God "implies" a
    doctrine of man, and so divine activity no longer contrasts
    with human inactivity.

29 SHEA, DANIEL B., JR. "Spiritual Autobiography in Early
    America." Ph.D. dissertation, Stanford University.
    Published as 1968.26.

30 SMITH, CLAUDE A[RCHIBALD]. "Jonathan Edwards and 'The Way of
    Ideas.'" Harvard Theological Review 59 (April):153-73.
        Contends that Edwards was forced "to strike out on his
    own" to explain divine revelation, going beyond Locke's
    narrowly based empiricism. Edwards had "a more active
    view" of the mind than Locke, asserting that the will
    depends upon man's judgment as well as his apprehension
    of good and that through the active power of the mind man
    "gained access" to the materials of revelation or the
    knowledge of God. That active power, perceiving the data
    experience in an ordered or aesthetic way, "links" man to
    Being or God.

31 SPONSELLER, EDWIN. Northampton and Jonathan Edwards. Faculty
    Monograph Series, no. 1. Shippensburg, Pa.: Shippensburg
    State College, 32 pp.
        Follows the career of Edwards at Northampton, amid the
    "friendly mountains" of the Connecticut Valley and through
    the "tragic" years following the Great Awakening. The
    "great events" of his ministry had to do with his prepara-
    tion for the revivals of 1734 and 1741; the crucial event
    was his rejection of the sacramentarian view of his late
    grandfather. Edwards, the "most brilliant son" of New
    England Puritanism, was "untimely born."

32 STARKEY, MARION L. "The Great Awakening." In her The Con-
    gregational Way: The Role of the Pilgrims and their
    Heirs in Shaping America. Garden City, N.Y.: Doubleday &
    Co., pp. 129-56.
        Traces Edwards's Congregational way from Yale to Prince-
    ton, noting the ironic role of the "newly redeemed young,"
    instruments of both his rise and his fall.

1966

33 Van de WETERING, JOHN E. "The Christian History of the Great
    Awakening." Journal of Presbyterian History 44 (June):
    122-29.
        Notes that the decision to publish Thomas Prince's
    Christian History was "probably triggered" by Edwards's
    suggestion that the progress of the revival should be re-
    corded fortnightly or monthly by a Boston minister "close
    to the press." It is "very likely" that Prince consulted
    Edwards before first publishing the "last major propaganda
    blast" of the Great Awakening.

34 WARREN, AUSTIN. The New England Conscience. Ann Arbor:
    University of Michigan Press, pp. 88-101 passim.
        Examines Edwards's autobiographical writings and True
    Virtue to plumb the conscience of a New England saint.
    The "Resolutions" and the Diary reveal Edwards's strong
    sense of duty and discipline, in private and public mat-
    ters, in intellect and in spirituality. The Personal
    Narrative details the "successive deepenings" of his
    conversion from an emotional to an intellectual to an
    affectional acceptance of the sovereignty of God and ends
    in a new sense of glory. True Virtue resolves his special
    experience into a general love of duty, an expression of
    the affections and the beauty of virtue. "Only the con-
    verted (who, viewed from God's side are the elect) are
    capable of loving the ought."

35 WHITTEMORE, ROBERT C[LIFTON]. "Jonathan Edwards and the
    Theology of the Sixth Way." Church History 35 (March):
    60-75.
        Concludes that Edwards is neither the panentheist nor
    mystical realist of Douglas Elwood (1960.3), the modern
    empiricist of Perry Miller (1949.9) nor yet the medieval
    biblicist of Vincent Tomas (1952.12), but rather a Chris-
    tian Neoplatonist, a "classical" theist, and a theologian
    of the sixth way. Of the ten ways to describe the rela-
    tionship of God to the universe, Edwards offers a version
    of the sixth way in which God is real and the universe is
    God's image or shadow. Edwards is "more the medievalist
    than the modern" because he stresses Being to the exclu-
    sion of Becoming. Such an ontology, at one with Anselm
    and Aquinas, marks Edwards "an important philosopher" as
    well as "an anachronism."

36 WILEY, MARGARET L. "Jonathan Edwards and Eighteenth-Century
    Simplicity." In her Creative Sceptics. London: George
    Allen & Unwin, pp. 168-202.

Discovers in Edwards the "great American master of the creative paradox," a skeptic "wrestling" with experience, rejecting the simplicity of American teleology and neo-classical rationalism. Edwards reverses the standard pattern of the skeptic—nescience, dualism, paradox, and doing in order to know—and solves problems by his "over-powering conviction, wrung from the depths of bitter experience," and by his litany of belief. Thus his scriptural sense, his theological concepts (especially his trinitarian views), his philosophical speculations are characterized by "oblique insights" and cast in paradox, much in the same manner as Spenser, Bacon, and Milton, Emerson, Melville, and James.

37 WINSLOW, OLA ELIZABETH. Foreword to her Jonathan Edwards: Basic Writings. New York: Signet Books, pp. vii-xxviii.
      Traces Edwards's career through his publications and suggests that he is still relevant, not doctrinally, but in the "depth and dimension" of his thought, in a preface to selections from his work (with headnotes).

38 _____. Review of Jonathan Edwards, by Alfred Owen Aldridge. American Literature 38 (March):127-28.
      Praises the flawless scholarship, the sympathetic interpretation, and the lucid exposition in A. O. Aldridge's "fresh inquiry" into Edwards's place in English philosophical and theological thought.

39 _____. Review of Jonathan Edwards: The Narrative of a Puritan Mind, by Edward H. Davidson. American Literature 38 (November):388-89.
      Recommends, with "occasional amendments," Edward H. Davidson's narrative of Edwards's "perpetual battle" between Calvinism and the new philosophy of Locke and Newton (1966.10).

40 WRIGHT, [CHARLES] CONRAD. "The Freedom of the Will." In his The Beginnings of Unitarianism in America. Boston: Beacon Press.
      Reprint of 1955.12.

1967

1 AHLSTROM, SYDNEY E., ed. Theology in America: The Major Protestant Voices from Puritanism to New-Orthodoxy. Indianapolis: Bobbs-Merrill Co., pp. 149-52.

1967

Characterizes Edwards as an "apostle" to the Age of
Reason, "the theologian of a vast international revival
and the chief intellectual ornament of its American phase."
Edwards synthesized the demands of the Platonic tradition
and the demands of the Enlightenment--pietism and science--
and made "the most impressive contribution" to Reformed
theology between John Calvin and Karl Barth.

2   ANON. Review of The Theology of Jonathan Edwards: A Reap-
    praisal, by Conrad Cherry. Ethics 77 (April):232.
        Finds that Conrad Cherry's "elaborate" study (1966.9)
    makes Edwards seem less remote.

3   BLANSHARD, BRAND. "Religion and Revolt." New York Times
    Book Review, 1 January, p. 3.
        Reviews Religion and the American Mind, by Alan Heimert
    (1966.17) and The Theology of Jonathan Edwards, by Conrad
    Cherry (1966.9) and finds the intellectual that Cherry
    writes of needed the evangelist that Heimert writes of to
    keep Edwards "in line."

4   BORGES, JORGE LUIS. Introduccion a la Literatura Norte-
    americana. [Buenos Aires]: Editorial Columba, pp. 11-12.
        Considers Edwards a complex Calvinist, in a brief
    survey. (In Spanish; transl. 1971.2.)

5   BUSHMAN, RICHARD L. From Puritan to Yankee: Character and
    the Social Order in Connecticut, 1690-1765. Cambridge,
    Mass.: Harvard University Press, pp. 209-11, 214.
        Includes Edwards among the moderates of the New Lights
    because he believed that experimental religion could exist
    within the established ecclesiastical order and that
    ministerial authority was vital to it. His emphasis on
    the new birth, both the necessary evidence of it and the
    effective preaching to bring it about, seemed radical to
    some, and at first few New Lights followed him. In time,
    he and his followers "hammered out" concepts of experi-
    mental conversion acceptable to most, though they lost
    those conservatives given over to the "regeneration of
    reason."

6   CARSE, JAMES [PEARCE]. Jonathan Edwards and the Visibility of
    God. New York: Charles Scribner's Sons, 191 pp.
        Considers the central fact of Edwards's thought and
    ministry to be his rejection of the "principle of private
    judgment" in religious and ethical matters for the
    "principle of visibility," in which a communal sense of

what appears to be becomes the source of action of the
will. The "final validity" of Edwards's thought rests
upon "a special knowledge" some men have that their greatest good lies in the visible God-man Christ and through
Him, God. Just as Christ is visible, so the saints, or
the effects of divine grace in them, must be visible to
others, and when joined to a profession of faith, something
"radically revolutionary" emerges. The church becomes a
community of men in the vanguard of "the long journey
toward the ultimate society." Edwards preached such
"radical this-worldliness" in all his sermons. He hoped
that a "smaller society" of visible saints would become
"the most apparent good" for the rest of civilization.
But he failed, as every other "great American prophet"
must fail: the "American journey is over."

7   _____. "Mr. Locke's Magic Onions and an Unboxed Beetle for
    Young Jonathan." Journal of Religion 47 (October):331-39.
    Reprints chapter 2 of 1967.6.

8   DAVIDSON, CLIFFORD. "Jonathan Edwards and Mysticism." Col-
    lege Language Association Journal 11 (December):149-56.
       Challenges the view that Edwards's mysticism is at odds
    with his reason, for he was part of a Puritan tradition
    which tried to unite piety and rationalism. His Christian
    experience is like that of the Puritan mystic Francis Rous
    in his Mysticall Marriage (1631); his spiritual sense is
    like the "spiritual sensation" of the Cambridge Platonist
    John Smith in his "The True Way or Method of Attaining
    Divine Knowledge" (Select Discourses, 1660). Edwards's
    theology, then, brings together feeling and thought,
    pietism and orthodoxy, in a "rigid rationalistic" form.

9   EVANS, W. GLYN. "Jonathan Edwards--Puritan Paradox."
    Bibliotheca Sacra 124 (January):51-65.
       Tries to explain the paradox of Edwards--scientist-
    revivalist, idealist-pragmatist, rationalist-emotionalist--,
    a "greatly gifted mind who squandered his talents on
    theological trifles." The answer to this "paradoxical
    pulpiteer" lies in his method of preaching. In those im-
    portant elements of public speaking--understanding, impres-
    sion, reaction, duration, and direction--Edwards was
    "amazingly effective," an articulate Puritan apologist
    and America's "greatest revivalist."

1967

10   FOSTER, MARY CATHERINE. "Hampshire County, Massachusetts,
1729-1754: A Covenant Society in Transition." Ph.D.
dissertation, University of Michigan.
    Calls Edwards's dismissal an "important" turning point
in the covenant society of Hampshire County. By limiting
church membership to the regenerate, Edwards provoked
strong opposition and a call for his removal from the
social leaders, and though they succeeded in keeping the
"form" of the old social covenant, they lost its "spiritual
vitality."

11   [GARRETT, ARTHUR.] "2[sic] College Presidents: of Princeton,
Yale: Jonathan Edwards and his Grandson Dwight." In his
AmeriChristendom. Portland, Ore.: Graphic Arts Center,
pp. 147-71.
    Renders Edwards's career (and Timothy Dwight's) in a
two-column folio format resembling verse.

12   GILLETTE, GERALD W. "A Checklist of Doctoral Dissertations
on American Presbyterian and Reformed Subjects, 1912-1965."
Journal of Presbyterian History 45 (September):203-21.
    Lists dissertations on Edwards, pp. 206-208.

13   GRANT, LEONARD T. "A Preface to Jonathan Edwards' Financial
Difficulties." Journal of Presbyterian History 45 (March):
27-32.
    Discovers a "yellowing" receipt of a loan from Samuel
Phelps to Edwards that attests to his financial difficulties in 1742 as a result of Northampton's "disenchantment"
with him and his revivals. Apparently, the town withheld
his salary in an attempt to force change, but Edwards
borrowed against it to sustain his family and his principles.

14   GUSTAFSON, JAMES WALTER. "Causality and Freedom in Jonathan
Edwards, Samuel Alexander, and Brand Blanshard." Ph.D.
dissertation, Boston University.
    Relates Edwards's concepts of causality and freedom to
those of Samuel Alexander and Brand Blanshard, finds all
share a theory of determined freedom, and argues that the
lack of moral responsibility renders them all unsatisfac-
tory. For Edwards, freedom is the ability to "execute
decisions which are the necessary consequents of their
causal antecedents."

15 HEIMERT, ALAN [EDWARD], and MILLER, PERRY, eds. Introduction
    to their The Great Awakening: Documents Illustrating the
    Crisis and Its Consequences. The American Heritage Series.
    Indianapolis and New York: Bobbs-Merrill Co., pp. xii-lxi.
        Claims that "all of Edwards' thinking embodied both the
    lessons and the aspirations" of the Great Awakening, in a
    source book of documents--many from Edwards--touching upon
    the revival of 1740, the beginning of the "evolution of
    the American mind" and the awakening of the "spirit of
    American democracy." Edwards shifts the center of man's
    regeneration from the earlier Puritan preparation of the
    saint to the immediate and "undifferentiated" perception
    of divine excellence through the experience of conversion,
    from introspection and contemplation to trial and action,
    from self to community. Edwards "divested" Calvinism of
    covenant theology and construed the "ultimate test" of
    sainthood to be man's promotion of God's "historical pro-
    gram," his salvation part of a "divinely-ordered sequence"
    of social redemption made real in America.

16 HOLBROOK, CLYDE A[MOS]. "Edwards and the Ethical Question."
    Harvard Theological Review 60 (April):163-75.
        Challenges the radical anthropocentrism, the "unbridled
    human autonomy" in ethics, of such contemporary moral
    philosophers as P. H. Nowell-Smith, Kai Nielsen, and W. G.
    MacLagan with Edwards's equally radical theocentrism.
    Edwards adopts Francis Hutcheson's concept of benevolence
    and the equality of the moral sense, but he rejects his
    "ultimate focus" in humanity. In True Virtue, God, or
    Being in general, is the "objective criterion," the moral
    and aesthetic object to which man must come seeking the
    harmony of consent.

17 JACKSON, FRANK MALCOLM. "An Application of the Principles
    of Aristotelean Rhetoric to Certain Early New England
    Prose." Ph.D. dissertation, University of Texas.
        Applies the principles of Aristotle's Rhetoric to
    Edwards's Sinners in the Hands of an Angry God, one of
    nine early American texts examined for their persuasive
    intention.

18 LONG, EDWARD LEROY, JR. Survey of Christian Ethics. New
    York: Oxford University Press, pp. 135-38.
        Compares Edwards's approach to the Christian moral
    impulse in True Virtue and Religious Affections to that of
    Augustine and Luther, but contrasts his use of philosophi-
    cal categories to theirs of biblical idiom in making his
    argument.

1967

19   LOVEJOY, DAVID S.   "Samuel Hopkins: Religion, Slavery, and
      the Revolution."   New England Quarterly 40 (June):227-43.
      Gauges Edwards's effect on Samuel Hopkins, who "lived,
      read, and prayed" at his Northampton home.   Though his
      view of slavery, for instance, parallels Edwards's, his
      ideas on his master's disinterested benevolence undergo
      substantial change.

20   LOWANCE, MASON IRA, JR.   "Images and Shadows of Divine Things:
      Puritan Typology in New England from 1600 to 1750."   Ph.D.
      dissertation, Emory University.
      Relates the "transformed" types of Edwards's Images or
      Shadows to Emerson and the transcendentalists, in a detailed
      examination of Puritan typology and its relationship to
      nineteenth-century symbolism.

21   McGLINCHEE, CLAIRE.   "Jonathan Edwards and Benjamin Franklin,
      Antithetical Figures."   In Studies on Voltaire and the
      Eighteenth Century, 56.   Edited by Theodore Besterman.
      Transactions of the Second International Congress in the
      Enlightenment, no. 2.   Geneva: Institut et Musse Voltaire,
      pp. 813-22.
      Compares, in the standard way, the careers of Edwards
      and Benjamin Franklin, the "initial literary stylists" of
      America, and their influence on the Enlightenment.   Ed-
      wards's influence was "limited" because he was retrospec-
      tive, Franklin's "far-reaching" because he was prospective.

22   McLOUGHLIN, WILLIAM G.   "The American Revolution as a Reli-
      gious Revival: 'The Millennium in One Country.'"   New
      England Quarterly 40 (March):99-110.
      Faults Alan Heimert's "monumental" study (1966.17) for
      considering the Great Awakening a "critical watershed,"
      for the history of American life from the beginning has
      been a history of pietism "in various formulations," not
      only that of Edwards.   Heimert's failure to distinguish
      between secular liberalism and religious liberalism under-
      mines the "important task" he performs in reestablishing
      the contributions of the Edwardseans to the founding of
      the Republic.   (An essay review.)

23   MILLER, PERRY.   Jonathan Edwards.   New York: Dell Publishing
      Co.
      Reprint of 1949.9.

24   _____. "Sinners in the Hands of a Benevolent God." In his
        Nature's Nation. Cambridge, Mass.: Harvard University
        Press, pp. 279-89.
        Marks the change in perception of God in America in the
        example of Edwards, from the grim terror of Sinners in the
        Hands of an Angry God to the ecstatic benevolence of True
        Virtue. The Enfield sermon endures as one of the "arch-
        symbols" of its time and temper because of Edwards's
        "simple, unflinching, unforgettable rhetoric." True
        Virtue, a "disturbing tract" for American Protestantism,
        offers to sinners the hands of a benevolent God, a God who
        later would lead them to glorious independence and social
        prosperity.

25   MORGAN, EDMUND S.   Review of Religion and the American Mind
        from the Great Awakening to the Revolution, by Alan
        Heimert. William and Mary Quarterly, 3d ser. 24 (July):
        454-59.
        Judges that the "enormous erudition" of Alan Heimert's
        study (1966.17) fails to prevent readings so wrenched from
        context and evidence that the world of Edwards becomes one
        "more of fantasy than of history."

26   O'BRIEN, JON, S.J. "The Architecture of Conversion: Faith
        and Grace in the Theology of Jonathan Edwards." S.T.D.
        dissertation, Pontifical Gregorian University.
        Traces Edwards's treatment of preparation, justifica-
        tion, and saving grace, and comments upon his doctrines of
        conversion from a Catholic point of view. On the theory
        of conversion, a Catholic would agree with Edwards that
        God prepares man, though the nature of grace is different;
        on actual conversion, a Catholic would agree about the
        change in man and the work faith and love in the process;
        on the "extent of renovation" in conversion and the
        absolute scheme of justification, however, a Catholic would
        have to disagree. Still, the "surprising agreements" be-
        tween Catholics and Edwards "stand as warnings" against
        attributing to all American Protestants of colonial times
        a thorough refutation of the Council of Trent. (The final
        chapter of the dissertation, separately published, appears
        under the above title.)

27   SPEARE, ELIZABETH GEORGE. The Prospering. Boston: Houghton
        Mifflin Co., pp. 283-331.
        Recounts Edwards's difficulties with the Williams family
        in Stockbridge, in a novel narrated by a fictional Eliza-
        beth Williams: "His failure was that he was not John
        Sergeant," the former minister.

1967

28 SUTER, RUFUS [ORLANDO, JR.] "The Philosophy of Jonathan
    Edwards (1703-1758)." In his Berkeley and Edwards.
    Studi e Ricerche di Storia della Filosofia, no. 85.
    Torino: Edizioni di Filosofia, pp. [3]-4.
       Revises the abstract of Rufus Suter's dissertation in
    Harvard's Summaries of Theses, 1932. (See 1932.13.)

29 _____. "The Word Indiscerpible and Jonathan Edwards." Isis
    58 (Summer):238-39.
       Notes that like others before him--Henry More, Isaac
    Newton, and Samuel Clarke--Edwards used indiscerpible in
    "Notes on Natural Science" to mean "unsplittable" as
    applied to the atom.

                            1968

1   AKERS, CHARLES W. Review of Jonathan Edwards and the Visi-
    bility of God, by James Carse. New England Quarterly 41
    (June):302-305.
       Finds that although James Carse (1967.6) knows his
    subject well, he distorts Edwards for New Left purposes.

2   CLEBSCH, WILLIAM A. From Sacred to Profane America: The
    Role of Religion in American History. New York: Harper &
    Row, pp. 85-86, passim.
       Underscores Edwards's appeal to the young in the North-
    ampton revival of 1734 and suggests that he "invented"
    the mainstay of evangelical religion in America, the youth
    group.

3   CONKIN, PAUL K[EITH]. "Jonathan Edwards: Theology." In
    his Puritans and Pragmatists: Eight Eminent American
    Thinkers. New York: Dodd, Mead, pp. 39-72.
       Considers Edwards's fusion of ethics and aesthetics in
    a revived piety and a sensationalist psychology "a highly
    original and very personal work of art" and critically
    important to subsequent New England philosophy, in a de-
    tailed explanation of his major work. His record and
    analysis of the revivals, Freedom of the Will, and the
    trilogy of his last years form "a vast intellectual homage
    to an overwhelming God" in an age of rising individualism,
    cold rationalism, and humanistic Arminianism. Edwards's
    notions of "temperamental determinism" and holy affec-
    tions, grace and alienation, idealism and trinitarianism,
    ontology and sociology, sin and virtue show "an outstand-
    ing coherence and consistency" and bear tellingly on
    twentieth-century existential Calvinism.

4   COWING, CEDRIC B. "Sex and Preaching in the Great Awakening."
    American Quarterly 20 (Fall):624-44.
       Argues that Edwards's revival in Northampton not only
    affected the young, women, and blacks, as is commonly held,
    but that the conversion experience was "very attractive" to
    men. Given the general sex ratios in New England churches
    then, it is "surely remarkable" that during 1729-1742
    Edwards's converts were fifty percent male. Moreover,
    fifty of the converts over age forty were men--hardly a
    youthful identity crisis--and there was a dramatic increase
    in the number of men confessing fornication. Whatever else
    the Awakening was socially or politically or theologically,
    by bringing men into church it "retarded the drift toward
    worldliness and sexual laxity."

5   DAVENPORT, FREDERICK MORGAN. "The New England Awakening Orig-
    inating with Jonathan Edwards." In his Primitive Traits in
    Religious Revivals. New York: Negro Universities Press.
       Reprint of 1905.2.

6   DAVIDSON, EDWARD H. Jonathan Edwards: The Narrative of a
    Puritan Mind. Cambridge, Mass. Harvard University Press,
    161 pp.
       Reprint of 1966.10.

7   DAVIS, THOMAS M. "The Traditions of Puritan Typology." Ph.D.
    dissertation, University of Missouri.
       Traces the development of typology from New Testament
    writers to the Puritans and finds that Edwards, though
    the historical traditions of that methodology cease with
    him, "partially utilized" typology in his symbolic render-
    ing of nature in Images or Shadows.

8   DELATTRE, ROLAND ANDRÉ. Beauty and Sensibility in the Thought
    of Jonathan Edwards: An Essay in Aesthetics and Theologi-
    cal Ethics. New Haven and London: Yale University Press,
    254 pp.
       Considers beauty, both primary and secondary, to be the
    "central clue" to the nature of reality for Edwards, es-
    pecially in his theological ethics, in a full-length study
    that explores the relationship of beauty to being, excel-
    lence, goodness, value, order, and unity, and explains the
    element of beauty as divine perfection in the trinity,
    creation, governance, and redemption. Reality, for Ed-
    wards, is manifest and encountered as good in forms of
    primary beauty of being's consent to being and as being
    in forms of secondary beauty of proportion and harmony.

1968

Forms of one are correlative with each other (for example,
excellence, benevolence, and love in primary beauty) and
coordinate to the other forms (for example, excellence and
existence, benevolence and complacence, love and self-
love). So, too, the understanding and the will are manifest and encountered at once as being and as good in the
aesthetic-affectional self with sensibility as the "key
to the quality" of both, the degree determining knowledge
or ignorance in the one and consent or dissent in the
other. For Edwards, the order of beauty and the order of
sensibility terminate in fullness or nothingness (being
and nothing, life and death) and are coordinate to the
order of God or being-in-general as spiritual and moral
good. Beauty is the "formulative, structural, inner first
principle" of being-itself and in its fullness God mani-
fests and communicates Himself in the trinity and in
creation and, importantly, to perceiving man.

9   DELATTRE, ROLAND A[NDRÉ]. "Beauty and Theology: A Reappraisal
of Jonathan Edwards." Soundings 51 (Spring):60-79.
    Considers Edwards's concept of beauty the "key" to the
moral and religious life, the "central clue" to divine
governance and to human freedom and responsibility. According to Edwards, God governs by His attractive power--
the beauty of the apparent good--and it is by this that He
is "primarily distinguished as God." Beauty, for Edwards,
is objective, structural, relational, and creative and
consists of primary attributes--the consent of being--and
secondary attributes--harmony and proportion. What is
"remarkable" in Edwards is that of the three stages in
man's knowledge of God--His natural perfections, His moral
perfections, and His beauty--God's grace, goodness, and
holiness may be known, yet His beauty may be "hidden from
view." Such perceptions of beauty place Edwards at the
beginning of an American theological tradition that reaches
to H. Richard Niebuhr, Albert Hofstadter, and others.

10 GAUSTAD, EDWIN SCOTT. The Great Awakening in New England.
Chicago: Quadrangle Books.
    Reprint of 1957.6.

11 GOEN, C[LARENCE] C[URTIS]. Review of Jonathan Edwards and
the Visibility of God, by James Carse. William and Mary
Quarterly, 3d ser. 25 (October):650-52.
    Considers James Carse's work (1967.6) "less a book than
a sermon" and believes "more straight-laced scholars" will
resent his "Kantian personalist-existentialist-Social
Gospel activist" Edwards.

12   GOODWIN, GERALD J.   "The Myth of 'Arminian-Calvinism' in
     Eighteenth-Century New England."   New England Quarterly 41
     (June):213-37.
         Challenges traditional interpretations of New England
     Puritanism that argue that Arminianism arose out of diluted
     or misdirected Calvinism--Anglicanism is the culprit--and
     that Edwards was America's "first authentic" Calvinist.
     Arminian-Calvinism "never existed," and Edwards's God
     Glorified is not, as some historians hold, "a crucial
     signpost" in American intellectual life, positing for the
     first time a Calvinism free of "the covenant or covert
     Arminianism."   The Great Awakening, which Edwards had
     much to do with, was the "climactic demonstration" of
     pure, dogmatic Calvinism.

13   LOWELL, ROBERT.   Interview with Frederick Seidel.   In Robert
     Lowell: A Collection of Critical Essays.   Edited by
     Thomas Parkinson.   Englewood Cliffs, N.J.:   Prentice-Hall,
     pp. 12-35.
         Recalls that he worked on a biography of Edwards,
     abandoned it when he became "numb," and wrote two poems
     derived from his research and Edwards's language, in
     Lowell's recollection of his stay at the Allen Tates'.

14   MEAD, SIDNEY E[EARL].   "Through and Beyond the Lines."
     Journal of Religion 48 (July):274-88.
         Attacks Alan Heimert's Religion and the American Mind
     (1966.17) for its inferential methodology--exchanging
     facts for the shadows beyond them--and its confounding of
     the religious with the political.   Perhaps the book may
     counter the neglect usually given the contribution to the
     Revolution of Edwards and his followers, but it has the
     "odor of Calvinist propaganda" about it and seems "an
     inordinately long doctoral dissertation that slipped past
     the committee."

15   MEREDITH, ROBERT.   The Politics of the Universe: Edward
     Beecher, Abolition, and Orthodoxy.   Nashville, Tenn.:
     Vanderbilt University Press, pp. 15-17, 136-37, 212.
         Notes the influence Edwards's theology exerted on the
     Beechers--Edward, Lyman, and Charles.

16   MILLAR, ALBERT EDWARD, JR.   "Spiritual Autobiography in
     Selected Writings of Sewall, Edwards, Byrd, Woolman, and
     Franklin: A Comparison of Technique and Content."   Ph.D.
     dissertation, University of Delaware.

1968

Analyzes the autobiographical writings of Samuel Sewall, William Byrd, John Woolman, Benjamin Franklin, and Edwards and concludes that only the last wrote a "specifically designed" spiritual autobiography in his Personal Narrative.

17   MORRIS, WILLIAM S[PARKES]. "The Genius of Jonathan Edwards." In Reinterpretation in American Church History. Edited by Jerald C. Brauer. Essays in Divinity, no. 5. Chicago: University of Chicago Press, pp. 29-65.
      Discovers Edwards's genius in his union of the rational and the empirical, a combination of the logic of Burgersdycke and the sensationalism of Locke, in an analysis of the foundations of Edwards's method and thought. The rational in Edwards functions along Burgersdyckean (not Ramean), synthetic lines of deduction and along Lockean, analytic lines of intuition and demonstration; the empirical functions as ideas of sensation, subject to strict logic and Scripture, so that even the sense of the heart, which is immediately self-evident, must be judged by "rational norms." Edwards counters the "agnostic and skeptical tendencies" in Locke's epistemology by affirming the primacy of Being and restoring objective real essences to morality and religion. Thus his logic is "severely" metaphysical and his philosophy and theology, "spiritual realism." And thus he is "a man of his age," sharing the importance of reason but insisting it was "the subject and not the cause of man's enlightenment."

18   NAGY, PAUL JOSEPH. "The Doctrine of Experience in the Philosophy of Jonathan Edwards." Ph.D. dissertation, Fordham University.
      Considers Edwards's philosophy to be a "systematic explication" of experience, with his idea of beauty, sense of the heart, and concept of grace at its center. Edwards is an "early exponent" of an American tradition of thought emphasizing experience rather than reason.

19   NEWLIN, CLAUDE MILTON. Philosophy and Religion in Colonial America. New York: Greenwood Press.
      Reprint of 1962.11.

20   PARKER, GAIL THAIN. "Jonathan Edwards and Melancholy." New England Quarterly 14 (June):193-212.
      Expands upon Joseph Crooker's psychological study (1890.3) by suggesting that Edwards's emphasis upon experimental religion was "clearly informed" by his knowledge of the history and disease of melancholy, a condition

he explored in himself in the 1720s and in others a decade later. That store of psychological theory and experience may have been "crucial" to his health and to his interpretation of similar crises in others. In Religious Affections, his mature analysis of melancholy, he went "beyond" Richard Baxter and Benjamin Colman to assert that melancholy held "sinister implications for the value of rumination itself."

21 PARKER, WILLIAM HENRY. "The Social Theory of Jonathan Edwards: as Developed in his Works on Revivalism." D.S.S. dissertation, Syracuse University.

Discerns in Edwards's works on revivalism a social theory based upon the Christian vision of a loving relationship among men, who freely subordinate their private ends to the universal Christian community, and likened to the social process outlined in George Herbert Mead's Mind, Self and Society. Thus in Personal Narrative, the saint, one of a "natural aristocracy," desires to extend his joyous experiences to the community at large in an act of love; in Religious Affections, the saint seeks to respond to the needs of others through trials of self-knowledge and love; and in True Virtue, the saint tries to reconcile diverse groups into a harmonious community through a common language of common social needs and love.

22 PIERCE, DAVID C[LARENCE]. "Jonathan Edwards and the 'New Sense' of Glory." New England Quarterly 41 (March):82-95.

Suggests that Edwards embraced two "fundamentally contrasting" forms of piety at once in Personal Narrative and that this may help explain the discontinuity frequently noted in his career. The first, based on his devotion to the absolute sovereignty of God, accounts for a God of order and restraint, an elect society of limitations, a holy commonwealth; the second, based on his delight in divine omnipresence in all creation, accounts for a God of space and enlargement, a world of vastness and variety, the widening imagination of nature enthusiasm. Edwards's new sense of glory, "unique" in the Puritan tradition, involves direct and unmediated experience and stresses the heart attentative to "its own motions" rather than to "inherited paradigms." What is called Edwards's mysticism thus has a "particular historical context" in the nature enthusiasts of the "new philosophy."

1968

23 REES, ROBERT A. "Seeds of the Enlightenment: Public Testi-
    mony in the New England Congregational Chruches, 1630-
    1750." Early American Literature 3 (Spring):22-29.
        Traces the history of the public profession of faith
    in New England and Edwards's reverting to it in the "last
    desperate moments of his decline and fall from ecclesias-
    tical glory." In part the difficulty of separating the
    genuinely converted from the merely moved during the
    Great Awakening may account for his change; in part his
    reversion to an earlier system may have been an attempt to
    moderate the excesses of the revival. Ironically, the
    reinstitution of public profession engendered liberalism,
    and so the "seeds planted in the conservative New England
    earth had proved to be dragon's teeth."

24 ROWE, HENRY KALLOCH. "Jonathan Edwards." In his Modern
    Pathfinders of Christianity. Freeport, N.Y.: Books for
    Libraries Press.
        Reprint of 1928.6.

25 SCHAFER, THOMAS A[NTON]. "Manuscript Problems in the Yale
    Edition of Jonathan Edwards." Early American Literature 3
    (Winter):159-71.
        Singles out the illegibility of the manuscripts as the
    "most pervasive and persistent" of all the problems facing
    the editors of the Yale Edwards, more troublesome than the
    disposition of the manuscripts, the inadequate catalogue
    of items, the very "size and richness" of his work. As
    Timothy Dwight remarked, Edwards kept "'one hand for him-
    self, another for his friends,'" so that his "homemade"
    shorthand becomes, increasingly in his later years, an
    "almost indecipherable cryptography." Compounding the
    difficulty of his "well formed but very small" script is
    a scarcity of punctuation and a capitalization "more or
    less erratic."

26 SHEA, DANIEL B., JR. "Jonathan Edwards and the Narrative of
    Conversion." In his Spiritual Autobiography in Early
    America. Princeton, N.J.: Princeton University Press,
    pp. 182-233.
        Reprints 1965.18 with additions.

27 TOWNSEND, HARVEY GATES. Philosophical Ideas in the United
    States. New York: Octagon Books.
        Reprint of 1934.10.

28   TUVESON, ERNEST LEE. Redeemer Nation: the Idea of America's Millennial Role. Chicago and London: University of Chicago Press, pp. 27-30, 55-57.

        Reads Edwards's History of Redemption as one of many American schemes for the redemption of society. Unlike Augustine, Edwards looks for redemption in this world-- a kingdom of God like Utopia--in an "appointed progression" of events. His radical theory of multiple parousia hints at a continuous apocalypse and a recurrent regeneration and suggests a profound change in Protestantism.

*29   TWEET, ROALD D. "Jonathan Edwards and the Affecting Style." Ph.D. dissertation, University of Chicago.

        Cited in Comprehensive Dissertation Index 1861-1972, 29:402.

30   WAGER, WILLIS. American Literature: A World View. New York: New York University Press, pp. 28-31.

        Suggests that Edwards's major work shares "common ground" with current philosophical realists.

31   WALKER, WILLISTON. "Jonathan Edwards." In his Great Men of the Christian Church. Freeport, N.Y.: Books for Libraries Press.

        Reprint of 1908.3.

32   WARD, ROBERT STAFFORD. "Still 'Christians', Still Infidels." Southern Humanities Review 2 (Summer):365-74.

        Rescues Ralph Waldo Emerson from the charge of heresy made by the Fugitives (see 1958.23) by linking him to Edwards as a "necessary and logical outgrowth" of Puritan orthodoxy, refined of its "fundamentalist dross."

33   WILLIAMSON, JOSEPH CRAWFORD. "The Excellency of Christ: A Study in the Christology of Jonathan Edwards." Ph.D. dissertation, Harvard University.

        Defines Edwards's idea of excellency as "consent, expressed as love" and relates the movement of consent from God to man and from man to God through Christ the receiver and giver of the Holy Spirit. Christ is "the supreme object and the supreme subject" of the relationship between God and man, the glorification of both man and God.

34   WINSLOW, OLA ELIZABETH. Review of Jonathan Edwards and the Visibility of God, by James Carse. American Literature 40 (November):400-401.

        Recommends James Carse's "new slant" on Edwards (1967.6) though not all his conclusions.

1968

35   WOOD, JAMES PLAYSTED. <u>Mr. Jonathan Edwards</u>. New York: Sea-
      bury Press, 166 pp.
          Considers Edwards "a poet, a mystic, a clear-eyed
      scholar, and . . . a pantheistic transcendentalist" against
      a background of incidental history and local politics in a
      biography and appreciation designed for the young. His
      dismissal, for instance, is set against a background of
      contending factions amid Northampton's "new world of the
      flesh and the dollar," a world that demanded not merely
      victory but "his blood." And the tenor of his mind derived
      from a Calvinist tradition rooted in a Puritan ministerial
      ancestry "on both sides" and nourished in the "rural Con-
      necticut" parish of his father. Edwards affected religion
      in America "lastingly, and in two different and contradic-
      tory ways": his monument of a rigid, somewhat altered
      Calvinism remains, and, through Emerson and his followers,
      his mystical, pantheistic spirit of "God as God" persists.

                              <u>1969</u>

1   ALDRIDGE, A[LFRED] OWEN. Review of <u>Jonathan Edwards: The</u>
     <u>Narrative of a Puritan Mind</u>, by Edward H. Davidson.
     <u>Seventeenth-Century News</u> 27 (Summer):32, 34.
         Finds Edward H. Davidson's study (1966.10) more solid
     and "far more credible" than Perry Miller's (1949.9).

2   ANON. "Think on These Things." <u>Covenant Companion</u> 58 (1 Jan-
     uary):4-5.
         Reprints a shortened version of Edwards's <u>Resolutions</u>
     to show its spiritual force and to offer it to others.

3   BORGES, JORGE LUIS. "Jonathan Edwards (1703-1758)." In his
     <u>El otro, el mismo</u> [The Self and the Other]. Buenos Aires:
     Emecé Editors, p. 155.
         Characterizes Edwards's world as a "Vessel of wrath" and
     his diety as "Another prisoner, God, the Spider," in a
     sonnet. (In Spanish; transl. 1972.4.)

4   BORMANN, ERNEST G. Review of <u>Jonathan Edwards: The Narrative</u>
     <u>of a Puritan Mind</u>, by Edward H. Davidson, and <u>Beauty and</u>
     <u>Sensibility in the Thought of Jonathan Edwards</u>, by Roland
     A. Delattre. <u>Quarterly Journal of Speech</u> 55 (April):202-
     203.
         Judges Edward Davidson's book (1966.10) to be of greater
     relevance to rhetorical critics than Roland Delattre's
     (1968.8), though both are as difficult to understand as
     Edwards himself.

5   BUSHMAN, RICHARD L. "Jonathan Edwards as Great Man: Identity,
    Conversion, and Leadership in the Great Awakening."
    Soundings 52 (Spring):15-46.
        Discovers in the "emotional congruities" of Edwards and
    the Great Awakening a compelling instance of Erik Erikson's
    model of the great man by reconstructing Edwards's identity
    and the general social condition. His father's compulsive
    traits, high hopes, and fear of destruction produce in
    Edwards an "exceedingly aggressive" conscience; three early
    essays reveal aspirations to succeed, "inward filthiness,"
    and an alienating tendency to carp. But his conversion
    resolves or sublimates these characteristics, and his
    ministry channels them into acceptable forms, both public
    and private. Thus shaped, Edwards's psychological struc-
    ture coincides with the emotional needs of his time--
    speculation threatens economic expansion, institutional
    authority clashes with personal ambition, litigation de-
    stroys friendships. Thousands of conversions testify to
    the coincidence. (Reprinted in 1977.7 and 1978.5.)

6   CARSE, JAMES P[EARCE]. Review of Jonathan Edwards, by Edward
    H. Davidson. New England Quarterly 42 (June):287-89.
        Questions Edward Davidson's understanding of "the living
    center" of Freedom of the Will in his reissued study of
    Edwards (1968.6).

7   CLIFT, ARLENE LOUISE. "Rhetoric and the Reason-Revelation
    Relationship in the Writings of Jonathan Edwards." Ph.D.
    dissertation, Harvard University.
        Analyzes Edwards's rhetorical aims and methods as in-
    fluences upon his use of Scripture. At times, Edwards uses
    Scripture as an appeal to reason and as a "major means" to
    establish doctrine; at other times, he relegates Scripture
    to rhetorical considerations in response to "challenges"
    to Calvinism. Only in his treatment of history does
    Edwards realize the "'ideal apprehension'" of reason and
    the affective mode in his rhetorical use of Scripture.

8   COLLINS, EDWARD M., JR. "The Rhetoric of Sensation Challenges
    the Rhetoric of the Intellect: an Eighteenth-Century Con-
    troversy." In Preaching in American History: Selected
    Issues in the American Pulpit, 1630-1967. Edited by
    DeWitte Holland. Nashville, Tenn.: Abingdon Press,
    pp. 98-117.
        Places Edwards between Charles Chauncy's reason and
    institutionalism and James Davenport's emotionalism and

1969

antinomianism. Edwards fused the intellect of the first
with the experience of the second under grace to yield the
tempered holy affections of true religion. Such "double-
edged form" brought orthodoxy and revivalism to bear upon
the common, crucial problem of regeneration.

9   COWAN, JAMES C. "Jonathan Edwards' Sermon Style: 'The Future
     Punishment of the Wicked Unavoidable and Intolerable.'"
     South Central Bulletin 29 (Winter):119-22.
         Offers Future Punishment as further testimony (see
     1949.1) that in sermonic organization and imagery Edwards
     was a conscious stylist. Edwards uses the conventional
     rhetorical devices of word coupling, balance, antithesis,
     alliteration, and assonance found in the Puritan plain
     style, but his use of sensational--that is, Lockean--
     imagery gives his sermon "emotional power" and the cumula-
     tive, accelerated structure an "immediacy of physical
     fact."

10   CROZIER, ALICE C. The Novels of Harriet Beecher Stowe. New
     York: Oxford University Press, pp. 19-21, 74-76, 118-31
     passim.
         Details the use Harriet Beecher Stowe made of her
     "decidedly ambiguous" relationship to Edwards. More con-
     cerned with the psychological and social consequences of
     his theology than with its doctrine, Stowe hated his
     inflexibility and rationalizing and was "enthralled" by
     his piety and passionate love of God, by his nobility.

11   DAVIDSON, EDWARD H. Review of Beauty and Sensibility in the
     Thought of Jonathan Edwards, by Roland A. Delattre.
     American Literature 41 (May):282-83.
         Finds Roland A. Delattre's "special kind" of study
     (1968.8) the "best statement" of Edwards's ontological
     unity and one that demonstrates affinities with contem-
     porary radical monotheism.

12   EMERSON, EVERETT H. Review of Jonathan Edwards: A Profile,
     edited by David Levin. Early American Literature 4, no. 2:
     109-110.
         Recommends David Levin's "intelligent" selections
     (1969.21).

13   GRABO, NORMAN S. "Jonathan Edwards' Personal Narrative:
     Dynamic Stasis." Literatur in Wissenschaft und Unterricht
     2, no. 3:141-48.

Examines the different structures of spiritual autobiography in Edwards's account of Abigail Hutchinson and Phebe Bartlet's conversion in Faithful Narrative and his own in Personal Narrative. The sketches in the first concentrate on the value and significance of experience rather than external events and develop linearly in Hutchinson and like "a branch erupting into blossom" in Bartlet. The second account differs from the first and from conventional forms in its use of several kinds of time simultaneously and in its circular treatment: Edwards's four periods of awakening develop into four concentric, interacting circles. Hence, by its limiting structure, Personal Narrative "intuitively betrays" the Great Awakening.

14 _____. Review of Jonathan Edwards and the Visibility of God, by James Carse. Early American Literature 4, no. 1:45-46.
    Finds James Carse's analysis (1967.6) at odds with Edwards's statements and the neglect of the supernatural a failure to deal with a "major dimension" of his thought.

15 HAND, JAMES ALBERT. "Teleogical Aspects of Creation: A Comparison of the Concepts of Being and Meaning in the Theologies of Jonathan Edwards and Paul Tillich." Ph.D. dissertation, Vanderbilt University.
    Compares Edwards and Paul Tillich on spirit ontology--Edwards synthesizes rationalism and enthusiasm, Tillich idealism and existentialism--and shows that both use contemporary cultural self-interpretation. But Edwards, lacking any "dialectical process of life" in his thought, develops a theology of consciousness and Tillich one of life framed by history.

16 HELM, PAUL. "John Locke and Jonathan Edwards: A Reconsideration." Journal of the History of Philosophy 7 (January):51-61.
    Insists that Edwards is not an empiricist and that he uses Lockean empiricism as "a model for religious experience," not as a theory of it, as Perry Miller mistakenly argues. For Edwards, virtue is cast in theistic paradigms of moral necessity, not only illustratively but evidentially. Though he makes use of Locke's language of "'sense,'" "'sensation,'" and "'new simple idea,'" Edwards does so to emphasize the "non-natural" character of the religious experience and to adapt, in a "radical" way, Lockean notions for purposes "entirely" his own. Any characterization of his account of the religious experience or of the "'sixth sense'" as Lockean or naturalistic is subject to "important qualifications."

1969

17   HOLBROOK, CLYDE A[MOS]. Review of <u>Beauty and Sensibility in</u>
      <u>the Thought of Jonathan Edwards</u>, by Roland A. Delattre.
      <u>New England Quarterly</u> 42 (June):310-12.
           Regards Roland A. Delattre's study (1968.8) "valuable
      and highly persuasive," but faults its attempt to make
      Edwards more consistent than he is.

18   JOHNSON, ELLWOOD GERD. "Some Versions of Individualism in
      American Literature and Thought." Ph.D. dissertation,
      University of Washington.
           Relates Edwards's concept of individualism found in the
      psychological preparation of the heart in <u>Religious Affec-</u>
      <u>tions</u> and <u>True Virtue</u> to later versions of that indigenous
      strain in Hawthorne, Emerson, Twain, Dos Passos, William
      James, and Faulkner.

19   JOHNSON, JAMES E. "Charles Finney and a Theology of Revival-
      ism." <u>Church History</u> 38 (September):338-58.
           Considers Edwards's awareness of conversion as "the
      great necessity" of the eighteenth century (and his
      sermons on justification) to be the foundation of the
      revival theology of the nineteenth century and Charles
      Grandison Finney's role in it.

20   KAUFMAN, ARNOLD S., and FRANKENA, WILLIAM K., eds. Introduc-
      tion to <u>Freedom of the Will</u>. Indianapolis and New York:
      Bobbs-Merrill Co., pp. ix-xl.
           Analyzes Edwards's defense of "'The Compatability
      Theory'" in <u>Freedom of the Will</u> by examining his linguis-
      tic method, in an introduction to a text that has only
      recently received "the philosophical appreciation it
      merits." Edwards argues for the compatability of deter-
      minism and moral responsibility by drawing upon common-
      sense rather than metaphysical usages of ordinary words.
      Though he shows "immense skill" and modernity in this
      method, problems persist: not only do contexts shift and
      meanings change, but the authority of common sense is
      questionable.

21   LEVIN, DAVID, ed. Introduction to <u>Jonathan Edwards: A Pro-</u>
      <u>file</u>. American Profiles. New York: Hill & Wang,
      pp. ix-xvii, xix-xxi, 257-59.
           Calls Edwards "the exemplary Puritan," fusing a rigor-
      ous intellect to a passionate piety; offers a brief
      biography and bibliography; and reprints selections from
      Samuel Hopkins's <u>Life</u> (1765.2), Williston Walker's <u>Ten</u>
      <u>New England Leaders</u> (1901.14), Henry Bamford Parkes's <u>The</u>

1969

Fiery Puritan (1930.10), Ola Elizabeth Winslow's biography (1940.21), Perry Miller's intellectual biography (1949.9), John E. Smith introduction to Religious Affections (1959.18), James Carse's Visibility of God (1967.6), Peter Gay's Loss of Mastery (1966.14), and Robert Lowell's "After the Surprising Conversions" (1946.3), and "Jonathan Edwards in Western Massachusetts" (1964.14).

22 LOVEJOY, DAVID S. Religious Enthusiasm and the Great Awakening. American Historical Sources Series. Englewood Cliffs, N.J.: Prentice-Hall, pp. 18-21.
Views Edwards and the Great Awakening from the perspective of religious enthusiasm. Edwards mistrusted enthusiasm, as did most men of his time, and so he "exploited" Brainerd's life to distinugish the true conversion experience from the false, the lasting effect from the short-lived. The "most profound" defense of the Awakening is Edwards's Distinguishing Marks.

23 LYNEN, JOHN F. The Design of the Present: Essays on Time and Form in American Literature. New Haven and London: Yale University Press, pp. 93-119 passim.
Suggests that Edwards's "perfect harmony" of the present time of self and the eternal time of God provides the clue to his theology, style, and influence, and a measure of the effect (along with Franklin) of the single point of view. Edwards tries to resolve the duality of God as transcendence and immanence in point of view, which accounts both for his reformulation of Puritan doctrines of will, causation, and sovereignty, and for "his subtle and often confusing ambiguity." Thus Edwards's art is central to his thought: he construes theology in a world he defines "poetically" and uses language, often through exact repetition, to "dominate and transform," converting reason into feeling, harmonizing self and nature. Edwards "clearly anticipates" Emerson, Poe, and others as a symbolist, but he regards a symbol as distinct from its meaning as well as continuous with it, as his point of view mandates.

24 MacLEAN, JOHN. History of the College of New Jersey, 1746-1854. New York: Arno Press.
Reprint of 1877.3.

25 MACPHAIL, ANDREW. "Jonathan Edwards." In his Essays in Puritanism. Port Washington, N.Y.: Kennikat Press.
Reprint of 1905.4.

1969

26   MINTER, DAVID L. The Interpreted Design as a Structural
      Principle in American Prose. Yale Publications in American
      Studies. New Haven and London: Yale University Press,
      pp. 72-77.
          Contends that Edwards's Personal Narrative alters the
      pattern of Puritan spiritual autobiography by "exploiting
      and extending" the conventional form, by changing its tone,
      mood, and focus, and by interpreting, "in a radical sense,"
      the recollected experience. Edwards "combines" the in-
      terpretation that he gives his conversion efforts (his
      "impotent design") with the divine judgment of it (God's
      "salvific design"). Each detail of his religious life
      forms a single pattern related to God's redemptive acts,
      so that for Edwards salvation becomes a "precise horizontal
      organization and planned vertical expansion."

27   OPIE, JOHN, JR. Introduction to his Jonathan Edwards and the
      Enlightenment. Problems in American Civilization. Lexing-
      ton, Mass.: D. C. Heath & Co., pp. v-viii.
          Considers Edwards "the most acute American analyst of
      the achievements of the Englightenment, far surpassing the
      perceptiveness of Franklin, Mayhew, Paine, and even Jeffer-
      son, in science, psychology, and philosophy," and reprints
      selections from Perry Miller's intellectual biography
      (1949.9), Vincent Tomas's "The Modernity of Jonathan Ed-
      wards" (1952.12), Clarence H. Fausts's "Jonathan Edwards
      as a Scientist" (1930.4), Theodore Hornberger's "The Effect
      of the New Science" (1937.4), Vernon Louis Parrington's
      "The Anachronism of Jonathan Edwards" (1927.2), Ola
      Elizabeth Winslow's biography (1940.21), Peter Gay's Loss
      of Mastery (1966.14), and Conrad Cherry's The Theology of
      Jonathan Edwards (1966.9).

28   PATRICK, WALTON R. "Melville's 'Bartleby' and the Doctrine
      of Necessity." American Literature 41 (March):39-54.
          Uses Edwards's Freedom of the Will and Priestley's
      Necessity to explicate a line in Herman Melville's
      "Bartleby" and to interpret the story.

29   RODDEY, GLORIA J. "The Metaphor of Counsel: A Shift from
      Objective Realism to Psychological Subjectivism in the
      Conceptual Cosmology of Puritanism." Ph.D. dissertation,
      University of Kentucky.
          Illustrates the shift of metaphor from objective to
      subjective realism as a consequence of the doctrine of
      election in a dozen Puritans, including Edwards, and Haw-
      thorne.

30   RUPP, GEORGE. "The 'Idealism' of Jonathan Edwards." Harvard
     Theological Review 62 (April):209-26.
         Contends that the "central and indeed decisive asser-
     tion" in Edwards's early essays is that God is "coexten-
     sive" with reality and space and that his "alleged" ideal-
     ism has its roots in his epistemology and his ontology.
     Edwards goes beyond Newton, Locke, and Berkeley in stress-
     ing the dependence of every thing, being, and event on
     divine energy and in connecting physics to metaphysics.
     Unfortunately, Edwards does not argue his case for ideal-
     ism "in detail," nor does he use "adequate verbal dis-
     tinctions" to differentiate between objects and ideas.
     Even so, there is a "measure of coherence" to his meta-
     physics not apparent at first glance.

31   RUTMAN, DARRETT B. Review of Jonathan Edwards: The Narrative
     of a Puritan Mind, by Edward H. Davidson. American His-
     torical Review 74 (April):1351-52.
         Considers Edward H. Davidson's Narrative (1968.6,
     reprinted) more appropriately an exegesis of Edwards's
     writings and as such "commendable," but it slights the
     continuities between Edwards and the past.

32   SCHAFER, THOMAS A[NTON]. "The Role of Jonathan Edwards in
     American Religious History." Encounter 30 (Summer):212-23.
         Assesses Edwards's effect upon American religious his-
     tory arising from his role in the Great Awakening. First,
     Edwards combined in himself both doctrinal correctness and
     vital piety "to a superlative degree," unlike earlier
     Puritans who kept head and heart "more or less" in balance;
     second, Edwards demonstrated, by precept and by example
     (at Stockbridge), the importance of missionary work;
     third, Edwards "promoted the ecumenical implications" of
     evangelism and fashioned a new eschatology for it; and
     fourth, Edwards set an "important precedent" for the vol-
     untary principle in rejecting the communion practice of
     the half-way convenant and suffering dismissal for it.
     Yet his "chief role" in the future may well lie in theo-
     logical ethics, and Religious Affections and True Virtue
     may become more famous than Freedom of the Will.

33   WAGGONER, HYATT H. "'Grace' in the Thought of Emerson,
     Thoreau, and Hawthorne." Emerson Society Quarterly, no.
     54, Part 2 (I Quarter):68-72.
         Complements Perry Miller's thesis of Emerson's relation
     to Edwards (1940.9) by exploring similar patterns of
     thought in Hawthorne and Thoreau. Edwards probably would

1969

have thought all three "ultimately heretical" on the subject of grace, but in fact they were close to the "central
meaning" of his divine and supernatural light, even if
their language was not. Emerson's version is the "most
mystical," Thoreau's the "most sensuous-aesthetic," and
Hawthorne's "at once the most humanistic and commonsensical
and the most 'other worldly.'"

34 ZIMMERMAN, LESTER F. "'And justify the ways . . .'--a Sug-
gested Context," in Papers on Milton. Edited by Philip
Mahone Griffith and Lester F. Zimmerman. University of
Tulsa Department of English Monograph Series, no. 8.
Tulsa, Okla.: University of Tulsa, pp. 57-66.
    Suggests that Edwards's Personal Narrative recounts a
conversion experience similar to Adam's in Milton's
Paradise Lost, Book X.

1970

1   BERCOVITCH, SACVAN. "Horologicals to Chronometricals: The
Rhetoric of the Jeremiad." In Literary Monographs, no. 3.
Edited by Eric Rothstein. Madison: University of Wisconsin Press, pp. 81-90.
    Links Edwards's eschatology to American jeremiads of
the seventeenth century and finds the "gradualistic
apocalypticism" of Some Thoughts, Humble Attempt, Distinguishing Marks, and especially History of Redemption,
"a more effective vehicle for the old historiography."
For him as for his forebears, individual salvation and
corporate success were counterparts of the divine work
of redemption. Edwards fashioned a "new angle" to the
earlier tradition by welding "the whole temporal progression into an organic whole" and, inadvertently, helped
secularize millennial hope into political destiny.

2   BRUMM, URSULA. "Jonathan Edwards and Ralph Waldo Emerson."
In her American Thought and Religious Typology. Trans-
lated by John Hoagland. New Brunswick, N.J.: Rutgers
University Press, pp. 86-108, passim.
    Translates 1963.4.

3   BUCKINGHAM, WILLIS J. "Stylistic Artistry in the Sermons of
Jonathan Edwards." Papers on Language & Literature 6
(Spring):136-51.
    Locates the strength of Edwards's sermonic style in
his "controlling the movement of language." Edwards
follows "closely" the Puritan homilectic tradition of

restraint and decorum, a prose unadorned and plain, but
adds a "peculiarly heavy kind of pacing" that gives
greater weight to punctuation and achieves a certain dignity and amplitude of rhythm. Through that natural style
Edwards was able to modify the "mechanical" Puritan
aesthetic and bring form and content together.

4   BUMSTED, J. M., ed. The Great Awakening: The Beginnings of
    Evangelical Pietism in America. Waltham, Mass.: Blais-
    dell Publishing Co., pp. 27, 142.
        Comments briefly on Edwards's role in the Great Awaken-
    ing and reprints from Faithful Narrative and his 7 May
    1750 letter to Peter Clark.

5   BUSHMAN, RICHARD L., ed. The Great Awakening: Documents on
    the Revival of Religion, 1740-1745. New York: Atheneum,
    pp. 110, 135-36.
        Introduces and reprints selections from Distinguishing
    Marks, True Virtue, and "The Northampton Covenant, 1742."

6   CARSE, JAMES P[EARCE]. "The Puritans, the American Dream,
    and the Modern Tyranny of Leisure." Presbyterian Life 23
    (1 May):7-9, 32-33.
        Uses Edwards as an example of the persistence of the
    American dream and an acknowledgement of its failure in
    an essay on the current loss of faith in the young.
    Edwards's millennial optimism "vanished" before his con-
    gregation's "spiritual rebellion" at the coming of the
    Kingdom.

7   CREMIN, LAWRENCE A. American Education: The Colonial Experi-
    ence, 1607-1783. New York: Harper & Row, pp. 266, 314-16.
        Characterizes the Great Awakening as a "large-scale"
    educational movement and Edwards's use of his church for
    teaching purposes as "novel."

8   DALLIMORE, ARNOLD A. George Whitefield. London: Banner of
    Truth Trust, 1:537-40.
        Records the meeting between Edwards and George White-
    field, reprints supporting documents, and attributes the
    distance between the two not to their theological or
    intellectual differences so much as to Whitefield's "deep
    disappointment" over his proposal to Elizabeth Delamotte.

9   DELATTRE, ROLAND A[NDRÉ]. "Beauty and Politics: Toward a
    Theological Anthropology." Union Seminary Quarterly
    Review 25 (Summer):401-19.

1970

Cites Edwards as an example of the generalization that
those who are sensitive to the aesthetic in human affairs
"tend to distort" the political, but suggests that his
consent to being has political as well as aesthetic
relevance.

10 _____ . Review of Jonathan Edwards: A Profile, edited by
David Levin. New England Quarterly 43 (March):169-72.
Recommends David Levin's selection (1969.21) for its
balance of biography, theology, and contemporary criticism.

11 DIXON, JOHN W., JR. Review of Beauty and Sensibility in the
Thought of Jonathan Edwards, by Roland A. Delattre.
Journal of Aesthetics and Art Criticism 28 (Summer):546-47.
Cautions aestheticians that Roland A. Delattre's study
(1968.8) is theological ethics, not philosophical
aesthetics, and that while the first half will be of "very
considerable interest" to them, the second part--the
theological consequences of Edwards's aesthetics--might
not.

12 GARRISON, JOSEPH M., JR. "Teaching Early American Literature:
Some Suggestions." College English 31 (February):487-97.
Suggests that only as students recognize the "other"
Edwards of Personal Narrative will they understand the
rhetoric of the imprecatory sermons. The two voices of
Personal Narrative--one before conversion dominated by
"I," active verbs, and images of confinement; the other
after conversion by passive verbs, "ecstatic metaphor
and the language of epiphany"--differentiate between
Edwards's prideful resistance to and his selfless affirm-
ation of God's sovereignty. Thus Sinners in the Hands of
an Angry God makes man aware not of a terrible God so much
as his own sin, finitude, and necessary submission to
divine justice.

13 HAROUTUNIAN, JOSEPH [G.] Piety versus Moralism. New York:
Harper & Row.
Reprint of 1932.5.

14 HOEDEMAKER, LIBERTUS A. The Theology of H. Richard Niebuhr.
Philadelphia: Pilgrim Press, pp. 33-38.
Finds in H. Richard Niebuhr's thought "a growing affinity and congruence" with major themes in Edwards based on
divine sovereignty--love, beauty, order, history. The
"heart" of Edwards lies in the "immediate relation" between the perception of reality and the religious affections, between divine presence and human behavior. To
put it briefly, "Edwards' anthropocentricism is built

on the foundation of theocentricism." Niebuhr's
rediscovery of Edwards is "one of the apects" of
his rediscovery of God.

15 HOLBROOK, CLYDE A[MOS]. "Editor's Introduction." In
     Original Sin. The Works of Jonathan Edwards, vol. 3.
     New Haven and London: Yale University Press, pp. 1-
     101.
          Traces the New England controversy about original
     sin and the sources of Edwards's thought; explains the
     arguments of Original Sin and the provenance of the
     text; and records its "mixed" reception since 1758, in
     an introduction to the thrid volume of the Yale Edwards.
     Edwards's defense rests on the observation that man
     still persists in sin, that sin results from his
     corrupt nature identified in Adam, and that he, not
     God, is the author of his deplorable state. The
     central doctrine, founded upon the "bedrock" of God's
     arbitrary and sovereign will, holds that as God unifies
     man's life, so he unifies the whole race of man by con-
     tinuously creating him identical with Adam, imputing his
     sin. Thus each man recapitulates the first fall. Ed-
     wards, "haunted" by John Taylor's The Scripture-Doctrine
     of Original Sin since it first appeared on the eve of the
     Awakening, ended his point-by-point refutation by burying
     him "under an avalanche of criticism."

16 JOHNSON, ELLWOOD [GERD]. "Individualism and the Puritan
     Imagination." American Quarterly 22 (Summer):230-37.
          Links Edwards's theory of the heart's preparation to
     the individualism of Emerson and William James, Twain and
     Whitman, as an instance of cultural continuity in Ameri-
     can thought and art. Individualism, or a man's ability
     to become a "prime cause," is "deeply imbedded" in theo-
     cratic Puritanism and found expression "most concretely,"
     if "rather accidentally," in Edwards's revision of the
     psychology of preparation for salvation. Concepts like
     isolation or innocence are "extensions"; terms like af-
     fections (Edwards), belief (Emerson), and attention
     (James) are "analogous." As well, each version of in-
     dividualism shares a response to determinism: the Puritan
     to predestination, the transcendentalist to historical
     necessity, the pragmatist to social determinism.

17 JOHNSON, THOMAS H[ERBERT]. The Printed Writings of Jonathan
     Edwards 1703-1758: A Bibliography. New York: Burt
     Franklin.
          Reprint of 1940.7.

1970

18 LASKOWSKY, HENRY J. "Jonathan Edwards: A Puritan Philoso-
    pher of Science." Connecticut Review 4 (October):33-41.
        Contends that Edwards's "sophisticated" principles of
    causality, derived from Newton and Locke, compare favora-
    bly with modern formulations. Edwards grafted Locke's
    notion that physical efficient causality acts through and
    within the mind to Newton's mechanistic, materialistic
    definition of cause. And so Edwards conceptualizes the
    causal relationship between the physical observable world
    of man and the mental unobservable world of God through
    "certain linguistic conventions," just as modern physicists
    do in the unobservable world of the atom.

19 LENSING, GEORGE. "'Memories of West Street and Lepke':
    Robert Lowell's Associative Mirror." Concerning Poetry 3
    (Fall):23-26.
        Cites Edwards as an example of Robert Lowell's use of
    others to define his "moral ambiguities and personal
    frailties" in his poetry.

20 LOWANCE, MASON I[RA], JR. "Images and Shadows of Divine
    Things: The Typology of Jonathan Edwards." Early Ameri-
    can Literature 5, Part 1 (Spring):141-81.
        Discovers a "spectrum of conservative-to-liberal
    typological exegesis" in Edwards, from History of Redemp-
    tion to Images or Shadows, from the linear and historical
    to the manipulated and Platonic, from type to allegory,
    as he tries to reconcile Nature and Scripture. In Images
    or Shadows, Edwards uses a new typology (based on Locke's
    empirical psychology) and endows natural objects with
    allegorical significance leading to spiritual truth.
    Such a "graduated movement" parallels the process of
    mystical revelation and thus accounts for calling Edwards
    a mystic or a pantheist.

21 MARSDEN, GEORGE M. The Evangelical Mind and the New School
    Presbyterian Experience: A Case Study of Thought and
    and Theology in Nineteenth-Century America. New Haven and
    London: Yale University Press, pp. 31-36, 177-79.
        Finds the influence of Edwards's evangelical message
    on nineteenth-century Presbyterian theologians to be the
    "moral revolution" necessary to regeneration. Particular-
    ly influential for such clergymen as Henry Boynton Smith
    (1815-1877) were his ideas on imputation and inability.

22 MARTY, MARTIN E. Righteous Empire: The Protestant Experi-
    ence in America. New York: Dial Press, pp. 79-80.
        Notes Edwards's millennialist thought.

23 MIEGS, JAMES THOMAS. "The Half-Way Covenant: A Study in
    Religious Transition." Foundations 13 (April-June):142-58.
       Connects Edwards's rebellion against the "loose system"
    of admission in his church and its "Arminian implications"
    to the Great Awakening and its response to the "radical
    deviation" from covenant theology (in a history of the
    half-way covenant). In his Qualifications, Edwards re-
    jects his grandfather Stoddard's and his own earlier com-
    munion practice for one limiting admission to professing
    Christians in complete standing. Hence his interest in a
    religion of self-examination is of a piece with his oppo-
    sition to the half-way covenant.

24 MILLER, PERRY. "Edwards, Locke, and the Rhetoric of Sensa-
    tion." In Perspectives in Criticism. Edited by Harry
    Levin. New York: Russell & Russell.
       Reprint of 1950.13.

25 MORRIS, WILLIAM S[PARKES]. Review of Jonathan Edwards: A
    Profile, edited by David Levin. Church History 39 (June):
    263-64.
       Finds that the "chief value" of David Levin's collection
    (1969.21) is Samuel Hopkins's Life of Edwards, long out of
    print, and that there is little else to recommend it:
    Levin's introduction is careless and excessive; James
    Carse "manifestly falsified" Edwards on immortality and
    the will; and Peter Gay is "ill-informed" and "woefully
    wrong" about almost everything.

26 NAGY, PAUL J[OSEPH]. "Jonathan Edwards and the Metaphysics
    of Consent." Personalist 51 (Autumn):434-46.
       Considers Edward's "unique" contribution is not his
    synthesis of the new philosophy and the old theology but
    his "highly original" theories of the sense of the heart
    and the consent to being. For Edwards, the "key" to all
    experience, to a unified view of man, nature, and God—
    "a new and interesting triad"—is consent realized
    through the heart. The world is at once physical and
    spiritual, utilitarian and aesthetic, material and moral,
    and communication (or "'conversation'") between its parts,
    between God and man, is experienced through holy affec-
    tions. "God communicates a concrete world of value, and
    man responds with concrete feeling."

27 NYE, RUSSEL B. American Literary History: 1607-1830.
    Borzoi Studies in History. New York: Alfred A. Knopf,
    pp. 70-73.

1970

Suggests that mysticism defines Edwards, sets him apart
from traditional Calvinism, and accounts for the contradictions in his thought.

28   OATES, STEPHEN B.   To Purge this Land with Blood: A Biography
of John Brown.   New York: Harper & Row, pp. 22-24.
Claims that Edwards, particularly his imprecatory
sermons, "powerfully" influenced John Brown.

29   O'MALLEY, J. STEVEN.   "Edwards and the Problems of Knowledge
in Protestant Tradition."   Drew Gateway 40 (Winter):54-79.
Locates Edwards's epistemology within the Reformed
tradition--knowledge is a public and immediate mental
activity, revealed in the Word, rather than a private and
interior one.   Edwards goes beyond Locke by asserting that
all mental activity and all externality are ideas and
not real substances and that knowledge is not so much the
perception of the agreement or disagreement of ideas as it
is the consistency of ideas with themselves or with God.
Reason, the only way to deal with things as they are, is
"at the heart" of man's humanness and God intends reason
to be passionate and the affections rational.   Edwards
developed "a cognitive basis for theology that was at once
philosophically sublime and corporately meaningful, for
the everyday world . . . provided the model for our
knowledge of God through the Word.

30   PARKES, HENRY BAMFORD.   "The Puritan Heresy."   In his The
Pragmatic Test.   New York: Octagon Books.
Reprint of 1932.12.

31   PATTERSON, ROBERT LEET.   A Philosophy of Religion.   Durham,
N.C.:   Duke University Press, pp. 92-94.
Notes that Edwards's emphasis on the aesthetic element
in the religious experience upset the Calvinist balance
between subjective illumination and objective revelation.

32   REYNOLDS, CHARLES.   "A Proposal for Understanding the Place
of Reason in Christian Ethics."   Journal of Religion 50
(April):155-68.
Cites Edwards as an example of a theologian whose ethical theory identifies God's point of view with the moral
point of view and with reason.   Edwards was first to use
Francis Hutcheson's impartial spectator or ideal observer
theory in an explicitly theological context, arguing that
God acted as an impartial spectator and that His moral
judgments were rational, not arbitrary.   Edwards realized
that the ideal observer was a "secular model" of God and
that as such could analyze moral concepts because God had
"conditioned meaning."

33   RUTMAN, DARRETT B., ed. The Great Awakening: Event and Ex-
         egsis. New York: John Wiley & Sons, pp. 25-26, 79 passim.
         Comments briefly on Edwards's role in the Great Awaken-
     ing; reprints selections from Faithful Narrative and Some
     Thoughts; and reprints part of Vernon Louis Parrington's
     "Anachronism" (1927.2), H. Richard Niebuhr's Kingdom of
     God (1937.7), Alan Heimert's Religion and the American
     Mind (1966.17), and Perry Miller's "Jonathan Edwards and
     the Great Awakening" (1952.4).

34   SEARL, STANFORD JAY, JR. "The Symbolic Imagination of Ameri-
         can Puritanism: Metaphors for the Invisible World."
         Ph.D. dissertation, Syracuse University.
         Remarks the relationship between Edwards's prose and
     the symbolic process of the plain style in Bradford,
     Winthrop, and Hooker.

35   SIMONSON, HAROLD P. Introduction to his Selected Writings of
         Jonathan Edwards. Milestones of Thought in the History of
         Ideas. New York: Frederick Ungar Publishing Co.,
         pp. 7-23.
         Examines Edwards's work serially and finds that sense
     is the "all-important" word summarizing his system of
     thought. For Edwards, religion was an experience, a re-
     generative experience founded upon a sense of God's
     reality, at once "overwhelming, intuitive, and immediate,"
     a sixth sense reorienting and changing the converted.
     Coherence lies in God--that is what God's sovereignty
     means--and religious certainty lies in the "direct per-
     ception" of Him. Edwards's Divine and Supernatural Light
     and Sinners in the Hands of an Angry God "reconstruct the
     divine and human antipodes" of his vision, a vision
     corroborating our own.

36   STEARNS, MONROE. The Great Awakening, 1720-1760. New York:
         Franklin Watts, pp. 14-22.
         Attributes to Edwards's love of God and the Great Awak-
     ening a reversal in the spiritual (and temporal) fortunes
     of the politically and financially oppressed of New Eng-
     land. Defying the river gods and the Boston merchants,
     Edwards brought the "unloved" to dignity, hope, and joy
     through religious revival. Enfield signalled the end of
     medieval religious superstition and the beginning of man's
     responsibility for his happiness and his salvation.

1970

37   STEPHENS, BRUCE MILTON.   "The Doctrine of the Trinity from
     Jonathan Edwards to Horace Bushnell: A Study in the
     Eternal Sonship of Christ."   Ph.D. dissertation, Drew
     University.
          Traces trinitarian doctrine from Edwards to Horace Bush-
     nell to show certain Christological developments.   The
     tension between the doctrine of imminent trinity and that
     of economic trinity is "broken" with the rejection of the
     eternal sonship of Christ.

38   STUART, ROBERT LEE.   "The Table and the Desk: Conversion in
     the Writings Published by Solomon Stoddard and Jonathan
     Edwards during their Northampton Ministries, 1672-1751."
     Ph.D. dissertation, Stanford University.
          Compares the function of the communion in Edwards and
     Solomon Stoddard and finds, though their differences were
     real, they were not nearly so great as Northampton or
     scholars have thought.   Stoddard took the table and the
     desk to be one--the Word dramatized was the Word pro-
     claimed--and so invited the unregenerate to communion as
     a converting ordinance.   Edwards subordinated the table to
     the desk and so kept all but the regenerate from the
     Supper.

39   WALKER, WILLISTON.   A History of the Congregational Churches
     in the United States.   New York: Burt Franklin.
          Reprint of 1894.5.

40   WERGE, THOMAS.   "Jonathan Edwards and the Puritan Mind in
     America: Directions in Textual and Interpretative Criti-
     cism."   Reformed Review 23 (Spring):153-56, 173-83.
          Supplements W. J. Burggraaff's bibliographical essay
     (1965.3) by remarking serially on English and American
     Puritan texts, criticism, and reprints, and concludes
     that Edwards, not Franklin, now seems "the dominant fig-
     ure" in America before the nineteenth century.   Of the
     work on Edwards appearing since 1965, Conrad Cherry's
     study (1966.9) seems the "most significant," challenging
     Perry Miller's (1949.9) but not replacing it.   Though more
     work will be done relating Locke and Newton to Edwards,
     the study of Edwards should benefit from the more general
     movement toward "defining the continuity" of Puritanism
     now underway.

1971

1   BERKOUWER, G. C. Sin. Grand Rapids, Mich.: William B.
    Eerdmans Publishing Co., pp. 460-61.
        Notes Edwards's doctrine of the double imputation of
    original sin.

2   BORGES, JORGE LUIS. An Introduction to American Literature.
    Translated and edited by L. Clark Keating and Robert O.
    Evans. Lexington: University Press of Kentucky, pp. 8-9.
        Translates 1967.4.

3   COLLINS, EDWARD M., JR. "The Rhetoric of Sensation Challenges
    the Rhetoric of the Intellect." In Sermons in American
    History: Selected Issues in the American Pulpit, 1630-
    1967. Edited by DeWitte Holland. Nashville, Tenn.:
    Abingdon Press, pp. 72-76.
        Reprints Edwards's Distinguishing Marks and Charles
    Chauncy's Enthusiasm Described and Cautioned Against as
    an illustration of the polarity between religion of the
    heart and religion of the head in eighteenth-century
    America. Edwards realized, as Chauncy did not, that a
    synthesis of both positions was necessary to the religious
    experience.

4   COOK, CALVIN W. Enthusiasm Re-visited. Grahamstown, South
    Africa: Rhodes University, 15 pp.
        Quotes Edwards's letter to the Princeton trustees about
    his unsuitability to preside over the College in order to
    "look again at his references" as agent and apologist for
    revivalism. In his Life of Brainerd, Edwards substantiates
    his belief that the revival was a genuine work of God, that
    it overcame nature, and that it produced extraordinary
    results from "unlikely elements." Both Edwards and Brain-
    erd discounted enthusiastic claims of "dreams, visions,
    and voices"; argued against "facile explanations" of
    social and psychological manipulation; and welcomed "the
    most shattering social implication" of divine grace in
    the new world: counted among the elect could be men and
    women of Northampton and Stockbridge, colonist and Indian.

5   COWING, CEDRIC B. The Great Awakening and the American
    Revolution: Colonial Thought in the 18th Century. Rand
    McNally Series on the History of American Thought and
    Culture. Chicago: Rand McNally & Co., pp. 45-51, 64-66,
    192-98, passim.

1971

Notes Edwards's role in frontier revivalism, the New
Lights controversy, and the Arminian heresy, in a survey
of the Great Awakening and its relationship to the Revolution. Though Edwards was "the pre-eminent," yet discriminating, apologist for Calvinist evangelism, he
neglected the lessons of experimental piety of the Awakening in his defense of Calvinism in Freedom of the Will and
Original Sin, and "ran counter" to the growing sense of
individual accountability.

6   DODDS, ELISABETH D. Marriage to a Difficult Man: The "Uncommon Union" of Jonathan and Sarah Edwards. Philadelphia:
Westminster Press, 224 pp.
Recounts the domestic life of the Edwardses as "a
parable for the befuddled woman," in a form neither scholarly (footnotes cannot explain "this intricate relationship") nor fictional ("an offense to the scrupulously
truthful Edwards"). The focus is more nearly on Sarah
than on Jonathan, particularly upon her emotional crisis
in January 1742. Sarah emerges from that a "changed and
liberated" woman, whom Jonathan, "previously her only
critic, was to consider a saint." The contrast between
them is remarkable: he is "socially bumbling," given to
"black patches of introspection"; she is "vibrant" and
"blithe." Truth to tell, "A genius is seldom an easy
husband."

7   ELLIS, JOSEPH J., III. "The Puritan Mind in Transition: The
Philosophy of Samuel Johnson." William and Mary Quarterly,
3d ser. 28 (January):26-45.
Identifies some commonly held philosophical points of
the Puritan Edwards and the Anglican Samuel Johnson--
immaterialism, idealism, causation, and so on--and their
desire to infuse New England religious thought with them.

8   EMERSON, EVERETT H. "Jonathan Edwards." In Fifteen American
Authors before 1900: Bibliographic Essays on Research
and Criticism. Edited by Robert A. Rees and Earl N.
Harbert. Madison: University of Wisconsin Press,
pp. 169-84.
Evaluates bibliographies, editions, and biographies of
Edwards and the important criticism of the last seventy-
five years and calls for "a general book" on his thought
incorporating the recent and difficult work of church
historians and theologians, in a bibliographical essay
for students of American literature.

9   FANT, CLYDE E., JR. and PINSON, WILLIAM M., eds. 20 Centuries
     of Great Preaching. Waco, Texas: Word Books, 3:41-55.
          Reprints several Edwards sermons, including Sinners in
     the Hands of an Angry God, the most famous of "all time,"
     and numbers him among the great and unforgettable in the
     history of the American pulpit. Edwards's life was one of
     continued social concern, defending the unpopular Indians
     and championing the common folk in "their struggle with
     injustice and oppression."

10   FAWCETT, ARTHUR. The Cambuslang Revival: The Scottish
     Evangelical Revival of the Eighteenth Century. London:
     Banner of Truth Trust, pp. 223-30 passim.
          Traces the cooperative feature of the missionary move-
     ment in the second half of the eighteenth century to
     Edwards's Humble Attempt and to his suggestion for a
     concert of prayer in the conclusion of Some Thoughts, in
     a detailed examination of its influence among Scottish
     divines.

11   GRABO, NORMAN S. Review of The Great Christian Doctrine of
     Original Sin Defended, edited by Clyde A. Holbrook.
     American Literature 43 (May):286-87.
          Welcomes Clyde A. Holbrook's "sturdy" introduction
     (1970.15) but faults his (and Yale's) editorial principles
     and practice, "living proof of Edwards's judgment of post-
     lapsarian man."

12   GRAY, JOSEPH M. M. "Jonathan Edwards, his God." In his
     Prophets of the Soul. Freeport, N.Y.: Books for Libraries
     Press.
          Reprint of 1936.7.

13   GRIFFIN, EDWARD M[ICHAEL]. Jonathan Edwards. University of
     Minnesota Pamphlets on American Writers, no. 97. Minnea-
     polis: University of Minnesota Press, 46 pp.
          Focuses upon three aspects of Edwards, "man, spokesman,
     and symbol," in a brief biography, seriatim analysis of
     his chief works, and estimate of his place in American
     literature, and draws upon current scholarship to set the
     problems and solve them. Edwards's life was dramatic--
     "some would say tragic"--marked by "odd turns" or by
     the "surprising conversions" of events and actions into
     blessings and catastrophes. His work from Sinners in the
     Hands of an Angry God to History of Redemption echoes with
     the "keynote" of his "radical distinction" between God and
     man--the Great Awakening provides "a fresh appreciation"

1971

of that distinction--and affirms again and again, as the
twentieth century has come to realize, that "man should
not be overly optimistic about his godly propensities."
His symbolic value lies in his role as "an American
artist," sharing with both Herman Melville and Nathaniel
Hawthorne that "cast of mind" which strikes the "uneven
balance" between good and evil, and as the dramatic
realization of "the pilgrim, struggling in his progress
but hopeful, always hopeful, of a glorious reception in
Zion."

14   HAUCK, RICHARD BOYD. A Cheerful Nihilism: Confidence and
     "The Absurd" in American Fiction. Bloomington: Indiana
     University Press, pp. 25-32.
          Claims Edwards perceived the world and man's place in
     it as absurd. The resolution to the "dilemma of rela-
     tivity" facing man lies in what Edwards calls the divine
     and supernatural light, an unmerited gift of God.
     Edwards solves the problem of the absurdist by attributing
     meaning to God by an act of faith, but he fails to show
     how to gain that faith.

15   HELM, PAUL, ed. Introduction to Treatise on Grace and Other
     Posthumously Published Writings, by Jonathan Edwards.
     Cambridge and London: James Clarke & Co., pp. 1-23.
          Contends, contrary to Perry Miller (1949.9) and Peter
     DeJong (1945.1), that Edwards's concept of grace is "a
     pivotal notion" in his theology and that his trinitarian
     views are orthodox and "quite explicitly" in the covenantal
     framework of Calvinism, in an historical, theological,
     and philosophical analysis of his Treatise on Grace, Ob-
     servations concerning the Trinity and the Covenant of Re-
     demption, and An Essay on the Trinity. Edwards offers a
     "modification" of covenant theology, though "clearly . . .
     within" it, because it "inadequately expresses" the imme-
     diacy and uniqueness of divine grace taught in the Bible.
     From his emphasis on those qualities of grace comes his
     opposition to the half-way covenant, his support of the
     revivals, his belief that the "new sense" could be tested
     in public, his denial of mysticism. In short, Edwards
     reaffirms "classic Puritan insistence on Word and Spirit."

16   HOFSTADTER, RICHARD. America at 1750: A Social Portrait.
     New York: Alfred A. Knopf, pp. 235-44.
          Considers Edwards "a pious frontier intellectual" who
     became "the most subtle and formidable" apologist for
     the Great Awakening, though George Whitefield was its
     "heart and soul." In his attempt to domesticate Locke

and Newton to New England needs, Edwards was not being
modern so much as "trying to be up-to-date." He can
hardly be said (as Perry Miller does) to be in the modern-
ist tradition of Hume and Voltaire, Franklin and Jefferson.

17 HOWARD, LEON. "The Creative Imagination of a College Rebel:
    Jonathan Edwards' Undergraduate Writings." Early American
    Literature 5 (Winter):50-56.
        Recounts Edwards's rebellion as a Yale undergraduate--
    physical at first in his rejection of New Haven for Weth-
    ersfield and intellectual later in his rejection of Ramus
    and Locke for the Port Royal logic--and his "extraordinary
    imaginative leap" from essays on spiders and rainbows to
    those on idealism and being. Edwards used The Art of
    Thinking rather than the categories of Ramus or the
    empirical induction of Locke to formulate his "greatest"
    intellectual achievements, "Of Being" and "Of the Preju-
    dices of the Imagination," moving "through philosophical
    idealism . . . to a rationalistic concept of abstract
    reality" independent of Locke's theory of ideas and
    stirred by the passion of a "student rebel."

18 KIMNACH, WILSON HENRY. "The Literary Techniques of Jonathan
    Edwards." Ph.D. dissertation, University of Pennsylvania.
        Portrays Edwards at work as a "conscious literary
    craftsman" in an investigation of his art and thought
    recorded in sermons, outlines, revisions, notebooks, and
    manuscript treatises. Edwards's desire for a theoretical
    basis for matters of style led him to important analyses
    of the nature of the mind, language, and communication.

19 LOUD, GROVER CLEVELAND. Evangelized America. Freeport, N.Y.:
    Books for Libraries Press, pp. 10-31.
        Reprint of 1928.5.

20 MILLER, GLENN THOMAS. "The Rise of Evangelical Calvinism:
    A Study in Jonathan Edwards and the Puritan Tradition."
    Th.D. dissertation, Union Theological Seminary.
        Characterizes Edwards's evangelical Calvinism as a
    "development" of the preparationist-Stoddardean tradition
    and traces it from his juvenilia to Religious Affections.
    Early indications can be found in his idealism and his
    conversion experience recounted in Personal Narrative.
    Later, in the cause of evangelism, he works through ideas
    on immediacy, the trinity, eschatology, and "invitational
    Christology." Still later, in the Great Awakening, he
    joins his theology of conversion to his millennialism and
    his typology.

1971

21 MILLER, PERRY. "Jonathan Edwards and the Great Awakening."
    In America in Crisis. Edited by Daniel Aaron. Hamden,
    Conn.: Shoe String Press.
        Reprint of 1952.4.

22 MURRAY, IAIN H. The Puritan Hope: A Study in Revival and
    the Interpretation of Prophecy. London: Banner of Truth
    Trust, pp. 151-52, passim.
        Notes the warm reception given Edwards's Humble Attempt
    in Scotland and among the founders of the Baptist Mission-
    ary Society (1792).

23 NAGY, PAUL J[OSEPH]. "The Beloved Community of Jonathan
    Edwards." Transactions of the Charles S. Pierce Society:
    A Quarterly Journal in American Philosophy 7 (Spring):
    93-104.
        Characterizes Edwards's theology as "essentially social"
    rather than individual and places him "at the beginning
    of a speculative tradition in American social thought."
    Edwards seeks a dynamic reconciliation of opposites, much
    like Ralph Waldo Emerson's each and all, based upon the
    "key concept" of consent to being. Society, for Edwards,
    is the "instrument as well as the end" of redemption, but
    "authentic," representative individualism, as a function
    of divine self-love and public affection, is the "corner-
    stone" of society.

24 PATTERSON, ROBERT LEET. The Role of History in Religion.
    New York: Exposition Press, pp. 24-29.
        Focuses upon Edwards's use of the "overlooked" aesthet-
    ic element in Calvin to fashion his eschatology. To
    Edwards, the fall, Israel, incarnation, resurrection, and
    judgment are connected cosmic events in time, and the
    spiritual enlightenment imparted by God guarantees their
    historicity and their beauty.

25 RICE, DANIEL F. "Natural Theology and the Scottish Philoso-
    phy in the Thought of Thomas Chalmers." Scottish Journal
    of Theology 24 (February):23-46.
        Suggests that Thomas Chalmers's reading of Edwards on
    philosophical necessity delivered him from the mechanistic
    and materialistic determinism of William Godwin's Politi-
    cal Justice to a religious piety based on an expanded
    vision of creation. In addition, his systematic theology
    is indebted to Edwards on the will, sin, holiness, and
    the affections.

26   RUDISILL, DORUS PAUL. The Doctrine of the Atonement in
      Jonathan Edwards and His Successors. New York: Poseidon
      Books, 152 pp.
          Examines Edwards's doctrine of the atonement, its
      divergence from traditional, New England penal theory and
      its effect upon the doctrines of Joseph Bellamy, Samuel
      Hopkins, and Stephen West, and later Edwardseans. Edwards
      modifies the penal theory that Christ satisfied distribu-
      tive justice by suffering "the precise quantity and the
      precise quality" of the elect throughout eternity by sug-
      gesting that God reconciled justice and mercy as a "pre-
      condition" to forgiveness. He abandons the quantum
      measure--Christ's capacity to suffer is far deeper than
      man's--and substitutes the nature of the passionate Christ
      and His relationship to God. Christ's suffering does not
      affect man's predicament so much as it illustrates that
      "all God's attributes may be effectually functional and
      compatible." As love, for Edwards, is the "all-controlling"
      attribute of God, Christ satisfies distributive justice by
      suffering and commutative justice by obedience. "It is
      scarcely possible for one to magnify and glorify the suf-
      fering of Christ more than Edwards does."

27   SANDON, LEO, JR. "H. Richard Niebuhr's Interpretation of the
      American Theological Tradition." Ph.D. dissertation,
      Boston University.
          Finds that H. Richard Niebuhr's interpretation of the
      American theological tradition constitutes the single most
      important influence in his constructive theology and that
      Edwards profoundly affected his value theory, his radical
      monotheism, and, "quite possibly," his Christology.

28   SHEA, DANIEL B., JR. Review of Beauty and Sensibility in the
      Thought of Jonathan Edwards, by Roland André Delattre.
      Early American Literature 5 (Winter):83-84.
          Suggests that the programmatic approach of Roland André
      Delattre's study (1968.8) "unintentionally drives a wedge"
      between the moral and the aesthetic in Edwards.

29   SLOAN, DOUGLAS. The Scottish Enlightenment and the American
      College Ideal. New York: [Columbia] Teachers College
      Press, pp. 48-53, 99-101.
          Recounts Edwards's relationship to Scotland, from his
      "close personal ties" to Scottish divines to his acquaint-
      ance with Scottish education and thought. Edwards early
      joined intellect and learning to a revivalist impulse--a
      key formulation in Scotland--and stressed understanding.

1971

Later he adapted Francis Hutcheson's study to his True Virtue, retaining his empirical psychology while rejecting his idea that true benevolence is possible in natural man.

30   SMITH, ELWYN A[LLEN]. "The Voluntary Establishment of Reli-
gion." In The Religion of the Republic. Edited by Elwyn
A. Smith. Philadelphia: Fortress Press, pp. 154-82.
Notes the influence of Edwards's concept of the volun-
tary upon Timothy Dwight, Lyman Beecher, and Nathaniel
Taylor, the new theocrats.

31   STEIN, STEPHEN J. "'Notes on the Apocalypse' by Jonathan
Edwards." Ph.D. dissertation, Yale University.
See 1977.28.

32   WHITTEMORE, ROBERT CLIFTON. "Jonathan Edwards." In his
Makers of the American Mind. Freeport, N.Y.: Books for
Libraries Press.
Reprint of 1964.25.

33   WILSON, DAVID S. "The Flying Spider." Journal of the History of Ideas 32 (July-September):447-58.
Calls "unwarranted" the critics' claim of uniqueness for
Edwards's youthful observations of flying spiders and shows
his essay to be a "felicitous and precocious" example of a
well-established genre in natural philosophy.

1972

1   ABELOVE, HENRY. "Jonathan Edwards's Letter of Invitation to
George Whitefield." William and Mary Quarterly, 3d ser.
29 (July):487-89.
Reprints Edwards's letter of invitation to George
Whitefield, 12 February 1740, a "fascinating" document of
the Awakening that clarifies Whitefield's motives and
reveals Edwards's temperament.

2   AHLSTROM, SYDNEY E. "Jonathan Edwards and the Revival of New
England Theology." In his A Religious History of the
American People. New Haven and London: Yale University
Press, pp. 295-313.
Surveys Edwards's work and discovers it to be a "monumental reconstruction of strict Reformed orthodoxy." From
his earliest writings on, Edwards remained "utterly captive" to the Synod of Dort, the Westminister Assembly,
and Puritan thought, though freed somewhat by the new

306

learning and by philosophical idealism. With his later, less polemical work--True Virtue and the End of Creation-- Edwards left Lockean psychology for the "great tradition" of Christian Platonism and a "genuine" mysticism. Perhaps always a "misunderstood stranger," he is more than any one of the five aspects others have claimed the "essential Edwards" from time to time: exegetical preacher, New England polemicist, experiential apologist, Christian ontologist, and sacred historian.

3 BASTAKI, SHAFIKAH A. A. "A Reconstruction of Jonathan Ed- wards' Volitional Theory in the Context of Contemporary Action Theory: An Examination of Freedom of the Will." Ph.D. dissertation, University of Pittsburgh.
     Reconstructs Edwards's concepts of actions and voli- tions, chiefly found in Freedom of the Will, into a "com- prehensive" theory of action in the context of post- Wittgensteinian discussions. Supplemented by recent volitional and pro-attitude theories of action, Edwards proves to be "consistent" and capable of answering charges of infinite regress and circularity.

4 BORGES, JORGE LUIS. "Jonathan Edwards (1703-1758)." In Selected Poems, 1923-1967. Edited by Normas Thomas DiGiovanni. New York: Delacorte Press, pp. 168-69.
     Translates 1969.3, by Richard Howards and Cesar Rennert.

5 COLACURCIO, ROBERT EUGENE. "The Perception of Excellency as the Glory of God in Jonathan Edwards: An Essay Toward the Epistemology of Discernment." Ph.D. dissertation, Fordham University.
     Recovers Edwards's epistemology of discernment through a fugal structure of related themes. What is implied in Edwards, though "nowhere to be found in the original source," is that the "beauty of God's holiness effects an order which has its pattern virtually imaged in the per- ception of God's excellency." Such beauty of the living God is beyond language but is powerfully present in the heart of the believer through the medium of the virtual image.

6 COLEMAN, ALEXANDER. "Notes on Borges and American Literature." TriQuarterly 25 (Fall):356-77.
     Examines Jorge Borges on Edwards in prose (1967.4) and poetry (1969.3) and offers the transposition of Edwards's symbol of the spider from dangling man to entrapped God as a good example of his "literary imposition" upon American writers.

1972

7   DAVENPORT, FREDERICK MORGAN. "The New England Awakening
    Originating with Jonathan Edwards." In his <u>Primitive
    Traits in Religious Revivals</u>. New York: AMS Press.
        Reprint of 1905.2.

8   DENAULT, PATRICIA. "Jonathan Edwards, the Great Awakener."
    <u>American History Illustrated</u> 6 (January):28-36.
        Recounts Edwards's career. Edwards's writing is an
    "atonement" for his lack of sociability, his views of
    the Great Awakening so singular neither side could fully
    accept them.

9   FIERING, NORMAN S. "Will and Intellect in the New England
    Mind." <u>William and Mary Quarterly</u> 3d ser. 29 (October):
    515-58.
        Traces the contention in the Great Awakening between
    Old Calvinist evangelicals like Edwards and Arminian lib-
    erals like Charles Chauncy to debates on will and intel-
    lect in the seventeenth century. There is a remarkably
    "close" correspondence between seventeenth-century
    Augustinian voluntarist ideas and those of Edwards, just
    as there is a similarity between seventeenth-century
    intellectualist ideas and those of Chauncy. (Indeed, the
    historical connection should temper the "exaggerated"
    claims of influence of Locke's sensationalism upon Edwards
    and others in the first half of the eighteenth century.)
    The Great Awakening is simply a recurrence of the "peren-
    nial opposition" of head and heart, intellect and will.

10 GAUSTAD, EDWIN SCOTT. <u>The Great Awakening in New England</u>.
    New York: Times Books.
        Reprint of 1957.6.

11 GOEN, C[LARENCE] C[URTIS]. "Editor's Introduction." In <u>The
    Great Awakening</u>. The Works of Jonathan Edwards, vol. 4.
    New Haven and London: Yale University Press, pp. 1-95.
        Examines the tracts and occasional pieces that show how
    Edwards "initially made his case" for the Great Awakening--
    <u>Faithful Narrative</u>, <u>Distinguishing Marks</u>, <u>Some Thoughts</u>,
    seven letters, and the preface to Joseph Bellamy's <u>True
    Religion</u>--and suggests that Edwards's analysis and pattern
    of the conversion experience becomes normative in America,
    in a survey of his role in the revivals and the contro-
    versy that ensued. By definition, revivalism is the
    necessary result of evangelical pietism, the very center
    of the Reformed movement, and Arminianism is a threat to
    the faith on which it rests. A "charismatic leader . . .

[of] a bewildered people," Edwards clinically observed the work of God in Northampton, refracted it through Locke, and published his findings in Faithful Narrative (its provenance detailed fully here). But there were "premonitions" of difficulty--the reaction to Whitefield, the Tennents, and Davenport--and Edwards's Distinguishing Marks, an attempt to find a middle way, unintentionally polarized matters further. A "saddened" Edwards braced against the critics' onslaught, published his "most ambitious" defense in Some Thoughts, but only widened the "veritable chasm" between him and Charles Chauncy. His letters to correspondents here and abroad serve as a "footnote" to his devotion to revivalism; his preface to True Religion, written reluctantly after his dismissal, a measure of the blame he took upon himself for his lack of judgment.

12 HALL, DAVID D. Review of The Great Awakening, edited by C. C. Goen. New England Quarterly 45 (September):455-57.
      Faults C. C. Goen's introduction (1972.11) for its emphasis on Edwards's challenge to Arminianism as the source of the Great Awakening in New England.

13 HAMILTON, JAMES EDWARD. "A Comparison of the Moral Theories of Charles Finney and Asa Mahan." Ph.D. dissertation, State University of New York at Buffalo.
      Remarks the influence Edwards and Thomas Reid had on the development of nineteenth-century academic orthodoxy, especially in the moral theories of Finney and Mahan.

14 HANKAMER, ERNEST WOLFRAM. "Das Politische Denken von Jonathan Edwards." Ph.D. dissertation, University of Munich. Published as 1972.15.

15 _____. Das Politische Denken von Jonathan Edwards. Munich: n.p., 292 pp.
      Traces Edwards's political thought from his anthropology through his ethics and predicates his "wahre Politik" upon passages in True Virtue, Qualifications, and several sermons. Edwards regards man's freedom to be moral rather than social, rooted in God's grace and independent of secular guarantees of social organization or social ideology. The primary dimension of man's existence is virtue; his end is freedom; but a free life is conditional on a free heart in God. (In German.)

1972

16 HOLIFIELD, E. BROOKS. "The Renaissance of Sacramental Piety
    in Colonial New England." William and Mary Quarterly, 3d
    ser. 29 (January):33-48.
        Notes that the rejection of Solomon Stoddard's admis-
    sions policies by Edwards and other ministers of the Great
    Awakening put an end to the sacramental renaissance.

*17 IRBY, JOE BEN. "Changing Conceptions of the Doctrine of
    Predestination in American Reformed Theology." Th.D.
    dissertation, Union Theological Seminary in Virginia.
        Cited in Comprehensive Dissertation Index 1861-1972,
    32:573.

18 JONES, JAMES W. "Reflections on the Problem of Religious
    Experience." Journal of the American Academy of Religion
    40 (December):445-53.
        Denies that religious experience is a function of "a
    sixth sense or a new faculty of sensation"; argues that
    it is an experiencing of "all of reality"; and compares
    Edwards's insights into the matter with those of Cardinal
    Newman, Deitrich Bonhoeffer, and Samuel Willard. For
    Edwards, the experience recounted in Personal Narrative
    is "the very fact" of faith realized as a new perception.
    His "'new sense'" experience enables man "to live in a
    world of plural experiences without loss of intellectual
    and psychological unity."

19 KEATING, JEROME FRANCIS. "Personal Identity in Jonathan
    Edwards, Ralph Waldo Emerson, and Alfred North Whitehead."
    Ph.D. dissertation, Syracuse University.
        Defines Edwards's concept of identity as both in a
    Lockean tradition--the mind is a passive receptor--and out
    of it--identity is founded in consciousness. Original sin
    forces Edwards to link man's identity not to his memory
    as in Locke, but to his soul and to God's saving grace.
    Emerson illustrates the Leibnitzean tradition of identity--
    the mind is an active participant. Whitehead combines
    both traditions.

20 KOLODNY, ANNETTE. "Imagery in the Sermons of Jonathan Ed-
    wards." Early American Literature 7 (Fall):172-82.
        Analyzes Edwards's "conscious artistic manipulation"
    of figurative language in three sermons--Sinners in the
    Hands of an Angry God, God Glorified, and The Peace which
    Christ Gives--and maintains that it is "characteristic of
    all" his sermons. Edwards uses images for "emotional per-
    suasion" and arranges them cumulatively to emphasize

divine power and to deny human power. The overall effect
of the images is "to force the listener to go through very
specific and analyzable emotional responses."

21 LEE, BRIAN. Review of Jonathan Edwards, by Edward H. Davidson; The Interpreted Design, by David L. Minter; and
Spiritual Autobiography, by Daniel B. Shea. Notes and
Queries, n.s. 19 (October):393-95.
    Compares the studies of E. H. Davidson (1966.10), D. L.
Minter (1969.26), and D. B. Shea (1968.26) by focusing
upon Edwards's Personal Narrative and finds that only Shea
offers a "convincing" analysis.

22 LEE, SANG HYUN. "The Concept of Habit in the Thought of Jonathan Edwards." Ph.D. dissertation, Harvard University.
    Analyzes Edwards's concept of habit and its functions.
Through it Edwards constructs a theory of experience fusing
sensation and the mind's activity and a theory of reality
positing being as actual and in process.

23 _____. "Jonathan Edwards' Theory of the Imagination." Michigan Academician 5 (Fall):233-41.
    Contends that Edwards's definition of habit, "drastically"
different from Locke's, gives the mind a real and active
role in experience without resorting to rationalist explanations or losing the empirical sensationalism of his
epistemology. He does this by making the imaginative power
of habit "a mediating principle" between the activity of
the mind and the sensations it passively receives, between
the intuitive or immediate mode of perception and the
rational or discursive. Thus the imagination of habit of
mind enables the self to achieve "unity and direction" and
describes in a "fresh way" the indwelling of the Holy Spirit.

24 LOGAN, SAMUEL TALBOT, JR. "Hermeneutics and American Literature." Ph.D. dissertation, Emory University.
    Contrasts, in part, Edwards's hermeneutics and Haw-
thorne's: Edwards restored Calvin's balanced scheme rather
than continue the technologia of seventeenth- and eighteenth-
century Puritans; Hawthorne failed to develop a coherent
hermeneutics and ends in narrative ambiguity.

25 LONG, GARY DALE. "The Doctrine of Original Sin in New England
Theology from Jonathan Edwards to Edwards Amasa Park."
Th.D. dissertation, Dallas Theological Seminary.
    Traces the doctrinal drift on original sin from mid-
eighteenth-century orthodoxy to late nineteenth-century

1972

heterodoxy; from the New Divinity School of Samuel Hopkins
and Joseph Bellamy to the New Haven School, the Andover
School, the Oberlin School, and New School Presbyterianism;
from Edwards to Edwards Amasa Park. Early rejection of
both the realistic and the representative union views of
Adam and posterity resulted in semi-Pelagianism and represents a complete departure from Edwards. The error stems
primarily from faulty exegesis, tactics of concealment,
and ambiguous language.

26   LOWANCE, MASON I[RA], JR. "'Images or Shadows of Divine
      Things' in the Thought of Jonathan Edwards." In Typology
      and Early American Literature. Edited by Sacvan Berco-
      vitch. [Amherst:] University of Massachusetts Press,
      pp. 209-44.
          Reprint of 1970.20.

27   LUDWIG, RICHARD M., ed. "Jonathan Edwards." In Literary
      History of the United States: Bibliographical Supplement
      II. Edited by Robert E. Spiller et al. New York: Mac-
      millan Co., pp. 149-50.
          Updates 1959.8.

28   LYTTLE, DAVID [JAMES]. "Jonathan Edwards on Personal Iden-
      tity." Early American Literature 7 (Fall):163-71.
          Defines personal identity in Edwards as "a generic
      unit of darkened thinking substance" and man's moral worth
      as part of that generic immateriality. He disregards
      individuation and considers insignificant the uniqueness
      of each soul, as outlined in Original Sin. Man is known
      by his relationship to God and not, as John Locke held and
      Edwards rejected, by his actions.

29   MILLER, GLENN T[HOMAS]. Review of The Great Awakening,
      edited by C. C. Goen. William and Mary Quarterly, 3d ser.
      29 (October):655-57.
          Values C. C. Goen's "crisp" introduction (1972.11) but
      finds that he "overstresses" the historical continuities
      of evangelicalism, thus robbing the Great Awakening of its
      newness, and that he "obscures the complex love-hate
      relationship" Edwards had with the Enlightenment.

30   NISSENBAUM, STEPHEN, ed. The Great Awakening at Yale College.
      American History Research Series. Belmont, Cal.: Wads-
      worth Publishing Co., p. 54.
          Comments about Edwards's career and his Yale commence-
      ment sermon, Distinguishing Marks, and reprints much of
      that first and "major analytic" examination of the

Awakening and all of his account of David Brainerd's
expulsion from the College.

31   REASKE, CHRISTOPHER R. "The Devil and Jonathan Edwards."
       Journal of the History of Ideas 33 (January-March):123-38.
       Traces and describes the devil as Edwards wrote of
       him from 1731 to 1750, from his "mild preoccupation"
       before the Great Awakening, to his "monomania" during it,
       to his "subdued awareness" after it. Edwards's conspicu-
       ous concern with the devil during the revival was due to
       his "somewhat melancholic mood," which deepened with his
       increased fascination. Thus the Awakening was a "catalyst,"
       releasing the "dark part of Edwards' psyche where the
       devil resided." His notions of Satan, at times "unortho-
       dox," derive from the Bible, Paradise Lost, and the work
       of John Flavel, and find expression chiefly in Distinguish-
       ing Marks, Some Thoughts, and Religious Affections.

32   _____. "An Unpublished Letter Concerning 'Sanctification' by
       Elisha Williams, Jonathan Edwards' Tutor." New England
       Quarterly 45 (September):429-34.
       Sees a "blurred foreshadowing" of Edwards's attack on
       Arminian rationalism and a "very real influence" on Ed-
       wards's views on sanctification in Religious Affections
       in an unpublished letter by Elisha Williams, Edwards's
       young tutor at Yale in 1719.

33   RIFORGIATO, LEONARD R. "The Unified Thought of Jonathan
       Edwards." Thought 47 (Winter):599-610.
       Finds in Edwards a related and consistent pattern
       blending his early thoughts about Newtonian cosmology
       into his later fully developed ideas of theology. The
       link between the two, and at once the basis for his
       ontology, derives from his trinitarian model of harmo-
       nious consent: God's expressed idea of Himself is con-
       sented to in love. Hence, man's conscious consent to
       being recapitulates creation.

34   SELDES, GILBERT. The Stammering Century. Gloucester, Mass.:
       Peter Smith.
       Reprint of 1928.8.

35   SERIO, JOHN N. "From Edwards to Poe." Connecticut Review 6
       (October):88-92.
       Notes similarities between Edwards and Poe in their
       "emblematic reading" of the natural world, their "preoc-
       cupation" with states of guilt, and their emphasis on
       the moral culpability of man in a determined universe.

1972

36   SHEA, DANIEL B., JR.   "Jonathan Edwards, Historian of Con-
      sciousness."   In Major Writers of Early American Litera-
      ture.   Edited by Everett Emerson.   Madison: University
      of Wisconsin Press, pp. 179-204.
          Considers Edwards's thought, "not as system, but as the
      expression of a profound experience of the interrelated-
      ness of things," coherent in his personality and revealed
      in progressive development.   Thus similar ideas about true
      faith and false enthusiasm, for example, run through
      Personal Narrative, Faithful Narrative, Some Thoughts,
      Life of Brainerd, and Religious Affections, but in each
      the focus shifts--from the young Edwards to Phebe Bartlet
      and Abigail Hutchinson to Sarah to Brainerd to an "imper-
      sonal biography of a saint"--and yields a critical per-
      spective on the psychology of mass movements, God's
      sovereignty, and man's vulnerability.   Edwards understands
      history in "multiple dimensions" and attempts to plot the
      complex relationship between the regenerate soul and an
      emerging America.   In doing so, he adumbrates later writers
      and contributes significantly to the "history of the
      American consciousness."

37   SHUFFELTON, FRANK CHARLES.   "Light of the Western Churches:
      The Career of Thomas Hooker, 1586-1647."   Ph.D. disserta-
      tion, Stanford University.
          Suggests Thomas Hooker's influence upon Edwards (in the
      final chapter).

38   SONTAG, FREDERICK, and ROTH, JOHN K.   The American Religious
      Experience: the Roots, Trends, and Future of American
      Theology.   New York: Harper & Row, pp. 41-48.
          Regards Edwards's systematic theology a failure in
      American terms because it had "little to do with" freedom
      of self-determination.   Even though he combines philo-
      sophical reflection with technical theology and measures
      religious experience by practical tests and acts--clearly,
      American traits--Edwards failed to elaborate his personal
      compassionate experience of divinity and of the religious
      affections into an "'American God.'"   And so his "true
      God remained unborn in his time."

39   STEIN, STEPHEN J.   "A Notebook on the Apocalypse by Jonathan
      Edwards."   William and Mary Quarterly, 3d ser. 29 (October):
      623-34.
          Describes in detail Edwards's unpublished private note-
      book on the Apocalypse--its appearance, history, composi-
      tion, and dating--and suggests its function and

significance at different times in his life: "as a
discursive commentary on the Revelation, as a copybook for
transcribing authors whom he found insightful on topics
related to apocalyptic, as a scrapbook for collecting
accounts from his reading in contemporary affairs and for
listing evidences of progress in God's kingdom, and as a
sketchbook for developing thoughts on eschatological
matters."

40 STUART, ROBERT LEE. "'Mr. Stoddard's Way': Church and
    Sacraments in Northampton." American Quarterly 24 (May):
    243-53.
        Considers Edwards's failure to note Solomon Stoddard's
    distinction between conversion and regeneration an "injus-
    tice" to his grandfather and a "disservice" to himself--
    his dismissal hinged on it--in an examination of Stod-
    dard's "ingenious" scheme of communion.

41 TALLON, JOHN WILLIAM. "Flight into Glory: The Cosmic
    Imagination of Jonathan Edwards." Ph.D. dissertation,
    University of Pennsylvania.
        Examines Edwards's modifications of the Puritan sym-
    bolic system concerning the natural world, man, God, and
    history. The world symbolizes the "interior reality" of
    God into which man tries to absorb himself. God's glory
    is illimitable and indefinable, and so history, as the
    "inevitable" fulfillment of His glory, is "meaningless"
    without it. "Thus the American imagination meets in
    Edwards a developmental dead end."

42 THOMAS, REUEN. Leaders in Thought in the Modern Church.
    Freeport, N.Y.: Books for Libraries Press.
        Reprint of 1892.3.

43 TOWNSEND, HARVEY G[ATES]. The Philosophy of Jonathan Edwards
    from his Private Notebooks. Wesport, Conn.: Greenwood
    Press.
        Reprint of 1955.10.

44 WATKINS, KEITH. "Original Sin." Encounter 33 (Spring):203-
    205.
        Reviews Clyde Holbrook's edition of Original Sin
    (1970.15); finds it "carefully edited, splendidly intro-
    duced, and handsomely printed"; sides with Edwards against
    John Taylor, his principal opponent in the treatise; and
    urges a wider audience to turn to it for it addresses our
    condition.

1972

45 WHITE, MORTON, ed. Documents in the History of American
    Philosophy: From Jonathan Edwards to John Dewey. New
    York: Oxford University Press, pp. 39-42.
        Reprints selections from Religious Affections and
    Freedom of the Will, summarizes the arguments, and calls
    Edwards "the first American philosopher of distinction,"
    through derivative of Locke and Calvin.

46 WHITE, MORTON. "Jonathan Edwards: The Doctrine of Necessity
    and the Sense of the Heart." In his Science and Sentiment
    in America: Philosophical Thought from Jonathan Edwards
    to John Dewey. New York: Oxford University Press,
    pp. 30-54 passim.
        Puts Edwards in the "middle band" of philosophy, com-
    bining logic in metaphysics with emotion in religion, in
    an examination of the dual nature of his philosophical
    work: the doctrine of necessity and moral judgment of the
    sinner in Freedom of the Will and the doctrine of grace
    and the heart of the saint in Religious Affections. Ed-
    wards took the theory of universal causation from Locke
    and Newton and rigorously applied it to the will, but he
    abandoned it and the "scientific mood" for the mystical
    one as he turned to the "superempirical" nature of grace.
    Thus Freedom of the Will shows "great intellectual power
    and skill," especially in distinguishing philosophical
    from ordinary necessity, and Religious Affections is "very
    obscure" and alogical, a pattern for transcendental
    thought.

1973

1   BAYM, MAX I. A History of Literary Aesthetics in America.
    New York: Frederick Ungar Publishing Co., pp. 1-4.
        Characterizes Edwards's aesthetics as mathematical--
    beauty and being are perceived proportionally and numeri-
    cally--and his relating physical to spiritual beauty as
    "close to" romantic.

2   BRUMM, URSULA. Puritanismus und Literatur in Amerika.
    Darmstadt: Wissenschaftliche Buchgessellschaft, pp. 87-94.
        Provides an Edwards bibliography of primary and second-
    ary works in English and a brief estimate. (In German.)

3   CAMPBELL, DENNIS MARION. "Authority and the Renewal of Theol-
    ogy in America: An Historical Study and Contemporary
    Critique." Ph.D. dissertation, Duke University.
    Published as 1976.14.

4   CHERRY, [CHARLES] CONRAD. "Promoting the Cause and Testing
     the Spirits: Jonathan Edwards on Revivals of Religion--
     A Review Article." Journal of Presbyterian History 51
     (Fall):327-37.
          Reviews The Great Awakening, edited by C. C. Goen
     (1972.11), finds Goen's "most valuable service" to be his
     restoration of Faithful Narrative from Edwards's annotated
     copy, but regrets the lack of "penetrating theological in-
     sights" into Edwards's critical role in the Awakening.
     The desk and the pulpit, theological analysis and evangeli-
     cal preaching, are complementary in Edwards and are brought
     together in the "graphic symbol," the concrete and vivid
     image that moves the whole man, mind and emotion, to
     regeneration. After Edwards, imaginative preaching de-
     clines to the "dour dogma" of Calvinism or the "bland
     moral lecture" of Unitarianism, and the correlation between
     theology and affections disappears.

5   CLEBSCH, WILLIAM A. American Religious Thought: A History.
     Chicago History of American Religion. Chicago: University
     of Chicago Press, pp. 11-68, passim.
          Contends that Edwards (and Emerson and William James)
     exchanged the moralistic spirituality of traditional Puri-
     tanism for the aesthetic spirituality of a native American
     experience, "turning the sense of duty to the sense of
     beauty," in an examination of his theology and psychology.
     Edwards insists that human experience is unitive--head and
     heart, understanding and will are one; that God's beauty
     and the world's beauty are "indivisible"; that theology
     and the religious experience, theory and practice are one;
     and that "the religious life equals the good life equals
     the beautiful life." Neither mystic nor pantheist,
     Edwards "knew and taught" holy beauty, testifying to
     outward and empirical spirituality, no longer inward nor
     mysterious.

6   DAVIDSON, JAMES WEST. "Eschatology in New England: 1700-
     1763." Ph.D. dissertation, Yale University.
          See 1977.8.

7   DAVIDSON, MARSHALL B., et al. The American Heritage History
     of the Writers' America. New York: American Heritage
     Publishing Co., pp. 50-52.
          Finds a "more engaging" Edwards in his natural obser-
     vations than in his polemics, in a brief estimate and
     sometime comparison to Franklin. (Illustrated.)

1973

8   FRASER, JAMES. "Interpreters of Our Faith: Jonathan Edwards."
     A.D. 2 (August):6-11.
          Offers a brief life of Edwards and six tests of the
     spirit from Religious Affections so that a new generation
     might know the signs of the visibility of the Word.

9   FULCHER, J. RODNEY. "Puritans and the Passions: The Faculty
     Psychology in American Puritanism." Journal of the History
     of the Behavioral Sciences 9 (April):123-39.
          Considers Edwards, in his adoption of Lockean empiricist
     psychology, a countervailing force to the divisive faculty
     psychology of conversion of seventeenth-century Puritans.
     Unlike them, Edwards fashioned a psychological theory that
     brought piety and intellect into balance instead of con-
     tention.

10   GRIFFITH, JOHN. "Jonathan Edwards as a Literary Artist."
     Criticism 15 (Spring):156-73.
          Rescues Edwards from becoming "a preserved specimen in
     the museum of American theology" by treating him as a
     literary artist, by exploring "his genius for creating
     psychological drama obliquely" and for manipulating dis-
     tractions and logic into "figurative reality." Personal
     Narrative can be read as a "poetic fiction," a bildungs-
     roman of lost youthful illusion and found mature reality,
     a "literary act of worship" rather than communication,
     with a sense of autonomy and independence about it. Like-
     wise True Virtue is "a work of literary art" rather than
     an "out-dated" religious tract, its architectonics and
     incantatory phrases evoking a "figurative universe" where
     such virtue exists. As a "symbolic paradigm of a mental
     universe" True Virtue is "a perfect work."

11   HEARN, ROSEMARY. "Stylistic Analysis of the Sermons of
     Jonathan Edwards." Ph.D. dissertation, Indiana University.
          Analyzes Edwards's sermonic structure and rhetoric and
     finds his style somewhat inconsistent with Puritan prac-
     tice, though "skillfully adapted and frequently lively."
     Responsive to the important issues of his time, Edwards
     often "manipulated" contemporary practice to suit his ends.

12   HEINEMANN, ROBERT L. "God, Man, and the Great Awakening."
     In America in Controversy. Edited by DeWitte Holland.
     Dubuque, Iowa: W. C. Brown Co., pp. 35-51.
          Cites Edwards as an exemplar of the orthodox view in
     the theological, ecclesiastical, and rhetorical issues of
     the Great Awakening. Edwards is a "valiant" defender of
     the old Calvinism, a firm believer in affective rather

than rational preaching. By insisting on election and experiential religion, Edwards fosters "individualistc and revolutionary" behavior, the hallmark of the Great Awakening.

13 HOLBROOK, CLYDE A[MOS]. The Ethics of Jonathan Edwards: Morality and Aesthetics. Ann Arbor: University of Michigan Press, 236 pp.

Contends that Edwards's ethics (and much else in his thought) can best be understood as an expression of his theological objectivism—his "well-nigh overwhelming conviction of God's centrality, power, and beauty"—and rendered coherent in sermons and treatises by his "aesthetic rhetoric," in a study of the major patterns of his thought and the relationship of ethics to aesthetics, the beauty of holiness. Although Edwards escapes panentheism by his "contrived differentiation" between subject and object and sometimes turns to theological subjectivism when it suits him, the "key concept" for him remains theological objectivism with its denial of utilitarianism and its ethics of "spontaneous virtue." To Edwards, moral beauty comes from the cordial consent of beings to Being, in the same manner as the Trinity consists in the "beauty of relationships"; ethical responsibility arises from the attraction of good and beauty in being to being, not from a sense of duty. An "adventurous thinker," Edwards brings Calvinism and Neoplatonism together in a world "replete with the beauteous evidences of God's presence."

14 JONES, JAMES W. The Shattered Synthesis: New England Puritanism before the Great Awakening. New Haven and London: Yale University Press, pp. 168-72, 176.

Narrows the debate between Edwards and Charles Chauncy, first, to questions about God and the world and, then, to questions about man in America. To Edwards, God was a mystery in a miraculous world; to Chauncy, God was orderly, rational, and predictable, as was the world. Edwards attacked Arminianism, in Freedom of the Will, not only as theology but as an expression of the American myth of the self-made man; Chauncy's defense was as political as it was moral.

15 LARSON, DAVID MITCHELL. "The Man of Feeling in America: a Study of Major Early American Writers' Attitudes toward Benevolent Ethics and Behavior." Ph.D. dissertation, University of Minnesota.

1973

Cites Edwards as an example of a major writer--Woolman,
Franklin, Crevecoeur, H. H. Brackenridge, and Brockden
Brown are the others--who adapts the man of feeling to
his ethical system of benevolence, in a study of the
change in sensibility in eighteenth-century America.

16   LEE, MARC FRANK. "A Literary Approach to Selected Writings
     of Jonathan Edwards." Ph.D. dissertation, University of
     Wisconsin, Milwaukee.
        Examines Edwards's sermonic style and finds, though it
     is formal and logical, that imagery and typology often
     inform it. But in End of Creation Edwards eschews images
     and creates a "beauty of intellectual and metaphorical
     design almost as a literary by-product of the pursuit
     after an ever-receding truth."

17   LOEWINSOHN, RON. "Jonathan Edwards' Opticks: Images and
     Metaphors in Some of His Major Works." Early American
     Literature 8 (Spring):21-32.
        Records Edwards's debt to Newton's Opticks in his use
     of metaphors of light and suggests that such metaphors
     provide a "coherence" to his work unavailable through
     other means. Edwards distinguishes between the light of
     common grace and the light of special grace, marking the
     first in conventional eighteenth-century figures and the
     second in images of light and vegetation. His reading of
     Newton results in the "crucial" reconciliation of God and
     man with nature, an "even more momentous" synthesis than
     that of head and heart derived from Locke.

18   LOWANCE, MASON I[RA], JR. "From Edwards to Emerson to
     Thoreau: A Revaluation." American Transcendental Quar-
     terly, no. 18, Parts 1-2 (Spring):3-12.
        Extends the "line of continuity" between Edwards and
     Emerson (see 1940.9) to include Thoreau, detecting a
     common pattern of the perception of nature and the symbol-
     ic expression of it in all three. The transcendentalists
     abandon Edwards's Biblical types and history for Platonic
     symbols and the eternal moment but retain his natural
     revelation, with this difference: revelation possible
     only to the saints in Edwards becomes available to the
     "transcendentally redeemed" in Emerson and Thoreau.
     Through the organic principle Thoreau unites symbol and
     idea, as earlier Edwards had through "doctrinal mysticism."

19   LOWELL, ROBERT. "The Worst Sinner, Jonathan Edwards' God."
     In his History. New York: Farrar, Straus and Giroux,
     p. 73.

Ends the octave of a sonnet with this:
But Jonathan Edwards prayed to think himself
worse than any man that ever breathed;
he was a good man, and he prayed with reason--
which of us hasn't thought his same thought worse?

20 MARTIN, JEAN-PIERRE. "Edwards' Epistemology and the New
Science." Early American Literature 7 (Winter):247-55.
Denies that the new philosophy of the eighteenth century materially affected Edwards's epistemology, for he
was in "ever so many ways . . . behind his times." Like
his speculative theology, his science was "embarrassingly
conservative"; his emphasis on experimental religion was
"merely" an American version of a "general European
stream" of enthusiasm, shunned by the century's intellectuals. Perhaps the greatness of Edwards lies in "his
effort to solve the Kierkegaardian antimony between the
esthetic and theological degrees of consciousness, not
by any new scientific method but by the harmonies of an
inherited epistemology."

21 MILLER, PERRY. Jonathan Edwards. Westport, Conn.: Greenwood Press.
Reprint of 1949.9.

22 MORSBERGER, ROBERT E. "'The Minister's Black Veil':
'Shrouded in a Blackness, Ten Times Black.'" New England
Quarterly 46 (September):454-63.
Suggests that, although he does not use Edwards's
dramatic career in any of his fiction, Nathaniel Hawthorne
deals with a "spiritual tension" in "The Minister's Black
Veil" best met in Edwards.

23 NAPLES, DIANE CLARK. "The Sensible Order: An Interpretation
and Critical Edition of Jonathan Edwards' Personal Narrative." Ph.D. dissertation, University of California,
Los Angeles.
Traces Edwards's Personal Narrative to his theories of
spiritual epistemology and developmental psychology "implicit" in his work. The stages of his religious growth
follow those detailed in Miscellany 782 and Religious
Affections, rather than standard Puritan conversion narratives, and may be construed in Jungian terms of centro-
version.

1973

24 NAUMAN, ST. ELMO, JR. <u>Dictionary of American Philosophy</u>.
   New York: Philosophical Library, pp. 87-97.
      Offers a life and bibliography of Edwards, an "impor-
   tant" contributor to the philosophy and psychology of religion, metaphysics, ethics, and epistemology, despite a
   "barbarous" Calvinism.

25 OLSEN, WESLEY A. "The Philosophy of Jonathan Edwards and its
   Significance for Educational Thinking." Ed.D. dissertation, Rutgers University.
      Uses Edwards's philosophy--particularly his psychology,
   aesthetics, and ethics--to gain insight into the educational thought of the Puritan period. Although no formal
   philosophy of education exists for his time, Edwards provides the "fundamental dispositions" toward man and nature
   important to it in <u>Freedom of the Will</u>, <u>True Virtue</u>, and
   <u>Religious Affections</u>. His sensational empiricism stresses
   individual learning; his consent to being, the unity of
   man and nature; and his ethics of harmony, the union of
   man and society.

26 PARKER, WILLIAM H[ENRY]. "Jonathan Edwards: Founder of the
   Counter-Tradition of Transcendental Thought in America."
   <u>Georgia Review</u> 27 (Winter):543-49.
      Sees Edwards's fusion of his supernaturalism, Locke's
   sensationalism, and Newton's empiricism as a challenge to
   the rationalist view of the central place of reason in
   human affairs. Edwards gives primacy to the reality of
   the religious affections at the expense of the understanding and marks the affections as the source of growth and
   change. Thus Edwards is a transcendentalist in the
   tradition of Emerson, William James, and Reinhold Niebuhr.

27 PFISTERER, KARL DIETERICH. "The Prism of Scripture: Studies
   on History and Historicity in the Work of Jonathan Edwards."
   Ph.D. dissertation, Columbia University.
      Published as 1975.13.

28 SCHEICK, WILLIAM J. Review of <u>The Great Awakening</u>, edited by
   C. C. Goen. <u>Thought</u> 48 (Summer):309-11.
      Commends C. C. Goen's "reliable" text and "accurate"
   introduction (1972.11) but finds "somewhat misleading"
   his understanding of Edwards's conversion pattern. Unlike
   the traditional system that dwelt on means, Edwards
   evaluated effects of the conversion experience, thereby
   resolving the "problematic" issue of preparation.

29   SCHULTZ, JOSEPH P. "The Religious Psychology of Jonathan
      Edwards and the Hassidic Masters of Habad." Journal of
      Ecumenical Studies 10 (Fall):716-27.
          Notes "remarkable similarities" between Edwards and the
      Habad masters of Hassidism in their attempts to join in-
      tellect to emotion in the religious experience and to
      distinguish "authentic religious fervor from sham enthusi-
      asm." Although their approaches differ, their analyses
      of the mind, the saints, the religious experience, and the
      mystic way are parallel.

30   SLOAN, DOUGLAS. Introduction to his The Great Awakening and
      American Education: A Documentary History. New York and
      London: [Columbia] Teachers College Press, pp. 30-37.
          Connects the shift to empiricism in American education
      to the experimental religion of Edwards and the Great
      Awakening. To Edwards, "all meaningful knowledge" com-
      bines the cognitive and affective powers of personality
      and draws upon sensible experience and empirical fact.
      His "strong pragmatic and utilitarian" thought finds its
      way into revivalist college curricula.

31   SLOTKIN, RICHARD. Regeneration Through Violence: The Myth-
      ology of the American Frontier, 1600-1860. Middletown,
      Conn.: Wesleyan University Press, pp. 103-106, passim.
          Parallels the sensationalist psychology and rhetoric of
      revival sermons such as Edwards's Sinners in the Hands of
      an Angry God to that of early American myth-tales such as
      Mrs. Rowlandson's A Narrative of the Captivity.

32   STENERSON, DOUGLAS C. "An Anglican Critique of the Early
      Rise of the Great Awakening in New England: A Letter by
      Timothy Cutler." William and Mary Quarterly, 3d ser. 30
      (July):475-88.
          Reprints a letter, 28 May 1739, from Thomas Cutler,
      rector at Yale, to Edmund Gibson, Bishop of London, re-
      counting the genesis of the Great Awakening and offering
      this portrait of Edwards: "He is very much emaciated, and
      impair'd in his health, and it is doubtful to me whether
      he will attain to the Age of 40. He was Critical, subtil
      and peculiar, but I think not very solid in Disputation.
      Always a sober Person, but withal pretty recluse, austere
      and rigid." Cutler also describes the beginnings of the
      revival and fears the excesses inherent in it.

1973

33 SWEET, WILLIAM W[ARREN]. Story of Religion in America. Grand
    Rapids, Mich.: Baker Book House.
        Reprint of 1930.14.

34 TATTRIE, GEORGE ARTHUR. "Jonathan Edwards' Understanding of
    the Natural World and Man's Relationship to It." Ph.D.
    dissertation, McGill University.
        Examines Edwards's views of the natural order and man's
    relationship to it, a community of purpose, unity, indi-
    viduality, and corporateness, subject to external authority,
    order, consent, and service. Such a community "partici-
    pates" in Being and thus shares with man a moral quality.
    Edwards's "unique" concept of the natural world has signi-
    ficance for the "ecological debate . . . now raging."

35 WAANDERS, DAVID WILLIAM. "Illumination and Insight: An
    Analogical Study." Ph.D. dissertation, Princeton Theologi-
    cal Seminary.
        Explores Edwards's theology for his psychological under-
    standing of illumination--especially in his treatment of
    the sense of the heart and the religious affections--;
    explains the analogy between insight and illumination in
    Edwards in terms of therapeutic, creative, and Gestalt
    insight; and relates data on perception, cognition, and
    mental health criteria to "evaluative themes in Edwards in
    constructing six new evaluative criteria."

36 WARCH, RICHARD. School of the Prophets: Yale College, 1701-
    1740. The Yale Scene: University Series, no. 2. New
    Haven and London: Yale University Press, pp. 93-95, 204-
    207, 301-303 passim.
        Comments briefly upon the relationship between Edwards
    and Yale, both as student and tutor, and the effect his
    training there had upon his thought and career. Only
    Edwards, of all Yale graduates before the Awakening,
    adopted the new learning and then only to "argue against
    its tendencies."

37 WEDDLE, DAVID LEROY. "The New Man: A Study of the Signifi-
    cance of Conversion for the Theological Definition of the
    Self in Jonathan Edwards and Charles G. Finney." Ph.D.
    dissertation, Harvard University.
        Finds the images of self in the theology of Edwards and
    Charles Grandison Finney reflective of their eras in Ameri-
    can religious life. Edwards's view of personal identity,
    derived in part from Locke, Newton, Shaftesbury, and Puri-
    tan piety, may be called "affectional-communal"; Finney's

theological anthropology, arising from nineteenth-century frontier America, may be called "volitional-individualist."

38   WESSELL, LYNN R[AY]. "Great Awakening: The First American Revolution." Christianity Today 17 (31 August):11-12, 21.
    Argues that Edwards and the Great Awakening "helped to promote" the American Revolution by creating a "passionate sense of community love" and by liberating men and women through the doctrine of disinterested benevolence. Inner experience replaces institutional formulations, religious expressions and feelings change, and the "Americanization of pietism as a revolutionary awakening" begins. Edwards's philosophy of holy love, socially realized, is "just as democratic" as Jefferson's political thought.

39   WHITE, MORTON. "Jonathan Edwards: The Doctrine of Necessity and the Sense of the Heart." In his Science and Sentiment. London and New York: Oxford University Press.
    Reprint of 1972.46.

40   WILSON, PATRICIA ANNE. "The Theology of Grace in Jonathan Edwards." Ph.D. dissertation, University of Iowa.
    Characterizes Edwards's theology of grace as a departure from "prevailing" Puritan concepts and a "return" to an Augustinian-Calvinist theology influenced by the metaphysics of the Cambridge Platonists. Edwards replaces preparation, human effort, and obedience to covenant law with an absolute sovereignty of divine grace operating upon totally passive man and acting wholly for God's glorification.

41   WINSLOW, OLA ELIZABETH. Jonathan Edwards, 1703-1758. New York: Octagon Books, 418 pp.
    Reprint of 1940.21.

42   ZIFF, LARZER. Puritanism in America: New Culture in a New World. New York: Viking Press, pp. 299-311.
    Weighs the effects upon the American mind and spirit of Edwards's revivalist temper and the "culture of expansion" that was Puritanism. Edwards justified revivalism, though not its anti-intellectual excesses, as a way "to lift Americans out of their sense of inconsequential provinciality by belittling the importance for their true selves of the economic and political institutions that had come to control their lives." By focusing upon a shift in psychic make-up rather than upon a rearrangement of social institutions, Edwards established the "characteristic

pattern" of American rebellion against oppressive daily
life. And he helped establish another pattern. Edwards
stressed emotion in writing as in life; Franklin stressed
reason; but neither "encouraged a confidence" in literature. American writers were to inherit this "ambivalence"
and a "deep distrust" of their vocation.

1974

1 ALLEN, ALEXANDER V. G. Jonathan Edwards. New York: Burt
   Franklin.
       Reprint of 1889.1.

2 ANDERSON, WALLACE E[ARL]. Preface to Of Insects, by Jonathan
   Edwards. New Haven, Conn.: Jonathan Edwards College
   Press, pp. [i-ii].
       Compares Edwards's earlier view of spiders as wonderful
   and wise in "Of Insects" to his later use of them as
   symbols of corruption and vileness. An edition of that
   work is newly transcribed from the manuscripts and super-
   sedes that of Egbert Smyth (1890.8).

3 BENNETT, JONATHAN. "The Conscience of Huckleberry Finn."
   Philosophy 49 (April):123-34.
       Uses Huck Finn, Heinrich Himmler, and Edwards to show
   the relationship between sympathy and "bad morality" and
   finds Edwards's morality to be "worse than Himmler's" in
   his approval of eternal damnation. Of course, Edwards
   never actually tormented the damned, but he never found
   "painful" another's suffering, never bore sympathy for
   them.

4 BERK, STEPHEN E. Calvinism versus Democracy: Timothy Dwight
   and the Origins of American Evangelical Orthodoxy.
   Hamden, Conn.: Shoe String Press, pp. 49-54.
       Traces the division in the followers of Edwards--Timothy
   Dwight among them--to a split in Edwards himself. In an
   earlier period Edwards was dominated by the heart, experiential and evangelical; in a later period by the head,
   rational and metaphysical. The New Divinity theologians
   followed either the experimental piety of the first phase
   or the scholasticism of the second.

5 BLIGHT, JAMES GEORGE. "Gracious Discoveries: Toward an Understanding of Jonathan Edwards' Psychological Theory, and
   an Assessment of his Place in the History of American
   Psychology." Ph.D. dissertation, University of New Hampshire.

1974

Discovers in Edwards's combination of rational-emotive
and proactive and reactive principles of human nature an
analogue to the multiple-processing model of contemporary
information-processing theorists and applies the model to
the successive stages of the conversion experience described by Edwards, in an estimate of his place in the
history of American psychology from colonial times to
William James.

6   CECIL, ANTHONY C., JR.   The Theological Development of Edwards
    Amasa Park: Last of the "Consistent Calvinists." Disser-
    tation Series, no. 1. Missoula, Mont.: Scholars Press,
    pp. 207-20 passim.
        Traces the career of Edwards Amasa Park, Edwards's "last
    'lineal disciple,'" as a mediating theologian in his at-
    tempt to reconcile the demands of intellect and feeling,
    divine sovereignty and human freedom, traditional Chris-
    tianity and the modern temper, Nathaniel Taylor and Jona-
    than Edwards.

7   CHERRY, [CHARLES] CONRAD.   The Theology of Jonathan Edwards:
    A Reappraisal. Gloucester, Mass.: Peter Smith.
        Reprint of 1966.9.

8   DELATTRE, ROLAND A[NDRÉ].   Review of The Ethics of Jonathan
    Edwards: Morality and Aesthetics, by Clyde Holbrook.
    New England Quarterly 47 (March):155-58.
        Calls Clyde Holbrook's study of Edwards (1973.13) "a
    great disappointment" for his failure to relate Edwards's
    ethics to his aesthetics and to accommodate both to his
    theological objectivism.

9   DEWEY, EDWARD HOOKER.   "Jonathan Edwards." In American
    Writers on American Literature. Edited by John Macy.
    Westport, Conn.: Greenwood Press.
        Reprint of 1931.8.

10 EDWARDS, JONATHAN, the younger. A Dissertation Concerning
    Liberty and Necessity. New York: Burt Franklin Reprints.
        Reprint of 1797.1.

11 FOSTER, MARY C[ATHERINE].   "Theological Debate in a Revival
    Setting: Hampshire County in the Great Awakening." Fides
    et Historia 6 (Spring):31-47.
        Defends Edwards's belief that the theological debate
    about justification by faith begun in the Connecticut
    Valley in November 1734 was "humanly speaking" the cause

327

of the revival that followed a month later and suggests
that the justification controversy was "much more fundamental" to the theological division following the Great
Awakening than either the debates about freedom of the
will and original sin or the Awakening itself. Edwards's
sermons on justification were effective in removing "every
hope outside of faith" for salvation and so stimulated the
need for conversion experiences provided by revivals.
Religious Affections, his "final evaluation" of the Awakening, reformulates the theology of religious experience
for New England and "still clarifies" it for us today.

12 HOLIFIELD, E. BROOKS. The Covenant Sealed: The Development
    of Puritan Sacramental Theology in Old and New England,
    1570-1720. New Haven and London: Yale University Press,
    pp. 228-29.
        Cites Edwards's communion practice as a rejection of
    both Solomon Stoddard's converting ordinance and Cotton
    Mather's "evangelistic sacramental piety."

13 LESNING, GEORGE S. "Robert Lowell and Jonathan Edwards:
    Poetry in the Hands of an Angry God." South Carolina
    Review 6 (April):7-17.
        Analyzes four Robert Lowell poems--"Mr. Edwards and the
    Spider" and "After the Surprising Conversions" in Lord
    Weary's Castle (1946), "Jonathan Edwards in Western Mass-
    achusetts" in For the Union Dead (1964), and "The Worst
    Sinner, Jonathan Edwards' God" in History (1973). Edwards's
    influence on Lowell is "preponderant and perplexing" and
    consistent over three decades of work: there is a per-
    sonal affinity--the Puritan preacher is like the exhorta-
    tive poet--and a "fundamental paradox." Edwards repre-
    sents a stern and disastrous morality that Lowell condemns
    yet a theocentric, apocalyptic, and historical vision he
    shares.

14 MARTY, MARTIN E. "The Edwardean Tradition." Christian Cen-
    tury 91 (2 January):18, 20-31.
        Reviews C. C. Goen's The Great Awakening (1972.11) and
    identifies the Edwardean tradition in evangelism--its
    optimism, worldliness, and sense of community--with the
    Social Gospel, the Secular City, and Progressive movements
    and contrasts it with the tradition of Dwight Moody and
    Billy Sunday with its pessimism and apocalypse. Yet Ed-
    wards's pattern probably belongs more to his times than
    ours, a world "largely irrecoverable," and his talent for
    "surprises" belongs to a manner out of date.

15 MUDGE, JEAN McCLURE. Review of Marriage to a Difficult Man,
      by Elizabeth D. Dodds. Journal of Presbyterian History
      52 (Spring):90–93.
          Considers Elisabeth D. Dodds's biography of the Edwards
      family (1971.6) a "veritably tract for the consecration of
      the domestic circle," a study in which "irrelevance joins
      inconsistency."

16 PARKMAN, EBENEZER. The Diary of Ebenezer Parkman, 1703–1782.
      First Part: 1719–1755. Edited by Francis G. Walett.
      Worcester, Mass.: American Antiquarian Society, pp. 52
      passim.
          Records the first meeting with Edwards on 15 September
      1738 following a Yale commencement and all subsequent
      meetings, conversations, readings, and notices, ending on
      28 December 1754 about Edwards's months–long illness at
      Stockbridge. (Parkman's frequent references to Edwards's
      death in 1758 have not been published as yet.)

17 SCHAFER, THOMAS A[NTON]. "Edwards, Jonathan." Encyclopaedia
      Britannica, 15th ed., 6:440–42.
          Considers Edwards "the greatest theologian and philoso-
      pher of American Puritanism," in a brief account of his
      life, works, and influence, and attributes renewed inter-
      est in him to the "cosmic sweep" of his thought with its
      emphasis on faith and love.

18 SCHEICK, WILLIAM J. "Family, Conversion, and the Self, in
      Jonathan Edwards' A Faithful Narrative of the Surprising
      Work of God." Tennessee Studies in Literature 19:79–89.
          Focuses upon the family motif in Faithful Narrative
      and its relationship to Edwards's concerns for conversion
      and the inner self. Edwards sought to restore the early
      Puritan sense of the family as "a principle of order, the
      basic unit, the very foundation of church and state" by
      indicting parents for the spiritual laxity of their
      children and by reasserting his "parental role" as spirit-
      ual father to the communal family. The well-ordered
      family proved, to Edwards, the only environment for con-
      version and offered, in its stability and isolation, a
      useful symbol of the inegrity of the inner self in a
      changing world.

19 SCHULTZ, JOSEPH P. "The Lurianic Strand in Jonathan Edwards'
      Concept of Progress." Judaica 30 (September):126–34.
          Traces the gradualism in Edwards's millenarian thought
      to the Lurianic Kabbalah of the sixteenth century. Unlike

1974

other millenarists, Edwards believes redemption to come,
not catastrophically nor miraculously, but gradually
through the cumulative and ameliorative effect of the
deeds of men. The Lurianic Kabbalah, "adapted to a Christian framework" and reaching Edwards through ill-defined
channels, is the source for the idea of continuous
progress in History of Redemption.

20 SELSAM, HOWARD. "Jonathan Edwards on the Freedom of the
Will." In Boston Studies in the Philosophy of Science,
XV. Edited by R. S. Cohen, J. J. Stachel, and M. W.
Wartofsky. Scientific, Historical and Political Essays
in Honor of Dirk J. Struik. Dordrecht, Holland, and
Boston: D. Reidel Publishing Co., pp. 391-402.
Characterizes Edwards as a "great philosopher almost
in spite of himself" by relating his Calvinism to Marxist
scientific materialism and Freedom of the Will to Friedrich Engels's Anti-Duhring: Socialism, Utopian and Scientific (1878). Edwards's "intuitively dialectical"
analysis of causation, freedom, and necessity fails only
in its individualistic, rather than its collective,
application.

21 SHEA, DANIEL B., JR. "The Art and Instruction of Jonathan
Edwards' Personal Narrative." In The American Puritan
Imagination: Essays in Revaluation. Edited by Sacvan
Bercovitch. London: Cambridge University Press, pp. 159-
72.
Reprint of 1965.18.

22 _____. "B. F. Skinner: The Puritan Within." Virginia
Quarterly Review 50 (Summer):416-37.
Draws parallels bwtween Skinner's Beyond Freedom and
Dignity and Edwards's Freedom of the Will in such matters
as rhetorical strategies, verbal behavior, and the "language of tropism." More broadly, both thinkers share the
Puritan proclivity to "imagine utopia while suspecting the
worst of human nature, and then, in the face of this
dichotomy, to seek infallible controls for bringing a
truculent world to moral attention." But Skinner lacks
Edwards's piety and enthusiasm and substitutes verifiable
works for free grace.

23 SIMONSON, HAROLD P. Jonathan Edwards: Theologian of the
Heart. Grand Rapids, Mich.: William B. Eerdmans Publishing Co., 174 pp.
Considers that the "central theme" in Edwards concerns
the sense of the redeemed and sanctified heart and its

preparation to experience God's glory, in a full-length study of his conversion experience, his role in the Great Awakening, his imagination and vision, his language, and his concepts of sin and salvation. That "heart-felt pietism" is at the core of the religious experience and transcends sense, reason, understanding, and aesthetics, enabling faithful man to perceive through "sanctified imagination" what is unknowable to natural man. For Edwards, religious language, an occasional rather than a sufficient cause for conversion, sets the emotional context for the experience and serves "to bridge knowledge and being, cognition and apprehension." Only through the sense of the heart, Edwards concludes, may man go beyond his tragic limitations--Edwards held that Calvinism was "experientially true"--and through Christ "come to possess all things."

24   SMITH, JOHN E. "Jonathan Edwards: Piety and Practice in the American Character." Journal of Religion 54 (April): 166-80.

Examines Edwards's "fidelity" to theological empiricism, principally in Religious Affections; his connection of piety to practice; and his contribution to "all forms" of religion in America. By specifying the evidences of genuine religion, Edwards turned the process from a subjective and immediate affair to one objective and discursive; by making the signs of conversion part of the "total bearing" of a person, not isolated as "enclosed states" of mind, Edwards pushed empiricism to pragmatism. Religious virtues, then, could be known only in and through active expression, and private experience, subject to valid testing, could be publicly assessed. Although Edwards was the "sworn enemy" of a religion of morality and good works, his system "opened the door" to just that development in American religion at the same time that it satisfied the practical bent of the American mind.

25   STAMEY, JOSEPH D. "Newton's Time, Locke's Ideas, and Jonathan's Spiders." Proceedings of the New Mexico-West Texas Philosophical Society (April):79-87.

Compares Edwards to Marx as philosophers resolving epistemological problems not on conceptual or theoretical grounds but on practical and ideological ones with decidedly social consequences. "For Marx, one had to create the truth by creating a classless society. . . . For Edwards, one has to enact the truth in human feeling." Like Marx,

1974

Edwards tried to reconcile the themes of determinism,
freedom, and providence, the impetus for Edwards arising
from his New England background and his understanding of
Locke's sensationalism and Newton's time.

26   STEIN, STEPHEN J.   "Cotton Mather and Jonathan Edwards on the
Number of the Beast: Eighteenth-Century Speculation about
the Antichrist." Proceedings of the American Antiquarian
Society 84 (October):293-315.
   Remarks the similarities between Edwards and Cotton
Mather's reception of Francis Potter's An Interpretation
of the Number 666 (1642) and concludes that, contrary to
Alan Heimert's assertion that anti-Catholicism waned after
the Great Awakening, such sentiments continued unabated
through the Revolution. In subscribing to the myth of the
Beast and Potter's square root formulas, Edwards and others
like him adopted a dualistic view of history and "significantly shaped America's religious and cultural heritage."

27   _____. "Jonathan Edwards and the Rainbow: Biblical Exegesis
and Poetic Imagination." New England Quarterly 47 (September):440-56.
   Discovers in the Biblical exegesis of his later years
a "delightfully different" Edwards, a creative poet quite
unlike both the stereotypical logician of custom and the
turgid exegete of his own day. His exegesis of the covenant of the rainbow (Genesis 9:12-17) found in No. 348 of
his "Notes on Scripture" is an "excellent" example of
Edwards's hermeneutics as he combines science and theology
through the four-fold medieval pattern of the literal,
allegorical, tropological, and analogical. For Edwards,
such an exercise offers a "convenient and congenial" way
of expressing dogma and provides a "synopsis of his
cardinal tenets."

28   STROUT, CUSHING.   The New Heavens and New Earth: Political
Religion in America. New York: Harper & Row, pp. 29-45,
passim.
   Traces Edwards's career, focusing upon his role in the
Great Awakening--"one of those notable conjunctions between
private needs and public anxieties"--and remarks the social
and political consequences of the revivals. Edwards's
"tragic overtones of hubris" are matched by the special
ironies of the Awakening, in which original intentions
were confounded: sincerity gave way to doubt, social
peace to public, legal battles, skepticism of learning to
the founding of colleges, and so on. At first "profoundly

nonpolitical," as Edwards understood it, the Great Awakening later "contributed to social conflict and change."

29 WEDDLE, DAVID L[EROY]. "Jonathan Edwards on Men and Trees, and the Problem of Solidarity." Harvard Theological Review 67 (April):155-75.
   Argues that Edwards uses the image of a tree and its branches as a type of the solidarity of sinners and of saints in interpreting the doctrines of original sin and the atonement and that such an organic metaphor differs "significantly" from the biological one of traditional Calvinism and the juridical one of covenant theology. For Edwards, the unity of the race arises as a "shared disposition" through a process of growth and development in history, not by Adam's infection nor by his headship; man's redemption arises through the ingrafting of Christ upon him. Edwards identifies the common disposition as a moral act in history, and thus he makes man a moral agent, at once generic and individual, in nature and in society.

1975

1 AHLSTROM, SYDNEY E. "Jonathan Edwards and the Revival of New England Theology." In his A Religious History of the American People. Garden City, N.Y.: Doubleday & Co. Reprint of 1972.2.

2 ANGOFF, CHARLES, ed. Jonathan Edwards: His Life and Influence. The Leverton Lecture Series. Rutherford, N.J.: Fairleigh Dickinson University Press, 65 pp.
   Prints the papers and records the remarks at a symposium on Edwards in the following order:
   Cherry, Conrad. "Imagery and Analysis: Jonathan Edwards on Revivals of Religion," pp. 19-28. Asserts that Edwards blended theological analysis with sensible imagery to evoke both understanding and emotion during the revivals. Described in Religious Affections as "affectionate knowledge," this coherent use of language serves to check both unthinking enthusiasm and unfeeling reason and is clearly at odds with the anti-intellectualism of later revivalists.
   Kimnach, Wilson H. "The Brazen Trumpet: Jonathan Edwards's Conception of the Sermon," pp. 29-44. Traces the growth and direction of Edwards's sermons from the early formal ones, imitative of his father and grandfather, to

those later ones given to sustained pursuit of an idea.
He early masters the formula of text, doctrine, and application, and the use of rhetorical and poetic devices to
pierce the heart. His later practice reflects a growing
desire to divorce the hortatory from the philosophical and
is best met in Sinners in the Hands of an Angry God. With
the end of the Awakening comes few sermons; with the Stockbridge years fewer still. Yet the sermonic form pervades
his major treatises, and he never found another to replace
it.

"Symposium: Leverton Lecture Series, April 18, 1973,"
pp. 45-65. Ranges widely and discursively over aspects
of Edwards's thought and career: his debt to Locke, his
millenarianism and affections, his social and political
awareness, his consistency and influence, his centrality
to American intellectual history. The panel, moderated
by Edward Cook, included Conrad Cherry, Wilson Kimnach,
Charles Wetzel, and Donald Jones.

3   BERCOVITCH, SACVAN. The Puritan Origins of the American Self.
New Haven and London: Yale University Press, pp. 152-63
passim.

Remarks the close relationship of natural theology to
federal teleology in the rhetoric of Edwards, one of a
long line of "solitary keepers" of the American dream
that includes Cotton Mather and Ralph Waldo Emerson.
Edwards's eschatology has a peculiarly American cast, his
typology a penchant for American figures. So Edwards
defines colonial progress in millennial terms and the
regenerate in new world images.

4   BOGUE, CARL W. "Jonathan Edwards and the Covenant of Grace."
Th.D. dissertation, Free University of Amsterdam.
Published as 1975.5.

5   _____. Jonathan Edwards and the Covenant of Grace. Cherry
Hill, N.J.: Mack Publishing Co., 312 pp.

Affirms Edwards's "rightful place" among Calvinist or
Reformed theologians in his acceptance of the correlation
between divine sovereignty and human responsibility acknowledged in the covenant of grace, in an examination of
the Calvinist framework and Edwards's notes, sermons, and
treatises. For Edwards, the covenant of grace and the
covenant of redemption are aspects of the unabrogated
covenant of works, but are distinctive, though not in a
substantive way, in this: the covenant of grace (between
Christ and man) is an "historical manifestation" of the

covenant of redemption (between God and Christ) and anal-
ogous to a marriage covenant, offered now and fulfilled
later. The covenant of redemption is eternal, as the
trinity is; the covenant of grace, because of man's participation, is becoming. Hence, divine sovereignty and
human responsibility meet in the covenant of grace, con-
sented to by man through faith. To see Edwards, as recent
commentators have, caught in an unresolved conflict or
contradiction in this is "inaccurate" and "superficial."

6   CLEBSCH, WILLIAM A. American Religious Thought: A History.
      Chicago History of American Religion Series. Chicago:
      University of Chicago Press.
         Reprint of 1973.5.

7   EVERSLEY, WALTER VERNON LLOYD. "Christus Gloria: An
      Aesthetic-Teleological Investigation of Atonement." Ph.D.
      dissertation, Harvard University.
         Attributes Edwards's use of some aesthetic-teleological
      ideas in his concept of the atonement to Athanasius,
      Anselm, and Calvin. Like them, he held the atonement to
      be an opportunity for man to find forgiveness of sin, but
      Edwards also held the atonement to be a means of "main-
      taining the relationship of a whole world order that con-
      tained man" and the ultimate purpose of all things to be
      the glory of God.

8   FIERING, NORMAN S. Review of The Ethics of Jonathan Edwards:
      Morality and Aesthetics, by Clyde A. Holbrook. William
      and Mary Quarterly, 3d ser. 32 (January):139-41.
         Finds Clyde Holbrook's thesis of theological objectivism
      "anachronistic, irrelevant, or superfluous," his analysis
      of Edwards's aesthetics no more informed than that of his
      ethics (1973.13).

9   GELPI, ALBERT [J.]. The Tenth Muse: The Psyche of the Ameri-
      can Poet. Cambridge, Mass.: Harvard University Press,
      pp. 47-50, 229-30.
         Compares Edwards's use of types and tropes, especially
      in Images or Shadows, to Edward Taylor's before him and
      Ralph Waldo Emerson's and Emily Dickinson's after him.

10 HAMILTON, JAMES E., and MADDEN, EDWARD H. "Edwards, Finney,
      and Mahan on the Derivation of Duties." Journal of the
      History of Philosophy 13 (July):347-60.

> Uses Edwards as a point of departure for examining some
> aspects of the moral philosophy of Charles Grandison Finney
> and Asa Mahan. Edwards's ethical theory in <u>True Virtue</u>
> is "essentially teleological" inasmuch as all duties of
> man are reduced to advancing being in general, and what is
> right is always a means, not an end, in achieving it.
> Though Finney rejected Edwards's Calvinistic determinism,
> he "followed" Edwards's teleological ethics; Mahan, on the
> other hand, identified Finney's view as a "variation" of
> utilitarianism and criticized it as such.

11   KIMNACH, WILSON H. "Jonathan Edwards' Sermon Mill." <u>Early</u>
<u>American Literature</u> 10 (Fall):167-77.
> Concludes, after inspecting 600 of his sermons, that
> Edwards revised them principally to meet the rhetorical
> demands of a different occasion or audience. Edwards was
> an "ingenious manipulator" of his materials, preaching
> some sermons (revised) as many as seven times, and kept a
> "carefully inventoried" sermon file and index. He used
> this "storehouse" to ease his pulpit burdens and the press
> of other work as well as to generate new sermons.

12   MARTIN, J. ALFRED, JR. "The Empirical, the Esthetic, and the
Religious." <u>Union Seminary Quarterly Review</u> 30 (Winter):
110-20.
> Lists Edwards and John Dewey among those American
> thinkers who approach religion empirically and who find a
> "strong and fruitful" affinity between the religious ex-
> perience and the aesthetic. Neither Edwards nor Dewey
> collapse the good into the beautiful or equate the reli-
> gious with the aesthetic, but both link the beautiful to
> the divine and express the "roots of faith" aesthetically.
> For Edwards the experience shows man to be a child of God,
> for Dewey a child of nature.

13   PFISTERER, KARL DIETERICH. <u>The Prism of Scripture: Studies</u>
<u>on History and Historicity in the Work of Jonathan Edwards</u>.
Anglo-American Forum, no. 1. Frankfurt: Peter Lang,
387 pp.
> Explores Edwards's understanding of history and his use
> of Scripture (and exegesis) as an historiographical mode,
> its sources and its consequences. For Edwards, Scripture
> was a prism--he used "the idea if not the term"--display-
> ing the "coherence of vision and variety," the configura-
> tion of the one and the many. As the historian of the
> revival, Edwards used Scripture as a prism to integrate
> the past and to suggest a model community; as the historian
> of redemption, Edwards used Scripture as a prism to develop

"a theory of communication which conceptualizes the vision and variety of history ontologically as well as historically."

14 SCHEICK, WILLIAM J. "The Grand Design: Jonathan Edwards' History of the Work of Redemption." Eighteenth-Century Studies 8 (Spring):300-14.
    Notes that Edwards considered his History of Redemption "innovative" because he treated history as an allegory of the conversion experience, the manifestation "in large" of the spiritual progress of the individual regenerative soul. Edwards combines nature, history, and the elect into a progressively harmonious whole and assumes for himself a prophetic persona, merging his private self of biography with the collective self of history, his individual covenant of grace with the historical covenant of redemption. "In a very real sense Edwards had come to think of himself as a luminary, like the prophets of old, shedding light on God's grand architectural design."

15 _____. Review of Jonathan Edwards: Theologian of the Heart, by Harold P. Simonson. Early American Literature 10 (Spring):95-96.
    Considers Harold Simonson's thesis about Edwards (1974.23) "unoriginal, uninspired and self-evident," a study unfit for a general or scholarly audience.

16 _____. The Writings of Jonathan Edwards: Theme, Motif, and Style. College Station: Texas A & M University Press, 176 pp.
    Explores the "progressive interiorization" of Edwards's concerns and the implications for his theology, his quest for identity, and his art, in a chronological review of the themes and structure, the motifs and style of his writings, from the juvenilia to the major works. Particularly, Edwards uses natural images to portray the inner self's immediate and vital perception of divine reality and uses images of the family to convey "the beautiful order inherent in God's grand design," reflected in the orderly relationship of communing Christians, of the minister as spiritual father, and of the marriage between regenerate man and Christ. Edwards experiments with the sermonic form to make it a more effective means of conversion, seeking to "arouse the whole man," intellect and will, to know grace intuitively and using images of light to symbolize both the heart's intuition and God's order. But uncertainty and "spiritual unrest" mark the conversion

process for Edwards, and may, in fact, be a sign of conversion. "In a sense Edwards' entire career pivoted on this
inner turmoil. His study of conversion became in effect
spiritual autobiography."

17   SIMONSON, HAROLD P. "Jonathan Edwards and the Imagination."
     Andover Newton Quarterly 16 (November):109-18.
         Insists that Edwards is "first and last a Christian
     theologian, not a literary artist," and that his theory
     of imagination is in keeping with Christian revelation,
     regardless of resemblances to Emerson, the Cambridge
     Platonists, or literary criticism, generally. Though he
     sometimes casts his theology in aesthetic terms, Edwards
     knew that natural imagination was inadequate to his concept
     of beauty and incapable of spiritual truth without the
     infusion of grace: "natural imagination embraces nothing
     unless the soul through faith first embraces God." So
     regenerate man sees a world not only symbolical but sacra-
     mental in a creative act of sanctified imagination.

18   STEIN, STEPHEN J.   Review of Jonathan Edwards: His Life and
     Influence, edited by Charles Angoff. New England Quarterly
     48 (September):443-45.
         Finds Conrad Cherry's lecture "unimaginative," Wilson
     Kimnach's "insightful," and the symposium clichéd, in a
     review of Charles Angoff's gathering (1975.2).

19   STRAUSS, JAMES D.   "A Puritan in a Post-Puritan World--Jona-
     than Edwards." In Grace Unlimited. Edited by Clark H.
     Pinnock. Minneapolis: Bethany Fellowship, pp. 242-64.
         Juxtaposes Edwards's "brilliant, if futile" account of
     free will and moral agency against modern notions of free-
     dom in a radically determined universe in Gödel's proof,
     Chomsky's transformational grammar, and D. M. McKay's
     model of free choice. Edwards's "lethal" fallacy lies in
     his ambiguous definition of the determination of the will.
     Thus he fails both to demonstrate the necessary connection
     between acts and motives and to reconcile moral agency
     with "any form" of radical determinism.

20   WATTS, EMILY STIPES. "The Neoplatonic Basis of Jonathan Ed-
     wards' 'True Virtue.'" Early American Literature 10
     (Fall):179-89.
         Suggests Thomas More's Enchiridion Ethicum as an early
     and important source for Edwards's "ultimate ethical defi-
     nitions" of excellency, virtue, and justice found in his
     True Virtue. Edwards's debt to More was substantial

though certainly not total: not only did Edwards have to
contend with the empiricism of Locke and the moral sense
philosophy of Shaftesbury in shaping his ethics, he also
disagreed with More on the source of the inclination to
love and on his emphasis on mind rather than sensibility.

21   WEDDLE, DAVID L[EROY]. "The Image of the Self in Jonathan
     Edwards: A Study of Autobiography and Theology." Journal
     of the American Academy of Religion 43 (March):70-83.
         Explores the relationship between the primary language
     of "identity" in Edwards's autobiographical writing and
     the secondary language of "ideology" in his theological
     writing (to use Erik Erikson's terms) and uncovers "a
     distinctive image of self," combining both the piety of
     obedience and the piety of adoration in a view "neither
     strictly legalist nor exclusively mystical." Edwards
     achieves a balance between the self as agent and as sub-
     ject, between universal moral order and immediate divine
     communion, in a "personal synthesis" focused on the divine
     beauty in Christ. Through his conversion experience, ex-
     pressed Personal Narrative, Edwards realized that his
     identity was of a piece with others "within a shared
     history," and so he broadcast that new image in his sermons
     and treatises. For Edwards, "religious autobiography is a
     form of theological argument."

22   WHALEY, HOWARD. "The First Great Awakening." Moody Monthly
     75 (June):47-49.
         Divides the Great Awakening, an "intercolonial, non-
     sectarian" movement, into three successive stages--the
     middle Atlantic, the New England, the Southern--and notes
     the role Edwards's sermons on justification played in the
     outpourings of God's spirit upon His church in America.

                              1976

1   ALLEN, ALEXANDER V. G. Jonathan Edwards. St. Clair Shores,
     Michigan: Scholarly Press.
         Reprint of 1889.1.

2   ANDERSON, QUENTIN. "Practical and Visionary Americans."
     American Scholar 45 (Summer):405-18.
         Uses Edwards as an example of the historical develop-
     ment and religious roots of personal authority and its
     importance to other visionary Americans--Emerson, Thoreau,
     Whitman--and the guilt of acquisition.

1976

3   ANON. "Sinners in the Hands of an Angry God." <u>Faith for the
        Family</u> 4 (July–August):21–22.
            Introduces and reprints selections from Edwards's
        <u>Sinners in the Hands of an Angry God</u>.

4   BEAM, CHRISTOPHER MERRIMAN. "Millennialism in American
        Thought, 1740–1840." Ph.D. dissertation, University of
        Illinois.
            Considers Edwards's millennialism (and that of the Ed-
        wardseans) as part of a unitary force of evangelism,
        republicanism, and nationalism that swept over America
        between the Great Awakening and the Civil War in a rush
        of moral fervor.

5   BLEDSOE, ALBERT T[AYLOR]. <u>An Examination of President
        Edwards' Inquiry into the Freedom of the Will</u>. St. Clair
        Shores, Mich.: Scholarly Press.
            Reprint of 1845.2.

6   _____ . <u>A Theodicy</u>. New York: AMS Press.
            Reprint of 1853.8.

7   BOARDMAN, GEORGE NYE. <u>A History of New England Theology</u>.
        St. Clair Shores, Mich.: Scholarly Press.
            Reprint of 1899.2.

8   BOGUE, CARL [W.]. "Jonathan Edwards on the Covenant of
        Grace." In <u>Soli Deo Gloria: Essays in Reformed Theology</u>.
        Festschrift for John H. Gerstner. Edited by R. C. Sproul.
        [Nutley, N.J.]: Presbyterian and Reformed Publishing Co.,
        pp. 134–45.
            Summarizes 1975.5.

9   BRAUER, JERALD C. "Puritanism, Revivalism, and the Revolu-
        tion." In <u>Religion and the American Revolution</u>. Edited by
        Jerald C. Brauer. Philadelphia: Fortress Press, pp. 22–23.
            Considers Edwards's vision of a new man in a new age in
        his <u>History of Redemption</u> an updated version of the chosen
        people theme and an indication of American "uniqueness and
        individuality" before the Revolution.

10 BREMER, FRANCIS J. "Jonathan Edwards and the Great Awaken-
        ings." In his <u>The Puritan Experiment: New England Society
        from Bradford to Edwards</u>. New York: St. Martin's Press,
        pp. 226–31.
            Sees little difference between Edwards's revival in
        1734 and earlier ones in Solomon Stoddard's Northampton

and in John Cotton's Boston except for the "sense of ex-
pectancy" fed by Edwards's Faithful Narrative. Yet to
understand the Great Awakening one must turn to Edwards
for his "accurate and favorable" insights.

11   BRYANT, MARCUS DARROL. "History and Eschatology in Jonathan
     Edwards: A Critique of the Heimert Thesis." Ph.D. dis-
     sertation, University of St. Michaels College (Canada).
        Disagrees with Alan Heimert's thesis that Edwards pro-
     vides a radical ideology for American nationalism, in a
     close analysis of Religion and the American Mind (1966.17)
     and its views of Edwards's evangelical Calvinism, es-
     chatology, anthropology, and sociology. What Edwards
     does offer is a commentary and critique of "nascent forms"
     of American millennial thought of a heavenly, not a
     worldly, kind.

12   BUMSTED, J. M., and Van de WETERING, JOHN E. What Must I Do
     to be Saved?: The Great Awakening in Colonial America.
     Berkshire Studies in History. Hinsdale, Ill.: Dryden
     Press, pp. 98-106, 118-21, passim.
        Includes Edwards, as well as Thomas Prince and Jonathan
     Dickinson, among the "moderates" in the Great Awakening,
     advocates of the revival as "the logical outgrowth of the
     past," of the covenant of grace as "an avenue" to conver-
     sion, of "ecstatic joy" as evidence of election. But
     Edwards's abandonment of the traditional steps to salva-
     tion for a number of signs (in Religious Affections)
     represents "a sharp departure" from an orthodox past.
     Although moderates insisted defensively that there was
     "nothing new" theologically or religiously in the revival,
     both their break with past practices and their "sophisti-
     cated acceptance" of Locke and Newton--Edwards's "singu-
     lar" role has been "exaggerated"--argued otherwise and
     threatened their position. Their critics fared no better:
     in his quarrel with Charles Chauncy, Edwards's uniting of
     affection and will represents "a truly modern" psychologi-
     cal view against a "medieval" faculty one.

13   BYINGTON, EZRA HOYT. "Jonathan Edwards, and the Great
     Awakening." In his The Puritan as a Colonist and Reformer.
     New York: AMS Press.
        Reprint of 1899.4.

1976

14   CAMPBELL, DENNIS M[ARION]. "Authority and the Sense of the
     Heart: Jonathan Edwards." In his <u>Authority and the</u>
     <u>Renewal of American Theology</u>. Philadelphia: United Church
     Press, pp. 5-19.
          Characterizes Edwards's theory of the sense of the heart
     as "supremely dysfunctional" to the social order and a
     threat to traditional, heirarchal authority. Edwards
     couples his belief in God's sovereignty with his conviction
     that God revealed Himself "personally, immediately, ex-
     perientially" through the affections of the heart, so that
     man's internal awareness of God became "certain and author-
     itative" and the "norm and content" of theology. Such a
     shift in the basis of authority "frontally challenged" New
     England's reliance on Scripture and tradition and "knocked
     the props out from under" the civil governance of society.

15   COCHRAN, ALICE COWAN. "Sin and Salvation in American Thought."
     <u>Perkins School of Theology Journal</u> 30 (Fall):1-14.
          Traces the evolution of American thought on sin and
     salvation from Edwards through the Mercersburg theologians,
     Horace Bushnell, and modern prophets of the social gospel.
     Edwards reflects the Dortian orthodoxy on election and
     rebrobation, and his promotion of and interest in revivals
     comes from his conviction of man's depravity and his hope
     for unmerited grace. Twentieth-century theologians argue
     a return to an Edwardsean orthodoxy but directed outwardly
     as collective redemption from social immorality and
     achieved, as in the past, in America.

16   CONKIN, PAUL KEITH. "Jonathan Edwards: Theology." In his
     <u>Puritans and Pragmatists</u>. Bloomington: Indiana University
     Press.
          Reprint of 1968.3.

17   CUSOLO, RONALD S. "The Return of Jonathan Edwards: A Bicen-
     tennial Reflection." <u>Nassau Review</u> 3:86-94.
          Urges that Edwards be restored to the pantheon of
     national heroes denied him because of "denominational
     barriers" and his opposition to the assumptions and impli-
     cations of the Enlightenment. Edwards countered the in-
     fallibility of reason, the self-sufficiency of man, and
     the sanctity of science with a belief in God and religion,
     a stand probably responsible for renewed interest in this
     "peerless prophet of our age."

18   D'AVANZO, MARIO L. "The Ambitious Guest in the Hands of an
      Angry God." English Language Notes 14 (September):38-42.
          Suggests Edwards's Sinners in the Hands of an Angry God
      as the philosophical, moral, tonal, and linguistic "frame
      of reference" for Nathaniel Hawthorne's "The Ambiitous
      Guest."

19   EMERY, ALLAN MOORE. "The Alternatives of Melville's 'Bartle-
      by.'" Nineteenth-Century Fiction 31 (September):170-87.
          Suggests Edwards's Freedom of the Will and True Virtue
      and Joseph Priestley's Doctrine of Philosophical Necessity
      Illustrated as glosses for Herman Melville's "Bartleby,
      the Scrivener."

20   EVANS, W. GLYN. "Jonathan Edwards: Puritan Paradox." In
      his Profiles of Revival Leaders. Nashville, Tenn.:
      Broadman Press, pp. 15-31.
          Reprint of (revised) 1967.9.

21   GARDINER, HARRY N[ORMAN], ed. Jonathan Edwards, a Retrospect.
      New York: AMS Press.
          Reprint of 1901.6.

22   GERSTNER, JOHN H. "An Outline of the Apologetics of Jonathan
      Edwards. Part I: The Argument from Being." Bibliotheca
      Sacra 133 (January-March):3-10.
          Considers Edwards "as orthodox in his view of reason as
      in everything else," in the first of four articles (see
      below) on his apologetics, perhaps "more idealistic, com-
      prehensive, and demonstrative" than some but well within
      the "general" tradition of both Bible and church. Edwards
      explains the doctrine of the eternal cause from "an empiri-
      cal a posteriori observation of the universe," seeing
      Eternal Being revealed as the eternal cause and proved as
      necessity, inasmuch as Nothing does not exist.

23   _____. "An Outline of the Apologetics of Jonathan Edwards.
      Part II: The Unity of God." Bibliotheca Sacra 133 (April-
      June):99-107.
          Continues an outline of Edwards's apologetics, by
      examining his doctrine of the unitary nature of being and
      the implications of pantheism. Edwards distinguishes
      Being and being in "degree and manner, not in substance";
      insists that there is only one Being, generating and glori-
      fying itself; but does not consider all being identical.
      His theology is "particularistic to the core," devoted to
      the eternal separation of heaven and hell, in which man's

1976

being is preserved but "everlastingly and painfully aware"
of its existence apart from God. Edwards was "pantheistic
by implication and panentheistic by intention."

24 ____. "An Outline of the Apologetics of Jonathan Edwards.
Part III: The Proof of God's Special Revelation, the
Bible." Bibliotheca Sacra 133 (July-September):195-201.
Continues an outline of Edwards's apologetics by examining his critique of the deists--he proved them not
"deficient in heart so much as soft in the head"--and his
doctrine of the necessity of special revelation. For
Edwards, it was foolish to expect reason to explain the
trinity, for example, when it could not explain the external world and it was "most unreasonable" to subject
the Word of God, the Bible, to the tests of reason. In
addition to general or natural revelation, special revelation is necessary, if at times "unreasonable" or para-
doxical, so that man might come to know God and His
salvific intentions.

25 ____. "An Outline of the Apologetics of Jonathan Edwards.
Part IV: The Proof of God's Special Revelation, the
Bible--Continued." Bibliotheca Sacra 113 (October-
December):291-98.
Concludes an outline of Edwards's apologetics by examining his proof of God's special revelation, which culmi-
nates in Christ and which exists with right reason in
"the most perfect harmony." The Bible simply requires
of finite man "a reasonable use of reason" to understand
God's revelation. Divine light gives man "divine apprehension" of the Bible, enables him to see the excellency
of doctrine, and creates, in turn, a need for even more
illumination. Grace and truth "work together" in his
sanctification: "The sight of God changes man into the
image of God."

26 HAZARD, ROWLAND G[IBSON]. "Review of Edwards on the Will."
In his Freedom of Mind in Willing. New York: AMS Press.
Reprint of 1864.3.

27 HENDRY, GEORGE S. "The Glory of God and the Future of Man."
Reformed World 34 (December):147-57.
Considers Edwards's solution to the problem of God's
glory and man's future, proposed in End of Creation, an
example of a non-traditional, alternate eschatology.
Edwards traces the destiny of redeemed man on an asymptotic
curve, an "eternal approximation to God," as he continues

through all time to approach nearer and nearer to God, finding happiness in his endless progress. Edwards avoids the "'fearful symmetry'" of Karl Barth's creature-creator annulling relationship by making man's "continuing creatureliness" compatible with the moment of his return to God. God's glory goes out from God and relates to that which is not God, the perfection of His glory returning as perfection raised to "a higher and ever higher" perfection.

28   HINDSON, EDWARD, ed. Introduction to Puritan Theology: A Reader. Grand Rapids, Mich.: Baker Book House, pp. 249-51.
     Reprints Edwards's "The Portion of the Wicked" and "The Portion of the Righteous" as illustrations of Puritan eschatology, which emphasizes judgment and eternal states but lacks speculation about "exact" fulfillment.

29   [HOPKINS, SAMUEL]. The Life and Character of the Late Reverend, Learned & Pious Mr. Jonathan Edwards, President of the College of New-Jersey. New York: AMS Press.
     Reprint of 1804.1.

30   HULL, AARLIE J. "Sarah and Jonathan Edwards." Herald of Holiness 64 (1 April):18.
     Tries to account for the "generations of productive, successful" descendants of Edwards by examining the family life in Elisabeth's Dodds's Marriage to a Difficult Man (1971.6).

31   LAURENCE, DAVID ERNST. "Religious Experience in the Biblical World of Jonathan Edwards: A Study in Eighteenth-Century Supernaturalism." Ph.D. dissertation, Yale University.
     Associates Edwards's precritical Biblical hermeneutics with his "peculiar perspective" of eighteenth-century currents of thought, developing his metaphysics of being out of Newton's physics and his supernaturalism out of Locke's sensationalism. The resulting visionary experience differs from Romantic expressions of the reality of spiritual truths and from Puritan preparationist models of conversion. Edwards came to believe that humiliation was an exercise of faith and that conversion was a gradual change of heart.

32   LEE, SANG HYUN. "Mental Activity and the Perception of Beauty in Jonathan Edwards." Harvard Theological Review 69 (October):369-96.

1976

> Finds the "key" to Edwards's epistemology, aesthetics, and ontology in his concept of habit, defined as "an active and real tendency to behavior or event of a determinate sort." For Edwards, mental activity was a spontaneous, immediate, nondiscursive, intuitive, and creative ordering of sense experience, a relational tending toward union of the knowing mind and the unknown world, idea and reality, and beauty and being. The aesthetic sense or sense of the heart is a habit of mind integrating sensation not mechanistically but organically in the modern manner.

33 LIPS, ROGER CAMERON. "The Spirit's Holy Errand: A Study of Continuities of Thought from Jonathan Edwards to Ralph Waldo Emerson." Ph.D. dissertation, University of Wisconsin, Madison.

> Explores the connection between Edwards and Emerson in thought and in language. Both dwelt upon the natural-spiritual dichotomy of man, psychological theories of the will and the intuition, and especially the nature of the spiritual experience: religious affections, the new sense, disinterested benevolence, and the "increasing union with the divine nature." Clearly, Emerson continues to "expound the Calvinist piety of his ancestors."

34 LLOYD-JONES, D. MARTYN. "Jonathan Edwards and the Crucial Importance of Revival." In The Puritan Experiment in the New World. Westminster Conference for Theological and Historical Study, 1976. Huntington, England: Wesminster Conference, pp. 103-21.

> Urges that Edwards be read on revivals--"No man is more relevant to the present condition of Christianity"--to know the essentials of the spirit, in a discursive address to the Westminster Conference, an unabashed tribute to Edwards, the "very zenith" of Puritanism, its "Mount Everest."

35 LUISI, MIRIAM P. "The Community of Consent in the Thought of Jonathan Edwards." Ph.D. dissertation, Fordham University.

> Considers the "basic insight" of Edwards's view of the convenant, consent, and community to be the "constitutional relatedness" of all being, in which the community of men, united through disinterested love to being in general, actively engages the self in the community of being. For Edwards, the archetype of such unity in community is the Trinity.

1976

36   McGIFFERT, ARTHUR C[USHMAN], JR. Jonathan Edwards. Creative
         Lives Series. New York: AMS Press.
         Reprint of 1932.10.

37   MAY, HENRY F. The Enlightenment in America. New York:
         Oxford University Press, pp. 49-50.
         Finds paradoxical Edwards's place in America: a product
      of the Enlightenment, he held reason "worthless" without
      divine light; the "greatest" figure of the Awakening, he
      was "least typical" of it; no founder of the American
      religious way of life, he "deeply" affected American
      culture.

38   MEYER, DONALD H. "Jonathan Edwards and the Reality of the
         Unseen." In his The Democratic Enlightenment. New York:
         G. P. Putnam's Sons, pp. 18-34.
         Considers Edwards "a significant representative figure"
      of the American Enlightenment, in an analysis of his ideas
      concerning the mystery of conversion (Personal Narrative),
      the nature of true religion (Religious Affections), and
      the question of human morality (Freedom of the Will and
      True Virtue). In a time not particularly congenial to it,
      Edwards tried to establish the legitimacy of the super-
      natural experience. In his attempt at reconciling tradi-
      tional pietism and the new philosophy and at engaging in
      a public dialogue as a "responsible intellectual" con-
      cerned with important social issues, he was very much a
      part of his time.

39   PANOSIAN, EDWARD M. "America's Theologian-Preacher." Faith
         for the Family 4 (November-December):12, 42-43.
         Traces the career of Edwards, a controversial figure
      then and now.

40   PARKES, HENRY BAMFORD. Jonathan Edwards, the Fiery Puritan.
         New York: AMS Press.
         Reprint of 1930.10.

41   SANDON, LEO, JR. "Jonathan Edwards and H. Richard Niebuhr."
         Journal of Religious Studies 12 (March):105-15.
         Discovers sources for H. Richard Niebuhr's radical
      monotheism and his value theory in Edwards, Niebuhr's
      "principal mentor" in the language of sovereignty and the
      language of being. Without Edwardsean motifs of divine
      sovereignty and being-in-relation, Niebuhr's constructive
      theology would have been quite different, a fact "explicitly
      acknowledged" by him and "implicitly demonstrable."

1976

42 SHAW, MARK R. "The Spirit of 1740." <u>Christianity Today</u> 20
    (2 January):7-8.
       Singles out Edwards (and his <u>Faithful Narrative</u>) for
    his role in revivalism in America and suggests that what
    occurred in 1740 was "nothing less than an inner American
    revolution, a spiritual declaration of independence that
    made political reshuffling thirty-six years later an
    inevitability."

43 SMITH, JOHN E. "Jonathan Edwards as Philosophical Theolo-
    gian." <u>Review of Metaphysics</u> 30 (December):306-24.
       Solves the "imposing enigma" of Biblical absolutism and
    philosophical speculation in Edwards by showing that
    Edwards "never" rested his arguments on the Bible "alone,"
    but that he "repeatedly" clinched them by philosophical
    concepts founded in reason and experience. His is a
    "subtle interweaving" of the "equally important" August-
    inian (later, Cambridge Platonic) tradition and Lockean
    epistemology into theological empiricism. Edwards's <u>Notes
    on the Mind</u> and <u>Miscellaneous Observations</u> reveal "origi-
    nality and critical acumen" in dealing with God's being,
    His existence, and man's "new sense" of glory; his <u>Reli-
    gious Affections</u> reveals him as a philosophical "interpret-
    er and mediator" of the logical and psychological elements
    of the emotions. In short, Edwards is "a major philosoph-
    ical theologian."

44 STORLIE, ERIK FRASER. "Grace and Works, Enlightenment and
    Practice: Paradox and Poetry in John Cotton, Jonathan
    Edwards, and Dogen Zenji." Ph.D. dissertation, University
    of Minnesota.
       Suggests a common thought and language runs through
    Edwards, John Cotton, and Dogen, the Zen master (1200-
    1253). All expressed the union of man's finite works with
    infinite grace in both logical and alogical discourse and
    in metaphors of unity gathered from the natural world.
    So Edwards's sense of the heart expresses that union and
    is perceived in metaphors, derived from Newton and Locke,
    of the "flowing, unified energy in fountain, sun, and
    tree."

45 STUART, ROBERT LEE. "Jonathan Edwards at Enfield: 'And Oh
    the Cheerfulness and Pleasantness. . . .'" <u>American Lit-
    erature</u> 48 (March):46-59.
       Corrects the received opinion that Edwards's <u>Sinners in
    the Hands of an Angry God</u> is pure imprecation by analyzing

1976

the "element of comfort" at critical points in the architecture of the Enfield sermon and finds a carefully wrought
tension between hope and fear there.

46 SWEET, LEONARD I. "Letter from Jonathan Edwards." Theology
    Today 33 (July):193-95.
       Prints an "unauthenticated epistle" by Edwards "from
    the beyond" dispelling the notion that Puritans had
    repressive ideas on sex and indicting the "stuffy" Vic-
    torians.

47 WAANDERS, DAVID W[ILLIAM]. "The Pastoral Sense of Jonathan
    Edwards." Reformed Review 29 (Winter):124-32.
       Claims that Edwards, hardly a pastoral model, dealt
    chiefly with pastoral problems in his writings, most
    evidently in Religious Affections where he "penetrated to
    the very core" of pastoral theology. In his psychological
    analysis of the religious experience, Edwards considered
    the sense of the heart "a fundamental dimension" of reli-
    gious affections--what we would call religious attitudes--,
    the means of apprehending theological realities, and the
    operative mode of grace. So Edwards designed a personality
    theory of religious affections where "knowledge had both
    an objective focus in Scripture and a subjective focus in
    human experience, in which understanding of human person-
    ality was essential to an understanding of genuine reli-
    gion, and where Christian virtues and conduct occurred
    within predictable patterns of personality structure
    shaped by scriptural principles."

48 WEDDLE, DAVID L[EROY]. "The Beauty of Faith in Jonathan
    Edwards." Ohio Journal of Religious Studies 4 (October):
    42-53.
       Questions the view of Roland Delattre (1968.8) and
    William Clebsch (1973.5) that for Edwards beauty is an
    aesthetic rather than a moral category. Faith is the
    "vision of, and consent to, the beauty of God," perceived
    as His moral perfection and expressed as "'visible sanc-
    tity'" in the lives of men. Thus Edwards provides a
    theological gloss to Erik Erikson's discussion of basic
    trust and mature care in Childhood and Society: both
    thinkers point to a "fundamental congruence, or beauty,
    in human existence."

49 _____. "The Democracy of Grace: Political Reflections on
    the Evangelical Theology of Jonathan Edwards." Dialog:
    A Journal of Theology 15 (Autumn):248-52.

1976

> Finds democratic implications in Edwards's evangelical
> call and millennial hope--for Americans, a new birth into
> a new age. The Great Awakening underscored national unity
> and democratic feelings by its "revolutionary" character-
> istics of universality, antinomianism, and pluralism.
> Edwards, its chief apologist, is a "test case for a re-
> visionist interpretation of the political implications
> of evangelical theology."

50 WESSELL, LYNN RAY. "The Relation between Religious Enlighten-
    ment and Politics in America: 1740-1840." Ph.D. disser-
    tation, Claremont Graduate School.
      Links Edwards's concept of disinterested benevolence
    (and his New Light successors) to the growth of communal
    morality during the Great Awakening and to the develop-
    ment of equalitarian politics before the Revolution, in
    a history of the religious enlightenment in America.

51 WESTBROOK, ROBERT B. "Social Criticism and the Heavenly City
    of Jonathan Edwards." Soundings 59 (Winter):396-412.
      Suggests that Edwards's social criticism was "self-
    consciously normative," arising from his millennial view
    that in time man's imperfect society would give way to a
    community of saints bound to God and each other in dis-
    interested benevolence. His hopes for an imminent
    heavenly city ended with the Great Awakening, and he had
    to admit that he would "probably never see it."

52 WRIGHT, [CHARLES] CONRAD. "The Freedom of the Will." In his
    The Beginnings of Unitarianism in America. Hamden, Conn.:
    Archon Books.
      Reprint of 1955.12.

53 YOUNGS, J. WILLIAM T., JR. God's Messengers: Religious
    Leadership in Colonial New England, 1700-1750. Baltimore:
    Johns Hopkins University Press, pp. 130-32.
      Cites Edwards as one of several ministers concerned
    with the role of a professional and educated clergy during
    and after the Great Awakening, notably in True Excellency
    (1744), Church's Marriage (1746), and Christ the Example
    (1750).

54 ZILBOORG, CAROLINE CRAWFORD. "The Speaking Self in American
    Puritan Literature: A Study in Genre and Rhetorical
    Continuities." Ph.D. dissertation, University of Wiscon-
    sin, Madison.

Examines the narrative voice of self assertion in American Puritan texts, Edwards's not-too-successful Personal
Narrative among them, and suggests later nineteenth-
century literary continuities.

1977

1 AHLSTROM, SYDNEY E. "The Romantic Religion Revolution and
   the Dilemmas of Religious History." Church History 46
   (June):149-70.
      Discovers the mind of a "proto-Romantic" in Edwards's
   reformulation of Calvinism in a natural context. Edwards
   took the views of nature of Descartes, Newton, and Locke,
   joined them to his orthodox faith, and fashioned a pantheism suggestive of Spinoza and Shaftesbury. Edwards's
   Personal Narrative is "testimony" to a rapture common
   to Romantics but quite unlike Puritan conversion narratives.

2 BATSCHELET, MARGARET SUSAN. "Jonathan Edwards' Use of
   Typology: a Historical and Theological Approach."
   Ph.D. dissertation, University of Washington.
      Suggests that two strains of typology, the "'Pauline'"
   and the "'Philonic,'" culminate in Edwards and are extended through his unique formulations of perception and
   reality into the "new and far-reaching" typology of Images
   or Shadows. Edwards uses Philonic typology--fulfillment
   in the soul of the regenerate, not in Scripture--to free
   Pauline typology of its Old Testament-New Testament
   relationship and to posit a typology of the elect, God's
   glory revealed in natural facts. Thus Edwards frames a
   "unique vision" of God and creation and regenerate man
   through typology.

3 BERNER, ROBERT L. "Grace and Works in America: The Role of
   Jonathan Edwards." Southern Quarterly 15 (January):125-34.
      Attributes Edwards's dismissal to his congregation's
   shift from a belief in the covenant of grace to a belief
   in the covenant of works. That shift is simply part of
   the more general one in America in the eighteenth century
   from a belief in what men are to what men do and finds
   expression in the twentieth century in such works as
   The Great Gatsby and Death of a Salesman. But the price
   of political and social equality is spiritual crisis:
   "our tragedy" has been that we have bought quantitative
   success at the expense of the quality of human experience
   Edwards had insisted upon.

1977

4   BOWDEN, HENRY WARNER. "Edwards, Jonathan." In his <u>Diction-</u>
    <u>ary of American Religious Biography</u>. Westport, Conn.:
    Greenwood Press, pp. 141-43.
        Stresses Edwards's mysticism rather than his doctrinal
    theology, in a short biography and estimate.

5   BUSHMAN, RICHARD L. "Jonathan Edwards and Puritan Conscious-
    ness." In <u>Puritan New England: Essays on Religion,</u>
    <u>Society, and Culture</u>. Edited by Alden T. Vaughan and
    Francis J. Bremer. New York: St. Martin's Press,
    pp. 346-62.
        Reprint of 1966.6.

6   _____. "Jonathan Edwards as Great Man." In <u>Encounter with</u>
    <u>Erikson: Historical Interpretation and Religious Bio-</u>
    <u>graphy</u>. Edited by Donald Capps et al. Missoula, Mont.:
    Scholars Press, pp. 217-52.
        Reprint of 1969.5.

7   CONFORTI, JOSEPH A. "Samuel Hopkins and the New Divinity:
    Theology, Ethics, and Social Reform in Eighteenth-Century
    New England." <u>William and Mary Quarterly</u> 34 (October):
    572-89.
        Accounts Samuel Hopkins's alteration of Edwards's
    ethics a response to social and demographic change in
    mid-eighteenth-century America rather than a sterile
    exercise in New Divinity metaphysics as it is generally
    thought to be. Hopkins found "serious flaws" in <u>True</u>
    <u>Virtue</u>--Edwards mixed aesthetics and ethics, yielded to
    moral rationalists, lacked social dimension--and, there-
    fore, modified it to foster social activism and "self-
    denying idealism" in an increasingly acquisitive,
    egocentric nation. His opposition to slavery and the
    slave trade is the simple consequence of his radical
    disinterested benevolence.

8   DAVIDSON, JAMES WEST. <u>The Logic of Millennial Thought:</u>
    <u>Eighteenth-Century New England</u>. New Haven and London:
    Yale University Press, pp. 150-60, 166-75, 217-21, passim.
        Traces Edwards's millennial thought chiefly in <u>Humble</u>
    <u>Attempt</u>, "Notes on the Apocalypse," and <u>History of Redemp-</u>
    <u>tion</u> and its consequences for conversion and the social
    order. Edwards's model for the last days changes somewhat
    over the years but always manages to combine gloom and
    hope, "central to the entire millennial rhetoric" of his
    time. External afflictions and inner conviction--the
    "crucial factor"--were "inseparable" parts of salvation,

but Edwards held that affliction might be achieved without the literal slaying of the witnesses (Revelations 11:7-12). He saw individual conversion as part of the larger, historical context of redemption--his History is New England's "grandest summary of the plan"--but such a view was "simply apolitical in its impact" and had little effect on social reform.

9   DELATTRE, ROLAND A[NDRÉ]. "Beauty and Politics: A Problematic Legacy of Jonathan Edwards." In American Philosophy from Edwards to Quine. Edited by Robert W. Shahan and Kenneth R. Merrill. Norman: University of Oklahoma Press, pp. 20-48.
       Explores the political implications of Edwards's concept of beauty, discovering in True Virtue and End of Creation a pattern of divine governance appropriate to a theory of human governance. The political order, like the personal one of virtue, is a kind of beauty based upon "the affectional consent of human beings to the plurality of human beings," in which conflict and quality are resolved collectively and freedom measured by spiritual beauty. As God in creation governs by communicating His beauty and by engendering a cordial response, so men govern responsively in beauty, moving through history toward the kingdom of God. "The constitution of a genuinely political order is a humanly crucial expression of a radically monotheistic commitment and of a cordial consent to the being and the beauty and the beautification of the wider orders of reality within which the modest scope of human responsibility is set."

10   DePROSPO, RICHARD CHRIS. "Nature and Spirit in the Writings of Jonathan Edwards." Ph.D. dissertation, University of Virginia.
       Examines Edwards on creation, providence, and grace in order to show how he consistently reconciled the secular philosophy of the Enlightenment with the conservative theology of Calvinism "without falsifying either."

11   DOUGLAS, ANN. The Feminization of American Culture. New York: Alfred A. Knopf, p. 74, passim.
       Compares Edwards's strictness as a father to parental authority models a century later, in an examination of the change from the intellectual rigor of eighteenth-century Edwardseans to their popular, sentimental, and feminized nineteenth-century counterparts.

12   EHLE, CARL FREDERICK, JR.   "Prolegomena to Christian Zionism
      in America: The Views of Increase Mather and William E.
      Blackstone concerning the Doctrine of the Restoration of
      Israel." Ph.D. dissertation, New York University.
          Places Edwards in an almost unbroken line of American
      millennialists seeking the restoration of the Jews to
      Palestine as a prelude to the second coming of Christ.

13   EMERSON, EVERETT [H.]   Puritanism in America, 1620-1750.
      Twayne's World Leaders Series. Boston: Twayne Publishers,
      pp. 148-50.
          Cites Edwards's role in the revivals, his leadership
      in shattering Congregational unity, and his effect upon
      a declining Puritanism in America. Though influenced by
      such Puritans as Thomas Shepard and Thomas Hooker, Ed-
      wards's thought, an amalgam of Calvinism and the Enlighten-
      ment, is "so original that it is misleading to call him a
      Puritan."

*14   ERDT, TERRENCE. "Jonathan Edwards on Art and the Sense of
      the Heart." Ph.D. dissertation, University of California,
      Santa Barbara.
          (Revision published by the University of Massachusetts
      Press, 1980.)

15   FYE, KENNETH PAUL. "Jonathan Edwards on Freedom of the Will."
      Ph.D. dissertation, Boston University.
          Locates the central premise of Edwards's Freedom of the
      Will in his argument of the causal principle or universal
      determinism. In Edwards, universal determinism and abso-
      lute determinism are "functionally equivalent, equally
      implausible, and . . . irrevocably tied" to the Calvinism
      he defended against Arminian attack.

16   GREVEN, PHILIP. The Protestant Temperament: Patterns of
      Child-Rearing, Religious Experience, and the Self in
      Early America. New York: Alfred A. Knopf, pp. 31-34,
      62-71, 75-81, 99-102, 127-33 passim.
          Cites Edwards as an example of the self-suppressed
      evangelical, in a study of three patterns and continuities
      of Protestant temperament (moderate and genteel are the
      others) derived from modes of child-rearing and attitudes
      towards self, passion, power, sexuality, and piety. Like
      other evangelicals, Edwards abases the self and denies the
      body in the quest for a new birth; governs his family by
      authoritarian means, just as he willingly submits to the
      absolute sovereignty and power of God; suppresses anger

and hostility beneath "a facade of compliance and obedience"; and, though he asserts the superiority of men and
harbors a fear of women, implies that to be saved (as the
bride of Christ) men have "to cease being masculine."
And like other evangelicals, Edwards was a purist, in
life, in the church and community, and in piety.

17   HATCH, NATHAN O. The Sacred Cause of Liberty: Republican
Thought and the Millennium in Revolutionary New England.
New Haven and London: Yale University Press, pp. 24-36,
170-73.
    Contrasts Edwards's apocalyptic expectations of the
Great Awakening with the "civil millennialism" of the
Revolution--the hope of conversion and religious piety of
the one, the hope of victory and religious liberty of the
other. Although Edwards thought the millennium would
probably begin in America, the decline of piety after the
Awakening led him, in Humble Attempt, to seek a transat-
lantic union and a broader apocalyptic vision through a
concert of prayer. Even later millennialists like Lyman
Beecher, despite their claims, show "little resemblance
to Edwards's apolitical millennialism."

18   KELLER, KARL. "Alephs, Zahirs, and the Triumph of Ambiguity:
Typology in Nineteenth-Century American Literature." In
Literary Uses of Typology. Edited by Earl Miner. Princeton, N.J.: Princeton University Press, pp. 274-314.
    Finds Edwards's (and Cotton Mather's) use of plebeian
types--allegorizing things personal or spiritualizing
things natural--"at the heart" of nineteenth-century American literature. The construct of type to antitype, common
in Edwards's formulation, remains in Emerson, Thoreau, Hawthorne, Melville, and Whitman, though they confuse and
misuse the terms and all b'.: abandon its theology.

19   KIMNACH, WILSON H[ENRY]. "Jonathan Edwards' Early Sermons:
New York, 1722-1723." Journal of Presbyterian History 55
255-56.
    Examines Edwards's unpublished sermons of his New York
stay to document his theological development and his
preaching experience. The sermons, linked by their common
concern for the experiential basis of the Christian life,
"clearly anticipate" the work of the 1730s. Although they
show a "naivete and rustic vitality," the sermons are
marked by a gifted, concrete imagination and quite often
the "hortatory dimension is overshadowed by the poetically
evocative."

1977

20   LOWANCE, MASON I[RA], JR. "Typology and Millennial Eschatol-
      ogy in Early New England." In Literary Uses of Typology:
      from the Late Middle Ages to the Present. Edited by Earl
      Miner. Princeton, N.J.: Princeton University Press,
      pp. 228-73.
          Discovers in Edwards's use of typology an "original
      epistemology"--Scripture joined to the Book of Nature,
      prophecy to millennial utopianism--in an examination of
      Edwards's unpublished writings on types and History of
      Redemption. Edwards extends types and relationships be-
      yond the traditional figures of the Old and New Testaments
      to embrace the revelation of divine images in nature and,
      through progressive prophetic fulfillment, in contemporary
      history as well. In setting the millennium before the
      apocalypse, Edwards provides a "radical justification"
      for the Great Awakening and for an emergent nationalism.

21   MANOR, JAMES. "The Coming of Britain's Age of Empire and
      Protestant Mission Theology, 1750-1839." Zeitschrift für
      Missionswissenschaft und Religionswissenschaft 61 (Janu-
      ary):38-54.
          Calls Edwards a "major" influence for foreign missionary
      zeal in Great Britain in the late eighteenth and early
      nineteenth centuries. His Humble Attempt and Life of
      Brainerd aided in the missionary awakening early on, but
      succeeding generations were caught up in his eschatological
      vision and his insistence upon immediate conversion.
      "Edwards' theocentricity, known existentially, opened the
      way for the anthropocentrism of the later generations of
      evangelicals seeking to come to terms with humanistic
      trends of their time."

22   MARTY, MARTIN E. Religion, Awakening and Revolution. Faith
      of Our Fathers, no. 4. Wilmington, N.C.: Consortium
      Books, pp. 68-69, 107 passim.
          Cites Edwards's surprise, recorded in Faithful Narra-
      tive, to support the view that the Awakening was "largely
      unintended and accidental" and comments on his millennial
      expectations.

23   MEAD, SIDNEY E[ARL]. The Old Religion in the Brave New
      World: Reflections on the Relation Between Christendom
      and the Republic. Berkeley: University of California
      Press, pp. 51-54.
          Notes that the theology of Edwards (and other revival-
      ists) "legitimated the privatization" of religion, under-
      mined institutional churches, and inadvertently contributed

to the revolution against all constituted authority.
Unlike earlier Puritans, there is little in Edwards about
social or political responsibility or theory.

24 MILLER, PERRY, ed. Images or Shadows of Divine Things.
    Westport, Conn.: Greenwood Press.
       Reprint of 1948.7.

25 PUDALOFF, ROSS J. "The Imposition of the Garden: Nature
    and the Natural in Early American Literature." Ph.D.
    dissertation, State University of New York at Buffalo.
       Cites Edwards's Sinners in the Hands of an Angry God
    as a "striking example" of an anti-pastoral, in a survey
    of three versions of pastoral in America, those of Byrd,
    Jefferson, and Thoreau.

26 RUTMAN, DARRETT B., ed. The Great Awakening: Event and
    Exegesis. Huntington, N.Y.: Robert E. Kreiger Publishing
    Co.
       Reprint of 1970.33.

27 SHEA, DANIEL B., JR. "The Art and Instruction of Jonathan
    Edwards's Personal Narrative." In Puritan New England:
    Essays on Religion, Society, and Culture. Edited by
    Alden T. Vaughan and Francis J. Bremer. New York:
    St. Martin's Press, pp. 299-311.
       Reprint of 1965.18.

28 STEIN, STEPHEN J. "Editor's Introduction." In Apocalyptic
    Writings: "Notes on the Apocalypse" and An Humble Attempt.
    The Works of Jonathan Edwards, vol. 5. New Haven and
    London: Yale University Press, pp. 1-93.
       Traces the apocalyptic tradition, the development of
    Edwards's "Notes on the Apocalypse" and its effect on his
    ministry and his millennialism, his theory of the apocalypse
    and his sources (Moses Lowman, Matthew Poole, and Humphrey
    Prideaux among them), and the provenance of the text and
    the related Humble Attempt, in an introduction to the fifth
    volume of the Yale Edwards. During his New York pastorate
    Edwards began a series of comments on Revelation in his
    "Theological Miscellanies"; in 1723 he started a separate
    notebook on the apocalypse; in 1739 he delivered a series
    of sermons on the redemption, "prima facie evidence" of
    his apocalyptic concerns; in 1743 he revealed in Some
    Thoughts a public and "atypical" commitment to millennial-
    ism; in 1748 he opened even more his private speculatons
    on the coming of the kingdom in Humble Attempt; in 1757,

1977

in his letter to the Princeton trustees, he wrote of his
plan for a systematic theology based in part on apocalyptic
materials of a lifetime. Thus Edwards's continuing
thought about the apocalypse reveals an "intriguing and
complex, but sometimes contradictory," mix of a speculative, private record and a discreet, public one.

29   _____. "Quest for the Spiritual Sense: the Biblical Her-
        meneutics of Jonathan Edwards." Harvard Theological
        Review 70 (January–April):99–113.
             Finds that Edwards's Biblical hermeneutics goes beyond
        the literal interpretation of traditional, Reformed exege-
        sis to a "multiplicity of levels," in an investigation of
        the manuscript Miscellanies and "Blank Bible." Throughout
        his life Edwards "strenuously resisted" challenges to the
        authority and centrality of the Bible mounted by rational-
        ists, enthusiasts, and Roman Catholics, and at his death
        left unfinished projects of that commitment in History of
        Redemption and The Harmony of the Old and New Treatment.
        His hermeneutics emphasizes the necessity of a spiritual,
        in addition to a literal, sense of the Biblical text, a
        spiritual understanding that comes from the efficacious
        working of grace as process and product and results in
        multiple interpretations based on symbol and metaphor,
        typology and allegory.

30   STROUT, CUSHING. "Young People of the Great Awakening: The
        Dynamics of a Social Movement." In Encounter with Erik-
        son: Historical Interpretation and Religious Biography.
        Edited by Donald Capps et al. Missoula, Mont.: Scholars
        Press, pp. 183–216.
             Cites Edwards's generational status and the young con-
        verts of Faithful Narrative as important elements in the
        psychology and sociology of the revivals.

31   TRACY, PATRICIA JUNEAU. "Jonathan Edwards, Pastor: Minister
        and Congregation in the Eighteenth-Century Connecticut
        Valley." Ph.D. dissertation, University of Massachusetts.
             Attributes Edwards's failure as pastor, his inability
        to persuade his flock "to share his vision," to his lack
        of ministerial training, his father's losing struggle for
        power, his grandfather's overwhelming example, and North-
        ampton's (and society's) growing rejection of ministerial
        authority. Edwards's revivalist spirit assured his posi-
        tion for a time, but after 1742 his disagreement with his
        congregation on matters of discipline and admission was
        so profound that they abandoned his "vision of holiness"
        and forced him to leave. (Revision published by Hill &
        Wang, 1980.)

32 WILSON, JOHN F. "Jonathan Edwards as Historian." Church
    History 46 (March):5-18.
       Uses Edwards's History of Redemption, "a homely but
    remarkable set of sermons," as an example of religious
    history writing and as the generic problem it presents.
    History, for Edwards and church historians generally, is
    the "basic modality of individual and collective exist-
    ence," founded upon the singularly important redemptive
    process and meaning and couched in scriptural types and
    prophecies. Peter Gay and his critically antiquated
    Edwards (1966.14) and Perry Miller and his spiritually
    modern Edwards (1949.9) both do him and his History of
    Redemption "less than justice."

33 _____. "Jonathan Edwards's Notebook for 'A History of the
    Work of Redemption.'" In Reformation Conformity and
    Dissent: Essays in Honour of Geoffrey Nuttall. Edited
    by R. Buick Knox. London: Epworth Press, pp. 239-54.
       Examines the physical characteristics and the content
    of three notebooks Edwards arranged in preparation for his
    History of Redemption and concludes, on the basis of in-
    ternal evidence, correlative material, and ink analysis,
    that he began "serious and concerted" work no earlier
    than spring 1755 and continued into summer 1757. If this
    is so, then three broader conclusions are possible: one,
    the History represents his "synthesized interests, re-
    sources, and issues" of the great work of the Stockbridge
    years; two, his letter to the Princeton trustees should
    be "read quite literally" as a genuine expression of his
    concerns and intentions; and three, the prospective work
    was a "theological programme" giving promise of "the
    fullest flowering of the English Reformed theological
    tradition."

34 WILSON-KASTNER, PATRICIA. "Jonathan Edwards: History and
    the Covenant." Andrews University Seminary Studies 15
    (Autumn):205-16.
       Compares Edwards's view of individual salvation and
    historic redemption with that of his English and American
    forebears and concludes that he rejects the covenant argu-
    ment of the Puritans for the determinist one of Calvin.
    Edwards holds that grace (or the Holy Spirit) is the "sole
    determining factor" for salvation in the individual and
    that redemptive history is simply the action of grace in
    time: human autonomy in individuals and in history finds
    no place in Edwards's scheme. Just as each saint express-
    es the glory of God, so history is determined by it totally
    and particularly.

1978

1 ANON. Review of Jonathan Edwards, Apocalyptic Writings,
   edited by Stephen J. Stein. American Literature 49
   (January):676.
       Recommends Stephen Stein's "learnedly and effectively
   edited" Edwards text (1977.28).

2 BANTA, MARTHA. Failure and Success in America: A Literary
   Debate. Princeton, N.J.: Princeton University Press,
   pp. 124-25, 299-301.
       Notes that Edwards, "God's historian of cause and
   effect," was able to transcend sinfulness and suffering
   through public profession and thus, like Henry Adams and
   Norman Mailer, turn failure into success.

3 BERCOVITCH, SACVAN. The American Jeremiad. Madison: University of Wisconsin Press, pp. 94-117, passim.
       Reprints 1978.4 with added detail.

4 _____. "The Typology of America's Mission." American Quarterly 30 (Summer):135-55.
       Traces Edwards's eschatology of America's mission to
   seventeenth-century millennialists and their union of
   secular history and the sacred prophecy of errand.
   Edwards differs from most Puritans in that he believes
   the apocalypse will come after a golden age rather than
   before it--a post-millennial idea of progress and gradual
   fulfillment--but, for the most part, he "simply drew out
   the implications" of their thought and "adopted wholesale"
   their vision of America. What he contributes is a logical,
   consistently worked-out scheme, emphasizing the corporate
   rather than the individual mission.

5 BUSHMAN, RICHARD L. "Jonathan Edwards as Great Man." In
   Religion in American History. Edited by John N. Mulder
   and John F. Wilson. Englewood Cliffs, N.J.: Prentice-
   Hall, pp. 105-24.
       Reprint of 1969.5.

6 CRAWFORD, MICHAEL J. "The Invention of the American Revival:
   The Beginnings of Anglo-American Religious Revivalism,
   1690-1750." Ph.D. dissertation, Boston University.
       Traces the evolution of religious revivalism to its
   common evangelical sources in America, England, and Scotland, and notes Edwards's connection to the developed
   "network" of revival thought and action.

7   ERDT, TERRENCE. "The Calvinist Psychology of the Heart and
     the 'Sense' of Jonathan Edwards." Early American Litera-
     ture 13 (Fall):165-80.
          Finds in the "standard lexicon" of Calvinist piety, not
     in the sensationalism of Locke, the source of Edwards's
     sense of the heart, sweetness, and excellency. Calvin's
     psychology of the heart and the will informs Edwards's
     view of regeneration as it does those of earlier Puritans,
     William Ames and Thomas Hooker among them, and does so,
     contrary to Perry Miller, "without reduction to rational-
     ism."

8   GÄBLER, ULRICH. "Die Anfänge der Erweckungsbewegung in Neu-
     England und Jonathan Edwards, 1734/1735." Theologische
     Zeitschrift 34 (March-April):95-104.
          Attributes the beginning of revivalism in New England
     to Edwards's active encouragement of youthful conversions
     and his graphic description of them, in an account of
     Faithful Narrative and its effects. The revivals of 1734
     and 1735 prepared the way for the Great Awakening five
     years later; fostered a spirit of unity and independence
     among the people, perhaps for the first time in their
     colonial past; and convinced Edwards of America's unique
     place in the scheme of redemption. (In German.)

9   GAUSTAD, EDWIN S[COTT]. Review of Jonathan Edwards, Apoca-
     lyptic Writings, edited by Stephen J. Stein. Journal of
     American History 65 (June):108-109.
          Praises Stephen Stein's "diligence, thoroughness, and
     prodigious scholarship" in his edition of Edwards's par-
     ticularly difficult manuscript text (1977.28).

10   GURA, PHILIP F. "Sowing for the Harvest: William Williams
     and the Great Awakening." Journal of Presbyterian History
     56 (Winter):326-41.
          Argues that William Williams, pastor at Hatfield,
     Massachusetts, and uncle of Edwards, "played an important
     part" preparing the Connecticut Valley for Solomon Stod-
     dard's harvests and Edwards's surprising conversions
     through his doctrinal and evangelical work.

11   HEIMERT, ALAN [EDWARD]. "The Great Awakening as Watershed."
     In Religion in American History. Edited by John N. Mulder
     and John F. Wilson. Englewood Cliffs, N.J.: Prentice-
     Hall, pp. 127-44.
          Reprints parts of chapter 2, "The Work of Redemption,"
     in 1966.17.

1978

12 HUTCH, RICHARD A. "Jonathan Edwards' Analysis of Religious
    Experience." Journal of Psychology and Theology 6
    (Spring):123-31.
        Appraises Edwards's analysis of religious experience--
    Faithful Narrative, Distinguishing Marks, Some Thoughts,
    and Religious Affections--in its cultural, historical,
    psychological, and theological contexts, and concludes
    that it is an "integrated experience of seizure," express-
    ing itself in the inclination of the heart. True religion,
    for Edwards, was a matter of the affections, "a unique
    meeting and blending of both heat and light."

13 JONES, CHARLES EDWIN. "The Impolitic Mr. Edwards: The Per-
    sonal Dimension of the Robert Breck Affair." New England
    Quarterly 51 (March):64-79.
        Details the Robert Breck affair, Edwards's role in it,
    and the effect upon his dismission. At the behest of his
    uncle, William Williams, Edwards wrote a "ferocious
    apologetic"--A Letter to the Author of the Pamphlet Called
    an Answer to the Hampshire Narrative (1737)--in defense of
    that lost cause nearly two years after the fact. Nine
    years later, Breck, now a senior member of the ecclesias-
    tical council called to hear the Edwards's affair, cast
    the decisive ballot for his dismissal.

14 MARINI, STEPHEN A. Review of Jonathan Edwards, Apocalyptic
    Writings, edited by Stephen J. Stein. New England Quar-
    terly 51 (September):444-46.
        Questions Stephen Stein's reading of Edwards's apocalyp-
    tic writings (1977.28) as "unconsummated intellectual
    passion": the texts both demonstrate Edwards's method of
    turning theological theory to ecclesiastical practice and
    explain the scriptural basis for his political vision.

15 MURPHY, SUSAN. "In Remembrance of Me: Sacramental Theology
    and Practice in Colonial New England." Ph.D. dissertation,
    University of Washington.
        Traces the doctrine of the covenant in New England
    theology from its Old Testament and Reformed sources to
    the half-way measures of the late seventeenth century to
    Edwards's communion practices, a return full-circle.

16 PIPER, JOHN. "Jonathan Edwards on the Problem of Faith and
    History." Scottish Journal of Theology 31 (June):217-28.
        Considers Edwards's view on faith and history, expressed
    in Religious Affections, in terms of the current discussion

of historical criticism and finds he is able to "hold together" the reasonableness and the spirituality of saving faith whereas contemporary theologians cannot. Edwards encourages historical argument for the truth of the gospel, recognizes its limitations (most men are incapable of historical analysis), but insists that faith must have "a just ground for certainty" if it is to be saving.

17 _____. "A Personal Encounter with Jonathan Edwards." Reformed Journal 28 (November):13-17.
    Narrates an academic theologian's three personal encounters with Edwards's work (before, during, and after seminary) and concludes that Freedom of the Will is "one of the world's greatest books," that End of Creation "captures the essence" of Edwards's theology, and that Religious Affections is "a very contemporary and helpful message."

18 STEIN, STEPHEN J. "Providence and the Apocalypse in the Early Writings of Jonathan Edwards." Early American Literature 13 (Winter):250-67.
    Locates the organizing focus of Edwards's comments on the four beasts of Revelation 4 in the theme of providence, in an examination of his early comments on the Apocalypse in "Theological Miscellanies," "Notes on Scripture," and "Notes on the Apocalypse," all written before mid-1724. The results of such an investigation of the manuscripts should caution scholars against "a monothematic portrayal" of Edwards's eschatological thought. Providence is "central" to Edwards (and to Reformed theology generally) and provides a "richer" theological construct than millennialism.

19 STOKES, ANSON PHELPS. Memorials of Eminent Yale Men. Northford, Conn.: Elliot's Books.
    Reprint of 1914.5.

20 WEBER, DONALD LOUIS. "The Image of Jonathan Edwards in American Culture." Ph.D. dissertation, Columbia University.
    Unravels the history of the image and meaning of Edwards for American culture by tracing the impact of his work and person on his contemporaries and "guardians" in the eighteenth century (Hopkins and Bellamy), his defenders and detractors in the nineteenth (Finney and Bancroft, Stowe and Holmes), and his rejection and restoration in the

1978

twentieth (Parrington and Miller). Edwards has "enraged
and inspired" his interpreters over two centuries of
American cultural history.

21 WEDDLE, DAVID L[EROY]. Review of Jonathan Edwards, <u>Apocalyp-
tic Writings</u>, edited by Stephen J. Stein. <u>Journal of
Religion</u> 58 (October):437-39.
Praises Stephen Stein's "insightful" introduction to
an important Edwards manuscript (1977.28).

22 WILLARD, MALINDA KAYE. "Jonathan Edwards and Nathaniel Hawthorne: Themes from the Common Consciousness." Ph.D.
dissertation, University of South Carolina.
Attributes the similarity of themes in Edwards and
Hawthorne to their commonly shared New England mind, a
synthesis of Augustinian piety and Calvinist dogma. Thus
the reconciliation of fate and freedom is treated in both
<u>Freedom of the Will</u> and <u>The Scarlet Letter</u>; the portrait
of fallen man in <u>Original Sin</u> and <u>The Marble Faun</u>, of
redeemed man in <u>Divine and Supernatural Light</u> and <u>The
House of Seven Gables</u>; and the discrepancy between appear-
ance and reality in man in <u>Religious Affections</u> and <u>The
Blithedale Romance</u>, in nature (as symbolism) in <u>Images or
Shadows</u> and the tales.

23 WILSON-KASTNER, PATRICIA. <u>Coherence in a Fragmented World:
Jonathan Edwards' Theology of the Holy Spirit</u>. Washington,
D.C.: University Press of America, 90 pp.
Focues upon Edwards's unifying theology of the Holy
Spirit, "a model of clarity and balance," in a study of
the workings of the Spirit in his religious milieu, in
in conversion, and in grace, and of its effects upon personal change, social ethics, and millennial expectation.
His theology demands that "we turn ourselves inside out,"
making God and the mystery of his relationship the center
of life. Edwards held that true religion came from each
man's personal relation with God, that his responsibility
to all other men arose from his service to God, and that
America was destined to be "a servant of God's glory in
the world."

24 _____. "God's Infinity and His Relationship to Creation in
the Theologies of Gregory of Nyssa and Jonathan Edwards."
<u>Foundations</u> 21 (October-December):305-21.
Contrasts the notions of divine infinity in Gregory of
Nyssa and Edwards and their effect on the nature of God's
creativity, man's freedom, and necessity, and suggests

that Edwards's theological system becomes "more comprehensible" as an adaptation of Gregory's Christian Neoplatonism. Gregory's God is "absolutely satisfied in his own society"; Edwards's God is neither free nor sufficient inasmuch as His internal glory is dependent upon external exercise. Human freedom, for Edwards, is "bounded" by God's necessity to create; for Gregory a "free God" freely creates men who freely choose. Although there is no evidence to show that Edwards ever read Gregory first hand--he probably learned of him from Puritan writers, his Yale tutor, and the Cambridge Platonists--there is in Edwards a "very real, though mediated dependence" upon Gregory.

Index

The index interleaves authors and titles; reprints follow first publication in parentheses, book reviews follow title entries. All subject entries are grouped alphabetically under Edwards, Jonathan, and include references to sources and influences, themes and events, works and categories of thought. Within the subject group appear, as well, headings such as Bibliographies, Biographies, Books, Dissertations, and General estimates.

The American Spirit in Letters
1926.8
American Sunday School Union
1832.1
The American Temper 1952.5
American Thought from Puritanism
to Pragmatism 1915.3
America's Coming-of-Age 1915.1
"America's Theologian-Preacher"
1976.39
"America's Unforgettable Philo-
sopher" 1940.6
Amerikanische Philosophie 1936.9
(1950.15)
"The Anachronism of Jonathan
Edwards" 1927.2
"An Analysis of the Rev. Jonathan
Edwards's Interpretation of
the Last Ten Verses, in the
Fifth Chapter of the Epistle
to the Romans" 1817.3
"'And justify the ways . . .'--
a Suggested Context" 1969.34
Anderson, Courtney 1966.3
Anderson, Paul Russell, and Max
Harold Fisch 1939.1
Anderson, Quentin 1976.2
Anderson, Wallace Earl 1961.2;
1964.2; 1974.2
Anderson, Wilbert L. 1903.2
"Andrew Fuller and Fullerism"
1963.5
Andrews, Charles M. 1929.7
(1929.1)
Andrews, Evangeline Walker 1929.7
Andrews, George Wakeman 1903.17
"Die Anfänge der Erweckungsbewe-
gung in Neu-England und
Jonathan Edwards, 1734/1735"
1978.8
"An Anglican Critique of the Early
Rise of the Great Awakening
in New England" 1973.32
Angoff, Charles 1931.1; 1975.2
Animadversions on Mr. Hart's Late
Dialogue 1770.5
Annals of the American Pulpit
1857.4

"Anthropological Roots of Jonathan
Edwards' Doctrine of God"
1952.1
Anti-Intellectualism in American
Life 1963.12
Antiquities, Historicals and
Graduates of Northampton
1882.2
"Antiquities of Stockbridge"
1870.7
"Aphorisms on that which is Indeed
Spiritual Religion" 1829.2
"The Apologetic Significance of
Jonathan Edwards' Doctrine of
Religious Experience" 1960.14
"Appendix," An Antidote Against
Deism 1801.1
"Appendix," Calvin on Common Grace
1928.4
"Appendix," The Duty and Interest
of a People 1736.1
"Appendix: Samuel Johnson and
Jonathan Edwards" 1901.5
"Appendix II: Review of Edwards'
History of Redemption" 1827.2
"An Application of the Principles
of Aristotelean Rhetoric to
Certain Early New England
Prose" 1967.17
"The Architecture of Conversion"
1967.26
"Arminianism in Massachusetts,
1735-1780" 1943.10 (1955.12;
1966.40)
"The Art and Instruction of Jona-
than Edwards's Personal Nar-
rative" 1965.18 (1974.21;
1977.27)
"Art Treasures in Connecticut"
1895.1
The Articles of Faith and Prac-
tice 1750.2
"Artist in Ideals" 1950.8
"The Artistry of Jonathan Edwards"
1949.1
"As to Jonathan Edwards" 1880.1
Ashley, Jonathan 1753.1
"Aspects of Idealism in Early New
England" 1930.6

Channing, William Ellery 1830.2; 1841.2

Channing, William Henry 1847.2

Chapell, F. L. 1903.18

Character and Opinion in the United States 1920.5

"Charles Finney and a Theology of Revivalism" 1969.19

Chase, Mary Ellen 1949.2

Chauncy, Charles 1743.2; 1785.1; 1856.4

"A Checklist of Doctoral Dissertations on American Presbyterian and Reformed Subjects, 1912-1965" 1967.12

A Cheerful Nihilism 1971.14

Cheever, George B. 1842.2; 1852.3 (1853.10)

Cherry, Charles Conrad 1965.4 (1966.9; 1974.7); 1965.5; 1973.4; 1975.2

Chesley, Elizabeth 1954.4

Child, Frank Samuel 1898.3

Children and Puritanism 1933.2

Chrisman, Lewis H. 1921.3

Christ in Theology 1851.1

Christian, Curtis Wallace 1965.6

The Christian and Civic Economy of Our Large Towns 1821.2

Christian Ethics 1955.3

"The Christian History of the Great Awakening" 1966.33

The Christian Preacher 1800.2

Christian Realism in Contemporary Thought 1940.5

"Christian Unity in Nineteenth-Century America" 1954.17

"The Christian Way of Life in the Religious History of New England" 1925.3

Christie, Francis Albert 1912.3; 1931.7

"The Christology of Jonathan Edwards" 1966.8 (1967.6)

"Christus Gloria: An Aesthetic-Telelogical Investigation of Atonement" 1975.7

Church and State in Massachusetts 1930.9

Church and State in the United States 1950.18

Church History of New England from 1620 to 1804 1839.4

The Church in America and its Baptism of Fire 1896.9

"Churches Celebrate 200th Anniversary of Edwards's Birth" 1903.3

Circular Letters 1798.1

Claghorn, George S. 1964.7

Clap, Thomas 1745.1-2

Clark, Daniel A. 1826.1

Clark, George 1789.2

Clark, George Pierce 1956.4

Clark, Irene Woodbridge 1903.19

Clark, Joseph S. 1858.7

Clark, Solomon 1882.2; 1891.2

Clarke, William Newton 1903.27

Classic Americans 1931.4

Classics of Protestantism 1959.4

Clebsch, William A. 1968.2; 1973.5 (1975.6)

The Clergy in American Life and Letters 1900.1

The Clergy of America 1849.2

Clift, Arlene Louise 1969.7

Clipsham, Ernest F. 1963.5

Clough, Wilson O. 1964.8

Cobb, Sanford H. 1902.2

Cochran, Alice Cowan 1976.15

Cohen, I. Bernard 1941.2

Coherence in a Fragmented World: Jonathan Edwards' Theology of the Holy Spirit 1978.23

Colacurcio, Robert Eugene 1972.5

Cole, Bertha Woolsey Dwight 1900.10

Cole, Samuel Valentine 1904.14 (1904.5)

Coleman, Alexander 1972.6

Coleridge, Samuel Taylor 1829.2

"The Collapse of the New England Theology" 1908.1 (1920.3)

Collins, Edward M., Jr. 1969.8; 1971.3

Collins, Varnum Lansing 1914.2

Collmer, R. G. 1956.5

The Colonial Origins of American Thought 1964.20

"A Colonial Parson's Wife, Sarah Pierrepont Edwards, 1710-1758, 'And a Very Eminent Christian'" 1950.22

Gambrell, Mary Latimer 1937.3
Gardiner, Harry Norman 1900.12-
13; 1901.6 (1976.21);
1903.27; 1904.7
Gardiner, Harry Norman, and
Richard Webster 1910.4
Garrett, Arthur 1967.11
Garrison, Joseph M., Jr. 1970.12
"Gathering of the Tribe of Jona-
than Edwards" 1870.3
Gaustad, Edwin Scott 1951.4
(1957.6; 1965.7; 1968.10;
1972.10); 1954.8; 1966.13;
1978.9
Gay, Peter 1966.14
Gelpi, Albert J. 1966.15; 1975.9
"Genealogy of a Famous Family"
1895.4
A General View of the Progress of
Ethical Philosophy 1832.5
(1835.4; 1842.5)
A General View of the Progress of
Metaphysical, Ethical, and
Political Philosophy 1822.6
A Genetic History of the New
England Theology 1907.3
(1963.9)
"Genius" 1855.5
"The Genius of Jonathan Edwards"
1968.17
The Gentle Puritan 1962.8
George, E. A. 1884.1
George Whitefield 1970.8
George Whitefield's Journals
1960.16
"German Influence on Religious
Life and Thought in America
during the Colonial Period"
1907.4
Gerould, James Thayer 1936.6
Gerstner, John H. 1956.6;
1957.7; 1960.5; 1976.22-25
Geschichte der Congregationalsten
in Neu-England 1842.7
(1857.5)
Gewehr, Wesley M. 1930.5
Gillett, Ezra Hall 1864.2;
1867.2-3; 1868.3
Gillette, Gerald W. 1967.12
Gilmore, Albert F. 1940.4

Giovanni, G. 1951.5
"A Glance at Edwards' View of
Reason" 1904.15
"Glimpses into Edwards' Life"
1903.44
"The Glory of God and the Future
of Man" 1976.27
The Glory of God in the Theology
of Jonathan Edwards 1962.14
"God, Man, and the Great Awaken-
ing" 1973.12
"God's Infinity and His Relation-
ship to Creation in the
Theologies of Gregory of
Nyssa and Jonathan Edwards"
1978.24
God's Messengers 1976.53
Godwin, George 1950.6
Godwin, William 1793.5; 1801.2
Goen, Clarence Curtis 1959.5;
1960.6 (1962.3); 1968.11;
1972.11
Gohdes, Clarence 1930.6; 1941.5
Goodwin, Gerald J. 1968.12
Gordon, George A. 1895.3;
1900.14 (1901.6); 1908.1
(1920.3)
Gordon, William 1762.4
Grabo, Norman S. 1969.13-14;
1971.11
"Grace and Works, Enlightenment
and Practice" 1976.44
"Grace and Works in America:
The Role of Jonathan Edwards"
1977.3
"'Grace' in the Thought of Emer-
son, Thoreau, and Hawthorne"
1969.33
"Gracious Discoveries: Toward
an Understanding of Jonathan
Edwards' Psychological Theory"
1974.5
"The Grand Design: Jonathan Ed-
wards' History of the Work of
Redemption" 1975.14
Grant, Leonard T. 1967.13
Gray, Joseph M. M. 1936.7
(1971.12)
Grazier, James Lewis 1958.9

417